SOFTWARE TOOLS AND TECHNIQUES FOR EMBEDDED DISTRIBUTED PROCESSING

SOFTWARE TOOLS AND TECHNIQUES FOR EMBEDDED DISTRIBUTED PROCESSING

by

Herbert C. Conn, Jr., David L. Kellogg, David J. Rodjak
Rodney M. Bond, States L. Nelson, Scott L. Harmon
Sue A. Johnson, William D. Baker, Paul B. Dobbs

General Dynamics Corporation
Fort Worth, Texas

np

NOYES PUBLICATIONS
Park Ridge, New Jersey, U.S.A.

Library of Congress Catalog Card Number 85-28422
ISBN: 0-8155-1062-4
Printed in the United States

Published in the United States of America by
Noyes Publications
Mill Road, Park Ridge, New Jersey 07656

10 9 8 7 6 5 4 3 2 1

Library of Congress Cataloging-in-Publication Data
Main entry under title:

Software tools and techniques for embedded distributed processing.

Includes bibliographies and index.
1. United States--Armed Forces--Weapons systems--Data processing. 2. United States--Armed Forces--Communication systems--Data processing. 3. United States--Armed Forces--Weapons systems--Automation. 4. United States--Armed Forces--Communication systems--Automation. 5. Electronic data processing--Distributed processing. 6. Computer software. I. Conn, Herbert C.
UF503.S64 1986 355.8'2'0285 85-28422
ISBN 0-8155-1062-4

Foreword

An investigation of the requirements for life-cycle support in embedded distributed processing systems and the specification of applicable software tools and techniques by life-cycle phase are presented in this book. Special attention has been given to tightly-coupled distributed processing systems.

The objective of this three-phase effort is: (1) the identification of hardware/software technology pertinent to the implementation of tightly-coupled embedded distributed systems; (2) the establishment of an integrated approach to the total life-cycle software development period, correlated with the applicability of existing/near-term software engineering methodology, techniques, and tools to each life-cycle phase; and (3) a definition of the functional design requirements necessary for far-term development of needed software engineering methodology, techniques, and tools. It should be noted that, while these studies were prepared for military use, they will also have practical, commercial use. A product of this substantial effort is the recommended design of a system support environment encompassing the integrated implementation of candidate software engineering tools.

The information in the book is from the following documents:

> *Distributed Processing Tools Definition—Hardware and Software Technologies for Tightly-Coupled Distributed Systems,* prepared by Herbert C. Conn, Jr., David L. Kellogg, and David J. Rodjak of General Dynamics Corporation for the U.S. Air Force Systems Command Rome Air Development Center, June 1983.
>
> *Distributed Processing Tools Definition—Application of Software Engineering Technology,* prepared by Herbert C. Conn, Jr., David L. Kellogg, Rodney M. Bond, States L. Nelson, Scott L. Harmon, Sue A. Johnson, William D. Baker, and Paul B. Dobbs of General Dynamics Corporation for the U.S. Air Force Systems Command Rome Air Development Center, June 1983.

Distributed Processing Tools Definition—An Integrated Software Engineering Environment for Distributed Processing Software Development, prepared by Herbert C. Conn, Jr., David L. Kellogg, States L. Nelson, Scott L. Harmon, and Sue A. Johnson of General Dynamics Corporation for the U.S. Air Force Systems Command Rome Air Development Center, June 1983.

The table of contents is organized in such a way as to serve as a subject index and provides easy access to the information contained in the book.

NOTICE

Contents and Subject Index

PART I
HARDWARE AND SOFTWARE TECHNOLOGY FOR
TIGHTLY-COUPLED DISTRIBUTED SYSTEMS

PART II
APPLICATION OF SOFTWARE ENGINEERING TECHNOLOGY

PART III
AN INTEGRATED SOFTWARE ENGINEERING ENVIRONMENT FOR DISTRIBUTED PROCESSING SOFTWARE DEVELOPMENT

Part I

Hardware and Software Technology for Tightly-Coupled Distributed Systems

The information in Part I is from *Distributed Processing Tools Definition—Hardware and Software Technologies for Tightly-Coupled Distributed Systems,* prepared by Herbert C. Conn, Jr., David L. Kellogg, and David J. Rodjak of General Dynamics Corporation for the U.S. Air Force Systems Command Rome Air Development Center, June 1983.

1. Technical Report Summary

General Dynamics Data Systems Division is under contract to Rome Air Development Center to conduct a study entitled Distributed Processing Tools Definition. The objectives of this study are to investigate the requirements for software lifecycle support of embedded distributed processing systems and then to specify tools and techniques pertinent to each lifecycle phase. This study is divided into three phases as illustrated in Figure 1-1. Phase I of the study has been completed, and its results are described in this Technical Report.

Two generic classifications of military systems are addressed in this study: weapon systems (including armament, aeronautical, and missile and space configurations) and communication systems (including command/control/communication and mission/force management type configurations). This classification is based upon characteristics inherent to each group (ref. Appendix A) and permits specification of requirements for software tools and techniques for a larger class of generic military systems.

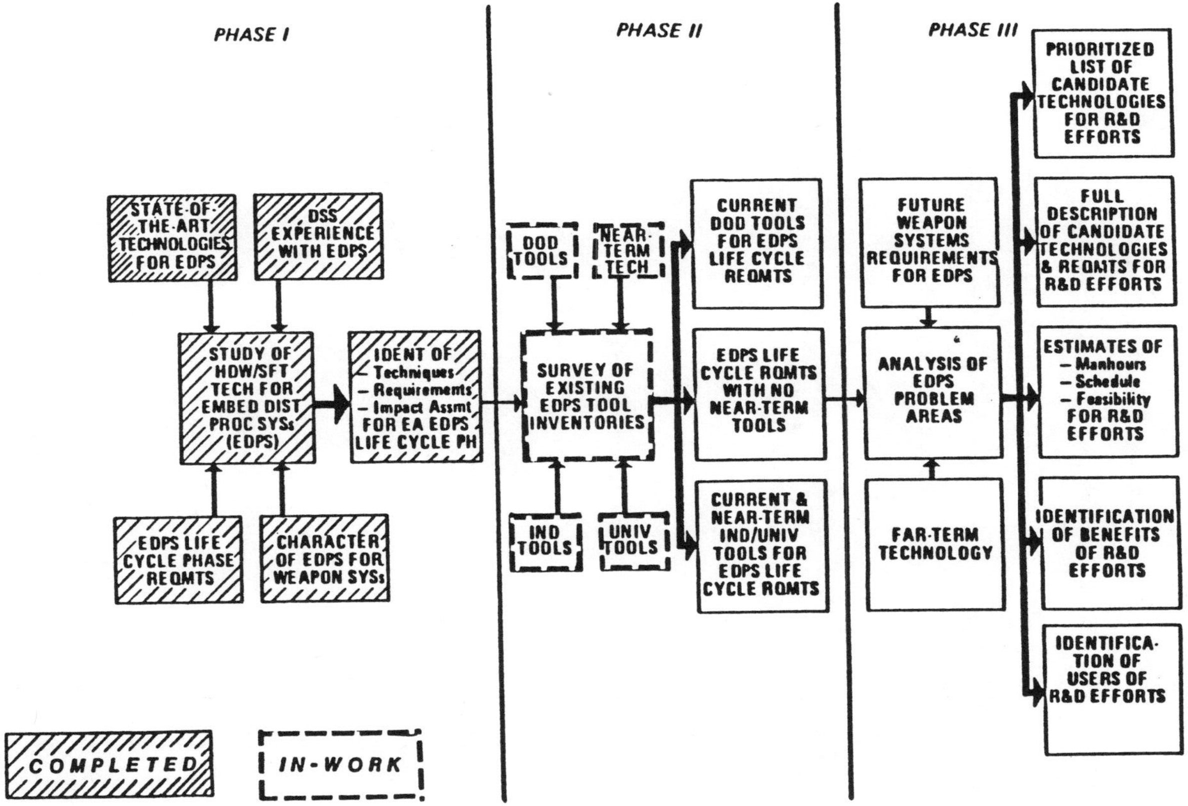

Figure 1-1 Overview of the Distributed Processing Tools Definition Study

The principal technical conclusion of the Phase I study is the requirement that software lifecycle phase support tools for embedded distributed processing systems must view the hardware and software from a total systems perspective. This perspective is accomplished by using the Concept of Object-Oriented Modularization (ref. Paragraph 6.0). Particular manifestations of the Concept of Object-Oriented Modularization applied to embedded distributed processing systems yield the following additional conclusions:

(1) Software tools must be small and integrated with larger environments; for example, the Ada Programming Support Environment or an Integrated Software Support Environment as proposed in the DOD Candidate R&D Thrusts for the Software Technology Initiative. In addition, these tools must be available at the beginning of the software development program (ref. Paragraphs 5.2.1, 5.2.2, and 5.2.7).

(2) Static analysis techniques may not be useful because of the probabilistic nature of distributed systems. This conclusion is corroborated by recent work of Dr. W. E. Howden (ref. Paragraphs 7.1.4 and 7.3.1).

(3) Rapid prototyping and impact analysis tools are critically needed (ref. Paragraphs 7.1.3 and 7.3.3).

(4) The real-time rendezvous and package set capabilities of the Ada language need further analysis in a distributed processing environment (ref. Paragraph 7.1.2 and Appendix B).

(5) Simulation of distributed hardware interconnections and networking must be done before the system is built because performance is critically dependent on these features (ref. Paragraphs 5.1.2 and 5.1.3).

In addition, the anticipated effects of static analysis, branch testing, and impact analysis techniques upon the lifecycle phases of embedded distributed processing systems are evaluated (ref. Paragraph 7.3). Finally, global timing and methods of distributed data base management have been identified as topics worthy of future research efforts.

Software lifecycle phase support tools are also required for communication systems (i.e., command/control/communication and mission/force management configurations). In such applications distributed processing has increased the importance of Object-Oriented Modularization (ref. Paragraph 6.0). Specific manifestations of such modularization are evident in the following conclusions concerning communication systems:

(1) Data distribution can vary throughout different levels of a multi-layered network. Object-Oriented Modularizations require alternative layering be examined (ref. Paragraphs 6.1 and 7.2.2).

(2) The performance behavior of multi-layered networks with distributed intelligence must be established before such networks are implemented (ref. Paragraphs 7.1 and 7.1.2).

(3) The capability to simulate a multi-layered network must become part of the Integrated Software Support Environment. (ref. Paragraphs 5.2.7 and 7.1.3).

Decision making concerning embedded distributed processing systems as well as communications systems requires knowledge of data movement and computational efficiency. Enough information must be known within specific real-time constraints to reach appropriate decisions. Subsequent functionality is a product of such decisions. Distributed processing functions are performed upon data bases residing within interconnected architectures. Growth in these data bases can force changes in their tightly-coupled architectures to accommodate increased information flow. The bottom line is functionality for both weapon systems and communication systems. The systems themselves can be viewed as interconnected hardware components but their functionality is a result of software. Using analytical techniques, such software can be validated and optimized. Without analytical techniques, the multiple processor operating system will allocate its resources. Under such an approach validation and optimization issues would not be addressed before the start of a weapon or communication system's operational software. Higher reliability at reduced costs and shorter development schedules would not be produced. Instead the emergence of a "fix it later" attitude would ensue. When real-time performance of both hardware and software is not considered at the outset, they will force subsequent consideration when problems inevitably occur. Proper analytical techniques anticipate and eliminate whole groups of validation and optimization problems. They also establish what performance can reasonably be expected from specific multiple processor configurations. Taken as a whole, these techniques become part of a support environment. The functionality of such a support environment can best be described as a configuration testbed. Although the issues addressed by an embedded system are different from a communications system, a single configuration testbed can accommodate both. In conclusion the need for testing command/control/communication systems and embedded distributed systems can be addressed by a single testbed built upon a programming support environment, e.g., the Ada Programming Support Environment. Such an effort is worthy of future research initiatives.

Phase II of the Distributed Processing Tools Definition Study will research industrial, university and Department of Defense tools that satisfy the requirements established in Phase I. Finally, Phase III will identify and describe candidate research and development efforts to solve any Phase I requirements not supported by a Phase II tool or technique.

2. Scope and Purpose of This Document

Projected military requirements for improvements in performance, reliability, and field maintainability of weapon and communication systems, indicate an increased utilization of embedded distributed processing technology. Software tools and techniques need to be identified and developed that support the already existing and future embedded distributed processing hardware. Consequently, General Dynamics Data Systems Division and Rome Air Development Center have contracted to conduct a study of software tools and techniques pertinent to embedded distributed processing systems (EDPS). This effort is entitled Distributed Processing Tools Definition (DPTD) study, and it is being conducted in three phases, namely:

Phase I - Study of Hardware and Software Technologies

Phase II - Survey of Existing Tools and Techniques

Phase III - Analysis of Problem Areas and Recommendation of Candidates for Research and Development Efforts.

The objectives of the DPTD study are to investigate the requirements for software lifecycle support of embedded distributed processing systems and then to identify and specify tools and techniques pertinent to each lifecycle phase. The availability of specifications for software tools and techniques to support embedded distributed processing systems will enable the tools to be developed prior to the start of the weapon or communication system operational software. This prior availability will result in higher reliability of the operational software at reduced costs and shorter development schedules.

The purpose of this document is to present the results of Phase I of the DPTD study in accordance with the requirements of paragraph 4.1.1 of the Statement of Work. The results of Phases II and III of the DPTD study will be concatenated to this Phase I report. The benefits of this approach are a smooth transition of the description of the results of the three phases for the reader and the opportunity to update previous sections as newer technologies are identified and deeper insights are gained into their impacts upon embedded distributed processing systems.

3. Introduction and Background

The gap between literature and practices is a chasm when viewed from the standpoint of distributed systems. While researchers advocate symbolic execution or proofs of correctness or even automated verification systems, currently operating distributed systems require hundreds of thousands of lines of computer code to be maintained. Consequently, the overriding commitment of the present is to maintain what has already been implemented. In most instances these systems have been developed without the benefit of automated verification. Static analysis has been limited to diagnostics produced by a typical compiler. Consistency checking and documentation about the definition, reference, and communication of data within a program has not been addressed. As processing is distributed over several nodes, dynamics become more important. Analysis of a program can be performed at the statement-level or through the examination of global execution. Most currently operating distributed systems have not been analyzed from a dynamic standpoint. These current systems accommodate a wide variety of hardware architectures and an even wider variety of software algorithms and data structures. The maintenance of these systems has grown too complicated for any one person to comprehend. However, their complexity continues to grow and their applications continue to expand. New techniques to cope with their increased complexity are beginning to emerge. Foremost among these techniques is the process of object-oriented modularization.

When implementing object-oriented modularization techniques individuals do not need to understand all modules within a distributed system. Although the idea is simple, its realization is often difficult. Obviously someone must know how all the modules of a system fit together. Furthermore, the operations in one module should not rely upon operations within another module unless very carefully controlled. These operationally independent modules characterize the object-oriented approach and distinguish it from the more conventional modularization techniques. The individual who performs the object-oriented modularization does not have to know the operational details in each module. Those details are decided by individuals who implement the specific modules.

Several factors contribute to the difficulty encountered during modularization. First, the modules in software are produced completely independent of the modules in hardware. The subsequent operational mix is sometimes mismatched. Hardware modularization takes place on a process basis. Each process is a module of concurrency with programs being constructed from one or more processes. If several processes are involved, communication between them becomes increasingly important. Such considerations originated within multiprogramming environments where each job could be viewed as a process. From multiprogramming the present methodology for implementing concurrency has evolved. As new hardware instruction sets are envisioned, they are implemented in terms of concurrency architectures. An example would be the MIL-STD-1750A Instruction Set Architecture implemented by RCA and TRACOR for Wright-Patterson Air Force Base. The CPU is subdivided into two pairs of General Processor Units (GPUs) and operates on an 8-bit slice architecture. The microcode is partitioned between the two GPUs and has no duplication. These partitions are accessed as needed and operate as concurrency modules. The instruction set of MIL-STD-1750A is accommodated through access to 16 different partitions or concurrency modules. To optimize a process requires knowledge of its access sequence. Of course such an approach emphasizes the importance of hardware modularization. Once the operating system has been written the emphasis on hardware modularization is downplayed. The importance of software and its associated algorithms and data structures is elevated. Object-oriented modularization is applied producing software with operationally independent modules. When these modules run concurrently, they can be viewed as concurrency modules within their respective hardware environments. Each such module exhibits its own efficiency with respect to access sequences on the hardware level. In most instances those access sequences are closely associated with the operating system. To bridge that gap between object-oriented modularization and hardware modularization requires a precise software tool. In the case of the MIL-STD-1750A implementation that tool was a derivative of SPICE which was developed at Carnegie-Mellon University. It is a message-based system containing two kinds of entities: messages (a collection of types and data) and ports (queues of messages). It does not emulate the object-oriented modularization but specializes in concurrency modules. Consequently, the implementation of the MIL-STD-1750A Instruction Set Architecture by RCA and TRACOR illustrates how modules in hardware are developed independently of modules in software.

Another difficulty encountered during modularization originates with scheduling. Production schedules for distributed systems are usually controlled by external factors. Such systems are usually components within larger systems; i.e., they are embedded. The schedules imposed by the larger systems take precedence over the embedded distributed processing systems. Despite this scheduling precedence, the need for object-oriented modularization persists.

Also, unless the interface between software modules is completely established, the subsequent software effort may be unclear.

Lack of clarity extracts a price later in the maintenance of the software system. Of course, clarity has its price too. More effort must be expended during the requirements study and preliminary design phase of the software development lifecycle. Such additional effort is a one time cost and it reduces the maintenance effort which is an ongoing cost. Consequently, unclear interfaces between software modules perpetuate a maintenance effort. The more complicated those interfaces, the larger the effort. Much can be avoided through an object-oriented modularization when software systems are initiated.

As distributed systems become more complex, a consensus concerning modularization has formed. It applies the principle of "information hiding" to distributed software procedures and data structures. Its basic idea is to group related procedures and their data structures together. The subsequent groupings comprise modules which can be viewed as either software or hardware; i.e., object-oriented modules or concurrency modules. Assuming the hardware stance is taken, related procedures refer to operational state transitions. Since computers are state-driven devices, their hardware transitions transform their internal operating states. Concurrency modules transform internal operating states in parallel and independently. Since such modules operate concurrently, the access problem among data abstractions is highlighted. Extra precautions must be taken to manage accesses to the same data by multiple concurrency modules. The tools to regulate access are in their infancy. In effect, the ability to produce concurrency modules has outstripped the present capability of simulation tools. Complicating the situation are software procedures which transform operating states by way of algorithms. Since these algorithms are usually expressed in higher order language statements, the operating transformations are more obscure. The subsequent tools available for access control are based upon logic and are divorced from considerations of hardware. Their analysis is static while the operational situation is concurrently dynamic. The problem has now been assigned the subsequent implementation of a higher order language, e.g., Ada. Whether the language can solve the problem has not been addressed because other issues must be resolved first. Until that language is implemented, the problem has simply been deferred. Despite the delay the access problem between concurrency modules remains significant.

Several programming languages are attempting to support "information hiding" modularization techniques. The latest such language is Ada which has been syntactically specified by the Department of Defense. Its implementation is underway but no validated compiler has yet been produced. Consequently, observations concerning its algorithms and data structures are constrained to its present syntactic definition. To make any observation assumes a future compiler will meet the syntactic specifications and will survive validation. Obviously the current definition of Ada is far removed from the actual state transitions within the concurrency modules of a computer. In instances of concurrency, Ada relies upon the rendezvous technique.

Under that technique, the fastest concurrent operation is completed and waits upon the slowest concurrent operation to complete. Consequently, all concurrent operations complete before processing is resumed. The programming location at which these concurrent operations await completion is called the rendezvous point. Actual wait time within a specific rendezvous depends upon the specific mix of concurrent operations. From the standpoint of an Ada compiler, these wait times are beyond the scope of object-oriented modularization. Such an observation is invalid from the standpoint of hardware concurrency modules. Unless such times are carefully delineated, the rendezvous becomes non-deterministic. In this document the non-deterministic concept will refer to a process whose outcome depends upon the choices and transitions made by the system components. This is in contrast to a deterministic process whose outcome depends only on the current system state. Such non-determinism is not acceptable within most military applications. The performance limitations of embedded distributed processing systems in most military applications must be known before implementation. Otherwise limits could be exceeded under catastrophic circumstances; e.g., battlefield conditions. Since Ada syntactic constructs accommodate non-deterministic situations, a problem is created for subsequent Ada Programming Support Environments (APSEs). The expectation that such APSEs will solve all instances of concurrency modularization is unrealistic. The state transitions available within hardware of the present and immediate future should be accessible from higher order languages like Ada. Otherwise the state transitions will be manipulated at the machine language level.

Obviously Very-Large-Scale-Integration (VLSI) devices capable of concurrent operations are impacting the marketplace. As more of these devices meet or exceed military specifications, the capability for embedded distributed processing systems increases. Beyond the present VLSI devices are the Very-High-Speed-Integrated-Circuit (VHSIC) technologies. Such technologies have as their objective the insertion of speed into defense systems. To achieve this objective, certain barriers must be overcome and subsystems must be built to demonstrate improved capability. Consequently, a VHSIC program has been created to address these barriers on a tri-service basis under the Under Secretary of Defense for Research and Engineering. In addition to the Air Force, Army, and Navy, the program involves the industrial and scientific communities. It has been subdivided into four phases: Phases 0, I, II, and III. While Phases 0, I, and II must operate consecutively, Phase III can operate concurrently. Phase 0 is the Study Phase which defines the work and generates a detailed approach. Phase I is subdivided into two efforts: one to implement electronic brassboards within three years and another to extend Integrated Circuit technology into submicron dimensions. Phase II is also subdivided into two parallel efforts: one provides subsystem demonstrations of the brassboards produced under Phase I and the other continues the submicron work begun under Phase I. Phase III addresses near-term efforts in key technologies which impact the total program. This particular phase is intended to encourage participation by universities and small businesses in very specific problems, e.g., advanced architecture and design concepts. The capability for modularization within VHSIC devices exceeds the current VLSI marketplace. The impact of VHSIC technologies on software languages is not completely understood. Several VHSIC Phase III contracts are addressing that issue. Results have not yet been generated. The non-deterministic nature of the present Ada rendezvous techniques is a crucial issue in VHSIC technologies. The reason rests with the capability of VHSIC hardware environments to provide ever-increasing concurrency modularization.

Furthermore, software produced by "information hiding" must reside in these new VHSIC environments. The near-term and far-term capability for concurrent operation will be enhanced significantly.

Appropriately defined object-oriented modules and concurrency modules proceed independently through their individual lifecycle phases. The reconciliation of these software lifecycle phases to hardware lifecycle phases is of paramount importance to "information hiding" modules. VLSI technologies are putting larger numbers of electronically active devices in hardware modules. As these numbers increase, the operational verification of each electronically active device becomes more difficult. The test phase of such high density VLSI hardware now depends upon statistical sampling techniques. When such hardware is released to the marketplace, its subsequent operation is non-deterministic or probabilistic. The Boolean logic accommodated by such hardware has seldom been completely tested before delivery to the customers. The future deliveries of VHSIC devices will only exacerbate the situation. The problem of marginally functional hardware modules has become the hidden problem of embedded distributed processing systems. Many compromises must be made before such equipment becomes functional. In most instances hardware deficiencies are subsumed by the software process itself. This creates a double bind for the software modularization effort. As software modules are designed and implemented, they may not run because of previously undetected hardware errors. If a software module does not run under such circumstances, is the problem attributable to hardware? Alternatively, the problem could lie with software. Furthermore, as a worst case, the problem could lie with both hardware and software. The end result of this situation is that the software development lifecycle phases are becoming the test phase for hardware modularization. Any discussion of software lifecycle phases must address the hardware testing issue. To ignore such an issue only compounds the problem faced by software modularization and development. An inventory of software tools must be accumulated to test the actual operation of hardware modules. Such a toolset serves the purpose of hardware quality assurance. Its objective would be the elimination of hardware problems within the subsequent software lifecycle phases. If the objective is achieved, software development costs should be reduced. Whether the reduction is temporary or permanent has not been established.

Assuming the quality of hardware modules can be assured, the subsequent software lifecycle phases need construction tools for separate software modules. Each tool should be associated with one or more lifecycle phases. Taken collectively all tools would cover the lifecycle spectrum: requirements tools, design tools, coding tools, testing tools, documentation tools, and maintenance tools. A clever design for such a toolkit would use "information hiding" concepts. Such concepts accommodate the trend toward increasing hardware modularization. Shrinking hardware modules present shrinking targets to the software development toolkits. These hardware modules are often overlooked by developmental toolkits. The present situation is summarized by the following observation. Tools for software lifecycle phases in distributed systems should operate within the distributed systems themselves. To accomplish such operation requires lifecycle tools to become smaller and more specialized. Such a trend runs counter to the current tool marketplace.

Currently available tools address a general systems orientation and combine several lifecycle phases together. The immediate result of such an orientation is to place tools in large uniprocessor configurations. The computer talent in such computer settings seldom appreciates the real-time problems of the distributed system. Ada suffers from the same orientation. Although capable of targeting small hardware modules, it must reside in an excessively large computer environment. In this large computer environment the modularization in the uniprocessor configuration itself is seldom evident. Unless the computer talent exerts extraordinary effort to discover how the large uniprocessor operates, the software tools it produces is not likely to exhibit such understanding.

Smaller and more specialized lifecycle tools can be combined into larger sets to accommodate a general systems orientation. The combination capability is provided by the process of software modularization. Current tools can be converted to these smaller and more specialized formats through additional analysis. Their components with respect to lifecycle phases have not been analyzed in sufficient detail. Upon completion of such an analysis, the resulting tools would be smaller and more specialized with respect to hardware modules. The optimal environment for these new toolkits is the emerging Ada Programming Support Environment (APSE). The intent of Ada has never been to reside in a distributed system but eventually it must. The current proponents of Ada subsets exhibit a distributed system orientation. As currently defined, Ada allows no subsetting. However, such constraints apply to the Dept. of Defense and the U.S. defense industry. The policy of U.S. allies is not as clearly delineated, e.g., Japan and France. To complicate matters Russia is even translating the Ada syntax. If an unauthorized subset of Ada succeeds quickly and impacts the marketplace, the continued insistence against subsetting may itself be called into question. In effect, the complete syntactic definition of Ada requires a very large uniprocessor to accommodate it. Subsets of the syntactic definition can easily be accommodated within the distributed environment itself; e.g., the Telesoft configuration. Systems are definitely becoming more distributed which means the argument for a distributed Ada is growing. Since Ada can be made sufficiently modular, it can eventually fit into a distributed system. Sufficiently modularized toolkits can also fit into distributed systems. Consequently, both Ada and a toolkit of highly specialized tools become part of an integrated software support environment. Obviously how well Ada accommodates itself to underlying hardware state transitions is of paramount importance. The future plans of the Department of Defense software efforts assume the availability of this integrated software support environment.

Subsequent sections will emphasize the importance of such an environment.

4. Characteristics of Distributed Processing Systems

The past several years have seen an increasing interest in the application of distributed computing systems, because a distributed processing system is one in which the computing functions are dispersed among several physical computing elements. These computing elements may be colocated or geographically separated. The distributed computing systems take many forms covering a diverse range of system architectures. In fact, the very term distributed processing may invoke radically different images of technology and problem solutions depending upon the user. To some, a distributed processing system is a collection of multiple computers or processing elements working closely together in the solution of a single problem. An example might be an Air Defense/Command Management system which is comprised of many data processing subsystems linked together by shared memory, communication lines/networks, or common buses. Each data processing center processes a subset of air/ground situation transactions and updates a portion of a common data base to develop a dynamic composite-air-situation picture against which force management can be exercised. Users of such systems are concerned with issues of hardware and software design, reliability, operating/executive systems, and how to optimally decompose programs and data bases. Figures 4-1 through 4-6 illustrate this type of modern distributed processing system in a generalized manner. Figure 4-1 shows the overall Air Defense Ground Environment (ADGE) System with Figures 4-2 through 4-6 showing the generic data processing elements in increasing detail. Since distribution of control is a key characteristic element of distributed processing systems, Figure 4-3 was included to highlight this characteristic.

To other users, a distributed system is a set of intelligent terminals located at the point of use to give local organizational elements more responsive computer support. These terminals perform most of the computing functions for the local group. When necessary the terminals communicate with remote host computers and each other for enhanced support. An example might be the remote Data Entry Display Stations (DEDS) shown in Figure 4-2 which could be located at weather control centers. To yet another set of users (e.g., aircraft pilots), distributed processing systems may mean a very tightly-coupled distributed system used for navigation, weapon delivery, or control of an aircraft.
Figure 4-7 illustrates this type of distributed system by showing the architecture of data processing systems

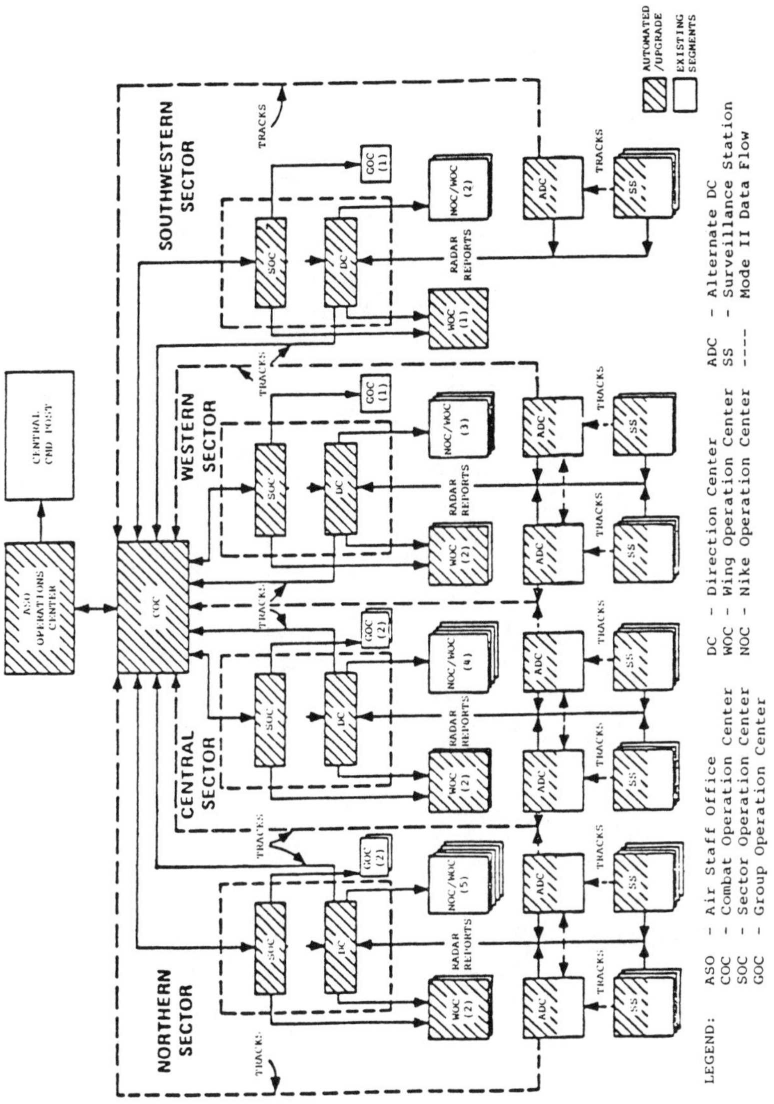

CENTRALIZED TRACKING – CENTRALIZED WEAPON CONTROL

Figure 4-1 General ADGE System

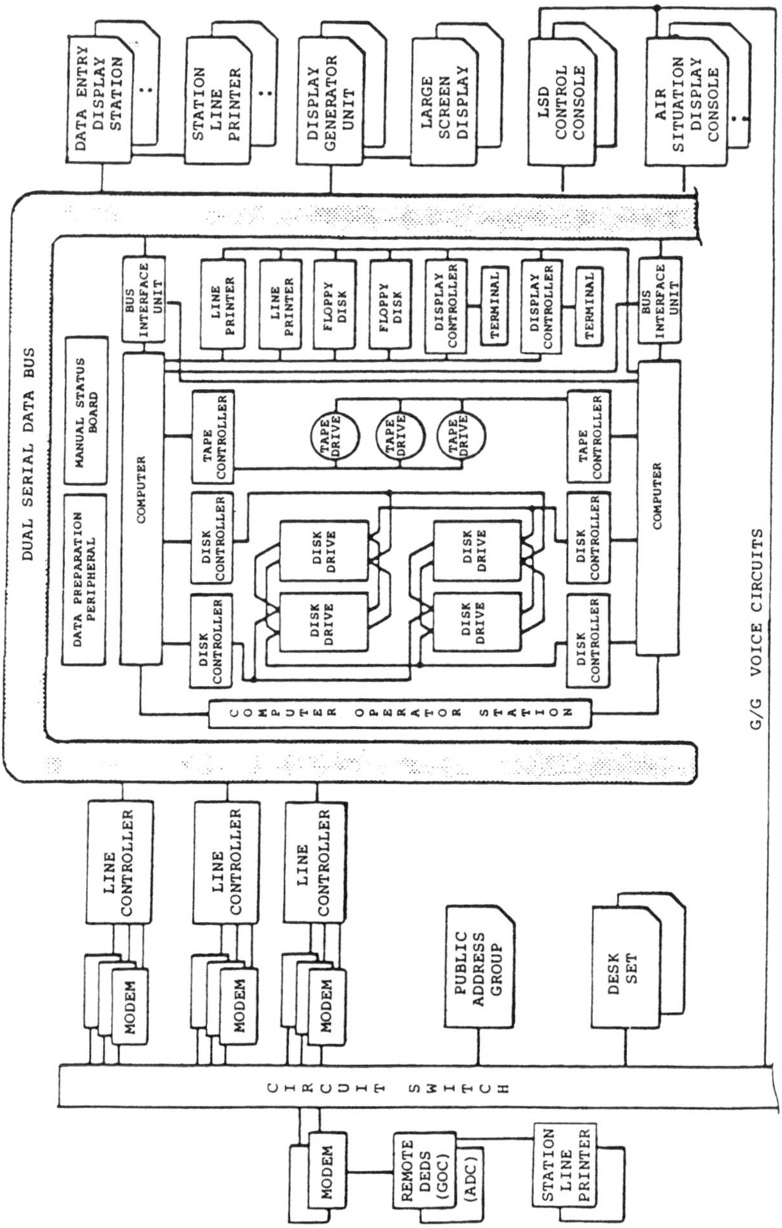

Figure 4-2 Generic Data Processing System for the Operation/Direction Center(s)

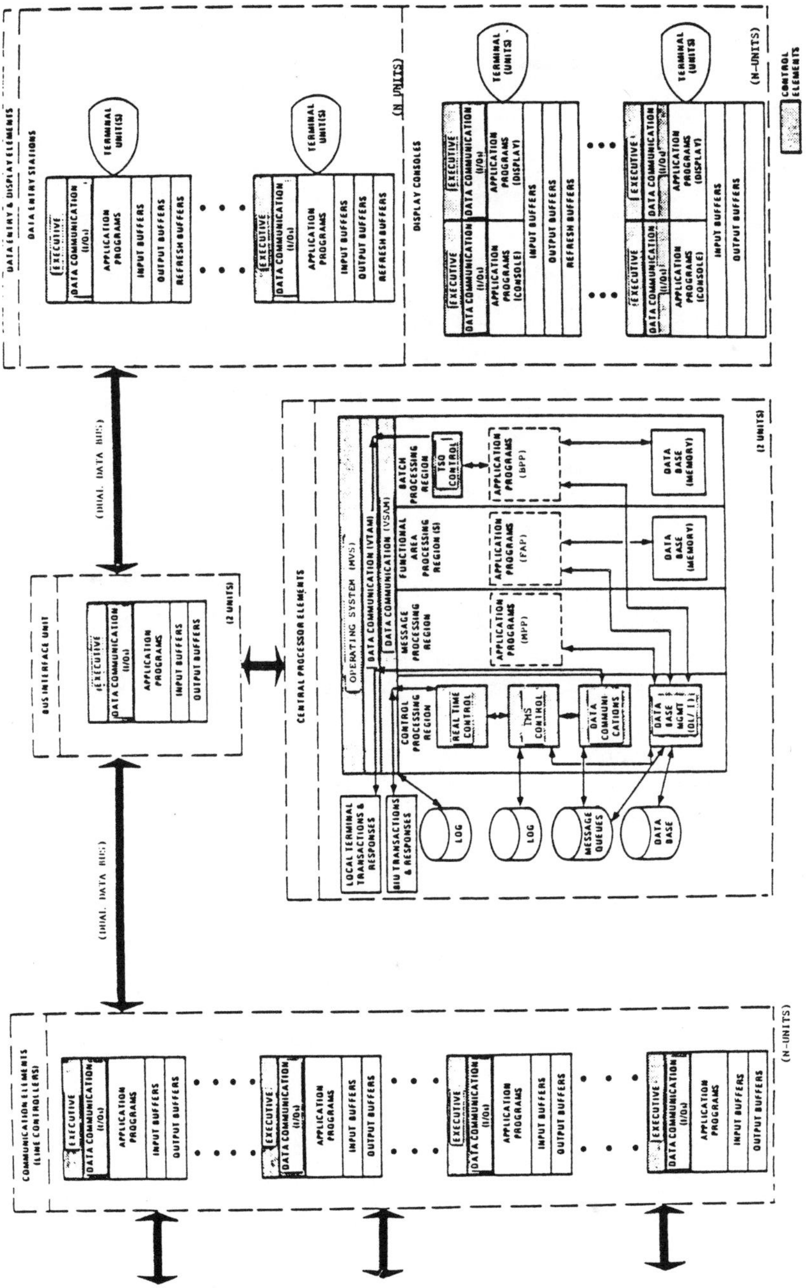

Figure 4-3 Distribution of Processing Control for the Operation/Direction Center(s)

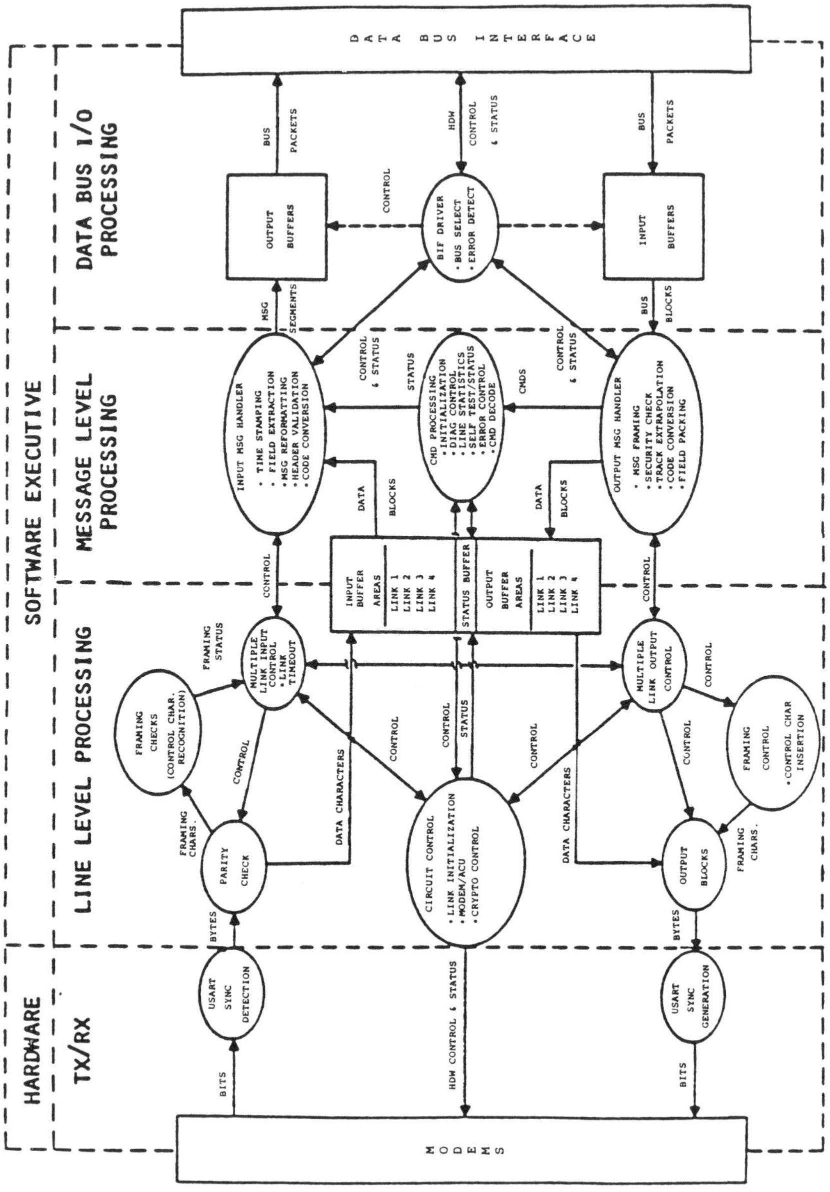

Figure 4-4 Generalized Line Controller Distributed Processing

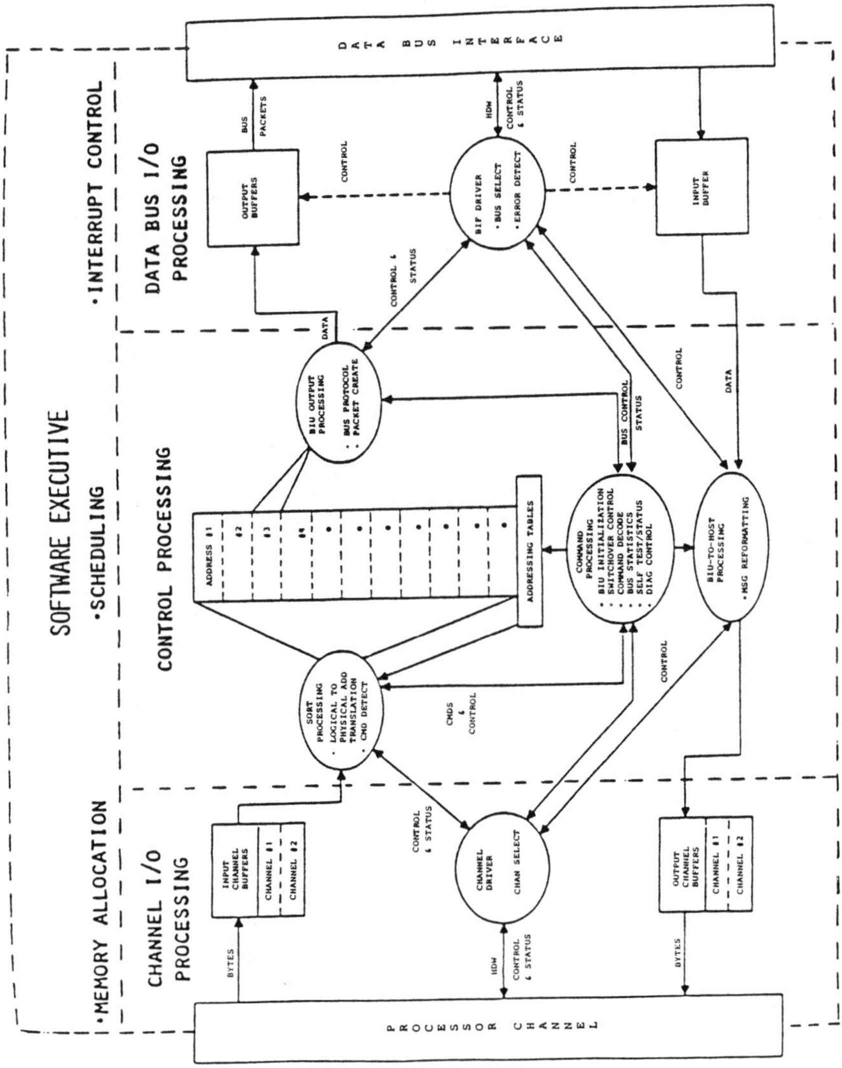

Figure 4-5 Generalized Bus Interface Unit Distributed Processing

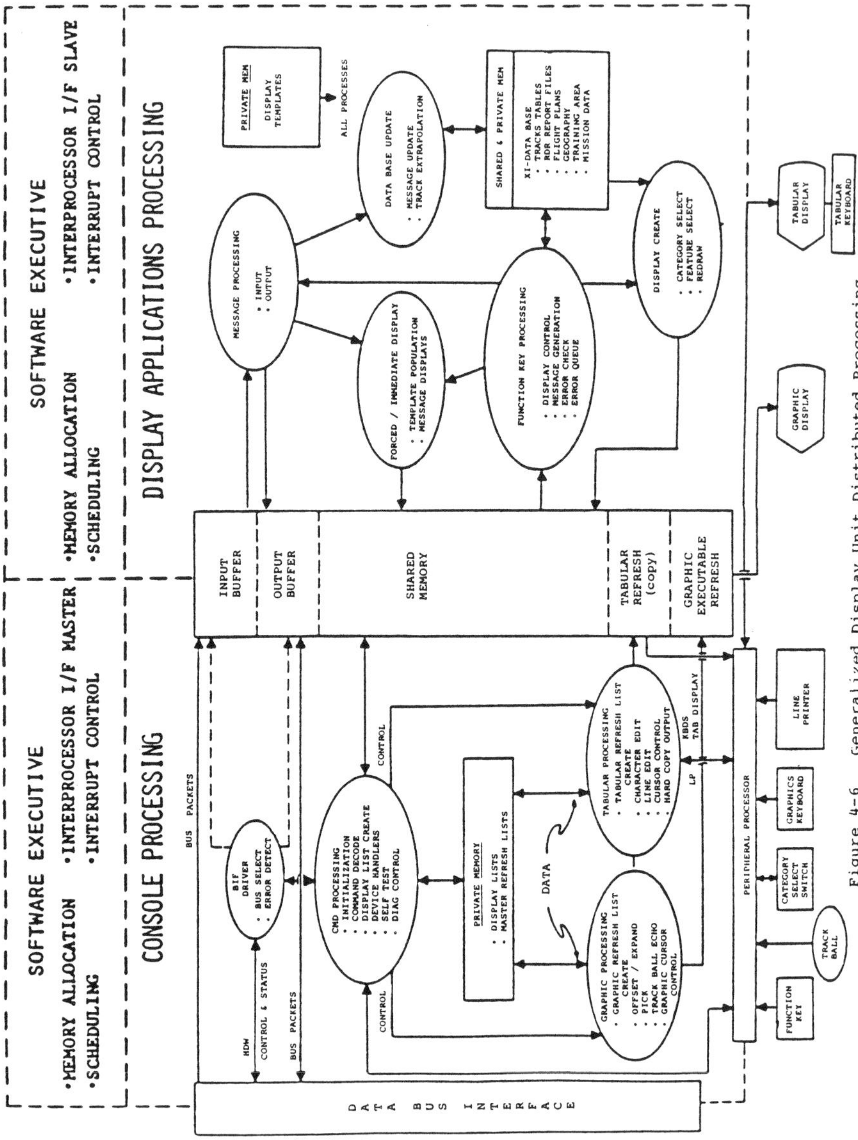

Figure 4-6 Generalized Display Unit Distributed Processing

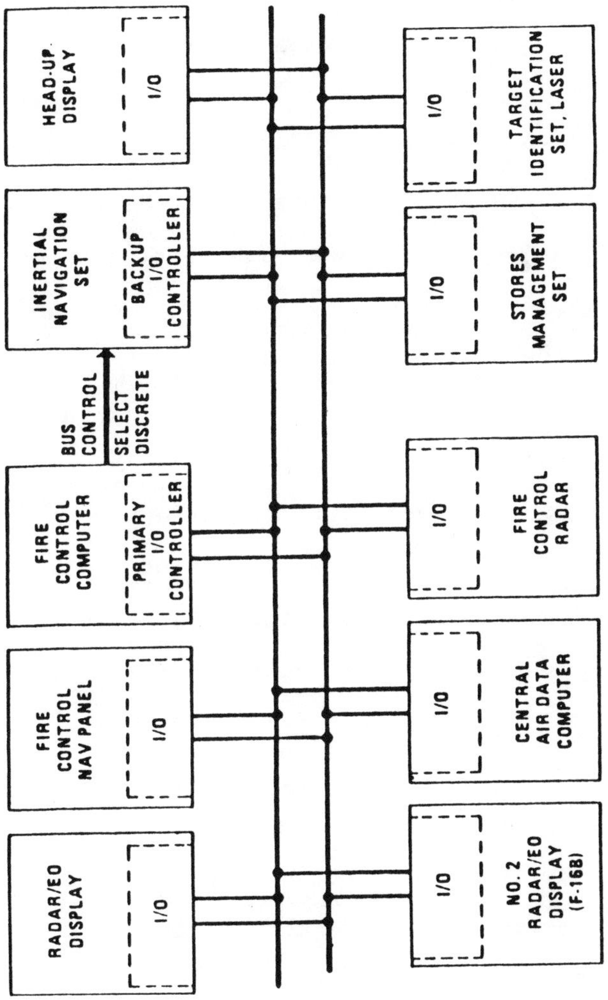

Figure 4-7 Distributed Data Processing Architecture for F-16 Aircraft

with MIL-STD-1553B Multiple Bus for the F-16 aircraft. The fire control computer is the systems integrator for this F-16 avionics and armament system. In this integration role, the fire control computer uses inputs from computer-controlled on-board sensor systems (e.g., radar, navigation, central air data computer, target identification set, etc.) to accomplish air-to-air and air-to-ground weapon delivery, navigation, fuel management, and stores management and control. Results of pertinent calculations are displayed on the radar E-O displays, NAV panels, and various other cockpit displays that are human-engineered for single-pilot operation. The F-16 system is unique in that it implements the standard military bus (MIL-STD-1553) with the latest version of this bus (MIL-STD-1553B) including additional subaddress modes, broadcast capability, improved noise rejection, and error-rate specifications. Use of this bus allows for distribution of the functional requirements to the various distributed computer systems and sensors.

As discussed previously, military computer systems span the spectrum from single microprocessors in "smart-bombs" or communications line controllers to multiple, distributed mainframes in world-wide Communication/Command/Control systems. These distributed processing systems can, however, be visualized as a region of a volume bounded by axes describing (1) distribution of hardware, (2) distribution of control, and (3) distribution of data bases. Figure 4-8 shows this volume as well as the relationship of uniprocessor systems to distributed processing systems. The particular use and performance, including reliability and maintainability, requirements of the computer system will determine where in the characteristic volume the system will be placed. Appendix A (Definition of the Scope of Embedded Distributed Processing Systems) discusses (1) the distribution of the various different types of military systems within this characteristic volume of Figure 4-8 and (2) the formulation of the various distributed processing systems into two high-level generic classifications: weapon systems and communication systems. Also presented in Appendix A (see Table A-1) are the key characteristics of the distributed processing systems which comprise these two generic categories.

The common thread linking the different types of distributed systems is the requirement to interconnect and communicate data and messages between the various processing elements. In many systems, serial communications lines are used as the interconnecting

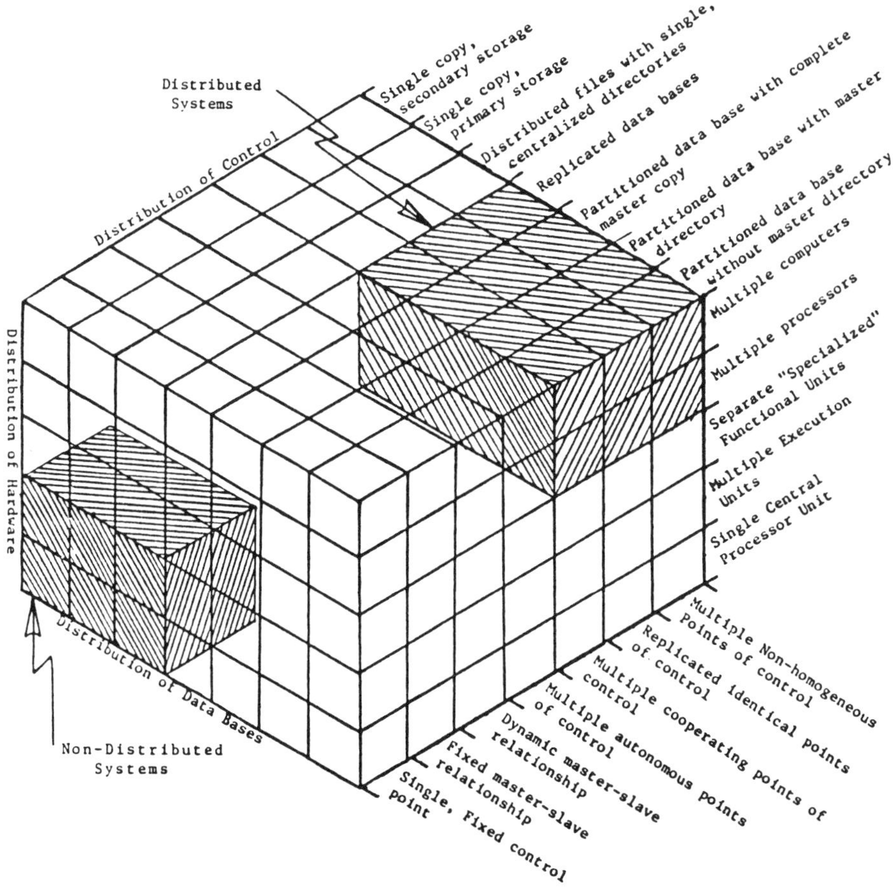

Figure 4-8 Characteristic Volume of Computer System Capabilities

links. For geographically dispersed systems, these links are usually provided by the common carriers or dedicated microwave systems. Hence, the designer of distributed systems is faced with significant communications issues. Generally, the analysis of these communications issues and interconnect technologies, with associated characteristics, is aided by grouping the various interconnect techniques and architectures into three generic classifications: 1) computer buses (elements geographically dispersed within 200 feet), 2) local area networks (elements geographically dispersed within 6000 feet), and 3) long haul networks (elements geographically dispersed over many miles). Figure 4-9 depicts the physical distance relationship for these communication networks. Table 4-1 identifies 12 common interconnect technologies, together with their performance, reliability, geographic distribution, and modularity and expandability characteristics that support maintainability. In addition to these interconnect topologies, a logical structure or protocol must be used to allow for meaningful communications. Protocol can be classified in five levels, not all of which exist in all networks:

(1) Line control procedures. This is the lowest level of protocol. It administers the physical transmission medium.

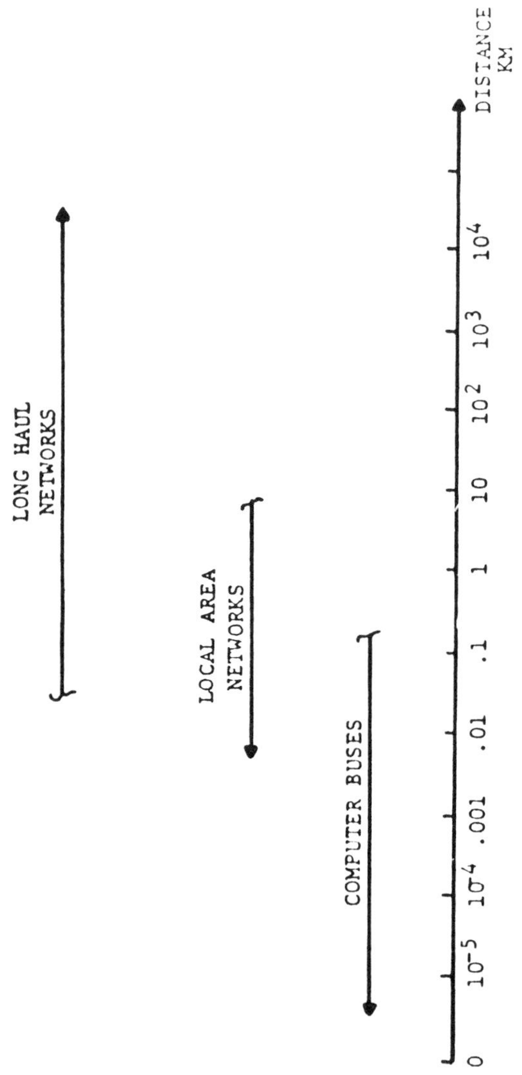

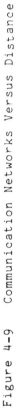

Figure 4-9 Communication Networks Versus Distance

Table 4-1 System Reliability Is a Driving Force for the Interconnect Technology

INTERCONNECT TECHNOLOGY		RELIABILITY	GEOGRAPHIC DISTRIBUTION	MODULARITY EXPANDABILITY	PERFORMANCE
COMPLETE INTERCONNECTION – THE COMPLETELY INTERCONNECTED ARCHITECTURE IS CONCEPTUALLY THE SIMPLEST DESIGN. IN THIS DESIGN EACH PROCESSOR IS CONNECTED BY A DEDICATED PATH TO EVERY OTHER PROCESSOR. COMMUNICATIONS COST BECOME PROHIBITIVE AS THE NUMBER OF PROCESSORS AND DISTANCES INCREASE.	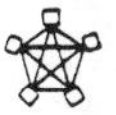	ONLY LOCAL PROBLEM IF MINI FAILS REDUNDANT PATHS FOR SINGLE LINK FAILURES (MAXIMUM)	UNLIMITED	FAIR NUMBER OF PORTS OF EACH MINI. • N - 1	TYPICALLY 2400-4800 bps 50 Kbps AND 1.544 Mbps POSSIBLE
PACKET SWITCHED NETWORK – MESSAGES BROKEN INTO PACKETS AND TRANSMITTED VIA AVAILABLE NODES. AT LEAST TWO PATHS EXIST BETWEEN ANY TWO COMPUTERS IN THE SYSTEM	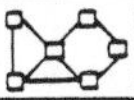	ONLY LOCAL PROBLEM IF MINI FAILS	UNLIMITED	GOOD	TYPICALLY 50 Kbps
REGULAR NETWORK – EVERY COMPUTER IS CONNECTED TO ITS TWO NEIGHBORS AND TWO COMPUTERS ABOVE AND BELOW IT. THE NETWORK GETS COMPLICATED IF THERE ARE VERY MANY COMPUTERS. THE "TREE" IS A HIERARCHICALLY STRUCTURED VARIATION WITH ANY PROCESSOR ABLE TO COMMUNICATE WITH ITS SUPERIOR AND ITS SUBORDINATES AS WELL AS ITS TWO NEIGHBORS	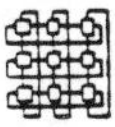	ONLY LOCAL PROBLEM IF MINI FAILS REDUNDANT PATHS FOR SINGLE CONNECT FAILURE	CAN BE UNLIMITED. TYPICALLY VERY LIMITED (10'S OF FEET)	POOR	TYPICALLY 3-5 Mbps
IRREGULAR NETWORK – THIS CONFIGURATION HAS NO CONSISTENT NEIGHBOR RELATIONSHIPS. IT IS COMMON IN GEOGRAPHICALLY DISPERSED NETWORKS WHERE COMMUNICATION LINKS CONTROL THE DESIGN	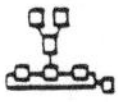	PARTIAL REDUNDANCY FOR LINK FAILURES (INCREASED RELIABILITY)	UNLIMITED	FAIR	TYPICALLY 2400-9600 bps
HIERARCHY – THIS CONFIGURATION IS USED IN PROCESS CONTROL AND DATA ACQUISITION APPLICATIONS. THE CAPABILITIES ARE SPECIALIZED AT LOWER LEVELS AND MORE GENERAL PURPOSE AT THE TOP.	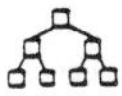	SYSTEM OPERABILITY REDUCED WITH SINGLE POINT FAILURE. MORE SERIOUS THE HIGHER UP THE FAILURE OCCURS.	UNLIMITED	GOOD	TYPICALLY 2400-9600 bps
LOOP OR RING – LOOP ARCHITECTURE EVOLVED FROM THE DATA COMMUNICATIONS ENVIRONMENT. IN THIS CONFIGURATION, EACH COMPUTER IS CONNECTED TO TWO NEIGHBORING COMPUTERS. THE TRAFFIC COULD FLOW IN BOTH DIRECTIONS, BUT CIRCULATING TRAFFIC IN ONE DIRECTION IS LESS COMPLICATED	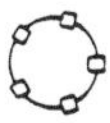	SYSTEM UNAFFECTED WITH SINGLE LOOP FAILURE FOR TWO-LOOP SYSTEM - CATASTROPHIC FOR SINGLE UNIDIRECTIONAL LOOP	LIMITED (100'S-1000'S OF FEET)	GOOD-LIMITED BY MINI ADDRESSSING CAPABILITY	PARALLEL UP TO 500 KILO WORDS/SEC SERIAL 1-3 Mbps
GLOBAL BUS – THE USE OF A COMMON OR GLOBAL BUS REQUIRES SOME ALLOCATION SCHEME FOR SENDING MESSAGES FROM ONE COMPUTER TO ANOTHER		ONLY LOCAL PROBLEM IF MINI FAILS CATASTROPHIC WITH BUS FAILURE	LIMITED (1000'S OF FEET)	GOOD	UP TO 50 Mbps TYPICAL 1-3 Mbps
STAR – THIS CONFIGURATION HAS A CENTRAL SWITCHING RESOURCE. EACH COMPUTER IS CONNECTED TO THE CENTRAL SWITCH. TRAFFIC IS IN BOTH DIRECTIONS	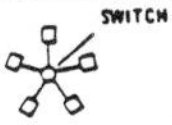	ONLY LOCAL PROBLEM IF MINI OR BUS FAILS. CATASTROPHIC IF SWITCH FAILS. SWITCH POSSIBLY LESS RELIABLE THAN BUS OR LOOP	LIMITED (1000'S OF FEET)	GOOD UNTIL SWITCH SATURATES	UP TO 3 Mbps
LOOP WITH SWITCH – THIS REFINEMENT OF THE LOOP PROVIDES A SWITCHING ELEMENT THAT REMOVES MESSAGES FROM THE LOOP, MAPS THEIR ADDRESSES, AND REPLACES THEM ON THE LOOP PROPERLY ADDRESSED TO THEIR INTENDED DESTINATION.	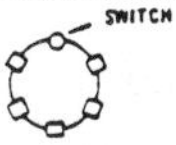	CATASTROPHIC IF EITHER SWITCH OR LOOP FAILS (REDUCED RELIABILITY)	LIMITED (100'S-1000'S OF FEET)	GOOD FAIR UNTIL SWITCH SATURATES	1-3 Mbps
BUS WINDOW – THIS CONFIGURATION HAS MORE THAN ONE SWITCH. MESSAGES MAY BE TRANSMITTED ON THE PATH THEY ARE RECEIVED OR ON ANOTHER. THE SWITCHES PROVIDE "WINDOWS" FOR PASSING MESSAGES BETWEEN BUSES.	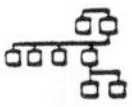	SERIOUS CONTENTION PROBLEMS. PARTIAL SYSTEM FAILURE IF SWITCH OR BUS FAILS	VERY LIMITED (10'S OF FEET)	POOR	200-500 KILO WORDS/SEC
BUS WITH SWITCH – THIS IS MORE LIKE THE GLOBAL BUS BECAUSE EACH COMPUTER IS CONNECTED TO THE CENTRAL SWITCH, AND TRAFFIC FLOWS FROM THE ORIGINATING COMPUTER TO THE SWITCH, AND FROM THE SWITCH TO THE DESTINATION COMPUTER. THE COMPUTERS SHARE THE PATH (BUS) TO SHARE ACCESS TO THE SWITCH.	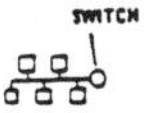	CATASTROPHIC IF BUS OR SWITCH FAILS	LIMITED (1000'S OF FEET)	GOOD FAIR UNTIL SWITCH SATURATES	UP TO 3 Mbps FOR SERIAL BUS
SHARED MEMORY – THE MOST COMMON WAY TO INTERCONNECT COMPUTER SYSTEMS IS TO COMMUNICATE BY LEAVING MESSAGES FOR ONE ANOTHER IN A COMMONLY ACCESSIBLE MEMORY. THE KEY CHARACTERISTIC IS THAT THE MEMORY IS USED AS A DATA PATH AS WELL AS STORAGE.		CATASTROPHIC IF MEMORY FAILS (MINIMUM)	VERY LIMITED (10'S OF FEET)	POOR-LIMITED TO NUMBER OF MEMORY PORTS	MEMORY SPEED 500 KW/SEC TO 3 MW/SEC

(2) Procedures to control data flow between communications processors (packet flow).

(3) Procedures to control data flow between a host computer and a communications processor.

(4) Procedures to allow flow between two distant host computers.

(5) Procedures to allow message flow between two user processes.

However, the particular categories of military systems most affected by technological advancements in embedded distributed processing include primarily the first two categories, local area networks and computer buses. The expansion of the von Neumann architecture within a multiprocess environment is typified by the diagram in Figure 4-10 and is characteristic of the interconnect technologies associated with the computer buses. Also in the computer bus technologies, the advances in Very-Large-Scale-Integration (VLSI) circuitry has offered new interconnect architectural alternatives which are shown in Figure 4-11 and are discussed in paragraphs 5.1 and 7.1. The key characteristic of the layered bus architecture is associated with its operation; in that, the communication between layers becomes probabilistic instead of deterministic as is the case with the von Neumann architecture. (Refer to paragraph 7.1.1 for a full explanation of this terminology.)

Local area networks (LAN) have evolved primarily from a need to provide data communication on a packet basis between increasingly intelligent terminals and host computer systems. The intelligent terminals are generally separated over larger distances than the internal workings of the computer buses, but at the same time these terminals are not nearly so distant as to require a communication link such as microwave or other long haul communication systems. Furthermore, LAN architecture and protocol is generally compatible with computer systems on a level not always achieved with long haul networks. Examples of the local area network are shown in Figure 4-2 and 4-3 in terms of the dual serial data bus. Dual bus topology is generally the preferred topology used with LAN systems since they offer acceptable performance and high reliability. Figure 4-12 shows some of the key advantages and disadvantages associated with the LAN bus topology. In a like manner, bus control strategies, examples of bus systems, and examples of transmission media are shown in Figures 4-13, 4-14, and 4-15, respectively. Table

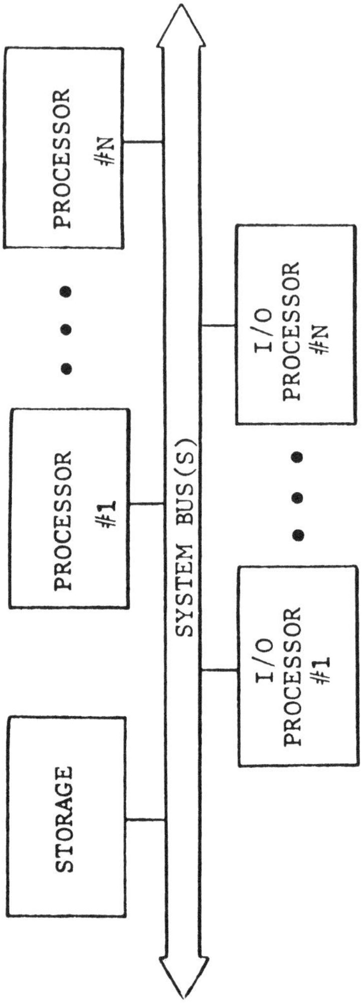

Figure 4-10 Expanded von Neumann Architecture

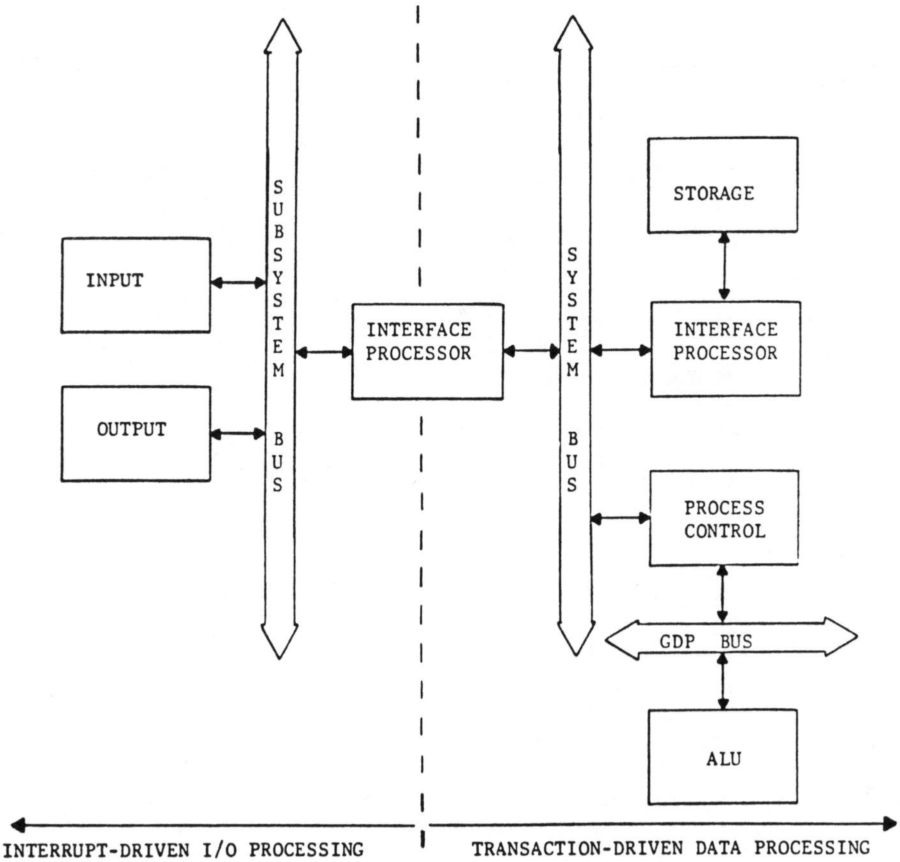

Figure 4-11 Layered Bus Architecture

4-2 is a compilation of the majority of LAN's currently available.

Six additional distributed processing characteristics which serve as motivations for the continued development of parallel (concurrent) processing systems are:

- Response time
- Flexibility
- Resource sharing
- Reliability
- Availability
- Transportability

The common denominator and ultimate result of improvements in these characteristics is improved overall system performance, usually measured also on the basis of cost effectiveness. These characteristics are further discussed as follows:

(1) Reliability - Redundancy, which is related to reliability, can be achieved in a relatively inexpensive manner in a distributed system since the entire system does not have to be replicated as is the case with a single computer. Only an incremental number of processors must be added to insure the

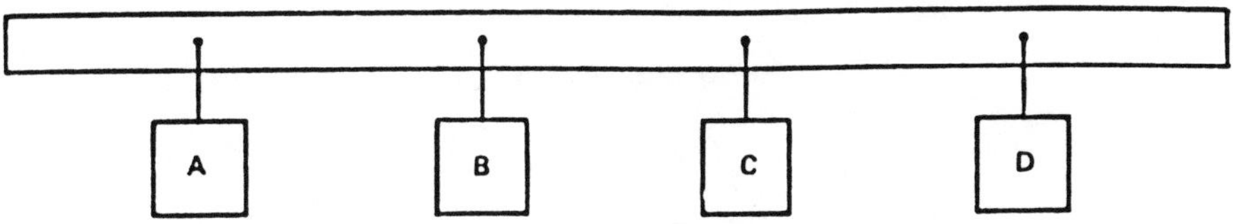

ADVANTAGES

- No Active Taps
- Interface Simplicity
- Fully Connected
- High Reliability (Distributed Control)

DISADVANTAGES

- Bandwith Limitations
- Probabilistic Access

Figure 4-12 Linear Bus Subnetwork Topology

Contention

- Transmit
- Listen before talk
- Listen while talk

Back Off Strategies

- Fixed delay
- Adaptive delay
- Random delay

Figure 4-13 Bus Control Strategies

- Ethernet (Xerox)
- Mitre-bus (Mitre)
- Ford net (FACC)
- NSC-hyperchannel (Network Systems)
- LCN (UNIVAC)
- CABLENET (AMDAX CORP.)

Figure 4-14 Examples of Bus Systems

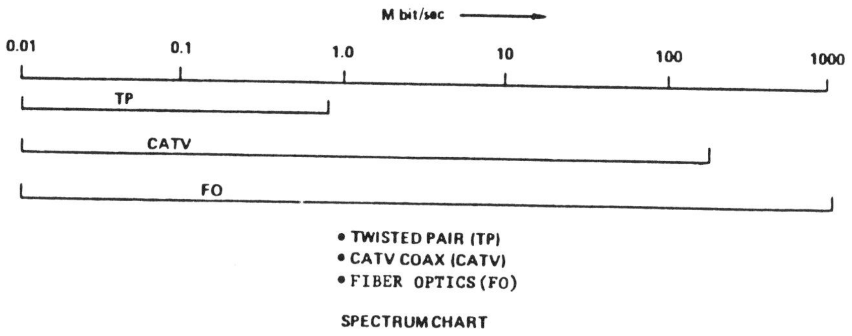

Figure 4-15 Transmission Media

Local Network	Company	Trans-Mission Medium	Max No. of Nodes	Network Archi-tecture	Access Scheme	Max length of Interno-dal trans-mission medium	Max Data Rate	Applications	Comments
Attached Resource Computer (ARC)	Datapoint Corp.	Broad-band coax/non-coherent infrared energy	255	Star	Proprie-tary	4 miles for coax. 1 mi.for infrared	2.5Mb/s	Office auto-mation, data processing	Each processor node can parti-cipate in up to 6 ARCs
Cluster/ One Model A	Nestar Systems Inc.	Baseband multi-conductor cable	64	Arbi-trary (bus, star, etc.)	CSMA/ CD	1000 ft	250 kb/s Low	Office auto-mation,person-al computers, general-purpose	Free-form topology due to low data rates
Distri-buted Operating Multi Access Inter Network (DOMAIN)	Apollo Computer Corp.	Broad-band coax	Several hundred	Ring	Token passing	3000 ft	12Mb/s Mb/s	Engineering scientific, CAD/CAM, gen-eral-purpose	Virtual file accessing, can page across network in a virtual en-vironment
ETHERNET	Xerox Corp.	Baseband coax	100	Bus	CSMA/ CD	2.5 km	10 Mb/s	Office automation	Maximum separa-tion between stations is 2.5 km.
HYPER-channel	Network Systems Corp.	Base-band coax	16 Low	Bus	CSMA/ CA	Unavail-able	50 Mb/s	Scientific, large computer centers	Link adapters allow a node to be attached to 4 independent trunk-to-trunk interfacing via microwave,fiber optics, and com-mon carrier lines.
HYPER-bus	*	*	*	*	Hybrid CSMA/CD (ACK)	*	6 Mbs		

Table 4-2 Typical Local Area Network Products

Local Network	Company	Trans-Mission Medium	Max No. of Nodes	Network Archi-tecture	Access Scheme	Max length of Interno-dal trans-mission medium	Max Data Rate	Applications	Comments
Modway	Modcon Div. of Gould Inc.	Base-band or broad-band coax, fi-ber optics	250	Arbi-tary (bus, star, etc.)	Token passing	15,000 ft	1,544 Mb/s	Data process-ing, process control	Compatible with microwave and satelite-commun-ications faci-lities for com-mon-carrier transmissions
WANGNET	Wang Labs	Broad-Band coax		Open Loop					
Utility Band	Wang Labs	"	7 Channels		None	N/A	N/A	Video	Supplies 7 channels to com-posite video equipment
Intercon-nect Band	"	"	32	"	None	N/A	9.6Kb/J		Modem
			16				64 Kbs		Modem
Wang Band	"	Broad Band coax	Many	"	CSMA/CD (802)	N/A	12 MHz		X.25 SDLC com-patible and CSMA/CD com-patible
Loosely coupled Network LCN	Control Data Corp.	Base Band coax	106	Trunk + Node	Rotating Priority Synchron-our mode TOKEN	3000 ft	50 MHz	Large Computers	Not x.25 compatible compares with Hyperchannel
IMUX	SCI, Systems	Base Band	100	Bus	Conten-tion	1000 ft.	10 MHz	Data Bus Systems	

Table 4-2 (continued)

Local Network	Company	Trans-Mission Medium	Max No. of Nodes	Network Archi-tecture	Access Scheme	Max length of Interno-dal trans-mission medium	Max Data Rate	Applications	Comments
Net/One	Unger-manu-Bass Inc.	Base-band coaz	250	Bus	CSMA/CD	4000 ft	4 Mb/s	OEM systems, data process-ing, scientific office auto-mation, pro-cess control	Intelligent net-work interface units can be programmed to interface to a wide variety of terminals
Omnlink	Northern Telecom Inc.	Broad-band coax	9 Low	Ring	Token passing	5000 ft	40 kb/s	Data process-ing, office automation	Each node can have indepen-dent and accessible files peripherals and processors
Primenet	Prime computer Inc.	Base-band coax	15 Low	Ring	Token passing	750 ft	10 Mb/s	Data process-ing, large computer centers	CCITT X.25-com-patible for interfacing to other networks over long dis-tances
Z-Net	Zilog Inc.	Base-band coax	255	Bus	CSMA/CD	2 km	800 kb/s Low	Office auto-mation, small business computers	Emulator pack-age allows data transfer between Zilog equipment and other vendors' equipment

Table 4-2 (Continued)

Local Network	Company	Trans-Mission Medium	Max No. of Nodes	Network Archi-tecture	Access Scheme	Max length of Interno-dal trans-mission medium	Max Data Rate	Applications	Comments
Localnet Systems 20 & 40	Sytek Inc.	Broad-band coax	256/ channel	Bus	CSMA/ CD	30 km	120 kb/s, 2 Mb/s	Distributed processing design auto-mation	Each channel has CSMA/CD accessing. Up to 120 channels per cable
Cablenet	Amdax Corp.	Coax Broad Band	16,000	Bus	Hybrid TDMA conten-tion	50 miles	14 MHz	Universal	Protocol Free
DPS	Litton			Loop	SDLC	200M	20 MHz		Main Computer tie-in using noses $100,000/ node - see Electronics July 14, 1981
MITRE X	MITRE	Coax Broad Band		Bus	Hybrid		1 MHz		LWT
Cambridge Ring	Cambridge Univ. (Logica Ltd. (Toltec Data, Ltd)	Twisted Pair cable Fiber Optic cable	15 Expand-able	Ring	Rotating Slots	100M Long Distances	10 MHz	For terminals, Computer tie ins	Will interface with most

Table 4-2 (Continued)

required degree of availability. Also simpler, and hence more reliable, software structures may be achievable in a collection of small distributed processors.

(2) Response time - The distributed system can be more responsive because direct access to a computer or processing element can be provided to smaller user communities. This responsiveness can take the form of reduced turn-around time in a batch environment and faster response times in a real-time environment.

(3) Flexibility - A distributed system in danger of overload can be expanded incrementally at low cost by the addition of more processors. Also a host computer system in danger of overload can be preserved by offloading functions onto smaller processors.

(4) Resource sharing - A distributed network of computing systems allows users at one location to take advantage of resources that are available at other locations. These resources could consist of programs, data buses, and computational power. Resource-sharing

networks allow load balancing, backup, and reduced duplication of effort.

(5) Availability - Enhanced system availability can be achieved in a distributed system by means of improved reliability and maintainability. Specifically, system maintenance functions can be performed in parallel with system operation, if appropriate redundancy in key system elements, such as processors, memory, displays and peripherals is also provided.

(6) Transportability - Redundancy also supports system transportability by providing the means whereby the system processes can be shifted to the various distributed data processor elements.

In summary, the grouping of (1) the distributed processing systems, (2) the interconnect technologies, and (3) the overall system characteristics has benefitted the Distributed Processing Tools Definition study by allowing the requirements for tools and techniques to be layered by classes of generic military systems with associated interconnect technologies.

5. State-of-the-Art Technologies

The scope of embedded distributed processing systems has grown too broad for the computer specialists of today to understand. These specialists concentrate on a single aspect of the whole instead of the whole itself. Until a new group of computing professionals assumes the more general viewpoint the specialist of today must be used. Their use requires some degree of modularization. Different groups of specialized individuals should be able to maintain separate modules without interfering with one another. This requires clever design of both hardware and software. Furthermore, the dichotomy between hardware and software is not clear within embedded distributed processing systems. A clever design in hardware impacts software and vice versa. The current situation is doubly serious because of the highly specialized nature of existing computing personnel. An obvious polarity exists within these personnel. Some prefer the hardware issues and gravitate to an engineering orientation. Others prefer software issues and gravitate toward real-time systems, operating systems, compilers, security, network systems, etc. However, such a polarity only indicates the knowledge gap which must be overcome by a new group of computer professionals.

Current organizations generally group their computing design efforts together. Their span of control ranges from a purely hardware orientation to a software orientation. The subsequent section acknowledges such an organization. In the following section, hardware technologies will be addressed. After those, a section on software technologies is presented. The issues raised in either section impact the other. Such cross correlation should be kept in mind as the sections are read.

5.1 Hardware Technologies

Modern embedded distributed processing systems are being influenced primarily by two hardware circuit technologies: (1) Very-Large-Scale-Integrated (VLSI) circuits and (2) Very-High-Speed-Integrated Circuits (VHSIC). In fact, these hardware technologies in conjunction with the current software crisis (software cost, reliability, and management) has caused a flurry of research during the past few years; and, this research has resulted in a number of technological advances that relate to the embedded distributed processing systems. Figure 5-1 illustrates the industrial trends in VLSI and VHSIC. The key technological advances can, generally, be grouped as follows:

- Development of algorithmically specialized processors; e.g., nxn mesh of interconnected microprocessors

- Development of new computer architectures; e.g., Intel iAPX432 computer system

- Development of specialized embedded processors with appropriate protocol to support local area bus networks; e.g., VLSI chips to support Ethernet.

5.1.1 Algorithmically Specialized Processors

Examples of algorithmically specialized processors include designs for (1) Logical Unit (LU) matrix decomposition which is the main step in solving systems of linear equations; (2) tree processors which are used in searching, sorting and expression

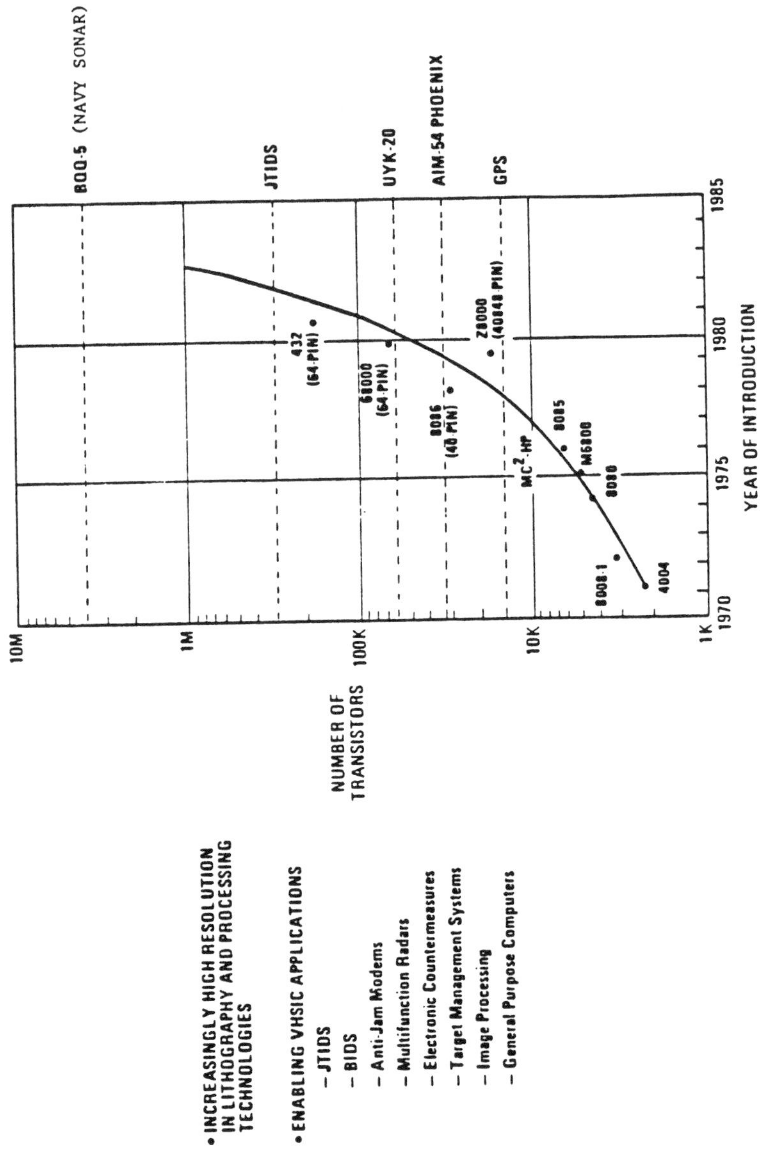

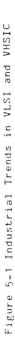

Figure 5-1 Industrial Trends in VLSI and VHSIC

evaluation; (3) dynamic programming matrix processors which are used for general problem solving; and (4) joint processors which are used for data base querying. Many researchers are, however, going to a more flexible approach which is to replace these dedicated processing elements with more general microprocessors and simply to program the algorithmically specialized processors. This solution is much more flexible since different components can use the same devices by changing programs and, with more recent research results, the interconnection patterns. Figure 5-2 shows some examples of the interconnection patterns used for specific functions. Figure 5-3 shows three examples of switch lattices which are used to reconfigure the matrices of general purpose microprocessor systems. The switch lattices are regular structures which are formed from programmable switches connected by data paths.

The Department of Computer Science personnel at Purdue University has developed a multimicroprocessor computer system (which is part of the research under the Blue CHiP Project) using this general processor and switching lattices network technology named the Configurable, Highly Parallel (CHiP)

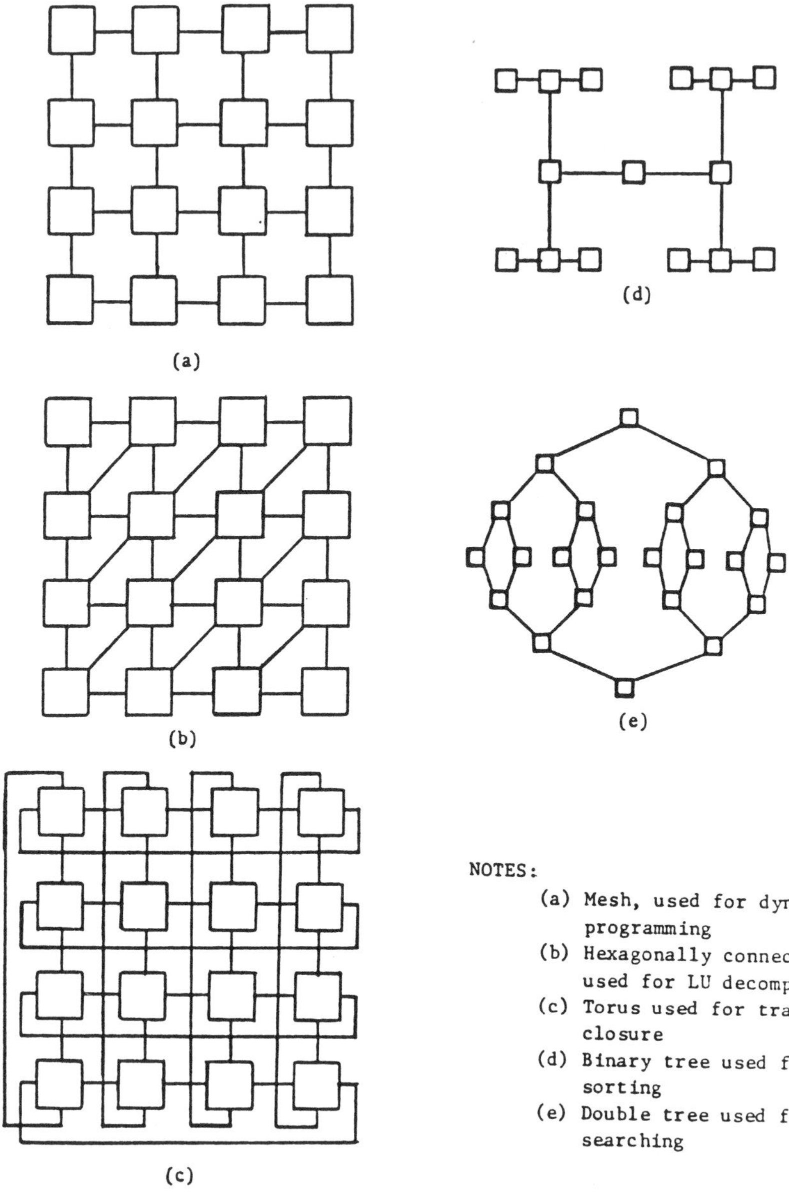

NOTES:

(a) Mesh, used for dynamic programming
(b) Hexagonally connected mesh used for LU decomposition
(c) Torus used for transitive closure
(d) Binary tree used for sorting
(e) Double tree used for searching

Figure 5-2 Interconnection Patterns for Algorithmically Specialized Processors

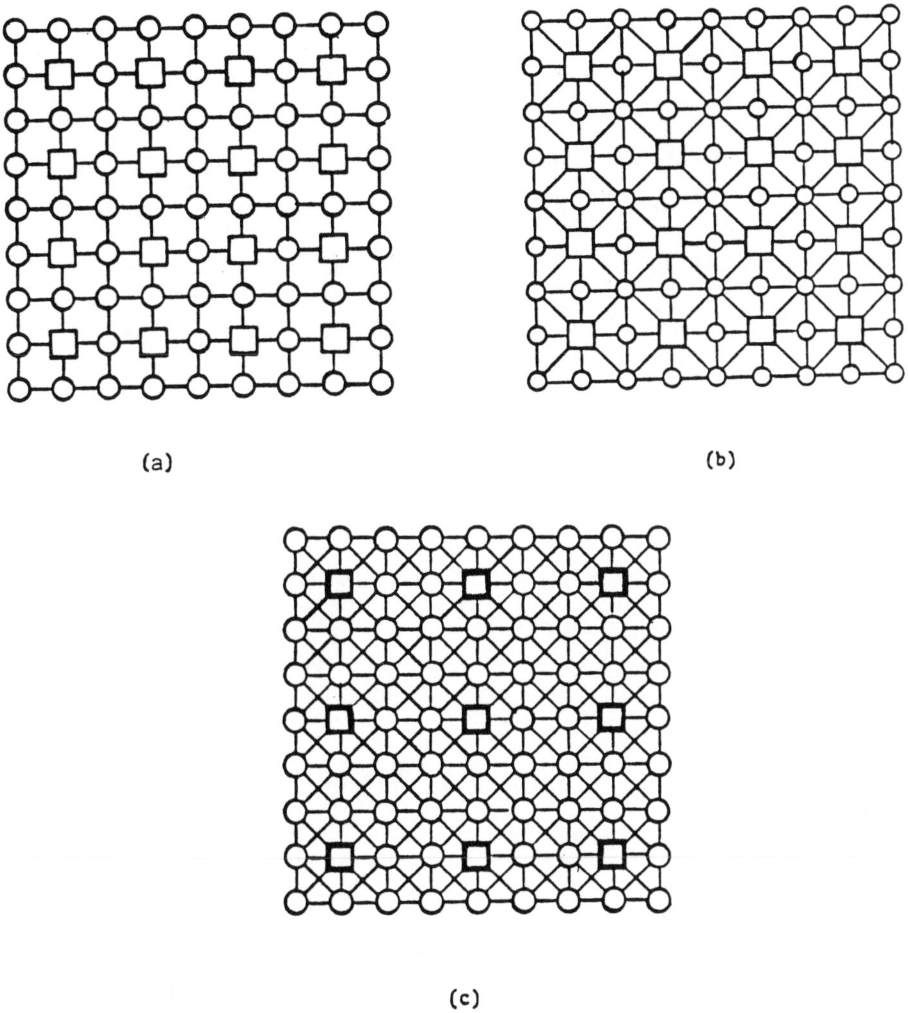

NOTE: Circles represent switches;
Squares represent processors

Figure 5-3 Three Switch Lattice Structures

Computer. The objective of this project is to provide the flexibility needed to compose general problem solutions while retaining the benefits of uniformity and locality that the algorithmically specialized processors exploit. The CHiP computer is a family of architectures each constructed from three components: (1) a collection of homogeneous microprocessors with associated memory, (2) a switch lattice, and (3) a controller. The switch lattice is the most important component and the main source of differences among family members; i.e., Figure 5-3(a), 5-3(b), and 5-3(c). The controller is responsible for loading the switch memory. CHiP processing begins with the controller broadcasting a command to all switches to invoke a particular configuration setting. For example suppose it is a mesh pattern (see Figure 5-2(a)) and a three switch lattice representation is used (see Figure 5-3). With the entire structure interconnected into a mesh, the individual microprocessor systems synchronously execute the instructions stored in their local memory. When a new phase of processing is to begin, the controller broadcasts a command to all switches to invoke a new configuration setting, say the one for a tree. With the lattice restructured into a tree interconnection pattern (see Figure 5-2(d)), the microprocessor systems resume processing, having spent only a single logical step in interphase structure reconfiguration. All three switch lattice structures of Figure 5-3 are capable of representing such an interconnection pattern. Other modes of operation include the operation of the microprocessor matrix with multiple instruction streams and multiple data streams. In this mode of parallelism, each processor takes its instructions and its data from its associated memory. As in the other mode, the interconnection network provides interprocessor communication. The overview of the CHiP computer family has been superficial, but it provided a context in which to present one hardware technological advancement category. Figures 5-4 and 5-5 show other system level architectures of the microprocessor matrix being used by the government, under support from System Development Corporation, at ARC Huntsville, Alabama.

5.1.2 Local Area Networks

In the area of other VLSI/VHSIC technology advancements, interconnect techniques/technologies are of vital importance to multiprocessor system

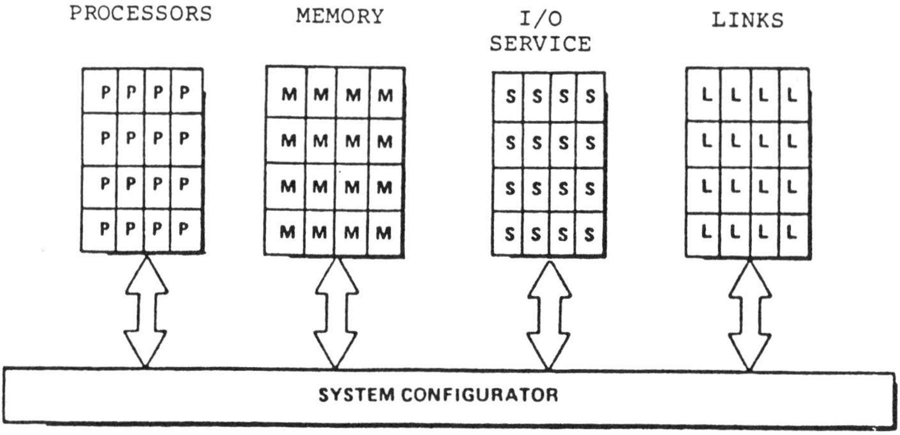

- OBJECTIVES
  - EMULATION OF DISTRIBUTED PROCESSING ARCHITECTURES
  - HIGH FIDELITY SIMULATION OF LWIRS SENSORS AND RADAR ANTENNA ELEMENTS
  - SUPPORT INTERFACES WITH SPECIAL-PURPOSE OPTICAL PROCESSORS
- FOURTH GENERATION MICROPROCESSOR HARDWARE
  - INTEL 8086
  - ZILOG Z8000
  - MOTOROLA MC 68000
- SYSTEM CONFIGURATOR
  - SWITCHING NETWORKS
  - PROGRAMMABLE INTERCONNECTION WITH BIT-SLICE

Figure 5-4 Multiple Microprocessor System

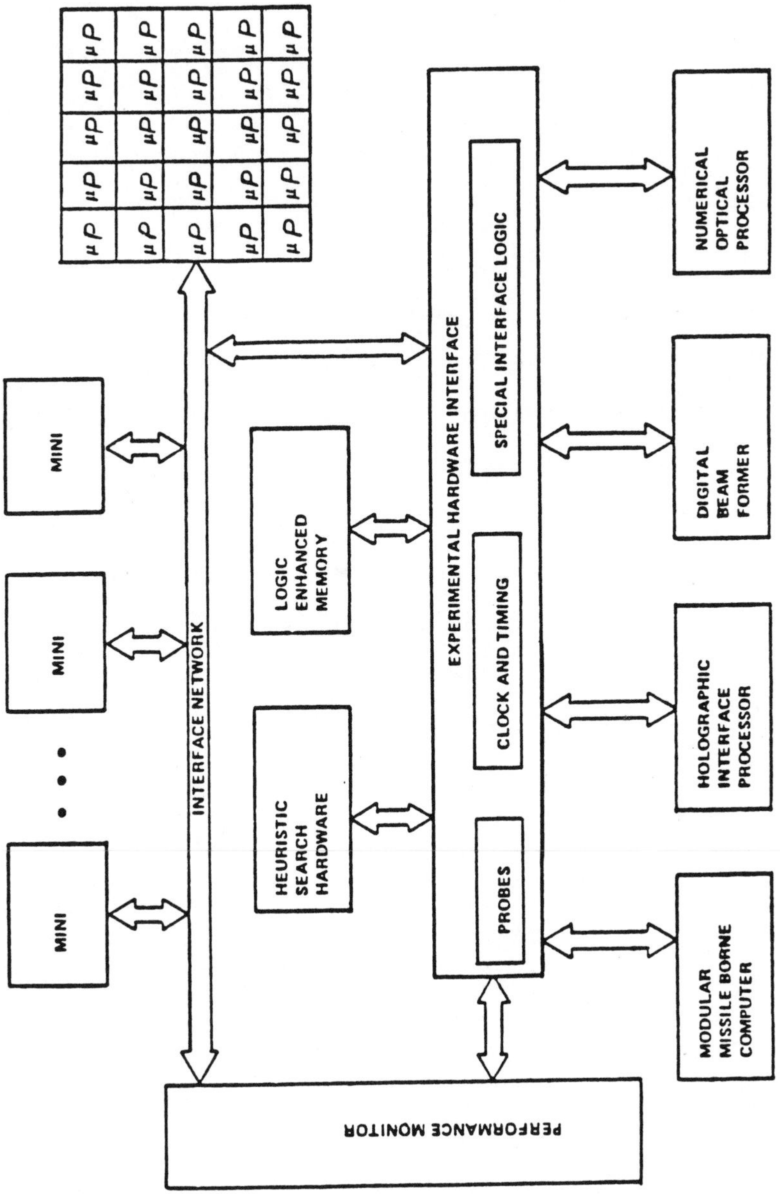

Figure 5-5 Advanced Data Processing Testbed - Laboratory Model Hardware

operation. In fact, all distributed data processing systems are characterized by the requirements to interconnect and communicate data and messages between the various processing elements. However, local area networks and computer bus technologies have increasingly occupied the attention of research workers. As discussed in paragraph 4.0, local area networks are data communications systems for the interconnection of terminal and distributed data processing elements that are within one building, in several buildings on the same property, or in close proximity; as contrasted with the more familiar local and long-haul networks for private lines, public switched services, and private switched systems. The total extent of a local area network may thus be as little as a few hundred meters, or as great as several kilometers. Furthermore, the characteristic that sets recently-announced local area networks apart from conventional local and long-haul networks is bandwidth. It is feasible and relatively inexpensive to implement bandwidths or data rates of 10 megabytes per second (Mbps) in local area networks. Because of (1) the varying views of local network designers and users in regard to the diversity of types of devices to the connected, (2) the need for consistency of local network protocols with mainframe protocols, and (3) the desire to interoperate local networks and various external networks, such as the packet-switched common carrier networks, standardized, off-the-shelf local area networks are somewhat limited. DEC, Intel, and Xerox are, however, developing a specification with associated VLSI chips to support Ethernet Carrier Sense Multiple Access with Collision Detection (CSMA-CD) method of control. Xerox provides the basic local network design; DEC contributes the system design expertise in the area of communication transceivers and mini-computer networks; and Intel supplies the expertise in the partitioning of complex communications functions into micro-computer systems and VLSI components. The main problem with Ethernet occurs when two stations begin transmitting at the same instant. Such an event wastes the channel for an entire packet time. In this method a station wishing to transmit listens first for channel clear, and then transmits if such is the case. Collision detection is also implemented for the case where two stations transmit simultaneously. The characteristics of this network include a 10-Mbps data rate, coaxial cable medium with 500 meter Computer Interface Unit (CIU) spacing, and a datagram link-level protocol. The VLSI/VHSIC technologies are allowing many other companies, such as Zilog, to follow suit with their network versions as well. As discussed previously, detailed discussions of the characteristics of various interconnects/networks are presented in paragraph 4.0.

5.1.3 Bus Technologies

Primary advances in the computer bus technologies, as related to embedded distributed processing systems, are computer architectures which are characterized by multiple computer buses. Detail discussions of these multiple bus architectures are presented in paragraphs 6.3 and 7.1.1.

5.1.4 New Computer Architectures - iAPX432

The Intel iAPX432 computer architecture includes, in addition to multiple buses, the total impact of the VLSI/VHSIC technologies on modern computer architectures. Figure 5-6 presents the Intel iAPX432 structure along with key features/characteristics. As noted on the figure, bus bandwidth limits system performance. Figure 5-

- INTERCONNECTIVITY USING BUSES
- DATA STRUCTURE ENCODING
  - Huffmann Code
  - Assumed Frequency of Occurrence
- BUS BANDWIDTH LIMITS PERFORMANCE
- USES Ada MODULARIZATION
- TRANSACTION DRIVEN ARCHITECTURE
  - Interface Processors Control Bus Traffic
  - Interface Processors Control Data FLow
- HIGHLY-CONCURRENT ARCHITECTURE
- VLSI PRODUCT

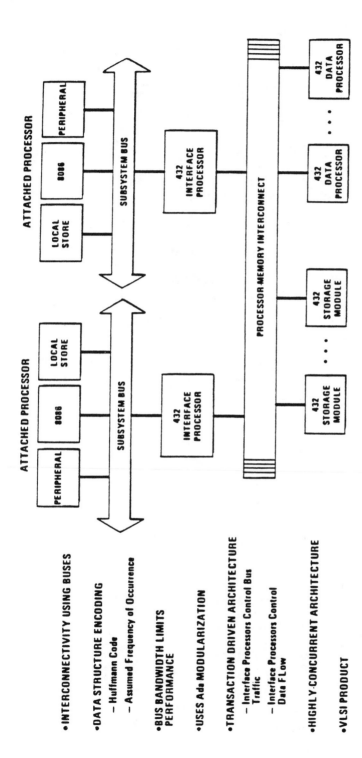

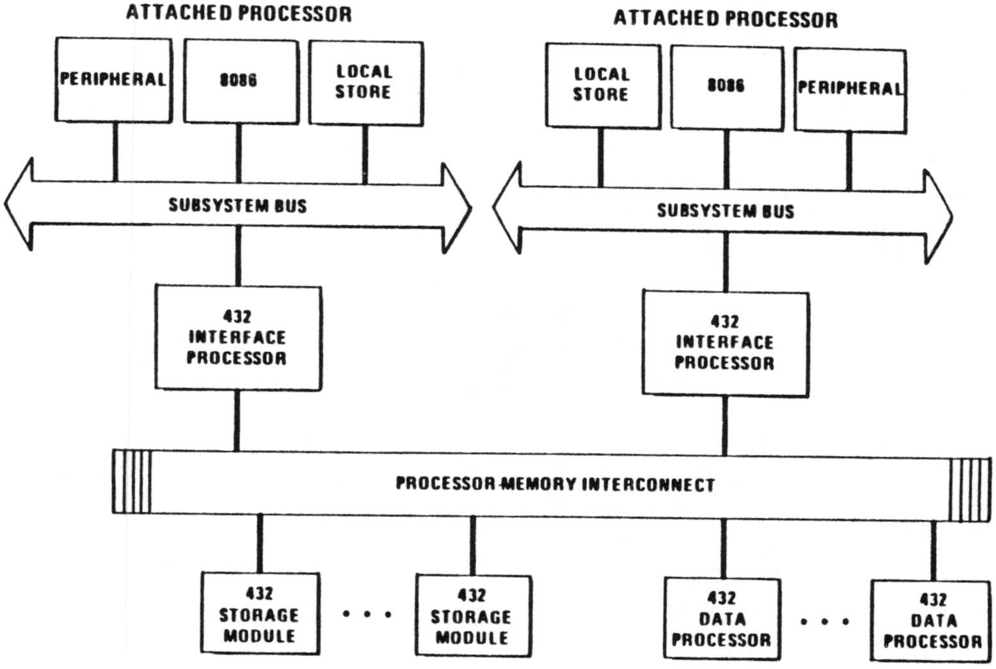

Figure 5-6 Intel iAPX432 Computer Structure

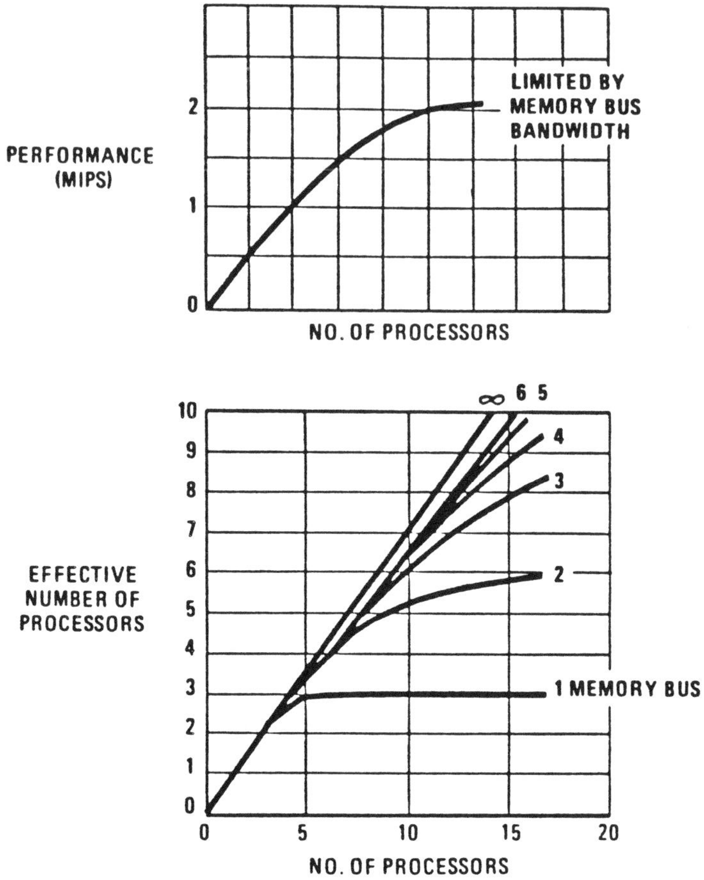

- BUS BANDWIDTH LIMITS PERFORMANCE

- INCREASING THE NUMBER OF BUSES, INCREASES INTERCONNECTIVITY PROBLEMS

- INCREASING INTERCONNECTIVITY, INCREASES CONCURRENT OPERATING CAPABILITY

- INCREASING CONCURRENT OPERATION, INCREASES DEMAND ON THE HOL FOR CONCURRENT SOFTWARE

Figure 5-7 Impact of Performance Planning for iAPX432

7 further illustrates this characteristic by showing that 2 million instructions per second (MIPS) is the upper throughput performance limit with current memory bandwidth and a single memory bus. The figure also shows the relationship of the effective number of processors versus the number of memory buses. As an example, a five processor configuration with only one memory bus would have throughput performance capabilities (measured in MIPS) of only three processors; whereas, two memory buses would increase the effective number of processors to about 3.5. However, a ten processor configuration would require two memory buses to achieve a five processor throughput. Figure 5-8 shows the performance of the Intel iAPX432 computer as compared to other computer types; and Figure 5-9 shows the new approach to hardware fault detection which can be implemented within Intel iAPX432 architecture. With this new hardware fault detection, the iAPX432 hardware can detect many different fault conditions, from attempting to execute data, to complex faults involving several processes. Once a fault is detected, the operation is aborted, and a complete description of the fault is reported. In a multiprocess system, a fault may cause one processor to suspend itself and begin

running diagnostics, but the other processors can usually keep the system operating.

In summary, advances in VLSI circuits and VHSIC technologies are having major impacts on modern embedded distributed processing systems. Specific impacts, on computer system capacity trends are itemized as follows:

- Increasing Programming Payloads
- Exceeding Requirements of Existing Military Standards
  - 1750A
  - 1553B
  - 1765 (Proposed)
- Increasing Tightly-Coupled Configurations
- Increasing Concurrent Hardware Operation
- Improving Error/Correction Capability

In a like manner, the impacts of VLSI/VHSIC technologies on computer timing trends are summarized as follows:

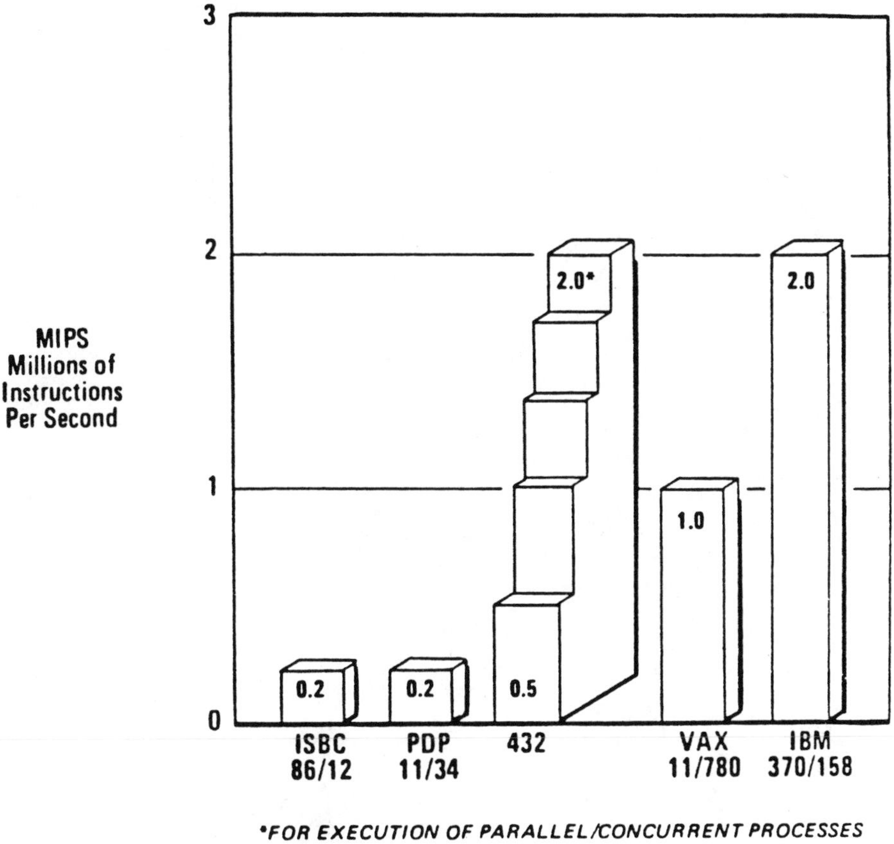

Figure 5-8 Performance Comparison

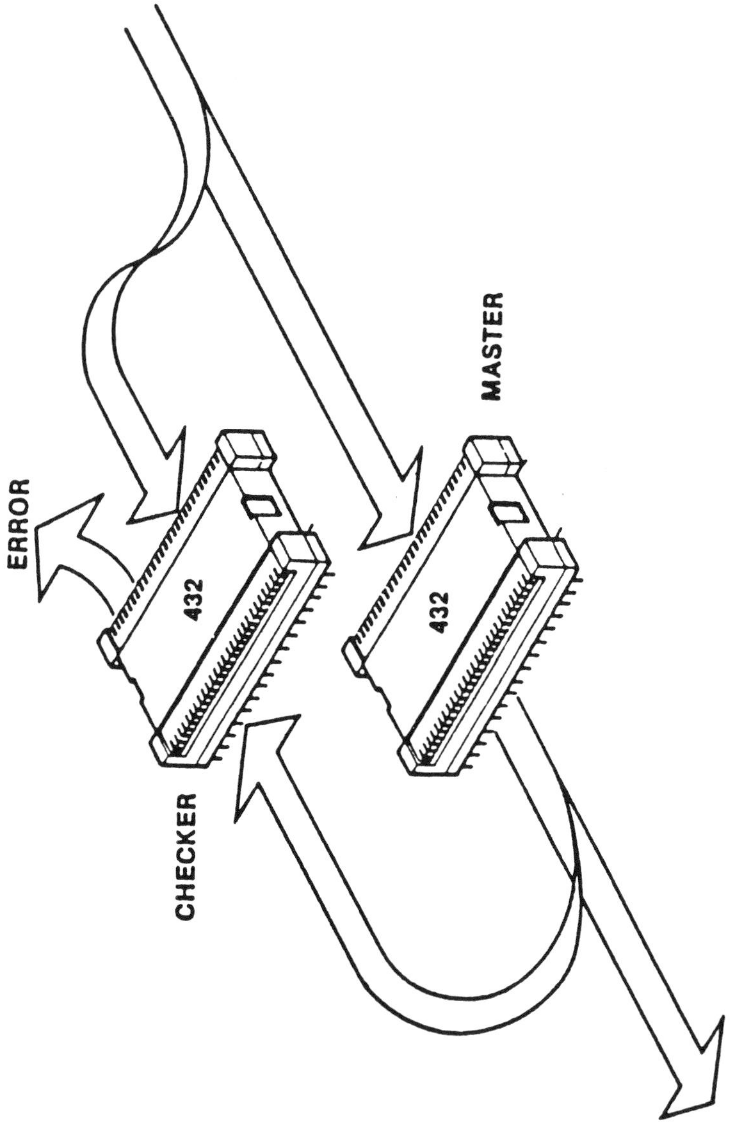

Figure 5-9 Hardware Fault Detection

- Faster Hardware Performance
- Increases in Concurrent Software
- Increases in Solution Complex Timing Problems
- Transparent Higher Order Languages (HOL) With Hardware-Related Timing Mechanisms
- Transaction-Driven Systems
- Highly-Distributed Intelligence with Independent Decision Making

5.2 Software Technologies

As the scope of embedded distributed processing systems continues to grow, their productivity becomes increasingly important. Software engineering is crucial to meeting that need. More manageable approaches to software development are essential. Important new aspects of software engineering address the following areas:

- Improved tools for software developments

- Improved facilities for software development
- Powerful specification and implementation languages
- Effective human interfaces with software
- Software performance engineering
- Appropriate modularizations
- Enhanced adaptability and reusability of modules
- Assurance of correctness.

Present embedded distributed processing systems are being implemented with VLSI components. Such components require their own internal operating systems which are usually implemented in microcode. Software development tools for these VLSI components can be characterized as inadequate. This characterization is not new. Users of large mainframes have long encountered inadequacies when they attempt to build integrated portfolios of applications programs upon a centralized data base. The availability of tools within the large mainframe environment has been scarce. In the VLSI environment such tools are virtually non-existent. Despite such obvious tool shortages embedded distributed processing systems continue to grow and expand. Underlying this growth and expansion is a universal desire to increase productivity. The problem comes in realizing that desire. The objective is difficult to achieve. Some degree of performance management must be applied in the initial stages of the design phase. Furthermore, performance management issues must continually be addressed throughout the remaining software development lifecycle phases. Subsequent sections will address the new aspects of software engineering which have been enumerated above in the present section.

5.2.1 Improved Tools for Software Development - Set(s) of Tools Covering Entire Lifecycle

The Ada Programming Support Environment (APSE) provides its own set of tools; i.e., compiler, debugger, linker-loader, editor, run controller, and configuration manager. With the growing use of object-oriented modularization such tools are not sufficient. Additional ones with carefully defined links to each phase of the software system lifecycle are required. Additional simulation tools would help. Examples would include simulators to simplify feasibility analyses, requirements languages, software specification languages, design languages, and static analysis. Most helpful would be formal verification tools, testing tools, change impact analyzers, and optimizers. Management aids for planning and control are also needed.

More than a single set of tools covering the entire lifecycle remains a distinct possibility. No single methodology seems to be emerging which means divergence might require several tool sets. Such divergence is not in concert with standardization. Consequently, unless a methodology offers an important feature which is unique, it should not be used as justification for an independent tool set.

Many individual tools establish development requirements of their own. Despite such need the subsequent concentration should be toward the complete tool set applicable throughout the lifecycle phases. The obvious benefit would be the reduction of errors but greater continuity would also be evident between the phases.

Several efforts have already been undertaken to develop a toolset for the entire lifecycle. One such effort is the Unix Programmer's Workbench (PWB) which possesses tools with crude compatibility. That compatibility derives from the byte-string nature of all Unix files which enables any tool to read the output from any other tool. Meaningful programming is another matter. Another effort is Maestro which exhibits clear compatibility as well as clear incompatibilities. Neither Unix nor Maestro contains the full spectrum of desired tools. Other efforts include the development environment CADES by ICL, USE by UCSF, Gandalf by CMU, and DREAM by the University of Colorado at Boulder.

5.2.2 Improved Facilities for Software Development - Programmer Workstation

The arrival of VLSI circuitry enables processing power and memory to be consolidated locally for use by programmers. The concept is to provide advanced graphics and displays in a single unit called a programmer workstation. These multi-media, multi-screen stations can provide powerful programmer/computer interfaces which can increase programmer productivity. One example of this approach is the SPICE workstation at Carnegie-Mellon University.

Workstations can provide an interface between the programmers and software engineers with their respective computer systems. The centralized computational power provides the data base management capability. Modularity of both hardware and software allows modification to match individual programmer need and the installation of updated technology. Standardized features and interfaces within the workstation can reduce training time for programmers assigned under new projects.

Considerable research into workstations is needed. Low cost configurations with appropriate modularity must be combined for ease of use by the programmer. Workstation software has yet to be established. Such software must be modified easily, portable, and capable of rapid installation.

Current interest in local area networks has heightened the interest in programmer workstations. Groups in human factors research and standardization are also interested in such workstations.

Many types of workstations are currently under development. Most prominent is SPICE at the Carnegie-Mellon University. Another is being developed by Xerox at its Palo Alto Research Center. The National Science Foundation is sponsoring Project Quanta at Purdue University to generate a problem solving environment.

5.2.3 Powerful Specification and Implementation Languages - Configurable, Highly Parallel Computers

Under von Neumann architecture used by uniprocessors, computer functionality can be changed simply by changing programs. This ability to change has become so familiar that it is now considered to be obvious and is seldom discussed. Structured programming has produced a top-down methodology ideally suited for this uniprocessor architecture. However, programs can be viewed from a variety of directions. In their most basic form they simply are sequences of operations on a group of data structures. Consequently, programs can be typified by two sets: 1) a set of data structures and 2) a set of operations on those data structures. Obviously such a view of programs does not necessarily imply von Neumann architecture. Furthermore, the top-down methodology of structured programming does not enjoy its previously favored status. This basic and more general view of programs was not important until computers were configured around data structures and their operations. With the advent of VLSI circuitry that point has now been reached.

Currently VLSI circuit technology provides the potential for highly parallel computers which do not rely on von Neumann architecture. These devices have parallel functionality which can be changed by changing programs operating in parallel. The original approach used by structured programming needs modification. In its place is an object-oriented modularization which emphasizes data structures. Each data structure is carefully delineated and the operations allowed on that data structure is precisely defined. The data structures themselves are strongly typed as are their allowable operations. Each module is handled as if it were a single entity.

VLSI circuit technology raises the following issues which must be addressed.

- Should algorithmically specialized processors be built focusing on computationally intensive problems?

- How should alternative architectures be evaluated?
- How should alternative software approaches be compared?

Several efforts are underway to examine the impact of configurable, highly parallel computers. One such effort is under Dr. Lawrence Synder of Purdue University under the sponsorship of the Office of Naval Research. Another is under Dr. Ron Krutz at Carnegie-Mellon University under the sponsorship of the VHSIC program. The impact of non-von Neumann architecture is not sufficiently known as far as software is concerned. Alternative software approaches become probabilistic under highly parallel configurations. Testbeds capable of comparing data structures and data structure operators need to be implemented immediately. Otherwise the problems will be addressed after they occur and under situations of duress.

5.2.4 Effective Human Interfaces with Software - Presentation and Manipulation

Human factors are important in achieving the best interface between machines and software engineers. These factors relate to the characteristics of problems being solved as well as the tasks being performed. Although such factors are not part of an automated program development environment, their presence or absence impacts that environment. Under a human factors approach the resources of local hardware, communications, and software tools are brought to bear on the basic needs of a programmer. The user interface is tailored to the semantics and usage patterns peculiar to each programmer.

The timesharing systems of today are not oriented to video and/or non-keyboard communications with high-bandwidth input/output. New systems must accommodate many different communications media, including audio, graphics, light pens, image processing, optical character recognition, and movable devices. As yet the necessary software to implement such highly interactive forms of human/computer interface has not been developed.

Several efforts are underway to improve the human factors associated with software engineering. Most are in the conceptual stage; e.g., the professional programmer based systems (PPBS) by DEC and the Automatic Software Generation System (ASGS) by John G. Rice. As concept becomes reality, the impact of improved human factors will complement software productivity.

5.2.5 Software Performance Engineering - Performance Management Techniques

Performance is one of the most important aspects of software quality. Among users of distributed processing services, it can be the difference between satisfaction and absolute rejection. High-performance internal support systems are vital to the routine operations of distributed networks. Without rapid response time, productivity is impacted. Extra time is required for implementation and extra effort is required to modify subsequent performance problems. Performance is not normally considered, but only when it becomes a problem. Performance management techniques must be applied from the initial design stage throughout the entire lifecycle.

Engineering for performance throughout the lifecycle has obvious advantages. The quality of a software product can be improved and productivity can be increased through such engineering. As a first analysis the following information is necessary:

- work-load specifications,
- software structure,
- execution environment,
- performance goal, and
- resource requirements.

The work-load specifications are derived from the users of distributed processing services. Software structure is established during the design phase. The execution environment anticipates a hardware configuration and an operating system. The performance goal is established by management in agreement with users. Resource requirements are derived projected usage levels. The relevance of results depends on the accuracy of information sighted previously.

Several efforts have been made to establish performance techniques. The longest standing such effort is under Dr. J. C. Browne at the University of

Texas and Information Research Associates. Under sponsorship of NASA Langley Dr. Browne has implemented a strategy to analyze software performance called ADEPT, i.e., A Design-based Evaluation and Prediction Technique. Extensions to ADEPT have been made and have been included in PAWS, a Performance Analyst Workbench System. Much remains to be done. More extensions need to be made if recent VSHIC architecture and software advances are to be accommodated. The impacts of non-deterministic, transaction-driven VLSI configurations are little understood. To avoid massive performance problems in the future the present trends must be completely understood in terms of performance management. To do otherwise would be unconscionable.

5.2.6 Appropriate Modularizations - Object-Oriented Modularization

Although the term object-oriented is new, its concept is not. Over a decade ago structured programming evolved a methodology which could produce partially independent modules of programming statements. The approach was top-down with semi-independent modules being broken down into submodules until program statements are eventually produced. Under an object orientation the characteristics of such a process change. Related programming statements are grouped around like data structures. The data structure is emphasized and the operations which can be allowed are carefully delineated. These structures are strongly typed as are their allowable operations. Data modules are handled as if they were single entities. The number of data types available are patterned to the needs of individual programs. The approach is bottom-up with data structures being combined to produce even more complex data structures. The structured programming and object-oriented techniques complement each other.

Object-oriented techniques have remained conceptual in scope since implementation requires support from a programming language. The strong typing capability complicates the language facilities. Each type of definition must support "visible" as well as "hidden" parts. Unless some parts remain "hidden" every user would be able to modify each definition. Consequently, the goal of an object-oriented implementation is to limit users to "visible" parts within definitions. This limited access has important implications. None of the popular languages implement such a concept with the exception of Ada. However, no validated Ada compiler has yet been produced. Complete implementations of object-oriented techniques await the arrival of these Ada compilers.

Ada packages for embedded distributed systems should receive special emphasis. The standardization of signal processing and navigational algorithms are distinct possibilities. Such standardizations have impact in command/communication/control systems. Packages for graphics can address line drawing, sub-screen manipulation, character manipulation, three-dimensional manipulation, shading, sealing, etc.

Proposed standards for certain usage areas such as data base management and graphics already exist. Other candidates for software standardization are already underway. The primary benefit to object-oriented modularization is the exploitation of commonality between various embedded computer systems. The resulting emphasis will be for rigid definition of language, portable compilers, and special language constructs for packaged software.

5.2.7 Enhanced Adaptability and Reusability of Modules - Integrated Software Support Environment

System adaptability is the ease with which changes can be made. At one extreme are systems with many capabilities which are fixed and not subject to change. The other extreme are systems with few features which are easy to modify. Such systems are good items for software toolkits. However, they do have problems. They must be recombined to fit the situation in which they are used. Depending upon the process, the recombination can be formidable. Beginning programmers find systems with many fixed capabilities easier to implement. Experts prefer systems with few, easily-modified features. Such capability for modification is offered by the integrated software support environment. Beginning programmers must undergo rigorous training in order to use it effectively. The integrated software support environment will evolve from the Ada Programming Support Environment. The environment should be easy to learn and equally easy to use. The thrust of such an environment is the generation of a compatible tool set covering the entire lifecycle. This thrust provides a framework for other thrusts.

The greatest potential exists for synergy between tools and in the cumulative improvement in production. The concept of monitoring accesses to specific tools is the beginning of a toolkit optimization process. The most frequently used tools can be cached for quick access. Furthermore, the more popular a tool becomes, the more general its access should be. The concept of reusable generic tools awaits the implementation of an integrated software support environment.

The foremost effort to implement an integrated software support environment is associated with the implementation of the Ada Programming Support Environment. A layer of structure will be needed between the APSE and sets of individual tools. Such a layer should support other languages besides Ada. It should provide standards for combined and hidden invocation, maintain data structures, and manage multiple representations. Within such an environment, different sets of tools based upon different methodologies can evolve.

5.2.8 Assurance of Correctness - Automated Verification Systems

The sooner an error is detected, the less it costs to repair. The activity associated with error detection is termed verification. Such activity validates the result of each successive step in the software development cycle. Validity is established by verifying the intent of the previous step has been satisfied by the results of the present step. The objective of an automated verification system is to detect and correct errors as rapidly as possible. New theory needs to be developed concerning the points at which various types of errors can be committed and detected. Practical methods need to be constructed for verification and detection. Errors obviously occur in all aspects of software development including requirements, design, and documentation. Knowing the earliest theoretical point at which verification can be done would help. If that earliest point could be established, the form of the verification itself could be determined. Once determined the verification might possibly be automated which would present the best of all possible worlds.

A number of efforts have already been undertaken to verify statements of requirements and design. Most prominent has been the University of Michigan and its Problem Statement Language/Problem Statement Analyzer (PSL/PSA). The approach acknowledges the best design and best code in the world will not do the job if the user requirements are not adequately stated. Without proper requirements definition, structured design and structured programming help disaster arrive more quickly. Consequently, PSL/PSA concentrates on the documentation associated with requirements definition and the difficulty of producing and managing manually generated documentation. The techniques used by PSL/PSA have been extended and revised by efforts originating elsewhere. These other efforts include TRW, Boeing, Hughes, and the Army Ballistic Missile Defense Advanced Technology Center. Additional efforts have been undertaken by High Order Software and Computer Sciences Corporation.

6. Object-Oriented Modularization

The concept of object-oriented modularization provides a high-level abstraction of the essential characteristics of embedded distributed processing systems, described in section 4.0, and the key features of the state-of-the-art hardware and software technologies, described in section 5.0. This abstraction plays a central role between these observed features and the specific requirements and techniques needed to support each lifecycle phase of embedded distributed processing systems that are described in section 7.0. It will be shown in section 7.0 that particular manifestations of object-oriented modularization are directly relatable to support of the embedded distributed processing system lifecycle phases. Hence, in this section 6.0 the concept of object-oriented modularization will be introduced, developed, and explained. Subsequent subparagraphs of this section will (1) indicate the relationship of object-oriented modularization to abstract data structures and information hiding, (2) extend the object-oriented modularization abstraction to hardware and software for embedded distributed processing systems, and, finally, (3) discuss the benefits of this viewpoint to embedded distributed processing systems.

6.1 Description of Object-Oriented Modularization

This section begins by defining the terms _object_ and _modularization_; then describes object-oriented modularization, and finally concludes with an example contrasting object-oriented modularization to conventional modularization.

An _object_ is an entity that contains information in an organized manner. This definition is purposefully general to enable its application to both hardware and software. For example, in software an object can be thought of as a data structure; viz, a simple variable or an array or a complex record. In hardware an object could be a register, an I/O buffer, or even a VLSI component of a larger system. An object has three additional characteristics that permit segregation of similar objects.

(1) Each object has defined for it a set of operations that manipulates the contained information.

(2) Each object can be addressed (referenced) as a whole.

(3) Each object has a label that tells the object's type.

Objects are a very useful concept in dealing with distributed systems and increasingly sophisticated hardware designs. For example, communications ports, schedulers, and support software packages can all be considered as objects. This viewpoint creates a unified framework for the discussion of requirements for embedded distributed processing systems. Previously, communication ports, schedulers, and support software packages were considered as separate entities - as being inherently different. Objects provide a higher level, consistent method for analysis, design, and implementation of these kinds of entities for embedded distributed systems.

Modularization is traditionally viewed as the partitioning of the hardware/software task based upon a stated criterion. There are many ways to modularize; by function, by interface communications, by priority, etc. This traditional concept of modularization can be directly extended to include "modularization by object". Here, the basis for the partitioning of the tasks is the creation of objects. Modularization is now more than a simple partitioning; it is the recognition and assignment of a particular responsibility associated with the object. Modularity is now raised to a higher-level commensurate with the object concept.

Combining these two definitions, object-oriented modularization is the segmentation of the hardware/software task based upon the responsibility and domain of extent of the identified objects. The key feature of object-oriented modularization is that each object executes its responsibility without the need to know of the details of the internal structure of other objects. The objects communicate amongst themselves in a very well defined manner. In an object-oriented modularized system, the internal representation of any module could change, and the other object modules would not have to be changed. This feature is a great benefit in the software maintenance environment. As an example contrasting conventional modularization with object-oriented modularization, consider Figure 6-1.

The conventional modules (M's) could, for example, represent major processing steps and the data structures (D's) are accessed by the modules. In conventional modularization, it is possible for a particular data structure, for example D1, to be accessed by more than one module. The disadvantage of conventional modularization is that whenever a module or data structure is changed, several other modules or data structures may also have to be changed. This single fact decreases the system reliability. However, in object-oriented modularization, the central theme is a one-to-one correspondence between object modules and their data structure. A change in a module or data structure affects only that module or data structure - no others. The internal details of object modules and data structures are shielded from other system elements. The resulting benefits are easier maintenance and improved reliability.

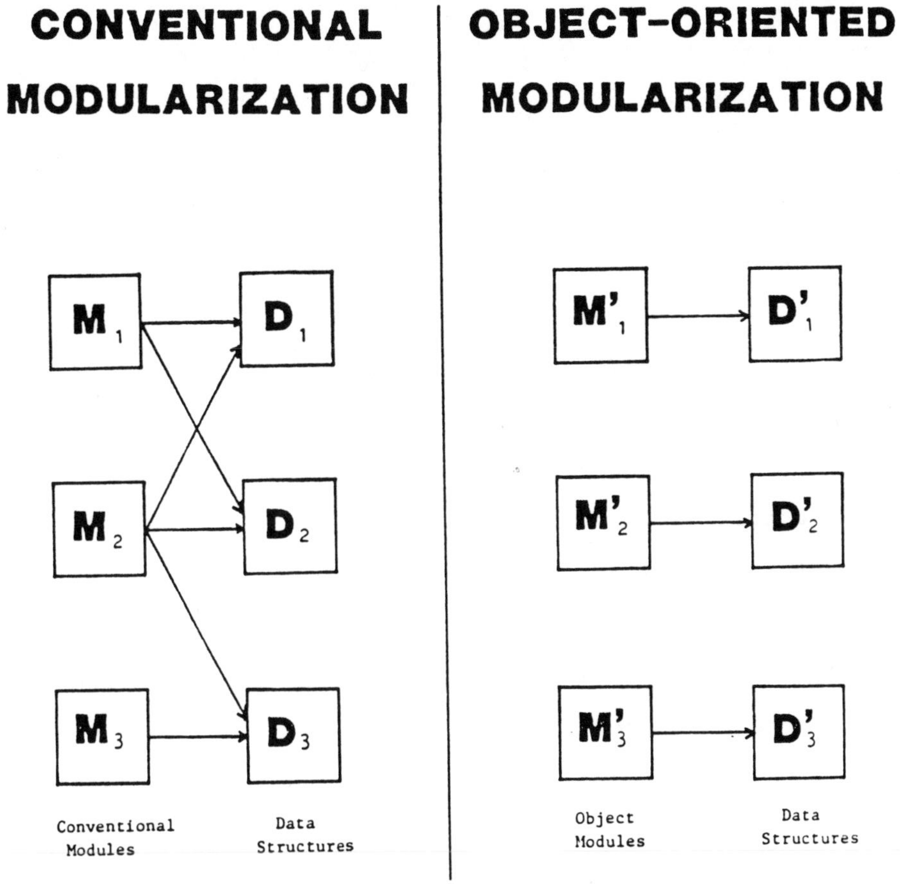

Arrows indicate data structures directly manipulated by the module.

Figure 6-1 Conventional Modularization Versus Object-Oriented Modularization

6.2 Relationship of Object-Oriented Modularization to Abstract Data Structures and Information Hiding

An abstract data structure defines a class of attributes that is completely characterized by the operations available on those attributes. The goal of an abstract data structure is to permit the expression of relevant details and the suppression of irrelevant details. In modern higher order languages it is desirable to provide the capability for user defined abstract data structures. This capability eases the programming task, makes the resulting code easier to understand, and provides a mechanism for the user to more easily communicate in a natural manner. Consequently, system reliability is enhanced. The particular implementation of the abstract data structure in a language is accomplished by the procedures and utilities that embody the defined operations.

The principle axiom of the Theory of Information Hiding as proposed by D. L. Parnas is that a software design methodology should shield information developed at one level of design from its use on another level of design. Consider two procedures A and B which do not reference each other directly. The Theory of Information Hiding states that the fundamental output (considered as level 1) of procedure A should not depend on the detailed implementation (considered as level 2) of procedure B. For example, if procedure B implements a stack operation by using a linked list and if the output of procedure A is to return the top item of the stack, then procedure A should not depend upon procedure B's linked list implementation. Procedure A only needs to know that procedure B provides a stack; how the stack is implemented is unimportant to procedure A. The detailed information of procedure B is "hidden" from procedure A. The benefit of this methodology is that if the implementation of procedure B changes, for example the linked list is replaced by an array or utilization of PUSH and POP hardware capabilities, procedure A remains unchanged.

The object-oriented modularization described in section 6.1 incorporates the main features of both abstract data structures and information hiding. Recall that each object has a set of operations defined for it that manipulates its information. This aspect directly draws from the domain of abstract data structures. As shown in Figure 6-1, the key feature of object-oriented modularization is to partition module, data structure pairs from other module, data structure pairs and thereby minimize the access of a particular data structure by more than one module. The effect is the same as information hiding; namely, changes to a particular module do not affect other modules. Hence, the object-oriented modularization is in concert with the current theories of abstract data structures and information hiding.

Object-oriented modularization is more than simply the amalgamation of abstract data structures and information hiding. Both of these concepts have traditionally been limited to software. However, the object-oriented modularization can also be applied to hardware elements. The key benefit here is that for embedded distributed processing system, object-oriented modularization provides a unifying concept for analysis and design at the hardware/software system level.

6.3 Example Application of Object-Oriented Modularization to an Embedded Distributed Processing System

As a concrete example of the application of the object-oriented modularization to an actual embedded distributed processing system, we shall examine the Intel iAPX432 System. The iAPX432 is a new product from Intel. It is a high technology device that is anticipated to have a profound impact upon the design of future embedded distributed processing systems. The design of the iAPX432 itself is an outstanding example of object-oriented modularization. For these reasons, it has been chosen to illustrate object-oriented modularization.

Figure 6-2 shows the top-level architecture of a typical product that would contain an embedded iAPX432 system to accomplish the product's application task. In addition, the most important objects are indicated, and these objects will be discussed in greater detail in the following subparagraphs.

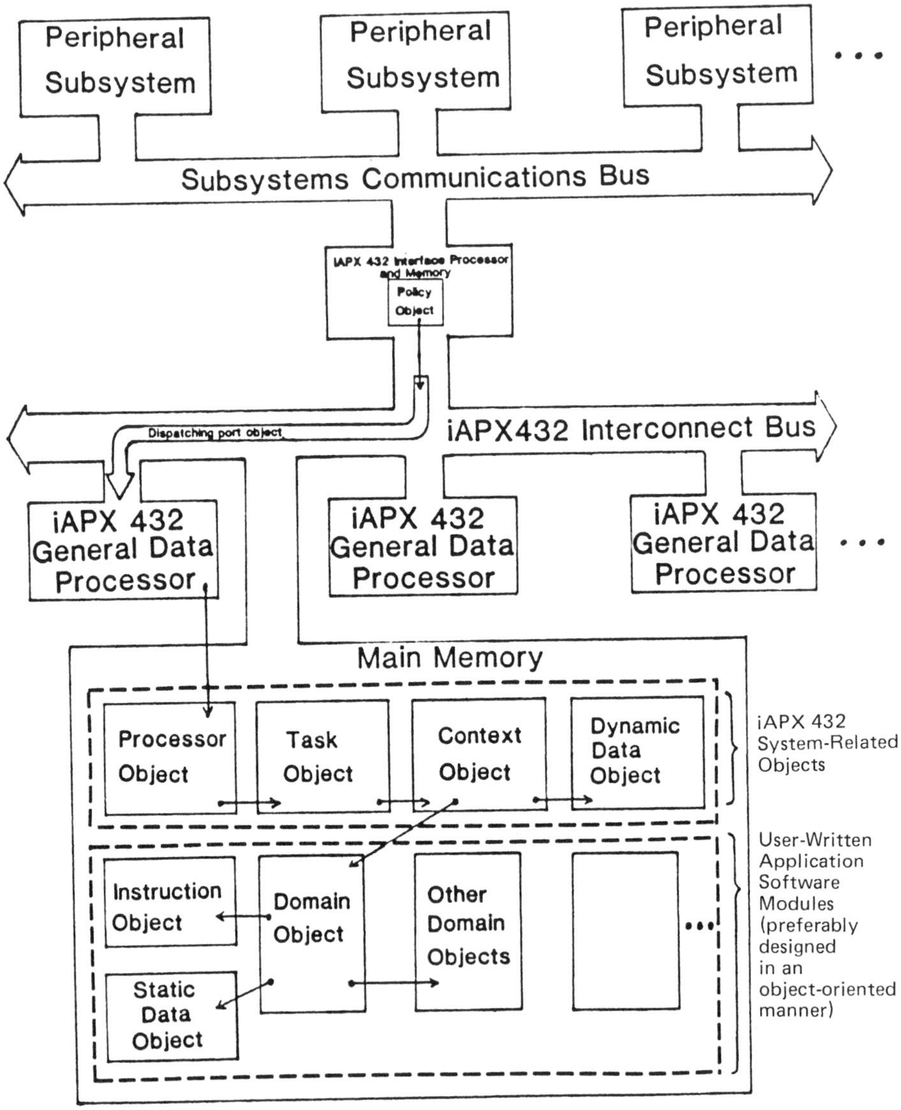

Figure 6-2 Top-Level Architecture and Objects in the iAPX432 System

The peripheral subsystems represent sensors, input/output devices, or functional units (e.g. inertial navigators, radars, line drivers, etc.), and these subsystems communicate via a common communications bus. The peripheral subsystems could also contain locally accessible memory. The interface processor is an intelligent link between the subsystems communications bus and the iAPX432 interconnect bus. The interface processor permits data transfer from the peripheral subsystems to iAPX432 main memory, and the interface processor contains the software for determining task execution priorities, scheduling, and dispatching (i.e., the policy object). Any number of iAPX432 general data processors can be put onto the interconnect bus and access main memory. Memory contention is resolved via the object-oriented modularization mechanisms in the iAPX432. The small arrow (--->) represents a reference of one object to another object. (Recall that two of the characteristics of an object are that it can be referenced as a whole and it has a label.) One object can access another object if and only if it contains an object reference. This mechanism provides protection of objects from other objects that do not have explicit access authorization.

The processor, task, context, and dynamic data objects are new concepts present in the iAPX432. The linkage of these objects minimizes erroneous access to software modules and provides a highly flexible capability that supports the dynamic environment needed for distributed processing. All of these objects are recognized by the iAPX432 hardware; hence, these object linkages do not degrade throughput. The application software modules reside, of course, in main memory. These modules are designed and coded by the user to accomplish the product's application task. The application modules are developed using standard practices of software engineering; preferably using the object-oriented modularization techniques described in section 6.1. The user application software (i.e. the domain objects) represents the bulk of main memory usage. The processor, task, context, and dynamic data objects are very minor tasks. The iAPX432 object-oriented modularization provides flexibility and protection for the user application software; it does not burden the software development activity.

6.3.1 Policy Object

The policy object has the responsibility of determining how the tasks to be executed are shared amongst the general data processors. Some typical criteria for policy decision are first-come-first-served, round-robin, priority, deadline, etc. Because the policy object must be tailored to the particular application, the policy object is implemented in software and resides in the interface processor. The scheduling and dispatching of tasks are accomplished in a manner consistent with the policy object. However, in order to increase throughput, the scheduling and dispatching functions are supported by hardware. The policy object contains a reference to the dispatching port object.

6.3.2 Dispatching Port Object

The dispatching port object is a hardware-recognized object that provides communications between the policy object and a particular general data processor. If all the processors are busy, the policy object can queue tasks in the dispatching port object awaiting a processor to become available. Likewise, if a processor is idle, it can wait at a dispatching port object for a task. Special hardware instructions SEND and RECEIVE provide rapid dispatching of tasks.

6.3.3 Processor Object

The processor object contains the information pertinent to a particular general data processor at each instance of time. Each processor has a processor object. The processor object contains information such as the processor status (e.g. running or waiting), diagnostic and machine check information, and an object reference to the particular task being executed. The object reference to the task being executed dynamically changes as the task being executed changes. Figure 6-3 shows an example of three processor objects at two points in time. At time t1, processor 1 is executing task B, processor 2 is halted, and processor 3 is executing task A. At a later time t2, processor 1 is still executing task B, processor 2 is now executing task C, and processor 3 is now halted. The processor objects dynamically changes as the tasks and processors are dispatched by the policy object. However, at each instance of time the status of each processor is completely determined by interrogation of its processor object. The processor object is referenced by the dispatching port object.

6.3.4 Task Object

The task object is the data structure that contains information about the task being executed; for example, the status of the task (running or waiting), how the task should be scheduled, and an object reference to the particular instance of the task being executed. The task objective is also a hardware recognized object to speed processing. Figure 6-4 shows how the task object changes as two tasks take turns running on a single processor. At time t1, task A is running and task B is waiting. At a later time t2, task A is now waiting and task B is now running.

6.3.5 Context Object and Dynamic Object

A task object can have more than one instance (or copy) of the procedures in memory at the same time; however, only one copy can be executing at a time in a particular general data processor. This

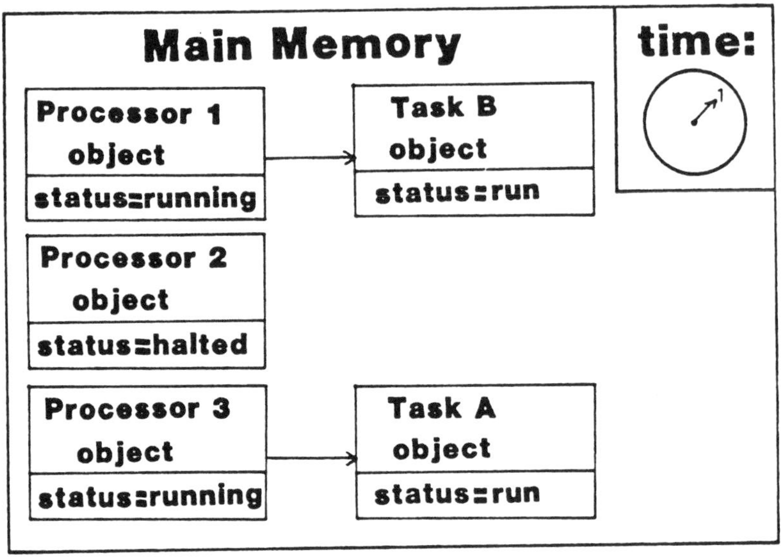

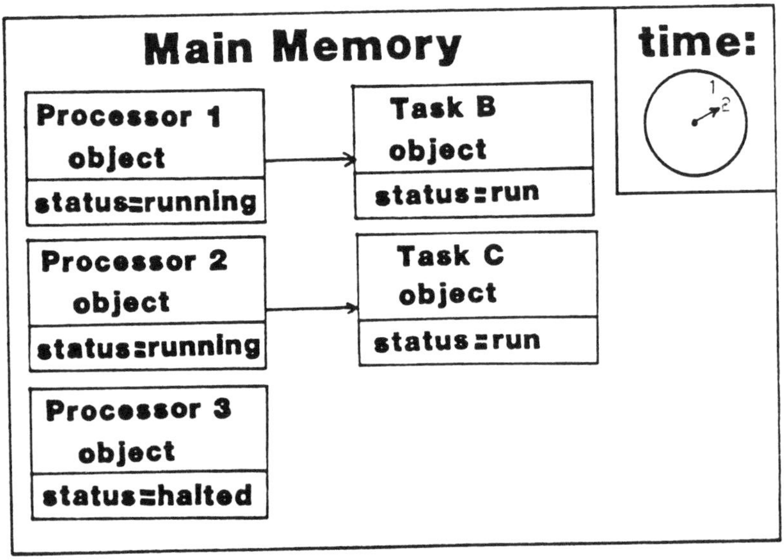

Figure 6-3 Processor Objects Snapshots at Two Instances in Time.

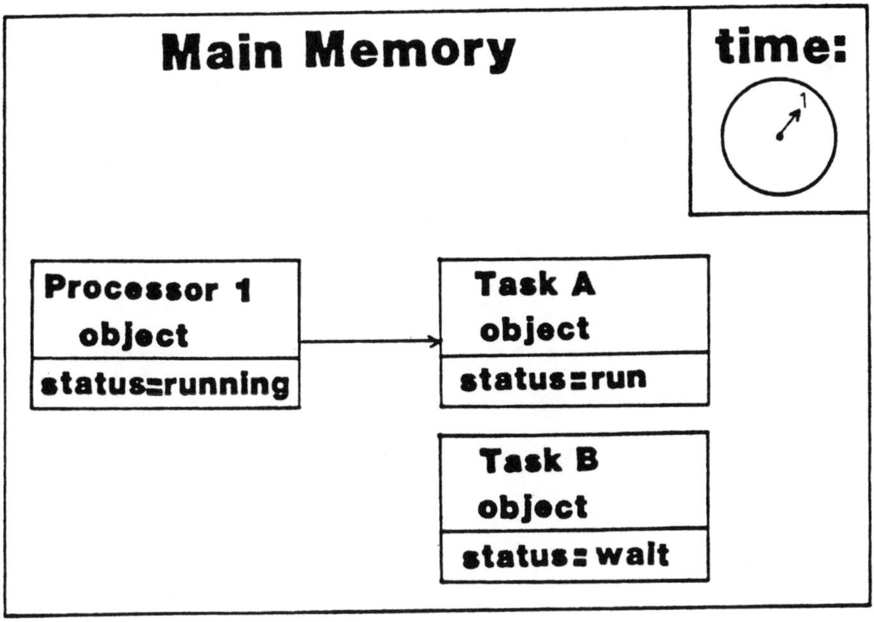

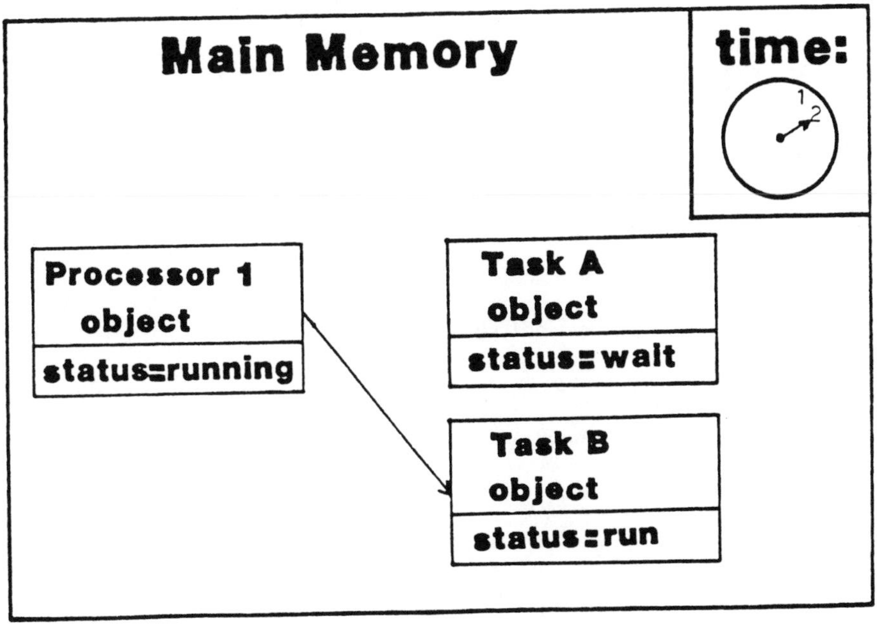

Figure 6-4 Task Objects Snapshots at Two Instances in Time.

situation commonly occurs for re-entrant procedures. A context object is the data structure that contains information pertinent to the particular instance of the task that is being executed. For example, the data contained in the context object includes an instruction pointer for this context, a stack pointer for this context, a return link to the task object, and references to all objects that can be accessed by this context. The context object is the fundamental vehicle for access of a particular instance of the task. Figure 6-5 shows how the context object changes in a typical subroutine calling sequence.

6.3.6 Domain, Instruction, and Static Objects

The domain object is a list of all the static object references to other applications modules, executable instructions, and static data. The object-oriented modularization is realized in the applications area by the structure of the modules and data structures written by the applications software engineer in accordance with the discussions presented in section 6.1. The domain object contains a reference to all of these objects. The instruction object contains only executable

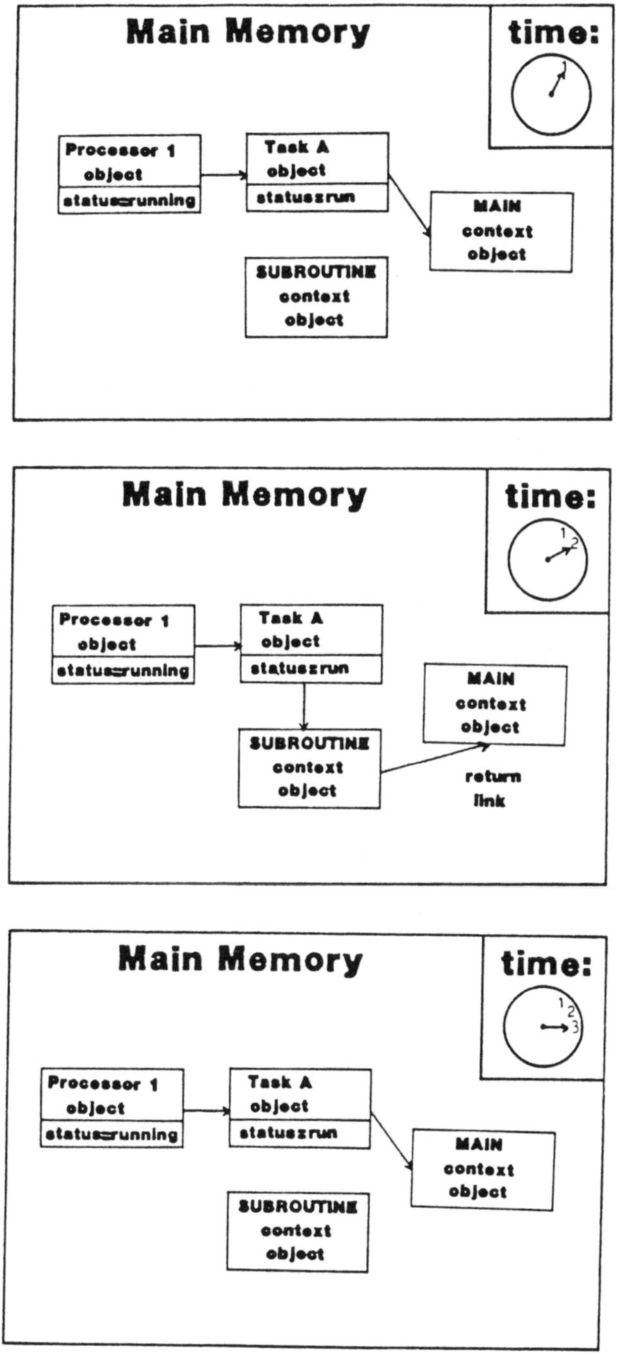

MAIN executing; before call

SUBROUTINE executing; after call

MAIN executing; after return

Figure 6-5 Changes in the Context Object During a Subroutine Calling Sequence.

instructions. The general data processor only uses the instruction object as a source of instructions to fetch and execute. The static data object contains static data that remains in memory after a particular context execution is complete. The instruction and static data objects are typically the end leaves of the iAPX432 object tree.

6.3.7 Summary of Benefits

The object-oriented modularization as exemplified by the iAPX432 has three distinct benefits. First, the object-oriented modularization is used in both the hardware and software. This approach provides a unified viewpoint to the entire iAPX432 system. It is anticipated that future embedded distributed processing systems must address the hardware and software as a total system. Object-oriented modularization provides a convenient, consistent, and flexible systems methodology. Secondly, frequently used objects (e.g., dispatching port, processor, task, and context objects) are supported by hardware capabilities to provide improved performance. Finally, the use of object references provides a flexible system that still incorporates careful control of object access. The control of object access is a vitally important problem in embedded distributed processing systems. The iAPX432 illustrates many of the problems of embedded distributed processing systems, and it is felt that the iAPX432 offers many viable solutions to these problems.

6.4 Benefit of Object-Oriented Modularization to Embedded Distributed Processing Systems

Embedded distributed processing systems are typically utilized in real-time, process control applications. These applications require a careful orchestration of the hardware and software; consequently, the hardware and software tasks must be viewed from a total systems standpoint. Object-oriented modularization as described in section 6 provides such a system level viewpoint. It is proposed that object-oriented modularization provide a central theme for the analysis, design, and implementation of embedded distributed processing systems. In section 7 we will explore specific manifestations of this object-oriented modularization theme and relate them to requirements and techniques to support the embedded distributed processing lifecycle phases.

7. Identification of Requirements and Techniques for Support of EDPS Life-Cycle Phases

Because of rapid advances in hardware technology both large and small computing systems will grow at an ever-increasing rate. The effective use of such systems will depend upon the ability of people to develop effective software. This software development must be of high quality and low cost. Because people have grown more expensive than machines, automation has an important role to play. The key element in that automation is the development of effective software tools. Major issues associated with the development of these software tools are as follows:

- the tools must form an integrated system which supports software throughout its lifecycle
- the role of breadboard models in requirements analysis and design phases of software development must be fully supported, and
- these tools must be developed under conditions which assure their successful use.

Much progress has been made in program development tools. However, much remains to be done on system construction tools. Tools are needed now to support independent specification and implementation of software modules.

The introduction of distributed systems on a large scale brings new challenges to the development of software. The design, development, testing and use of these systems demand increased simulation testing and more analysis tools in software development. In many hardware development activities, the product design phase requires the development of breadboard versions to investigate the difficult issues of system construction. A great need exists to quickly assemble and test breadboard versions. Performance needs to be analyzed and software design solidified before implementation begins.

7.1 Specific Manifestations of Object-Oriented Modularizations

Under object-oriented modularization the process of programming is transformed into a generic activity. Related programming statements are grouped on the basis of data structures. Operations are defined in terms of their impact on specific data structures. Both data structures and operations are strongly typed as to whether they are permissible or not. Furthermore, access to specific data structures can be tightly controlled. Once access has been accomplished, permission to change the accessed data structure may or may not be granted. If permission is not granted, the data structure is considered to be private. If allowed, the structure is visible. Graduations of access are a powerful tool under object-oriented modularizations. Data files and programs themself are handled as if they were individual data structures. A bottom-up orientation is possible with data structures being combined to form more complex structures. This emphasis on data structures demands an appreciation based upon experience. Novice programmers will undoubtedly prefer the simplicity of individualized programs and file structures. To program generically, more rigor is required. Object-oriented modularizations have many manifestations. Their consequences are only now being understood. The following paragraphs only begin to document such manifestations. Undoubtedly many more manifestations will be added as experience is gained. Most importantly an effort to gain needed experience must start immediately.

7.1.1 Deterministic Versus Probabilistic Systems

Von Neumann architecture within a uniprocessor environment is typified by Figure 7-1. Obviously the configuration is comprised of five functional components connected by a systems bus. The bus is somewhat misleading since its operation is not straightfoward. It is a combination of three distinctly different buses itself. Those three parts are a control bus, an address bus, and a data bus. Each has its characteristic architecture. The control bus is obviously the agent of the Process Control function within the von Neumann architecture. It instructs the actions to be taken by all the other functions within the architecture. Input and Output functions either place data on the data bus or take data off the data bus. Of course what action is performed is under the direction of the control bus. The Arithmetic Logic Unit or ALU performs either the arithmetic or logic required by the Process Control function. The results are usually placed on the data bus for subsequent usage within the architecture; e.g., Output or Storage.

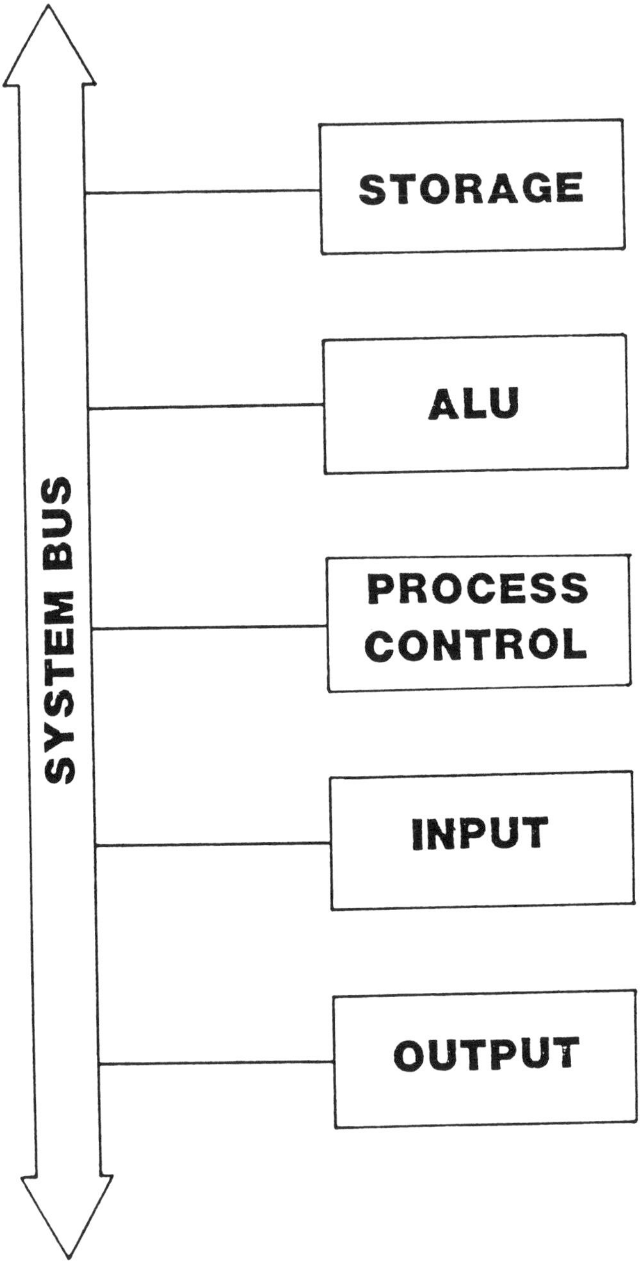

Figure 7-1 Von Neumann Architecture in Uniprocessor Environment

The Storage function either takes data from the data bus and places it in the location designated by the address bus or vice versa. The action taken is directed by the control bus. In summary the Systems Bus represents the concerted action of its three components.

Data flow between functions within a von Neumann architecture requires the use of registers. In effect such registers represent the beginning and ending points for the System Bus function. Since each register can be thought of as a "box" whose contents can be filled or emptied, the System Bus can be visualized as a postal service system. Each "box" is a mailbox in which letters are either delivered or dispatched. Such an analogy is valuable to illustrate certain architectural problems. When a letter is needed, it may not have arrived at its mailbox. Worse yet, the letter which was previously dispatched may not have been picked up and erroneously be misinterpreted as newly-arrived. In uniprocessor configurations which tend to be von Neumann in nature, the architectural problems are easy to avoid. The straightforward architecture illustrated previously can be expanded to exhibit the necessary mailboxes. Figure 7-2 illustrates this expanded von Neumann architecture.

Such expansions offer new architectural alternatives. The advances by Very-Large-Scale-Integration (VLSI) circuitry are exploring these alternatives. As a result, concurrent operations are becoming commonplace. Intelligence is being expanded to new architectural locations within von Neumann architecture. As an example, the mailboxes alluded to previously can assume their own intelligence. More appropriately they can be termed intelligent Interface Processors. Each such processor has its own von Neumann architecture with its own Input/Output being provided by either the System Bus or other von Neumann components. Furthermore, the actual computational process within a von Neumann architecture can be separated from the input/output process. In effect, two buses are introduced under such an arrangement: a system bus and a periphery bus. Figure 7-3 illustrates such an architecture. It is exemplified in the marketplace by the INTEL iAPX432 micromainframe. What emerges in such architectures is a layering of specialized buses. Figure 7-3 represents the architecture of a layered bus architecture.

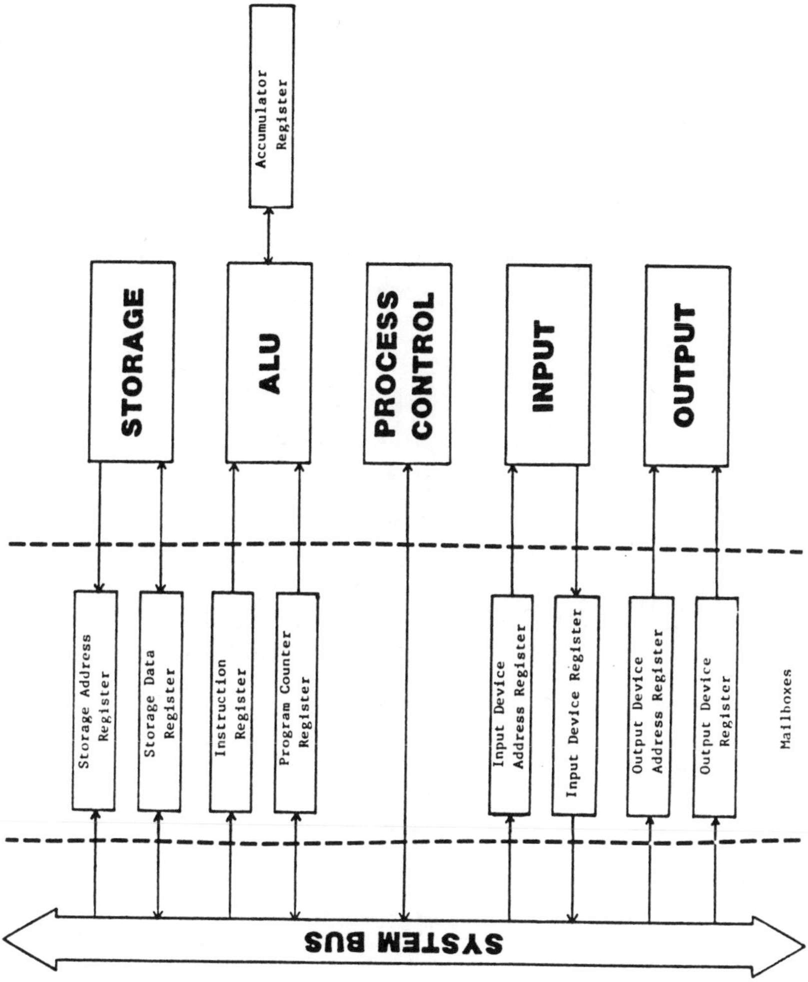

Figure 7-2 Von Neumann Architecture with Registers

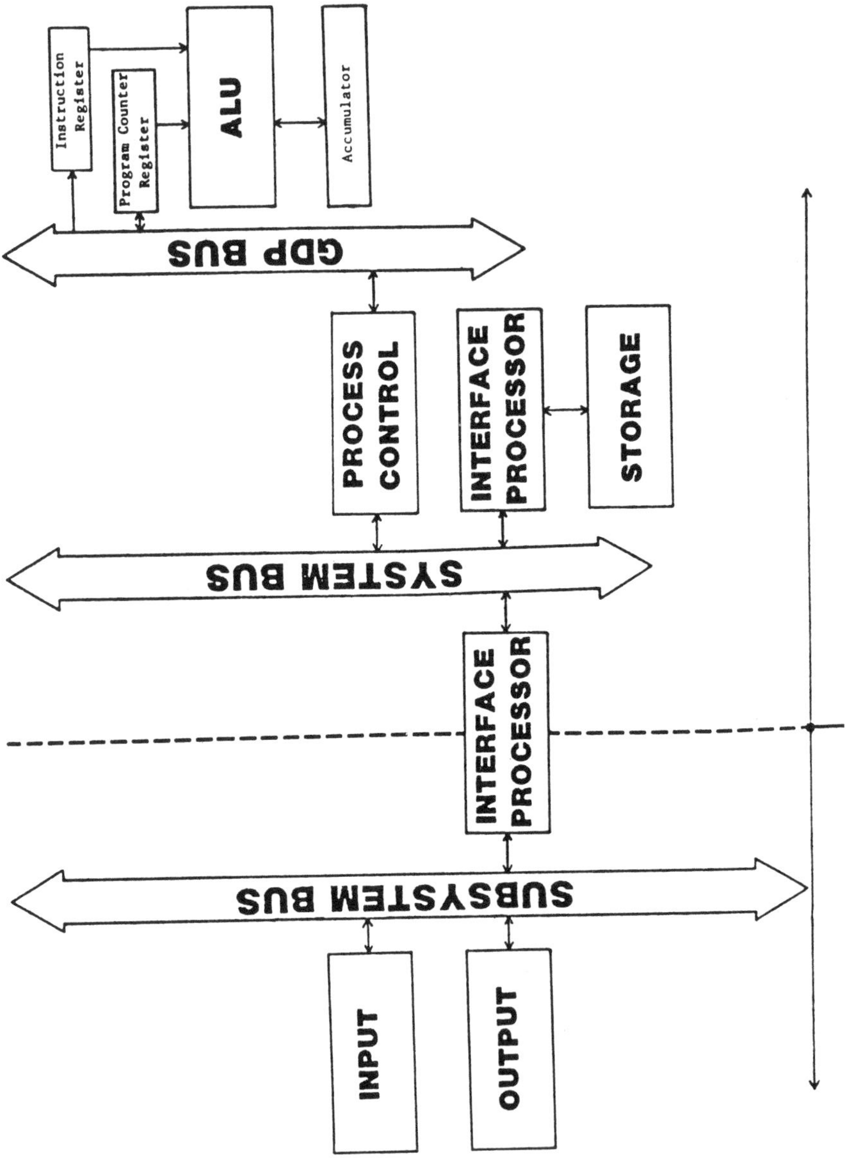

Figure 7-3 Layered Architecture of the iAPX432

The important property of layered bus architecture concerns its operation. The communication between layers becomes decidedly non-von Neumann or probabilistic. Such a phenomenon is enabled by the way the different buses are operating. Each is capable of operating independently of the other with communication occurring within mailboxes. At the topmost level the device appears to be interrupt-driven. However, at lower levels the device becomes transaction-driven which is the preferred architecture for distributed processing applications. Transactions occur independently of one another without an assumed interrupt schema. Such a philosophy has been adopted by the communications used with satellites and packet switching radio networks. New channel allocations have been implemented around open system, transaction-driven interconnect architectures. Projected advances in VLSI circuitry and Very-High-Speed-Integrated Circuitry (VHSIC) are adopting open system architectures to accommodate distributed systems. As a consequence, the operation is becoming more probabilistic. Various layers within the architecture can be operating independently of one another. Furthermore, components within a single interconnect level may also be operating independently of one another. To comprehend the operation of such configurations requires a knowledge of an underlying probability distribution. Not only must the transactions to be processed be known but their probability of occurrence must also be known. This requirements is new and very necessary in the emerging non-von Neumann architecture. The more layers of independently operating buses implemented, the more probabilistic subsequent operation becomes. Tools developed for von Neumann architecture are confronted with a non-von Neumann operation. The applicability of assumed von Neumann tools has yet to be established. Software tools are lagging behind VLSI and VHSIC developments. The situation needs to be corrected.

7.1.2 Global Timing

Advances within VLSI circuitry and the emerging VHSIC technology are enabling transaction-driven architectures to be implemented. In such architectures the predictability of time divided multiplexing is not available. Transactions either occur or they do not. Such operation accommodates a degree of spontaneity never before achieved.

When spontaneity is accommodated, a whole new approach must be applied. Transactions can overlay one another and compete for the same system resources. In the worst case transactions occur simultaneously with one another. Under such circumstances not only must transactions be processed but their overlap or coincidence must be recognized. In the case of either overlap or coincidence, the offending transactions must be reissued. If they are reissued, some means to assure they do not overlap or coincide a second time must be implemented.

Configuration throughputs have traditionally been modelled through the use of queuing networks. Such networks implement multiple job classes, mixed architectures, and hierarchical models. However, the underlying assumption remains von Neumann architecture which connotes a uniprocessor structure. As that architecture becomes more probabilistic and less von Neumann, the problem of timing becomes more acute. Characteristically the problem is either addressed directly or ignored completely. The easier solution is to ignore it completely which amounts to a "fix-it-later" attitude. By far the more rigorous approach is to confront it directly. Performance and global timing must be considered in the initial design stage and complicates subsequent software effort. The requirement for simulating different Poisson distributions is evident. Poisson mathematics is normally not addressed during the system lifecycle phases. However, Poisson distributions are mathematical tools available for the consideration of different probability density functions. Such functions underlie messages transmitted between independently operating bus structures within distributed architectures. As layered buses become more prevalent, the importance of the underlying message distribution functions is increased.

Presently available queuing networks can simulate multiple job classes, mixed architectures, and hierarchical models. However, each assumes an underlying Poisson distribution which does not vary. What is needed is the ability to vary the Poisson as well. When that variability is accomplished, the consequences of global timing can be appreciated. In the absence of such capability, purely software techniques are assumed to be valid with little or no justification. An example is the software technique called rendezvous within the Ada syntax definition. By virtue of its syntactic definition, such a technique may or may not accommodate subsequent operational distributions within the bus architecture of a particular system. In effect, by defining the rendezvous from a syntactic standpoint the whole issue of global timing is relegated to a "fix-it-later" approach. The current situation can be likened to the absence of ability to measure. Since global timing is not measured, the assumption is that it does not pose a problem. Until an architecture throttles itself there may not be a problem. But if the architecture ever does throttle, the problems are immense. They are much larger than necessary since their occurrence could have been avoided by including global timing as a design phase activity. The subsequent absence of problems should serve as justification for putting timing in the design phase within the system lifecycle phases.

7.1.3 Rapid Prototyping

System requirements have always been difficult to formulate. The difficulty is even encountered when similar automated applications are attempted. However, the similarity does provide information that normally is not available during the system requirements phase. It enables a quick prototype to be constructed to aid in the development of additional system requirements. This alleviates some of the problems usually faced by users and analysts when they attempt to specify complete sets of requirements. However, the present situation concerning such prototyping is not clear. The proliferation of differing software support environments has obscured its usefulness. When software support environments begin to standardize their capability, the importance of rapid prototyping will increase. This standardization is scheduled to proceed under the Ada implementation effort with the DOD. Once the Ada Program Support Environment (APSE) is implemented, rapid prototyping can demonstrate a reduction in time needed to produce requirements as well as an improvement in their quality.

An underlying question in rapid prototyping is what can best be ignored by the prototype. Many design details seem to be extraneous during the requirements phase. As Ada techniques become more widely known, this question becomes even more subtle. Because of the syntactic approach taken to global timing considerations by Ada, the design details previously thought to be extraneous may, in fact, not be. A suspicion begins to grow that clever deferring by Ada definers may complicate subsequent rapid prototyping efforts. As an adjunct to this line of reasoning, the applicability of rapid prototyping itself may be changing. As Ada usage grows, the capability for rapid prototyping becomes far more important. Not only must Ada programs be written but their subsequent interaction with the Integrated Software Support Environment (ISSE) must be known completely prior to the design phase; i.e., during the requirements phase. Obviously the language of choice to implement a rapid prototyping system should be Ada. Furthermore, once implemented, the prototyper should become part of the APSE.

A parallel effort to the development of a rapid prototyper for an ISSE should be the capability for simulating the ISSE. Such simulation would provide numbers or measurements which could be used to determine if an application is feasible or not. If not feasible, the effort could stop at that point. If feasible, the requirements phase could be addressed through the use of a rapid prototyper.

Such an approach simplifies the design of a prototyper since that prototyper does not have to handle impossible situations.

The use of rapid prototyping promises to improve the quality of requirements analysis. Subsequent systems should demonstrate improved relevance and usefulness.

Presently many companies are claiming competence in rapid prototyping based upon their efforts in general data base management systems. Components of such systems which come into play are configuration managers and specialized data storage and retrieval mechanisms. In most instances the storage involves hierarchical structures containing simulation parameters which are subsequently compared to each other. Rapid prototyping capability is closely related to the verbs contained in the data base management systems. However, such expertise may not apply when the APSE is implemented. Much of the capability claimed within a general data base management system will be offered by the APSE which offsets some of their expertise claimed in rapid prototyping. In effect, Ada ushers in an entire new set of circumstances for rapid prototyping.

7.1.4 Static Analysis Techniques

Static analysis techniques refer to the validation and verification techniques in which the analyst examines software without executing it. In its general sense it applies to all types of software products like designs, specifications, etc. In its restricted sense it applies only to data flow through a program in an attempt to detect anomalies like references to uninitialized variables. Until static analysis can be made to work in the restricted sense, it can not work in a general sense. Consequently, the following comments are limited to the restricted sense.

The best known early work on static analysis has been done by Osterweil and Fosdick. They built a system called DAVE which analyzed Fortran programs for data flow anomalies. It detected possible references to uninitialized variables and the assignment of value to a variable not referenced by the remainder of a program. Several criticisms have been levelled at DAVE. First, it carries out data flow analysis one variable at a time rather than simultaneously for all variables. Second, it non-selectively prints out too much data. Third, it is too large which may, in fact, pertain to the use of Fortran. Fourth, it is too slow and requires too much computer time. However, these criticisms can be ameliorated by viewing DAVE as a prototype product of a research project as opposed to a production line tool.

The research project which produced DAVE has enabled Fosdick and Osterweil to study the relationship between data flow in static analysis and data flow in program optimization. They were the first to observe data flow algorithms developed for optimizations could also be used for static analysis. The basic idea is that variables can be in different states and that operations such as value assignment and referencing can change those states. The set theory resulting from their observations is useful to the extent it indicates how existing well defined and efficient data flow algorithms can be used for static analysis. It is not useful as an end unto itself. The gen, kill, live, and avail sets are not good vehicles for the discussion of static analysis in general. However, this is not just a shortcoming of the work done with DAVE. No general problem-oriented approach to static analysis is presently available. Several ideas are beginning to emerge. First, static analysis can be viewed as a kind of program execution mechanism which operates in different programming language semantics. The analysis done on HAL/S for NASA is an example of such an effort. Such an approach needs to be applied to Ada constructs before its exception handling capability creates semantic problems within existing hardware configurations. Another idea is the abstract computation type which includes patterns of operators. Applying a set theory of its own will serve to verify and validate static data flow through programs. The end result would be to discriminate legal operator pattern sets from illegal operator pattern sets.

Distributed processing introduces massive complications in static analysis. The reason involves asynchronous processes. This enables referencing and defining of variable values in parallel processes. This, in turn, enables ambiguous variable definitions due to multiple variable definitions within parallel tasks. Underlying these problems is the problem of synchronization. Taylor has attacked the problem in a stepwise manner. He first examined concurrent programs with no interprocess communication. Upon completion of that highly restrictive case, Taylor examined the rendezvous technique of Ada. What has resulted from this effort has been the determination of whether or not a syntactically possible rendezvous violates the semantics of synchronization. The end result has been the realization that arbitrary systems of concurrent processes can not be analyzed efficiently using static analysis techniques. Although static analysis has been demonstrated to be an effective error detecting mechanism for analyzing single programs, they may or may not be applicable to concurrent programs. Their applicability rests upon the synchronization properties of the distributed system. An interesting adjunct to such a conclusion would be a future study of different kinds of process scheduling with different capabilities for distributed processing structures.

7.2 Relationship of Manifestations to EDPS

The increasing density of electronically active devices on VLSI semiconductors is fueling a revolution. More and more compute power is being squeezed into less and less space. The limiting factor is the speed of light which means quicker response times for new, smaller devices. VHSIC technology optimizes response times by shrinking circuitry within specialized hardware structures. In a sense, compute power is being distributed within its own architectures. So much power is being distributed that problems are generated in three general directions. First, access to all this new power is becoming increasingly difficult. Controlling that access is no longer trivial. Access can be used to perform a task within a given architecture or it can be used to modify the operating characteristics themselves. These operating characteristics are functions of hardware distribution which introduces another general consideration. How the compute power is distributed within hardware is becoming more important. As single buses are replaced by multiple buses, how information flows within an architecture is sometimes obscured. The von Neumann characteristics of a single processor are transformed into configurations displaying probabilistic characteristics. Working around these probabilistic characteristics emphasizes the importance of a third general consideration; i.e., the distribution of data bases. The architecture of a particular data base should parallel the operation of the hardware architecture which contains it. Obviously magnetic tape data structures would not be expected to operate optimally within disc architectures. Taken as a group, considerations concerning the distribution of control, the distribution of hardware, and the distribution of data bases are becoming increasingly important. The subsequent paragraphs will examine specific manifestations of such considerations within embedded distributed processing systems.

7.2.1 Support of EDPS by Object-Oriented Architecture

Current trends indicate significant departures from the usual von Neumann architecture of the present. Multiple processor configurations are becoming more prevalent and interconnect networks are offering unprecedented increases in their throughput. How to take advantage of these advances is becoming a growing problem. First, users must comprehend the advantages offered by such architectures. Such knowledge is in short supply. Second, suppliers of such architectures must explain their advances to the marketplace. These explanations are becoming more subtle and the required communication talent increasingly rare. Third, present commitments to existing architectures make revolutionary innovation difficult to learn. Simply maintaining existing architectures is a full time job requiring great technical expertise. Such workforces have little time to spend assessing revolutionary breakthroughs. In the absence of assessment the breakthroughs continue with a quickened pace. The suppliers are driven into popularity contests within the marketplace. In some instances single suppliers produce products which compete with one another; e.g., the IBM System/38 and the IBM 4300. Such antics exacerbate the problem. When single suppliers introduce innovative products competing with one another in identical marketplaces, the situation is out of control. Assessments which should originate within the marketplace have not occurred. Consequently, fragmentation occurs driving the suppliers to more innovation, more breakthroughs, and more chaos. One of the true ironies of such circumstances is the emerging role of colleges and universities. In attempts to remain abreast of the accelerating breakthroughs, groups of faculty and students concentrate on the assessment of specific revolutionary breakthroughs. In some instances they may even design and implement them; e.g., Ada and Diana. When the breakthroughs are introduced to the marketplace, the workforces acquired by that marketplace to assess them are recruited from the originating faculty and students. Attempts to adapt the breakthrough to specific needs within the marketplace rest upon these newly acquired workforces. Such workforces seldom appreciate the needs of the marketplace. Producing the revolutionary breakthroughs is a full time job with little time available for assessments within unknown marketplaces. As new generations of innovative researchers proceed to the marketplace, they are replaced by new faculty and new students. Neither has allegiance to existing architectures or ways of doing things. Consequently, they offer ideal test-beds for the development of revolutionary innovation. The present cycle works so well that colleges and universities have increasing difficulty in attracting and keeping competent computer faculty members. The marketplace pays a premium for the talent which understands revolutionary breakthroughs.

The job migration phenomenon mentioned above is particularly evident within the embedded distributed processing marketplace. Talent to maintain existing commitments is extremely scarce. Consequently, talent to assess technological breakthroughs is virtually non-existent. Significant departures from existing methodologies have few advocates but in the absence of independent assessment, revolutionary breakthroughs are being produced and adopted. The reorientation of existing workforces is becoming imperative. The adoption of an object-oriented modularization approach expedites this reorientation. Only with such an orientation can be consequences of non-von Neumann architecture be grasped. The understanding of a distributed system becomes more generic. The conceptualization of interconnect buses and their architectures is heightened. The emerging importance of distributed data bases is clarified. In fact, the object-orientation of the data bases themselves becomes evident. In summary, the performance of embedded distributed processing systems will be enhanced by object-oriented modularization. This will be evident in faster response times, increased flexibility, massive resource sharing, increased reliability, wider availability, and highly transportable systems. Failsafe architectures and operation will be the hallmark of distributed systems of the future. Underlying all such architectures and operations will be object-oriented modularizations.

7.2.2 Object-Oriented Modularizations and State-of-the-Art Technologies

The multi-layered architecture produced by VLSI circuits and VHSIC technologies has consequences far beyond simple departures from the von Neumann architecture of uniprocessors. It affects geographic location, data base partitioning, and system control. When multi-layered architecture is combined with multiple processors, the situation can become non-deterministic. Many of the operating characteristics of the past are being transformed in the present. Genuine multiprocessing hardware now exists. Each component operates independently of the other configuration components. They operate simultaneously. The network connecting all components is highly sophisticated and operates at a variety of levels. Each layer typifies a different level of abstraction. In the International Standards Organization's (ISO) Open Systems Interconnection (OSI) there are seven levels of abstraction. These are presented in Figure 7-4. The lowest level is physical and involves the movement of bits within a network.

Obviously, the next lowest level is grouping bits into frames. The frames can be grouped into packets for the third level of abstraction. Taken as a group these first three levels comprise the communication subnet boundary which exists for every architecture. Four additional layers have been provided for higher levels of abstraction. At the highest level is the application layer which is not transparent to network users. This is the level at which most users interface with the network. Ethernet is an example of communications alternatives which embody the OSI suggested by the ISO. As multi-layered architectures become prevalent, the operation of tightly-coupled buses approximates the operation of an OSI model. This layering effect is evident in the architecture of the iAPX432

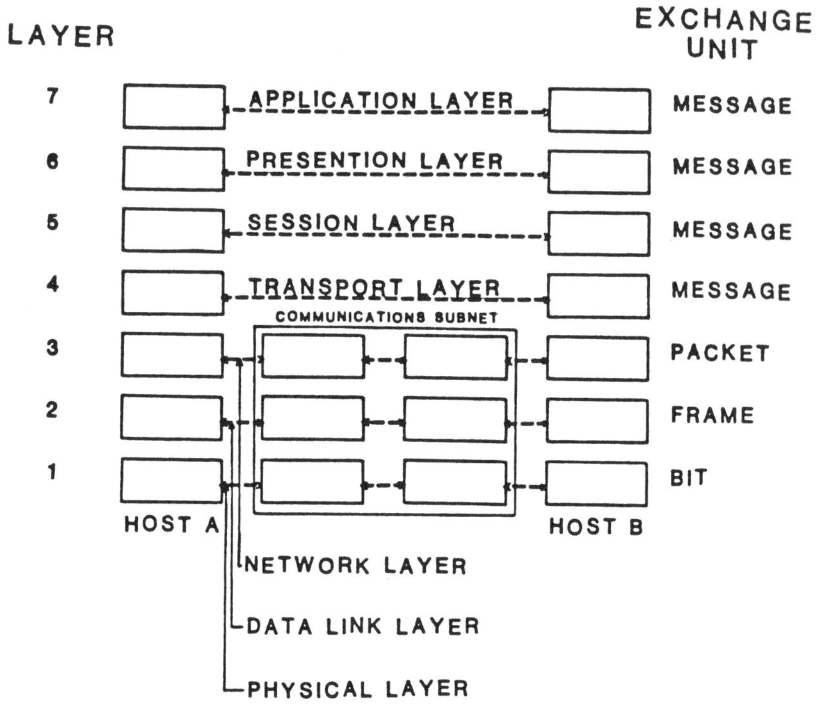

Layer 7 - the application layer encompasses information peculiar to the network's end users. It is the only layer which is not transparent to the user.

Layer 6 - the presentation layer translates messages between the various formats, codes and languages generated by different network residents.

Layer 5 - the session layer handles the logical exchange of messages between network stations.

Layer 4 - the transport layer manipulates message transport between end users like computers and communication networks.

Layer 3 - the network layer controls the switching and routing of messages between nodes to effect transparent data delivery.

Layer 2 - the data link layer regulates the coding and decoding of data packets for reception and delivery over data communication lines. It also performs error detection and can provide correction services.

Layer 1 - the physical layer incorporates the mechanical, electrical and functional characteristics of the line between network nodes.

Figure 7-4 International Standards Organization's Open Systems Interconnection Model

and is presented in Figure 7-5. In the previous analysis of the iAPX432 architecture the layers above the interface processor were interrupt-driven while those below were transaction-driven. Such an observation is tantamount to stating levels 4 to 7 are interrupt-driven and levels 1 to 3 are transaction-driven. Much of the knowledge needed to operate the multi-layer architecture of the iAPX432 is provided by a thorough knowledge of the OSI model.

In effect, the breakthroughs of VLSI and VHSIC technologies are forcing an understanding of the OSI model and its ramifications upon the marketplace. Object-oriented modularization is valuable because it enables applications (i.e., layer 7 issues of the ISO model) to be implemented without loss of control. As more power is distributed throughout EDPS networks the issues remain unchanged. The object-oriented approach by Ada will prove extremely valuable in future multi-layer, distributed architectures. Hence, immediate effort should concentrate upon thorough understandings of multi-layered architectures, open system interconnects, and Ada application packages. The subsequent integrated software support environments

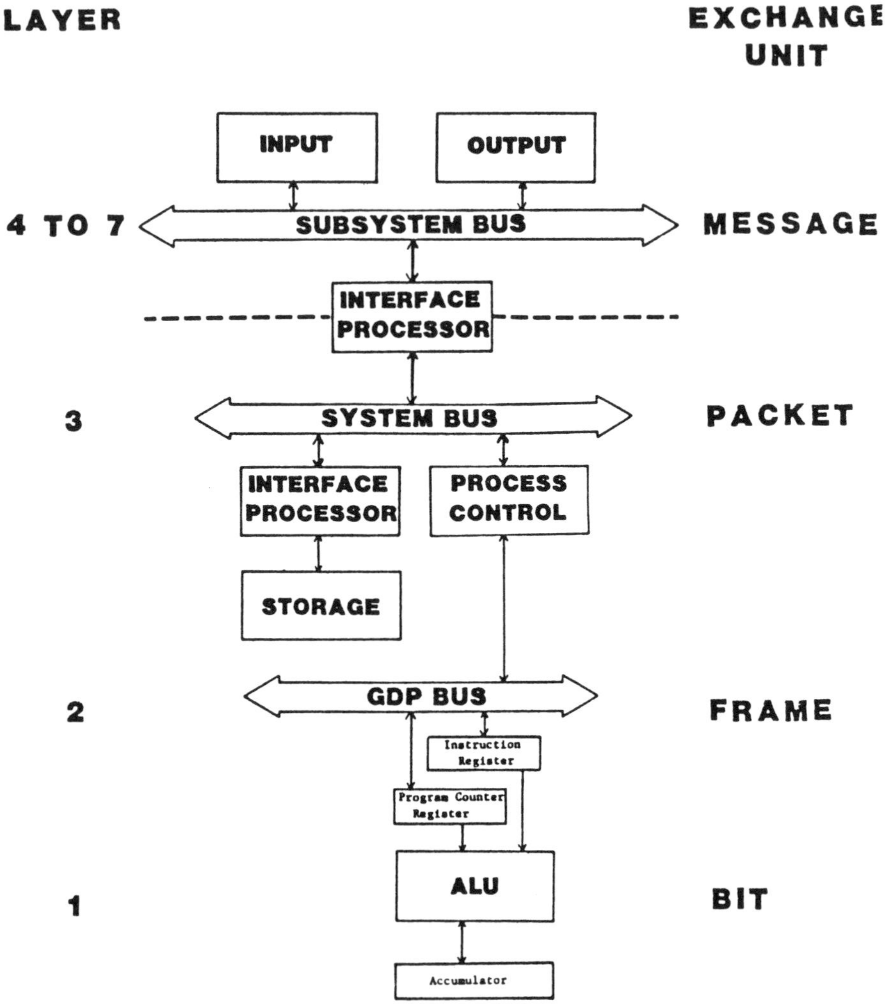

Figure 7-5 Open Systems Interconnections of the iAPX 432

should accommodate effort from all three directions. The largest unresolved problem remains distributed data base structures and their parallel algorithms. Such environments have simply not been sufficiently available to resolve the problem. Advances in VLSI and VHSIC technologies virtually assure the ready availability of such environments in the immediate future. The subsequent section addresses the highly technical and complex issue of tractability within such environments. The problem is so new that basic issues must again be examined.

7.2.3 Benefits of Object-Oriented Modularization to EDPS

The evolving environments of multi-layered architecture loosen the present constraints placed on computing power. Access to computational power is becoming commonplace. Communication networks with parallel structures are being implemented on a global basis. Data bases and their inherent structures are stored wherever needed. The cost of software has become greater than the cost of hardware. All these factors impact embedded distributed processing systems.

To combat costs and expedite development, an integrated software support environment remains essential. Before such an environment is realized the Ada program support environment is necessary. The commitments to the APSE have been made. Ultimately all advances are contingent upon the applications which are to be implemented. The most valuable technique during these implementations is object-oriented modularizations. However, this technique has its shortcomings as well. Most significant is the matter of tractability; i.e., whether the solution can be automated under all conditions. In effect, the absence of constraints introduces the tractability problem. The order of computation becomes increasingly important. Fewer constraints mean more alternatives for state transitions. Some orders of computation become indeterminant. The technical term is NP-complete. This problem was not encountered as often in uniprocessor architectures. Static analysis techniques had the problem in the uniprocessor environment. The problem with static analysis has increased with distributed systems.

In summary, object-oriented modularization solves many software problems within embedded distributed processing. It also raises other issues concerning tractability. The problems can be solved if they are recognized but this recognition is becoming increasingly subtle. New techniques are beginning to emerge and will be discussed in the subsequent phases of the Distributed Processing Tools Definition study.

7.3 Categorization of EDPS Requirements and Techniques by Lifecycle Phase

The Ada Programming Support Environment (APSE) provides an initial set of tools. They include a compiler, a debugger, a linker-loader, an editor, a run controller, and a configuration manager. Additional tools will be needed. Furthermore, each phase of the software system lifecycle must be addressed. As each new application is developed, where the software is used must be determined. Once that environment has been established, whether the requirements can be achieved by allocating an acceptable level of resources must be determined. If an unacceptable level of resources is required, why continue? Assuming the requirements phase issues can be resolved, the design phase should carefully weigh several more issues. An expected level of performance should be calculated. Such a calculation can be used to satisfy an expected level of performance. It verifies a proposed configuration and isolates what parts of the subsequent system must be monitored very closely. As the design phase continues, the impact of each change on the expected levels of performance must be carefully documented. Careful documentation will refine the expected performance. With each refinement the expected performance will become more realistic. During the coding phase, alternative ways to achieve the same operating expectations should be compared. As unforeseen problems are encountered, they should be carefully documented. Each critical component should be carefully monitored during the testing phase. The trade-off between resource requirements and critical component performance should be established as a matter of record. The documentation phase is aided by the compilation of adequate documents throughout the previous phases. When modifications are requested, the maintenance phase should assess the effect of each modification. From these assessments a long-range configuration requirements plan can be accumulated for the future.

In summary, performance is a primary consideration throughout the lifecycle. When requirements are being defined and the initial software design is being formulated, a performance analysis verifies the feasibility and desirability of the functional architecture. Once feasibility and desirability have been verified, the actual configuration required to support the new application is determined. Such a determination establishes the power required from the support hardware as well as the operating system software. Configuration and design are not separate issues. Design depends upon requirements while configuration depends upon design. Therefore, several iterations of requirements-design-configuration activities are usually needed before the best combination is known. The subsequent sections will illustrate this process.

7.3.1 Static Analysis of Concurrent Programs

The problems of referencing undefined program variables are compounded by asynchronous processes. Related problems include:

- referencing and defining variable values in parallel processes
- ambiguous variable definition due to multiple variable definitions in parallel tasks
- waiting for synchronization with a process which has already been guaranteed to have terminated
- waiting for synchronization with a process which may never have been scheduled, and
- the illegal scheduling of a process in parallel with itself.

Taylor studied concurrent programs in which there was no interprocess communication in his first paper on the subject. Such programs could schedule and then wait for completion of processes but concurrently running processes could not explicitly communicate with each other or affected each other's progress while running except through access to shared global variables.

Subsequent effort by both Taylor and Osterweil on concurrent programs can be carried out in an efficient way -- provided the programs require no interprocess communication. Furthermore, the programs disallow run-time determination of which processes will be scheduled. A related restriction is that the directed graph model of the process invocation structure of either program must be acyclic. Recursive subroutine calls are not allowed.

In addition to his work with Osterweil, Taylor has investigated different synchronization primitives. In particular, he studied the rendezvous mechanism of Ada. This mechanism allows interprocess communication and synchronization precluded previously. Taylor argues a flow model describing the set of possible flows of control through the system of simultaneously operating processes must be completed before static analysis can be performed. When single programs are examined, many of their syntactically possible flows are semantically infeasible. In single programs a flow path is infeasible if no set of input data exists which can satisfy the set of branch conditions occurring along its path. When concurrent programs are examined, their infeasible paths occur because of the semantics in the synchronization primitives. An example would be a process with two "calls" on an entry in another process and that second process waiting at the entry point for a call. If the two processes contain no cycles, the second call can never be synchronized with the entry point. In general, efficient static analysis for arbitrary systems of concurrent processes can not be constructed.

Depending upon the synchronization properties of the distributed system, the construction of data flow analysis algorithms may or may not be feasible. The work by Taylor indicates efficient algorithms for the general case can not be constructed. Taylor and Osterweil have shown efficient algorithms can be constructed for special situations in which the run-time determination of process scheduling is tightly constrained. When the scheduling of processes and the process interaction can be made deterministic, efficient static analysis algorithms can be constructed to detect a wide variety of possible data flow and process scheduling anomalies. Table 7-1 indicates the anticipated effect of static analysis techniques on EDPS lifecycle phases.

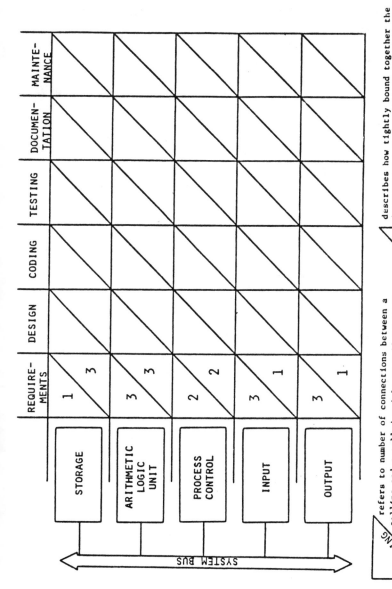

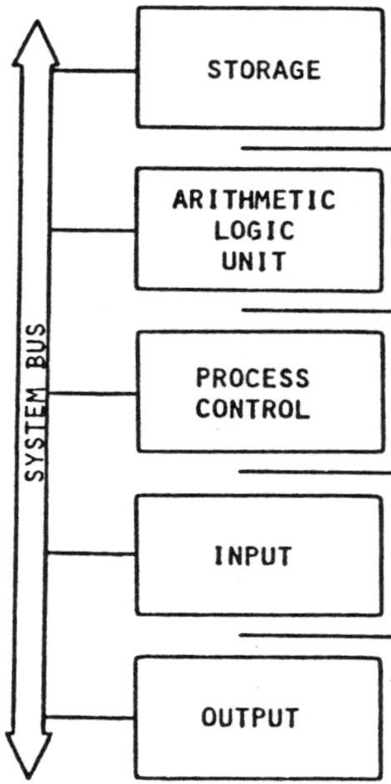

	REQUIREMENTS	DESIGN	CODING	TESTING	DOCUMENTATION	MAINTENANCE
STORAGE	1 / 3					
ARITHMETIC LOGIC UNIT	3 / 3					
PROCESS CONTROL	2 / 2					
INPUT	3 / 1					
OUTPUT	3 / 1					

COUPLING refers to number of connections between a calling and a called module as well as to the complexity of those connections. "1" means low coupling. "2" means average coupling. "3" means high coupling.

COHESION describes how tightly bound together the instructions are within a module. If module does more than one discrete task the instructions in that module are not bound very closely to each other. "1" means strong cohesion. "2" means average cohesion. "3" means weak cohesion.

Table 7-1 Effect of Static Analysis Techniques on EDPS Lifecycle Phases

Additional work concerning different kinds of process scheduling (e.g., non-deterministic or probabilistic) and interaction capabilities is required. Such scheduling and interaction presently exist within various kinds of distributed processing structures.

7.3.2 Branch Testing

Branch testing is the most common form of testing in which program structures rather than black box functional specifications are used to guide the testing efforts. The goal is to construct test data in such a way that every program branch is executed at least once. The method is appealing and tests all parts of the program. Furthermore, it is easy to audit and provides each programmer with criterion for a complete set of tests. However, many errors go unfound because every branch is usually tested only once. Attempts have been made to extend the method by requiring the testing of combinations of branches or classes of program paths. The problem with these extensions is that their number becomes very large, very quickly. The number can be reduced by relying upon the data flow relationships between program constructs. As an example, some test may cause the execution of two statements s1 and s2 if the first (s1) defines the values required by the second (s2). Otherwise s1 and s2 could be tested separately with two different tests.

The difficulties of extending branch testing to more powerful methods have caused a re-examination of functional testing. If a systematic approach to requirements specification is used, rules for identifying functions to be tested can be developed. Empirical evidence indicates that many errors can be found using a systematic approach to functional testing. Such errors cannot be found by branch testing alone. The best approach is probably a complimentary one using both functional testing and branch testing.

The techniques that have been developed for single, non-distributed programs or systems can obviously be applied to individual components within a distributed system. The special properties of distributed systems make them more difficult to test and require the development of additional test data generation techniques. Single programs can be thought of as being at a certain point in computation when the flow of control reaches that associated point in the program. To test such computations, test data must be constructed to reach that point in the program. In a distributed system several programs must cooperate to produce the desired effect. The state of the system becomes increasingly important because certain computations can only be performed while in an appropriate state.

The role of computation states in a distributed system affects testing in two principle ways:

- detailed systematic documentation of system states is absolutely necessary and

- the condition under which a system or program can change states must be known.

Much such information comes from design. Consequently, systematic design specification is more important for distributed systems than for non-distributed ones. The anticipated effects of branch testing techniques on EDPS lifecycle phases are indicated in Table 7-2.

	REQUIREMENTS	DESIGN	CODING	TESTING	DOCUMENTATION	MAINTENANCE
STORAGE				3 / 1		
ARITHMETIC LOGIC UNIT		1 / 3		3 / 2	3 / 1	
PROCESS CONTROL		1 / 3		2 / 3	3 / 3	
INPUT				1 / 1		
OUTPUT				1 / 1		

SYSTEM BUS

COUPLING refers to number of connections between a calling and a called module as well as to the complexity of those connections. "1" means low coupling. "2" means average coupling. "3" means high coupling.

COHESION describes how tightly bound together the instructions are within a module. If module does more than one discrete task the instructions in that module are not bound very closely to each other. "1" means strong cohesion. "2" means average cohesion. "3" means weak cohesion.

Table 7-2 Effect of Branch Testing Techniques on EDPS Lifecycle Phases

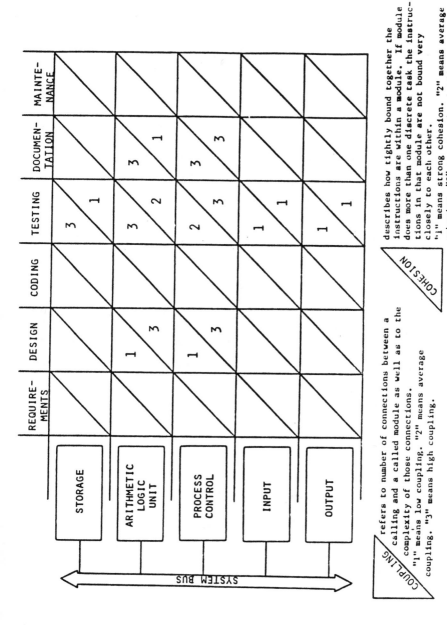

7.3.3 Impact Analysis

When a system object is altered there is always the danger that the change will have unforseen effects due to a forgotten relationship between the object which was changed and other objects. Automated impact analysis can be used to avoid this problem if relationships between objects are recorded in a machine readable format. There is a wide variety of kinds of objects and relationships.

Source code is the most commonly available object for impact analysis. A traditional cross reference testing tool can be thought of as a very simple impact analysis aid. Impact analysis tools can range in sophistication from tools that are as simple as cross reference listers to tools which are capable of complex data flow analysis.

Interesting, powerful tools can be built for source code impact analysis. It is important, however, to construct tools which are cost effective for dealing with real maintenance problems that really occur rather than with imagined problems whose principal appeal is that they can be attacked using an elegant methodology. For this reason it is suggested that research on impact analysis tools focus on studies of maintenance problems and on studies of the types of changes that are commonly made to source code.

Maintenance problems that arise due to changes in source code can be due not only to change itself but to bad design and imprecise specifications. Studies of maintenance problems should consider how the problems can be avoided with different design and specification methods. This is necessary in order to avoid building impact analysis tools for dealing with problems which might be avoidable through the use of better software development techniques. Structured design, for example, emphasizes the use of modular decompositions in which there is low inter-module coupling and high module cohesion. Parnas' design emphasizes the hiding of design decisions (e.g., data structure implementations) inside modules. Both methods are useful for reducing the potential effects of change and in reducing the need for elaborate impact analysis techniques and tools.

The special problems of doing impact analysis on distributed systems source code will include those of doing static analysis on distributed systems source code. In order to determine data dependencies between parts of a system it is necessary to do data flow analysis. The special problems of doing data flow analysis on distributed systems code are described in the static analysis critique. The limitations on distributed system structure which are necessary to allow data flow analysis to be carried out efficiently must be very carefully considered in any proposal to construct a change impact tool for distributed systems.

In distributed system design it is necessary to consider not only software design but also the hardware configuration onto which the software must be mapped. The effects of changes on hardware are likely to impact the design of a distributed system more than the design of a non-distributed system. It is necessary to model both the software system and the hardware resources in order to do automated impact analysis. It is also necessary to consider timing and synchronization, and to construct models for these. Table 7-3 shows the anticipated effect of impact analysis upon the lifecycle phases of EDPS. Little research has been completed on the representation of this kind of information for distributed systems and any proposed research into impact analysis for distributed systems should include resources for studying first the primary problems of design and requirements representations.

	REQUIREMENTS	DESIGN	CODING	TESTING	DOCUMENTATION	MAINTENANCE
STORAGE	3 / 2	3 / 3				2 / 3
ARITHMETIC LOGIC UNIT	1 / 3	2 / 3				1 / 2
PROCESS CONTROL	1 / 1	1 / 3				1 / 2
INPUT						1 / 1
OUTPUT						1 / 1

SYSTEM BUS

COUPLING refers to number of connections between a calling and a called module as well as to the complexity of those connections. "1" means low coupling. "2" means average coupling. "3" means high coupling.

COHESION describes how tightly bound together the instructions are within a module. If module does more than one discrete task the instructions in that module are not bound very closely to each other. "1" means strong cohesion. "2" means average cohesion. "3" means weak cohesion.

Table 7-3 Effect of Impact Analysis Techniques on EDPS Lifecycle Phases

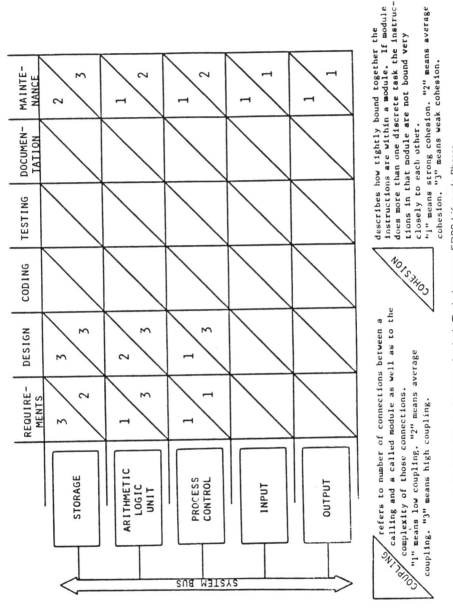

8. Remaining Work to be Accomplished in the Distributed Processing Tools Definition Study

The Distributed Processing Tools Definition (DPTD) study is divided into three phases:

- Phase I - Study of Hardware and Software Technologies
- Phase II - Survey of Existing Tools and Techniques
- Phase III - Analysis of Problem Areas and Recommendation of Candidates for Research and Development Efforts.

This report includes the results of the Phase I study only. The hardware and software technologies pertinent to embedded distributed processing systems have been analyzed and their requirements and impacts have been categorized with respect to the software life cycle phases. This categorization of requirements and impacts forms the basis of the Phase II survey. In Phase II, industrial, university, and Department of Defense software tools and techniques will be researched, and we will identify those tools and techniques that satisfy the lifecycle phase support requirements established in Phase I. Also in Phase II we will denote as problem areas those Phase I lifecycle requirements that are not supported by tools or techniques. Finally, in Phase III these problem areas will be analyzed and a prioritized list of candidate research and development efforts to solve the problem areas will be recommended. These candidate efforts will be fully described with estimates of manhours, schedules, technical feasibility, benefits, and probable users. Phase III completes the DPTD study.

The results of the tools survey will be submitted to RADC in an interim technical report upon the completion of Phase II. This report will be concatenated to the Phase I report. The benefits of this approach are twofold. First, the phases of the DPTD study are closely linked, and each phase builds upon the preceding phase. The understanding of the work completed to date on the DPTD study requires an understanding of the previously accomplished work. It is easier for a reader to understand the results if they are all bound in a single volume with smooth transition between phases. Secondly, in the course of the study modifications and updates can be easily incorporated. These updates arise because of recent technological advances or deeper insight gained in a particular area during the course of the study. Modifications to the text of previously submitted reports will be summarized in a list of page changes and change bars will be inserted in the text denoting the affected portions. Therefore, the final technical report for the DPTD study will be submitted to RADC in a single volume that reports the results of Phases I, II, and III.

Appendix A: Definition of the Scope of Embedded Distributed Processing Systems

Military computer systems span the spectrum from single microprocessors in "smart-bombs" to multiple, distributed mainframes in world-wide communications systems. The particular categories of military systems most affected by technological advancements in embedded distributed processing include: (1) armament, (2) aeronautical, (3) missile and space, (4) command/control/communication, and (5) mission/force management systems. The analysis of the impact of technological advancements upon these five categories of systems is aided by grouping the five categories into two, higher-level, generic classifications. The armament, aeronautical, and missile and space systems will be classified as weapon systems, and the command/control/communication and mission/force management systems will be classified as communication systems. These generic classifications are based upon common characteristics of the members within each class. These common characteristics are defined later in this appendix. Hence, in this technical report we will use the generic classifications of weapon systems and communication systems, and it is understood that observations and conclusions pertinent to a generic classification apply to all members of the class.

Distributed processing systems can be visualized as a region of a volume bounded by axes describing (1) distribution of hardware, (2) distribution of control, and (3) distribution of data base. Figure A-1 shows this volume.

The portion of this volume characterized by a single CPU, a single, fixed executive controller, and a single copy of the data base represents the common uniprocessor systems of today. Moving toward multiple computers, multiple operating systems, and partitioned data bases is characteristic of fully distributed processing systems. Weapon systems and communication systems occupy different regions within the characteristic volume, but are definitely within the distributed processing domain. Figure A-1 shows the relationship of uniprocessor systems to distributed processing systems and where weapon and communication systems fit in these descriptions.

The differences between weapon systems and communication systems are rooted in implementation of the

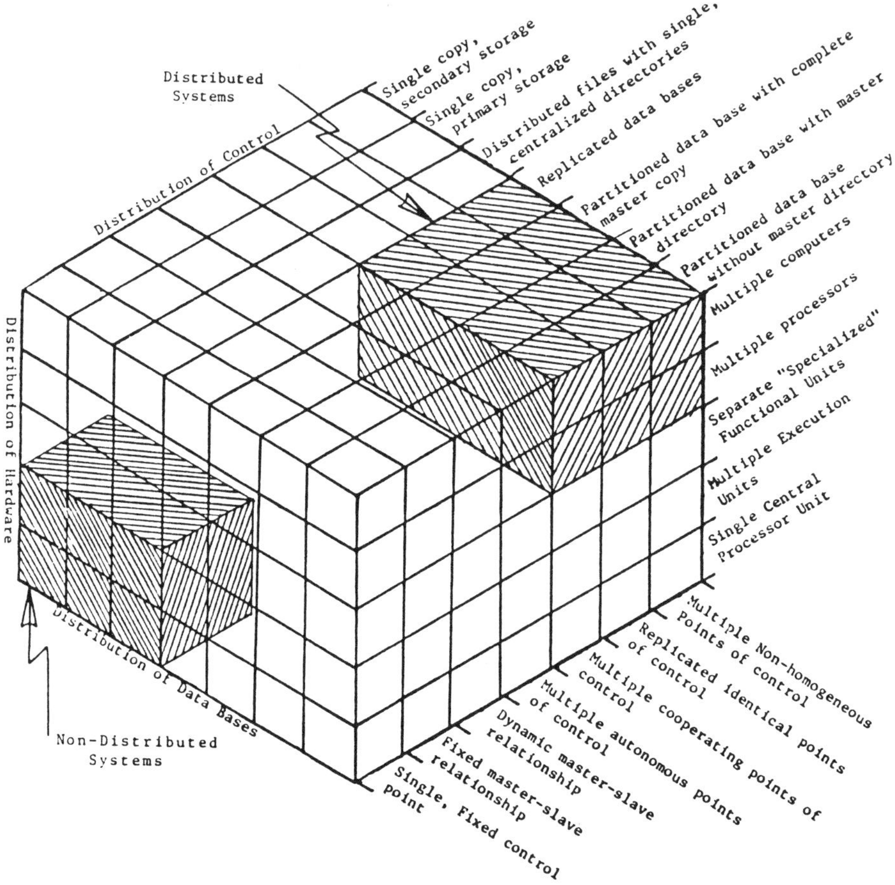

Figure A-1 Characteristic Volume of Computer System Capabilities

following two key features of distributed processing environments:

(1) the degree of human interaction required by the hardware/software system

(2) the timing constraints of system operation.

Weapon systems must require human decision before a weapon is released; for safety requirements a system should not automatically switch from a non-attack situation to an attack with weapons launch capability without explicit human consent. However, once this consent is acknowledged, the hardware/software system must execute in real-time because of the speeds associated with targets and launch platforms. Therefore, prior knowledge of system state transitions is a prerequisite for weapon systems mode design. Other characteristics of weapons systems that are commensurate with these two features are shown in Table A-1.

In contrast, communication systems permit a higher degree of automation without human intervention. If no human response is received the system can automatically queue messages or resend the transmissions to provide backup capability. Consequently, the system mode design is often interrupt driven with queuing permitted. The system timing constraints are often near real-time; that is, between one millisecond and one second. Table A-1 lists the characteristics of communication systems. A study of Table A-1 shows that both weapon systems and communication systems strongly exhibit features of distributed processing; however, there are significant differences within this distributed processing domain to warrant the two generic classifications of weapon systems and communication systems that we have identified.

In summary the grouping of armament, aeronautical, and missile and space systems into the generic classification of weapon systems and the grouping of command/control/communication and mission/force management into the generic classification of communication systems recognizes the differences between the groups and benefits the distributed processing tools definition study by specifying the requirements for tools and techniques for a larger class of generic military systems.

Table A-1

Characteristics of Weapon and Communication Embedded Distributed Processing Systems

CHARACTERISTICS	CLASSIFICATION	
	WEAPON SYSTEMS (Armament & Aeronautical & Missile & Space)	COMMUNICATION SYSTEMS (Command/Control Communications & Mission/Force Management)
Timing Constraints	Real-Time (usually less than a few milliseconds)	Near Real-Time (usually between milliseconds and several seconds)
Spatial Constraints	Close physical proximity (often less than 1000 feet) of components	Large geographical separations (often more than 100,000 feet) of components
System Mode Design	All transitions between system states are a priori known to satisfy safety requirements	System state transitions are often interrupt/transaction driven with queuing permitted and may be random
Data Transfer	Usually relatively small quantities of data transferred at high data rates	Very large amounts of data transferred

Table A-1 (Continued)

CHARACTERISTICS	CLASSIFICATION: WEAPON SYSTEMS (Armament & Aeronautical & Missile & Space)	CLASSIFICATION: COMMUNICATION SYSTEMS (Command/Control Communications & Mission/Force Management)
Hardware/ Software Resources	Hardware and software functions are often distributed to special-purpose, dedicated units	Usually a multiplicity of general purpose hardware components (disks memories, CPU, etc.) and software must be transparent to hardware peculiarities
Operating System	Minimum size with limited capabilities for support of system mode designs	High-level, very capable system that integrates and controls the distributed components
System Component Interconnection	Highly standardized communication protocols to permit easy add on of new units to bus	"Cooperative autonomy" whereby the various system components work largely independently but in a coordinated manner under the control of the operating system
Cohesiveness	Tightly-coupled	Loosely-coupled to fully distributed

Table A-1 (Continued)

	CLASSIFICATION	
CHARACTERISTICS	WEAPON SYSTEMS (Armament & Aeronautical & Missile & Space)	COMMUNICATION SYSTEMS (Command/Control Communications & Mission/Force Management)
Backup Capability	System degradation must be predictable	System degradation is minimized by redundant data processing elements and communication links
Security	Security must be maintained at the entire system level because the weapon system must be isolated from external manipulation	Security must be maintained within the individual components because of extensive communication links to the external environment

Appendix B: Rationale for the Selection of ADA as the Higher Order Language to Study for EDPS

Ada has now been adopted by the Department of Defense. As far as the United States Air Force is concerned, Ada is scheduled for introduction and use by 1983. By 1986 all new embedded distributed processing systems must use Ada. Present strategy relies upon the continued use of JOVIAL (J73) until sufficient development time has been provided for Ada.

The Office of the Under Secretary of Defense for Research and Engineering (OUSDRE) has been assigned responsibility for planning the Software Technology Initiative (STI) of the Department of Defense. Subsequent coordination also rests with OUSDRE. The present is particularly propitious for a concerted and concentrated effort on Ada. All candidates for short-term research initiatives must emphasize technology transfer, standardization of software environments, tools, packages, workstations, and preliminary results from thrusts whose payoffs occur later. In summary they must produce reusable Ada packages within integrated software support environments which are themselves dependent upon Ada. As presently envisioned, the integrated software support environment of the future will evolve from or be incorporated by the Ada Programming Support Environment (APSE). Active efforts are underway to design and implement the APSE. All future software tools concerning embedded distributed processing systems must link to the APSE. The consequences of Ada will be felt throughout the entire industry as well as all the Federal Government. The integrated software support environment provided by Ada will provide important contributions for many years.

Meeting the overall goals of the Ada effort depends upon the wide availability of effective support environments. In particular these environments must be rigorously engineered to support Ada throughout the software life cycle phases. Specific features of such environments include:

- layered approaches to maximize subsequent portability of tools;
- completely engineered Ada compilers which produce high quality object code;
- comprehensive basic toolsets;
- careful separation of roles between hosts and targets;

- user friendly interfaces;
- sophisticated database techniques; and
- complete sets of control tools.

Many attempts at integrated software support environments have been made. Few have succeeded. The fragments of both the successful and unsuccessful attempts still exist and are constantly being used. All these remainders need to be converted to the integrated software support environment that Ada enables. The tools of this emerging environment have yet to be developed. Most are generic in nature and will probably exhibit unique properties. All will be developed through the system lifecycle phases. Consequently, of primary importance to embedded distributed processing systems is a complete understanding of Ada and what its impact will be on the software development lifecycle. Subsequent effort within the Distributed Processing Tools Definition Study for RADC will concentrate upon Ada. The justification for such a concentration is offered in the preceding remarks.

List of Abbreviations

ADEPT	- A Design-based Evaluation and Prediction Technique
ADGE	- Air Defense Ground Environment
ALU	- Arithmetic Logic Unit
APSE	- Ada Programming Support Environment
ARC	- Advanced Research Center
ASGS	- Automatic Software Generation System
CADES	- Computer Analytical Design Evaluation System
CHiP	- Configurable, Highly Parallel
CIU	- Computer Interface Unit
CMU	- Carnegie Mellon University
CPU	- Central Processor Unit
CSMA-CD	- Carrier Sense Multiple Access with Collision Detection
DAVE	- Documentation, Analysis, Validation and Error-detection
DEC	- Digital Equipment Corporation
DEDS	- Data Entry Display Stations
DOD	- Department of Defense
DPTD	- Distributed Processing Tools Definition
DREAM	- Design Requirements Evaluation Analysis Method
EDPS	- Embedded Distributed Processing Systems
E/O	- Electro/Optical
GPU	- General Processor Unit

HAL/S	- Hierarchical Analysis Language/System
HOL	- Higher Order Language
ICL	- International Computers Limited
I/O	- Input/Output
ISO	- International Standards Organization
ISSE	- Integrated Software Support Environment
LAN	- Local Area Network
LU	- Logical Unit
Mbps	- Megabytes per second
MIPS	- Million Instructions Per Second
NASA	- National Aeronautics and Space Administration
NAV	- Navigation
NP	- Non-deterministic Polynomial
OOM	- Object-Oriented Modularization
OSI	- Open Systems Interconnection
OUSDRE	- Office of the Under Secretary of Defense for Research and Engineering
PAWS	- Performance Analyst Workbench System
PPBS	- Professional Programmer Based System
PSA	- Problem Statement Analyzer
PSL	- Problem Statement Language
PWB	- Programmer's Work Bench
STI	- Software Technology Initiatives
TRW	- Thompson Ramo Woolridge
UCSF	- University of California at San Francisco
VHSIC	- Very High Speed Integrated Circuits
VLSI	- Very Large Scale Integration

Bibliography

1. Aho, A.V., Hopcroft, J.E., and Ullman, J.D., The Design and Analysis of Computer Algorithms, Addison-Wesley Publishing Co., Reading, Mass., Oct., 1975.

2. Andrews, D.M. and Bensen, J.P., An Automated Testing Methodology and Its Implementation, Proceeding of the Fifth International Conference on Software Engineering, San Diego, 1981.

3. Barbe, D.F., VHSIC Systems and Technology, Computer, Feb., 1981.

4. Barnes, J., et al, United Kingdom Ada Study Final Technical Report, London, Dept. of Industry, 1982.

5. Bernstein, P.A. and Goodman, N., Concurrency Control in Distributed Data Base Systems, ACM Computing Surveys, June, 1981.

6. Boehm, B.W., Some Experience With Automated Aids to the Design of Large Scale Reliable Software, IEEE Transactions on Software Engineering, Vol. SE-1, 1975.

7. Browne, J.C., The Performance Analyst's Workbench System, Information Research Associates, Austin, Texas, Apr., 1981.

8. DeMarco, T., Structured Analysis and System Specification, Yourdon, N.Y., 1978.

9. Deutsch, M.S., Software Project Verification and Validations, IEEE Computer, Apr., 1981.

10. Ferris, David, Micro Software Trends in the Business and Professional Environment Conference, Anaheim, Calif., Nov., 1981.

11. Fosdick, L.D. and Osterweil, L.J., Data Flow Analysis in Software Reliability, Computing Surveys, Vol. 8, 1976.

12. Gutz, S., Wasserman, A.I., and Spier, M.J., Personal Development Systems for the Professional Programmer, Computer, Vol. 14, No. 4, Apr., 1981.

13. Hansen, P.B., Testing a Multiprogramming System, Software Practice and Experience, Vol. 3, 1973.

14. Hennell, M.A., Woodward, M.R., and Hedley, R., On Program Analysis, Information Processing Letters, Vol. 5, 1978.

15. Horejs, J., Finite Semantics for Program Testing, Scripta Fac. Sci. Nat. U.J.E.P. Brunensis, Mathematical 1, Vol. 9, 1979.

16. Howden, W.E., Methodology for the Generation of Program Test Data, IEEE Transactions on Computers, C-24, 1975.

17. Howden, W.E., Life Cycle Software Validation, Computer, Feb., 1982.

18. Howden, W.E., Applicability of Software Validation Techniques to Scientific Programs, ACM Transactions on Programming Languages and Systems, Vol. 2, 1980.

19. Howden, W.E., Functional Program Testing, IEEE Transactions Software Engineering, Vol. SE-7, 1980.

20. Howden, W.E., Functional Testing and Design Abstraction, Journal of Systems and Software, Vol. 1, 1980.

21. Howden, W.E., Contemporary Software Development Environments, Communications of the ACM, Apr., 1982.

22. Ichbiah, J.D., et al, Reference Manual for the Ada Programming Language, U.S. DoD, July, 1980.

23. Intel Corporation, iAPX432 Object Primer, manual order number 171858-001 Rev. B., Santa Clara, CA., 1981.

24. Intel Corporation, Introduction to the iAPX432 Architecture, manual order number 171821-001, Santa Clara, CA., 1981.

25. Korel, B. and Laski, J.W., A Data Flow Oriented Program Testing Strategy, Institute of Control Systems, Ul.Armii Czerkuonej 101, Katowice, Poland, 1980.

26. Krutz, R.L., A Hierarchical Design Approach for VHSIC, VHSIC Briefs (Phase 3 Projects), OUSDRE, Oct., 1981.

27. LeBlanc, R.J. and MacCabe, A.B., An Introduction to Data Abstraction, School of Information and

Computer Science, Georgia Institute of Technology, Atlanta, Georgia.

28. Liskov, B. and Zilles, S., Programming with Abstract Data Types, Project MAC, Massachusetts Institute of Technology, Cambridge, Massachusetts.

29. Mhatre, G., VLSI: The Challenge, Electronics Engineering Times Technology Strategies, Nov., 1981.

30. Miller, E.F. and Melton, R.A., Automated Generation of Test Case Data Sets, Proceedings 1975 International Conference on Reliable Software, L.A., 1975.

31. Myers, G.F., The Art of Software Testing, Wiley Interscience, N.Y., 1979.

32. Ntafos, S.L., On Testing With Required Elements, Dept. of Math. Science, U. of Texas at Dallas, 1981.

33. Osterwald, L.J., A Software Lifecycle Methodology and Tool Support, U. of Colorado at Boulder, Boulder, Colorado, Apr. 1979.

34. Osterweil, L.J. and Fosdick, L.D., DAVE - A Validation, Error Detection, and Documentation System for FORTRAN Programs, Software Practice and Experience, Vol. 6, 1976.

35. Panzl, D.J., Automatic Software Test Drivers, Computer, Vol. 11, 1978.

36. Parnas, D.L., On the Criteria to be Used in Decomposing Systems in Modules, Communications of the ACM, Vol. 15, No. 12, Dec., 1972, p. 1053.

37. Parnas, D.L., Information Distribution Aspects of Design Methodology, IFIPS-71, North Holland, 1971.

38. Redwine, Samuel T., Siegel, Eric D., and Berglass, Gilbert R., Candidate R & D Thrusts for the Software Technology Initiative, DoD, May, 1981.

39. Reifer, D.J. and Trattner, S., A Glossary of Software Tools and Techniques, Computer, Vol. 10, No. 7, July, 1977.

40. Rice, J.G., Build Program Technique: A Practical Approach for the Development of Automatic Software Generation Systems, John Wiley & Sons, 1981.

41. Riddle, W.E. and Fairley, R.E., Software Development Tools, Berlin, Springer-Verlag, 1980.

42. Ryer, M. and Belmont, P.A., Building the First Ada Compiler - Planning Ahead, AIAA Computers in Aerospace III Conference, Oct., 1981.

43. Siegel, H.J. and Smith, S.D., An Interconnection Network for Multimicroprocessor Emulator Systems, IEEE, June, 1979.

44. Smith, Connie, Software Performance Engineering, Computerworld, Dec. 7, 1981.

45. Smith, C.U., The Prediction and Evaluation of the Performance of Software from Extended Design Specifications, IPAD Project Report No. 2, NASA, Aug., 1980.

46 Snyder, L., Introduction to the Configurable, Highly Parallel Computer, ONR Report CSD-TR-351, May, 1981.

47. Stucki, L.G., Automatic Generation of Self-Metric Software, Proceedings IEEE Symposium on Computer Software Reliability, N.Y., 1973.

48. Stucki, L.G., New Directions in Automated Tools for Improving Software Quality, Current Trends in Programming Methodology, Vol. 27, Prentice-Hall, 1977.

49. Taylor, R.N. and Osterweil, L.J., Anomaly Detection in Concurrent Software of Static Data Flow Analysis, IEEE Transactions on Software Engineering, Vol. 6, 1980.

50. Taylor, R.N., Complexity of Analyzing the Synchronization Structure of Concurrent Programs, U. of Victoria, Dept. of Comp. Sci., 1981.

51. Teichroew, D. and Bastarache, M.J., PSL User's Manual, U. of Michigan, ISDOS Working Paper No. 98, March, 1975.

52. Yourdon, E. and Constantine, L., Structured Design, Prentice-Hall, Englewood Cliffs, N.J., 1979.

Part II

Application of Software Engineering Technology

The information in Part II is from *Distributed Processing Tools Definition—Application of Software Engineering Technology,* prepared by Herbert C. Conn, Jr., David L. Kellogg, Rodney M. Bond, States L. Nelson, Scott L. Harmon, Sue A. Johnson, William D. Baker, and Paul B. Dobbs of General Dynamics Corporation for the U.S. Air Force Systems Command Rome Air Development Center, June 1983.

1. Technical Report Summary

General Dynamics Data Systems Division is under contract to Rome Air Development Center to conduct a study entitled Distributed Processing Tools Definition. The objectives are to investigate the requirements for software life cycle support in embedded distributed processing systems and to specify applicable software tools and techniques by life cycle phase.

1.1 Project Overview

The study is divided into three phases which are illustrated in Figure 1-1. Phases I and II of the study have been completed, and their results are described in the present Technical Report.

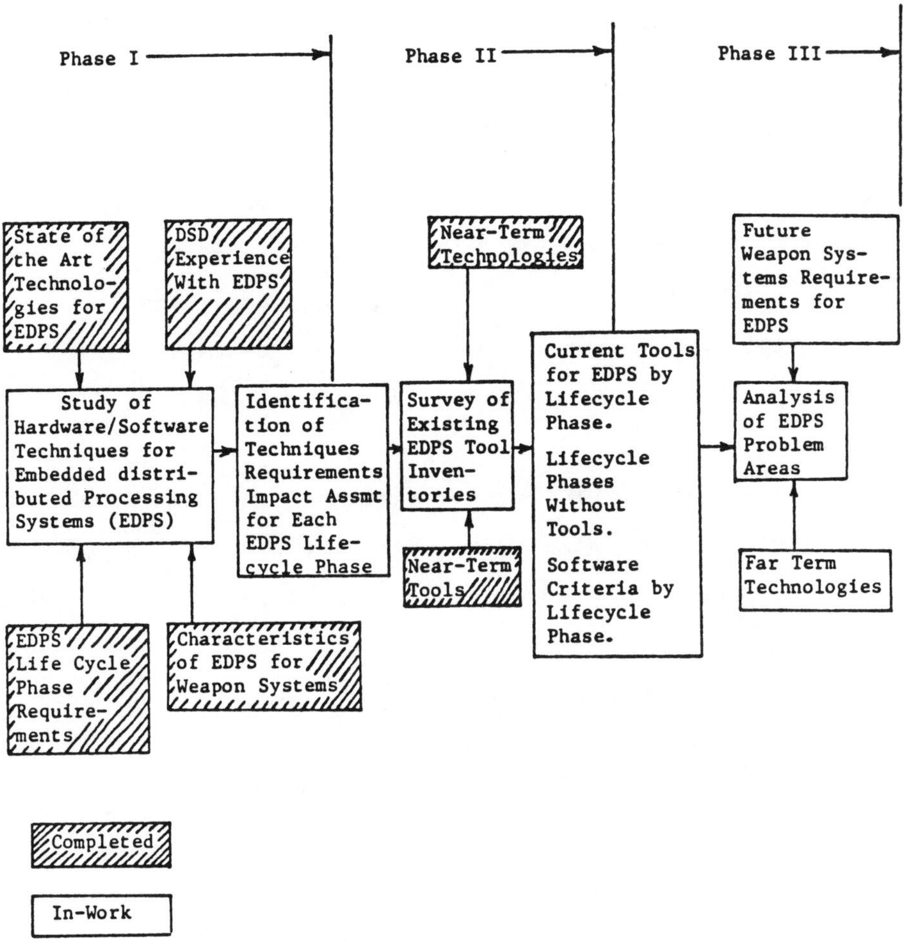

Figure 1-1 Overview of the Distributed Processing Tools Definition Study

1.2 Phase II Conclusions

The principal technical perspective used in the following conclusions assumes a combined system functionality for hardware and software. Embedded distributed processing systems require both to be operable at the same time. Each conclusion is followed by a reference to its appropriate discussion in the Technical Report.

1) Development of Distributed Processing Systems is best supported by an Integrated Software Support Environment (ISSE) (see paragraph 3.0).

2) It is economically efficient to make ISSEs for distributed processing open-ended (see paragraph 3.0).

3) Efficient static analysis of deterministic systems is possible (see paragraph 3.1).

4) Further research is needed on static analysis of nondeterministic systems (see paragraph 3.1).

5) Ada will require a cross-reference tool with extensive capabilities (see paragraph 3.1.1).

6) Ada will require static analyzers for its concurrency constructs (see paragraph 3.1.1).

7) The requirements and design phases must be heavily stressed and further automated to build cost efficient and reliable distributed systems (see paragraph 3.2).

8) Rapid prototypers and simulators are necessary support for distributed processing system designers (see paragraph 3.2).

9) An automated requirements tool consisting of a requirements interface processor, a requirements document generator, a requirements analyzer, and a requirements language translator has proven to be useful during the requirements phase and should be further developed for distributed systems (see paragraph 4.2.1).

10) The design phase is virtually poverty-stricken with regard to tools. The only tools available currently in this area are program design language processors, even though this phase is one of the most important in determining the overall quality of the finished system (see paragraph 4.2.2).

11) The tools of the coding phase can be divided into two categories: tools dealing with languages and tools dealing with standards. The tools dealing with languages exist for any usable high level language, with the possible exception of checkout compilers. Since the functions of a checkout compiler overlap both the coding and the testing phase, checkout compilers should be developed where possible. Standards auditors and formatters should be developed to enhance consistency of code (see paragraph 4.2.3).

12) The tools of the testing phase are concerned with checking for adherence to requirements and design and resolving coding errors. Referring to Table 4-2, all needed criteria for the life cycle phase of testing (Table 4-1) have been enhanced. Due to the applicability of the testing tools to other phases, criteria not identified as needed have been enhanced in the testing phase. Testing has an abundance of tools; however, tools should be more concerned with distributedness of the software (see paragraph 4.2.4).

13) The tools of the maintenance phase consist of a version generator, rapid reconfiguration, and report generator. Many criteria are not addressed in the maintenance phase (Table 4-2) according to the

prescribed criteria in Table 4-1. More tools should be developed to satisfy the requirements since it is the phase ensuring the continuation of quality throughout the life of the software (see paragraph 4.2.5).

14) The operations phase has few tools since it is usually a user phase with little software engineering activity; however, tools should be developed to ensure operational quality of the system. Comparing Table 4-2 with the required criteria for the operations phase in Table 4-1, the diagnostic analyzer and system builder enhance less than one-half of the criteria. Criteria such as control of data access and ease of use, which are critical user criteria, need to be addressed by new tool development (see paragraph 4.2.6).

15) Knowledge-based systems will be components of far-term artificial intelligence techniques both in development support systems and in operational application systems. Near-term tool definition should take into account the potential for integration into future highly intelligent systems (see paragraph 3.2.4).

2. Scope of Embedded Distributed Processing Systems

Distributed processing systems can be characterized by their position within a three-dimensional space. Each axis of that space can be used to separate the non-distributed environment from its distributed counterpart. The first of these axes concerns the distribution of hardware. It ranges from a single central processor unit to multiple computers. The single central processor unit is characterized by one control unit, one arithmetic logic unit, and one central memory. The multiple computers are characterized by multiple general purpose central processing units which have their own control units, arithmetic logic units, central memories, and input/output systems. Several configurations lie somewhere between these two extremes. In summary, the five following generic hardware configurations have been isolated and are in common use.

1) Single central processor unit characterized by
   - i) one control unit
   - ii) one arithmetic logic unit and
   - iii) one central memory.
2) Multiple execution units characterized by
   - i) one control unit
   - ii) mutiple, identical arithmetic logic units

and

iii) possibly multiple, independent central memories.

3) Separate "specialized" functional units characterized by
   - i) one general purpose control unit and
   - ii) multiple arithmetic logic units or processing units
     - a) some may be specialized units
     - b) each is limited and
     - c) all may be identical general purpose units.

4) Multiple processors characterized by
   - i) multiple control units
   - ii) multiple arithmetic logic units
   - iii) possibly multiple, independent, central memories and
   - iv) a single, coordinated input/output system.

5) Multiple computers characterized by
   - i) multiple general purpose central processing units with their own control unit, arithmetic logic unit, central memory, and input/output system.

Distributed processing systems are usually composed of multiple processors and multiple computers which are the fourth and fifth generic hardware configurations. The non-distributed environment is typified by the single central processor unit and multiple execution units which are the first and second generic configurations.

The second axis within the three-dimensional space concerns the distribution of control. It ranges from a single, fixed point of control to multiple control points which are not necessarily homogeneous but which cooperate on the execution of a task. In all there are seven categories of generic control:

1) Single, fixed control point;
2) Fixed master-slave relationship;
3) Dynamic master-slave relationship;
4) Multiple points of control which are totally autonomous;
5) Multiple points of control which cooperate on the execution of a task which has been subdivided into sub-tasks;
6) Replicated, identical points of control cooperating on the execution of a task; and
7) Multiple control points which are not necessarily homogeneous but which cooperate on the execution of a task.

Distributed processing systems are usually typified by the top three categories of generic control, i.e., multiple points of control, replicated points of control, and multiple control points. Conversely, non-distributed processing systems are characterized by the bottom two categories, i.e., single control points and fixed master-slave relationships.

After an examination of only two of the three dimensions, several obvious observations can be made. First, the movement within the marketplace has been and will continue to be from single processors to multiple processors. As these multiple processors become more prevalent, non-distributed control policies become questionable. Second, as individual nodes reach parity within multiple processor configurations, choosing one node over another for control purposes is increasingly difficult to defend. Third, configurations which run without an overriding executive are now possible. In summary, the multiple processor configurations have complicated the present situation.

The third and final axis within the three-dimensional space concerns the distribution of data bases. In terms of complexity it ranges from a single copy data in secondary storage to a completely partitioned data base without a master file or director. Many gradations exist between these two extremes. To date approximately seven generic categories of distributed data bases have been isolated. The first three are associated with centralized data bases while the last four are associated with the emerging distributed data bases.

Centralized data bases include:

1) single copy, secondary storage;
2) single copy, primary memory; and
3) distributed files with single, centralized directories.

Distributed data bases include:

4) replicated data bases;
5) partitioned data base with a complete master copy;
6) partitioned data base with a master directory; and
7) partitioned data base without a master file or directory.

File structures must not only accommodate the serialized requests from a single processor but must also accommodate the concurrent requests from several processors.

When all three axes of the three-dimensional space are considered, the spatial location of distributed processing is clearly different from non-distributed or centralized processing. That difference is illustrated in Figure 2-1. Such distributed processing systems are usually components within larger systems, i.e., they are embedded.

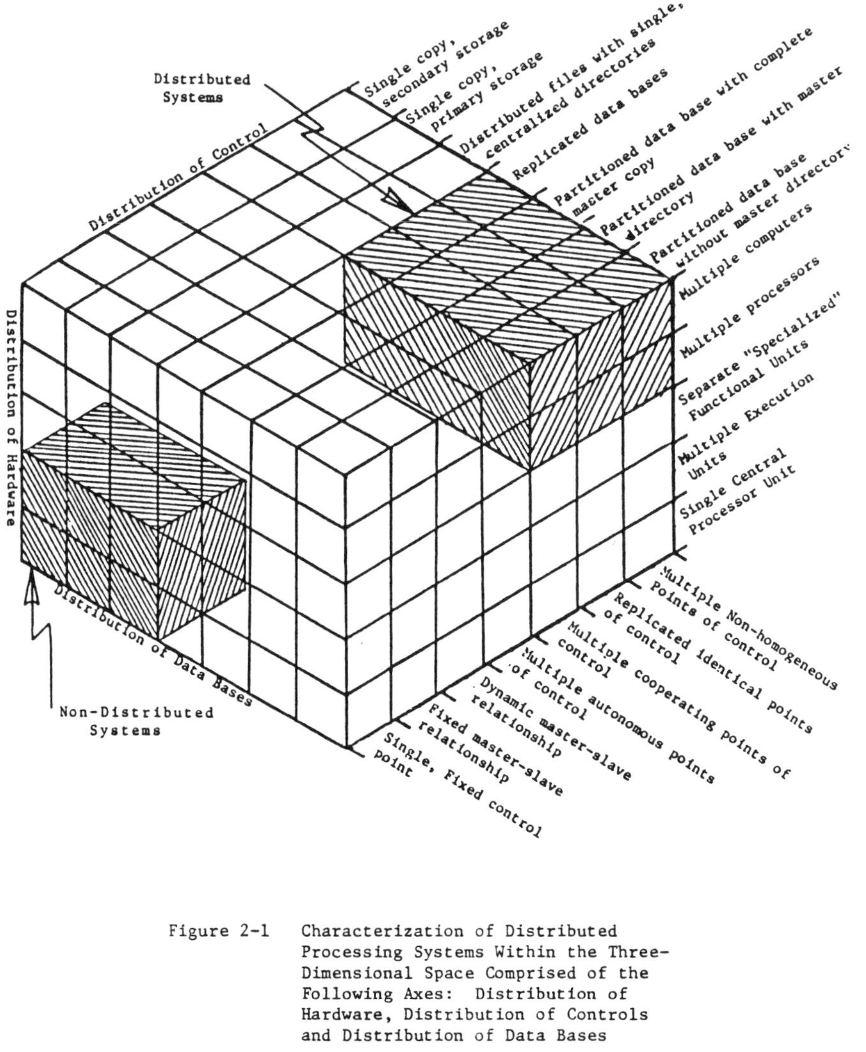

Figure 2-1 Characterization of Distributed Processing Systems Within the Three-Dimensional Space Comprised of the Following Axes: Distribution of Hardware, Distribution of Controls and Distribution of Data Bases

The application functions performed by these larger systems commonly take precedence over their embedded components. Examples would include large mainframes composed of tightly-coupled multiple processors. The users of such mainframes are seldom aware of their embedded components and assume a centralized environment. Of course the tools available to such users are designed to operate in a centralized environment. The capability of a tightly-coupled, concurrently-operated environment is seldom made available to users because of a shortage of tools. Despite this shortage, decision making concerning embedded distributed processing systems requires mastery of data movement and a solid understanding of computational efficiency. Enough information about the distribution of hardware, control, and data bases must be known within appropriate real-time constraints in order to reach informed decisions. The functionality of the final product depends upon these informed decisions.

Because of inter-relations between axes, the analogy of a three-dimensional space can only be carried so far. Hardware, control, and data bases are not independent of one another in a distributed processing environment. A change in one impacts the other.

Growth in data bases can and does force change in tightly-coupled hardware to accommodate increased information flow. As tightly-coupled hardware changes, the control process is impacted. The bottom line remains functionality despite what happens to either the data base, hardware, or control. That functionality represents a massive tradeoff between hardware and software. Furthermore, each one of these tradeoffs can be characterized by its position within the inter-related, three-dimensional space.

2.1 Increased Distribution of Hardware

As distributed processing systems are winning wide acceptance within the marketplace, their ability to move and efficiently process large amounts of data has attracted military interest. Current military computer systems span the spectrum from "smart bombs" and bullets to global communications systems. The resultant military applications fall into two very large generic classifications:

1) Weapon systems and
2) Communications systems

Included within weapon systems are armament, aeronautical, missile, and space applications. Included within communications systems are command/control/communications applications as well as mission and force management functions. Each category occupies a characteristic position within the three-dimensional space whose axes are the distribution of control, the distribution of hardware, and the distribution of data bases. These positions are presented in Figure 2-2.

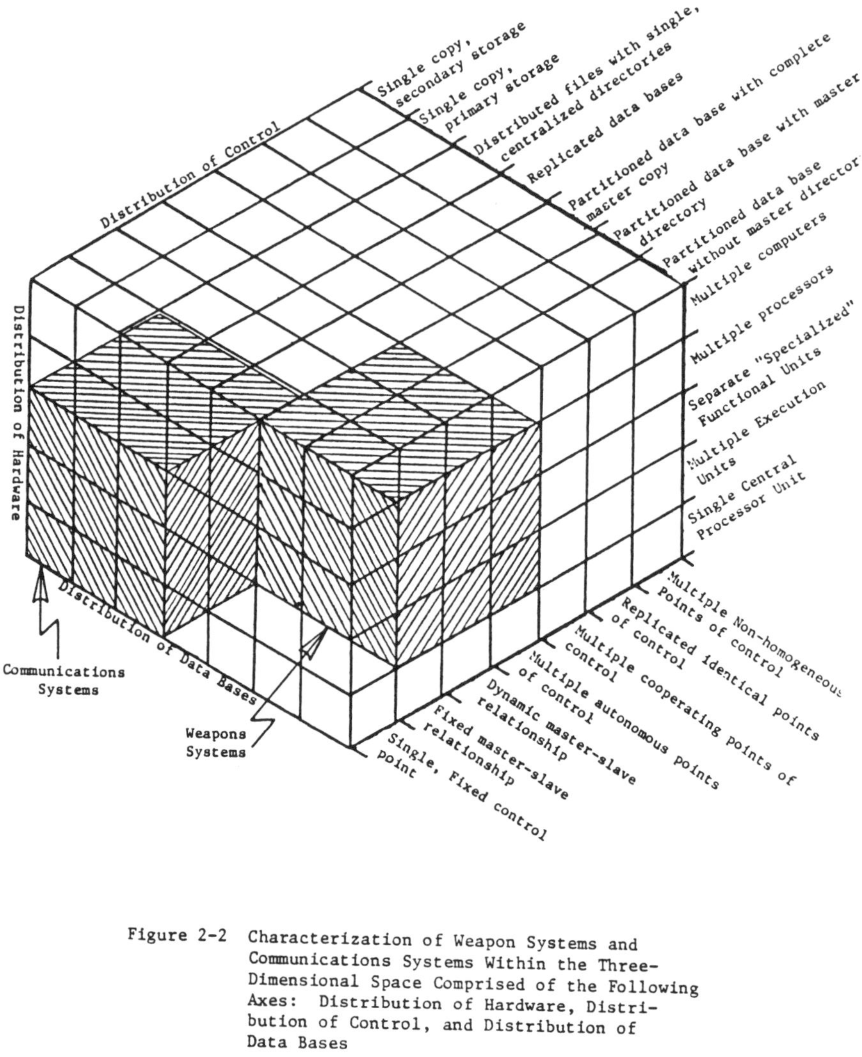

Figure 2-2 Characterization of Weapon Systems and Communications Systems Within the Three-Dimensional Space Comprised of the Following Axes: Distribution of Hardware, Distribution of Control, and Distribution of Data Bases

Currently the communications systems contain the characteristics of non-distributed systems. However, growth is occurring and such systems are expanding their capability. Dynamic master-slave relationships and separate "specialized" functional units are beginning to appear. Furthermore, distributed files with single, centralized directories are beginning to appear in some leading-edge communications systems. Notably the connections remain loosely-coupled and are exemplified by command/control/communications systems. Such loose-coupling results from the constrained bandwidth of the connection technologies currently in use. However, these technologies are undergoing great change. Bandwidths are increasing and as they increase, the capability for tighter-coupling is enabled. Possibly replicated data bases with multiple processors will be available in the near term.

Currently weapon systems lie somewhere between the non-distributed and distributed technologies. Their connections are more tightly-coupled than the communications systems. Although their bandwidths are usually greater than communications systems, they are not as high as the distributed systems. As a consequence, some of the capability of distributed systems is not available in current weapon systems. The reason lies in the control functions. By their nature, weapon systems must be tightly controlled. A stores management system may inventory, fire, and update a particular weapon system's status. However, that same system is not fail-safe and must verify its action beforehand through the concurrence of a control system. Its actual operation is characteristic of an embedded system, not a completely distributed system. In the near term, weapon systems will retain their present orientation. Completely fail-safe operation of distributed systems remains a concept for future implementation.

2.1.1 Weapon Systems

Advanced weapon systems are becoming increasingly complex and rely upon computers and embedded processors to operate. One example is provided by self-contained surface mobile weapon systems used by the Army. Such systems rely heavily upon an internal fire control computer and an embedded navigation system to provide operational direction. As newer systems evolve, an increasing number of remote functions are being incorporated. One such function is a remote operating console which requires more tightly-coupled data bases and a high level of data exchange. Traditional methods of fault detection and isolation no longer apply in such configurations.

Failures can occur and remain undetected simply because of sheer complexity. An example would be a minor logic error which occurred intermittently within the internal fire control computer. If a sufficient number of errors were generated, the weapon's accuracy would be destroyed. Since the problem is intermittent, routine maintenance would probably not perceive it.

Intermittent malfunctions are a problem for weapon systems in general, not surface mobile systems in particular. If these malfunctions occur at a critical time during an engagement, the effectiveness of a weapon system may be nullified. The internal fire control computer in a self-contained surface mobile weapon system illustrates how important a malfunction can be. Its embedded navigation system could have shifted modes from target search to target track when a malfunction caused the reverse shift. Instead of directing the system to the target, the fire control computer begins to search for that target. Observing such a phenomenon from the remote operating console does not alleviate the situation. To regain the lost target tracking mode, some sort of direct intervention must be initiated. Alternative modes of optical sighting and infrared detection schemes are often activated. In any case, the preferred action is to resolve and correct the malfunction source. This involves the direct detection and isolation of faults in real-time which is no trivial matter. Compounding the problem in our example is the implementation of a mode shift. Such a shift is related to the distribution of control. The embedded navigation system is capable of directing the fire control computer to the target but needs the concurrence of the fire control computer itself. This concurrence is a fail-safe mechanism to assure adequate operation of the surface mobile weapon system. In essence, the fire control computer concurs on the changes in operational modes. As illustrated, the ability of this computer to override the embedded navigation sytem can also create problems. What emerges is a need for new software tools.

Real-time fault isolation requirements are being satisfied in aircraft systems as well as spacecraft systems. The approach used by both systems is system redundancy through the use of multiple processors. When malfunctions occur, the redundant system automatically activities itself to maintain the operational mode and the same level of performance. The problem with such an approach is cost. The architecture in surface mobile weapon systems simply cannot afford the extra cost for redundancy. Consequently, software tools must be relied upon to accomplish the same objectives as system redundancy. These objectives are two in number:

1) provide real-time fault detection and advise a console operator of his alternatives and
2) achieve real-time fault isolation and retain specific failure parameters to diagnose the intermittent malfunctions.

As weapon systems have grown more complex, the verification of software has assumed greater importance. Missile systems provide a good example of evolving complexity. The transition from ballistic capability to cruise capability requires significantly greater amounts of software to be written and verified. General Dynamics has studied various software verification techniques and determined some of their shortcomings. In the context of weapon systems these shortcomings include computational overflows and program time constraints. Other methods of verification are required to address such problem areas, e.g., program testing based upon realistic simulations. Such realistic simulations can be used to verify more than computational overflows and program time constraints within weapon systems application software. Both software verification techniques and realistic simulations can be used to detect the following types of software errors:

1) Input conversion problems;
2) Output conversion problems;

3) Mathematical calculation problems;
4) Logic decision problems;
5) Path analysis problems;
6) Mathematical precision problems;
7) Lack of computational precision;
8) Initialization problems; and
9) Switches in operational modes.

Testing efforts based upon realistic simulations are clearly related to the distributions of hardware and control. The software verification techniques ignore the distribution of hardware but concentrate on the distributions of data bases and control.

As the complexity of weapon systems increases, the distribution of hardware also increases. The use of multiple processors has already been referenced. Such processors are usually tightly-coupled since they share common resources, e.g., the same data base. Viewed from the standpoint of statistics, such resource sharing increases the degrees of freedom over which a weapon system can operate. State of the art realistic simulations can now accommodate six degrees of freedom, i.e., six parameters can vary concurrently. The more de-centralized a system becomes, the greater its degrees of freedom. Extremely complex weapon systems require rigorous software testing.

If the actual operation of such weapon systems is to be avoided, realistic simulations and software verification techniques become extremely important. In a sense, the complexity of weapon systems will be constrained to our ability to verify their software or to simulate their subsequent operation realistically.

2.1.2 Communication Systems

Advanced communication systems are becoming increasingly complex and rely upon computers and embedded processors to operate. Such systems include command/control/communication applications as well as mission and force management functions. From the standpoint of users such systems seem to be loosely-coupled or completely uncoupled. From the standpoint of network designers, such systems are becoming tightly-coupled. Both viewpoints are valid although they seem to be contradictory. An explanation can be developed through an examination of Figure 2-3 concerning the nodes and links within a generic network system. Several levels of communication take place concurrently within such a system. The most essential layers concern the operation of the network itself. In the example this includes the network hosts X, Y, and Z. Their communication links comprise the backbone or trunk of the network. They incorporate the lowest three levels of the International Standards Organization Open System Interconnection Model devoted to the movement of bits, frames, and packets. These backbones or trunks support the next three layers of the Open System Model which, in turn, support the user node requirements for the transport, interaction, and presentation of information. In the context of user applications the communication appears to be loosely-coupled or completely uncoupled because of the operation of those presentation, session, or transport layers. However, the backbones or trunks operate in a tightly-coupled format, i.e., resources are shared between network nodes.

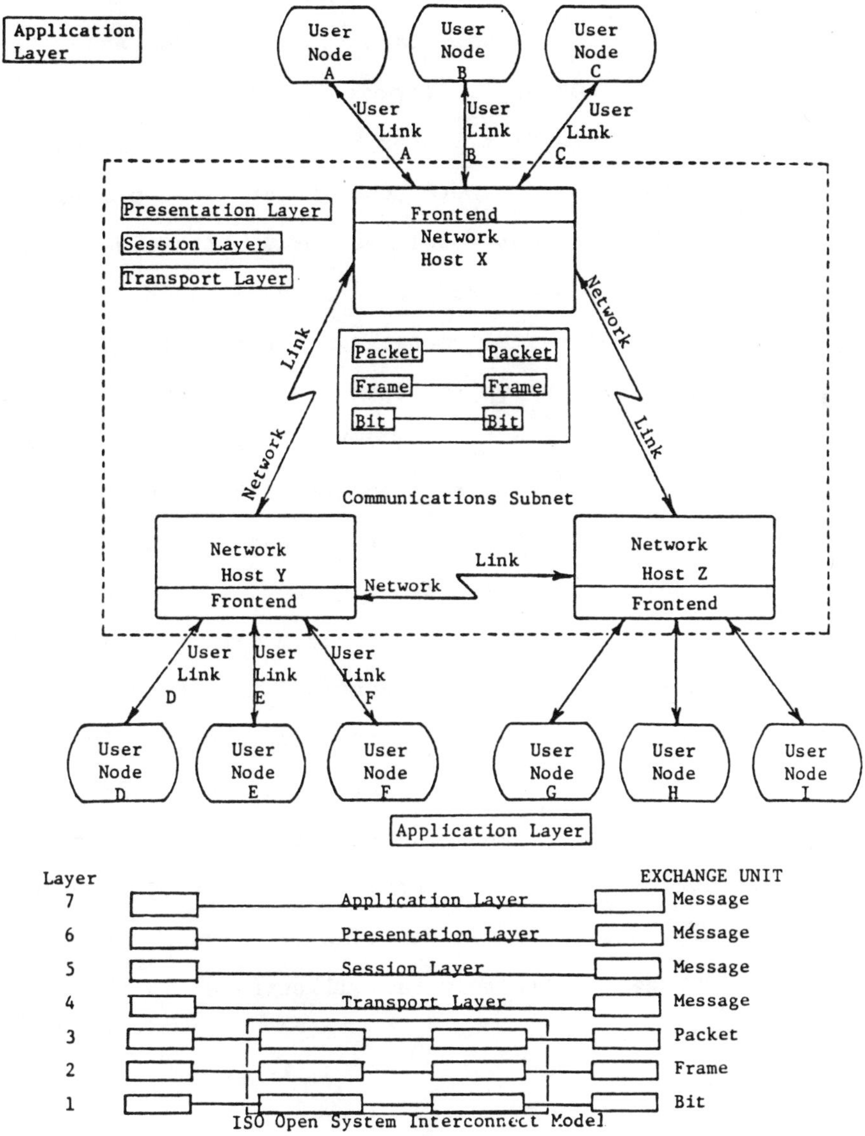

Figure 2-3 Classification of Nodes and Links Within a Network System

In the context of Figure 2-3, software is operating at several different locations. Each location addresses a particular layer or set of layers within the Open System Model. Growth within distributed systems can be measured in terms of increased computational power being placed at these strategic locations within networks. Starting from the standpoint of a user, several observations can be made concerning the software operating characteristics of various implementations of the Open System Interconnection Model. The first location at which significant computational power is encountered occurs at the network host level. Each host has its own front end to support a variety of user nodes. Two types of software are evident at this juncture. One resides upon each network host and addresses the computational function. The other resides within the front end of each network host and within the user nodes serviced by the front end of that particular host. It addresses the management functions of formatting and routing messages, nodal commands, transferring data, and updating status information. The differences between these two types of software are illustrated in the following table.

Network Host Front End and User Nodes Functions

Computational Functions	Management Functions
Requires data in binary format	Handles data in one of several transmission codes
Requires uncompressed data	Data compressed for efficient transmission
Processes complete blocks of data	Data transmitted in bit-by-bit serial format
Processes only data	Transmits data and line protocol information
Controls own timing	Handles a variety of timings dependent upon devices and operator speeds.

Obviously communication software between the network host and its user nodes must accommodate both the computational and management functions. It does so by addressing the problem at a variety of levels. The first is the physical interface itself. It concerns how the network host actually transfers the bits and frames between itself and the user nodes it services. These are the first two layers of the Open System Interconnection Model. The second level used to address the software problem concerns line control. It uses the bits and frames of the physical interface to direct the flow of information the network host and its user nodes. When software satisfies the physical interface and line control requirements, the first three layers of the Open System Interconnection Model have been implemented between the network host and its user nodes. These layers are called the communication subnet. A variety of such subnets are available within the communications marketplace, e.g., IEEE 802 interfaces and Ethernet. The third level used to address the communications software problem concerns control of the network. Whereas the previous two levels usually operate within loosely-coupled and uncoupled formats, network control usually does not. Such control addresses communication between individual network hosts. Within this level, resources are usually shared and software operates concurrently on the various network hosts. In effect, this level parallels the first level of the physical interface between an individual network host and its user nodes. The major difference is that this third level deals with the physical interface between network hosts themselves. When this latter interface operates, the network backbone or trunk is implemented. The efficiency of that backbone or trunk is a product of how the physical interface between network hosts is used. The software addressing that issue occurs within the fourth level of abstraction in the approach to communication software. At this level a network operating system resides. It distributes control, operates the various network hosts, and distributes the network databases. Obviously such software operates within a concurrent environment and is tightly coupled. In summary, the following four levels of abstraction are used to address the communication software between the network hosts and their respective user nodes.

1. Physical Interface (loosely-coupled or uncoupled)
2. Line Control (loosely-coupled or uncoupled)
3. Network Control (tightly-coupled and concurrent)
4. Operating System (tightly-coupled and concurrent)

The following diagram relates these levels of abstraction to one another.

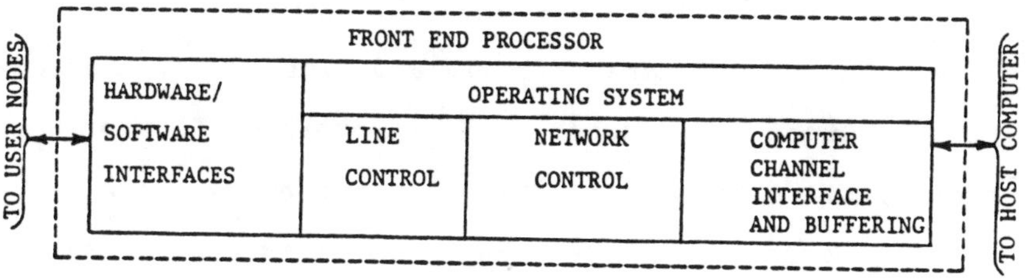

Information flows between the individual network hosts and their respective user nodes via the user line interface. Such flow can be accomplished through hardware itself or software driving such hardware. Software drivers serve to transmit control information to user nodes and monitor traffic conditions. The software drivers at the line control level actual regulate those traffic conditions being monitored at the line interface level. They do not concern themselves with message content but simply concentrate on the movement of packets, frames, and bits.

Network control software performs the formatting function. It creates a single data stream and imposes a message structure upon the subsequent information flow between network hosts. This latter flow is managed by the network operating system which can range from single routine handling peripheral devices to very complex routines handling concurrent environments. The sophistication required of a network operating system is related to the hardware topology. Some of the most notable network topologies follow:

1. fully connected topology
2. generalized tree topology,
3. minimal spanning tree (MST) topology.
4. bus topology,

5. loop (or ring) topology
6. single-center,single-star (SCSS) topology,
7. single-center, multidrop (SCMD) topology,
8. multicenter, multistar (MCMS) topology, and
9. multicenter,multidrop (MCMD) topology.

The decreasing cost of hardware favors the implementation of MCMS and MCMD topologies. Two examples of an MCMS are presented in Figure 2-4 while a two-level, hierarchical MCMD is presented in Figure 2-5. Such network topologies require very sophisticated software operating systems. However, such topologies are characteristics of the marketplace in general and not the military in particular. Bus topologies will continue to be popular within the military architecture because they emphasize single processor architectures. The bus structure is a simple and economical interconnection between processing elements and memory modules in a multiprocessor architecture. As a consequence, bus structure are widely chosen during the design of local computer networks based upon distributed control.

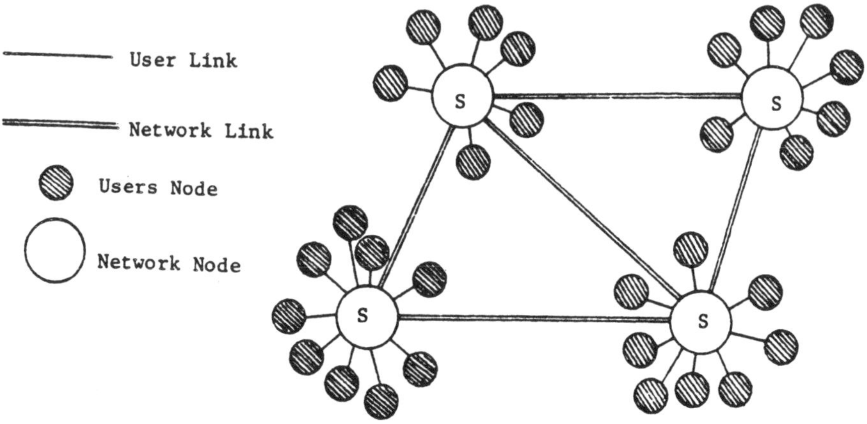

A two-level, hierarchical MCMS topology

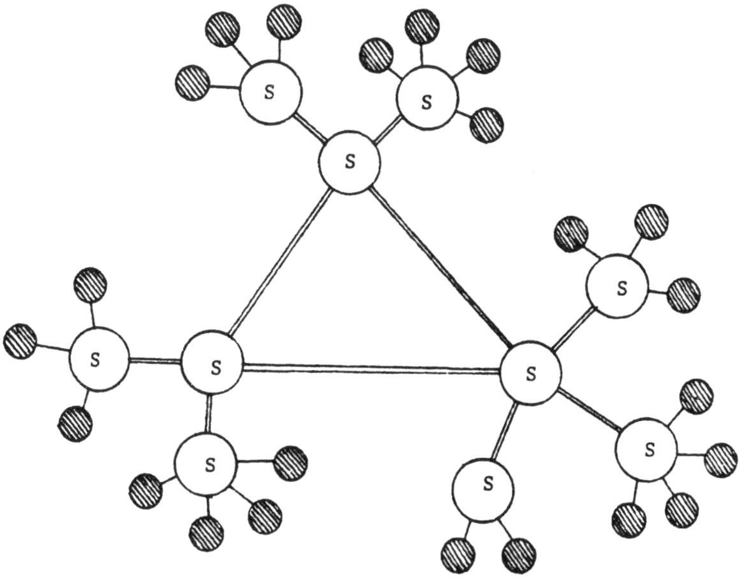

A three-level MCMS topology

Figure 2-4 Two Examples of a Multicenter, Multistar Topology

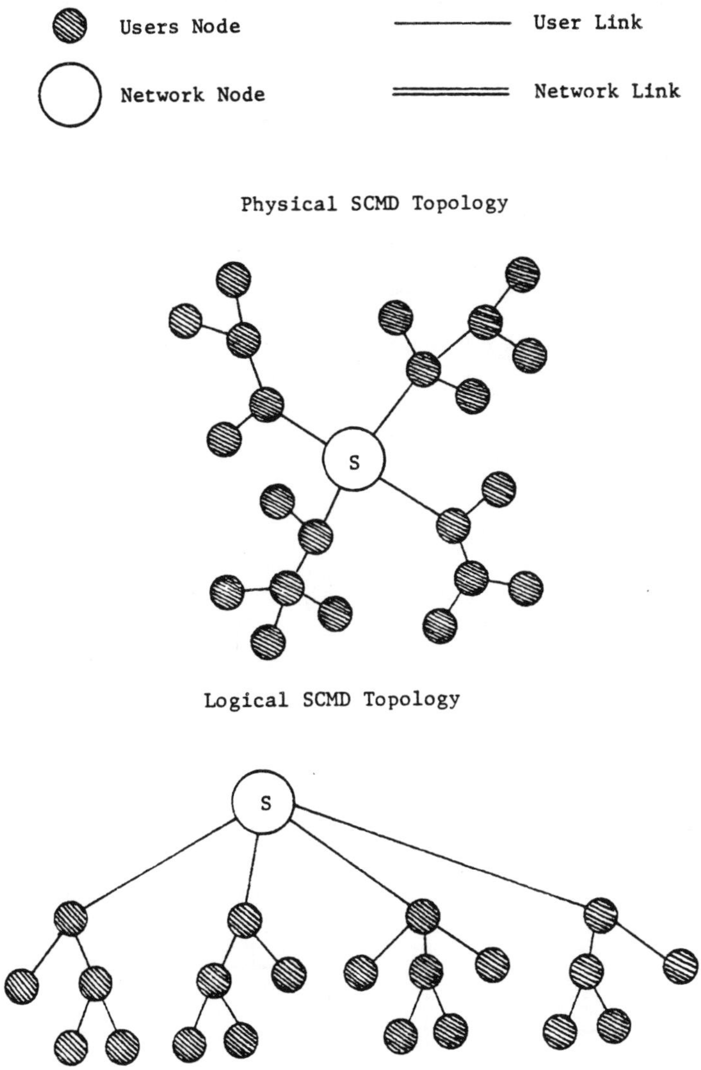

Figure 2-5 A Single-Center, Multidrop Topology

A distributed bus topology is presented in the following diagram.

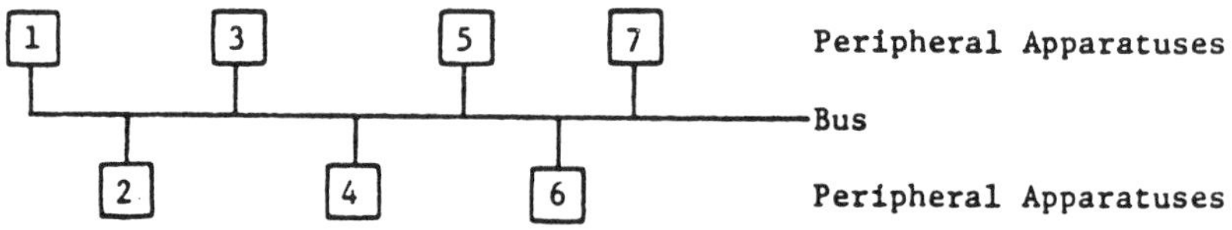

In most instances, the bus itself is controlled by a central controller which is illustrated in the following diagram.

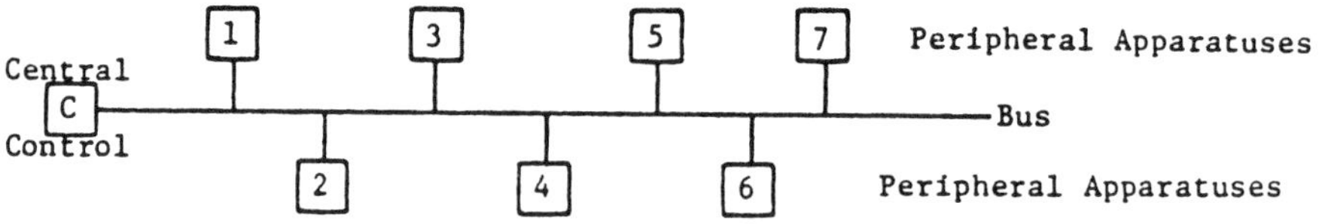

The military situation is typified by advancements within sensors. As more sensors are involved and newer sensors come on-line to existing force management systems, the data rates within existing networks increase. The effect is to shorten decision times. Since the increased data must be accommodated within shorter times, the counter-force capacity must be increased. As this additional capacity becomes available, newer sensors come on-line and the cycle starts again. In such an environment three issues become apparent:

1. What type of system is involved?
2. What kind of distribution is involved?
3. Who is going to use the system?

Each issue impacts the definition of software tools. The force management decision making process can be viewed in

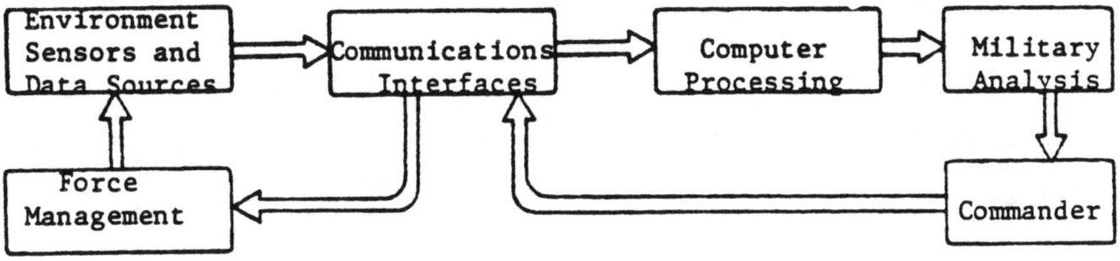

Each situation requiring a decision has two extremes. Furthermore, conflicts between these extremes must be resolved in shorter periods of time. Different decision making scenarios are being studied through simulation, e.g., the Martin Marietta Advanced Modeling System. However, the bottom line returns to network architecture considerations. Figure 2-6 presents such architectural considerations as well as the generic diagram of the military command/control/communication system of the future. The complexity of such a system will be constrained to our ability to verify its software or to simulate its subsequent operation realistically.

2.2 Increased Distribution of Control

Figure 2-7 presents the two levels of control evident in a distributed processing system. In current technology the network operating system resides in only one host and is not replicated throughout all hosts. The Bolt, Beranek and Newman Jericho system is an example. However, replicated copies of the network operating systems present a worst case analysis for consideration. The network level of resource allocation represents the highest level of resource allocation.

a) Architectural Considerations in a Command/Control/Communication System

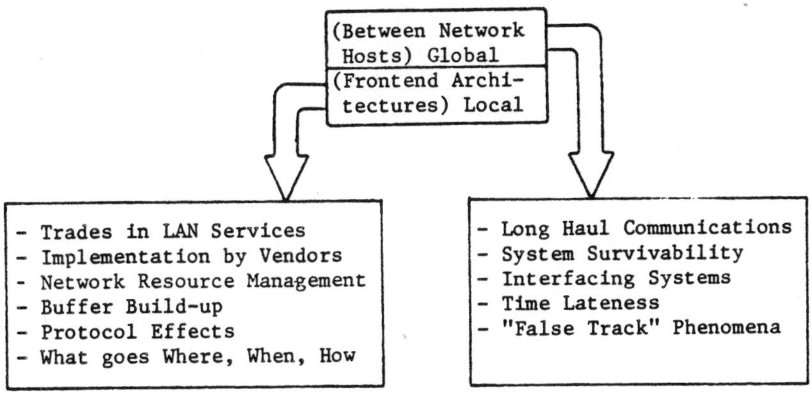

b) Trends in Networking and Command/Control

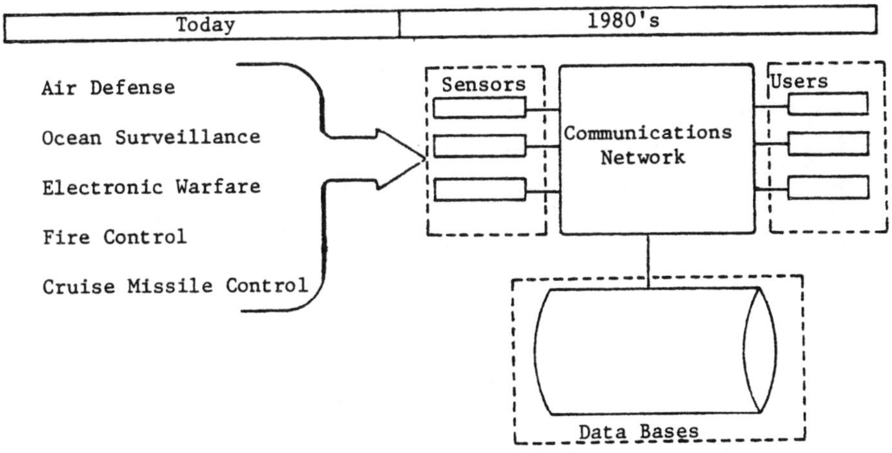

Figure 2-6 Architectural Considerations and Trends in Command/Control/Communication Systems

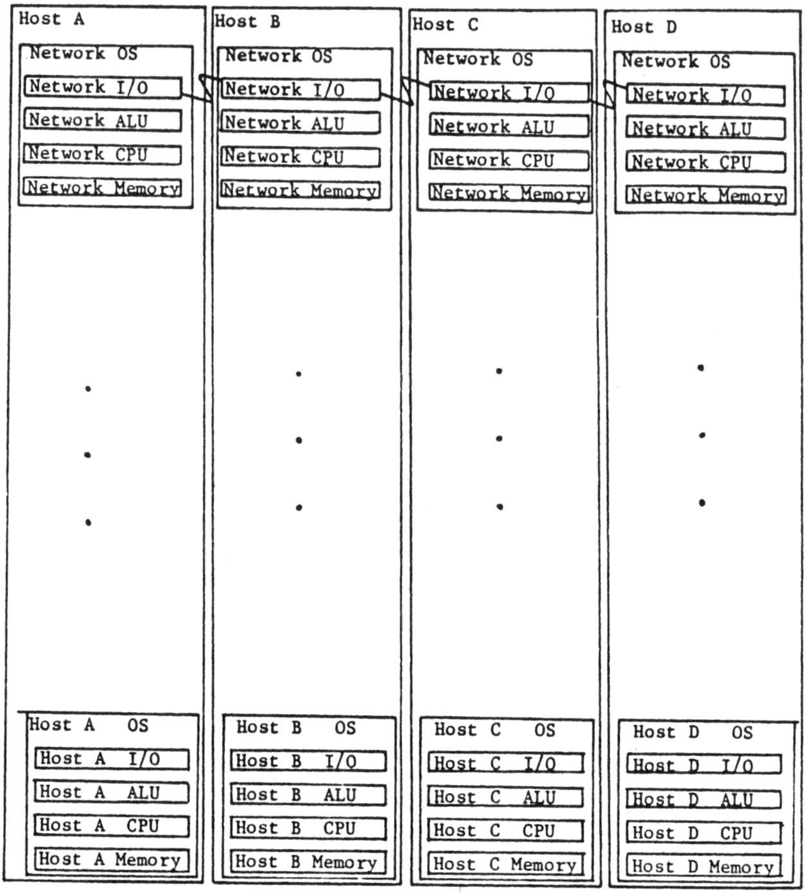

Issues: Should a centralized computer have systemwide executive control to limit the kind of processing which can be embedded in remote I/O systems? Should the network impose little restriction on the physical dispersal of processing and not achieve global executive control?

Figure 2-7 The Two Levels of Control Within a Distributed Processing System

Consequently, work flow is controlled at that level, i.e., jobs are submitted at the network operating system level. In such an architecture the language capability at the network level is a high level one. Consequently, the network operating system itself must not only allocate network resources but also translate its instructions into the operating levels within each network node. To accomplish such objectives is not a trivial task. The leading edges of several issues must be resolved. Object-Oriented Modularization must be applied on two levels simultaneously, i.e., at the network operating system level and at the nodal operating system level. Conventional Modularization is precluded by the concurrent operating characteristics of the distributed architecture itself. In summary, two great issues arise:

1) Should control be centralized and to what extent? and,

2) What restrictions should be placed upon dispersion?

2.2.1 System-Wide Control With and Without Centralization

Figure 2-7 presented the two levels of distributed processing control. In effect, a single applications environment is presented to the network user. From the standpoint of that user a job is submitted and it is executed. The architecture could just as easily have been a uniprocessor as opposed to several uniprocessors configured into a network (provided execution does not require the concurrent operation of several uniprocessors). The issues faced within the network operating system should remain transparent to the user. To illustrate the complexity being handled by the network operating system, a generic job is submitted on one of the network hosts. Figure 2-8 presents the resultant modularization performed on that job by the network operating system. The job could have been submitted by any node within the network, i.e., Host A, Host B, Host C, Host D, etc. From an executive standpoint the network operating system apportions the job to be performed over the nodes in the network. When more than one node is used the relationship between segments becomes all-important. Since each node operates independently of other nodes, the sequence by which segments are completed determines the validity of results.

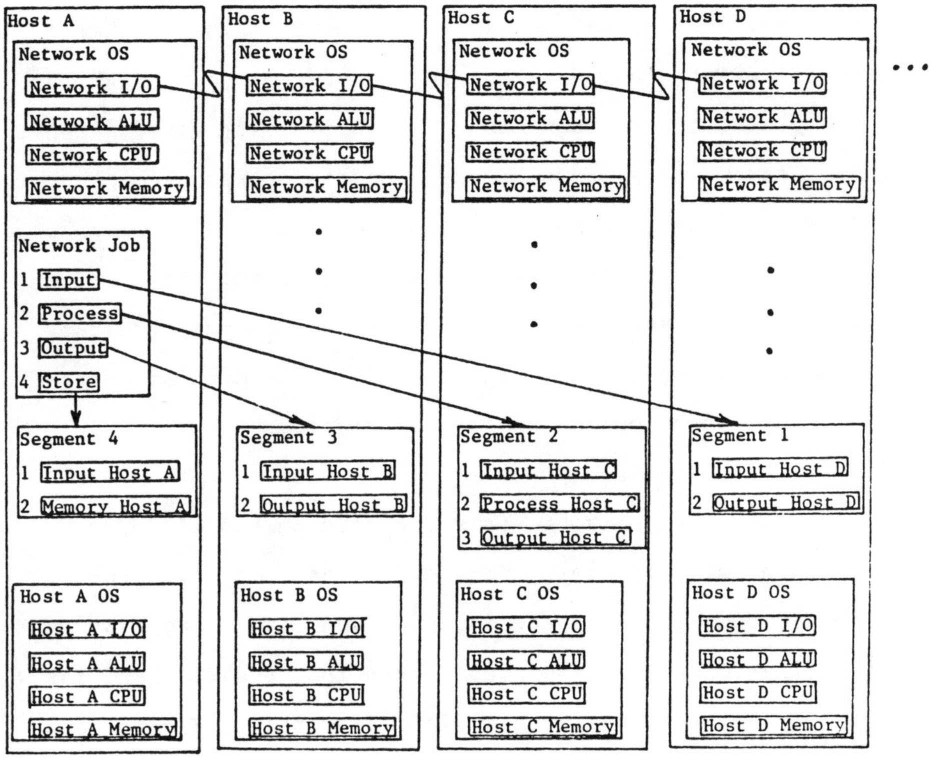

Figure 2-8 Segmentation of a Job Submitted to the Network Operating System

Such sequencing is termed serialization. In the example the assumed serialization is that Segment 1 is completed before Segment 2 which is completed before Segment 3 which is completed before Segment 4. The difficulty enters when many network jobs produce many segments operating concurrently throughout the various nodes of the network. Serialization becomes difficult to maintain. As traffic increases, the serialization problem becomes greater. How the network operating system handles the problem determines subsequent operating characteristics.

Underlying the network is a specific number of nodes at any given point in time. Each node has its own intelligence and probably has its own nodal operating system. In a classic sense these nodal operating systems address the Von Neumann functions of I/O, Processing, Memory, and ALU within each node. Consequently, each node exhibits its own serialization problem. Of course serialization at the nodal level is constrained to sequencing segments exclusively within that particular node. Such sequencing may or may not meet the requirements of the network operating system. How that particular sequencing is satisfied raises the issue of centralized control versus dispersed control. The situation is characterized by Figure 2-9.

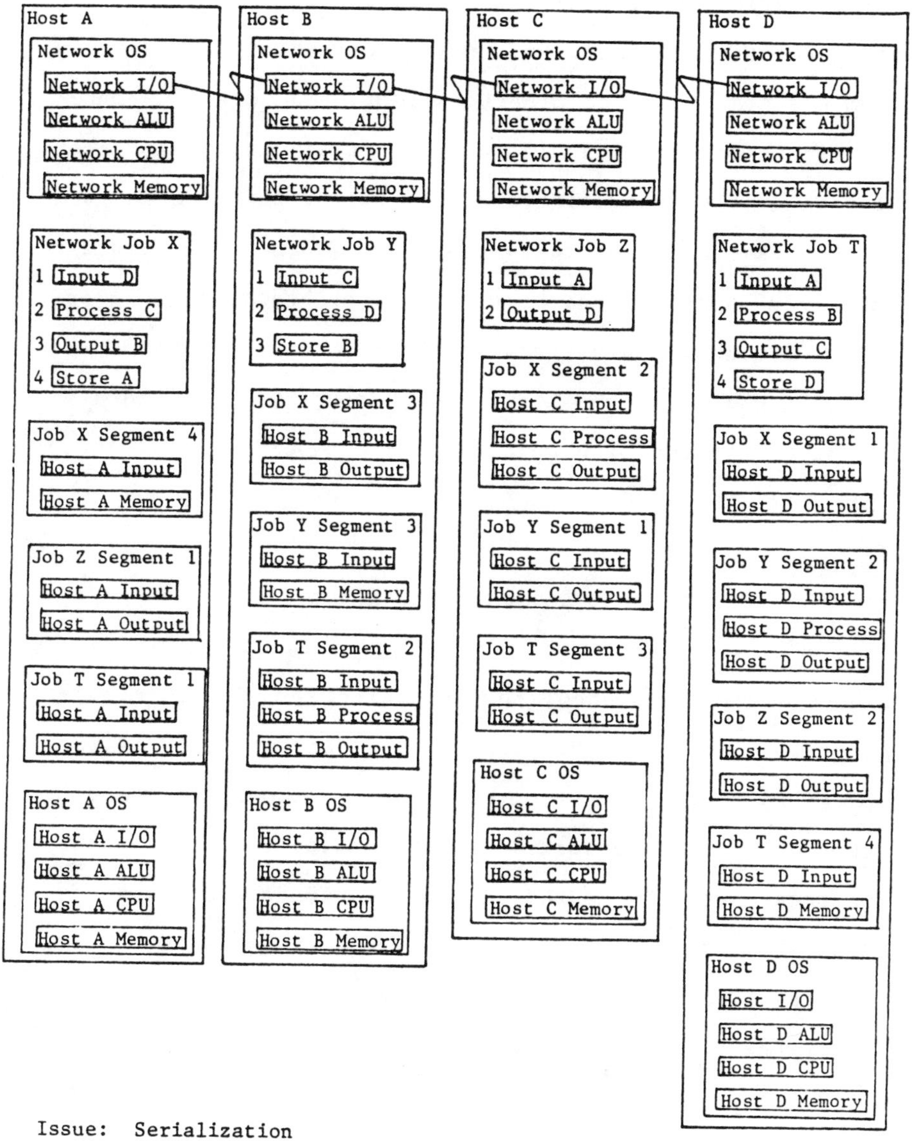

Figure 2-9 Multiple Segmentation on Multiple Hosts Within a Network Operating System

Serialization is normally performed within each particular node exclusive of the other nodes. Consequently, ordering from the standpoint of a network requirements is an abnormal situation. In most instances this situation has been controlled by delegating a single host within the network as the network operating system host. In such a context this new host exerts control throughout the network for subsequent queueing of its own host and the others as well. In effect, the network operating system delineates the kind of processing which can be embedded in the remote input/output systems.

2.2.2 Replication to Combat Degradation

Figure 2-7 presented the two levels of distributed processing control. Replicated versions of the network operating system were presented throughout the various hosts within the network. The reason for such replication concerns network degradation. Individual hosts may come up as well as go down without impacting the network. If the architectural philosophy is to allow such coming and going, new problems are created. The resources presented to a network job vary from job to job. Worse yet, the resources may vary within a network job. Such variance impacts the network operating system as well as the individual host operating systems. To accommodate it is a nontrivial task.

Tightly-coupled resources within a particular local-area-network have the same problem. Accesses to those resources may vary as a local-area-network job stream is processed. The access structure may vary with time, e.g., one processor may go down while its shared memory and another processor continue to function. In fact, the access structure may change during the operation of a single job. To accommodate this coming and going of access structures is also a nontrivial task.

In a concurrently operating environment the resources that stay have knowledge of the operating environment while the resources that go, do not. When such resources return, their knowledge must be updated if they are to assume parity within the operating network. Furthermore, what happened to their network tasks while they were gone? In general, the fewer restrictions imposed on the dispersal of computational power in a network, the more important such questions become. If strong centralized control is not exerted within a network, new kinds of problems arise to accommodate concurrency and degradation.

One alternative to solve the coming and going problem is to build software environments which automatically generate pending tasks for network nodes as they return to service. The same approach seems feasible in software applications for the concurrent environment. In Figure 2-9 the multiple segmentations on various hosts of a network operating system were presented. Using the same tasking, an auxiliary directory can be implemented on each host. That directory can be used by a host to determine the location of tasks allocated for a specific host when that host returns to service. The auxiliary directory is illustrated in Figure 2-10. Assume Host B went down. From jobs accumulated on the remaining hosts, B can assemble its pending tasks from the auxiliary directories when it returns to service. The following table can be constructed.

Auxiliary Directory	Network Job	Instruction
Host A	Job X	3
Host D	Job T	2

Inserting the execution of pending network operating system instructions into a proper sequence is a nontrivial task. Serialization is difficult enough but serialization with network components coming and going is extremely rigorous.

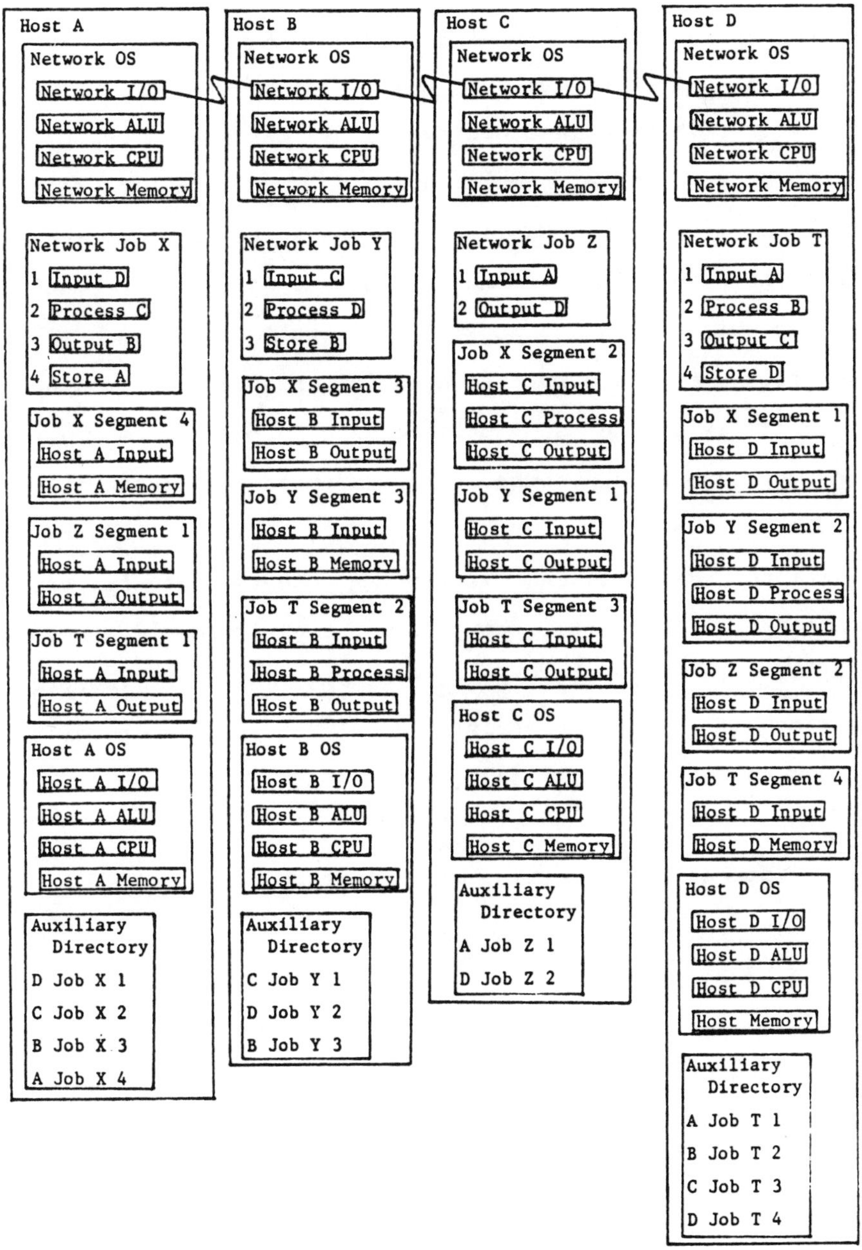

Figure 2-10 Multiple Segmentation on Multiple Hosts Within a Network Operating System Using Auxiliary Directories

However, such coming and going is part of the real world. Consequently, the capability for a network operating system to accommodate degradation and regeneration is an important attribute of a concurrently operating environment. Software designed and implemented for such an environment must rely upon such capability being available. Otherwise the software itself must address degradation and regeneration within its operating environment. Such tools are relatively rare but the need for them is great. Many tradeoffs exist when such problems are addressed. A major consideration is the number of operational restrictions to put into place. Each restriction constrains the computational dispersement within a network. Whether the configuration is loosely-coupled or tightly-coupled matters little. The issues are the same. As each tradeoff is made, it should be carefully documented to enable users to understand its full consequence.

2.3 Increased Distribution of Data Bases

Figure 2-11 presents the four levels of control which impact data bases within a distributed processing system. In current technology the DBMS resides on only one host and is not replicated throughout all hosts.

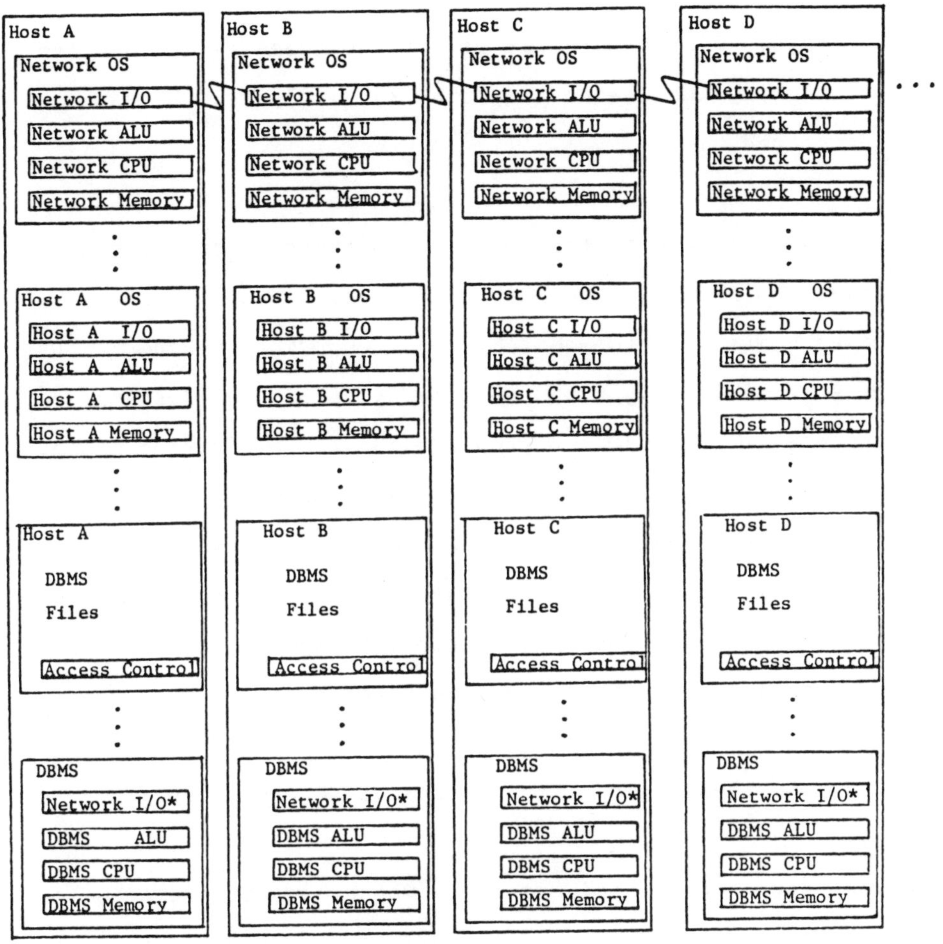

* Note DMBS I/O depends upon the Network I/O

Figure 2-11 The Four Levels of Control Which Impact Data Bases Within a Distributed Processing System

However, such replication represents a worst case analysis. Furthermore, as particular nodes may come and go within the network, such an analysis is not too farfetched.

An important relationship exists between distributed data bases and network operating systems. Since such data bases must accommodate input/output throughout the network, they rely upon the network operating systems to accomplish such I/O. Beyond I/O their similarities cease. However, they share several issues in common. In fact, their approaches to such issues must remain compatible with one another. Much work on the compatibilities between network operating systems and distributed data base management systems remains to be done.

2.3.1 Serialization Under Increased Segmentation

The four levels of control which impact the specific host's operating system, the DBMS files residing on each host, and the DBMS itself. These are presented in Figure 2-11. However, that particular presentation does not convey the relationship of the DBMS to serialization and segmentation. To illustrate these concepts Figure 2-12 has been developed.

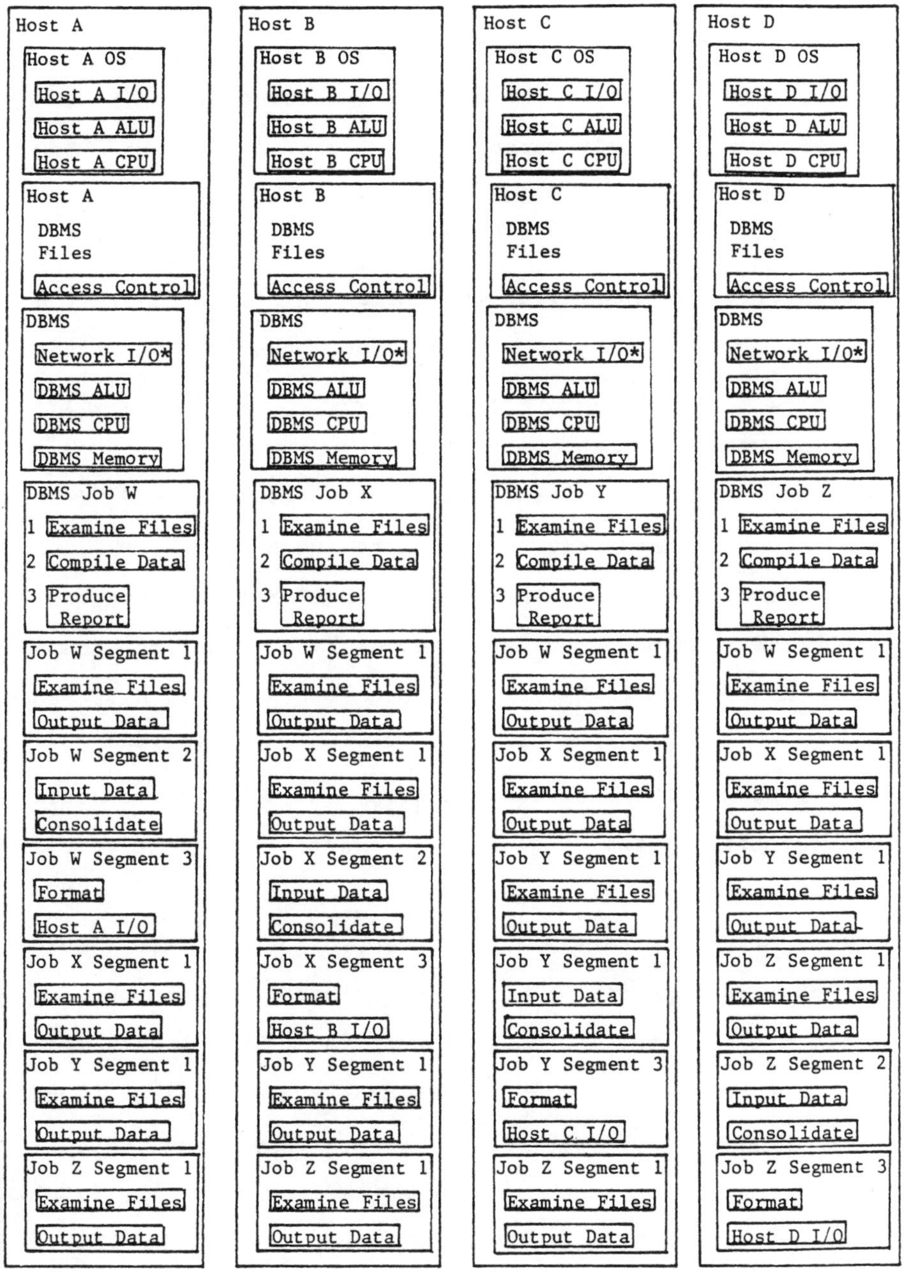

* Note DBMS I/O depends upon the Network I/O (not pictured).

Figure 2-12 Segmentation of DBMS Jobs Throughout a Distributed Processing System Network

Included in its presentation are the specific host's operating system, the DBMS files residing on each host, and the DBMS itself. The network operating system is excluded since its only purpose is to provide network I/O for the DBMS.

Similarities exist between the operation of a DBMS and the network operating system. Both accept jobs throughout the network. Consequently, the process of modularization/segmentation of these network level jobs remains essentially unchanged. In Figure 2-12 four separate jobs have been submitted to the network at four separate locations. Assuming the DBMS files have been dispersed throughout the network, each job requires searches by each of the separate processors. Once a search has been completed the results must be consolidated over all processors. Once consolidated, the data is formatted and outputed on the originating processor. Obviously the processors need to be carefully orchestrated since they are tightly-coupled from the standpoint of a DBMS. Such an observation is valid even if the actual network operating system architecture is loosely-coupled. Resource sharing within a DBMS can usually be classified as tightly-coupled despite the network operating system. Under such circumstances serialization is not a trivial problem. Serialization from the standpoint of the network operating system can be achieved while serialization within the DBMS goes unaddressed.

To queue the pending segments within individual network hosts from the standpoint of a DBMS requires some network-wide knowledge of the DBMS. Current state of the art exerts such knowledge by applying a single DBMS located on a single processor of a network for control and processing of all DBMS jobs. Such central control obviously constrains the DBMS to a non-distributed, batch-oriented approach. The alternative is obvious but how to establish system-wide DBMS control is not. One key rests with the DBMS files themselves. Access control to those particular files is a means whereby queuing may be accomplished. If the file structures themselves are provided decision-making capability, they can determine when more than one segment is demanding access. They can insure only one segment is operating within them at any given time. Whether this access control interferes with the DBMS serialization from a negative standpoint is a function of how the DBMS is attempting to serialize its segments on a network-wide basis. Both efforts must be carefully orchestrated and designed to operate concurrently.

Since decision-making capability can be supplied the file structures, it can also be supplied the DBMS segments themselves. How these separate intelligences are combined and orchestrated is the subject of much current research. Much remains to be done before such techniques become available in the marketplace. Currently such software resides in the ROMs of the very few hardware products being marketed as database machines. In any case, the distributed architecture is a generation away in computer technology.

2.3.2 Access Control

By its nature a DBMS in a distributed processing environment is tightly-coupled. Its DBMS files are a memory resource shared throughout the nodes of a network. In effect, each node is a processor capable of accessing that DBMS memory regardless of location. Figure 2-12 presented the worst case analysis for a distributed processing network involving four nodes. Each node can accommodate a DBMS job concurrently with every other node. Serialization is a problem summarized in the previous section. However, other problems also exist and are characteristic of distributed networks. Individual hosts may come up as well as go down without impacting the network. If those hosts also control DBMS storage, their presence or absence definitely impacts the DBMS throughout the network. Two areas are of specific concern to the

DBMS viewpoint: file storage and the DBMS modules themselves. In a truly decentralized architecture the DBMS modules are replicated at each node to enable nodes to come and go without impacting each other. However, if those particular nodes also control some aspects of DBMS storage, what becomes of that storage? Obviously if its controlling node goes down, it is no longer available to the network. Consequently, even though the network can continue to operate, a data base request involving its missing file would be severely impacted. The mere presence or absence of a node within a network is not enough for a DBMS to continue to operate. The DBMS storage controlled by those present or absent nodes must be known at all times. The network operating system can gracefully degrade itself while the DBMS may not. Basic issues on a distributed or decentralized DBMS have yet to be resolved. One is the location of tightly-coupled DBMS file storage. As nodes come and go, DBMS files may migrate to stay within an active distributed processing network. Not only is access controlled within such an environment but the files themselves must be capable of migration when nodes go down. Otherwise the DBMS will have limited application to the distributed or decentralized environment.

3. Integrated Software Support Environments

Because of their inherent complexity, distributed processing systems are best supported by an integrated software support environment (ISSE). Such an environment provides economy of support through tools which work in conjunction with one another. This eliminates the need for obviously redundant tools which are characteristic of the non-integrated support environments. Integrated support environments also provide tool sets which can be used to address specific problems. The modular nature of such tool sets provides a flexibility which allows problems to be subdivided into object-oriented task statements. Such statements are compatible with emerging languages like Ada, Pascal, and Jovial. Another desirable characteristic of integrated support environments is their open-ended nature. As particular applications need new tools, they can be added. Tools to characterize particular target structures and/or operations can also be added when needed. This capability to add new tools as they are developed makes such environments easy to update and helps prevent their obsolescence.

Open-ended integrated software support environments do have their liabilities as well as their previously mentioned assets. As new tools are added to such environments, extreme care must be exercised. Unless these new tools are added properly, their subsequent use and recall within the integrated environment can be severely curtailed. In such a case, the advantages of the integrated environment will be lost. The probability of such an occurrence is lessened by the inherent simplicity of the tools themselves. Integrated support environments encourage simpler tools since tasks are accommodated by straightforward combinations of less complex tools. As individual tasks are accommodated exclusively by their own tools, tool complexity increases. Although such tools would be difficult to add to an integrated environment, they are precisely the type of tools which are noncharacteristic of it. Consequently, the extreme care which must be exercised when adding new tools to an integrated environment is offset by the simplicity of those tools. What appears to be a liability becomes an asset when the tools remain sufficiently simple. In summary, the utility of an integrated software support environment is a direct result of the simplicity and/or complexity of the tools it contains.

3.1 Impact of Ada

The major impact of Ada is the standardization thrust which accompanies its introduction. As a new language, it also has the impact of any new language which is characterized by the change in features that it provides in comparison to other available languages. Additionally, to meet the DoD objectives connected with the introduction of Ada, the language alone is insufficient and must be supported by a comprehensive integrated software support environment.

The standardization associated with the Ada language is being infused into the required support environment. To facilitate standardization the support environment has been divided into three components: 1) the KAPSE (Kernel Ada Programming Support Environment) which is the host dependent portion of the environment software, 2) MAPSE (Minimal Ada Programming Support Environment) which consists of a minimal comprehensive tool set, and 3) APSE (Ada Programming Support Environment) which is a full environment based upon a particular MAPSE. The KAPSE Interface Team is tasked with standardizing the definition of the KAPSE Interface. Once a standard is established, tools designed to it will be portable to any system with a standard KAPSE. The task of establishing an APSE on a new host will be reduced to constructing a KAPSE for the new host which meets the standard and a code generator for the Ada compiler that is targeted to the new host, along with a rewrite of any target dependent Runtime Support Library routines. This done, the moving of source code of any desired APSE tool to the new host and compiling on that new host is greatly simplified.

Since Ada is a new language it will require the development of the various language dependent tools that are generally available for existing languages. This set of tools is expected to change slightly as Ada was designed to help programmers avoid the known common mistakes. The Ada compilers will be required to provide some checks (previously done by separate tools) in regard to types and range constraints. Ada compilers are also expected to produce set/used listings. A relatively new area for language tools will be the analysis of the concurrency constructs which are available in Ada. Taylor studied the use of the rendezvous mechanism which is used in Ada. His research indicates that it will not be possible to construct efficient algorithms in the general case where no restrictions are placed on the synchronization structure. His work indicates that algorithms can be constructed in certain clases of special situations. The principal feature of these special situations is restrictions in the runtime determination of the scheduling of processes. When the scheduling of processes and process interaction can be made deterministic, then efficient static analysis algorithms can be constructed to detect a wide variety of possible data flow and process scheduling anomalies. Additional research needs to be conducted to ascertain if there are restrictions on nondeterministic scheduling and interaction, which will yield classes for which efficient static analysis algorithms can be constructed.

3.1.1 Host Programming Support

The Host is the system on which a major portion of development and maintenance is carried out. This is the system on which the integrated software support environment resides. Thus to support an APSE a KAPSE must be developed for the host system. Then a MAPSE must be developed which will include tools such as command language interpreter, compiler, linker, loader, symbolic debugger, editor, formatter, database management system, and configuration manager. Additionally an APSE for distributed processing systems will be extended with tools to assist a programmer with handling aspects specific to distributed systems. As Ada matures as a standard, APSE tools will be moved from host to host. The most portable will be generic tools which analyze Ada programs without using implementation or target dependent information. In the near-term many tools exist which are applicable and usable without change. Although these are not written in Ada and therefore cannot reside in an APSE, they can be hosted on the same host as an APSE and be used to augment the capabilities available.

There are also existing tools which can easily be modified to recognize the Ada constructs pertinent to their analysis without a complete rewrite. For the near-term, it will be economical to modify these in the language in which they are presently written. Later, when it becomes necessary to rewrite them in Ada in order to facilitate their installation in an APSE, any desirable modifications which have been discovered during their interim use can be included.

For tools that require significant extensions or rewrites in order to be applicable to Ada, it may be desirable to have them written in Ada. Due consideration must be given, however, to the availability and suitability of Ada environments in which to develop those tools. A cross reference generator for Ada will be required to accommodate the multiple compilation units which Ada supports. In conjunction with this it will need to be able to generate listings by unqualified names and by qualified names. It will need to distinguish overloaded names and indicate which instance is referenced in each case. Resolving overloaded references may be too complex for rudimentary cross-reference tools as some cases are context sensitive and require extensive analysis. In an APSE a compiler can resolve the overloading and store the necessary information such that a cross-reference generator can access it and quickly generate any desired cross-reference listing with any desired level of qualification. Additionally, certain "referenced by" listings will require that a compiler store information in the data base for the modules referenced by the module it is actually compiling. A similar tool, the call tree generator, also has to obtain information which may span several compilation units. This may also be facilitated by the compiler recording pertinent information in the data base.

Static analyzers will be required to process Ada statements in doing many of the now traditional analyses. This will include detection of references to uninitialized variables. It may be desirable that it also be capable of indicating when default initialization is invoked, as Ada has the capability of defining a default initialization for data types. The strong data types in Ada have relegated to the compiler the checking of the legality of data types, the consistency of use of variables, and type matching of parameters. Other data analysis will include the detection of dead definitions of variables. This will need to provide the capability to specify any variables which are memory mapped I/O ports in order that analysis reports will be meaningful.

A relatively new area for static analyzers will be the Ada concurrency constructs. The element of concurrency also adds complexity to previously mentioned static analysis of uninitialized variables and dead definitions of variables. Problems that arise are situations in which a variable is global to two or more concurrent tasks, with referencing occurring in one task and definition occurring in another. The referencing may occur prior to the definition due to a lack of synchronization. Another similar situation is when two tasks may define the common variable, but it may be indeterminate as to which definition will occur first. Again, due to a lack of synchronization, static analyzers will need to be able to analyze the concurrent structures to detect and flag these situations.

Another class of problems is involved with the scheduling and rendezvous of concurrent tasks. Ada may have eliminated the possibility of scheduling a task in parallel with itself; however, it does permit multiple copies of identical tasks, and they may be allocated using an identical name, but the name can only indicate the last task allocated. The Ada synchronization mechanism the rendezvous can permit a number of anomalies. A task may attempt to rendezvous with an unscheduled task, this is not an error in Ada as the task may eventually be scheduled. Static analyzers will be needed to detect when tasks attempt rendezvous with tasks that will never be scheduled. A task may also attempt to rendezvous with a terminated task or a task which terminates prior to servicing the call. This will generate a runtime exception in Ada. It will, therefore, be desirable to have a static analyzer to indicate where and under what circumstances this situation can occur. It is also possible that a task enter a state in which it will never service certain of its entries. Other tasks which attempt to call those entries will wait forever. Situations of this sort need to be detected by a static analyzer. Ada has a restriction that a block, subprogram body, or task body may not be left until all dependent tasks have terminated. This may lead to situations in which a task is deadlocked because a dependent task is in a nonterminating state or cannot proceed to termination because it is waiting on an event which will not occur. Detecting these situations with a static analyzer is desirable. As previously mentioned, this will be difficult for programs in which the scheduling of tasks is nondeterministic.

A similar class of problems deals with the allocation and termination of tasks. In Ada, tasks are not necessarily dependent on the block, subprogram body, or task body in which they are allocated. It is, therefore, possible to allocate a task using a local variable, then exit and lose any means of accessing that task. This is not always an error, as the intention may be to start up an independent active task with which no additional interaction will be required. This may even occur at the main program level, as a task may be dependent on a library package, and therefore, may not be required to terminate prior to the completion of the main program. Such an occurrence generates an operational task which appears to be an orphan, i.e., it has no living parents. A static analyzer should easily be able to discover the tasks which belong in the above mentioned categories and provide a list of them for consideration. Another scheduling problem can occur when an unlimited number of tasks can be generated without requiring that any terminate. These situations are difficult to dissect with a static analyzer as they are quite often very dependent on external stimulus. A static analyzer should, however, be able to flag these areas for further examination. A thorough static analysis of task scheduling would produce statistics on how many of each type of task could be in each queue. An analysis this thorough is ambitious even for deterministic scheduling cases and likely impractical for many nondeterministic schedules. The problem of orphan tasks exacerbates the situation.

3.1.2 Target Programming Support

Ada's main impact on the Target Programming Support is that it is a language that supports concurrent aspects in programs. There are several features that current research has recognized as required to support distributed processing. They are: 1) a basic software unit for distribution, 2) a means of exchange of information between units, 3) a means of synchronization between units, 4) a control structure to handle nondeterminism, and 5) a kernel to interface between high level program language and hardware. Ada provides its particular brand of each of these features.

One is a basic software unit for distribution which is embodied by the task in Ada. They may be specified at compile time or allocated dynamically at runtime. The Ada loop construct permits a run forever version of a task. However, a task may terminate by completing its code or by a terminate statement in a selective wait statement. It can also be the object of an abort statement. The maximum permitted number of active tasks is limited only by available resources. There is some control over resource utilization provided to the programmer through the specification of storage space allotment for a task or task type. The interrelationship between tasks is hierarchical as each task is dependent on the block, subprogram body, task body, or library package in which it or its access type is declared. Calling another task, however, is limited only by visibility rules. Thus a programmer has a great deal of discretion in the call structure he utilizes. The call mechanism known as the rendezvous in Ada is a well defined synchronized interaction mechanism. Another means of interaction would be via global variables for which there is no implicit control other than normal scoping rules.

A second necessary feature is a means of exchanging information between tasks. This is supported by the above mentioned rendezvous in Ada. This high order language construct hides the hardware configuration from the program level software. It utilizes the very powerful and general technique of message passing. Automatic buffering is not provided; therefore, the first task ready to communicate is blocked until the other task is ready.

Because of this blocking, the rendezvous also satisfies the third required feature which is a means of synchronization. In Ada the rendezvous is not required to include a parameter list for message passing, thus parameter passing overhead is not imposed on rendezvous used simply for synchronization. An additional feature included with the Ada rendezvous is a critical region of code which is guaranteed to be executed prior to the calling task being released to proceed with its own execution.

The fourth feature required is a control structure to accomodate nondeterminism. This is provided by the selective wait construct in Ada. There are additional select constructs which provide for conditional and timed delay on rendezvous requests. Conditions may also be associated with each possible rendezvous in the selective wait construct.

The fifth feature is a kernel to act as an interface between high level program language and the hardware. A kernel, because of its interface role, is extremely sensitive to the hardware characteristics as well as the language. The Ada language definition does not address the kernel. Ada is intended to be used on a variety of target systems; therefore, a specific target system hardware has not been defined. There is a move to define specific kernels by developing formal requirement specifications for Ada Target Machine Operating Systems for the target machines used in military systems.

In the distributed processing environment, the target operating systems must provide not only an interface to the hardware but must also support an interface to the distributed structure of the entire target system environment. It must correlate the Ada tasks, which are software units for distribution, to the distributed processing units in the hardware system. This a non-trivial problem and has a multitude of possible solutions. Some possibilities are one Ada task per processor, or any number of Ada tasks running indiscriminately or any number of identical processors, or selected groups of Ada tasks running on specific different processors. There are other more complex possibilities such as systems which permit Ada tasks to migrate from processor to processor via sub-program calls. Particular associations between tasks and processors supported by individual target systems will vary greatly. For this reason system designers will need modeling tools to support rapid prototyping and simulations in order to try out various possibilities and make intelligent decisions concerning the best target system for each specific application.

Scheduling of tasks is another aspect which must be supported by the target operating system. This can vary greatly both with what is supportable by the particular target system and with the requirements of the particular application program. In some systems scheduling may be deterministic, in others nondeterministic. In conjunction with scheduling, allocation of resources to tasks may be static or dynamic. Complications arise when tasks in one process can initiate or invoke the scheduling of tasks in another processor. In some systems the control of resources will reside solely within the network operating system. In other systems there will be a need for Ada implementation pragmas which will provide limited control of resources to the application program level. Again, modeling of resource allocation will need to be supported so that various schemes may be evaluated by the designers prior to commitment to a particular scheme for implementation.

Another level of support in the operating system is for the intertask communication embodied by the rendezvous in Ada. The operating system must provide an interface between this software communication mechanism and the actual hardware communication between distributed processors. The solutions available here are closely tied to how tasks have been distributed throughout the system.

If tasks have been assigned one for one to processors then the software rendezvous can be implemented directly by the hardware communication mechanism. In systems using a homogenous structure of identical processors the rendezvous could be supported strictly at a software level, thus only indirectly affecting hardware processors through its affect on task queue status. For all the other various system structures the rendezvous support may require more customizing in order to accommodate rendezvous between tasks residing in the same processor or processor group, and to accommocate rendezvous between tasks in separate processors either identical or of diverse types. Passing rendezvous information between processors is complicated by the blocking nature of the rendezvous since in most cases it is desirable that only the task and not the processor be blocked. These types of interactions will not only need to be prototyped during early states of design, but also need to be exercised in a full scale simulation or on the actual target system during the coding and implementation phase in order to tune the software to provide the desired response.

3.2 Design and Development Considerations

With the near-term certainty of distributed computing systems, as both host and target, much attention must be given to the methods and vehicles used for system development. The development of distributed systems is in some ways similar to the development of conventional, centralized systems, but in many ways far different. Workshops must be aware of the fact that environments that support centralized systems development cannot simply be "massaged" slightly to accommodate distributed systems development. Rather, an ISSE must be built for the specific types of distributed systems to be developed.

As discussed in section 2.1, the current military systems range from centralized to what can be termed "moderately distributed" (see Figure 2-2). For the near-term then, tools needed to build very loosely coupled systems need not be included in a military ISSE.

The rest of this section deals with the types of tools and methodologies that are of prime importance for building an ISSE for military use. First, some overall policies and basic tool requirements are presented. Then, the specific impact of distributed operating systems, interconnection architectures, and data bases is presented.

Design methodologies and the methods by which these methodologies are conceived must be altered to reflect the nature of distributed systems development and the problems inherent to it. The main responsibility for prevention, detection, and correction of errors must be assumed by the requirements (taken here to mean both requirements specification and analysis) and design phases of the software life cycle (see Figure 3-1). Conversely, the coding, testing and maintenance phases must be relieved of as much of the responsibility for system soundness as possible. The main reasons for this are:

1) EASE OF CORRECTION & DETECTION - If errors are detected and corrected in the requirements and design phases, much less effort is required to correct these errors than after they are "hard-coded" in the implementation phase.

2) COMPLIANT SOFTWARE - Traditional error correction and detection (coding, testing, maintenance phases) leads directly to noncompliant software which can radically shorten the system's life.

A more detailed discussion of these issues follows.

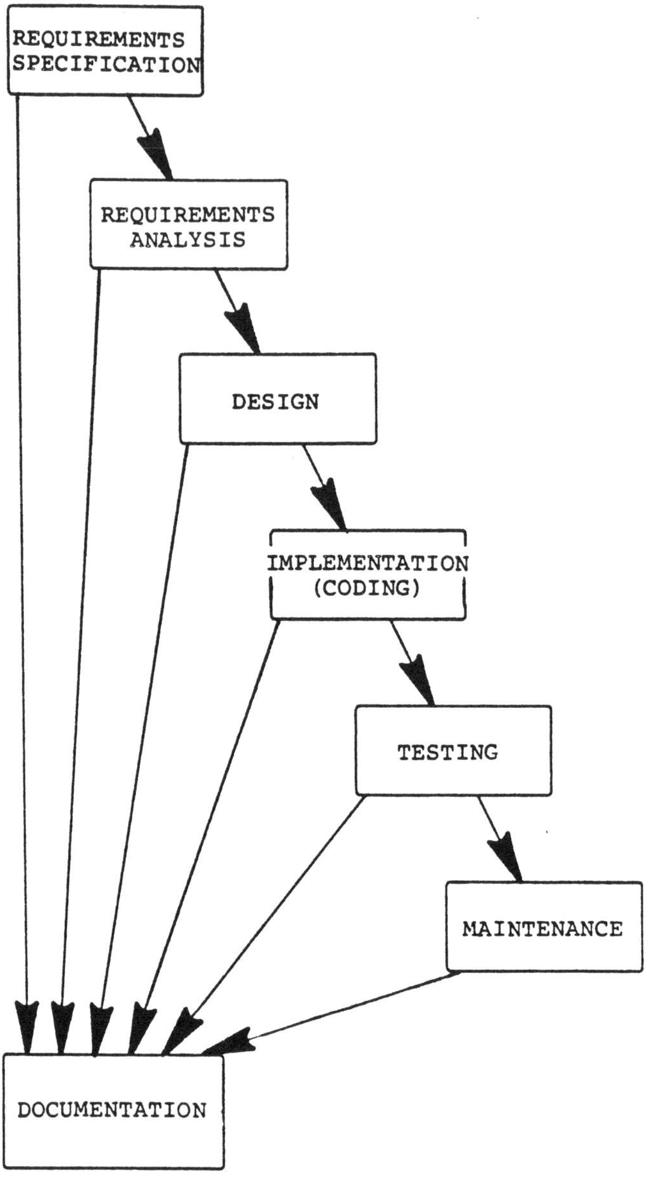

Figure 3-1 Generic Life Cycle Phases

Since the definition of distributed systems states the presence of more than one node, once the software is coded it becomes truly distributed. Software errors usually impact other elements of software (and usually other nodes), and therefore, error detection and correction requires the identification and correction of any and all software impacted by that error. For example, if it is decided that a data type be changed, then a maintenance programmer must find all statements and declarations that reference that type and update them accordingly. This task is extremely time consuming, and system degradation is almost certainly accelerated. When the software is distributed over many nodes, totally repairing an error is a very difficult task for a programmer to perform without the aid of tools, and may leave the system in worse shape than before. If the error is detected in the requirements or design phase, correction is far easier and system integrity is maintained much longer.

The insurance of software compliance, or implementation that complies with its design, is another argument for shifting error detection and correction "upward" in the software life cycle. If errors are detected and corrected after the final design, it is easy for the software to become noncompliant and, therefore, not as maintainable as it should be.

This upward shift of responsibility in the software life cycle must be implemented by development methodologies and the framework used to form these methodologies. This framework must be designed to produce methodologies that place special emphasis on the requirements specification, analysis, and design phase of the software life cycle.

With the importance of design methodologies recognized, we can proceed to a discussion of the creation of an ISSE that sufficiently supports production of distributed systems. This ISSE will be composed of a standardized minimal tool set (see section 3.1), as well as all the tools necessary to accommodate any and all methodologies that might be developed. The remainder of this section discusses the major tool needs and sketches outlines of their design.

There exist several areas of tool classifications that need improvements or extensions to make them useful to the software engineer who is building a distributed system. Many of the tools that exist now and were designed for use on centralized systems development lend themselves well to distributed systems as well. It is not that old tools will no longer be useful in the distributed environment, but rather that more tool support will be needed due to the non-deterministic nature of concurrent software. The areas of particular need are:

1) AUTOMATED SPECIFICATION LANGUAGE/ANALYSIS - Network communications are not specifically addressed by any current specification language, and this area should be the one most stressed for tool development.

2) STATIC/DYNAMIC ANALYSIS - The existing tools need to be extended to tell programmers when the possibilities exist for certain concurrent software phenomenon.

3) SOFTWARE INTERRELATIONSHIPS - The internodal dependencies of all software in a distributed system need to be permanently catalogued to reduce time and cost related to the testing maintenance phases.

A more detailed discussion of these areas follows.

The methods currently used to assist in the systems requirements and design phases are insufficient to fully support development of distributed systems. Since it is of paramount importance to give the development of distributed systems maximum support at the requirements and design phases, new methodologies and tools must be developed to further automate these phases. Automation of these phases is the key to making the design methodologies as useful as they should be. Specifically, they must address the issues of protocol definition and bulk data communications, to assist in determining optimum networking methods. These tools must also produce reports that are easily reviewed and modified by humans and then fed back to the computer to be reanalyzed. So-called "Feedback Development" must be used when developing distributed systems.

Once the requirements and design phases have been completed, the programmers charged with implementation of the defined system must be provided with tools to aid them in producing sound distributed software. If the methodology being used is a good one, the programmer will be provided with a specific design with all of the distributed processing considerations already addressed and resolved.

The problems arise when program errors inherent to distributed processing occur and no testing tools exist to detect or prevent them. For example, orphan spawning (see section 3.1.1) and deadlock are two of the problems that arise in distributed software and further study is required to specifically address these problems. Static analysis techniques such as path analysis can be extended to tell programmers when the possibility for these phenomena exists, and the programmer can then investigate further. For example, if a programmer wants to test his code for orphans, static test tools (extensions of existing ones, that is) can analyze the program and identify points in the code where orphan processes might be spawned and which processes they might be. Because of the non-deterministic nature of distributed software, current static analysis tools can do no more than this. Dynamic analysis tools also need to be extended to allow for detection of orphan processes via instrumentation schemes.

Finally, the problem of software interdependency must be addressed. Distributed software that is non-deterministic operates as separate autonomous entities, and maintenance is extremely difficult. When one area or module of software must be altered, the impact on other modules is usually far reaching and unpredictable. Since maintenance represents approximately 75% of the software life cycle, and even more in the distributed environment, tools and methods must be incorporated into any ISSE to help categorize software interdependencies. Although tools that manage these types of software interdependencies exist, there are several shortcomings with them. First of all, the data is not managed by computer, and usually takes the form of a post-mortem listing. Therefore, no categorization is performed and no easy cross-reference ability exists. Second, the only way to build an accurate final copy of the relationships is to manually update when modules are recompiled. In a large distributed system, this task represents quite a problem. Therefore, a tool must be developed to completely automate these data collection and management functions. Figure 3-2 depicts a tool that makes use of the symbol table built by the compiler to collect software dependency data. This tool builds and maintains a permanent data base consisting of this symbol table information. This data base can then be queried interactively by programmers or evaluated by the static analysis tools of the ISSE. Programmers could then determine all of the changes required to repair a problem and avoid hasty and ill-advised "patches".

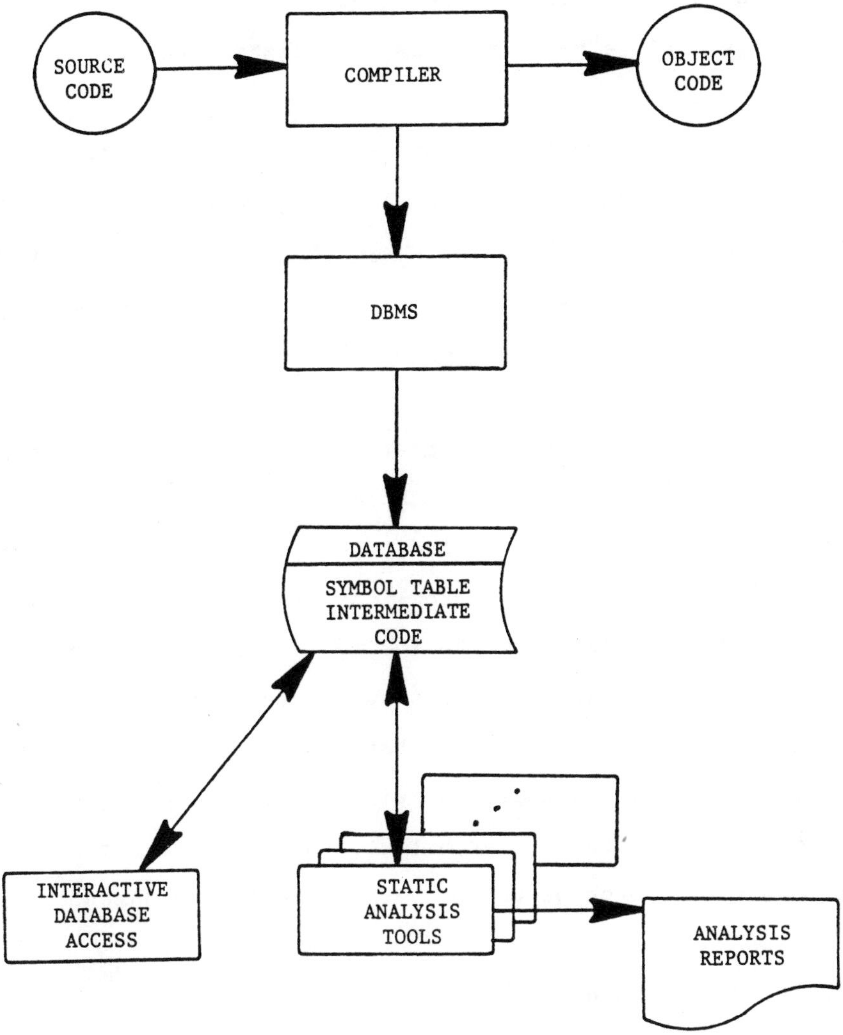

Figure 3-2 Data Flow Diagram of Generic Software Dependency Tool

This technique would greatly slow the phenomenon of "software rot", a major problem with distributed software.

These tools designed and added to a standardized tool set will allow for more efficient and complete distributed system design and development. Most importantly, the methodologies adapted by a particular workshop should all be totally supportable by any such ISSE.

Any ISSE built to support distributed systems design and development should have the characteristics outlined by the preceeding section. Also, the specific types of distributed systems to be created has an impact on which tools comprise the ISSE. Following is a discussion of the three most important variables used in describing distributed systems. The military's near-term target computer systems are analyzed with respect to operating systems, interconnect architectures, and data bases, and the impact of each of these on the ISSE is presented.

3.2.1 Distributed Operating Systems

Distributed Operating Systems (DOS) are the entities that coordinate the activities of many concurrently functioning processors and other resources. The scope of this section is limited to a discussion of DOSs only and not individual

Constituent Operating Systems (COS). Distributed processing considerations only impact COSs when it is being determined how much, if any, of the COS responsibilities will be relegated to the DOS when designing a network. This section also limits its discussion to the military's current and near-term distributed systems technology, e.g., low to mid-range distribution of control (see section 2.1). The basic functions of a DOS and its design considerations are discussed with respect to the military's two basic distributed processing areas: communications systems and weapons systems.

Although communications systems and weapons systems occupy mutually exclusive volumes in the distributed processing three-space pictured in Figure 2-2, the design and development considerations of the DOSs for these systems are very similar. The functions which both types of systems must provide are the same, though these functions vary in relative importance. Three basic functions are:

1) Resource management (including data transfer/communications)

2) Fault tolerance/recovery

3) Transparency of system control.

Resource management is the main function of executive control (DOS). This is the function of sending messages and coordination of the different nodes of the network. These resources consist of all the separate entities of the network to be united into a single functioning whole. Communications systems executive control typically manages a large quantity of data transfer devices, e.g., satellite communication links, packet radio controllers, as well as the standard types of nodes. It is important for most communications systems to be easily reconfigured, relocated or added to quickly, so the executive control must lend itself to this dynamic resource configuration. Weapons systems, by contrast, are more static in their configuration but their resources demand a high level of coordination by the DOS. This is because of the stringent real-time environments in which they operate. For instance, up to date information on the state of all processor queues must be kept or quickly obtainable to insure the high throughput of time-critical tasks. So, though in each environment (communications, weapons) the DOS must place emphasis on different resource management issues, the same basic functions are performed by each type of DOS.

Fault tolerance and recovery is another main function of the DOS and, like resource management, receives different emphasis depending on the type of system. Extreme fault tolerance is usually required of weapons systems and the DOS must be designed to accommodate this. High replication of hardware and a highly distributed DOS, usually with multiple autonomous points of control, insure this high level of fault tolerance. In the case of communications systems, where faults can be tolerated relatively more often, more emphasis is placed on quick, state-resuming recovery. In these systems, though hardware is often replicated, the DOS is uaually of a dynamic master-slave nature. This usually takes the form of one processor possessing all the DOS modules and functioning as master, but upon an abend, one or more "slave" processors are capable of assuming possession of the DOS modules and becoming master. In this environment, the DOS is charged with the responsibility of maintaining a high degree of state information in its local tables for efficient recovery purposes. Also the various network nodes (especially communications processors) are designed to retain recent data transmissions for a short time in case the current master abends and another processor must assume master status. In this way, fault recovery can occur with a minimum of state information lost.

The network operating system must also provide transparency of system control (a virtual machine layer) to all user and most applications programs. The exception to this is found in some embedded weapons systems, when applications must be programmed using knowledge of the network configuration. In these real-time systems, the DOS functions mostly as a communications supervisor, turning much of its responsibility over to the application software. But usually the DOS must provide a level of transparency allowing user and application to proceed without specific information about the different network nodes. Reference by name, rather than address, is an example of this. In communications systems, this DOS function enables packages of messages to be sent by users to people without concerning themselves with the specific location and routing information. Flexible DOS protocol techniques implement these communications and allow for easy reconfiguration of the network. Likewise, the DOS in most weapons systems allows for applications software to be designed and run as processor-independent code. Also, interprocessor communications are handled by the DOS allowing, for instance, an application program to reference data without knowing which of many data bases it is stored on. Such flexibility serves to greatly enhance fault tolerance and retard system degradation.

The design and development of these distributed operating systems is quite obviously complex and the overall performance of the resultant network depends highly on the soundness of this design and development effort. As is the case with distributed target software development, DOS design and development must be accomplished within an ISSE. The extensions to be made to the ISSE discussed in sections 3.0 and 3.2 in order to accommodate DOS development are few. The need for tools and methodologies in the requirements specification phase, the requirements analysis phase, and the design phase, is particularly pressing when developing DOS software. Specifically, simulation tools that expose the operating characteristics of models of proposed DOSs must be incorporated into the ISSE. Several simulation tools exist today that test the operating characteristics of most of the network models being proposed. The only shortcoming is in simulating interfacing between nodes that are not compatible as far as protocols and data structures. The encoding, decoding, and transmission of data between nodes using non-standardized protocols needs to be simulated accurately in order to satisfactorily evaluate proposed models in the design phase.

Beyond the need for this added simulation capability, the ISSE discussed in earlier sections will prove to be sufficient to support the design of distributed operating systems. When development of the DOS is conducted separately from the development of applications software targeted for the same system, i.e., most weapons systems, the same methodologies and ISSE will be sufficient to provide sound support to both efforts.

3.2.2 Interconnect Architectures

The means in which various components of a network are interconnected has a direct and profound impact on overall system performance. The schemes for interconnection, or interconnect architectures (IA), can vary greatly from system to system. Therefore, system designers must be provided with the means to fully evaluate the advantages and disadvantages of various proposed architectures before committing manhours of labor to implementation and detailed design. This function must be provided by the ISSE (see section 3.0). This section discusses various ways of classifying IAs and the types of tool support needed within an ISSE for modeling, prototyping and simulating these IAs. Note that specific architectures and design criteria are not addressed in this section. Rather, software design and support considerations are the primary concerns. Finally, this section discusses some second-level issues of the interconnection of various networks and the problems in designing tools to support these types of architectures.

Several major researchers have made attempts to categorize different types of IAs. The one common factor between these attempts is a range in IA design from very loosely-coupled architectures to very tightly-coupled ones. The various ways this continuum is broken into distinct classifications is not important to this discussion. What is important is the fact that there exist different classifications of IAs, and tool support must be grouped in the same classifications.

Figure 3-3 illustrates a proposed grouping of support tools. For each IA category, IA , a corresponding group of tools, TG , must be provided in the ISSE.

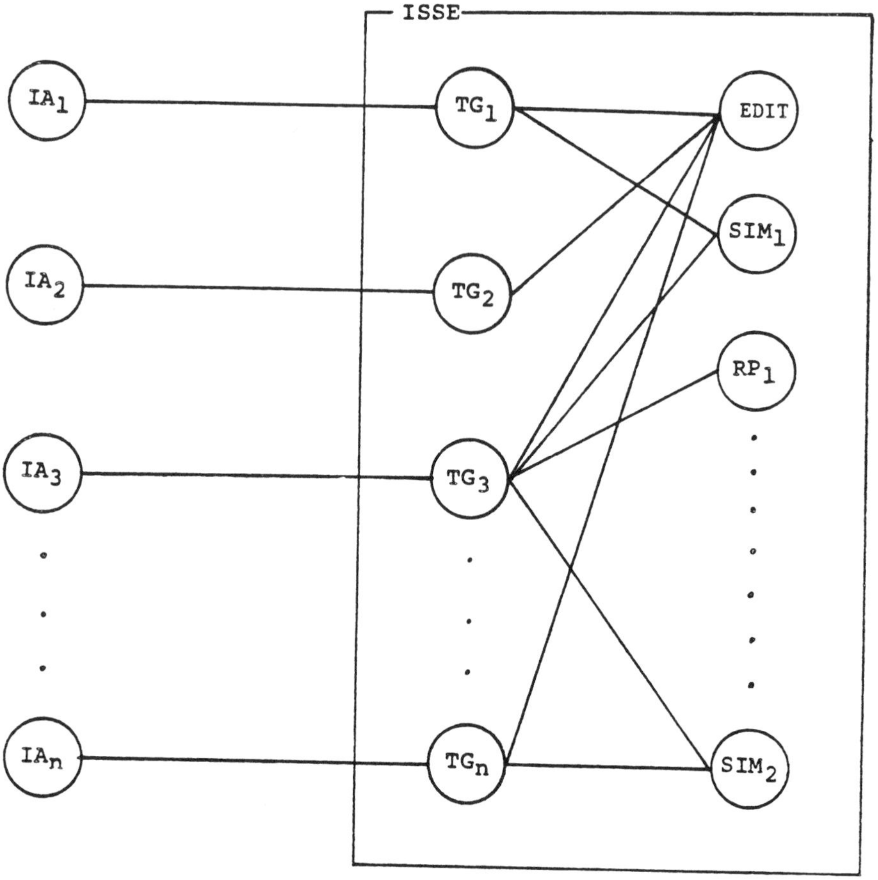

LEGEND

IA_i = INTERCONNECT ARCHITECTURE
TG_i = TOOL GROUPING
ISSE = INTEGRATED SOFTWARE SUPPORT ENVIRONMENT
SIM_i = SIMULATOR
RP_i = RAPID PROTOTYPER

Figure 3-3 Tool Support for Interconnection Architecture Classifications

Different tool groups may consist of many of the same tools. For example, the analysis and design of IA can be completely supported by TG . This group may consist of a text editor, one or more simulators, a rapid prototyping tool, etc. Some or all of these tools may also be part of another tool group, but the union of all the tool groups is the total set of tools needed to support any IA design.

As indicated above, the requirements phase of the software life cycle is where most of the tools to support IA design are required. Specifically, rapid prototyping, simulation and modeling techniques and methodologies must be refined/developed to support the entire spectrum of IA possibilities. There are several aspects of distributed architectures that suggest changes required to simulation tools. The remainder of this section deals with these issues.

The current general method for iterative modeling is top-down. That is, a model of the overall system is developed, then simulated, and from the results of the simulation a new, more specific model is developed. This process continues until the results are sufficient to make sound design decisions or until the simulator tool(s) being used can get no more specific. Unfortunately, the latter is usually the case. For this reason, and because networks are becoming increasingly complex and layered (e.g., networks within networks), it will be necessary to use simulation tools to simulate various nodes of a distributed system while the overall system is itself being simulated by a tool using the data from the nodal simulators. Take, for example, the design of a distributed system consisting of four major nodes, A, B, C, and D. Each of these nodes is in turn a network of its own and may or may not be implemented already. It is extremely advantageous to be able to test different IAs before deciding on a final configuration for the overall network. To this end, the four nodes A, B, C, and D can be simulated while another tool concurrently simulates the operation of the entire system using the simulation of A, B, C, and D as inputs. As stated earlier, the tools picked for incorporation into the ISSE must be able to support the design of the entire spectrum of IAs. Also, they must be capable of operating concurrently together as any level of a proposed network. Much further study needs to be done in this field before tools that possess this functionality can be built.

Keeping the ultimate goal of a highly functional, modular set of simulators in mind, a repertoire of simulators can be built up in ISSEs. There already exist network simulators which are quite flexible and powerful. They need to be extended to reach the desired goal of functionality. Such extensions are necessary within the near-term time frame.

3.2.3 Data Bases

In section 2.3.1 a discussion of data bases in the context of a decentralized system was presented. However, such a discussion is incomplete until the impact of data bases within the target environments is discussed. These target environments are the weapon systems problems. State of the art development systems involving host-to-target downloading characteristically operate on a point-to-point basis. In other words, a single target's program is developed and downloaded from the host environment. When programs for more than one target are involved, they are developed on a sequential basis for one target after another. Underlying such approaches is an implicit assumption that targets themselves are controlling their own resources, e.g., memory and mass storage. In reality such control is often shared, e.g., two targets accessing the same memory buffer. This happens in a tightly-coupled architecture and when it occurs the data base can be described as the contents of that shared memory buffer. The complicating factor is that such a data base is not under the complete control of either target. Furthermore, when one target goes down, the other continues to operate as long as the memory buffer functions. If that memory buffer malfunctions, both targets lose access to the data base. Of course the data base could be important enough to be provided redundant storage, i.e., an alternative memory buffer in which to reside. In either instance, the applications development environment of a multiple target configuration is not a straightforward use of point-to-point communications between host and target.

Application programs residing within targets manage the databases controlled by those targets. Such management addresses the following issues:

- how the databases are structured;
- how interconnects between targets are accomplished;
- how the "typical" application is accomplished;
- how the data model is structured;
- how the targets are synchronized;
- etc.

The key motivation behind such environments is high data base availability and accessibility. When data bases are shared between targets, the objective is to increase accessibility while enhanching reliability. In fact, the reliability of a system composed of several targets is greater than the reliability of each single target. However, such gains in reliability extract a price in terms of data base software. The data bases must remain accessible even though targets malfunction. Coping with such failures is not an easy task. Furthermore, efficiency suffers when more and more coping takes place. A graceful degradation is required which departs from the point-to-point orientation between host and target. To illustrate the problem Figure 3-4 presents a redundant DBMS scattered throughout a network composed of four targets. Jobs submitted to the network have been segmented. Auxiliary Directories are provided for each network job for backup purposes. Each directory associates itself with a particular host and documents the source of that host's segments. In case that host goes down, a backup Auxiliary Directory is provided on an alternative host. This duplicate directory can be used to regenerate the original host's Auxiliary Directory when it returns to the network. The threesome composed of the DBMS job, the Auxiliary Directory, and the Auxiliary Directory Backup, address network tasking but ignore the distributed data base problem. Consequently, Figure 3-4 includes DBMS files associated with each host and provides redundant backup. That backup resides on a different host within the network, i.e., the same host providing the Auxiliary Directory backup. Under such an architecture the ingredients for graceful degradation of both the network operating system and distributed data bases are evident. When such degradation is perceived becomes important. Obviously Auxiliary Directories and their backups should be updated coincidentally. Point-to-point communication does not achieve such coincidence. When Host A originates a segment for Host B it updates the Auxiliary Directory for Host B as well. However, updating of the duplicate Auxiliary Directory on Host C should be done coincidentally. In point-to-point schemata Host A updates Host B and then Host C.

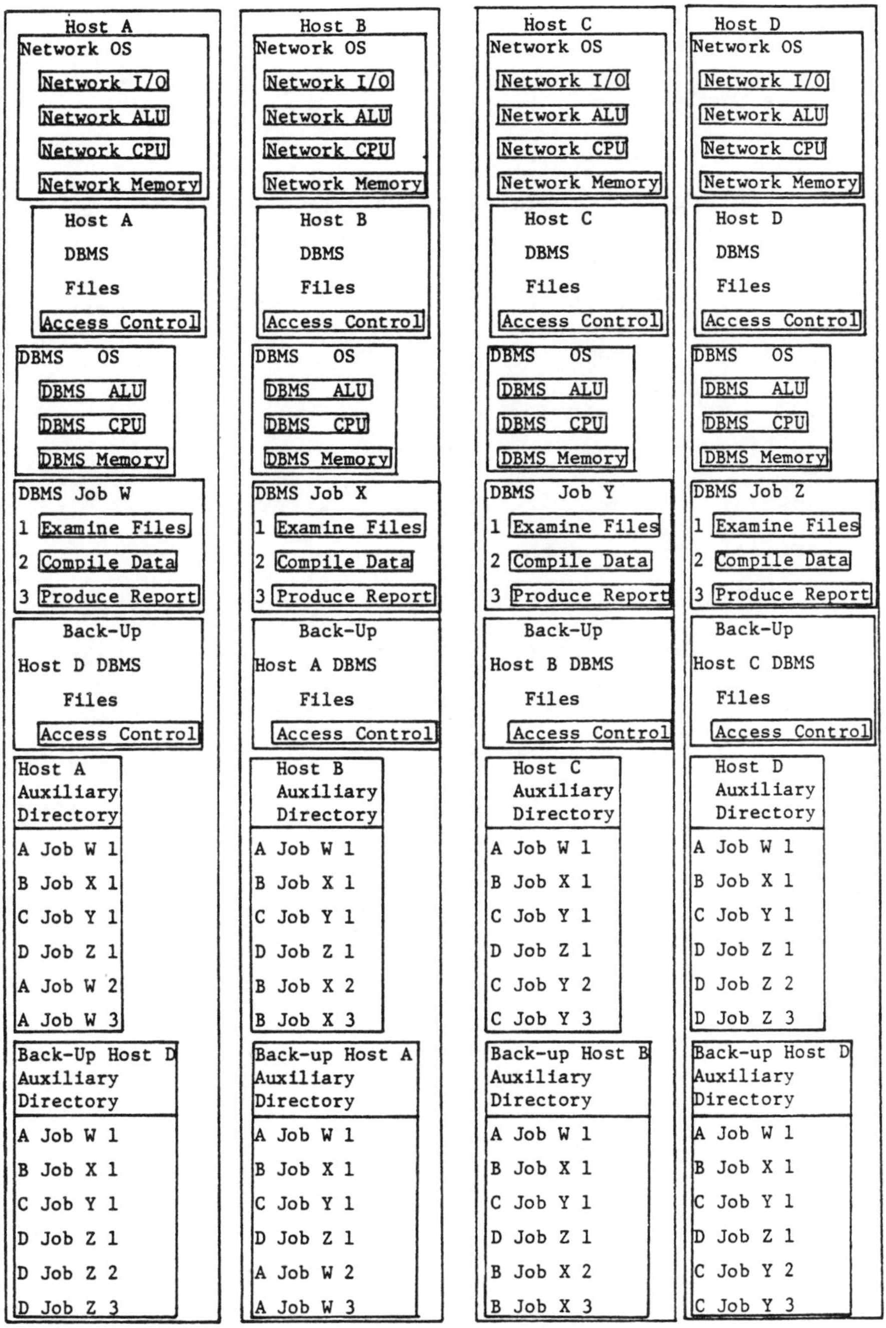

Figure 3-4 DBMS Job Segmentation and Redundant DBMS File Storage

The same observation can be made of the distributed data base. In both instances, a reliable broadcast approach must be implemented.

The structure behind DBMS jobs is presented in Figure 3-5. Note the tight-coupling of examinations to the DBMS files controlled by each host. Whereas individual hosts can compile and produce reports, the very tight coupling across all partitions is required within truly de-centralized data bases. Under circumstances of graceful degradation, some of the nodes within Figure 3-5 will disappear. How long their disappearance is tolerated and what happens while they are gone is a decentralized data base problem. It involves failure detection, partitioning, and the operating around missing nodes. Tools to develop such architectures and software systems are not readily available. File allocation schemes within distributed DBMS approaches lack generality. User demand for joining the relations between two targets is not being addressed. Complete synchronization with sufficient redundancy is also not being addressed. Finally, tools to reassign DBMS files to different hosts and locations within network operating systems are not sufficiently general in their scope.

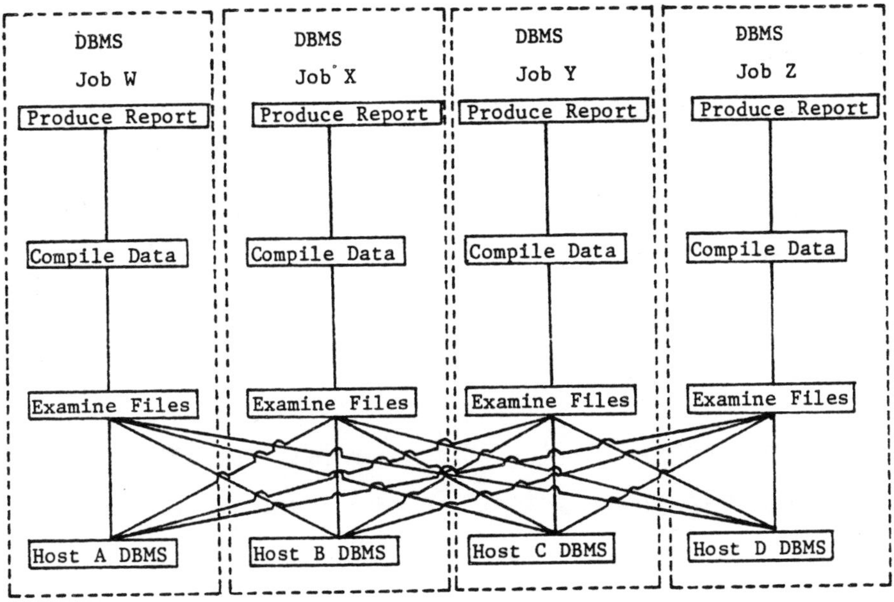

Figure 3-5 Hierarchical Structure of the DBMS Jobs

3.2.4 Intelligence in Environments

The term "intelligent" has begun to appear in discussions of automated environments. While the term often signifies merely a high degree of functional automation, it increasingly refers to a set of characteristics bearing on issues of adaptability, action on incomplete information, heuristics for search and evaluation, and organized knowledge of application domains and of programming language rationale.

Exploration of these issues in depth has implications for far-term generic techniques in distributed processing. Therefore, most of the discussion of sophisticated artificially intelligent tools in this report appears in Section 5. Nevertheless, there is a place in the present section for a preliminary discussion of intelligence in support environments which will serve as a bridge between near-term design and development considerations on one hand and far-term tools and techniques on the other. In this section we mainly want to point out that near-term tool definition should consider ease of integration with intelligent systems of the future.

Although intelligent development support systems may be designed essentially independently of evolving concepts of intelligence in the operational systems, both systems will employ the same generic technology. For example, in the design of an application system, there likely will be an integrated intelligent toolkit to synthesize strategies for an intelligent application (e.g., decomposition of a task definition and assignment to distributed components). One implication for near-term tool definition is that the tool's potential support for or enhancement to intelligent systems should be addressed. For example, it will be desirable to address the tool's potential support for the type of knowledge base that will be the foundation of future intelligent systems. Further, it will be profitable to consider the relation of support tools to the predictable characteristics of evolving intelligent run-time support systems for application programs.

4. Near-Term Generic Tools

This section of the report serves to correlate information known about existing software tools and the software development life cycle, as well as to propose tools which will be needed in the near future. The tools proposed will provide support to new projects in the area of distributed processing, a complex and evolving aspect of computer science.

Two basic approaches were available to identify requirements for new tools. The first approach would be to survey all tools; to identify the functionality of each tool with respect to the life cycle; and to determine if any aspect of the life cycle had not been addressed. This approach was not chosen primarily because of the unnecessary work that would be performed in evaluating the capabilities of functionally redundant tools.

Additionally, the task's complexity would be high because the search would entail looking for a functional characteristic that is a member of the set of all characteristics of software without knowing what the members of the set were.

The second approach consisted of a chronological reversal of the first approach. The characteristics of software are used as the basis for investigation of tools. Knowing the characteristics of software, a single (not all) tool can be found which enhances or evaluates those characteristics. If no tool can be found, that characteristic becomes a basis for tool development. The redundancy of the first approach would disappear because only a single tool-to-characteristic evaluation would be required; and the complexity of the first approach would be decreased because the starting point would be a known set of characteristics. Attempts will not be made to evaluate criteria that might be decreased when one or more other criteria are enhanced. Obvious relationships will be identified, but extensive evaluation will not occur.

4.1 Definition of Criteria and Life Cycle Phases for Software

This section contains definitions of the criteria for judging software characteristics which we have chosen, and the software life cycles to which they apply. The criteria were chosen after a study of the criteria defined in RADC-TR-80-109, "Software Quality Metrics Enhancements", by General Electric, and a slide presentation made by Boeing at the Distributed Processing

Technology Exchange Meeting at RADC on 18-20 May 1982. The list of criteria developed by these companies was much longer and more detailed than required for the purposes of this report, so categories of criteria were combined and deleted, and new definitions were written for those which were left. The life cycle phases used in this report are also a somewhat smaller set than sometimes used, since it was felt that this less detailed breakdown was more in keeping with the needs of the report.

4.1.1 Software Life Cycle Phases

The development of software requires that it progress through a life cycle consisting of requirements, design, coding, testing, maintenance and operation. The first four phases are concerned with the creation of the software. The latter two phases are concerned with the quality and reliability of the existing software. The following subsections are concerned with the definition of each of the life cycle phases.

4.1.1.1 Requirements Phase

The specification of system requirements is the first step in the software development life cycle. This phase begins with the statement of a problem to be solved and ends with a specification of what the system to solve the problem must look like. The goal of this phase is to clearly define and document the set of criteria by which a program will be ultimately examined for adherence to the specifications. The specification and documentation of the requirements of a system can be partially automated through the use of software tools. These tools allow the development of requirements specification documents using defined methodologies and analysis of the specifications for data flow and control sequences.

4.1.1.2 Design Phase

The second step in the software development life cycle is to develop an implementation for the previously established requirements. This ideally takes the form of a complete design that provides both an outline of the functional components of the system to be implemented and an explanation of how the requirements specifications will be met using the outlined system. This would additionally provide for precise, accurate and orderly transitions between the requirements design and coding activities. To this end the detail of the resulting design must be sufficient so that an implementors decisions cannot interfere with the ultimate satisfaction of specified requirements.

4.1.1.3 Coding Phase

Following or possibly overlapping the design phase is the implementation (coding & debug) phase. This phase is generally a manual process though defined methodologies do exist to help organize and improve the activity such as structured programming, and bottom-up and top-down implementations.

4.1.1.4 Testing Phase

The testing phase is a validation process that examines the implemented system to insure that the initial requirements are met. This process should additionally include tests to insure the quality and reliability of the system. This has become especially important as systems continue to grow in size and complexity. As with the other life cycle phases this process may overlap the previous (code and debug) phase. The two main elements of testing and quality assurance are static and dynamic testing both of which are characterized by the virtual necessity for the use of automated tools.

4.1.1.5 Maintenance Phase

The maintenance phase is a process continuing throughout the life of the software to ensure quality and reliability. Maintenance begins when changes in the software are required by management or when errors are found by the user during the operation of the software. When maintenance begins, it may require additional requirements, design, coding and testing. Since 75% or more of the time is spent in the maintenance phase, this phase is critical in the life cycle of software. It necessitates that effective tools exist to aid the software support personnel to provide timely and effective maintenance.

4.1.1.6 Operations Phase

The operations phase is that user-oriented phase in which software performs its planned and required function. With the aid of documentation and error-reporting tools, the user is provided the capability for monitoring and interacting with operatonal software to assure intended functionality is reached. When errors occur, they are either identified as user-originated or reported to software support personnel for correction. The operations phase requires correct documentation and effective error-reporting tools. User capability for monitoring and interacting with operational software is not required for embedded weapon systems. Such capability is more characteristic of communication systems.

4.1.2 Tool Criteria

The following definitions concern criteria for judging software characteristics. The criteria will be used to choose a minimum set of generic tools for the software life cycle phases.

Traceability - A program is traceable (exhibits traceability) if a thread exists to tie the modules of the program back through design to requirements. Traceability can exist independently in two directions: from requirements to the program, and from the program's modules to the requirements. In order to be fully traceable a program must exhibit traceability in both directions. Traceability must include design. That is, whatever design documents were retained as program documentation must be included in the thread.

Consistency - A program exhibits consistency if the requirements, design, and implementation techniques and notation are uniform throughout. Use of standardized languages and techniques are necessary to insure consistency.

Fault Tolerance - A program is fault tolerant if it is capable of operating in a consistent manner in spite of program errors, errors in input data, and hardware malfunctions. Total fault tolerance is an impossible goal, since there are hardware malfunctions and program errors from which no recovery is possible. The degree of fault tolerance which is desired and the actions to be taken under various conditions should be specified in the requirements document.

Simplicity - A program exhibits simplicity if each individual module is coded in an understandable manner, and the modularity has been established with consideration to a specific method, i.e., data structure, control flow, functionality, etc.

Modularity - A program is modular if its structure consists of highly independent modules. A module is independent if it could be implemented in a different manner without affecting the other modules of the program.

Functional Generality - A program or a module exhibits functional generality if its functions are not unnecessarily restricted. One example would be a routine to produce a line of print. If the line length is passed as a parameter rather than being "hard coded", the routine will be more general at a cost of very little additional complexity.

Expandability - A program is expandable if it is easy to add new functions, to enhance its current functions, or to increase the amount or types of data handled.

Instrumentation - Instrumentation provides the user and/or the maintainer with information on the operation of the program. For the user, it generally means status information. For the maintainer, it means such information as how many times a particular function is called, how data is distributed among differing types, and records of type and frequency of errors.

Resource Utilization - Resources utilization is the measure of how well a program conserves system resources. These resources include time, memory and external storage. How much priority is given to the conservation of each of these resources is a function of the requirements of the system.

Control of Data Access - Control of data access reflects two conflicting requirements: ease of access and restriction of access to sensitive data. Program data should be easily accessible to all modules and users who need it.

Ease of access is especially important in distributed systems where the user may be physically distant from the data being accessed. However, modules which do not need a particular datum and users who are not authorized to have specific information should be prohibited from access. In addition, a requirement may be that the system keep records of attempted and successful accesses to sensitive data.

Ease of Use - Ease of use measures the amount of effort which must be put forth to operate the system. It includes simplicity of input preparation, simplicity and understandability of operator commands, understandability of output data, and the amount of training required for new users of the system.

Independence - A program's independence is determined by the extent to which it relies on a specific hardware system or a specific underlying software system (operating system or run time system). A program is more independent when those functions which must be made specific to most hardware or software are isolated in lower level modules or are parameterized to allow easy change during system builds.

Commonality - A program exhibits commonality to the extent that standard interfaces are used between modules and that standard data formats are used. An effect of commonality should be the development of reusable software.

Compliance - A compliant program meets all the requirements laid down for it. This includes, but may not be limited to, normal processing, error handling, response time, memory/resource usage, and the accuracy of results.

Clarity - A program exhibits clarity through its documentation, including its internal documentation, to the extent that that documentation is readable and understandable.

Virtuality - A program exhibits virtuality if the user is not required to have a knowledge of the hardware implementation in order to run the system. Such things as the number and type of auxiliary storage devices, the amount of main storage, and even the type of CPU should be transparent to the user.

Distributedness - Distributedness is the extent to which elements of the system are logically and/or geographically separated. The word elements as used above includes both software and hardware. Software specific considerations are distribution of control, interconnect architectures, and data bases.

4.1.3 Correlation of Life Cycle Phases and Criteria

The correlation between life cycle phases and the criteria is given by Table 4-1. Almost all criteria apply to the initial phases from requirements through coding. The criteria that do not apply to requirements (simplicity, modularity, and functional generality) all deal specifically

SOFTWARE LIFE CYCLE PHASES	TRACEABILITY	CONSISTENCY	FAULT TOLERANCE	SIMPLICITY	MODULARITY	FUNCTIONAL GENERALITY	EXPANDABILITY	INSTRUMENTATION	RESOURCE UTILIZATION	CONTROL OF DATA ACCESS	EASE OF USE	INDEPENDENCE	COMMONALITY	COMPLIANCE	CLARITY	VIRTUALITY	DISTRIBUTEDNESS
REQUIREMENTS	✓	✓	✓			✓	✓	✓	✓	✓	✓	✓	✓	✓	✓	✓	✓
DESIGN	✓	✓	✓	✓	✓	✓	✓	✓	✓	✓	✓	✓	✓	✓	✓	✓	✓
CODING	✓	✓		✓	✓	✓			✓		✓	✓	✓	✓	✓	✓	✓
TESTING	✓							✓	✓					✓			✓
MAINTENANCE	✓	✓	✓	✓	✓	✓	✓	✓	✓	✓	✓	✓	✓	✓	✓	✓	✓
OPERATIONS			✓					✓	✓	✓	✓			✓		✓	

Table 4-1 Life Cycle Phases vs. Software Quality Criteria

with design and coding. Criteria that do not apply to coding (fault tolerance, expandability, instrumentation and control of data access) are areas which have already been settled by design and requirements. The testing phase is concerned with measuring compliance, which includes resource utilization. This is accomplished with the use of instrumentation. Traceability and distributedness must be maintained through this phase. The operations and maintenance phases affect all criteria.

4.2 Correlation of Tools to Criteria

This section contains a list of generic tools with their definitions. Each tool is related to the life cycle phase of its primary use. Criteria enhanced by each tool during its primary life cycle phase are discussed (refer to Table 4-2).

Table 4-2. Software Quality Criteria vs. Software Tools

SOFTWARE TOOLS (by Life Cycle Phase)		TRACEABILITY	CONSISTENTY	FAULT TOLERANCE	SIMPLICITY	MODULARITY	FUNCTIONAL GENERALITY	EXPANDABILITY	INSTRUMENTATION	RESOURCE UTILIZATION	CONTROL OF DATA ACCESS	EASE OF USE	INDEPENDENCE	COMMONALITY	COMPLIANCE	CLARITY	VIRTUALITY	DISTRIBUTEDNESS
Requirement	AUTOMATED REQUIREMENTS DOCUMENT GENERATOR							+										
	AUTOMATED REQUIREMENTS ANALYZER		+												+	+		
	AUTOMATED LANGUAGE TRANSLATOR	+	+											+				
	REQUIREMENTS INTERFACE PROCESSOR			+			+	+	+	+		+			+		+	+
	RAPID PROTOTYPER														+			
Design	CALLING TREE GENERATOR															+		
	CROSS REFERENCE GENERATOR															+		
	STRUCTURE CHECKER															+		
Coding	OPTIMIZING COMPILER									+					+			
	CROSS COMPILER				+				+	+					+			
	LINKER/LOADER					+				+				+	+			
	CHECK-OUT COMPILER								+									
	STANDARDS AUDITOR		+		+										+			
	FORMATTER		+		+													
	MENU GENERATOR											+						
Testing	COMPLETION ANALYZER								+						+			
	STUB GENERATOR						+											
	MUTATION TESTER								+						+			
	PATH FLOW ANALYZER								+						+			
	STORAGE DUMP								+									
	ASSERTION CHECKER	+	+		+										+	+		
	RESOURCE MANAGEMENT ANALYZER									+					+			
	CORRECTNESS ANALYZER	+	+						+						+			
	SYMBOLIC DEBUGGER								+						+			
	HISTORICAL FILE GENERATOR								+									
	INTERFACE MAPPER					+								+				
	VARIABLE MAPPER								+									
	CONNECTIVITY ANALYZER					+												
	REACHABILITY ANALYZER					+												
	TIMING ANALYZER								+	+					+			
	USAGE COUNTER								+									
Maintenance	VERSION GENERATOR	+						+			+					+		
	RAPID RECONFIGURATOR			+	+					+				+				
	REPORT GENERATOR											+						
Operations	DIAGNOSTIC ANALYZER			+						+								
	SYSTEM BUILDER					+												

Software Quality Criteria (columns)

4.2.1 Requirements Tools

4.2.1.1 Automated Requirements Document Generator

This tool generates a requirement by accepting an implementation independent specification couched in a formalized language, performs processing to format requested output, and then generates the output in graphic or textual representations as required. Expandability is enhanced when new requirements are generated during the maintenance phase.

4.2.1.2 Automated Requirements Analyzer

Assuming the requirements are specified in a formalized language, this tool will provide checks for completeness, consistency, and redundancy of information given. Compliance is enhanced since the completeness of the specification is checked, and clarity is enhanced by not allowing redundant names or functions.

4.2.1.3 Automatic Language Translator

One of multiple languages is selected to be the target language for the implementation independent specification. This tool then automatically translates the specification into a compilable program in that language. Traceability, consistency, and commonality are all enhanced by this tool. Simplicity and clarity would probably be decreased by this tool.

4.2.1.4 Requirements Interface Processor

This tool is a front end to the automated requirements document generator. Its function is to provide user-friendly access and use of the tool as well as provide a powerful modification capability to support rapid prototyping and simulation. Multiple data entry techniques, such as graphic representation, menu representation, default selection, etc. should be supported. Criteria enhanced indirectly include ease of use, resource utilization, compliance, fault tolerance, functional generality, expandability, instrumentation, virtuality, and distributedness since these may be modeled during development of the requirements specification (assuming an analyzer and translator are present). No criteria are directly enhanced by this tool since the final product could achieve the same status through manual methods of analysis and documentation over an extended period of time.

4.2.1.5 Rapid Prototyping

This process involves automating the labor intensive portions of feasibility studies through computer simulation and modeling techniques.

4.2.2 Design Tools

4.2.2.1 Program Design Language (PDL) Calling Tree Generator

A calling tree generator is similar in operation to a cross reference generator, but is restricted to subprogram names rather than all identifiers. The output is arranged in the opposite manner to that in which cross reference shows where a particular name is used, that is, that C is called by A and B, while the calling tree shows that A calls B and C. This different orientation makes a valuable addition to documentation, increasing clarity.

4.2.2.2 PDL Cross Reference Generator

A cross reference generator accepts as input a design expressed in PDL and produces as output a listing of all points of definition and all references which can be retained as documentation, thus improving clarity.

4.2.2.3 Structure Checker

A structure checker for PDL is a program that accepts as input a design expressed in PDL and produces as output the same PDL with its structures checked for correctness and completeness. Structure here refers to programming language structures such as if-then-else, begin-end and the case statement. Since PDL may be kept as documentation for the finished product, clarity is improved by this process.

4.2.3 Coding Tools

4.2.3.1 Optimizing Compilers

Optimization is a compiler function which improves the quality of the machine language code produced by the compiler. Most optimizations improve both speed of execution and the size of the executable program. They therefore improve resource utilization. In extreme cases of memory size limits or response time constraints, optimization may be required for compliance. Six common optimizations are: constant propagation, common subexpression elimination, strength reduction, code motion, dead code elimination, and the elimination of induction variables. Constant propagation occurs when the optimizer recognizes computations for which all data is available. Since the data is available, the compiler can do the computation, providing its result as a constant. Therefore, the time and code required to compute the result during execution is saved. Common subexpression elimination takes place when the compiler recognizes that the same result will be computed in two or more places. (To derive the same result, not only must the expressions be the same except possibly for commutivity, but the data must be the same.) The compiler saves the result from the first computation, and uses it to replace the code required for the subsequent computations. Strength reduction occurs when the compiler is able to replace an arithmetic operation with another operation which requires less time. A good example would be the replacement of X squared by X times X. Dead code is any part of a program which will never be reached during execution. This sort of code is sometimes created by an if statement whose test always has the same result. If the compiler can detect this situation, it can eliminate the if test and the unreachable code, saving both time and memory. Code motion and the elimination of induction variables are both loop optimization techniques. The compiler can often find expressions whose result is the same for each iteration of the loop. These expressions are called loop invariants. Code motion is the removal of these expression from within the loop, and their placement just before the loop, where they will only be executed once. Induction variables are variables whose values vary in a linear fashion during execution of the loop. Not all induction variables are part of the source code. A FORTRAN example might be:

```
      REAL X(10), Y(10)
      DO 10,I=1,10
      X(I)=0
   10 Y(I)=0
```

There are three induction variables in this code segment: I and the offsets used to address elements of the arrays X and Y. If a real occupies 4 address units of storage, the expression for the offset into X is (I-1)*4. The expression for Y is the same. A good compiler might first recognize these two as the same and eliminate the second computation. (common subexpression elimination). It might then realize that it could get the same result by setting the offset to zero outside the loop and adding four to it on each loop pass. (strength reduction). Finally, it might realize that it does not need both the offset and I, since it can determine loop termination by testing the value of the offset. Therefore, it could eliminate I from the loop (elimination of an induction variable). Two types of loop optimization which are rarely used are loop unrolling and loop jamming. Loop unrolling can only be done when the number of times a loop will be executed is known. It consists of duplicating the body of the loop a number of times in order to eliminate some of the tests for loop termination. This technique saves time, but invariably wastes space. Loop jamming can take place when two loops have the same indices and no result of the first loop is used in the second. The two loops are merged into one. A (trivial) example might be:

```
      REAL X(10),Y(10)
      DO 10,I=1,10
 10   X(I)=0
      DO 20,I=1,10
 20   Y(I)=1
```

Which might be merged into:

```
      REAL X(10),Y(10)
 DO 10,I=1,10
      X(I)=0
 10   Y(I)=1
```

All of the above optimizations save time. Most of them also save space, with the exception of loop unrolling and possibly code motion.

4.2.3.2 Cross Compiler

A cross compiler is a compiler which is hosted (runs) on a type of machine different from that for which it generates code. Usually this means that the host machine is a mainframe or a mini computer and the target machine is a microprocessor. Cross compilers allow the use of larger, more complex compilers (which may be required for complex languages such as Ada or PL/I) than could be hosted on the target. The features of the cross compiler can then include optimization and/or the options of a checkout compiler. Therefore cross compilers may indirectly improve instrumentation, resource utilization, and compliance, while also improving ease of development. A cross compiler makes it possible to use a more complex compiler (or a compiler for a more complex language) than might be available on the target system. It may improve resource utilization, simplicity, and compliance.

4.2.3.3 Linker/Loader

The normal functions of a linker/loader are to allow the usage of external routines and to allow programs to be loaded in different locations (relocation). These functions increase commonality, and modularity. In addition, some linker/loaders may provide facilities for overlaying program segments. Overlaying allows different program segments to occupy the same memory locations, with each segment being read in as it is needed. This improves one facet of resource utilization (space) at the expense of another (time). It may be required for compliance.

4.2.3.4 Checkout Compiler

Checkout compilers provide special services during the compilation of programs which assist during program checkout. Options in the compiler provide for automatic printing of variables each time their values change, for automatic trace of subprogram calls, or for collection of other statistics such as the amont of time spent in each routine. In other words, a checkout compiler adds instrumentation.

4.2.3.5 Standards Auditor

A standards auditor (code auditor) takes as input a source program in some specific language and produces a report detailing violations of some set of programming standards. By enforcing standards, it improves consistency, simplicity, and clarity. (Clarity is improved because the use of procedure headers may be part of the standard being enforced.)

4.2.3.6 Formatter

A formatter is a program which takes as input a source program in some specific high order language and rearranges the input source into some specified format, enforcing standard indentation conventions and other standards for layout of the program on the printed page. It therefore improves the consistency of the program. Since understandability is improved by proper indentation, the simplicity of the program is also improved.

4.2.3.7 Menu Generator

A menu generator is designed to provide optimum usefulness and versatility in data entry by utilizing video display terminals. A user-defined form, or mask, for data manipulation on the display area improves ease of use. Since the mask resembles a printed form, data is placed into the form by filling in the appropriate blanks on the screen.

4.2.4 Testing Tools

4.2.4.1 Completion Analyzer

A completion analyzer (or coverage analyzer) provides data that shows how thoroughly the source code has been exercised during the testing with respect to the testing goals which provides compliance and adds instrumentation.

4.2.4.2 Stub Generator

A stub generator provides substitutes during testing for modules which have not been coded. Testing of individual modules is thus made much easier. This tool enhances functional generality.

4.2.4.3 Mutation Tester

A mutation tester constructs a set of mutants of the target program which will test a program's compliance. A mutant is a program statement which has been transformed in such a way as to effect typical program errors. A programmer could test a program with the assumption that the current state of the program is a mutant of the correct one.

4.2.4.4 Path Flow Analyzer

A path flow analyzer is a software technique which provides instrumentation and compliance by scanning the source code in order to design an optimal set of test cases which exercise the primary paths in a software module.

4.2.4.5 Storage Dumps

Storage dumps provide program/system status and selected data values which contribute to instrumentation.

4.2.4.6 Connectivity Analysis

Connectivity analysis is used to identify the direct program paths between any two sections of code within a program, segment tracing, which provides a measure of modularity of the program.

4.2.4.7 Reachability Analysis

Reachability analysis is used to identify the specific program paths, direct or indirect, exercised in order to reach a specific module, subroutine or section of code within a program which provides a measure of modularity of the program and distributedness of the system of programs. It can also be used to identify unreachable modules and "dead" code.

4.2.4.8 Timing Analyzer

A timing analyzer reads the executable code and produces a report showing program segment invocation hierarchy and the actual execution times per complete program segment cycles. Instrumentation, resource utilization, and compliance are measured with respect to the timing in the operation of the program.

4.2.4.9 Symbolic Debugger

A symbolic debugger is used to enhance instrumentation. Since testing is the process of determining whether or not errors or faults exist in a program, debugging is an attempt to isolate the source of a problem and to find a solution with snaps of variables and absolute identifiers which enhances compliance.

4.2.4.10 Historical File Generation

Historical file generation provides instrumentation by the generation of accumulated execution statistics for all test cases including blocks executed, paths taken, modules invoked, etc.

4.2.4.11 Interface Mapping

Interface mapping is used to measure commonality with respect to the identification of program interfaces such as called and calling modules or modules involved in interprocess communications and the verification of the range and limits of the module parameters. It is useful for the analysis of modularity, a module's impact on other modules, and the identification of data abstractions from subroutine calls, function calls and macros.

4.2.4.12 Variable Mapping

Variable mapping provides information with respect to the definition and use of the individual variables in the program and may provide actual values and initialization, during execution of the program. Instrumentation is measured with respect to the information provided.

4.2.4.13 Assertion Checker

An assertion checker is used to check a program's critical requirements for compliance with the results derived by dynamic analysis. It enhances the simplicity and maintainability of the program and improves the traceability and consistency of the software. By inserting assertions concerning the value or condition of program variables in the program code, assertion checking may be applied to error detection activities, understanding program behavior and clarity through documention of the program's critical requirements.

4.2.4.14 Resource Management Analysis

Resource management analysis dicatates resource utilization for the purpose of compliance in processing requirements such that programs and data should be allocated the minimum amount of time and storage that is necessary. When additional amounts are needed, they are acquired and released dynamically.

4.2.4.15 Correctness Analyzer

A correctness analyzer determines the traceability between a program's total response and the stated response in the functional requirements and between the program as coded and the programming requirements. Measuring the program's response helps to determine instrumentation and compliance.

4.2.4.16 Usage Counter

A usage counter reads the executable code and collects usage data during program execution such as the number of times each executable statement, branch and subroutine calls were executed. Instrumentation is measured with respect to how many times a particular statement, branch or subroutine is executed.

4.2.5 Maintenance Tools

4.2.5.1 Version Generator

A version generator is a system to track and control changes to files (source, object or text) associated with software development which enhances the control of data access, provides expandability, and ensures traceability in the maintenance life cycle. The system should be able to store, update and retrieve files including audit trails as well as maintain historical records on all versions controlled for the purpose of complete program documentation and clarity.

4.2.5.2 Rapid Reconfiguration

Rapid reconfiguration is an automated process by which a system is rebuilt after changes which provides fault tolerance. All file dependencies and processes (resource utilization, common memory, compilations, preprocessing, etc) are specified in a hierarchical manner such that a change in one module can easily and quickly be related to changes required in other modules which provides commonality and simplicity.

4.2.5.3 Report Generator

A report generator consists of methods for customized formatting of generated output to provide ease of use and improve resource utilization.

4.2.6 Operations Tools

4.2.6.1 Diagnostic Analyzer

A diagnostic analyzer measures the capability of the system to perform its functions in accordance with design requirements, even in the present of hardware failures. If the system functions can be performed in the event of faults, the system is partially fault tolerant when design specifications are not met with respect to the time required or the storage capacity required to complete the job. Fault tolerance is provided by the use of redundant resources, resource utilization, for upgraded system reliability and protection.

4.2.6.2 System Builder

A system builder identifies all required programs, and it compiles, links, relocates and produces an object file for execution which enhances modularity.

4.3 Recommended Near-Term Tools and Their Flowcharts

There are five tools which affect the requirements phase. They are the Automated Requirements Document Generator, the Automated Requirements Analyzer, the Automatic Language Translator, the Requirements Interface Processor, and the Rapid Prototyper. The Automatic Language Translator directly enhances traceability, consistency, and commonality. The Automatic Requirements Analyzer enhances consistency and compliance. All other criteria influenced are influenced indirectly (see Table 4-2).

The design phase, in which decisions are made which affect the most criteria, is almost devoid of automated tools. There exist several useful methodologies which were developed mostly for use in the business data processing sphere, but none of them have been satisfactorily automated. Some of the tools discussed for the requirements phase extend into the design phase, but the act of design still remains a manual (or even cerebral) art. The tools which apply to this phase which will be discussed here all fall into the class of program design language processors, and are generally found as a single tool rather than individually. All three tools (a calling tree generator, a cross reference generator, and a structure checker) are concerned with the production or checking of documentation, therefore the only criterion affected is clarity.

Tools for the coding or implementation phase can be divided into two areas: tools affecting source code, and tools affecting object code. The tools affecting source code are the menu generator, the standards auditor, and the formatter. The menu generator helps coders to lay out and design screens and menus for interactive input. By doing this it affects ease of use of the finished project. Both of the other tools affect consistency and simplicity of the source code, and the standards auditor also affects compliance if coding standards are specified in the requirements. The tools affecting object code are the optimizing compiler, the cross compiler, the linker/loader, and the checkout compiler. The first three of these all affect compliance and resource utilization by making programs more time and/or space efficient. The cross compiler also affects simplicity and possibly instrumentation if it has some of the features of the checkout compiler. The linker/loader affects commonality and modularity as well. The checkout compiler adds instrumentation only.

During the maintenance phase, all decisions made prior to this phase are either maintained or changed with respect to errors detected in either operations or requirements and design changes requested by management. Maintenance is accomplished with a generic maintenance tool comprised of a set of specific maintenance tools which provide correction of errors and requested changes in documentation and programs by modification, addition or removal of functions. Additionally, tools must be provided after error correction or requested changes. Replication of programs and documentation is ensured by the specific maintenance tools providing redundancy in distributed processing systems.

The criteria relating to redundancy in requirements and documentation are traceability, commonality, and clarity. The criteria relating to maintenance activities such as error correction are resource utilization, control of data access and fault tolerance. Since approximately 75% of the software life cycle is devoted to maintenance, it is necessary for a generic maintenance tool to enhance the aforementioned criteria as well as enhance ease of use, expandability and simplicity.

With reference to Table 4-2, the aforementioned criteria are enhanced by the version generator and rapid reconfiguration. Version generation provides an audit trail for maintenance of programs and their data dependencies. Using this audit trail, rapid reconfiguration automates rebuilding of a system. Additionally, the report generator enhances ease of use during the maintenance of programs. The combination of these specific maintenance tools forms a minimum generic maintenance tool.

During the testing phase, compliance and instrumentation are the important criteria measured by the specific testing tools as shown in Table 4-2. In order to determine the specific testing tools which are part of a generic testing tool, tools which enhance either or both of the criteria, compliance or instrumentation, should be considered.

The main group of specific testing tools which may be a part of a minimum generic testing tool should enhance both compliance and instrumentation. This group consists of a completion analyzer, mutation tester, path flow analyzer, correctness analyzer, timing analyzer and symbolic debugger. As shown in Table 4-2, these specific testing tools also enhance other criteria such as traceability and consistency in the correctness analyzer and resource utilization in the timing analyzer. The additional criteria improve the minimum generic testing tool which enhances compliance and instrumentation.

A secondary group of specific testing tools which may be a part of a generic testing tool are those which enhance either compliance or instrumentation, but both of the criteria are not enhanced. The tools which enhance compliance, not instrumentation, are an assertion checker and resource management analyzer. Similarly, the tools that enhance instrumentation, not compliance, consist of a usage counter, historical file generator, variable mapper and storage dump (see Table 4-2). Additionally, the assertion checker enhances traceability, consistency, simplicity, and clarity, and the Resource Management Analyzer enhances resource utilization. The additional enhancements further improve the generic testing tool.

A generic testing tool is composed of its minimum requirements if it consists of the main group of specific testing tools which enhance both instrumentation and compliance. The tool is improved if the secondary group of specific testing tools, enhancing either instrumentation or compliance, is added. A combination of the main and secondary groups of specific testing tools form a generic testing tool during the testing phase.

During the operations phase, programs must be capable of operating in a consistent manner with recovery from hardware malfunctions and program errors unless there is no recovery; therefore, a generic operations tool should enhance fault tolerances. Additionally, resource utilization and modularity should be enhanced since programs should conserve system resources. The specific operations tools comprising the generic operations tool should enhance the previously mentioned criteria.

Referring to the specific operations tools in Table 4-2, a diagnostic analyzer and a system builder form a minimum generic operations tool. A system builder, linking all of the programs in a system for execution, enhances modularity. Since a diagnostic analyzer measures the capability of the system of programs to perform its functions in accordance with design requirements, it enhances resource utilization and fault tolerance. Since these specific operations tools enhance the prescribed criteria, they form a minimum generic operations tool.

Compiler Generation Tools

The following tools are somewhat restricted in their application, although the first two could be used to read and parse other forms of command input. Their primary application, though, is the construction of compilers.

Lexical analyzer generators accept a description of the base elements of a language, which are called tokens, and generate tables to be used by a standard program in the recognition of tokens. A token is a sequence of characters which can be treated as a single logical entity. Tokens include keywords such as IF and GOTO, numbers, identifiers and special symbols such as = or <=. The lexical analyzer reads characters until it has recognized a token and then returns the type and value of the token.

Syntax analyzer generators accept a description (called a grammer) of a language and produce tables for use by a syntax analyzer. Syntax analyzers accept tokens from the lexical analyzer and parse the language into larger constructs. This action is somewhat analogous to the actions of an English student in diagramming a sentence. For example, if the lexical analyzer returned the tokens "article", "adjective" and "noun", then the syntax analyzer would recognize that these tokens comprise a "noun phrase". At a later phase the "noun phrase" might be combined with a "verb phrase" and another "noun phrase" into a "transitive sentence". In terms of a programming language, this means that a syntax analyzer would combine "identifier", "assign", "identifier", "plus" and "identifier" into "assignment statement". The compiler then takes this information to generate an intermediate representation of the program.

Code generator generators take as input some form of a description of a target machine and a description of the intermediate representation mentioned above. They produce as output tables and/or code for use by a standardized code generator. The code generator takes the intermediate representation of a program and converts it into target machine language. These tools are currently not fully developed, although some industrial use has taken place.

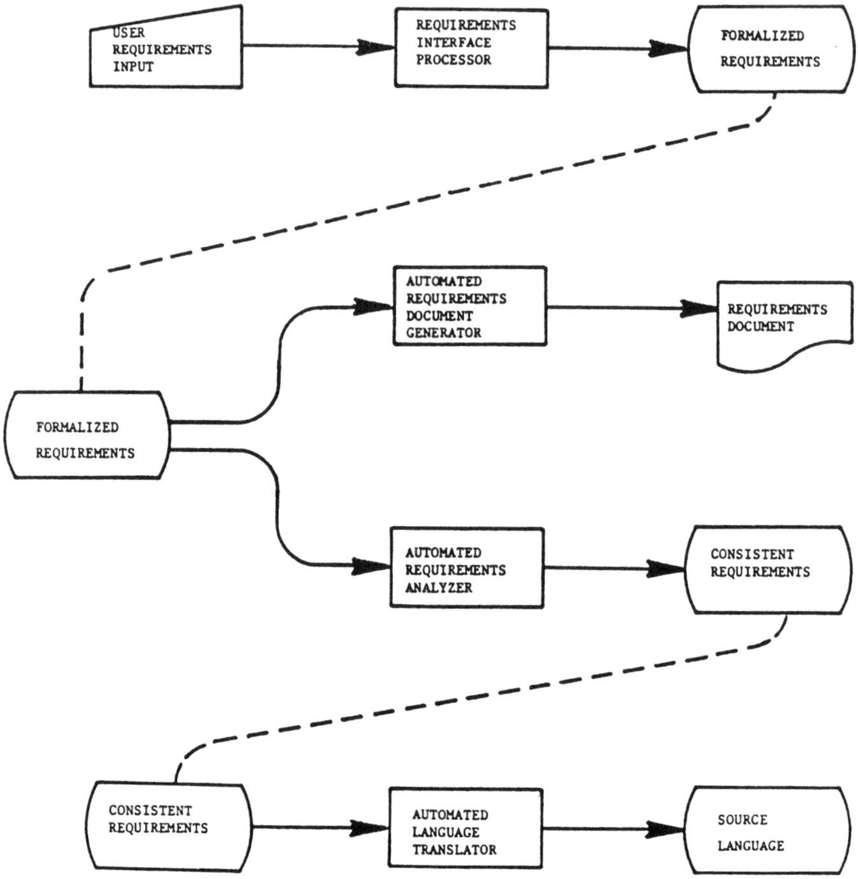

Figure 4-1 Generic Requirements Tool Flowchart

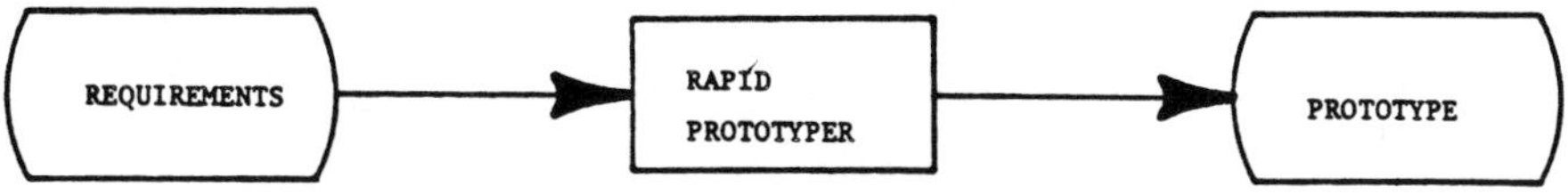

Figure 4-2 Rapid Prototyper Flowchart

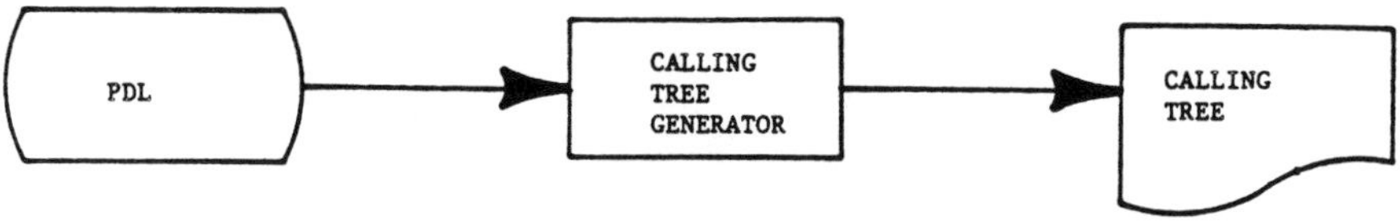

Figure 4-3 Calling Tree Generator Flowchart

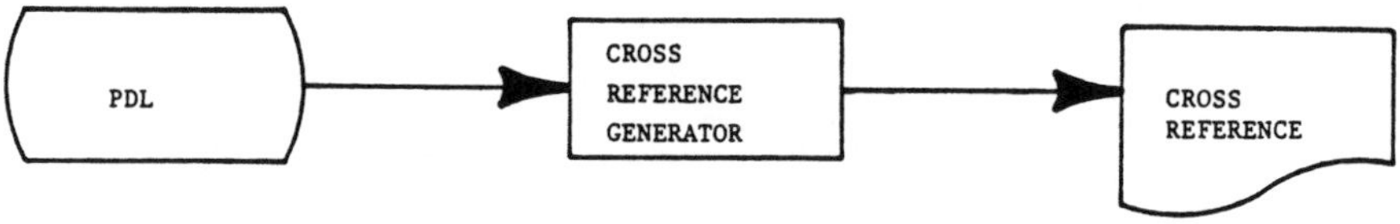

Figure 4-4 Cross Reference Generator Flowchart

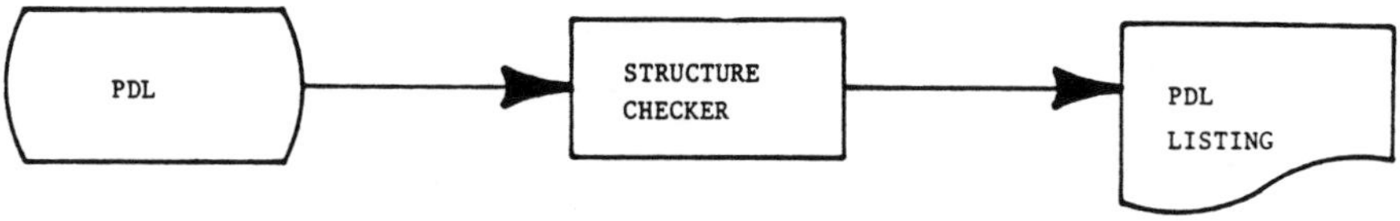

Figure 4-5 Structure Checker Flowchart

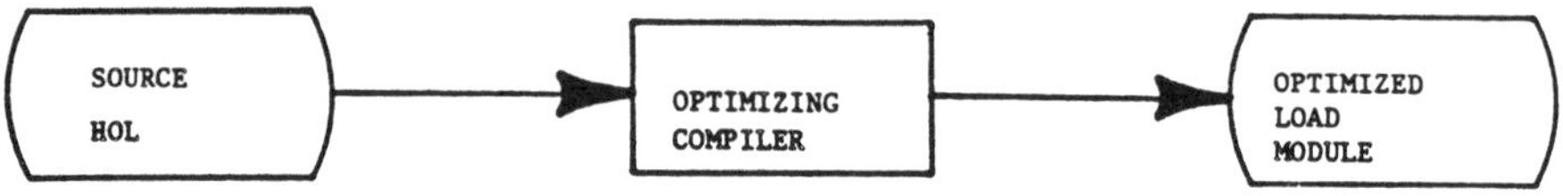

Figure 4-6 Optimizing Compiler Flowchart

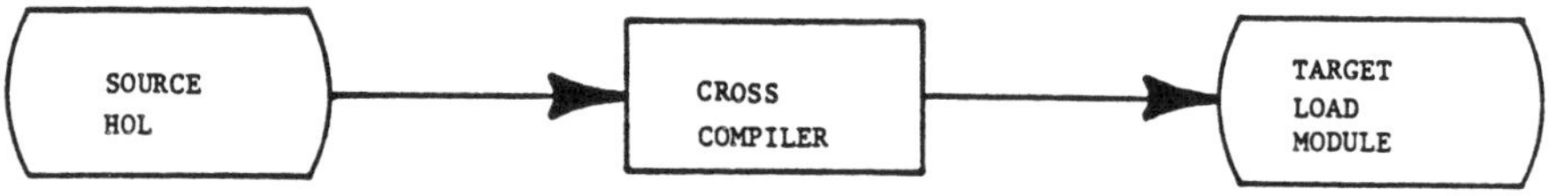

Figure 4-7 Cross Compiler Flowchart

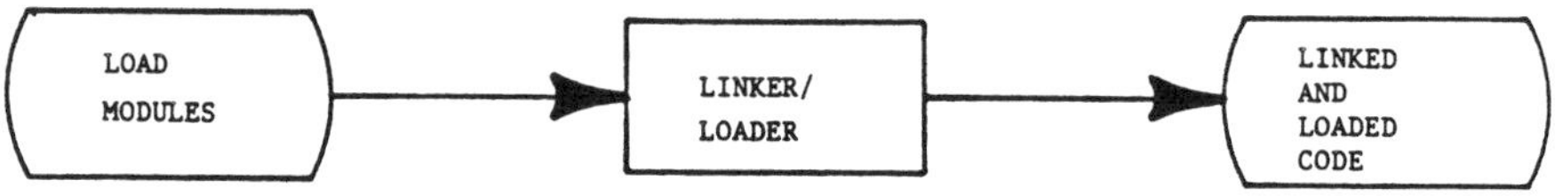

Figure 4-8 Linker/Loader Flowchart

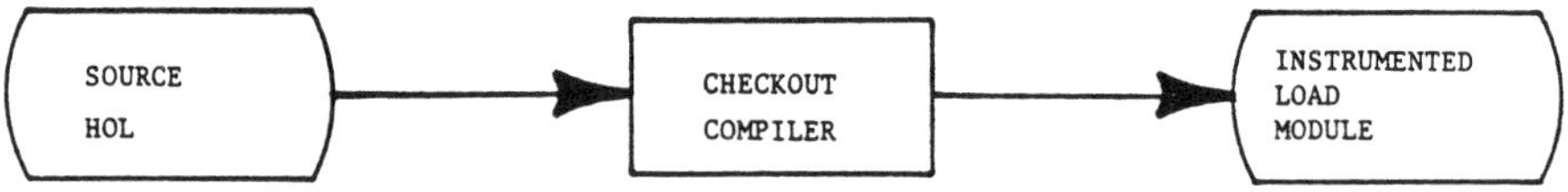

Figure 4-9 Checkout Compiler Flowchart

Figure 4-10 Standards Auditor Flowchart

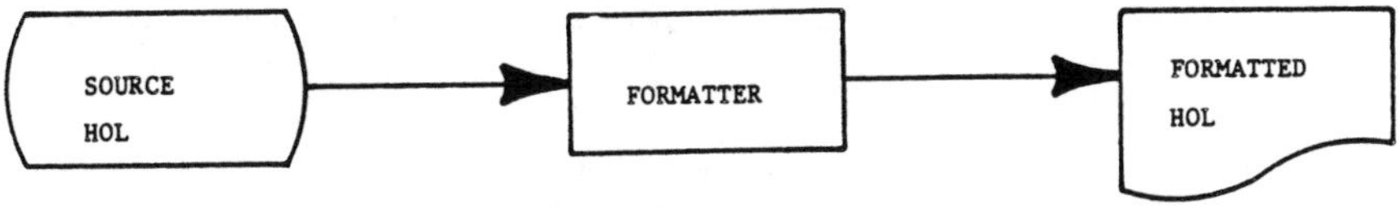

Figure 4-11 Formatter Flowchart

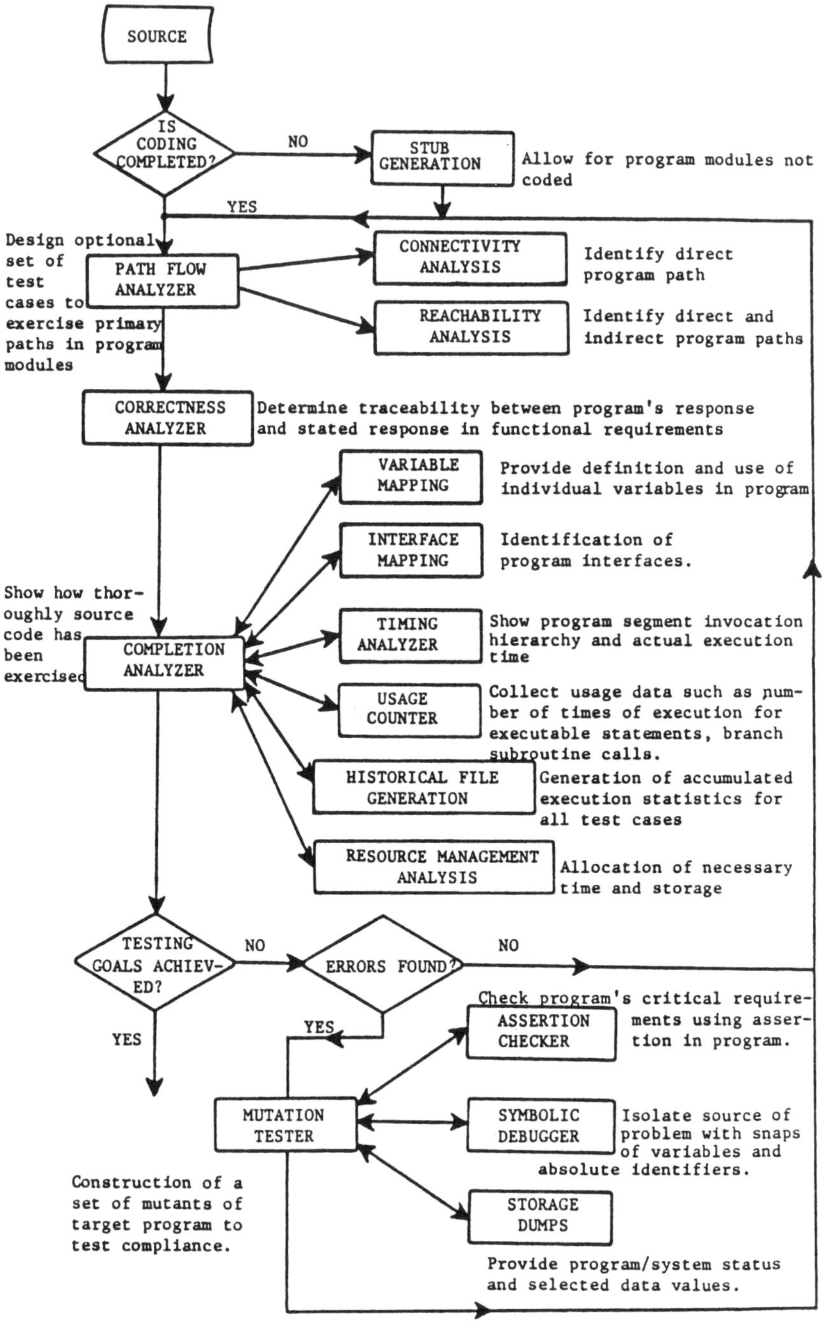

Figure 4-12 Testing Tools Flowchart

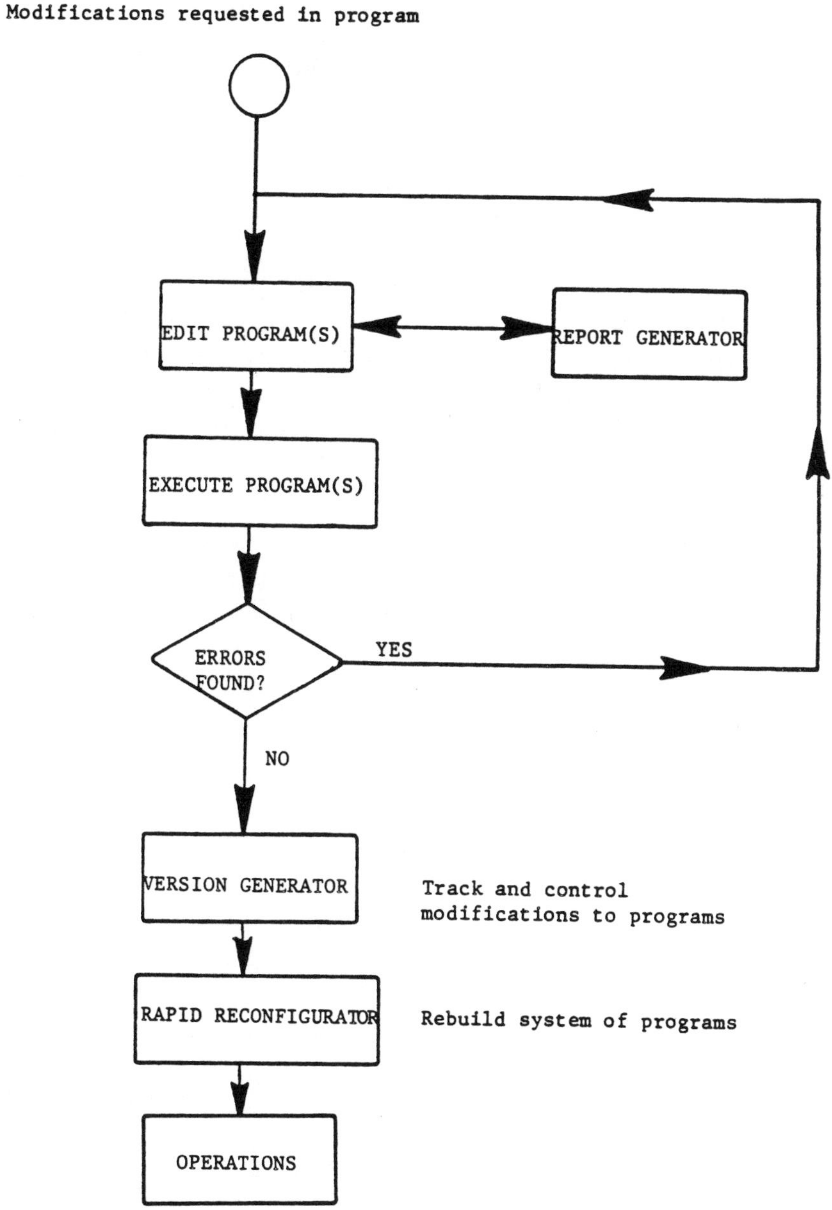

Figure 4-13 Maintenance Tools Flowchart

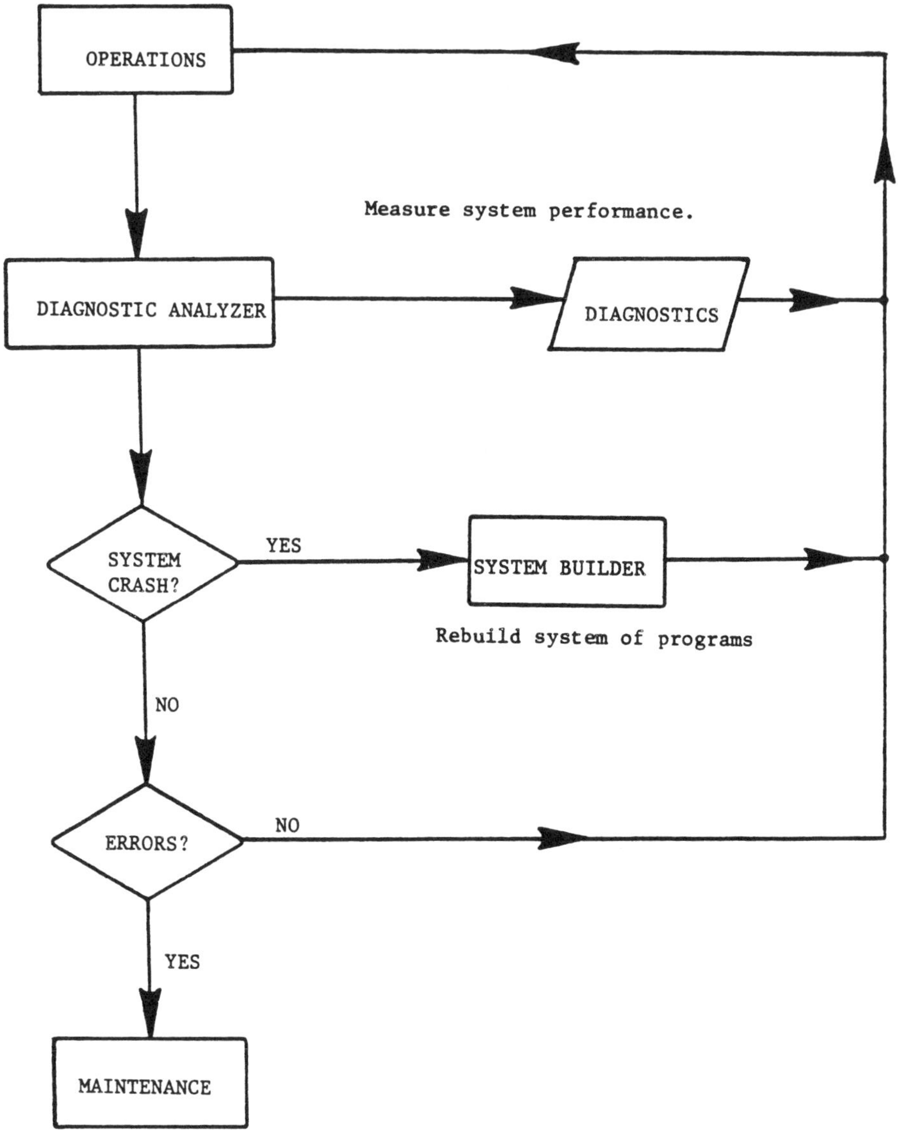

Figure 4-14 Operations Tools Flowchart

4.4 Near-Term Generic Tools Conclusions

In this section, conclusions are drawn based on Tables 4-1 and 4-2. Each life cycle phase was examined to determine whether any criterion applicable to that phase was not enhanced by any of the tools assigned to that phase. These criteria were then used to determine areas where further tool development is needed. The tables were also examined to determine if any criterion which was not applicable to a phase was enhanced by one of the tools assigned to that phase. Tools were grouped according to the phase in which they are more frequently used; however, some tools are used in other phases. For example, the checkout compiler was assigned to the coding phase with the other language tools, but its use overlaps into the testing phase. Because of these overlaps, criteria which were not applicable to a particular life cycle phase may be enhanced by tools assigned to that phase.

In the first life cycle phase, requirements, all applicable criteria are covered except control of data access and independence. It may be that these are difficult criteria to enhance at this early stage. This would certainly seem to be true of independence, but some sort of tool for evaluating the requirements for control of data access would seem to be needed.

The design phase is poverty-stricken with regard to tools. The only tools which exist enhance clarity of documentation. This would be a fertile area for the development of tools to automate the many design methodologies that exist.

The tools available for the coding phase do not address several criteria. These criteria are traceability, functional generality, independence, clarity, virtuality, and distributedness. Major emphasis should be placed on traceability and distributedness for new tool development.

The coverage of the testing phase shows the fact that most of the emphasis to date in tool development has been on testing tools. All criteria appropriate to this phase have been addressed.

There are eight applicable criteria which were not addressed for the maintenance phase. The basic problem in maintenance is to retain good qualities already present in the software. Those criteria not addressed are: consistency, modularity, functional generality, instrumentation, independence, compliance, virtuality, and distributedness. This lack of coverage is bad because of the fact that experience shows that approximately 75% of the budget spent on any piece of software is spent in the maintenance phase. The situation is somewhat ameliorated by the fact that many of the tools assigned to other phases can be applied during the maintenance phase.

A reasonable conclusion to be reached from this is that the present emphasis in tool development needs to be changed. The testing phase is probably sufficiently covered, but more research and development needs to be spent on designing tools for the design and maintenance phases. In addition, the criterion of independence is not addressed in any phase; therefore, it looms as a potential area for exploration and development.

5. Far-Term Generic Techniques

Distributed processing systems are best supported by an integrated software support environment. Much of the current development effort within the Department of Defense is directed toward such an environment. The subsequent cost savings provide justification for many on-going projects, e.g., the Ada Program Support Environment and various Integrated Software Support Environments. Present emphasis is on implementation as quickly as it can be achieved. However, this overlooks the more subtle long range impact such implementation will have. Why implement integrated software support environments in the first place? Are cost savings alone enough to justify them? Do they provide value-added to the computer users? These and a host of other questions are not addressed. Problems are currently arising within these computer user communities which should be addressed. One such problem concerns the almost apocryphal aspects behind knowledge based systems. An increasing number of computer users are justifying all sorts of new data bases based upon an enhancement to a knowledge based system. Of course a precise definition of what is meant by knowledge based system is usually not addressed. As these undefined levels of expectation become more common within the user community, the relationship of integrated software support environments to knowledge based systems becomes increasingly important. Once implemented, the contribution to specifically defined knowledge based systems by integrated software support environments must be made explicit. This contribution is a function of the emerging role of artificial intelligence. Actual computer intelligence will become evident within the databases and operations of the computer environment. In large part, the success of distributed processing systems will be circumscribed by their ability to contribute to the knowledge based systems of users. The bottom line remains functionality, and what users want is functional knowledge based systems. Consequently, the generic techniques required by distributed processing systems of the future concern knowledge based functionality. Tools not presently envisioned will be required. ISSEs will not be enough. Intelligent and adaptive integrated software support environments will be required. Under present circumstances, the distributed processing environment is complex. Under such future requirements, the complexity multiplies itself. Techniques which will become the tools of tomorrow are going to require artificial intelligence (AI). Although the present only hints of the future, the following observations concerning AI are evident.

The prime far-term generic tool and technique for highly complex systems, including distributed processing systems, will be the application of artificial intelligence. Intelligent components will be a feature of both developmental support systems and the operational systems. Such components will thus support the total software life cycle as well as serve to mediate the complexity of distributed system functions. The most persuasive rationale for the appropriateness of AI is precisely in the potential for managing complexity.

The overall integrating concept here is that of a knowledge based system (KBS). The realization of a KBS is of course somewhat different in the two application areas under discussion (support environments and operational systems). In support (host) environments, the KBS is the foundation of the "intelligent programmer's assistant". In operational (target) systems, intelligence and its supporting knowledge bases function as features of operating systems and data base management. Thus in distributed processing, this knowledge and intelligence will itself be distributed as a system component. Of course, the design of intelligent systems may itself by carried out on an intelligent development system.

Definitions of artificial intelligence usually emphasize the emulation of human cognitive abilities in such tasks as problem solving, symbol manipulation, and operations on incomplete or inaccurate information. Implicit in this emphasis is the assumption of the (metaphorical) ability to "understand". Understanding, in turn, is dependent on an appropriate and adequate representation of knowledge.

The types of knowledge represented and manipulated in a KBS will vary according to whether the KBS pertains to a support environment or to an operational system (though there may be overlap in the content of the two types). A support environment will optimally include detailed knowledge of the application domain(s) (and will include a means for acquiring knowledge about application domains). The design target may be a total system design including hardware/software partitioning, or it may be an application program for an existing target system. In the latter case, knowledge of the target configuration would be part of the knowledge base.

Further, an intelligent support system will have a sophisticated understanding of the application programming language. Any compiler for the language will of course have "knowledge" (but little "understanding") of the syntax and semantics of the language. Various types and levels of intelligence are candidates for incorporation into an intelligent compiler (embodying a knowledge of the pragmatics of the language) and an associated compile-time (and run-time) debugger. (Some of these will be discussed in more detail below.) Understanding of the language (and of the target system) will be useful in other development tools as well, such as a requirements analyzer which outputs source code text. Here the understanding comes into play in selection of appropriate language constructs and facilities. For example, an intelligent encapsulation mechanism (e.g., for packages in Ada) could define classes of objects to be packaged together, using heuristics guided by knowledge of the language rationale, the application domain, and measures of software quality. If low-level objects are specified in a requirements language, this automatic package definition can be viewed as the generation of a high-level, more abstract object.

As indicated above, the representation of knowledge is a fundamentally important issue in KBS development. Representation schemes include production rules (a set of conditions together with a conclusion, perhaps with an attached confidence level), frames, and scripts. Detection of true conditions in production rules may involve heuristic evaluation. An important aspect of knowledge representation is the association of teleology (purpose) with raw information. Inclusion of purpose aids an intelligent system in evaluation of the relevance of information to a task or problem.

Intelligence in knowledge-based, expert consulting systems will provide decision aids throughout the system life cycle. This will be valuable in any activity where the consequence of experimental adjustment of system parameters needs to be evaluated. An example is impact analysis of requirements or design changes, where what is desired is an evaluation of the severity of a proposed change. AI techniques can be used to search the knowledge base for relevant conceptual connections. Efficient heuristics could make feasible an interactive dialogue with the decision-maker. The search process in this example may be sufficient but not exhaustive. Once a change decision has been made a detailed analysis of affected system entities will be necessary. In this case, search will be exhaustive, but can be intelligently guided to avoid blind search.

A further desirable component of the knowledge base for decision aids will be the inclusion of quantitative and qualitative software metrics. This will enable an intelligent dialogue with program designers in which alternative design features can be evaluated against criteria of goodness. The decisions of the designer can feed back into the knowledge base so that future decisions can be more fully automated. A mature design knowledge base will be useful in rapid system prototyping.

Support tools of the future will be used in designing and implementing target systems with artificially intelligent components. A principal motivation for the use of AI techniques in distributed processing is the management of the inherent complexity of such systems. Since intelligent support systems and intelligent components of target systems will use the same generic technology, it is less expedient to detail the intelligent functions in the target systems. Likely there will be beneficial technology exchange in AI between tool development activity and applications program techniques. For the sake of completeness, we will lastly consider some important potential applications of AI in the target systems.

Local operating systems will require intelligence to direct decisions based on incomplete state information for resource management and for recovery. Intelligence can be applied to nondeterministic scheduling and task allocation in concurrent software. Application algorithms may be automatically partitioned and distributed to separate processors for parallel execution.

There will be intelligent components of data base management. Intelligent retrieval will make use of inferencing capacity and of strategies for merging schemas of distributed data bases. An emerging concept is that of active data bases, which will report evolving patterns of interest. Finally, natural language processing will be a feature of the user interface.

List of Abbreviations

AI	Artificial Intelligence
ALU	Arithmetic Logic Unit
APSE	Ada Programming Support Environment
COS	Constituent Operating System
DBMS	Data Base Management System
DoD	Department of Defense
DOS	Distributed Operating System
IA	Interconnect Architectures
IEEE	Institute of Electrical and Electronic Engineers
I/O	Input/Output
ISSE	Integrated Software Support Environment
KAPSE	Kernel Ada Program Support Environment
KBS	Knowledge Based System
KIT	KAPSE Interface Team
MAPSE	Minimal Ada Program Support Environment
MCMD	Multi-Center, Multi-Drop
MDMS	Multi-Center, Multi-Star
MST	Minimal Spanning Tree
PDL	Program Design Language
RADC	Rome Air Development Center
ROM	Read Only Memory
SCMD	Single-Center, Multi-Drop
SCSS	Single-Center, Single-Star

Bibliography

1. Andrews, D. M. and Melton, R. A., FAVS: FORTRAN Automated Verification System User's Manual, General Research Corp. Report CR-1-754/1, April, 1980.

2. Baklovich, E., Decentralized Systems. Computer Science Technical Report, University of Connecticut, AD/A099 195, Storrs, Connecticut, 1980.

3. Barr, A. and Feigenbaum, E. A., editors, The Handbook of Artificial Intelligence, Los Altos, CA, William Kaufman, 1981.

4. Benoit, John W. and Selander, J. Michael, Knowledge-Based Systems as Command Decision Aids, First U.S. Army Conference on Knowledge-Based Systems for C^3I, 1981.

5. Clark, Lori A. et al, Toward Feedback-Directed Development of Complex Software Systems, University of Massachusetts, Amherst, Massachusetts.

6. Cook, R. P., A Review of the Stoneman APSE Specification, Consulting Report, June, 1982.

7. Cook, R. P., How To Write a Distributed Program, Consulting Report, June, 1982.

8. Cook, R. P., Kernel Design for Concurrent Programming, Consulting Report, June, 1982.

9. Daley, P., Modeling of Distributed Command/Communication/Control Intelligence Systems, RADC Distributed Processing Technology Exchange, May, 1982.

10. Department of Defense, Reference Manual for the Ada Programming Language, July, 1980.

11. Donahoo, J. D. and Swearinger, D., A Review of Software Technology, RADC-TR-80-13, February, 1980.

12. Drazovich, Robert J. and Payne, J. Roland, Artificial Intelligence Approaches to Information Fusion, First U.S. Army Conference on Knowledge-Based Systems for C^3I, 1981.

13. Enslow, P., Performance of Distributed and Decentralized Control Models for Fully Distributed Processing Systems, RADC-TR-82-105, May, 1982.

14. Enslow, P., Support for Loosely-Coupled Distributed Processing Systems, RADC Distributed Processing Technology Exchange, May, 1982.

15. Feng, Tse-Yun and Wu, Chuan-lin, Interconnection Networks in Multiple-Processor Systems, RADC-TR-79-304, December, 1979.

16. Findler, N. V., editor, Associative Networks: The Representation and Use of Knowledge by Computers, New York, Academic Press, 1979.

17. First U.S. Army Conference on "Knowledge-Based Systems for C³I", Ft. Leavenworth, Kansas, 4-5 November, 1981.

18. Forsdick, Harry C., et al, Distributed Operating System Design Study, RADC-TR-81-384, January, 1982.

19. Fortier, P. J. and Leary, R. G., A General Simulation Model for the Evaluation of Distributed Processing Systems, Annual Simulation Symposium, November, 1981.

20. Gannon, C. and Brooks, N. B., JOVIAL J73 Automated Verification System Functional Description, General Research Corp. Report CR-1-947, March, 1980.

21. Giese, C., Research and Development Plan for Ada Target Machine Operating System (ATMOS) for the Ada Bare Target Machine, AJPO/U.S. Army AIRMICS, April, 1982.

22. Gorney, L., Queueing Theory: A Problem Solving Approach, Petrocelli Books, 1982.

23. Green, Cordell, A Knowledge-Based Approach to Rapid Prototyping, Software Engineering Symposium: Rapid Prototyping, 1982.

24. Hayes-Roth, Frederick, Artificial Intelligence and Expert Systems, A Tutorial, First U.S. Army Conference on Knowledge-Based Systems for C³I, 1981.

25. Jensen, D., Decentralized System Control, RADC Distributed Processing Technology Exchange, May, 1982.

26. Jensen, E. Douglas, The ARCHONS Project, RADC Distributed Processing Exchange, October, 1981.

27. Joobbani, R. and Siewiorek, D. P., Reliability Modeling of Multiprocessor Architectures, Carnegie-Mellon University, Pittsburg, PA, 1979.

28. Kemp, G. H., Debugging Embedded Computer Programs, GDPD Technical Memorandum, March, 1980.

29. McCall, J. A. and Matsumoto, M. T., Software Quality Metrics Enhancements, RADC-TR-80-109, Volumes I and II, April, 1980.

30. Melton, R., Grunburg, G. and Sharp, M., COBOL Automated Verification System: Study Phase, RADC-TR-81-11, March,1981.

31. Post, J., Quality Metrics for Distributed Systems, RADC Distributed Processing Technology Exchange, May, 1982.

32. Reinstein, H. C. and Hollander, C. R., A Knowledge-Based Approach to Application Development for Non-Programmers, IBM Palo Alto Scientific Center, July, 1979.

33. Saponas, T. G., Distributed and Decentralized Control in Fully Distributed Processing Systems, GIT-ITC-81/18, December, 1981.

34. Sharma, R. L., deSousa, P. J. T., and Ingle, A. D., Network Systems, Van Nostrand Reinhold Data Processing Services, 1982.

35. Sharp, M., Melton, R. and Greenburg, G., COBOL Automated Verification System Functional Description, General Research Corp. Report CR-2-970, November, 1980.

36. Stenning, V., et al, The Ada Environment: A Perspective, Computer, June, 1981.

37. Tanenbaum, A. S., Computer Networks, Prentice-Hall, Englewood Cliffs, NJ, 1981.

38. Taylor, R. N., Complexity of Analyzing the Structure of Concurrent Programs, University of Victoria Department of Computer Science, 1981.

39. Taylor, R. N. and Osterweil, L. J., Anomaly Detection in Concurrent Software by Static Data Flow Analysis, IEEE Transactions on Software Engineering, Volume 6, 1980.

40. Thomas, R., Distributed Personal Computer-Based Information Systems, RADC Distributed Processing Technology Exchange, May, 1982.

41. Wolfe, M. I., et al, The Ada Language System, Computer, June, 1981.

42. Ziegler, K., A Distributed Information System Study, IBM System Journal, Volume 18, Number 3, 1979.

Part III

An Integrated Software Engineering Environment for Distributed Processing Software Development

The information in Part III is from *Distributed Processing Tools Definition—An Integrated Software Engineering Environment for Distributed Processing Software Development,* prepared by Herbert C. Conn, Jr., David L. Kellogg, States L. Nelson, Scott L. Harmon, and Sue A. Johnson of General Dynamics Corporation for the U.S. Air Force Systems Command Rome Air Development Center, June 1983.

1. Technical Report Summary

1.0 TECHNICAL REPORT SUMMARY

General Dynamics Data Systems Division is under contract to Rome Air Development Center to conduct a study entitled Distributed Processing Tools Definition. The objectives are to investigate the requirements for software life cycle support in embedded distributed processing systems and to specify applicable software tools and techniques by life cycle phase. Special attention has been paid tightly-coupled distributed processing systems. Furthermore, such tight-coupling has been examined in applications concerning current and projected weapons systems applications as well as Command/Control/Communications systems.

1.1 PROJECT OVERVIEW

The study is divided into three phases which are illustrated in Figure 1-1. All three phases have been completed and their results are described in the present Phase III Technical Report.

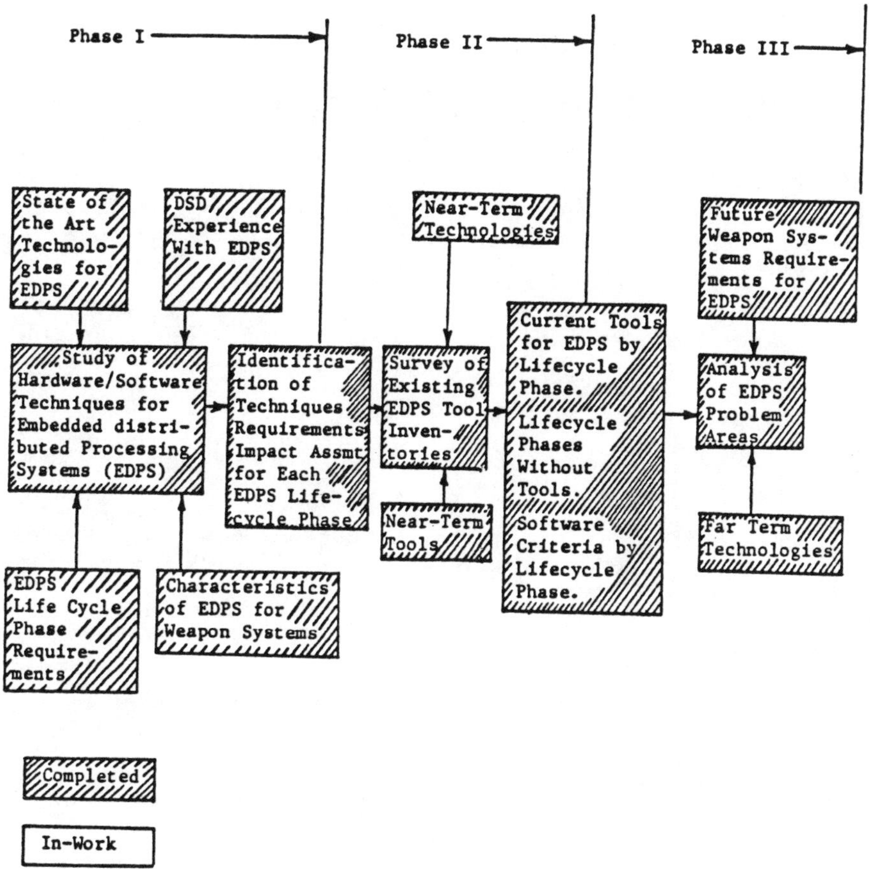

Figure 1-1 Overview of the Distributed Processing Tools Definition Study

1.2 PHASE III CONCLUSIONS

The principle technical perspective used in the following conclusions assumes a combined system functionality for hardware and software. Embedded distributed processing systems require both to be operable at the same time.

1) Development of Distributed Processing Systems is best supported by an Integrated Systems Support Environment (ISSE).

2) An ISSE requires the support of a powerful Data Base Management System (DBMS).

3) The operation of a highly-integrated tool of an ISSE may be meaningless outside its ISSE.

4) Most tools addressing distributed processing in an ISSE are highly-integrated.

5) The process of translating design specs into program descriptions needs formal definition before automation can be considered.

6) Feasibility study during design phase requires a set of highly-integrated simulation tools.

7) Tools of the implementation or coding phase must be integrated about a specific compiler.

8) The major aspects of distributed processing which most impact the design of tools are concurrency, distributedness, and fault tolerance.

2. Scope of Embedded Distributed Processing Systems

Distributed processing systems can be characterized by their position within a three-dimensional space. Each axis of that space can be used to separate the non-distributed environment from its distributed counterpart. The spatial location of distributed processing is clearly different from non-distributed or centralized processing. That difference is illustrated in Figure 2-1. Such distributed processing systems are usually components within larger systems, i.e., they are embedded.

The first of three axes concerns the distribution of hardware. It ranges from a single central processor unit to multiple computers. Five generic configurations have been isolated and are in common use.

1) Single central processor unit characterized by one control unit, one arithmetic logic unit, and one central memory.

2) Multiple execution units characterized by one control unit; multiple, identical arithmetic logic units; and possibly multiple, independent central memories.

3) Separate "specialized" functional units characterized by one general purpose control unit and multiple arithmetic logic or processing units.

4) Multiple processors characterized by multiple control units; multiple arithmetic logic units; possibly multiple, independent, central memories; and single, coordinated input/output systems.

5) Multiple computers characterized by multiple general purpose central processing units with their own control unit, arithmetic logic unit, central memory, and input/output system.

Distributed processing systems are usually composed of multiple processors and multiple computers, i.e., the fourth and fifth generic configurations. Non-distributed or centralized processing systems are usually composed of a single central processor unit and multiple execution units, i.e., the first and second generic configurations.

The second of three axes concerns the distribution of control. It ranges from a single, fixed point of control to multiple control points whichare not necessarily homogeneous but which cooperate on the execution of a task.

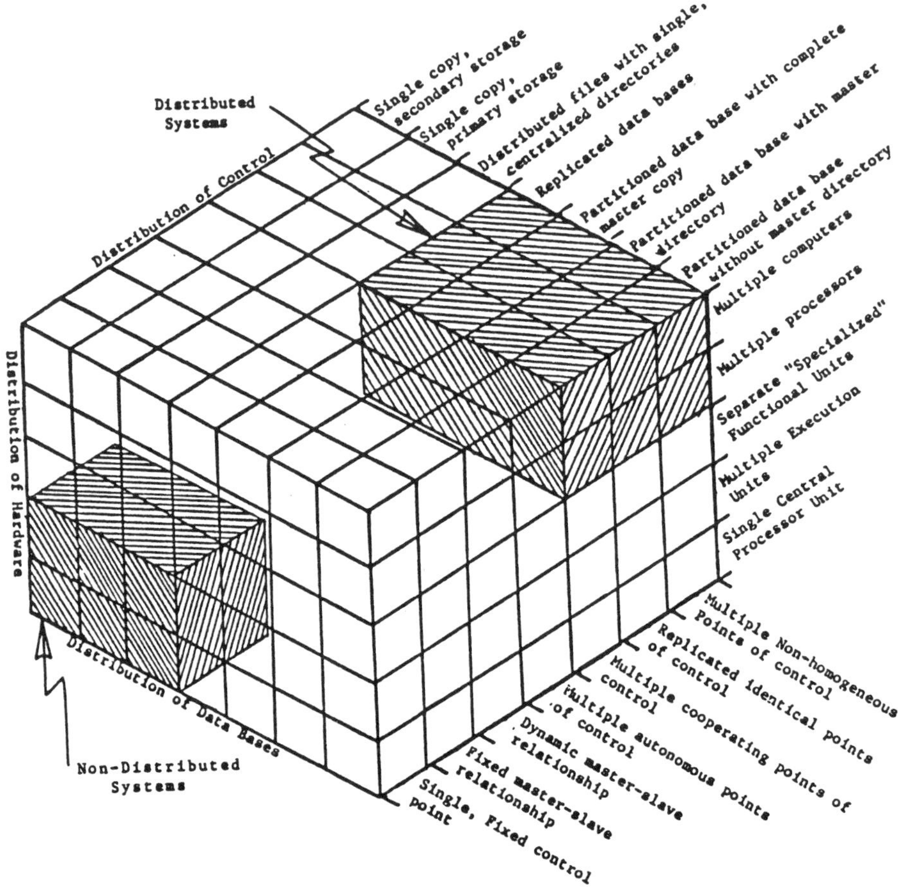

Figure 2-1 Characterization of Distributed Processing Systems Within the Three-Dimensional Space Comprised of the Following Axes: Distribution of Hardware, Distribution of Controls and Distribution of Data Bases

Seven generic control categories have been isolated and in common use:
1) Single, fixed control point;
2) Fixed master-slave relationship;
3) Dynamic master-slave relationship;
4) Multiple points of control which are totally autonomous;
5) Multiple points of control which cooperate on the execution of a task which has been subdivided into sub-tasks;
6) Replicated, identical points of control cooperating on the execution of a task; and
7) Multiple control points which are not necessarily homogeneous but which cooperate on the execution of a task.

Distributed processing systems are usually characterized by the last three generic control categories, i.e., multiple points of control, replicated points of control, and multiple control points. Non-distributed or centralized processing systems are usually characterized by the first two generic control categories, i.e., single control points and fixed master-slave relationships.

The third and final axis concerns the distribution of data bases. In terms of database complexity it ranges from a single copy database in secondary storage to a completely partitioned data base without a master file or directory. Many gradations exist between these two extremes. To date seven generic categories of distributed data bases have been isolated:
1) single copy, secondary storage;
2) single copy, primary memory;
3) distributed files with single, centralized directories;
4) replicated data bases;
5) partitioned data base with a complete master copy;
6) partitioned data base with a master directory; and
7) partitioned data base without a master file or directory.

Distributed processing systems are characterized by the last four categories of data bases,i.e., replicated, partitioned with master copy, partitioned with master directory, and partitioned without master directory. Non-distributed or centralized processing systems are characterized by the first three categories of data bases, i.e., single copy in secondary storage, single copy in primary storage, and distributed files with centralized directories.

Based upon the three-dimensional representation presented in Figure 2-1, the following observations can be made. Movement within the computer marketplace has been and will continue to be from single processors to multiple processors. As multiple processors become more prevalent, non-distributed control policies become questionable. As individual nodes reach parity within multiple processor configurations, choosing one node over another for control purposes will be increasingly difficult to defend. Configurations which run without an overriding executive will become increasingly available. File structures must not only accommodate serialized requests from a single processor but also concurrent requests from several processors. In summary, multiple processor configurations have complicated the present situation.

Application functions performed within larger systems commonly take precedence over the embedded components. Examples include large mainframes composed of tightly-coupled multiple processors. The users of such mainframes seldom appreciate the embedded components and assume a centralized environment. The tools available to such users are also designed to operate within a centralized environment. In summary, the capability of a tightly-coupled, concurrently-operating environment is seldom made available to users because of a shortage of tools for such an environment. However, despite this shortage, decision making involving embedded distributed processing continues and knowledge about its computational efficiency must be achieved. Enough information about the distribution of hardware, control, and data bases must be kown within appropriate real-time constraints in order to reach informed decisions. The functionality of a final product depends upon such informed decisions.

The analogy of a three-dimensional space in Figure 2-1 can only be carried so far. Inter-relations between the axes of that space are evident. Hardware, control, and data bases are not independent of one another in a distributed processing environment. Change in one impacts another. Furthermore, growth in data bases can and does force change concerning hardware and control. The bottom line remains functionality despite what happens along any of the three axes. In effect, functionality represents the constant tradeoff between hardware and software. Finally, each of these constant tradeoffs can be characterized by its position within the inter-related, three-dimensional space.

2.1 FUTURE WEAPON SYSTEMS

Advanced weapon systems are becoming increasingly complex and rely upon computers and embedded processors to operate. One example is the self-contained surface mobile weapon systems used by the Army. Such systems rely upon an internal fire control computer and an embedded navigation system to provide operational direction. Another example is the F-16 avionics systems. Such systems currently stand-alone and vertically integrate hardware, software, and interfaces. The primary integrator is the pilot. As speeds, threats, complexity, and workloads increase, the pilots find less time for necessary integration functions. As a consequence, new approaches to sensor blending and automation are being implemented. These emphasize a horizontal architecture which operates in parallel and concurrently. The embedded processors themselves perform the simpler tasks of integration without distracting the pilot. In effect, the role of a pilot is undergoing change. In the past, he has been the system integrator. In the future, he will be the weapons system manager.

As newer weapon systems evolve, an increasing number of remote functions are being incorporated, e.g., the Integrated Communications, Navigation and Identification Avionics system. One such function is a remote operating console which requires access to tightly-coupled data bases and an extremely high rate of data exchange. Traditional methods of fault detection and isolation no longer apply in such configurations. Failures can occur and remain undetected simply because of complexity. An example would be an intermittent logic error within an internal fire control computer of a weapon system. If a sufficient number of errors are generated, the weapon's accuracy could be compromised. Since the problem is intermittent, routine maintenance would probably not perceive it. Another example is a malfunctioning communications satellite. If the malfunction is sufficiently intermittent,few alternatives exist.

In general, intermittent malfunctions are a problem for weapon systems. If the malfunction occur at a critical time during a military engagement, the effectiveness of a weapon system may be nullified. The internal fire control computer in a self-contained surface mobile weapon system illustrates how important a malfunction can be. Its embedded navigation system could have shifted nodes from target search to target track when a malfunction causes a shift back to target search. Instead of directing the weapon system to the target, the fire control computer begins another search for it. Observing such an activity from a remote operating console does not alleviate the situation. The lost tracking mode is usually regained through some form of direct intervention, e.g., optical sighting or infrared detection schemes. In any case, the preferred action is to resolve and correct the malfunction at its source. To accomplish such action, faults must be detected and corrected in real-time which is not a trivial matter.

Real-time fault isolation requirements are being satisfied in aircraft and spacecraft systems. The approach involves system redundancy through the use of multiple processors. When malfunctions occur, the redundant system automatically activates itself to maintain the current operational mode at the same level of performance. Such an approach costs money and in most weapons systems that money is simply not available, e.g., the surface mobile weapon systems. Consequently, less costly software tools are used to replace the preferred redundancy. The objectives are as follows:
1) provide real-time fault detection and advise the console operator of his alternatives and
2) achieve real-time fault isolation and retain failure parameters for subsequent analysis.

As weapon systems grow more complex, software verification assumes greater importance. Missile systems provide an example of evolving complexity. Their transition from ballistic to cruise capability requires significantly greater amounts of software. General Dynamics has studied various software verification techniques and determined some of their shortcomings with respect to cruise missile production. Those shortcomings include computational overflows and program time constraints. Usual software verification techniques do not detect such shortcomings. Consequently, other methods of verification are required to address such problem areas, e.g., program testing based upon realistic simulations. Under rigorous simulation, the computational overflows and program time constraints within weapon systems software can be detected. Both software verification techniques and realistic simulations can be used to detect the following types of software errors:
1) Input conversion problems;
2) Output conversion problems;
3) Mathematical calculation problems;
4) Logic decision problems;
5) Path analysis problem;
6) Mathematical precision problems;
7) Lack of computational precision;

8) Initialization problems; and
9) Switches in operatonal modes.

Testing efforts based upon rigorous simulation address problem areas associated with hardware and control. Software verification techniques ignore hardware but concentrate on problem areas associated with control and data bases. Consequently, the best approach in sophisticated weapons systems is a combination of rigorous simulation and software verification.

As the complexity of weapon systems increase, the distribution of hardware also increases. The use of multiple processors is increasing and their shared resources are becoming more tightly-coupled. These shared resources apply not only to hardware but to data bases as well. From the statistical standpoint, resource sharing increases the degrees of freedom over which a weapon system can operate. For simulations to remain rigorous, these new degrees of freedom must be accommodated. Currently, state of the art simulation systems can accommodate six degrees of freedom. As new degrees of freedom are introduced by multiple processing, rigorous simulation and software verification become increasingly important when the only alternative is operation of the weapon system. If a complex weapon system exceeds six degrees of freedom, its excess must be addressed by software verification techniques. The operation pairing of rigorous simulation with software verifications will become increasingly important. In a sense, the complexity of future weapon systems will be constrained by our collective ability to verify their software and to rigorously simulate their subsequent operations.

2.2 FUTURE COMMUNICATIONS SYSTEMS

Advanced communication systems are becoming increasingly complex and rely upon computers and embedded processors to operate. From the user standpoint, such systems appear to be loosely-coupled or completely uncoupled. From the network design standpoint, such systems are becoming tightly-coupled and requiring expanding bandwidths. Although both viewpoints appear to be contradictory, they are valid. Several levels of communication take place concurrently within such systems. These are conceptualized by the International Standards Organization Open System Interconnection Model. Seven interconnect layers are envisioned by the model; 1) the application layer; 2)the presentation control layer; 3) the session control layer; 4) the end-to-end transport control layer; 5) the network control layer; 6) the link control layer; and 7) the physical control layer. Communication links between computers involve the movement of information on levels five through six of the interconnect model, i.e., physical/electrical control, link control, and package/network control. These levels apply to the respective movement of bits, bytes, and strings. Network architecture is based upon such movement and several alternative architectures are currently available, e.g., x.25, SNA and DECNET. The pipeline in which such movement of information occurs is termed the communication backbone or trunk. These backbones or trunks support the remaining interconnect layers, i.e., the end-to-end transport layer, the session control layer, the presentation control layer, and the application layer. The user standpoint of a communcation system is based upon the operation of these remaining layers supported by their respective backbones or trunks. Consequently, the user observation of a loosely-coupled or completely uncoupled communication system is based upon the layers supported by the backbones or trunks. The network designer observation of a tightly-coupled communication system is based upon the layers within the backbones or trunks.

Software within advanced communication systems operates at a variety of locations and on several interconnect layers concurrently. Each location within such systems addresses a particular interconnect layer or a set of interconnect layers. Growth in distributed systems is evident in the increased computational power being placed at strategic locations within communication systems. As computational power increases at specific locations, the software operating characteristics of the communication system can be changed. When one or more network hosts are involved, the increased computational capability generates the need for wider bandwidth between hosts. This wider bandwidth is associated with the communication backbone or trunk. Each network host commonly supports a variety of local nodes on the frontend it maintains for the backbone or trunk. As computational power is increased within particular local nodes, wider bandwidth is needed between those nodes and their respective network host frontends. In effect, as computational power is increased in the periphery of communications systems, the bandwidths between the impacted components and the backbone or trunk must also be increased. If bandwidths are not increased, the operational isolation of the computationally more powerful components will increase. In a general sense, advanced communication systems are increasing the computational power of their periphery. In the context of military applications like C^3I, the operation of such communication systems has been uncoupled, i.e., major components operate in comparative isolation. As computational power increases on the periphery, the comparative isolation of major components is enhanced. The sharing of tactical information within C³I architectures is very definitely affected. As computational power is increased within the periphery, the processed tactical information available at the periphery also increases. If this new tactical information is to be shared with other locations within the network, the sharing process is constrained by the bandwidths themselves. Just as importantly, the architectural software is also affected. The operational software for the periphery may no longer reside at centralized locations within the architecture. Programs for the periphery may become so large that they can no longer be downloaded within allowable time constraints, i.e., the bandwidth is no longer wide enough. Under such conditions, centralized data bases and centralized control are no longer sufficient. In their place are distributed data bases and distributed control. How these objectives will be satisfied is presently unclear. However, the advanced communication systems of the future will require such capability because of the increased computational power being inserted into the peripheries.

2.3 FAR TERM TECHNOLOGIES

Distributed processing systems are best supported by an Integrated System Support Environment. Much of the current development within the Department of Defense is directed toward such an environment. Such undertakings are thought to be justified from the standpoint of subsequent cost savings. However, justification can also be argued from a value-added standpoint. Regardless of the cost savings, the subsequent operation of software produced under an Integrated Systems Support Environment will be enhanced and comparatively error free. If such operation is achieved, the software produced by such a process will have value-added during the testing, operation, and maintenance phases of the software development lifecycle.

By design, an Integrated Systems Support Environment spans all phases of the software development lifecycle. As a consequence, it addresses the various levels of abstraction inherent within that development lifecycle. Starting from the most abstract level which occurs during the requirements phase, the ISSE must support transitions to increasingly lower levels of abstractions which culminate in executable object code which must be tested and maintained. Much highly skilled effort is required to move a software product through the various levels of abstraction evident in the software development lifecycle. As the occurrence of complex software systems increases, a concept concerning software development systems has gained currency. that concept deals with the creation of an ISSE which operates on a high level of abstraction and performs the high-skilled effort required to move such high level abstractions to executable object code. Without the intervention to highly-skilled humans, such an ISSE would have to possess its own knowledge base, i.e., the ISSE would be a knowledge based system (KBS).

In support environments like an ISSE, the KBS is the foundation of an "intelligent programmer's assistant". For software being developed for downloading to targets, the support environment must have very specific knowledge concerning target operation and must have its own data base management system. As a consequence, all sorts of new data bases are being justified in terms of an assumed relevance to a KBS. A precise definition of a KBS has yet to be developed. As the levels of expectation are raised, the relationship between an ISSE and KBS becomes increasingly important. To design an intelligent ISSE requires specific definition of its KBS component. What emerges in such a situation is a role for artificial intelligence. Actual computer intelligence will become evident in the databases and operations of the computer environment. In large part, the success of distributed processing systems will be measured in terms of their contribution to knowledge based systems. The bottom line remains functionality and what users want is functional knowledge based systems. Consequently, future generic techniques required by distributed processing systems must concern themselves with knowledge based functionality. Tools not presently envisioned will be required. ISSEs will not be enough. Under present circumstances, the distributed processing environment is complex. Under future requirements, that complexity multiplies itself. Techniques which will become the tools of the future are going to require artificial intelligence.

Intelligence in knowledge-based, expert consulting systems will provide decision aids throughout the system life cycle. This will be valuable in any activity where the consequence of experimental adjustment of system parameters needs to be evaluated. An example is impact analysis of requirements or design changes, where what is desired is an evaluation of the severity of a proposed change. AI techniques can be used to search the knowledge base for relevant conceptual connections. Efficient heuristics could make feasible an interactive dialogue with the decision-maker. The search process in this example may be sufficient but not exhaustive. Once a change decision has been made a detailed analysis of affected system entities will be necessary. In this case, the search will be exhaustive, but can be intelligently guided to avoid blind search.

A further desirable component of the knowledge base for decision aids will be the inclusion of quantitative and qualitative software metrics. This will enable an intelligent dialogue with program designers in which alternative design features can be evaluated against criteria of goodness. The decisions of the designer can feed back into the knowledge base so that future decisions can be more fully automated. A mature design knowledge base will be useful in rapid system prototyping.

Support tools of the future will be used in designing and implementing target systems with artificially intelligent components. A principal motivation for the use of AI techniques in distributed processing is the management of the inherent complexity of such systems. Since intelligent support systems and intelligent components of target systems will use the same generic technology, it is less expedient to detail the intelligent functions in the target systems. Likely there will be beneficial technology exchange in AI between tool development activity and applications program techniques. For the sake of completeness, we will lastly consider some important potential applications of AI in the target systems.

Local operating systems will require intelligence to direct decisions based on incomplete state information for resource management and for recovery. Intelligence can be applied to nondeterministic scheduling and task allocation in concurrent software. Application algorithms may be automatically partitioned and distributed to separate processors for parallel execution.

There will be intelligent components of data base management. Intelligent retrieval will make use of inferencing capacity and of strategies for merging schemes of distributed data bases. An emerging concept is that of active data bases, which will report evolving patterns of interest. Finally, natural language processing will be a feature of the user interface.

3. Integrated Systems Support Environment

Because of their inherent complexity, distributed processing systems are best supported by an integrated systems support environment (ISSE). Such an environment offers economy of support through tools which work in conjunction with one another. The environment also provides tool sets which can be used to address specific problems within the software development lifecycles. Most importantly the environment provides a consistent frame of reference in which planning can take place. Figure 3-1 presents the functional diagram of an ISSE in an abbreviated format.Approximately 25 tools are presented in the Figure 3-1. Study indicates the existence of approximately 20 additional tools in an ISSE. However, the ones presented in Figure 3-1 represent the most important tools and are linked to subsequent discussions of specific lifecycle phases. The subsequent sections discuss generic C^3I architecture in terms of the ISSE. Upon completion of discussions concerning communication subnets, fault isolation, and software debugging, the actual ISSE is discussed in detail.

3.1 GENERIC C^3I ARCHITECTURE

From the standpoint of distributed processing, a military command post uses a communications network to consolidate and display information. Such consolidation commonly involves several military missions. The subsequent actions taken by the battle staff within the command post are largely dependent upon the information supplied by its communications network. Information flow within such a network is so important that it produces a set of requirements unique to the military command situation. Some of these requirements are presented in the following list.

- The information consolidated and displayed for a military command post must be accurate since subsequent military action depends upon it.

- Once a military mission produces information for an appropriate command post, that information must not be misplaced by that command post.

- The communications network within a command post must not fail since its failure would entail the loss of access to information.

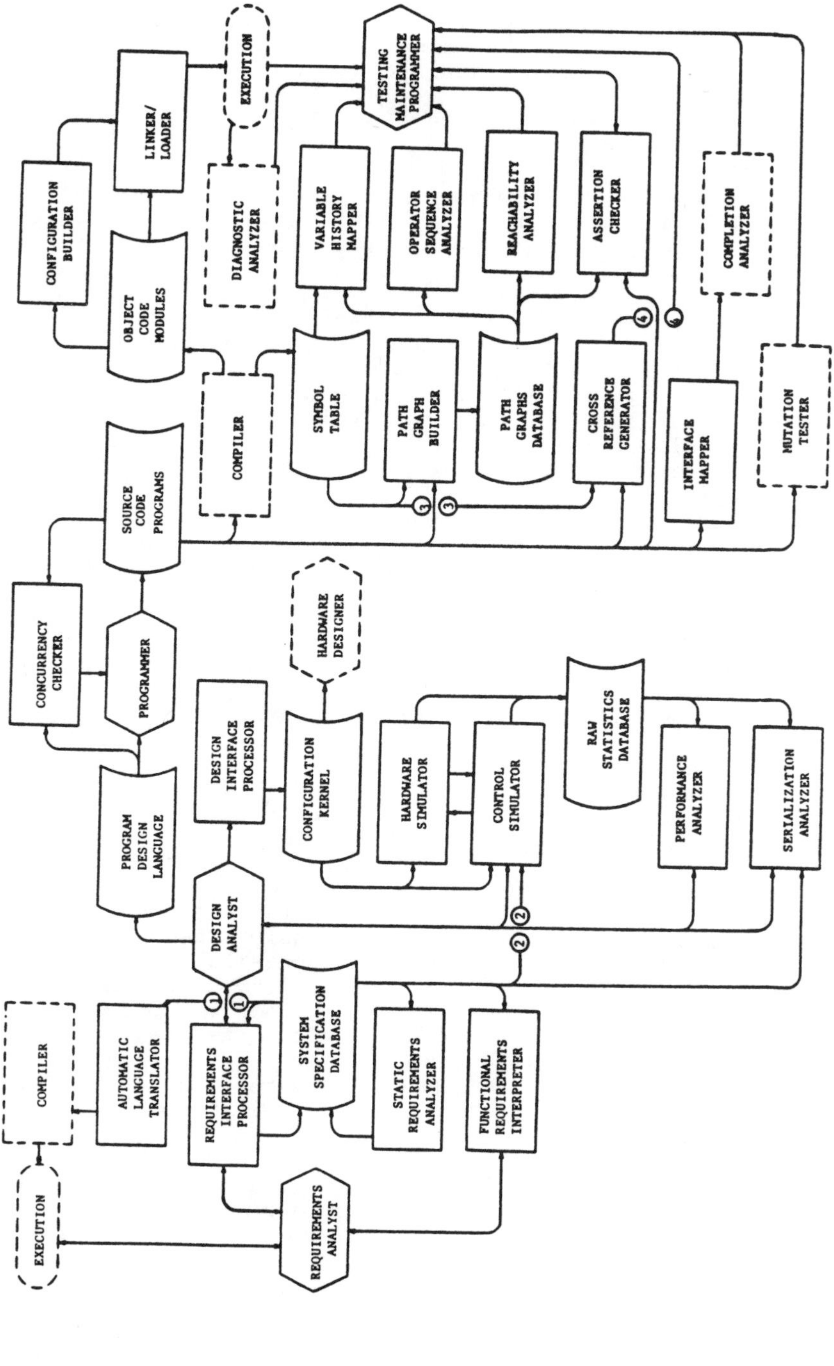

FIGURE 3-1 INTEGRATED SYSTEMS SUPPORT ENVIRONMENT FUNCTIONAL DIAGRAM

- If faults occur within the communications network of a command post, they must be isolated and operations must continue despite their presence.

- Regardless of what causes a fault, software must continue to function.

Such requirements are obviously difficult to satisfy. With a C³I architecture, the twin issues of fault isolation and software debugging are of overriding importance.

Although fault isolation and software debugging do not impact an Integrated Systems Support Environment (i.e., an ISSE) they do impact how such an environment is used. Tools contained in the ISSE must be able to develop and implement software for a target C³I architecture. Such software should be able to isolate faults and detect error conditions as it operates. Of course such behavior takes place within the target C³I architecture itself. Consequently, the ISSE must be able to simulate target architectures with great precision if software capable of isolating faults and detecting error conditions is to be produced. Furthermore, such software will need to be maintained and operated within its target architecture which reinforces the need for precise simulation within the ISSE. The software lifecycle phases introduce yet another consideration. Tools for the requirements and design phases should be available within the ISSE. Coding, testing, maintenance, and operation phases should have tools available within the ISSE and within the target C³I architecture itself. The ISSE should be capable of producing those tools available within the target C³I architecture itself. If such capability is offered by the ISSE, its contained simulation of the C³I architecture must be very precise. In most applications the C³I architecture is simply not available for troubleshooting hardware faults or software bugs. Those problems are to be anticipated and avoided as much as possible through the use of an ISSE with extraordinary simulation capability. Not only must software be produced within an appropriate C³I architecture but it must continue to operate in the presence of faults. Consequently, simulation and performance analysis assume great importance within an ISSE for C³I architectures. Such tools do not arise spontaneously within the context of an ISSE. The ISSE itself must be designed and shaped around the presence of such tools. Implementation of the tools themselves and the ISSE itself is not a trivial activity. Each tool must be rigorously related to every other tool and the framework of the ISSE must support the combined requirements of all tools. As an initial step, these relationships and the framework in which they operate must be described at a functional level before efforts at design and implementation are undertaken. The subsequent three sections address functional descriptions of C^3I architectures from the standpoint of their underlying communication subnets, their capability for fault isolation, and their capability for software debugging. Each is an important consideration and represents a generic characteristic of a C^3I architecture.

3.1.1 Underlying Communications Subnet Boundaries

A military command post uses its version of a Local Area Network (i.e., an LAN) to consolidate and display information from one or more of its military missions. Such consolidation and display does not impact the information contained within any of the component missions. In other words, the consolidation and display of information by a military command post is passive in nature.

Information across several military missions is constantly being compared by battle staffs within their respective command posts. The purpose behind such comparisons is to use information contained in one military mission as verification for information contained in another military mission. Anomalies do exist between information contained in different military missions. An example would be two over-the-horizon radar stations with overlapping scans. Both stations may not perceive the same phenomena within the overlap area. Some sort of reconciliation process must be accomplished to determine what the real situation is. In most instances, this reconciliation occurs at the command post level in C^3I applications. Furthermore, the reconciliation itself is usually produced by direct human intervention.

Based upon its consolidation and display of information across one or more military missions, a command post battle staff issues orders to the field. Dispatching these orders is not a passive activity. Consequently, the LAN within a command post is exemplified by two modes of operation. One mode is passive and involves the consolidation and display of information across one or more military missions. A second mode is extremely active and involves the dispatching of military orders to the field. These counterbalancing modes of operation are characteristic of a C^3I architecture.

Requirements for a military mission are usually defined and implemented within a very specialized architecture.

At the national and global levels these specialized architectures reflect the characteristics of their military missions. Even at the highest levels the need to consolidate and display information across military missions persists. Consequently, the LAN to support a command post must be specific enough to accommodate a very specialized mission architecture and general enough to accommodate alternatives to that architecture. The interface between the LAN and a specialized mission architecture approximates the characteristics of a communications gateway. The flow of information within that gateway is particularly important. Flow from the military mission to the command post is passive with respect to mission activity. Flow in the opposite direction is no longer passive. The command post issues instructions to particular military missions which may or may not impact the way those missions are acquiring data. This capability to issue instructions goes far beyond the characteristics of a gateway. Instead, the LAN serves as a frontend processor for the pertinent mission architecture. As each order is transmitted, its subsequent acceptance or rejection by the pertinent architecture must be verified by the command post LAN. Such transmission and validation is characteristic of a C^3I architecture.

Communication between specialized mission architectures and a command post LAN involves two underlying communication subnet boundaries. An Air Defense Ground Environment (i.e. an ADGE) serves as an example and is presented in Figure 3-2. The two modes of information flow within the ADGE military mission are clearly evident. Underlying each mode is an implemented communications subnet boundary. As long as the movement of packets, frames, and bits is constrained to a single military mission with its specialized communications subnet, no problem exists. However, command posts can seldom constrain themselves to a specialized architecture accommodating only one military mission. Under certain conditions, the command post must be capable of expansion to several military missions with a variety of specialized architectures. To provide such capability, a standardized command post architecture needs to be developed at the level of an LAN. If such standardization occurred, a very reliable set of interconnect buses could be implemented within the command post LAN. Much current effort within C^3I applications is attempting to establish the needed standardization. What emerges from such effort is a layered architecture based upon the LAN requirements of a command post. The architecture is presented in Figure 3-3 and is currently under development at the North American Air Defense installation at Colorado Springs, Colorado. The dichotomy between the internal

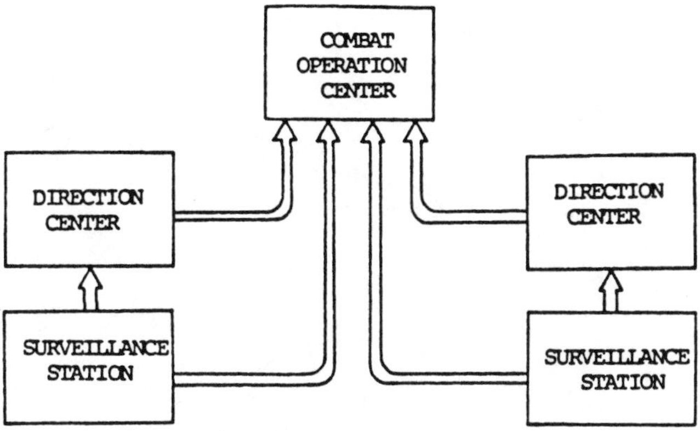

a) Radar Tracking Information to Command Post

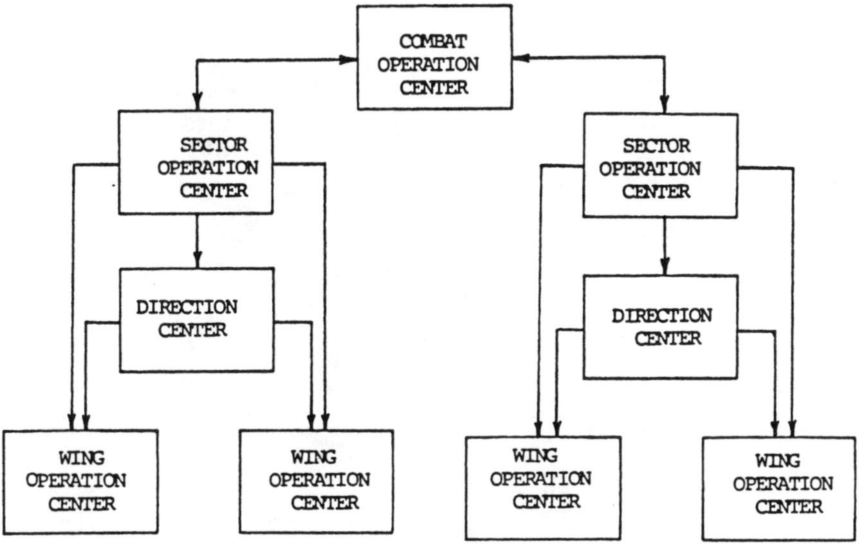

b) Dispatching Orders from the Command Post

Figure 3-2 Generic Air Defense Ground Environment with Two Modes of Information Flow

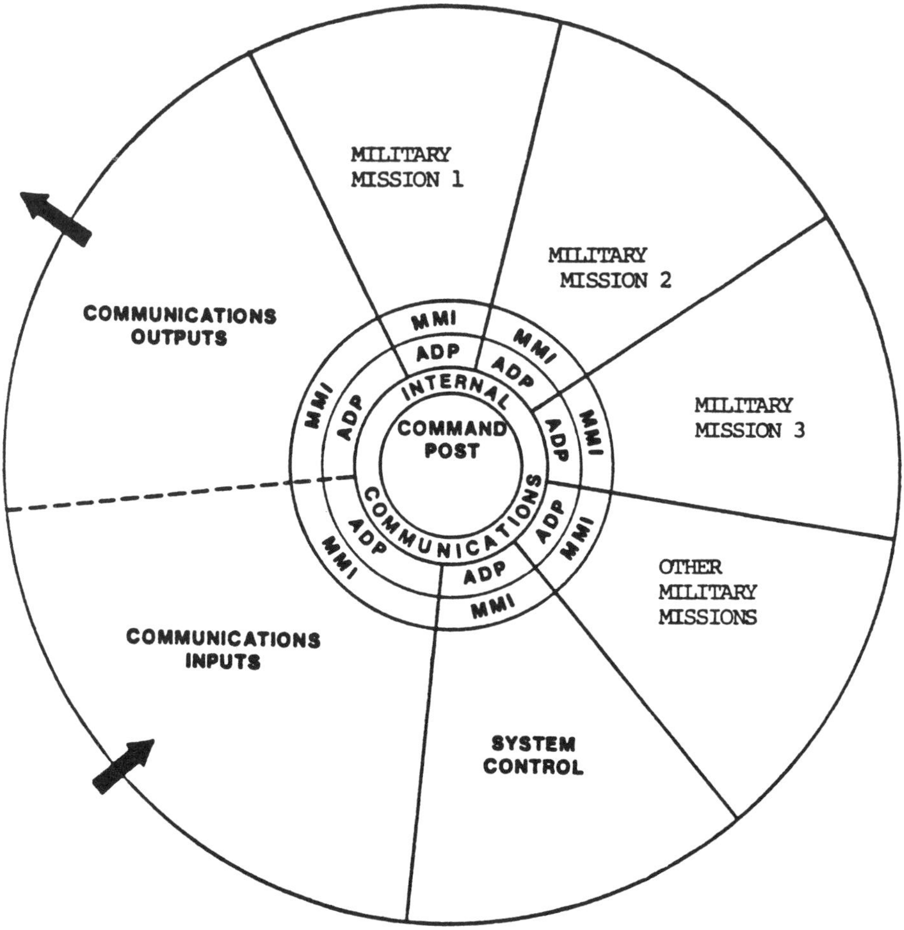

MMI - ManMachine Interface
ADP - Automated Data Processing

Figure 3-3 Layered Architecture of a Command Post Local Area Network (LAN)

communications of the command post and individual military missions is evident. In this particular representation, the command post communications with the external environment have the same architecture can be replicated and expanded to address additional military missions. Of course the upper limit of such expansion is constrained by the bandwidth of the internal communications of the command post. As that bandwidth is approached or exceeded, the command post either has to increase bandwidth or introduce a second layer of internal communications. The simplest alternative is to increase bandwidth but sometimes the wider bandwidth technology is not available. Consequently, the less desirable introduction of a second layer must be used. This second layer introduces coordination problems and requires the use of tightly-coupled resources within the command post LAN. Logical connections the combined communications subnets are unclear and susceptible to timing problems. In such a situation, the importance of simulation and performance analysis is emphasized. The time such simulation and performance analysis should be accomplished is during the requirements and design phases of the software development lifecycle. Tools to address subnet boundaries and timing constraints should be available during the requirements and design lifecycle phases. Such emphasis of these two phases is characteristic of a C^3I architecture. Failure to acknowledge this new orientation will introduce operational and maintenance problems in the subsequent lifecycle phases.

In summary, several characteristics of a C^3I architecture have been discussed. The counterbalancing modes of operation have been presented. The transmission and validation of orders has also been discussed. The emerging emphasis on requirements and design lifecycle phases has been presented. In each instance, an underlying communications subnet boundary is involved. The implementation of these subnet boundaries requires the use of various levels of abstraction. Dependent upon the consistency between abstractions throughout all characteristics of a C^3I architecture, subsequent software efforts may be helped or hindered. The power of an ISSE to simulate target architectures with great precision will definitely help in the development of C^3I communications subnet boundaries.

3.1.2 FAULT ISOLATION

Before either a hardware or software fault can be isolated, it must be detected. Assuming such detection can be accomplished, architectures which take advantage of it can be designed and implemented. In some instances, continued operation may not be possible even though a fault can be detected. In any case, the detection itself is important information and should be stored for future study and reference.

Current C³I architectures are emphasizing the detection of hardware and software faults. Such emphasis originates a demand for simulation and performance analysis seldom encountered in the software lifecycle phases. In effect, the ability to detect faults must be simulated during the design phase. This requirement impacts the way an ISSE is used by the design analyst. Under normal circumstances, the design analyst maps system specifications into configuration primitives and initiates a simulation based upon those primitives. Under fault conditions, the design analyst maps specific malfunctions into configuration primitives and initiates a simulation based upon fault isolation strategies within those configuration primitives. The level of detail addressed within an ISSE mushrooms when malfunctions are examined. For every detected fault, an alternative architecture be defined by the design analyst. How well this definition is accomplished within the ISSE depends upon the individual design analyst. In effect, the design analyst receives the level of detail he has previously been able to enter. Whether this detail is sufficient and represents reality is not addressed by the ISSE.

A realistic assessment of the severity associated with each detected fault depends upon the design analyst. As a consequence, how real a simulation is also depends upon the design analyst. The strategy used to circumvent detected faults depends upon the assumed severity of those faults. If the severity is understated, the strategy will probably be insufficient. However, such insufficiency will not be evident during requirements analysis and system design within the system lifecycle phases. If severity is overstated, the strategy may be needlessly complicated. In such an instance, the strategy itself may lead to additional faults when implemented. However, these additional faults will also not be evident during the requirements and design phases of the system lifecycle. An appropriate classification of severity is particularly important to C³I architectures. The next generation of such architectures should be able to use its assessment of fault severity to suggest action to be taken by its attendant staff. The man-machine interface to such architectures will be particularly user-friendly.

Fault detection from a software standpoint is not as clearcut as fault detection from a hardware standpoint. The detection of software faults by software is a paradoxical situation. For example, if software indicates it is failing, how does a user know its indication is correct? In the case of embedded processing, this paradox is avoided by concentrating on complete validaton and verification of software. Under such a procedure every path and branch within the logic structure of the software is examined individually. Every conceivable set of circumstances is used to test these branches. C³I architectures pose an entirely different problem which is closely akin to the paradoxical situation. Validation and verification with C³I architectures are not as clearcut as validation and verification in embedded architectures. As a consequence, simulation and performance analysis assume greater importance to C³I architectures than to embedded architectures. Whereas embedded architectures can rely upon complete validation and verification of application software, C³I architectures have marginal validation and verification capability and must rely upon simulation and performance analysis. Once installed, the C³I architecture must continue to operate despite the detection and presence of faults. This particular specification is extremely difficult to achieve and, in turn, increases the importance of good simulation and performance analysis. The impact of this increased importance on the ISSE is obvious. Powerful simulation and performance analysis tools must be available in the ISSE to support the needs of C³I architectures.

Fault detection from a hardware standpoint is implemented from two different directions. First, the hardware itself must be able to detect a fault when it occurs. Second, based upon that detection, software must be able to isolate the impact of that fault and initiate an alternative processing strategy. Some current configurations have reduced this second course of action to firmware, i.e., hardware. In any case, hardware fault isolation avoids the paradox encountered by software fault isolation through relying upon software to determine its subsequent operational strategy. Such software can be completely verified and validated prior to use within either an embedded architecture or a C³I architecture. Consequently, the simulation and performance analysis capability of an ISSE serves only to check previous validation and verification effort on behalf of such software.

In some applications in distributed processing, the requirement for fault tolerance is so stringent that additional confirmation of a system's operating characteristics are desired prior to installation in the real environment. This need can be met with a separate test facility. Separate test facilities can be quite expensive as they require equipment identical to that used in the real environment. Thus test facilities are an area in which significant cost trade-offs occur and usually a customized subset of the real environment is selected. This subset often requires augmentation with special equipment to mimic or dummy load the absent portions of the environment. When used in conjunction with an ISSE, a rapid link between the ISSE and test facility is useful for downloading software. Depending on the capabilities included in the test facility it may be desirable to use the rapid link for passing information back to the ISSE for processing with analysis or debug tools.

In summary, fault isolation does not impact an ISSE as much as how that ISSE is to be used. Tools within the ISSE are used to develop and implement software for target C^3I architectures. All lifecycle phases within those target architectures must be addressed but the last two phases of maintenance and operations are extremely important to fault isolation. Not only must software be produced within an appropriate C^3I architecture, but that software must continue to operate in the presence of faults. Consequently, tools for simulation and performance analysis assume greater importance in an ISSE for C^3I architectures. Furthermore, such tools are not linkely to arise spontaneously within an ISSE unless a great deal of effort has been devoted to their creation. For an ISSE to be used successfully in embedded architectures and C^3I architectures it must recognize the dichotomy between the two. ISSE tools supporting distributing processing must also acknowledge this dichotomy because it determines the specifications for a man-machine interface to the ISSE. Previously these specifications have not been taken into account in the design and implementation of an ISSE for distributed processing purposes.

3.1.3 SOFTWARE DEBUGGING

Software debugging does not impact an ISSE as much as how that ISSE is used. Its tools must support the development and implementation of software for distributed processing applications. This would include both embedded weapons systems and C^3I architectures. All software development lifecycle phases must be supported by the ISSE. For specific applications the following three questions must be answered by the design analyst before subsequent coding and testing is begun.

1. Is the proposed software architecture valid?

2. Will the proposed software architecture operate correctly?

3. Does the proposed software architecture satisfy the requirements specifications?

In embedded systems and C^3I architectures these questions are sometimes difficult to answer during the design phase. The C^3I architectures pose the greatest difficulty since they must continue to operate in the presence of faults. Such operation is extremely difficult to design and implement. Furthermore, such architectures operate concurrently and in parallel. The usual procedures of validation and verification used on embedded systems software do not apply in C^3I architectures. What does apply is a much higher emphasis on simulation and performance analysis. The validity of a software architecture depends upon its operational circumstances within a C^3I configuration. For a design analyst to establish validity he must be able to examine software architecture under a variety of circumstances. Each set of circumstances is represented by a single simulation. The correct operation of a software architecture depends upon a performance analysis of its operational circumstances within a C^3I configuration. The design analyst establishes correct operation by analyzing the performance of a software architecture under a simulated set ofcircumstances. This examination by the design analyst is an interactive process. The determination of whether a software architecture satisfies a specific set of application requirements is a judgmental process exercised by the design analyst. All the previous simulations and performance analyses performed by the design analyst should be takeninto account. Much of the determination depends upon the exerience factor of the individual design analyst. In most applications C^3I architectures operate concurrently and in parallel. They commonly control several mission-oriented processes simultaneously. Information flows through such architectures along concurrent and parallel paths. At various points along a path, information is processed in a manner characteristic of that particular path. When one path ceases to operate within a C^3I architecture, an alternate path must be made available to ensure continued operation. Two problems are posed by such a requirement. First the architecture itself must be capble of perceiving when information flow along a particular path has stopped. Second, the software must be capable of correcting the situation and continuing to run. This ability to continue operation is an extremely important characteristic of the C^3I environment. In cases when continued operation is impossible, orderly degradation must be achieved under the direction of softwre.

The converse problem to an orderly degradation is an orderly regeneration of a C^3I architecture that has suffered some sort of shutdown. The shutdown itself could either be in whole or in part. Two problems are posed by such a requirement. First the architecture itself must be capable of informing its software that additional capability has become available. Second, the software must be able to take advantage of the new capability. Compleications increase when tightly-coupled databases are involved. Within the C^3I environment, the speed with which a system is regenerated after a shutdown is extremely important. The longer the shutdown, the wider the window of vulnerability from a military standpoint.

With the C^3I architectures the operation of software is concurrent and parallel. Such operation usually contains rendezvous points which may malfunction for a variety of reasons, e.g., hardware faults, incorrect semaphores, etc. When a rendezvous is not completed, what does the software do? Furthermore, can the software perceive when a rendezvous is not completed? Such questions must be answered within an C^3I environment because software deadlock and shutdown must be avoided at all costs.

Perhaps the most unique aspect of C^3I architectures concerns how their software perceives itself. In architectures like embedded processors, a system user and/or maintainer supplies information concerning the operation of their own software. In other words, C^3I software must monitor its own operation to perceive the presence or absence of software malfunctions. When a software malfunction is perceived, the software must either correct it or work around it. In any case, subsequent maintenance should corrct the situation. How such maintenance corrects the situation while the C^3I architecture continues to operate is unclear. Most likely such operation will require duplication within both hardware and software.

In summary, software debugging does not impact an ISSE as much as how that ISSE is used. The validation of software for C^3I architectures emphasizes the importance of simulation and performance analysis within the ISSE. The communication between the software and hardware within a C^3I architecture must be bi-directional. Whenever hardware perceives a malfunction, that perception should be reported to software for the initiation of an operational alternative. Whenever a partial shutdown has been repaired, the software should contol the regeneration process within the hardware. Within the C^3I environment, the validity of software, its operational correctness, and its appropriateness are non-trivial issues. Each of these issues impacts the way an ISSE is used. Under current conditions, an ISSE supporting the needs of embedded architectures is much easier to envision than one supporting C^3I architectures. Within embedded architectures procedures already exist which can be used to address validity and verification. Consequently, the ISSE for embedded architectures does not need to duplicate what these validation and verification procedures already provide. However, such procedures are not available to C^3I architectures and the ISSE cannot ignore such issues. Although the issues cannot be ignored, they may remain unresolved even after an ISSE has been implemented. Failure to resolve such issues will not make them disappear. Therefore, software debugging within C^3I architectures will remain a long term problem. Some debugging problems will be ameliorated by an ISSE while others will not. The complete elimination of software debugging as a problem awaits advances in the formal theory behind distributed processing architectures.

3.2 ISSE FUNCTIONAL DESCRIPTION

As software becomes more complex, the difficulty it presents during the requirements and design phases also increases. Errors introduced during these phases have ramifications far beyond the software itself. Important projects can be delayed and valuable time lost simply because requirements and design errors were unintentionally introduced.

For too long, activity within the requirements and design phases has been viewed as an art, not a science. As distributed processing has evolved, many works of art have been created. However, such approaches have extracted a high price since their subsequent operation and maintenance have exceeded all expectations. Current effort is devoted to the creation of an environment in which reliable cost estimates can be generated. Such an environment would necessarily address all lifecycle phases and would transform the requirements and design phases into a science, not an art. Such an environment is called an Integrated System Support Environment (i.e., an ISSE) and is justified by the money it can save.

The ISSE can be discussed using various levels of abstraction throughout any or all the system lifecycle phases. As a starting point, the requirements and design phases

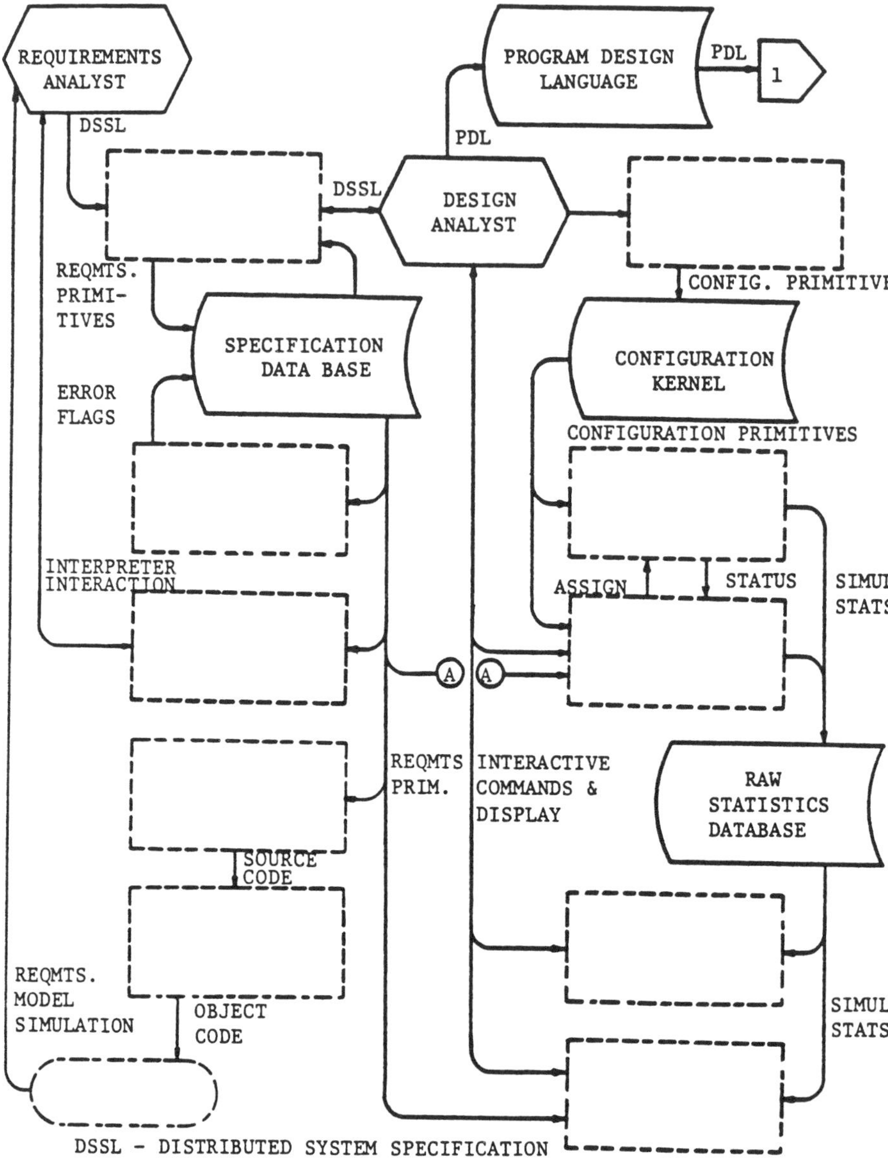

DSSL - DISTRIBUTED SYSTEM SPECIFICATION LANGUAGE
DSDL - DISTRIBUTED SYSTEMS DESIGN LANGUAGE
PDL - PROGRAM DESIGN LANGUAGE

FIGURE 3-4 UNDERLYING COMMUNICATIONS SUBNET FOR THE REQUIREMENTS AND DESIGN PHASE OF AN ISSE

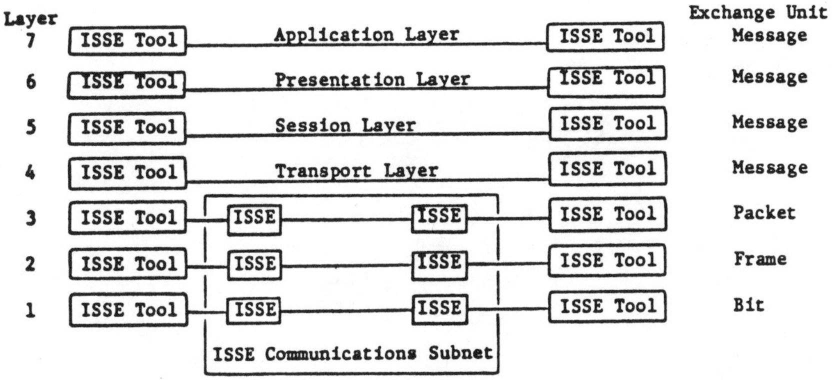

Messages to be transported by the underlying communications subnet within the requirements and design phases of an ISSE:

Distributed Systems Specification Language
Requirements Primitives
Error-Flagged Requirements Primitives
Error Flags
Interpreter Interactions by Requirements Analyst
Source Code
Object Code
Requirements Model Simulations
Distributed Systems Design Language
Configuration Primitives
Simulation Statistics
Complete Flags
Requirements Primitives/Node
Interactive Commands by Design Analyst
Initiation Commands by Design Analyst
Consolidated Displays for Design Analyst
Program Design Language
Concurrency Listing for Design Analyst (Programming Phase)

Figure 3-5 Transport Layer Messages Required During the Requirements and Design Phases of an ISSE

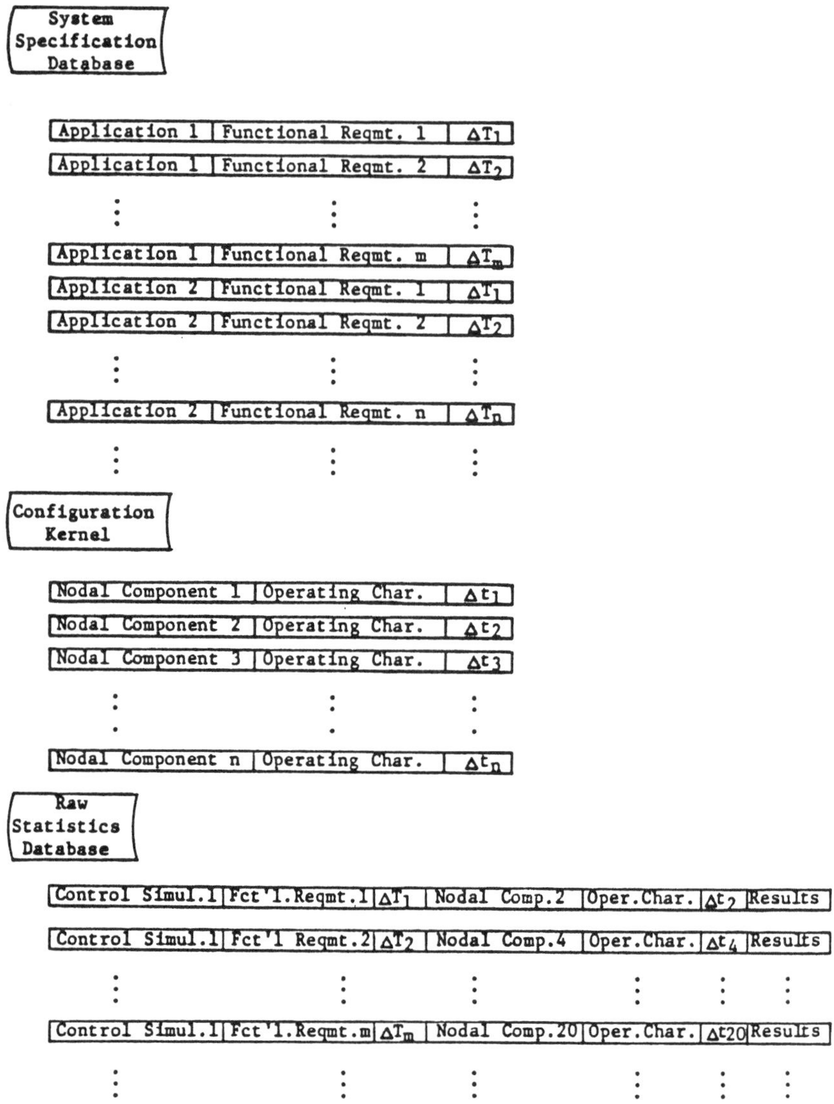

Figure 3-6 ISSE Databases Required to Support the Requirements and Design Phases

will be discussed first with special emphasis on an underlying communication network. Figure 3-4 presents the underlying structure and databases it contains without elaborating on the tools themselves. A variety of messages must be supported within the transport layer of an ISSE. A list of these messages is presented in Figure 3-5 along with an International Standards Organization's representation of the various architectural layers within an ISSE. Within the requirements and design phases, the ISSE communications subnet must transport at least 18 different types of messages, several databases must also be maintained, i.e., the system specification database, the configuration kernel, the raw statistics database, and the Program Design Language database. How these fit within an ISSE is presented in Figure 3-4. Of the four databases, the first three are most closely associated with the requirements and design lifecycle phases. As a consequence, these three databases are presented in Figure 3-6 with examples of the records they contain. The storage and retrieval mechanisms for these databases are not addressed because they represent ISSE implementation details. However, such implementation details do impact the underlying communications subnet since the database query structures would have to be accommodated within the transport layer.

After a brief study of Figures 3-4, 3-5, and 3-6, a wide variety of architectural alternatives becomes apparent. Several observatons should be made about these alternatives before actual implementation of an ISSE is attempted. Although only two lifecycle phases have been examined thusfar, the presence of three different databases are closely related, they should reside in the same ISSE implementation domain. Such a recommendation will also be made concerning specific groupings of tools within the ISSE. Unless appropriate groupings are made within suitable implementation domains, accessing could become a problem. The three data-bases already mentioned serve to illustrate the point. They are accessed by several different tools within the ISSE. However, each tool is functionally related to the other tools accessing the same database, e.g., one tool may be simulating while another is estimating. In effect, a database serves as a common starting point from which several functionally related tools start. Consequently, each must access the same database and the tools as well as the database should reside in the same implementation domain. If they do not, the starting point accesses must be implemented across partitions with protocols operating between such partitions. In such instances new problems arise during implementation of the ISSE. Not only must the tools within the ISSE be implemented but the protocols between the various partitions of the ISSE must also be implemented. Such an architecture complicates the necessary implementation of an underlying communciations subnet boundary and the transport layer within the ISSE.

The implementation domain for the requirements and design phases of the ISSE can be different from the implementation of the remaining phases, i.e., coding, testing, maintenance, and operation. The common point between these two groupings is the program design language database presented in Figure 3-4. The offpage connector included in that figure connects to the identically numbered connector in Figure 3-7. Consequently, the programmer in the coding phase starts with output from the design phase in the form of a program design language database.

Various levels of abstraction are at work within the coding, testing, maintenance, and operation phases. But regardless of the level of abstraction used, the implementation of an ISSE supporting these phases requires an underlying communication network. Such an network supplies the necessary transport medium for messages between tools and provides access to the necessary databases. In these last four lifecycle phases, a total of four databases are used, i.e., the program design language database, the source code database, a symbol table database, and an archival storage database. Messages which must be supported by the communications subnet of the ISSE within the coding, testing, maintenance, and operation phases are presented in Figure 3-8. Within these phases the communicatons subnet must transport at least 16 different types of message. When compared to the messages presented in Figure 3-5, only two are duplicated in Figure 3-8. Consequently, a total of at least 32 messages require support from the communications subnet throughout all software system lifecycle phases.

In addition to supporting 16 messages throughout the coding, testing, maintenance, and doperation phase, the ISSE must also support three databases, i.e., the source code database, the symbol tables database, and the archival storage database. These three databases are presented in Figure 3-9 plus an additional one called the Program Design Language pseudo-code database. This latter database has been included because it is the common point between the requirements/design implementation domain and the coding/testing/maintenance/operationimplementation domain. The observations made previously about the requirements/design domain can also be made about the coding/testing/maintenance/operation domain.

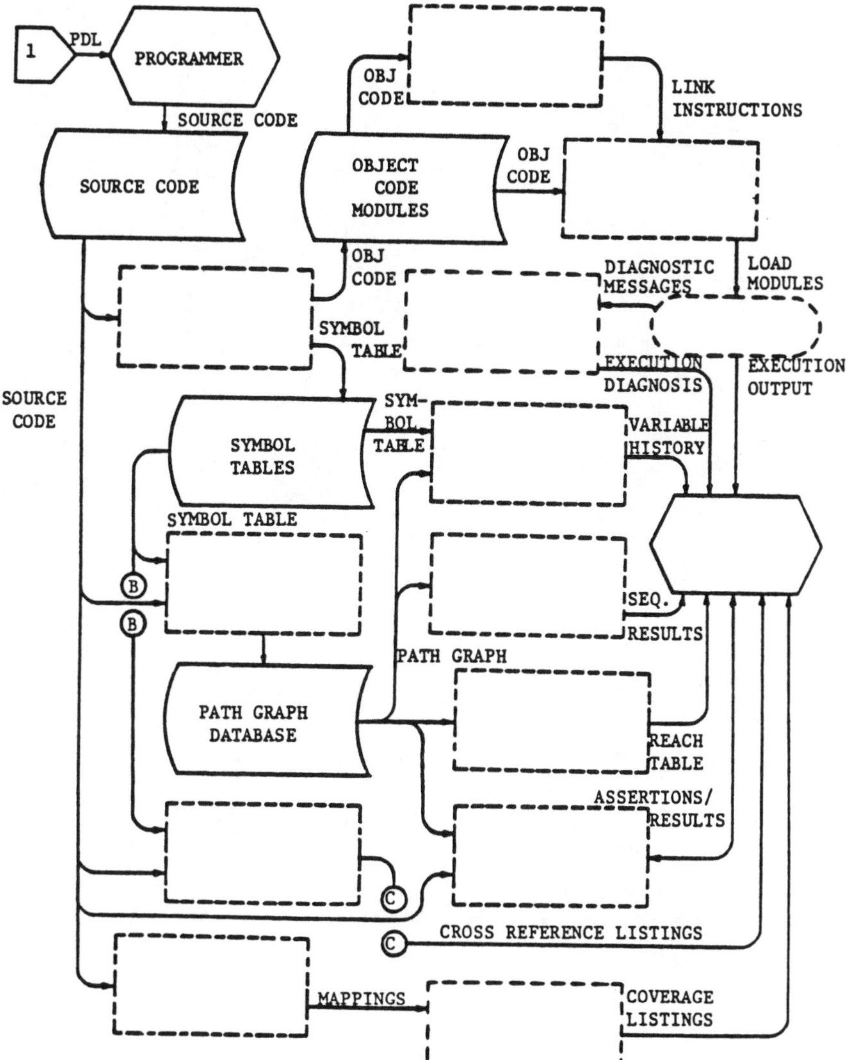

PDL - Program Design Language

Figure 3-7 Underlying Communications Subnet for the Coding, Testing, Maintenance, and Operation Phases of an ISSE

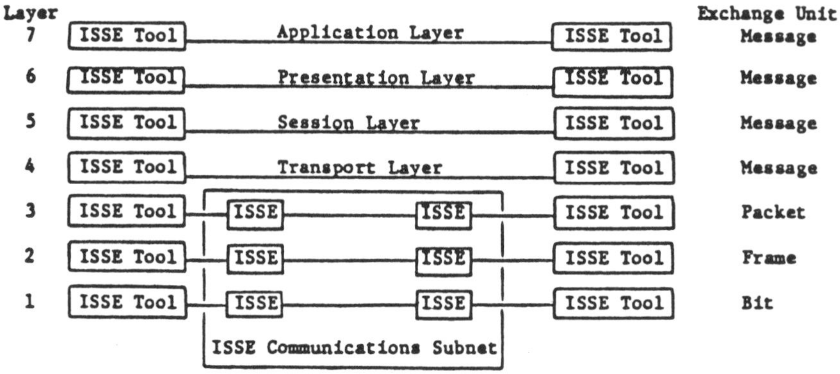

Messages to be transported by the underlying communications subnet within the Coding, Testing, Maintenance, and Operations phases of an ISSE:

Program Design Language
Program Source Code
Concurrency Listing for Programmer
Relocatable Code
Symbol Tables
Object Code Modules
Execution Modules
Program Execution Data
Execution Diagnostics
Path Graph
Connectivity Tables
Reachability Tables
Cross Reference Listings
Mappings
Coverage Listings
Assertion Tables

Figure 3-8 Transport Layer Messages Required During the Coding, Testing, Maintenance and Operation Phases of an ISSE

PDL
Pseudo-Code

Application 1	Fct'l.Reqmt.1	Nodal Comp. Id.	Program Description
Application 1	Fct'l.Reqmt.2	Nodal Comp. Id.	Program Description
⋮	⋮	⋮	⋮
Application 1	Fct'l.Reqmt.n	Nodal Comp. Id.	Program Description
⋮	⋮	⋮	⋮

Source-Code

Application 1	Source Code
Application 2	Source Code
⋮	⋮
Application n	Source Code

Symbol
Tables

Program	Program Object	Location
Program	Program Object	Location
⋮	⋮	⋮
Program	Program Object	Location

Archival
Storage

Program	Object Code
Program	Object Code
⋮	⋮
Program	Object Code

Figure 3-9 ISSE Databases Required to Support the Coding, Testing, Maintenance, and Operation Phases of an ISSE

The subsequent descriptions of tools fit into the functional description for the ISSE presented throughout Figure 3-4, 3-5, 3-6, 3-7, 3-8, and 3-9. As each tool is described, the boxes which have been left blank within Figure 3-4 and 3-7 will be filled in one at a time. A total of 19 tools will be specified for distributed processing applications by the ISSE. Twenty-seven others will be described more generally since they can address central or distributed processing applications by the ISSE. Upon completion of 46 descriptions, recommendations concerning implementation priorities will be presented.

3.2.1 SOFTWARE LIFECYCLE PHASE

Various levels of abstraction underlie the software development lifecycle phases. The highest level occurs during the requirements phase while the lowest occurs during operations and maintenance. As an application moves through the development process, it starts at a high level of abstraction and becomes less abstract as it proceeds through the lifecycle phases. In effect, the boundaries between lifecycle phases can be viewed as transformations between different levels of abstraction. To state there are three generic lifecycle phase (e.g., requirements, design, and implementation) is equivalent to asserting there are three levels of abstraction. An ISSE which supports all three phases must consequently contain tools which address three different levels of abstraction. Within such a frame of reference, the process of software development can be viewed from two complementary standpoints. First, the development process expresses the transformations involved in moving from an initial high level of abstraction to successively lower level of abstraction. At the lowest level of abstraction, executable code is produced. Second, the development process expresses the generation of executable code. Both views produce executable code but the first view is more pertinent to the construction of an ISSE. Understanding transformations between levels of abstraction is particularly important to the understanding of tools within an ISSE. The development of an application must proceed in the proper progression of transformations through the levels of abstraction. Once an application has been developed, any modifications to be introduced must enter the development progression at the earliest applicable point. Throughout the development progression through the levels of abstraction the proper tools in the ISSE must be called into play at the appropriate time for each tool's use. Furthermore, tools within an ISSE must be understood before they are used. Reaching that understanding is not as easy as simply producing executable code. In fact, the use of an ISSE to expeditiously produce executable code will make the development process more difficult. However, such difficulty should not preclude the use of an ISSE since that difficulty has always been there. It has simply been ignored in the rush to produce executable code. A better approach embodied in the ISSE is to make the difficulty visible and enable executable programs to be designed with a high level of confidence.

The highest level of abstraction occurs during the requirements phase. During that time, a requirements analyst is attempting to generate a set of system specifications representing a particular application. Several tools are availble within the ISSE to help the requirements analyst, e.g., the Requirements Interface Processor (RIP), the Static Requirements Analyzer (SRA), the Automatic Language Translator (ALT), and the Functional Requirements Interpreter (FRI). During this phase, the requirements analyst formulates an initial architecture to address the particular application. Included in this architecture are beginning and end points as well as functions and times to be satisfied within each node. Individual nodes are determined on the basis of functional cohesiveness. As a consequence of the initial architecture, antecedent, concurrent, and subsequent relationships between nodes are determined. Whether these relationship can be satisfied and maintained is established during the design phase. Figure 3-10 presents an example of an initial architecture proposed by a requirements analyst. The architecture is presented both graphically and in tabular form. The previously mentioned tools available within the ISSE to help the requirements analyst can be discussed in terms of Figure 3-10. An overall framework for these tools within the requirments phase is presented in Figure 3-11.
The Requirement Interface Processors (RIP) provides a user-friendly interface to the requirements analyst as system specifications are entered. Communication between the RIP and requirements analyst is accomplished through a Distributed System Specification Language accommodating both textual descriptions and graphics which have been illustrated in Figure 3-10. The RIP uses its communication with the requirements analyst to establish files pertaining to each specific application within the ISSE System SpecificationDatabase. Such files contain a proposed nodal architecture with its associated time requirements; the relationship between each node and the proposed architecture; and the processing that takes place at each node within that proposed architecture. Once established, these files are available within the System Specification Database to other tools within the ISSE.

NOTE:
Following representations are contained in the

ISSE
System
Specification
Database

a) Graphic Representation

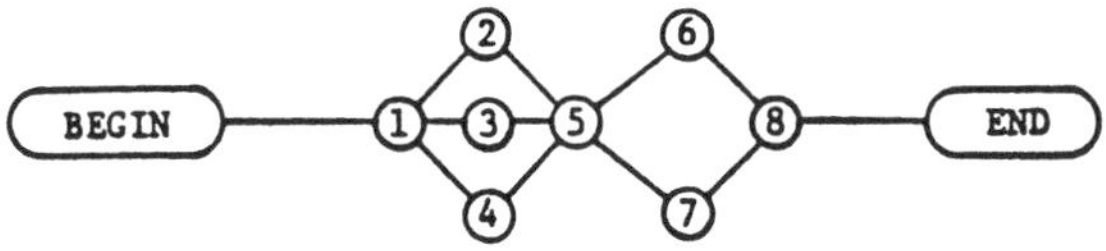

b) Tabular Representation

PER EACH APPLICATION

PRIMITIVE NODAL REQUIREMENTS	REQUIRED TIMES	ANTECEDENT NODES	CONCURRENT NODES	SUBSEQUENT NODES
① (Input-Processing-Output)	ΔT_1	BEGIN	-	2,3,4
② (Input-Processing-Output)	ΔT_2	1	3,4	5
③ (Input-Processing-Output)	ΔT_3	1	2,4	5
④ (Input-Processing-Output)	ΔT_4	1	2,3	5
⑤ (Input-Processing-Output)	ΔT_5	2,3,4	-	7
⑥ (Input-Processing-Output)	ΔT_6	5	7	8
⑦ (Input-Processing-Output)	ΔT_7	5	6	8
⑧ (Input-Processing-Output)	ΔT_8	6,7	-	END

Logically Equivalent I/O Structures

BEGIN=Input (1)
Output(1)=Input(2); Output(1)=Input(3); Output(1)=Input(4)
Output(2)=Input(5); Output(3)=Input(5); Output(4)=Input(5)
Output(5)=Input(6); Output(5)=Input(7)
Output(6)=Input(8); Output(7)=Input(8)
Output(8)=END

Figure 3-10 Initial Architecture Proposed by the Requirements Analyst during the Requirements Phase

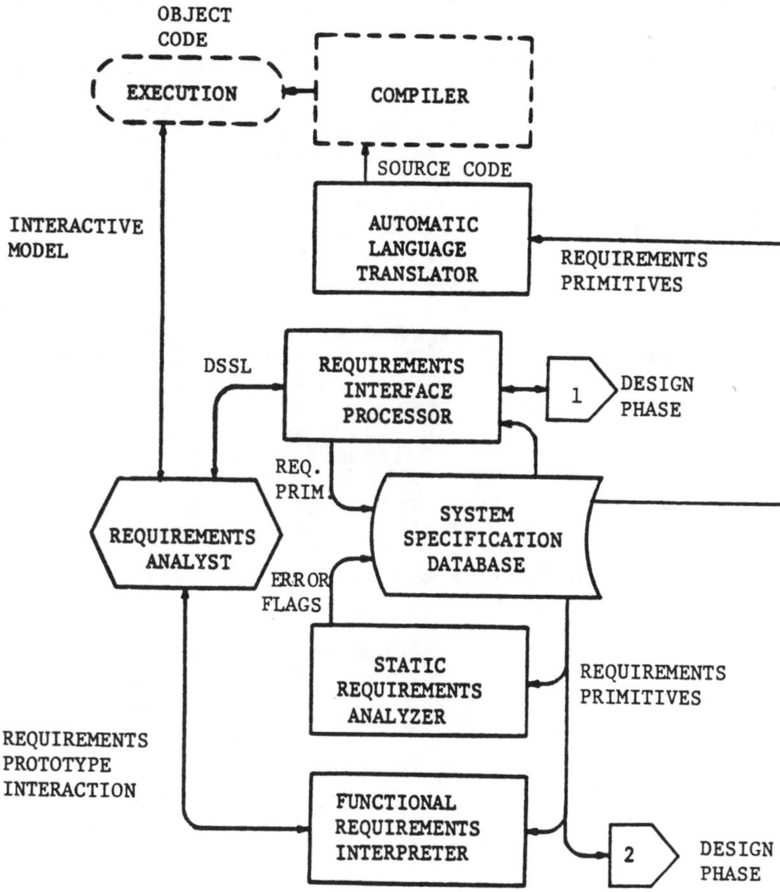

DSSL - DISTRIBUTED SYSTEM SPECIFICATION LANGUAGE

FIGURE 3-11 Tools within the ISSE Available for Use by the Requirements Analyst

The Static Requirements Analyzer (SRA) is initiated by the requirements analyst or the design analyst via pass through commands received and transmitted by the RIP. The SRA examines the textual and graphic descriptions of a particular application and flags erroneous specifications. The SRA annotated text and graphics are restored in the System Specification Database for subsequent retrieval by the RIP. Such subsequent retrieval is under the direction of either the requirements or design analyst. During its examination, the SRA performs a data flow analysis, a completion analysis, a consistency check, and a structure check.

The Functional Requirements Interpreter (FRI) is initiated and interacts with the requirements analyst. It analyzes the System Specification Database files for a particular application previously described using the Distributed Systems Specification Language. The FRI produces simulated output for the requirements analyst to determine if application requirements are being satisfied. Path analysis reports between functions of an application simulation are also generated by the FRI. As each function within a particular application is complete,d the FRI issues a report as to its success or failure with respect to specific application requirements.

The Automatic Language Translator (ALT) is initiated by the requirements analyst and maps the description of a particular application within the System Specification Database into a compilable code representation of itself. An executable model of the application requirements is produced by the ALT. The subsequent coding of nodal components are implementation details addressed during the coding phase. In effect, the only details available during the requirements phase at its high level of abstraction are a listing of functionally cohesive nodes remaining to be implemented. Whether the time constraints will be satisfied within the suggested architecture of the requirements analyst will be established during the design phase.

The next highest level of abstraction occurs during the design phase. During this phase, the design analyst is attempting to map the functional requirements expressed for a particular application and stored in the System Specification Database into various architectural alternatives. Several tools are available within the ISSE to help the design analyst, e.g.,the Design Interface Processor (DIP), the Control Simulator (CS), the Hardware Simulator (HS), the Performance Analyzer (PA), and the Serializaton Analyzer (SA). The use of such tools within

ISSE
System
Specification
Database

Application Representations (Requirements Phase):

a) Graphic Representation

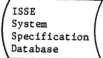

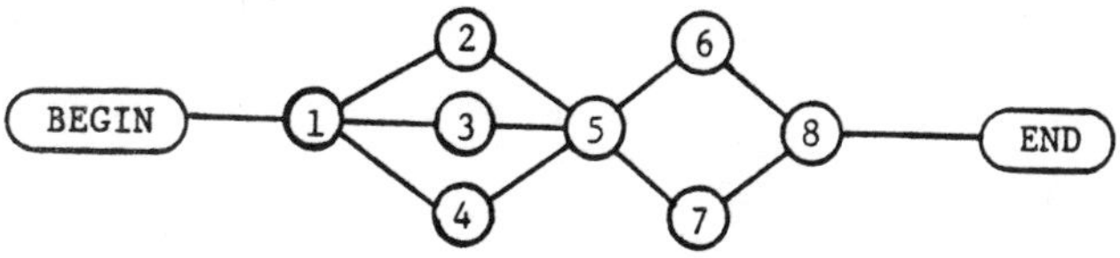

b) Tabular Representation

Functionally Cohesive Requirements	Times	Antecedent Nodes	Concurrent Nodes	Subseq. Nodes
1 (Input-Processing-Output)	ΔT_1	BEGIN	-	2,3,4
2 (Input-Processing-Output)	ΔT_2	1	3,4	5
3 (Input-Processing-Output)	ΔT_3	1	2,4	5
4 (Input-Processing-Output)	ΔT_4	1	2,3	5
5 (Input-Processing-Output)	ΔT_5	2,3,4	-	7
6 (Input-Processing-Output)	ΔT_6	5	7	8
7 (input-Processing-Output)	ΔT_7	5	6	8
8 (Input-Processing-Output)	ΔT_8	6,7	-	END

ISSE
Configuration
Kernel

Component Processing Characteristics

Component Number	Component Descriptions	Times
1	(Input-Processing-Output)	t_1
2	(Input-Processing-Output)	t_2
3	(Input-Processing-Output)	t_3
⋮	⋮	⋮
n	(Input-Processing-Output)	t_n

Figure 3-12 Contents of the ISSE System Specification Database Compared to the ISSE Configuration Kernel

the design phase depends upon access to two separate databases maintained by the ISSE, i.e., the System Specification Database and the Configuration Kernel. The contents of these databases are presented in Figure 3-12. The design analyst must map the contents of the System Specification Database for a particular application onto a proposed hardware architecture based upon the components cataloged in the Configuration Kernel. Such a mapping reduces the level of abstraction evident in the requirements phase and is characteristic of the design phase. During the requirements phase, the requirements analyst dealt with functionally cohesive requirements which must be satisfied and only a general knowledge of what functions must operate concurrently. At best, only an intuitive idea of an architecture existed during the requirements phase. However, the design analyst uses that intuitive idea as a starting point and addresses implementation issues in the design phase. Recommendations concerning concurrency and parallel operation are only tentative during the requirements phase. They are established for subsequent implementation during the design phase. The process of establishing an implementation architecture is what the design analyst does. As a basis for the process, the design analyst initiates a Configuration Kernel containing the basic building blocks for subsequent use in alternative architectures.

The ISSE tools provided a design analyst for the initiation of a Configuration Kernel is the Design Interface Processor (DIP). The DIP allows the design analyst to input the Configuration Kernel information required by particular simulations. Such input is parsed, tokenized, syntactically verified, and entered into the Configuration Kernel by the DIP. The generic information entered into the Configuration Kernel is presented in Figure 3-12. Basically each building block is described with its unique identifier, its operating characteristics, and its actual performance time. The operating characteristics include information concerning input, processing, and output. The performance time is the interval required by the component from initiation of input to production of output. Figure 3-13 presents the timing constraints produced by the requirements phase example of Figure 3-12. A particular architecture proposed by the design analyst to address the requirements phase example is also presented in Figure 3-13. Components from the Configuration Kernel are configured on a node-by-node basis by the design analyst. The components are represented by squares within Figure 3-13. What emerges is an architecture which is described to a much greater detail during the design phase, i.e., the level of ab-

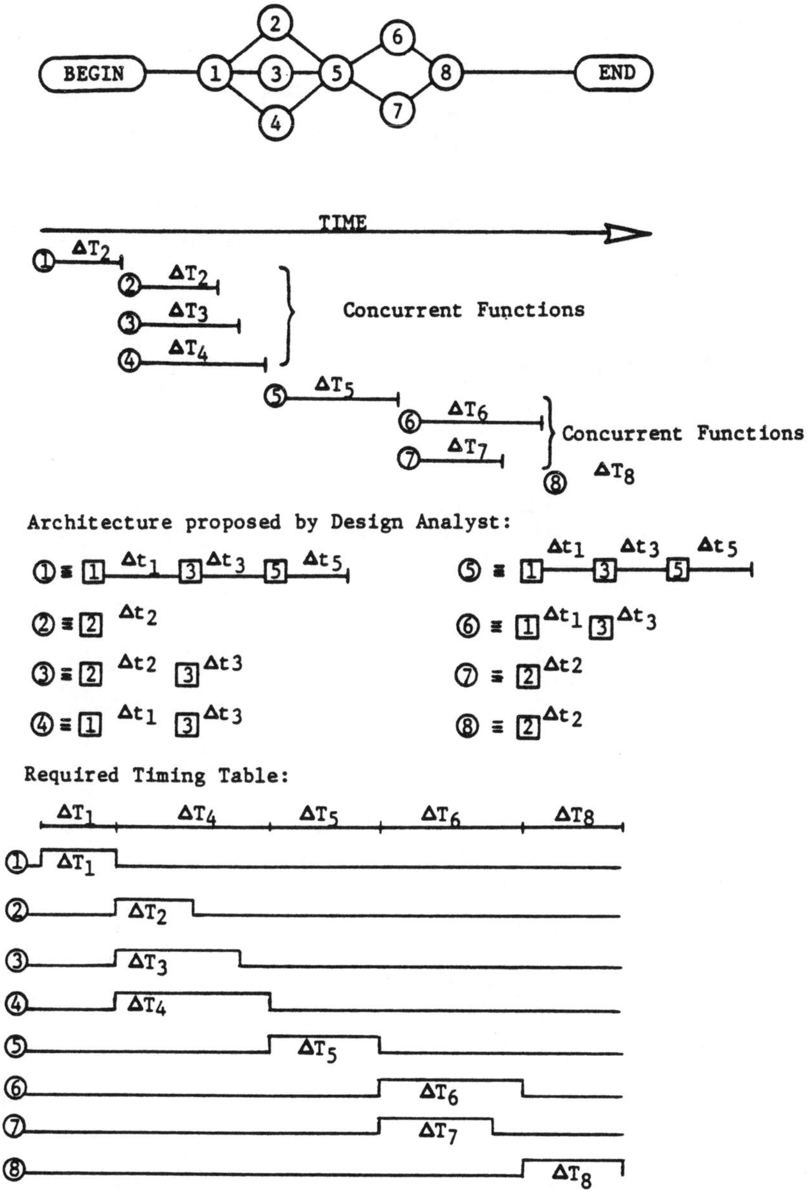

Figure 3-13 Requirements Phase Timing Table Constraints

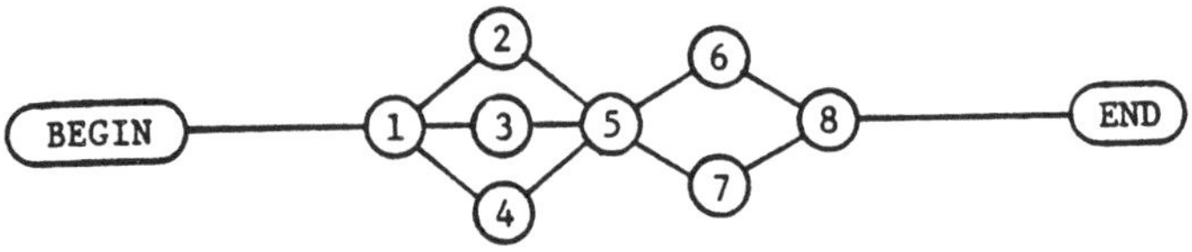

a) Graphic Representation of an Application during the Requirements Phase (Highest Level of Abstraction)

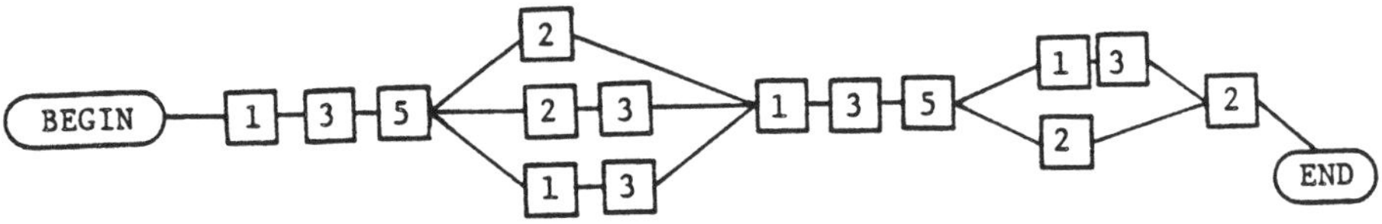

b) Graphic Representation of the above Application during the Design Phase (Next Highest Level of Abstraction)

Figure 3-14 Different Characterizations of the Same Example Within the Requirements and Design Phases

straction from the requirements phase has been reduced in the design phase. The example presented in Figure 3-12 and examined in Figure 3-13 is re-examined in Figure 3-14. The requirements phase characterization of the example uses circles while the design phase characterizaton uses squares. Both characterizations are presented in Figure 3-14. The primary difference between the two characterizations concerns their relations to the next phase within the software development lifecycles, i.e., the coding phase. Each node within the requirements phase represents a functionally cohesive application requirement with its appropriate time constraint which must be satisifed by the design architecture. Each node within the design phase represents a processing requirement which must be satisfied by actual programs to be written during the coding phase. The coding itself presents an implementation detal not addressed during the design phase. In effect, the design phase establishes what programs must be written and how fast they must operate. The details of the actual programming itself are delayed until the coding phase. As a consequence, the design analyst reconciles the functional requirments to specific architectures and constrains subsequent programming effort to particular instances of those architectures. Specific tools within the ISSE which assist the design analyst can be discussed in terms of the framework presented in Figure 3-15. Such a framework represents the ISSE tools which are implemented to address the design phase.

The Design Interface Processor (DIP) has already been described. It primary function is to provide a user-friendly interface to the design analyst as component descriptions are entered into the Configuration Kernel. Once these descriptions have been entered, the other tools provided by the ISSE for the design phase can be used. Of these remaining tools, the most significant is the Control Simulator (CS). The design analyst is provided the capability to exercise alternative architectures by the CS. Each alternative can be tested as to feasibility, performance, conformity to requirements, and other specifications generated during the design phase itself. For operation, the CS requires access to the component descriptions of the Configuration Kernel as well as the system specifications for an application within the System Specification Database of the requirements phase. The control procedures for the simulation itself are entered into the CS interactively by the design analyst prior to initiation. Based upon these interactions, the CS orchestrates the subsequent operation of the Hardware Simulator (HS) and itself throughout a subsequent simulation. The simulation data produced by both the CS and HS is entered

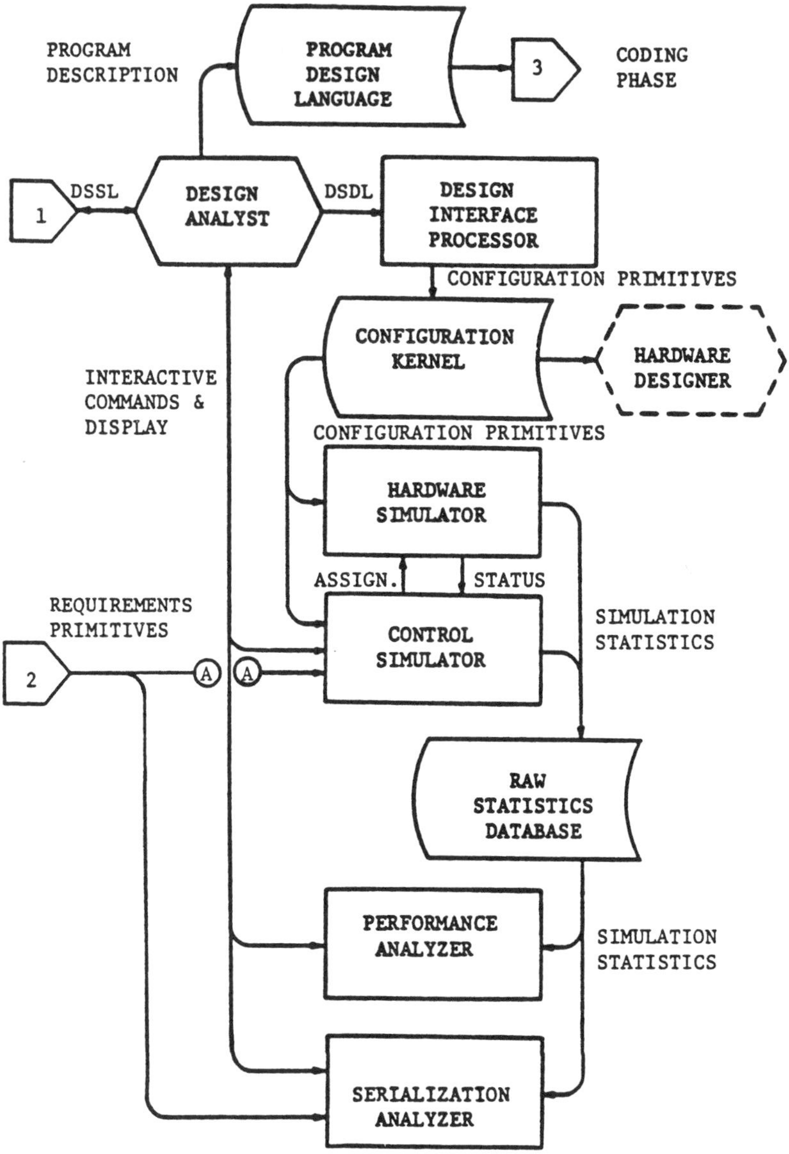

DSSL - DISTRIBUTION SYSTEM SPECIFICATION LANGUAGE
DSDL - DISTRIBUTED SYSTEM DESIGN LANGUAGE

FIGURE 3-15 Tools within the ISSE Available for Use by the Design Analyst During the Design Phase

into the ISSE Raw Statistics Database for subsequent use by other tools within the design phase.

The Hardware Simulator (HS simulates the execution of an application requirement assigned to it by the CS. Its simulation uses the component descriptions previously entered by the design analyst into the ISSE Configuration Kernel through the DIP. Simulation results by the HS are entered into the ISSE Raw Statistics Database for subsequent use by other tools within the design phase.

The Performance Analyzer (PA) consolidates simulation data previously generated and entered into the ISSE Raw Statistics Database by the HS and CS. The consolidation is initiated by a command to the PA from the design analyst. The PA constructs a consolidated display for the design analyst concerning the particular simulation under consideration.The operation of the PA, CS, and HS complement one another. Information contained in three ISSE databases is also used collectively by these tools. The databases are the Configuration Kernel, System Specification Database, and Raw Statistics Database.

The Serialization Analyzer (SA) consolidates the simulation data produced during the design phase with the functional requirements data produced during the requirements phase. The design analyst uses the SA consolidation to determine if functional requirements time constraints have been satisfied by a proposed architecture. That proposed architecture was previously entered by the design analyst through interaction with the CS. Functional requirmeents generated during the requirements phase are accessed by the CS and mapped into an architecture proposed by the systems analyst. Using the subsequent mapping, the CS initiates a series of simulations through the HS. As the HS completes each simulation, the results are entered into the Raw Statistics Database. Proposed architectures are entered into the Raw Statistics Database by the CS. Subsequent operation of the SA depends upon information from both the HS and CS in the Raw Statistics Database.

The coding phase occurs after the design phase and uses a much lower level of abstraction. Figure 3-16 presents the increasing level of detail within the coding phase in terms of program block diagrams per component included within the architecture produced in the design phase. The architectural example used within Figure 3-16 originated in Figure 3-12 and was carried through Figures 3-13 and 3-14. The component numbers used within the graphic representation of the architecture in Figure 3-16 refer to

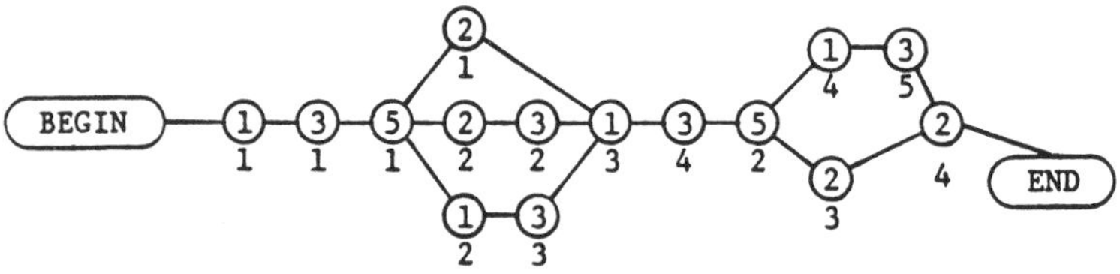

a) Graphic Representation of an Application Produced during the Design Phase

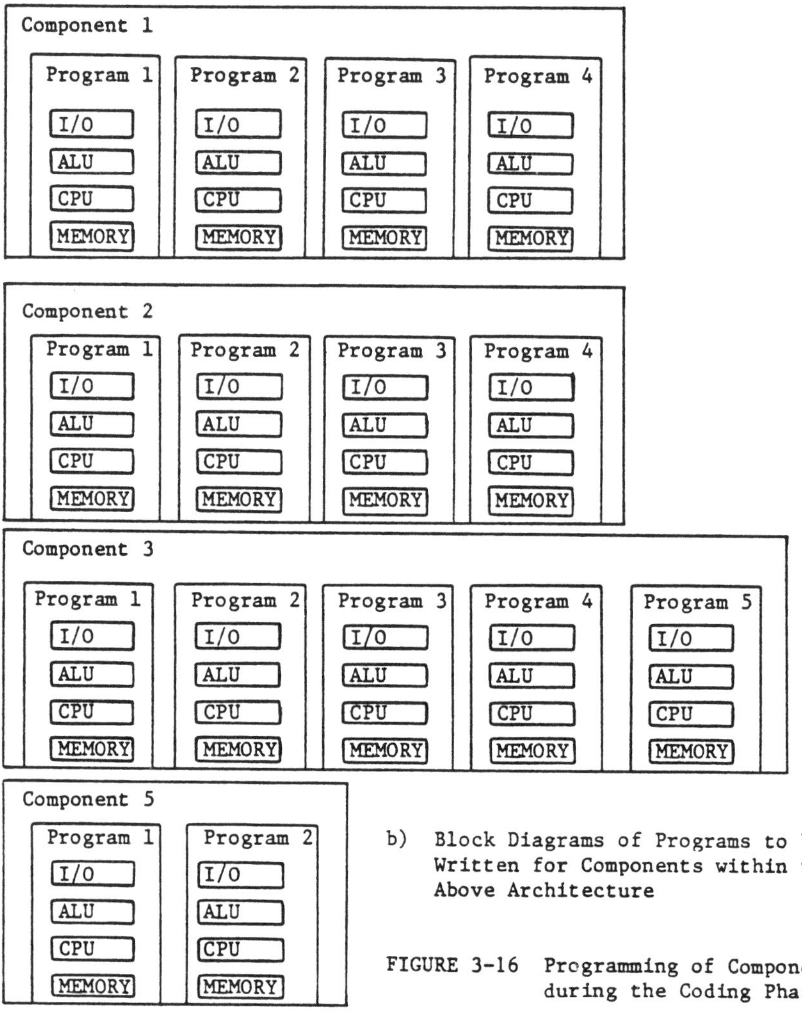

b) Block Diagrams of Programs to be Written for Components within the Above Architecture

FIGURE 3-16 Programming of Components during the Coding Phase

component identifiers used in the ISSE Configuration Kernel Database. Each component must host several programs to satisfy the functional requirements within the architecture. The block diagrams of Figure 3-16 group the various programs for a particular component together. Each program is implemented during the coding phase. Assuming a satisfactory architecture has been produced during the design phase, each program within a component presented in Figure 3-16 should be a functionally cohesive module with its own input/output, arithmetic logic operations, central processing operations, and memory usage. The source code programs to accomplish such cohesion are implementation details to be completed in the coding phase.

Specific tools are included within the ISSE to assist the coding phase. These tools are presented in an ISSE framework for the coding phase in Figure 3-17. Two databases are evident within the coding phase. The first concerns source code programs and the second, symbol tables for those source code programs after they have been compiled. The most important tool within the coding phase is the compiler. The ISSE can support a variety of compilers and should not be viewed as preferring one over another. The higher levels of abstraction in the previous phases, i.e., requirements and design, are supported by the ISSE regardless of what compiler is used during the coding phase. Functional modularization and architecture are decided before commitments to compilation are made. Such decisions are not easy and can be ignored in the rush to produce executable code. However, explicitly ignoring such decisions means the coding phase itself generates its own functional modularization and architecture under the unpredictable constraints of programmers. Such an approach does not engender confidence in the system development process.

After the compiler, the most useful tool within the coding phase is the Concurrency Checker (CC). Both design analysts and programmers alike can find use for such a tool. It accepts either a program design language description of what program are to do or source code of the programs themselves. The tool performs several distinct and separate functions. Its initial function is to parse the constructs of the input language which can be either a program design language or a source program. State tables for modules within the input language are constructed after the parsing has been completed. The relationships between modules themselves are used to construct a systems level state table by the CC. Possible interaction between modules include activations of different tasks, sending/receiving messages to/from external tasks,

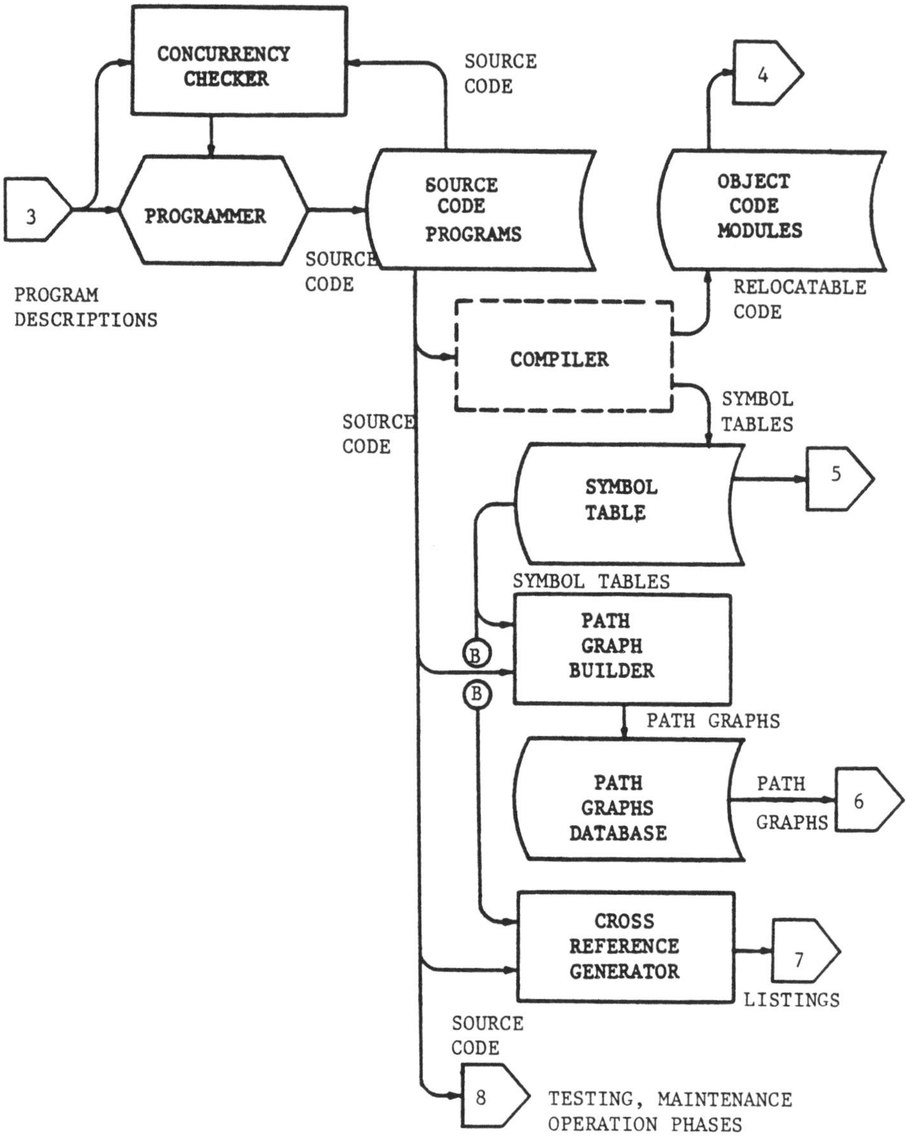

FIGURE 3-17 Tools within the ISSE Available for Use by the Programmer during the Coding Phase

deactivation of tasks, and terminations of tasks. At the system level, the CC detects database deadlock and references prior to initialization. In summary, the CC addresses problems inherent to distributed systems and concurrent architectures.

The remaining tools, i.e., the Path Graph Builder (PGB) and Cross Reference Generator (CRG), of the coding phase require the compilation of source code prior to their use. Such compilation produces a symbol table of recognized program variables and constants as well as the assigned or implied attributes of those variables and constants. The PGB processes program source code in conjunction with program symbol table information to produce a representation of the primary data flow paths through particular software modules. Information about data flow is particularly important to the subsequent phases of testing, maintenance, and operation.

The CRG processes program source code in conjunction with program symbol table information in response to requests from programmers. Subsequent maintainers and testers also find the CRG information to be useful. The CRG uses program source code as a context in which the program symbol table is cross referenced. Since the symbol table is produced by a compiler, the depth of information supplied by the CRG depends directly upon that compiler. As a consequence, the selection of a particular compiler can be influenced by the need for cross referencing, e.g., highly concurrent architecture with parallel operation.

The last two phases of the generic lifecycle are testing and maintenance. Their levels of abstraction involve the same detail as the previous implementation or coding phase. Various ISSE tools are available to address these two phases. The pertinent ISSE tools are presented in Figure 3-18. The tools within each phase are essentially the same. What discriminates one phase from another is how the tools are used. Obviously the same tool can be used to test or to maintain software, e.g., the Assertion Checker (AC). The only phase not addressed by the ISSE is the operations phase. Since operations take place within an actual target system itself, the ISSE can only simulate that system during the design, implementation and testing phases. Operational problems are addressed during the maintenance phase of the ISSE. In effect, the ISSE supports the requirements, design, implementation, testing, and maintenance phase to eliminate problems during the operation of a target system.

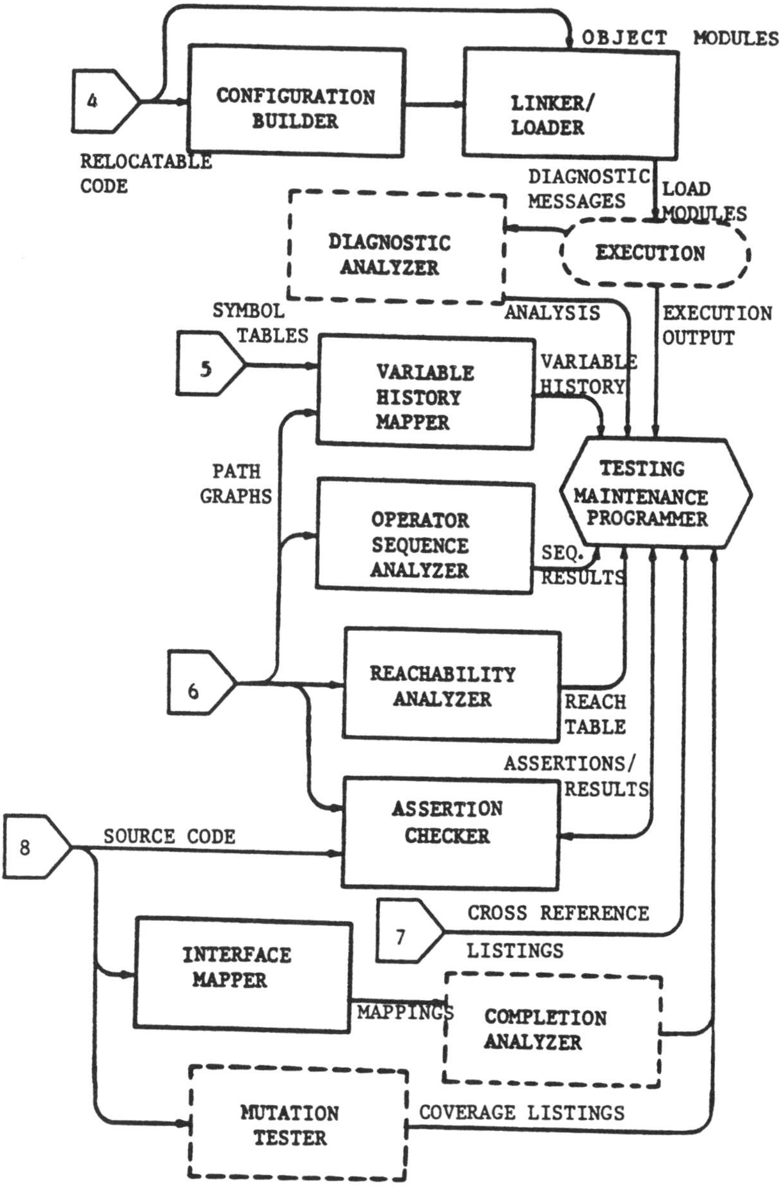

FIGURE 3-18 Tools Within the ISSE Available for Use by the Programmer During the Testing and Maintenance Phases

The testing and maintenance phases include the following ISSE toolset as a minimum: a Configuration Builder (CB), a Linker/Loader (LL), a Diagnostic Analyzer (DA), a Variable History Mapper (VHM), a Reachability Analyzer (RA) an Assertion Checker (AC), a Mutation Tester (MT), an Interface Mapper (IM), an Operator Sequence Analyzer (OSA) and a Completion Analyzer (CA). The subsequent sections describe each tool in the general framework of an ISSE.

As input, the Configuration Builder (CB) uses relocatable object-coded modules from the implementation or coding phase. Within each module are external references to other modules addressing the same application architecture. The particular architecture under consideration by the CB was established during the design phase. From these external references within a particular architecture, the CB constructs a dependency table which can be used to integrate all appropriate modules into a single architectural model. As output, the CB uses its dependency table to produce an architectural model. The CB also makes its dependency table available to other tools within the ISSE.

Once the CB produces a dependency table, the Linker/Loader (LL) can access it to perform the actualintegration of appropriate modules into an application model. Each modules has been previously compiled and is retrieved as executable object code by the LL. Cross references between modules are resolved by the LL. The output of the LL is an executable model of an application architecture. The behavior of a target architecture is modeled by the LL since the LL is a tool within the ISSE which resides upon a developmental host.

Once an architecture has had its configuration built and its executable object code linked, the subsequent model can be executed. Behavior of the particular target architecture is simulated on the developmental host containing the ISSE toolset. During this simulated execution, behavioral statistics are accumulated as input to a final testing tool of the ISSE. That tool is a Diagnostic Analyzer (DA) which consolidates the various statistics into an analysis for the testing and maintenance programmer. Assuming the behavioral statistics adequately approximate the operation of the particular target architecture under consideration, the analysis produced by the DA approximates a performance analysis of the architeture. Of course an actual performance analysis of the operating target architecture must await for implementation of the architecture itself, i.e., the operations phase which is outside the scope of an ISSE.

One of the databases produced during the implementation or coding phase concerned the symbol tables produced by action of acompiler. Of course the ISSE itself can support a variety of compilers which means the subsequent contents of the symbol table database is somewhat difficult to predict. In any case, the Variable History Mapper (VHM) tool of the testing and maintenance phases uses the contents of the symbol table database as part of its input. The balance of its input is provided by the Path Graph Builder (PGB) of the implementation or coding phase. The latter input represents primary data flow paths through the architecture under consideration to the VHM. Subsequent processing by the VHM enables it to correlate the architectural process flow with the symbol table information of the former input. As output to the testing and maintenance programmer, the VHM produces its own symbol table information concerning the initialization, use, and availability of variables within the operation of an architecture.

The Reachability Analyzer (RA) uses the path graphs produced by the Path Graph Builder (PGB) of the implementation or coding phase as input. Using these path graphs, the RA determines what variables control the flow of execution within an architecture. The RA examines conditions of entrance and exist to every module within a particular architecture. Through the analysis of such conditions, the RA analyzes how each module within an architecture is accessed and exercised. Such information is particularly valuable during the testing and maintenance phases.

The Assertion Checker (AC) uses source code for a particular architecture as its input. Within the various modules of source code, its operation is very similar to the RA. Whereas path graphs are available to the RA, such information is unavailable to the AC since compilation fo the source code has not been accomplished. Operation of the AC enables assertions concerning values of variables to be entered into the source code of the particular architecture enables the assertions ot be either denied or satisfied. Denials are reported to the testing and maintenance programmer as source code violations. As a consequence, the programmer can enter more assertions into the AC for subsequent determination during execution. Such capability provides a testing and maintenance programmer with greater understanding of program behavior and clarifies critical requirements within particular architectures.

The Mutation Tester (MT) uses the source code of apar- ticular architecture as its input. The various modules of source code are examined individually by the MT. Using the MT, a testing and maintenance programmer can in- dividually mutate the input conditions of each module and observe what processing pathologies are produced. Each processing pathology is associated with its own set of software errors. By using the MT, a testing and main- tenance programmer can develop a qualitative estimate of the compliance within an particular architecture.

The Interface Mapper (IM) uses the source code of a par- ticular architecture as its input. The modules within that architecture are examined singly by the IM. Specific attention is paid to the interfaces between these modules. The IM characterizes each interface between a module and its architectural environment in terms the data abstrac- tons transmitted and received. From these characterizations, a testing and maintenance programmer can assess whether thedegree of modularization is suf- ficiently functonal. The mapping of interfaces produced by the IM is used as input by the ISSE Completion Analyzer (CA). From this input, the CA is able to generate how much each module within a particular architecture has been exercised and how compliant each module is. In effect, the CA analyzes the coverage provided individually and collectively by the modules within a particular architecture. The subsequent coverage listing is provided the testing and maintenance by the CA for subsequent action.

3.2.2 DISTRIBUTED PROCESSING IMPACTED SUBSET

This section presents the subset of the entire ISSE that is directly impacted by distributed processing applications. The subset includes tools from all of the software development lifecycles and represents a set of tools needed to fully support the development of dis- tributed processing systems. Not every tool needed, however, has been explicitly defined in this section; this is because many tools considered to be basic support (e.g. editors, file managers, DBMSs) are treated later in sec- tion 3.2.4. All the tools discussed in this section are tools that are either (1) existing tools needing exten- sions due to the nature of distributed processing ap- plications or (2) new tools requiring the implementation of new or recently developed techniques

Several factors were considered in order to determine the tools to be included in this subset. First, the dominant problem areas for distributed C^3I systems in operation were researched. Along with this research, the historical weaknesses of conventional software support environments for centralized systems were studied. Another point of consideration was the future trend of distributed C³I systems and their changing requirements. With this information taken into consideration, it is felt that the subset arrived at and described in this section will lend the support needed to develop working, highly fault-tolerant C³I systems for a wise variety of applications.

The major aspects of distributed processing which were found to impact tool function are concurrency, distributedness, and fault tolerance. The concurrency aspect impacted tools with the problem of the serialization order of concurrent functions. This problem also involves timing characteristics of functions. Also involved with concurrency is serialization of data accesses by parallel processes. A new feature which is introduced because of concurrency is a synchronization structure to provide control between parallel processes. Availability of a new feature impacted tools by requiring extensions to handle it, and also provided the opportunity for a new tool specialized to analyze the new structures. Distributedness impacted tools with the questions that arise about internodal calls to distributed functions and internodal references to distributed data. These include how to denote or specify them, what level of support, and what restrictions apply. Fault tolerance impacts tools due to the increased emphasis that is placed on it for most distributed processing applicatons. Additionally, there is a proliferation of possible faults introduced by distributed processing. These are dependent on the pattern of connectivity and the redundancy included in a designed architecture. Thus a distributed architecture introduces failures such as a processor node failure or a internodal communication path failure, which impact the fault tolerance of a system. The particulars of the impact of distributed processing on a specific tool is further discussed in the description of each tool in the following section.

3.2.2.1 TOOL SPECIFICATIONS

A total of nineteen (19) tools impacted by distributed processing are described in the subsequent sections.

Each tool described in this section is presented in a format derived from "Type B5, Computer Program Development Specification" from MIL-STD 490, appendix VI and "figure 3-04, Program Specification" from DOD7935.1-5. This format is presented in figure 3-19. Section (1) provides an

1. INTRODUCTION

   Brief identification of the program giving some sort of nomenclature and a list of abbreviations

2. FUNCTIONAL SUMMARY

   - Describe tool in sufficient detail to clarify how it fits into the ISSE
   - Describe separate functions of modules within the tool (if applicable).
   - List criteria addressed by the tool and how they are dealt with.
   - Describe specifically how the tool addresses distributed processing

3. BRIEF DESCRIPTION (IF APPLICABLE) OF EXISTING TOOLS EXHIBITING SIMILAR FUNCTIONALITY

   - List tools and vendors
   - Briefly describe their features

4. SUMMARY OF IMPROVEMENTS

   Comparison to features identified in (3). Discussion shall include:

   A. Functional improvements (new capabilities)

   B. Existing desirable capabilities.

   C. Elimination or reduction of existing capabilities no longer needed.

5. TOOL SPECIFICATION (THIS SECTION SHOULD INCLUDE FLOW DIAGRAM)

   A. Identification of I/O Elements

      Names of possible (distinct) sources/sinks. Include what is being produced/consumed at each sink/source.

   B. Form of I/O Elements

      Discuss each distinct type of I/O (i.e. PDL, source code, RSL). Include important features specific to the operation of the tool.

   C. Logical function of I/O Elements

      Functional (as opposed to actual) content of the tool. Specifically, what meaning does each type of I/O have for each sink/source.

Figure 3-19. Outline for Functional Description of Tools

overview, listing such things as which life cycle the tool is to be used in, its slight functional description and abbreviations used throughout the description. Section (2) is the functional summary, and by reading it the reader can gain a good knowledge of how the tool is to accomplish its task. This section is usually the longest and most detailed. Sections (3) and (4) outline existing tools and technologies and the extensions required are given. Finally, section (5) outlines the I/O of the tool. Each tool section (secs. 3.2.2.1 thru 3.2.2.19) also contains Input - Process - Output (IPO) charts for a graphical representation of the functional description. Each tool's position within the ISSE is also shown in each section in the form of a context diagram. Each context diagram shows all tools with an immediate interface with the tool being described as well as all associated databases and their logical connections. If a tool appears in a context diagram depicted as a dashed box, then that tool is shown in the correct place but is not a member of the impacted subset being described in this section.

This section is meant to present the subset of tools impacted directly by distributed processing. Each functional description is not meant as a replacement for high-level design specifications; rather, each is a generic description of a particular tool's capabilities and it's role within the overall ISSE.

3.2.2.1.1 REQUIREMENTS INTERFACE PROCESSOR

1. INTRODUCTION

The Requirements Interface Processor (RIP) provides the interface for entering system specifications. The following abbreviations are used:

DBMS	Database Management System
DSSL	Distributed System Specification Language
ISSE	Integrated System Support Environment
REVS	Requirements Engineering and Validation System
RIP	Requirements Interface Processor
RLP	Requirements Language Processor
RPS	Requirements Processing System
RSL	Requirements Statement Language
SSDB	System Specification Database

2. FUNCTIONAL SUMMARY

The Requirements Interface Processor (RIP) provides an interactive interface for use by the requirements analyst to enter requirements into the System Specification Database (SSDB). It is also available for the design analyst to access the information in the SSDB. The input takes the form of a formal Distributed System Specification Language (DSSL). This DSSL must include a set of primitives sufficient to support C^3I applications. This includes the expression of requirements for concurrency, distributedness, redundancy, security, access, capacity, serialization, fault tolerance, etc. In C^3I certain functions must be accomplished concurrently without interfering with each other. Also particular functions may be required to be distributed to certain locations. A need for redundancy of data and functionality sometimes occurs. Security is a very important and sensitive issue as many C^3I applications utilize classifed information. Access requirements arise occasionally due to elements of the system being distributed. Capacity and its distribution become an issue as these requirements must be known to facilitate the allocation of resources to locations during design. The requirements for serialization of functions must be clearly expressable, particularly for concurrent functions distributed to different locations. Special considerations must be made during design to insure that proper synchronization will occur to effect the required serialization. Fault tolerance can be adversely affected so easily in a distributed system, that it is very important the requirements for fault tolerance be well established at the outset. It is also desirable that the vocabulary of the DSSL be extensible so that it may be customized for particular C^3I applications. This customization permits the analysts to easily express the specifications by using application terms which may be more complex than the primitives.

The RIP receives the input DSSL statements, checks them for proper syntax, reduces them to primitives, performs a superficial consistency check against previous entries in the SSDB, and enters them into the SSDB. These DSSL statements may represent requirements specifications of a system, declarations of primitives, or definitions of primitives. Thus the ability to add or modify primitives is available. This can be used very advantageously to accomplish a progressive specification of requirements, from a high level abstraction to a detailed low level description. This ability to change primitives is very powerful and must be controlled; therefore, a locking mechanism must be provided in order to restrict this capability to only authorized personnel.

As the RIP is interactive, it provides display capability. It cannot only echo DSSL entries as they are made but can also recall from the SSDB entries made previously and display them as DSSL statements. Errors, both those the RIP detects as it processes DSSL statements and those detected and entered in the SSDB by other tools, must be displayed in conjunction with the offending entries.

Another feature to improve useability is graphics. Many aspects of requirements can be displayed in graphical form. The RIP provides the automated mapping between graphics and the more common textual form. This permits entering requirements in one form and checking by examination of the other form. Alternating between forms during entry is also viable. Thus the RIP serves to provide an efficient means for inputing the requirements of distributed processing applications in C^3I.

A secondary function of the RIP is to provide a means for inputing into the SSDB the necessary modeling definitions of the primitives. These definitions are needed by the Automatic Language Translator when transforming a SSDB description of an application into an executable model.

3. BRIEF DESCRIPTION OF EXISTING TOOLS EXHIBITING SIMILAR FUNCTIONALITY

Some of the tools which perform similar functions are the Requirements Language Processor (RLP) in the Requirements Processing System (RPS), the RSL translator of REVS, the PSA statement analyzer and the editors in USE.IT. All of these tools accept textual input with the RLP being the most flexible in its acceptance of multi-lingual applications-oriented requirements languages. REVS and USE.IT are also capable of using graphics for their inputs. All three store the processed input for later access by other tools in their system. The translator of REVS stores the information in a relational database for use by a variety of other requirements tools in SREM.

4. SUMMARY OF IMPROVEMENTS

A. Functional improvements (new capabilities)

An expanded requirements specification language to include the primitives necessary to support distributed processing applications. The integration of this into an ISSE and the establishment of a SSDB which is compatible with a large variety of analysis tools. These tools should be capable of providing support through both the requirements and design phases of the life-cycle.

B. Existing desirable capabilities

The flexibility exhibited by existing specification languages should be preserved. Graphics capability will provide a more desirable interface package in the ISSE.

5. TOOL SPECIFICATION

A. Identification of I/O Elements

The input to the RIP can be either in graphical form or in a syntactical language extended with an application specific vocabulary. The RIP translates the input into specification primitives which are stored in the SSDB for use by other requirements tools.

B. Form of I/O Elements

Inputs - User-friendly vocabulary for expressing conceptual requirements (DSSL) or graphics.

Outputs- Entries in SSDB relational database representing specification requirements.

C. Logical Functions of I/O Elements

Inputs - Requirements analyst specifies conceptual requirements to be tested further for consistency and completeness.

Outputs - System specifications in the SSDB in a compatible form for processing by other tools.

REQUIREMENTS INTERFACE PROCESSOR

INPUT

REQUIREMENTS SPECIFICATION LANGUAGE

CUSTOMIZABLE PER APPLICATION NEEDS

MAPPABLE TO PRIMITIVES

INCLUDE CONSTRUCTS FOR DESCRIPTION OF DISTRIBUTED APPLICATIONS

ex. "RSL", "AXES", "PSL", INPUT FOR "RLP"

PROCESS

ASSURE SYNTACTICALLY CORRECT

ASSURE CONSISTENCY WITH PREVIOUS ENTRIES

TRANSLATE INTO PRIMITIVE FORM FOR INCLUSION IN SYSTEM SPECIFICATION DATABASE

ex. "REVS" TRANSLATOR, "RLP", "PSA" STATEMENT ANALYZER

OUTPUT

SYSTEM SPECIFICATION IN PRIMITIVE FORM FOR DATABASE

ex. "ASSM", "PSA" DATABASE, "RLP" DATABASE

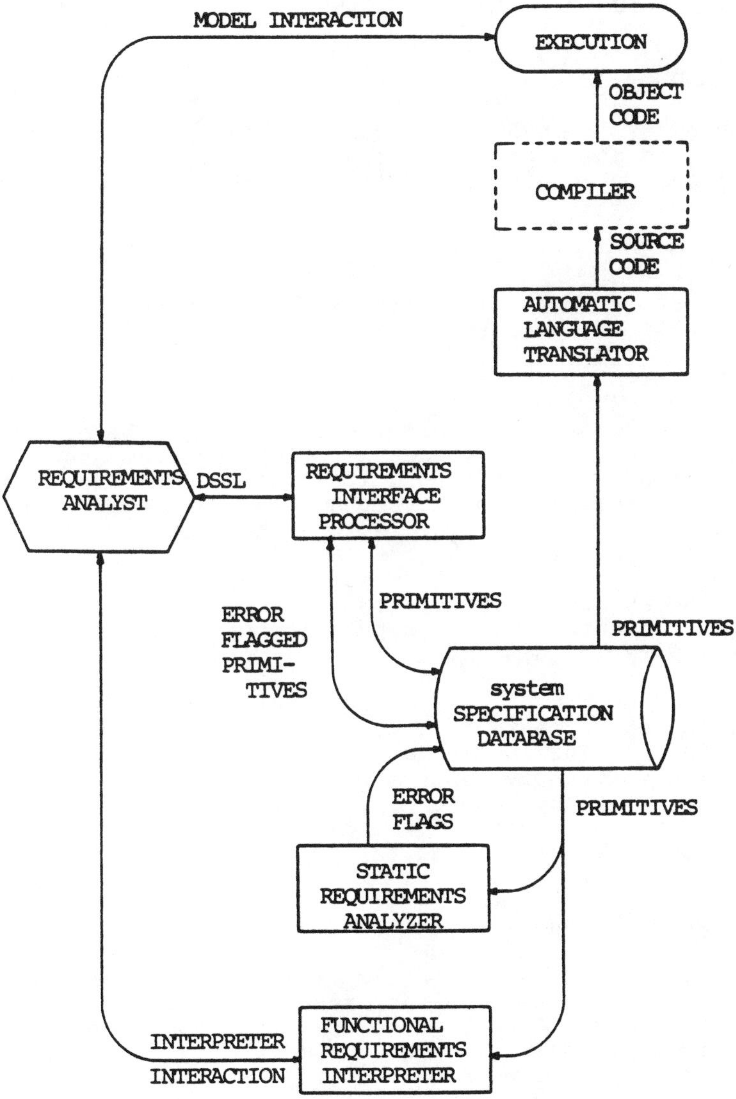

DSSL - DISTRIBUTED SYSTEMS SPECIFICATION LANGUAGE

3.2.2.1.2 AUTOMATIC LANGUAGE TRANSLATOR

1. INTRODUCTION

The Automatic Language Translator (ALT) is used in the requirements phase of the software life cycle. The abbreviations used in the following discussion are listed below:

DSSL	Distributed System's Specification Language
RIP	Requirements Interface Processor
SSDB	System Specification Database
RAT	Resource Allocation Tool

2. FUNCTIONAL SUMMARY

The ALT accommodates the requirements analyst by providing feedback with respect to the specified requirements. The requirements, as specified in the SSDB through the RIP by the requirements analyst, and the primitive transformations, as specified in the SSDB by authorized personnel, are combined by the ALT. The ALT combines the two in the form of output source code to be run on the host. The ability of the requirements analyst to check the requirements using output source code provides a feedback-directed design.

The ALT functions as a translator of the software application requirements to a compilable source code form of the DSSL. The translation occurs by mapping the requirements to equivalent source code constructs using primitive transformations from the SSDB. The primitive transformations, which provide low-level functional resolution, are specified through the RIP prior to using the ALT.

Criteria Addressed

Since the ALT accommodates feedback-directed design through requirements modeling, several software criteria are satisfied. Checking the specified requirements with the output compilable source code aid in checking compliance. Requirements modeling establishes the consistency of techniques and checks the degree of fault tolerance and the actions to be taken under various conditions. The documentation provided by the modeling output enhances clarity and traceability.

Distributed Processing Considerations

In C^3 environments, specialized primitives will be necessary to express requirements for software applications. New primitives will also be necessary to accommodate distributed processing. Authorized personnel can establish additional primitives in the SSDB prior to requirements modeling. Using the standard and additional primitives in the SSDB, the requirements constructs for C^3 distributed processing applications can be mapped to equivalent, compilable source code.

3. BRIEF DESCRIPTION OF EXISTING TOOLS EXHIBITING SIMILAR FUNCTIONALITY

An example of an existing tool exhibiting the characteristics similar to the ALT is the RAT portion of USE.IT (Higher Order Software). The input to USE.IT is a functional description of a system which is required to be complete and non-redundant. The output is a FORTRAN-66 direct implementation of the functional description.

4. SUMMARY OF IMPROVEMENTS

A. New capabilities (functional improvements)
The ALT must have the ability to allow for primitives specific to distributed processing.

B. Existing Desirable Capabilities
An existing tool, USE.IT, has the capability to utilize a library of primitives which can be augmented when necessary. It also has the capability to produce compilable source code for an executable model directly from the statement of the requirements.

5. TOOL SPECIFICATION

A. Identification of I/O Elements
The input to the ALT has two forms, the DSSL and the primitive transformations. The DSSL is generated by the requirements analyst through interaction with the RIP and the primitive transformations are established in the SSDB by the requirements analyst. The output of the ALT is high-level language source code for processing by coding phase tools.

B. Form of I/O Elements

Inputs:

Transformation Primitives - source code constructs to model the primitives.

Specification Primitives - reduction of DSSL to level of primitives.

Outputs:

Source code - High level language statements and declarations.

C. Logical Function of I/O Elements

Inputs:

Specification Primitives - provides a complete description of all distributed systems' requirements which have been checked previously for consistency and completeness.

Transformation Primitives - provide for the model the necessary information for mapping requirements primitives to source code.

Outputs:

Source Code - high-level language representation of the requirements customized for implementation on the host system.

AUTOMATIC LANGUAGE TRANSLATOR

INPUT

SPECIFICATION PRIMITIVES -

DISTRIBUTED SYSTEMS REQUIREMENTS CHECKED BY THE RIP

TRANSFORMATION PRIMITIVES -

INFORMATION FOR MAPPING REQUIREMENTS TO SOURCE CODE

PROCESS

MAP REQUIREMENTS

SPECIFICATION PRIMITIVES TO EQUIVALENT HIGH LEVEL LANGUAGE SOURCE CODE (COMPILABLE) TO BE RUN ON HOST

OUTPUT

COMPILABLE,

HIGH-LEVEL LANGUAGE SOURCE CODE TO BE RUN ON HOST

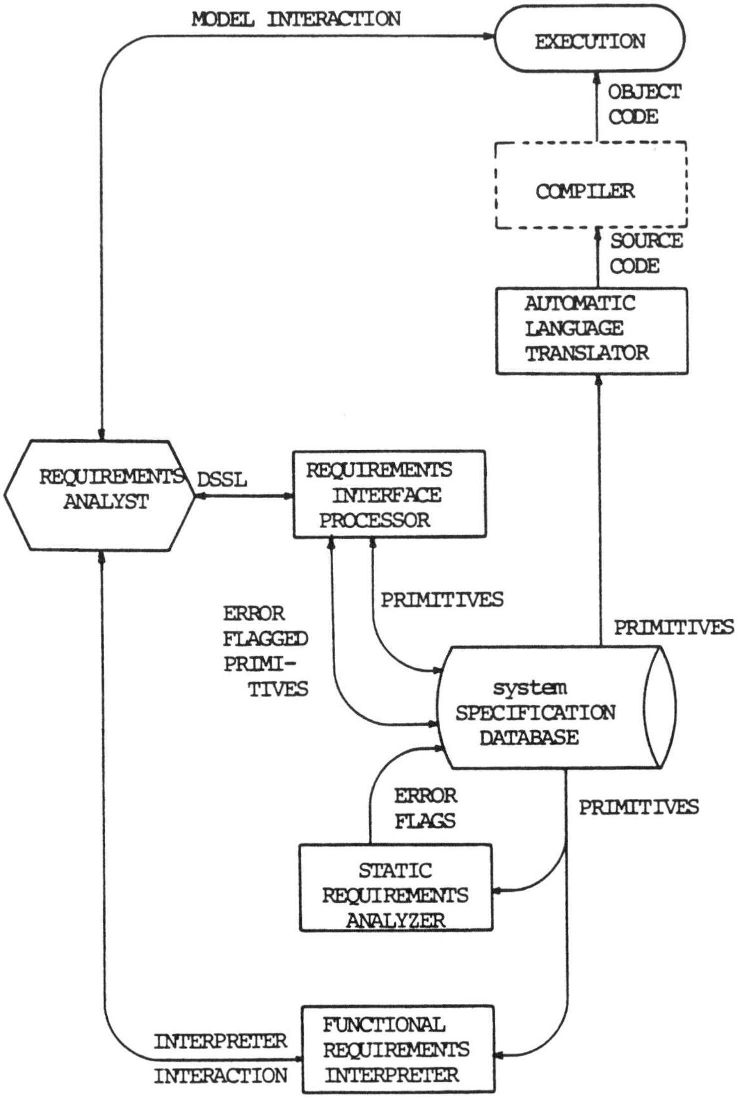

DSSL - DISTRIBUTED SYSTEMS SPECIFICATION LANGUAGE

3.2.2.1.3 STATIC REQUIREMENTS ANALYZER

1. INTRODUCTION

SRA	Static Requirements Analyzer
BMD	Ballistic Missile Defense
DBMS	Database Management System
ISSE	Integrated System Support Environment
REVS	Requirements Engineering and Validation System
RIP	Requirements Interface Processor
SREM	Software Requirements Engineering Methodology
SSDB	System Specification Database

2. FUNCTIONAL SUMMARY

The Static Requirements Analyzer (SRA) is available for use by the requirements analyst and designer to analyze a proposed software system. Distributed Systems' Specifications in their primitive form are accepted as input from the SSDB. These specifications are converted to their primitive form and stored in the SSDB by the RIP. The SRA analyzes the primitives for errors and only flags erroneous specifications. These errors are updated in the SSDB to output error listings.

The SRA performs the functions of data flow analysis, completion analysis, consistency checking, hierarchy checking and structure checking. Data flow analysis is used to detect potential and definite errors in data use and accumulates information with respect to the flow of each data item. It operates in the same manner as data flow analyzers for programming languages except for the complication of concurrency of path specifications allowed in DSSL. The analysis is concerned with data usage errors such as data usage prior to value assignment and the assignment of values for a data item in more than one path. Since the SRA will update the SSDB with data usage analysis, reports could be generated concerning the lifetime and usage of data.

Completion analysis assures that all references are resolved. The consistency of references is ensured by consistency checking. Structure checking examines the requirements for proper branching and rejoining of paths, usage of only one structure per node, and proper termination of all paths. Since all of the results of the aforementioned analyses are updated by the SRA in the SSDB, the RIP can access the SSDB to produce error reports.

Criteria Addressed

Since the SRA accommodates feedback-directed design through its multi-faceted analysis, several criteria are enhanced. The consistency of the specifications for the proposed system is analyzed by the SRA by consistency checking. Data flow analysis and structure checking establish the clarity of the specification. Completion analysis ensures compliance to the proposed system by checking for the completeness of the specifications.

Distributed Processing

Since distributed processing primitives can be expressed at a high level of abstraction, the SRA must support this level of abstraction. This capability enables the application of the SRA prior to design. The SRA must be capable of analyzing the information represented in the distributed processing primitives such as parallel data flow and concurrent functions. Since the distributed processing primitives represent the requirements at a high level of abstraction, the details of the primitives are implemented in the subsequent phases of the software life cycle.

3. BRIEF DESCRIPTION OF EXISTING TOOLS

Three products exhibiting similar functionality are the automated tools portion of REVS (SREM, TRW Defense and Space), ANALYZE of USE.IT (Higher Order Software), and Problem Statement Analyzer (PSA) of PSL/PSA (University of Michigan). All of these products process a description, or model, of the requirements for a proposed system and provide the requirements analyst feedback on the quality of these requirements. This feedback takes the form of error messages or requested reports displayed to the analyst in textual or graphical form. Several other standard-type functions are provided by this group of tools. Among these functions are structure checking, hierarchy checking, and checking for consistency and completeness. REVS also provides a feature for data flow analysis, and PSA generates comparison reports analyzing the similarities between input requirements and output requirements.

4. SUMMARY OF IMPROVEMENTS

A. Functional Improvements (new capabilities)

The SRA must accommodate the concurrencies inherent in distributed processing in the structures that are needed for describing the specification of the system. Requirements are expressed in primitives, a high-level of abstraction which permits requirements analysis early in the software life cycle. More specifically, the data flow analyzer part of the SRA must be capable of analyzing parallel data paths through the system. Also, the structure checker portion of the SRA must be able to check the validity of the concurrency as expressed in the SSDB. The SRA should provide a flexible workbench in which the functional modules may be invoked in any allowable combination. The execution of functional modules must be constrained to a sequential order. The interrelationships of functional modules within the SRA may dictate specific ordering.

B. Existing Desirable Capabilities
All of the existing features listed in section 3 should be included in the SRA. The important consideration for improvement is the level of modularity of the functions themselves. The design analyst should be able to envoke any of the functions he wants, in any order, without being forced to contend with the full functionality of the tool unless he so specifies. This is made possible through the decoupling that takes place by having the SRA directly interface with the SSDB only. The SRA should not alter any of the original specifications in the SSDB, but rather produce copies of the specification with corrections and error messages appended.

5. SPECIFICATIONS OF THE I/O OF THE TOOL

A. Identification of I/O Elements

The capability for I/O to the SRA is enabled when a SSDB is established by the RIP. The RIP functions both as the I/O source and I/O sink to the SRA. The I/O is buffered through the SSDB and read/write security is provided by the DBMS of the ISSE.

B. Form of I/O Elements

Inputs:
SSDB - record data structures received from the RIP.

Outputs:
SSDB - annotated record data structures compatible with the input data structures received from the RIP.

C. Logical Functions of I/O Elements

Inputs:
SSDB - provides a description of the requirements for a system in primitives.

Outputs:
SSDB - provides the results of the analysis as an appendage to the requirements description in the SSDB file.

STATIC REQUIREMENTS ANALYZER

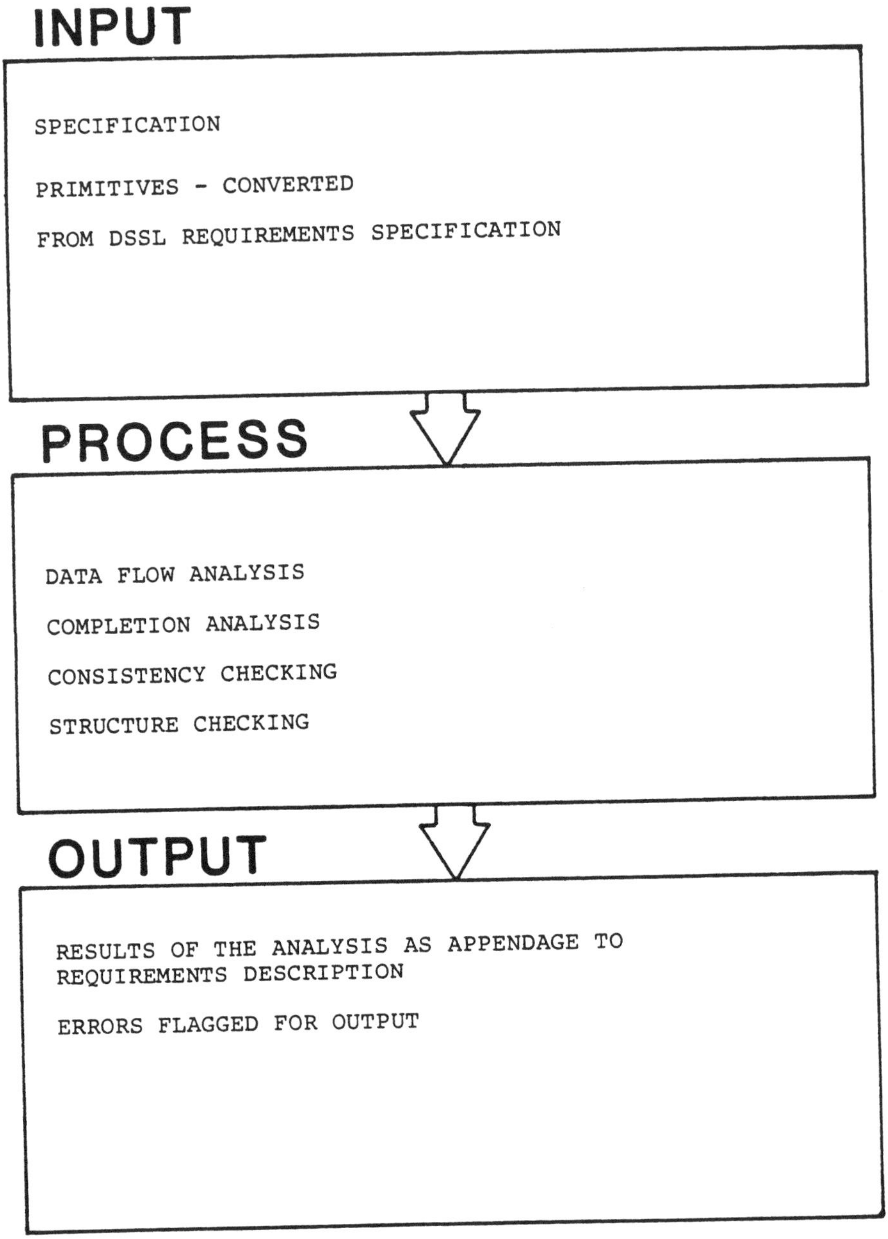

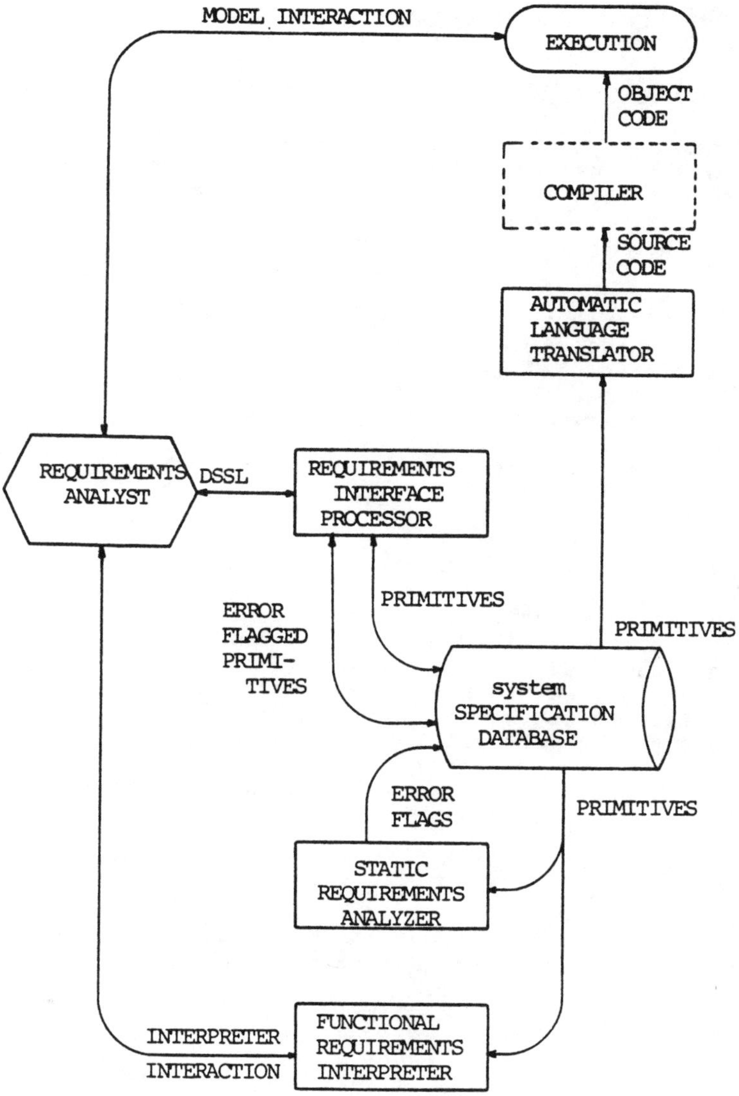

DSSL - DISTRIBUTED SYSTEMS SPECIFICATION LANGUAGE

3.2.2.1.4 FUNCTIONAL REQUIREMENTS INTERPRETER

1. INTRODUCTION

The Functional Requirements Interpreter (FRI) is designed for use in the requirements phase of the software lifecycle. This tool assists the requirements analyst in establishing a sequence of functional operations which satisfy a set of application requirements.

DSSL	Distributed System Specification Language
FRI	Functional Requirements Interpreter
ISSE	Integrated Systems Support Environment
MMI	Man Machine Interface
RIP	Requirements Interface Processor
SRA	Static Requirements Analyzer
SSDB	System Specification Database

2. FUNCTIONAL SUMMARY

The FRI analyzes the SSDB primitives for a particular application previously described using DSSL. Execution of the FRI is interactive with initiation and interaction by the requirements analyst. The FRI produces simulated output for the requirements analyst to determine if application requirements are being satisfied. Path analysis reports between functions of an application simulation are also generated by the FRI. As each function within a particular application is completed, the FRI issues a report as to its success or failure with respect to specific application requirements.

A particularly important function of the FRI concerns timing constraints. A process composed of a sequence of functions to be completed within a specified period of time is annotated throughout the FRI simulation. Another important function of the FRI concerns the construction of functional transition tables for subsequent use in the modeling activity of the FRI. Obviously the FRI must maintain a user-friendly MMI for the requirements analyst. Through this MMI, the requirements analyst constructs a table-driven path from an initial function to a final function to satisfy specific application requirements.

The FRI addresses several software quality criteria. The first is functional generality because its structure reflects the required functionality of an application. Applications themselves can be viewed as a sequence of functions. The requirements analyst specifies the initial function and the FRI must accommodate all subsequent linkages desired by that analyst in its structure. Furthermore, the FRI must also accommodate alternative linkages to demonstrate a limited degree of fault tolerance within specific applications. When a desired degree of fault tolerance has been achieved, the ease of use within a particular application has been enhanced. The underlying structure of the FRI realizes modularity as well as expandability.

The FRI addresses hardware criteria in its acknowledgement of real-time constraints. Such constraints are applied by the FRI after a specific application has been expressed as a sequence of one or more functions. Each function is expressed in terms of an object oriented module whose activity is functionally cohesive. The activity must be completed within a specified period of time regardless of whether it is performed by hardware, software, or a combination of the two. The expression of any application in terms of functionality makes the subsequent determination of feasibility much easier to accomplish during the design phase.

3. BRIEF DESCRIPTION OF EXISTING TOOLS EXHIBITING SIMILAR FUNCTIONALITY

Numerous tools designed to address rapid prototyping are in various stages of development. However, few are being actively marketed.

A system called GIST developed at the University of Southern California addresses some of the issues assigned to the FRI. However, GIST views an application in terms of a closed system of behavior which is characterized by a finite sequence of state transitions. Such a view is roughly equivalent to functionality addressed by the FRI GIST differs from the FRI in its use of a multi-dimensional approach to satisfy all possible applications. Dimensions are associated with techniques, data structues, and efficiencies. The FRI addresses each application on an individual basis. The technique, data structure, and efficiency required by that application drives the FRI.

Another rapid prototyping system is under development by the Army Institute for Research in Management Information and Computer Sciences (AIRMICS). Its approach has been evolved from research at Georgia Institute of Technology. A Problem Statement Language (PSL) is used to describe a particular application's requirements. Such activity is equivalent to the usage of DSSL within the ISSE. Once the PSL description has been completed, subsequent emphasis is on performance within the particular application's architecture. Such an emphasis is similar to a feasibility testbed. AIRMICS currently examines fully distributed or uncoupled architectures. The subsequent integration of their approach into an ISSE will not be easy.

Perhaps the most relevant system currently addressing rapid prototyping is the GTE Feature Simulator. It interprets and executes requirements specifications which have previously been validated and translated by a Requirements Language Processor. This parallels the operation of an RIP and an FRI within the ISSE. The Feature Simulator can serve as a rapid prototyper of a real-time system. It simulates the functional characteristics of an application while modeling real-time constraints. If the subsequent behavior is inappropriate, the specifications can be changed by the GTE Feature Simulator. Such capability will also be offered by the FRI and integrated into the ISSE.

4. SUMMARY OF IMPROVEMENTS

A. Functional Improvements (new capabilities)

The FRI must be able to analyze a particular application expressed in SSDB primitives. The analysis is controlled by the requirements analyst. As a consequence, operation of the FRI has been decoupled from the SSDB. Each application description contained in the SSDB has been compiled previously through the use of the DSSL. The independent relationship between the FRI, the SSDB, and the DSSL is particularly useful in the ISSE. How useful depends upon the expertise of the requirements analyst. These tools passively wait for the requirements analyst to initiate their use. Based upon its interaction with the requirements analyst, the FRI is constrained to the requirements phase. The information it generates is not accessible during the design phase. This completely uncouples the FRI from subsequent lifecycle phases. Such a relationship enhances the ISSE.

How well the FRI addresses time constraints also depends upon the expertise of the requirements analyst. The analyst must have properly delineated the functionally cohesive modules within a particular application before he can expect meaningful timing analysis. Furthermore, the transitions between functionally cohesive modules must be described in sufficient detail to accomplish a timing analysis. A beginning point and an ending point must be specified. The FRI will not provide a timing analysis unless requested.

B. Existing Desirable Capabilities

Decoupling the input of the FRI from the output of the RIP by way of the SSDB is desirable within the ISSE. Such decoupling is available within the GIST system at the University of Southern California and within the Feature Simulator of GTE. However, such decoupling is vertical in nature since it isolates one functionally cohesive module from another within the same lifecycle phase of the ISSE. Another type of decoupling occurs in the horizontal direction since it isolates functionally cohesive modules of one lifecycle phase from functionally cohesive modules in another lifecycle phase. Such horizontal decoupling occurs within the Feature Simulator of GTE and should be retained in the ISSE. Isolation from the vertical and horizontal standpoints is particularly important to the architecture of the ISSE.

C. Elimination or Reduction of Existing Capabilities no Longer Needed

The FRI must establish vertical as well as horizontal isolation to meet architectural requirements of the ISSE. Marketplace products invariably span more than a single lifecycle phase. Furthermore, such products are frequently coupled to other products. As a consequence, implementation of the ISSE is slowed.

5. TOOL SPECIFICATION

A. Identification of I/O Elements

The capability for I/O to the FRI is available through interaction with the requirements analyst. Input to the FRI is also available through access from the SSDB. Only the requirements analyst can serve as a sink to the FRI.

B. Form of the I/O Elements

Inputs: The data structures originally produced by the RIP comprise the record structures within the SSDB. These record structures are annotated by the SRA. All application inputs are provided by the requirements analyst.

Outputs: Annotated data structures are provided the requirements analyst. At his discretion, he may choose to enter an alternative set of data structures directly into the FRI.

C. Logical Function of I/O Elements

Inputs: The SSDB contains a description of application requirements in terms of system primitives. The requirements analyst may also describe application inputs to the FRI in accordance with a specific behavior. Such inputs must be expressed in terms of system primitives.

Outputs: The requirements analyst receives the interpretation of application requirements as generated by the FRI.

FUNCTIONAL REQUIREMENTS INTERPRETER

INPUT

FUNCTIONAL DESCRIPTION OF APPLICATION FROM SSDB. ORIGINALLY EXPRESSED IN DSSL BY REQUIREMENTS ANALYST AND DECOMPOSED INTO REQUIREMENTS PRIMITIVES BY THE RIP

INTERACTIVE I/O WITH REQUIREMENTS ANALYST TO CONTROL MODELING: INCLUDING ANY I/O REQUIRED BY MODEL

INTERPRETIVE DEFINITION OF REQUIREMENTS PRIMITIVES FROM SSDB

PROCESS

INTERPRETIVE EXECUTION OF FUNCTIONAL REQUIREMENTS AS PROMPTED BY ANALYST INTERACTION IN ACCORDANCE WITH DEFINITIONS AVAILABLE IN THE SSDB

OUTPUT

MODELING RESULTS IN FORM OF INTERACTIVE I/O WITH ANALYST

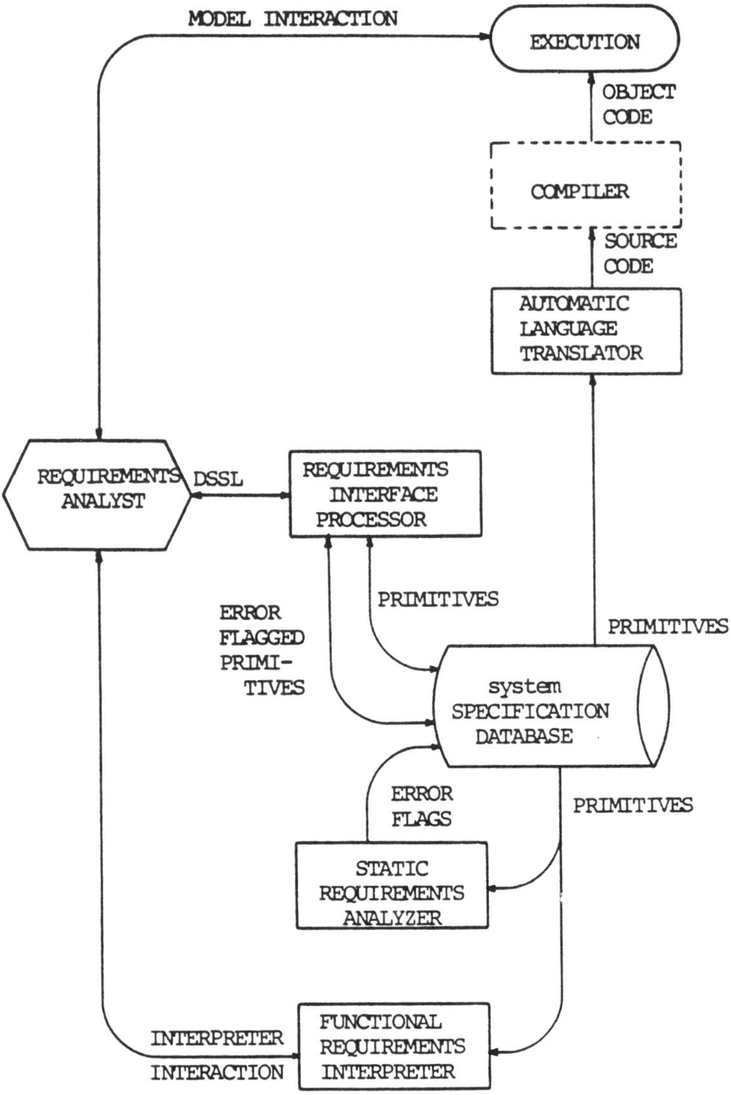

DSSL - DISTRIBUTED SYSTEMS SPECIFICATION LANGUAGE

3.2.2.1.5 DESIGN INTERFACE PROCESSOR

1. INTRODUCTION

The Design Interface Processor is for use in the design phase of the software lifecycle. It's main function is to provide the designer with an input interface to the hardware and control simulators.

A list of pertinent abbreviations follows:

CK	Configuration Kernel
CS	Control Simulator
DIP	Design Interface Processor
HS	Hardware Simulator
NOS	Network Operating System
SSDB	System Specification Database

2. FUNCTIONAL SUMMARY

The DIP allows the designer to input to the CK information required for simulation. The HS and CS then reference this information in the CK during the subsequent simulation of the proposed system. Both simulators make read references to the CK but do no writing; the DIP is the only source of input to the CK.

As stated earlier, the DIP provides the designer with an input interface to the CK and therefore the simulators that read from the CK. The inputs from the designer must all be parsed, tokenized, syntactically analyzed, and stored on the CK by the DIP. That is to say, the DIP performs the same function on inputs of varying content. These various inputs are described below:

- Control Inputs. The designer must enter in to the CK the various NOS control strategies required by the CS. Basically, this input consists of the algoritms to be used during the simulation with regard to network task scheduling, nodal task scheduling, file set management, control distribution, and other characteristics of NOS control.

- Configuration Architecture. The Configuration Architecture is the designer's description of the hardware and its properties to the CS. This description consists of; the connectivity of the network,i.e., what communications channels are available and how they're used, the mapping of control commands to configuration primitives, and assignments of software functions to hardware nodes or homogenous classes of nodes.

- Interpretations of Configuration Primitives. This allows the HS to carry out the simulation by manipulating the data structures representing the simulated system according to these interpretations.

- Interpretations of the Requirements Primitives in Terms of the Configuration Primitives. The CS uses these interpretations to translate a given requirement primitive into it's appropriate set of configuration primitives. This set of configuration primitives varies depending on which processor or set of processors the requirements primitive is targeted for simulated execution on.

The DIP influences several criteria concerning the end product. A list of these criteria accompanied by the ways the DIP effects them follows:

Traceability - The DIP provides the means for the designer to enter mapping from requirements to configuration primitives.

Modularity - The mapping selected and entered into the DIP by the designer is the first cust at design modules.

Functional Generality - the mapping of requirements primitives to the same configuration primitives is a sign of functional similarity and provides candidates for functional generality in the design.

Resource Utilization - the control inputs entered via the DIP represent the designer's proposal for handling resource utilization.

Distributedness - the configuration architecture entered via the DIP describes the proposed distributedness.

The DIP has several direct impacts on the distributed nature of the product it helps to produce. The tool aids the designer in testing different strategies for all aspects of network control and for different hardware and connectivity configurations. Based upon the results of the simulation, the designer can choose the most suitable target configuration and NOS policies on which to implement the application previously described by the requirements analyst.

3. BRIEF EXPLANATION OF EXISTING TOOLS EXHIBITING SIMILAR FUNCTIONALITY

Several tools exist that perform functions that overlap those of the DIP (see functional description of the RIP), however the input these tools process and the subsequent functions they perform vary greatly from the tool being described here. The areas of overlap include:

- Condensing an input to a tool-processible form and storing it on a database and,

- Parsing, tokenizing and syntactical checking of an input stream.

4. SUMMARY OF IMPROVEMENTS

A. Functional Improvements (New Capabilities)

The ability to parse, tokenize and syntactically analyze the input to the DIP is a new capability since this input is unique. This allows the simulators to be decoupled from the specification of the input while assuring the simulators of its correctness.

B. Existing Desirable Capabilities

The parsing, tokenization and syntactical analysis of input from the designer is an existing functionality of current tools which needs to be retained. Several tools perform these functions, on different inputs of course, as well as building a database from the information they process. Syntactical analysis is unique for every separate input, but poses no significant problem once the input scheme has been totally defined.

5. TOOL SPECIFICATION

A. Identification of I/O Elements

The input, which is functionally divided into NOS control strategies, interpretations and function-to-node assignments, is produced exclusively by the designer. The output may either be directed back to the designer providing feedback concerning the input or to the CK via its access routines.

B. Form of I/O Elements

Inputs

- Pre-determined language for expressing NOS control strategies

- Interpretations - List of relationships expressing translations from (1) requirements primitives to configuration primitives, (2) control primitives to configuration primitives, and (3)configuration primitives to actual simulation instructions.

- Function to Node Assignments - Names of application functions as specified in the SSDB that need to be associated with particular kinds of hardware or specific nodes.

Outputs

- Feedback to the designer - Error messages and listings.

- CK - The DIP builds the CK via its access routines for subsequent use during simulation.

C. Logical Function of I/O Elements

Inputs

- NOS control strategies. The CS is informed as to the NOS strategies the designer wishes to simulate. These include scheduling algoritms, (both network level and nodal level), file management strategies, resource allocation schemes, etc.

- Interpretations. The CS is informed as to the interpretations of the requirements primitives and control primitives. For each of these primitives, the interpretation consists of a list of configuration primitives which, when sent to the HS for simulated execution, achieve the intent of the original primitive. (this process is not unlike macro-expansion). The interpretations for the configuration primitives are similar, but stated in terms of actual simulator instructions.

- Function to Node Assignment. This is a list of hardware nodes or homogenous classes of hardware nodes that a particular software function (requirements primitive) must be constrained to execute on. The designer must have knowledge of the names of the functions as given in the SSDB to make these assignments.

Outputs

- Feedback to the designer. The designer receives feedback when the input he submits to the DIP is syntactically incorrect. The exact form of this output is an implementation consideration.

- CK. The DIP must build and update the CK as the designer establishes the inputs to the similators mimicking the target environment.

DESIGN INTERFACE PROCESSOR

INPUT

- CONFIGURATION ARCHITECTURE FROM PROGRAMMER/ MAINTAINER
- CONTROL STRATEGIES FROM PROGRAMMER/MAINTAINER
- DEFINITIONS OF CONFIGURATION PRIMITIVES IN TERMS OF EXECUTABLE SEGMENTS
- MAPPING OF REQUIREMENTS ELEMENTS TO DESIGN NODES

PROCESS

- CONDENSE INPUTS INTO FORM SUITABLE FOR STORAGE ON MASS STORAGE AND SUBSEQUENT RETRIEVAL BY HS & CS

OUTPUT

- CONDENSED FORM OF INPUTS FOR STORAGE ON CK

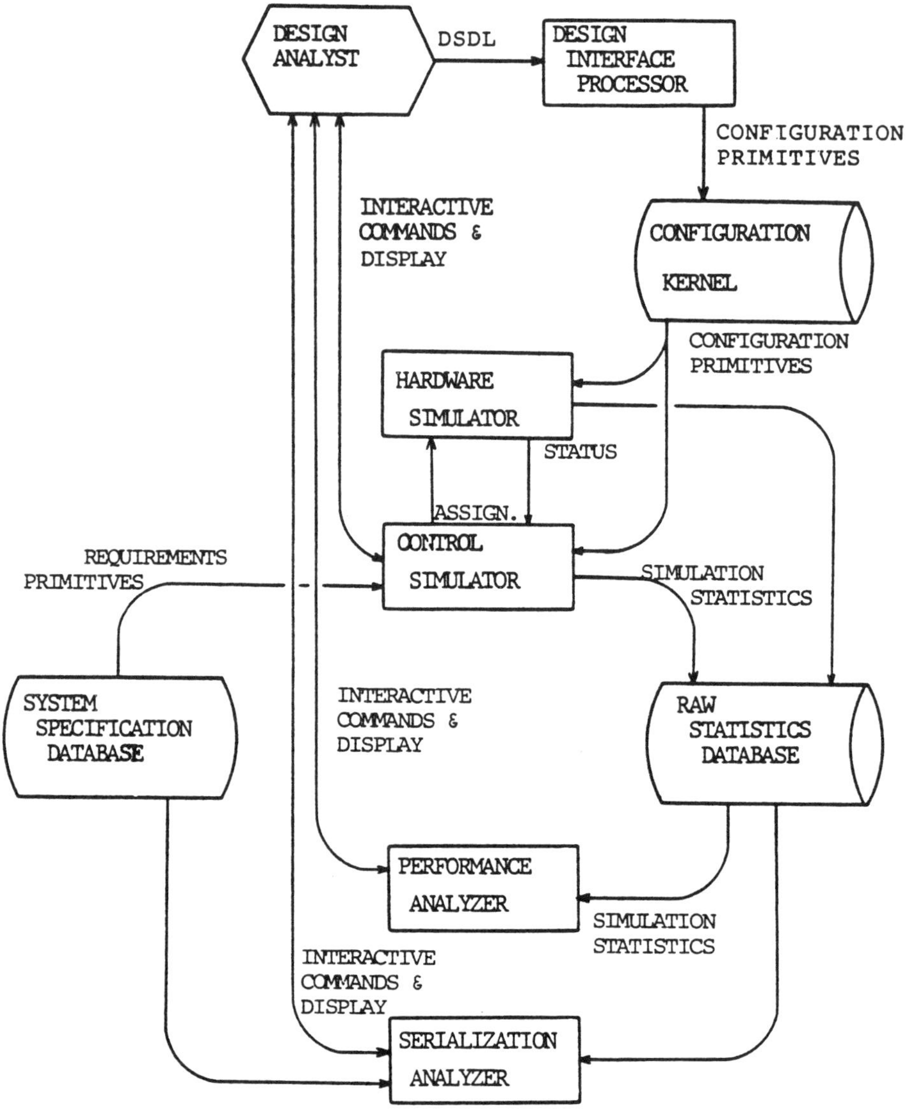

DSDL - DISTRIBUTED SYSTEM DESIGN LANGUAGE

3.2.2.1.6 CONTROL SIMULATOR

1. INTRODUCTION

The Control Simulator (CS) is designed for use in the design phase of the software lifecycle and is part of a set of four tools which provide the designer the ability to simulate his designs interactively and gather statistics about the performance of his design.

Abbreviations

CK	Configuration Kernel
CS	Control Simulator
DSSL	Design System Specification Language
HS	Hardware Simulator
NOS	Network Operating System
PA	Performance Analyzer
RSDB	Raw Statistics Database

2. FUNCTIONAL DESCRIPTION

The CS is for use in the design phase of the software lifecycle. The designer is provided with the capability to exercise his designs, both hardware and software. These designs may be tested with respect to feasibility, performance, conformity to requirements, and other measurements preferably gathered in the design phase. The CS requires as input the configuration architecture stored in the CK, the application description stored in the SSDB as DSSL primitives, and the specification of control methods to be used during the simulation. The CS provides output to the HS in the form of requriements primitves per node and to the PA in the form of raw simulation data. Since the CS has interactive operation by the designer, this provides I/O to the simulation of the application and overall simulation control.

The first function of the CS consists of interactive commands for the initiation of simulation where the simulation set-up includes reading information from the CK. An operational function of the CS includes retrieving application primitives from the SSDB and determining nodal assignment in conjunction with the configuration architecture and the proposed scheduling algoritm. The CS may also initiate control processes to compute scheduling assignments and other NOS overhead functions. The CS then passes the information to the HS for simulated execution of the primitive, the HS simulates the execution of the primitive accepts the results, updates the control information in local data structures, and finally the HS reports results of its simulation back to the CS. An ongoing function of the CS is the accumulation of raw simulation data for later analysis by the PA.

The CS is the first point in the software life cycle to test fault tolerance of the software design. Feedback is provided with respect to what the design is going to accomplish which ensures compliance to the requirements. Since requirements are input to the CS, the feedback strengthens traceability. The CS aids in optimization of resource utilization and allows the designer to evaluate the destributedness of the implementation. In designing control of data access, the simulation tests file reservation and directory implementation schemes.

There are several aspects of network control that the CS must simulate. The CS does this by having its "world" maintained by the HS as it simulates the execution of commands. The CS makes reference to this world and makes control decisions just as the eventual product will do. Some of the major aspects of network control that the CS must be provided information about in order to carry out its simulation are discussed below:

Connectivity - provides the CS with sufficient detail to define substructures which assist in accommodating a unit failure.

Resources and their Availability - A list of resources available to the system, where they are located, what entities are responsible for their control, and a list of which processes allowed access to them.

Communication strategies - Controls distributed communication strategies; e.g., broadcasting, packet-switched, message-switched, etc.

Directory Maintenance - maintenance procedures (where and when) for the distribution of directories (partitioned and distributed, single centralized copy, replication of identical copy)

Naming Conventions - provides decoupling between application and environment.

Resource Information Gathering Techniques - Methods for gathering information on resource availability and how that information is maintained (e.g., single-centralized, multiple copies, partititioned).

Function to Node Allocation Scheme (Scheduling Algorithm) - In the case that a particular software function (expressed in the SSDB) must be bound to a particular hardware node or set of nodes, the designer must specify this to the CS either in the SSDB description of the application or in the CK.

3. BRIEF DESCRIPTION OF EXISTING TOOLS EXHIBITING SIMILAR FUNCTIONALITY

For the study of executive control in the study entitled Distributed and Decentralized Control in Fully Distributed Processing Systems, Georgia Institute of Technology constructed an original simulator for the examination of different control model behavior. The simulator provides for user interaction and hardware description. While specific nodes are being simulated, the simulator supports communication between executive processes. During the simulation, the application is capable of actions such as compute, send or receive a message, loop back to a previous command a specific number of times, or terminate.

Another simulator available is ISPS developed by Carnegie-Mellon University. ISPS describes the interface between and behavior of abstract hardware units. The interface or external structure of the abstract hardware units relates to the number and types of information carriers for storage and transmission between the units. The behavior of the abstract hardware units is defined by procedures specifying the sequence of control and data operations in the machine.

4. SUMMARY OF IMPROVEMENTS

A. Functional Improvements (new capabilities)

The CS will use as its "load" or application the actual description of that application defined during the requirements phase, expressed in DSSL, and stored on the SSDB by the requirements analyst. This is a functional improvement in the sense that the load will not be "described" for simulation in terms of its characteristics, but will actually be specified by the designer and simulated on the CS and HS to provide a more realistic simulation. Moreover, each function within the requirements specification will have associated with it a time interval, t, determined by the requirements analyst specifying the time in which the function must be completed in order to meet real-time constraints. Likewise, each configuration primitive will have associated with it a t, entered by the designer, denoting the time required to execute that primitive on the proposed hardware. The CS then assigns specific functions to specific nodes and sends cumulative timing data to the RSDB for analysis by the PA.

The control simulator should also allow the designer the ability to simulate hardware failures and to observe the subsequent performance of the simulated system. The designer can interactively request that a specific hardware fault be simulated and that the CS should reconfigure the system to reflect the hardware fault. The scheduling algoritom will then attempt to schedule around the failed unit and the designer can observe the fault tolerant properties of his proposed network operating system. This type of simulation is particularly important to the development of C I applications, as extremely high fault tolerance is usually required.

Another functional improvement to the CS is the ability to simulate interprocessor communications. This ability is limited in existing simulators, where time delays are used only to simulate the sending of a message over a communication link. The CS assembles a message and places it in a "to be sent" queue, the HS "executes" the instruction (add to queue), and the time delay associated with the operation (the t as entered by the designer) is accumulated for analysis. Interprocessor communication is explicitly simulated and the designer is afforded the opportunity to test various software communication schemes and queuing strategies.

B. Existing Desirable Capabilities

Several features possessed by the tools mentioned above and others need to be incorporated into the CS, a list of the most important of these features is presented below.

- Timing Analysis - This is the estimation of the time required to perform specific functions. C I applications often impose real-time constraints on systems and extensive timing analysis is needed to evaluate proposed designs.

- Load Analysis - Load analysis is the measurement of software structure traffic throughout the simulation. Some examples of structures requiring analysis are message queues at each node, ready task queues at each node, task set size (this is an indication of page set size), and service request pending queues for system wide resources.

- File Allocation Simulation - The file system manager proposed for implementation by the designer is simulated by this feature. The availability status of the total file set is monitored through the simulation. This information helps the designer conclude whether his file management strategy is efficient enough to meet space requirements while at the same time reducing wait times for processes requesting file space. Again, this design consideration, which falls into the more general category of resource allocation strategies, is of particular importance to the C I application. The CS collects this information by logging the times that processes remain on the queues designated as "waiting-for-file allocation."

C. Elimination or Reduction of Existing Capabilities no Longer Needed

Because of the existence of the application description in the SSDB, there is no need for the simulator to require that a description of the load be placed on the running system. The description of the application describes this load implicitly to the CS and HS and eliminates the need for the designer to specify characteristics about the user community such as type of work being requested, ratio of computation to I/O, or resource requirements.

5. TOOL SPECIFICATION

A. Identification of I/O Elements

The designer initiates the CS using interactive commands. The primitive form of the application description, originally expressed in DSSL, is input from the SSDB as application functions. The Configuration Architecture, describing the Hardware configuration, is input from the CK and used by the CS to resolve the mapping of software functions to hardware nodes. Using the various control strategies entered earlier by the designer, the CS provides requirements primitives with their associated hardware nodes to the HS. When the HS has simulated the execution of a specific requirements primitive on its associated node, it reports the results to the CS to trigger further simulation. The CS interactively supplies messages to the designer requesting information to be input to the simulation. Raw simulation data is output to the RSDB for further processing by the PA.

B. Form of I/O Elements

Input - Application primitives from the SSDB; configuration architecture description from the CK; control strategies as established by the designer; results of the simulation of requirements primitives per node from the HS; interactive input required from the designer.

Output - Requirements Primitives per node to the HS; Simulated application output and requests for input to the designer; Raw simulation data to the PA.

C. Logical function of I/O Elements

The proposed application, expressed in DSSL primitives is stored in the SSDB for input to the CS. In order to determine scheduling assignments and communicate requests to the HS, the CS utilizes the Configuration Architecture description of the processors, communication links, and their respective interface characteristics, as well as the control strategies the designer wishes to simulate. Upon determination of these assignments, the CS transmits the requirements primitive with its respective nodal assignment to the HS for execution simulation. When the HS completes it simulation, it reports the results to the CS allowing the update of its internal data structures with the simulation results and status.

The interaction with the designer provides basic I/O required by the simulation execution and intermediate and final results of the simulation. Results, raw statistics, are output to the RSDB for further processing by the PA to provide the designer with a formatted analysis of the proposed design simulation.

CONTROL SIMULATOR

INPUT

APPLICATION PRIMITIVES - PROVIDES FUNCTIONAL BREAKDOWN OF APPLICATION

CONFIGURATION ARCHITECTURE - PROVIDES INFORMATION FOR ASSIGNMENT OF APPLICATION FUNCTIONS TO CONFIGURATION CAPABILITIES FOR ACCOMPLISHMENT

DESIGNER INTERACTION - PROVIDES CONTROLLING INSTRUCTIONS AND SIMULATES INPUTS NEEDED BY APPLICATION

HS RESULTS - KEEPS CS ABREAST OF SIMULATION PROGRESS

PROCESS

READ SET-UP INFO. FROM CK: NAMELY CONTROL METHODS, CONFIGURATION ARCHITECTURE

RETRIEVE APPLICATION PRIMITIVES FROM SSDB ONE AT A TIME, MAKE NODE ASSIGNMENTS

INITIATE CONTROL PROCESSES WHEN NECESSARY

PASS INFORMATION TO HS FOR SIMULATION OF EXECUTION OF PRIMITIVE

ACCUMULATE RAW SIMULATION DATA FOR LATER ANALYSIS BY PA

OUTPUT

INSTRUCTIONS TO HS - PROVIDES REQUIREMENT PRIMITIVES TO BE SIMULATED AND THE NODAL ASSIGNMENT FOR THE SIMULATION

DESIGNER INTERACTION - RETURNS SIMULATED APPLICATION OUTPUT, PROVIDES PROMPTS FOR NEEDED APPLICATION INPUTS, PROVIDES MESSAGES ABOUT SIMULATION PROGRESS

RAW SIMULATION DATA - PROVIDES COMPLETE STATISTICS ABOUT SIMULATION TO THE PA FOR ANALYSIS

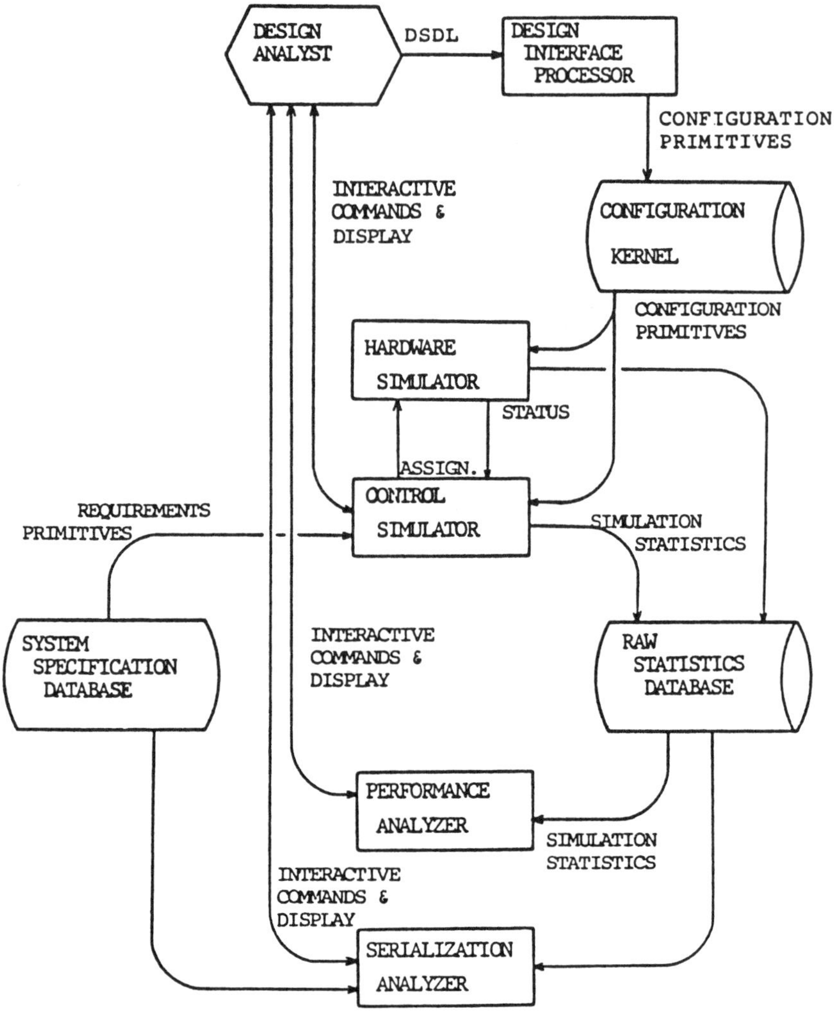

DSDL - DISTRIBUTED SYSTEM DESIGN LANGUAGE

3.2.2.1.7 HARDWARE SIMULATOR

1. INTRODUCTION

The Hardware Simulator is designed for use within the design phase of the software lifecycle. It simulates the operation of processing nodes using descriptions previously entered by the design analyst. The application requirements expressed during the requirements phase are assigned to processing nodes by the Control Simulator. The subsequent operation of particular processing nodes is simulated by the Hardware Simulator under the direction of the Control Simulator. Hardware Simulator output is provided the Control Simulator and the Performance Analyzer.

List of Abbreviations include:

HS	Hardware Simulator
CS	Control Simulator
PA	Performance Analyzer
CK	Configuration Kernel
DIP	Design Interface Processor
SSDB	System Specification Database
ISSE	Integrated System Support Environment

2. FUNCTIONAL SUMMARY

The HS simulates the execution of an application requirement assigned to it by the CS. Its simulation uses the processing node description previously entered by the design analyst into the CK. Simulation results are provided the CS and the PA.

The design analyst may want to examine more than one alternative at a particular processing node. A separate description for each alternative must be placed in the CK by the design analyst. Subsequent simulations will use these previously entered alternatives one at a time.

The level of analysis produced by the HS cannot exceed the level of detail contained in the CK. That level of detail in the CK was previously established by the design analyst himself when he entered processing node descriptions by way of the DIP. Different processing nodes can be described at different levels of detail within the same simulation.

The HS is used by the CS to characterize the processing paths within a specific hardware architecture. An analysis of each node along a processing path is performed one node at a time by the HS. Progress along each path is directed by the CS working interactively with the design analyst.

Dependent upon the application, a processing node may perform logical or arithmetic operations on a specific data structure. The HS obtains an initial data structure from the interaction between the design analyst and the CS. In effect, the CS directs the initial data structure from the design analyst to the appropriate simulation of a particular processing node. When the HS completes its simulation of that particular processing node, the final data structure is passed to the CS for appropriate referral to either the next processing node simulation or the design analyst.

The HS addresses several software quality criteria. The CS establishes a processing thread from the requirements specifications to individual simulations performed by the HS. Consistency is established through the mapping of requirements specifications from the SSDB into the processing node descriptions maintained on the CK. This mapping is implemented by the CS as it directs the operation of the HS. Modularity is implemented through the operational breakdown between the HS and the CS. The modules within the HS are devoted to the operational simulation of specific processing nodes. Each module is functionally cohesive. Because of the structure of the HS, it exhibits expandability. New processing functions can be added to the description of any processing node. Control of access is exhibited by the HS since it alone can use processing node descriptions to simulate hardware operation. Commonality is present since the HS is part of the ISSE and can be accessed by any other tool within it.

The HS does not specifically address distributed processing. Such considerations are addressed by tools which access and use the HS, e.g., the CS and the PA. Specific distributed architectures are addressed within the CS by its assignment of application requirements primitives to specific processing nodes as well as its simulation of control strategies. The subsequent simulation of these processing nodes is done by the HS.

3. BRIEF DESCRIPTION OF EXISTING TOOLS EXHIBITING SIMILAR FUNCTIONALITY

A system called ISPS developed at Carnegie-Mellon University exhibits the closest similarity to the HS. It is a computer description language which can be used for automated design, software development, hardware debugging, and automatic generation of machine relative software. The aim of ISPS is to describe computers and other digital systems. ISPS describes the interface and behavior of abstract hardware units.

Within an ISSE the HS simulates the behavior or processing nodes using descriptions previously entered into the CK by the design analyst. The interface between processing nodes is addressed by the CS. Consequently, the ISPS couples two functions together that are separated in the ISSE. However, ISPS does keep these two functions within the same lifecycle phase, i.e., the design phase. For use within an ISSE, parts of ISPS would have to be functionally separated which is equivalent to vertical decoupling within the design phase. Furthermore, the ISSE places hardware descriptions within the CK for use by a variety of tools, e.g., the HS and the DIP. The CK provides a special purpose database to the ISSE.

4. SUMMARY OF IMPROVEMENTS

A. Functional Improvements (new capabilities)

The HS must be able to simulate the operation of a particular processing node from the nodal description maintained in the CK. The CS initiates the operation of the HS by providing information concerning what processing node needs to be simulated and what operations that node must perform. Based upon the information supplied by the CS, the HS retrieves the appropriate nodal description from the CK and starts the processing node simulation. The HS assumes control of the simulation once it is initiated. When the simulation of a single action is complete, the HS informs the CS while reporting the simulation statistics to the PA. In effect, the CS and HS operate as a pair. The CS initiates the HS which, in turn, restarts the CS when the processing node description is complete. The advantages of such an architecture are twofold. First, the HS does not have to concern itself with mapping specific applications requirements to particular processing nodes. Second, the CS does not have to concern itself with the hardware simulation of a particular processing node once a specific applications requirement has been assigned to it. The subsequent construction of both the HS and the CS has been simplified.

B. Existing Desirable Capabilities

The ISPS system currently at Carnegie-Mellon University has some of the attributes mentioned in the HS but it also contains attributes of the CS. These need to be separated for use within the ISSE. The end result of the separation process would be two versions of the ISPS which parallels the utility of the HS and CS respectively. Provided ISPS can be subdivided and transported, its properties could prove valuable to the HS and CS.

C. Elimination or Reduction of Existing Capabilities no Longer Needed

The capabilities of systems like ISPS at Carnegie Mellon University need to be constrained to single life cycle phases, i.e., the design phase. In addition, the functions performed need to be decoupled into modularly cohesive tools within the ISSE, i.e., the CS and the HS.

5. TOOL SPECIFICATION

A. Identification of I/O Elements

The capability for input to the HS by the design analyst is available from two different directions. However, both are indirect. One is through the DIP by way of the CK while the other is through the CS. Since the CS offers interactive capability to the design analyst, input from the CS to the HS would probably have a higher usage level. Various hardware descriptions are entered into the CK for subsequent use by the HS. Use by the HS is under the initiation control of the CS.

The capability for output from the HS is available through the PA or the CS. Output is initiated by the HS itself.

B. Form of I/O Functions

The HS uses hardware descriptions of specific operating nodes previously entered into the CK by the design analyst. These hardware descriptions are in terms of Register Transfer Machine representations.

The CS provides information to the HS in terms of application requirements primitives to be satisfied at a particular operating node. These requirements primitives are mapped into functionally cohesive representations within the Register Transfer Machine of the pertinent operating node.

As output, the HS produces two types of information. First, it indicates to the CS that its simulation of a particular operating node is complete. Second, it produces raw statistical data generated during simulation for the PA.

C. Logical Function of I/O Elements

The hardware descriptions available to the CK for access by the HS serve as the source for subsequent Register Transfer Machine representations. The application requirements primitives to be satisfied at a particular operating node is provided by the CS. It serves as a logical mapping of application requirements to particular processing nodes.

The output provided the PA by the HS is statistical in nature. These statistics are subsequently used by the PA to generate performance characteristics. The output provided the CS by the HS is a flag indicating completion of the simulation.

HARDWARE SIMULATOR

INPUT

REQUIREMENTS PRIMITIVES - NODE ASSIGNMENT ALREADY RESOLVED BY CONTROL SIMULATOR

MAPPING OF REQUIREMENT PRIMITIVES TO THE CONFIGURATION PRIMITIVES OF THEIR RESPECTIVE NODES

DEFINITIONS OF CONFIGURATION PRIMITIVES WITH ASSOC. CHARACTERISTICS I.E. TIME SPACE, ETC.

ex. ISPS

PROCESS

MAINTAIN INTERNAL DATA STRUCTURES AS REQUIRED BY DEFINITIONS OF CONFIGURATION PRIMITIVES

RECEIVE REQUIREMENTS PRIMITIVES ROUTED BY CONTROL SIMULATOR, CARRY OUT THEIR SIMULATION IN ACCORDANCE WITH NODAL ASSIGNMENT

ACCUMULATE STATISTICS DURING SIMULATION, I.E. TIME, SPACE, QUEUE LENGTHS, ETC.

RETURN REPORTS TO CONTROL SIMULATOR

ex. ISPS

OUTPUT

RAW SIMULATION STATISTICS - STORED IN DATA BASE FOR USE BY PERFORMANCE ANALYZER

CONTROL REPORTS TO CONTROL SIMULATOR TO PROMPT PROGRESSION OF SIMULATION

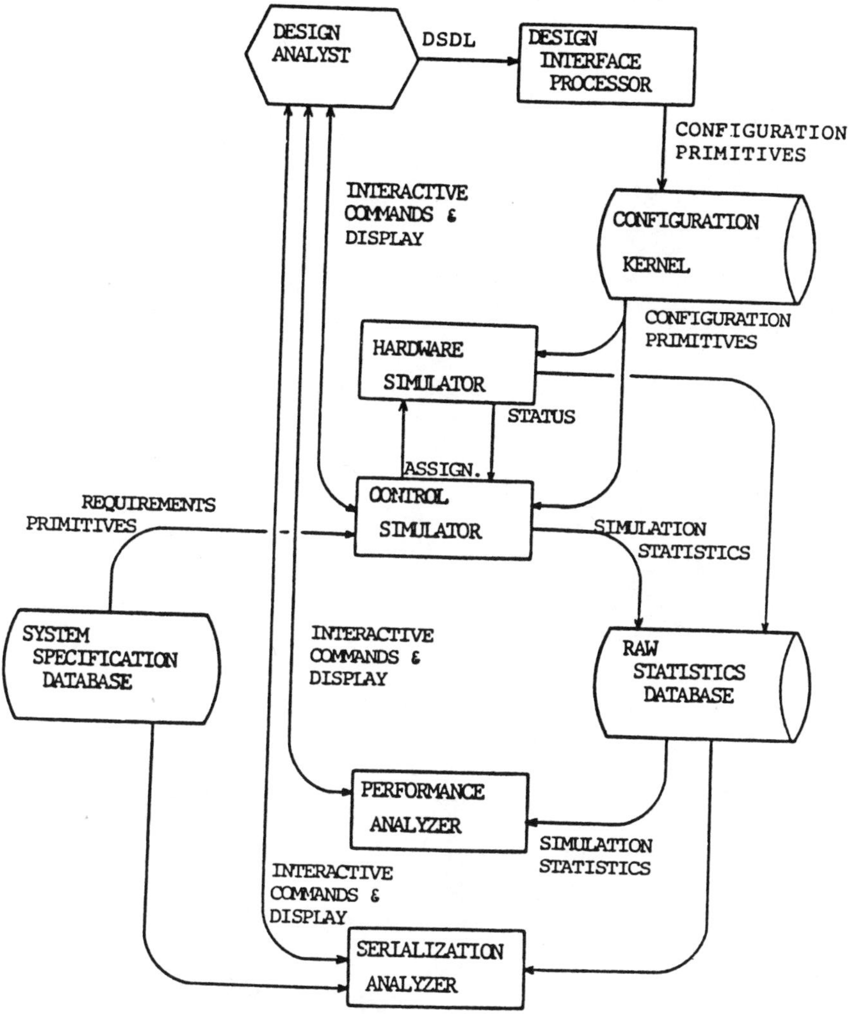

DSDL - DISTRIBUTED SYSTEM DESIGN LANGUAGE

3.2.2.1.8 PERFORMANCE ANALYZER

1. INTRODUCTION

The Performance Analyzer is designed for use in the design phase of the software lifecycle. It consolidates the simulation data produced by the Control and Hardware Simulators and presents its consolidation to the design analyst. The operation of the Performance Analyzer is invoked by the design analyst. Output from the Control and Hardware Simulators is temporarily stored in a Raw Statistics Database within the Integrated System Support Environment for subsequent use by the Performance Analyzer.

List of abbreviations include:

PA	Performance Analyzer
CS	Control Simulator
HS	Hardware Simulator
RSDB	Raw Statistics Database
ISSE	Integrated System Support Environment
SSDB	System Specification Database
CK	Configuration Kernel
SA	Serialization Analyzer

2. FUNCTIONAL SUMMARY

The PA consolidates simulation data produced by the CS and HS for the design analyst. The raw simulation data produced by the CS and HS is stored in the RSDB for subsequent use by the PA. That subsequent use is triggered by the design analyst when he initiates the PA. Within the architecture of an ISSE, the PA directly uses data produced by the CS and HS to consolidate a presentation for the design analyst. However, to accomplish such an objective, the PA must have indirect access to data stored in the SSDB and CK which is provided by the CS and HS respectively. The CS maps the requirements specifications contained in the SSDB onto processing nodes to be simulated by the HS. The HS maps the requirements specificatons assigned by the CS into particular processing node descriptions contained in the CK. The timing constraints that apply to each processing node are also contained in the CK. As the CS and HS perform, their simulation statistics are entered into RSDB for subsequent retrieval and use by the PA. In summary, the operations performed by the PA, CS, and HS complement one another. In addition, they have coupled their operation to the exchange of information through three databases within ISSE, i.e., the SSDB, CK, and RSDB.

Functionally, the PA consolidates the mapped application requirements of the CS with the nodal simulations of the HS. Information used in that consolidation is available through the RSDB. The design analyst initiates operation of the PA. Once initiated, the PA retrieves the appropriate information from the RSDBand consolidates it. The architecture of an application is supplied through information supplied by the CS. That architecture had its origin in the applications requirements mapping performed by the CS when a particular architecture was examined by the design analyst. Based upon that particular architecture, individual nodes were simulated by the HS and their simulation statistics entered into the RSDB. The pertinent architecture was entered into the RSDB by the CS. Time constraint information concerning the operation of specific nodes was previously entered by the design analyst into the CK. Those constraints were accessed by the HS on node-by-node basis and entered into the RSDB as specific nodes were simulated. Such time constraints are included in the consolidated report produced by the PA.

The PA addresses several software quality criteria. It enhances traceability by associating the nodal architecture expressed by the CS with the specific nodal operating characteristics produced by the HS. Once established, this traceability carries into the subsequent lifecycle phases. The PA contributes to consistency between the requirements and design phases. The translation of applications requirements into requirements per node into specific nodal simulations into performance analysis is closely monitored by the PA. Distributedness is enhanced by the PA since it enables various logical and geographic architectures to be studied. How well distributedness is applied to an application is a function of the design analyst.

The PA addresses distributed processing through the architectures it can analyze. The timing constraints of each particular architecture constructed by the PA are consolidated from information generated by the HS. Various alternatives for logical as well as geographic separation can be examined by the PA. Each alternative depends upon the expertise of the design analyst since the information required must be made available through the CS and HS. That particular information has to be entered by the design analyst prior to the initiation of the PA.

3. BRIEF DESCRIPTION OF EXISTING TOOLS EXHIBITING SIMILAR FUNCTIONALITY

A system called PAWS which stands for Performance Analyst's Workbench System is currently being marketed by Information Research Associates and provides some of the desired functionality. Designed as a stand-alone product, PAWS offers a high level model description language which can represent a wide variety of computer system features. As PAWS operates, performance statistics are generated for the design analyst. The design analyst can reapply PAWS to any number of subsequent changes in the model. The consolidation of performance statistics is very similar to the consolidation performed by the PA.

System Development Corporation maintains a configuration testbed which uses an architecture description language exhibiting some of the functionality characteristic of the PA. The language provides the design analyst with capability to describe arbitrary distributed architectures. Based upon the description, an experiment is constructed to execute, monitor, and evaluate the proposed architecture. Such activity within the experiment is very similar to the operation of the PA.

A variety of languages have been developed to address the problem of simulation. Several of these languages offer some of the functional characteristics associated with the PA. The GPSS or General Purpose Simulation System developed by IBM represents the relationship such languages have to the functional characteristics of the PA. While the PA is application-driven, the GPSS is process driven. Within a process, discrete events occur and move through the architecture simulated by GPSS. Such operation is roughly equivalent to an application requirement moving through the CS being simulated on the HS, and consolidated by the PA. To approximate a particular application by a process to drive a GPSS simulation is sometimes difficult for a design analyst. In effect, the expertise of the design analyst determines the success of his effort to use GPSS for the simulation of a particular application.

4. SUMMARY OF IMPROVEMENTS

A. Functional Improvements (new capabilities)

The PA has been decoupled from two functions performed elsewhere within theISSE. As a consequence its structure has been simplified and its operation made more straightforward. It operates on information previously generated and stored by the CS and HS in the RSDB. It is initiated by the design analyst and consolidates the information provided by the RSDB in an integrated output for the design analyst. Architectural information concerning an application is supplied by the CS. Such information had its origin in the requirements phase when a list of application requirements was compiled by the requirements analyst. The subsequent transformation of those application requirements into specific nodes within a particular architecture by the CS moved them into the design phase. Such a transformation clearly delineates the difference between activity within the requirements phase from activity within the design phase. Since the PA obtains the benefit of such information generated by the CS without having to generate it, the structure of the PA is simplified. In like manner, the subsequent simulation of each specific node by the HS also simplifies the PA. Once the CS and HS have completed their operations within a particular architecture, the task remaining for the PA to perform involves the consolidation of information. The consolidation works from the bottom up and constructs an integrated picture of the time constraints and processing operations occurring throughout a particular application architecture. How far down the consolidation starts is a function of how much detail has been previously entered by the design analyst. Consequently, the detail contained within a particular consolidation never exceeds the detail entered by the design analyst. Such a capability is particularly important to the implementation of top-down design.

B. Existing Desirable Capabilities

Previous examples mentioned in the section concerning existing tools possess several desirable characteristics. Perhaps the most desirable is their delineation of the design phase from the requirements phase. However, such a delineation depends greatly upon the computer languages used to implement such tools. The PAWS product marketed by Information Research Associates is based upon FORTRAN. The System Development Corporation architecture description language is based upon a VAX 11/780 operating system and isits own language. GPSS provided by IBM is strongly proprietary and depends uponan IBM environment to operate. In each instance the language used in the construction of the tool may or may not support the delineation between the requirements and design phases. A consistent decoupling between these phases must be implemented within the framework of an ISSE. The efforts mentioned above have only begun this decoupling process. Their beginnings have been most desirable but their implementations need to be advanced. One such advancement would be the use of a single language, e.g., Ada.

Just as important as decoupling activities between phases is the ability to decouple activities within a particular phase. Such capability is very important to the construction of an ISSE. The separation of activities between the CS, HS, and PA was proposed with such an objective in mind. Few existing products offer such capability within the design phase.

C. Elimination or Reduction of Existing Capabilities no Longer Needed

Existing products need to be tightly constrained within the lifecycle phase most pertinent to their operation. This would involve reducing some of the capability claimed within the marketplace. However, the subsequent use of such scaled-down tools would be greatly simplified. The justification for such a reduction rests with the implementation of an ISSE.

5. TOOL SPECIFICATION

A. Identification of I/O Elements

Input to the PA by the design analyst depends upon what he wants to do. If he wants to initiate the PA, his input is direct. However, if he wants to generate architectural information for subsequent use by the PA, hisinput is indirect and by way of the CS. If he wants to generate nodal operating descriptions, the input is via the CK and HS. In both instances of generating either architectural information or nodal operating descriptions, the information is entered into the RSDB for subsequent access and use by the PA.

Output from the PA is undirectional. Information provided by the HS and CS is consolidated and presented to the design analyst. Aside from the initiation of the PA, the design analyst does not interact with the PA.

B. Form of I/O Elements

Input from the design analyst to initiate the PA is in the form of a START command. Input from the CS is in the form of an applications requirements mapping to a specific architecture. Input from the HS is in the form of nodal hardware descriptions and time constraints. Input from the RSDB is in the form of the CS information, the HS information, and the linkages between the two.

Output to the design analyst is in the form of a tabular consolidation of information provided by the CS and the HS. The timing information provided in the consolidated report is also transmitted to the SA.

C. Logical Function of I/O Elements

Input from the HS serves as a source for Register Transfer Machine representations and time constraints for the subsequent consolidation by the PA. Input from the CS serves as a source of information concerning applications requirements to be met at each node within a specific architecture. Input from the RSDB links the CS and HS inputs together.

Output to the design analyst serves as a summary of the performance to be expected from a particular architecture under consideration. Additionally, the time constraint information serves as a source of information for the SA.

PERFORMANCE ANALYZER

INPUT

RAW STATISTICS. SIMULATION DATA ACCUMULATED BY HS & CS

INITIATION REQUEST BY DESIGNER DESIGNATING DATA TO BE ANALYZED AND SPECIFYING RESTRICTIONS IF ANY ON ANALYSIS TO BE PERFORMED

ex: PAWS internal data accumulated

PROCESS

CONSOLIDATE DATA FROM BOTH HS & CS; COMBINING AS NECESSARY TO PROVIDE STATISTICS ON AN APPLICATION FUNCTION LEVEL

CORRELATE DATA FROM RELATED FUNCTIONS OR OCCURRENCES

COLLATE TIME ORDER ACCOMPLISHMENT OF SIMULATED FUNCTIONS

EXTRACT PERTINENT DETAILS IN RESPONSE TO REQUEST

ex. PAWS

OUTPUT

DISPLAY OF SIMULATION RESULTS AS GLEANED BY ANALYSIS OF STATISTICS ACCUMULATED BY HS & CS

ex. PAWS OUTPUT, GPSS OUTPUT

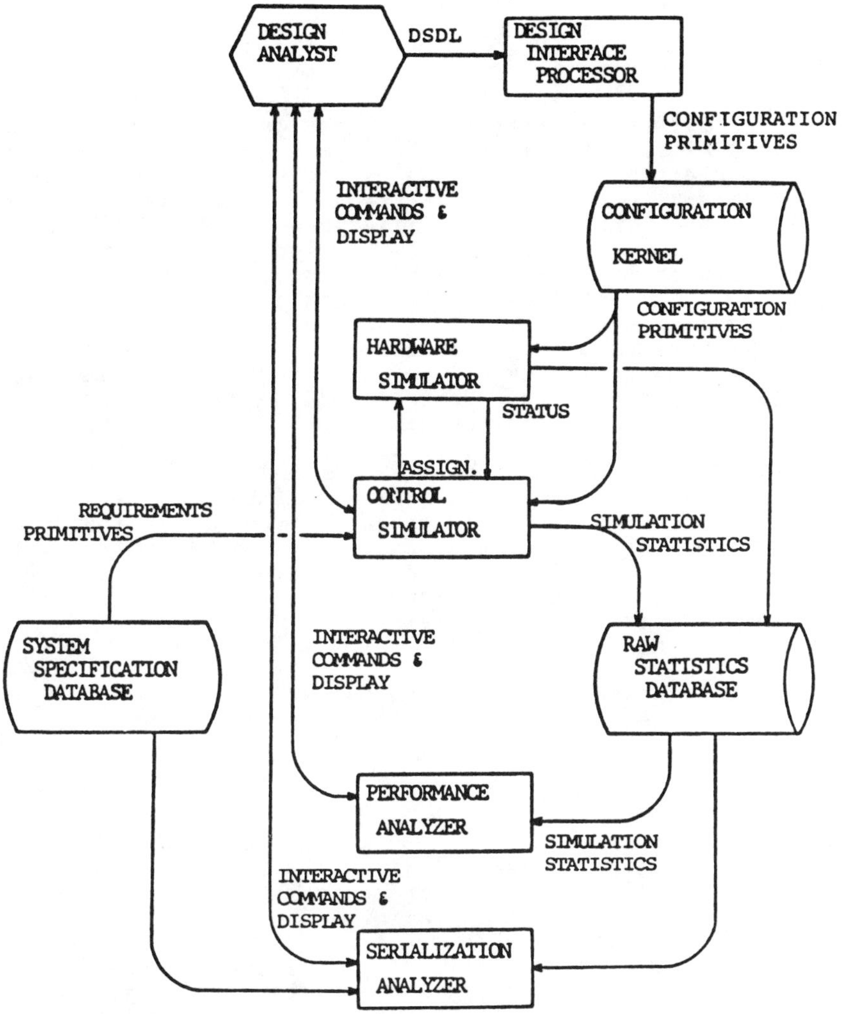

DSDL - DISTRIBUTED SYSTEM DESIGN LANGUAGE

3.2.2.1.9 SERIALIZATION ANALYZER

1. INTRODUCTION

The Serialization Analyzer is designed for use in the design phase of the software lifecycle. It consolidates the simulation data produced by the Control and Hardware Simulators with the functional requirements data produced during the requirements lifecycle phase. The consolidation is presented to the design analyst and addresses whether the functional requirements time constraints are satisfied by a particular architecture proposed by the design analyst and simulated by the Control and Hardware Simulators. Operation of the Serialization Analyzer is invoked by the design analyst. Simulation data from the Control and Hardware Simulators is made available to the Serialization Analyzer through storage in the Raw Statistics Database of the Integrated System Support Environment. Functional requirements time constraints are made available to the Serialization Analyzer through storage in the System Specification Database of the Integrated System Support Environment. Subsequent discussion of the Serialization Analyzer will use the following abbreviations:

SA	Serialization Analyzer
CS	Control Simulator
HS	Hardware Simulator
RSDB	Raw Statistics Database
ISSE	Integrated System Support Environment
SSDB	System Specification Database

2. FUNCTIONAL SUMMARY

The SA consolidates the simulation data produced during the design phase with functional requirements data produced during the requirements phase. The design analyst uses the SA consolidation to determine if functional requirements time constraints have been satisfied by a proposed architecture. Of course that proposed architecture was previously entered by the design analyst through interaction with the CS. The functional requirements generated during the requirements phase were accessed by the CS and mapped against the nodal architecture proposed by the systems analyst. Using the subsequent nodal mapping, the CS initiated a series of nodal simulations through the HS. As the HS completed its simulation of a particular node, that node's description and operating characteristics were entered into the RSDB. The proposed nodal architecture was also entered into the RSDB by the CS. Subsequent operation of the SA depends upon both sources of information being available within the RSDB. Included in the operating characteristics of each nodal simulation are the operating time constraints applicable to that node. Operation of the SA also requires access to the functional requirements of the subject application already stored in the SSDB. Included in the functional requirements descriptions are the required timing constraints which must be satisfied for those functions. The consolidation process which takes place within the SA determines if the functional requirements time constraints are satisfied by the proposed nodal architecture and the operating characteristics of its nodes. To accomplish this consolidation the SA depends upon the presence of two databases within the ISSE, i.e., the RSDB and SSDB. Their presence decouples the SA from the requirements phase and the operation of either the CS, HS, or PA.

Functionally, the SA consolidates information from the CS, HS, and SSDB to determine if functional requirements time constraints have been met by a proposed architecture. The information from the CS and HS has been previously entered into the RSDB. Consequently, the SA actually consolidates information from the RSDB and SSDB. From a functional standpoint, the SA implements a retrieval from the RSDB and a retrieval from the SSDB. The structure within the SSDB links a particular application to specific functionalrequirements which must be satisfied. The structure within the RSDB links each specific functional requirement to a nodal architecture with each node in that architecture linked to its operational simulation. The consolidation of information between the SSDB and RSDB consists of a comparison between the functional requirements time constraints and the simulated operating characteristics of a proposed architecture. Once the consolidation has been accomplished, the SA exhibits its results to the design analyst and indicates the completion of its analysis. The SA is initiated by the design analyst and can be used as often as needed. The level of detail produced by the SA is constrained to the detail contained in the SSDB and RSDB.

The SA addresses several software criteria when it is applied within the design phase. The traceability of the final product is enhanced since the functional requirments expressed by the requirements analyst are mapped by the design analyst into the RSDB via the CS and HS. The comparison of time constraints within the SA relies upon the traceability of proposed architecture to initial requirements. Independence with a final product is enhanced since the SA requires the explicit delineation between functional requirements satisifed by hardware and functional requirements satisfied by software. This delineation between hardware and software is entered into the RSDB before the SA is initiated. Compliance of the final product is enhanced since each functional requirement for a particular application must be mapped into a proposed architecture which satisfies each requirement. The satisfaction is verified by the SA. Distributedness is enhanced within the final product since the SA requires decisions concerning distribution of control and interconnect architectures before it can be initiated.

The SA addresses distributed processing through the proposed architectures it can examine. The nodal architecture suggested by the CS and simulated by the HS is verified by the SA from the standpoint of hardware and the control of that hardware. Specific architectural components with timing or control problems are isolated by the SA.

3. BRIEF DESCRIPTION OF EXISTING TOOLS EXHIBITING SIMILAR FUNCTIONALITY

The SA is a tool unique to distributed processing applications. Its position within the design phase of an ISSE is a new development. No tools exhibitingits unique characteristics are currently available within the marketplace.

4. SUMMARY OF IMPROVEMENTS

A. Functional Improvements (new capabilities)

No tools having the characteristics of the SA are currently available within the marketplace. The functionality provided by the S is a new development with new capabilities. The SA consolidates the simulation data produced during the design phase with functional requirements data produced during the requirements phase. Such a consolidation is used by the design analyst to determine if the functional requirements time constraints have been satisfied by a proposed architecture. Specific architectural components with timing or control problems can be isolated by the SA. Various architectural alternatives can be examined by the design analyst through repetitive use of the CS, HS, and SA.

B. Existing Desirable Capabilities

No tools having the characteristics o f the SA are currently available within the marketplace.

C. Elimination or Reduction of Existing Capabilities no Longer Needed

No tools having the characteristics of the SA are currently available within the marketplace.

5. TOOL SPECIFICATION

A. Identification of I/O Element

Input to the SA by the design analyst is exercised when the SA is initiated. In addition to a start command, information concerning files within the RSDB and SSDB must be submitted by the design analyst. The information about the RSDB is an indirect reference to previous runs by the CS and HS. Information about the SSDB is an indirect reference to previous runs of tools within the requirements phase.

Output from the SA is a consolidation of simulation data produced by the CS and HS with the functional requirements produced during the requirements phase. Aside from its initiation, the SA does not offer interactive capability to the design analyst.

B. Form of I/O Elements

Input from the SSDB is generated from a database retrieval linking a required application to its functional requirements. Input from the RSDB is generated from a database retrieval linking the functional requirements of a particular application to a proposed nodal architecture including operational descriptions and simulations of each node.

Output from the SA is a tabular presentation tailored to the needs of a design analyst. Specific architectural components with timing or control problems are highlighted.

C. Logical Function of I/O Elements

Input from the SSDB represents the functional requirements which must be satisfied for a particular application. Input from the RSDB represents a proposed architecture which is thought to meet or exceed the necessary requirements. The SA verifies whether those necessary requirements have been met or exceeded. Output from the SA indicates the problem areas within the proposed architecture to the design analyst.

SERIALIZATION ANALYZER

INPUT

RAW STATISTICS - FROM SIMULATIONS CARRIED OUT BY HARDWARE AND CONTROL SIMULATORS INCLUDING TIMING AND ORDER OF EXECUTION CARRIED OUT

REQUIREMENTS PRIMITIVES FROM SSDB INCLUDING ANY REQUIRED ORDERING OF EVENTS

INITIATION REQUESTS FROM DESIGNER SPECIFYING WHAT DATA TO ANALYZE AND DISPLAY INFORMATION DESIRED

PROCESS

CORRELATE SERIALIZATION OCCURRING IN SIMULATION VERSUS ALLOWED BY REQUIREMENTS

CONSOLIDATE STATISTICS IN RSDB;I.E. CALCULATE TOTAL TIMES PER APPLICATION FUNCTION FOR COMPARISON TO REQUIREMENTS

OUTPUT

DISPLAY OF REQUESTED INFORMATION GLEANED FROM DATA-BASES AND RESULTING FROM ANALYSIS OF DATA

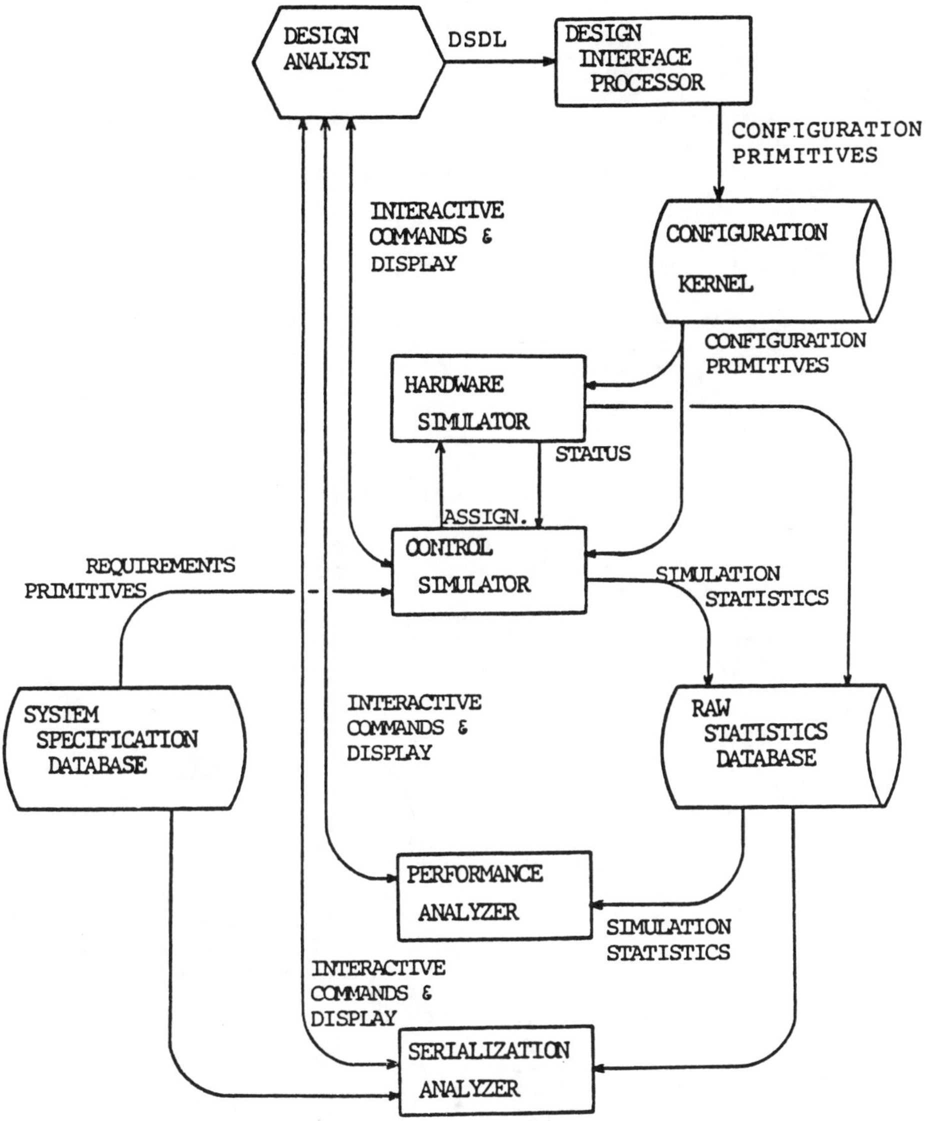

DSDL - DISTRIBUTED SYSTEM DESIGN LANGUAGE

3.2.2.1.10 CONCURRENCY CHECKER

1. INTRODUCTION

The Concurrency Checker is designed for use both in the design and coding phases of the software lifecycle. This tool assists the designer in validation of the concurrent constructs of the design.

List of Abbreviations:

C^3	Communications, Command, Control
CC	Concurrency Checker
DBMS	Database Management System
ISSE	Integrated Systems Support Environment
PDL	Program Design Language

2. FUNCTIONAL SUMMARY

Since the CC is for use in both the design and coding phases, designers and coders alike may use the tool at different times. This is made possible because the tool is to accept either a pseudo-code or one of several source languages. The tool is invoked by the user and directed to process pseudo-code or source code from files controlled by the DBMS of the ISSE. Its output is feedback to the user in the form of listings and therefore has no direct interaction with other tools of the ISSE.

Several distinct and separate functions exist within the tool itself. The initial function of the CC is to parse the constructs of the input language (again--either source or pseudo-code). This input language must support concurrency constructs required for distributed processing applications. After parsing, the CC must build state tables for each module of the program as well as a systems level state table. In the module state table, each state is defined by a set of module interactions that can occur next. Any one of the possible module interactions causes movement to the module's next state. A module can also go into an inactive state, since all tasks might not be active simultaneously. The possible means of interaction between modules of the program (causing the state transitions) are: activation of another task, sending or receiving messages to/from other tasks, deactivation of another task, and termination of the task.

After the CC builds the individual modules' state tables, it goes on to build the system level state table. The system level state table is comprised of each task's state within the system. A change in the system state table is determined by a change in one or more of the module state tables. The tool associates with each task's state any data shared with other tasks, thus allowing it to detect data access anomalies in the program. These anomalies, such as database deadlock and reference prior to initialization, are inherent problems to distributed systems design and it is difficult for a programmer/designer to avoid them without the aid of an automated tool such as the CC.

The CC also analyzes data accessed by more than one task for some common errors and indicators of problems. Some of these errors are:

- Improper initialization variables that are referenced before being assigned a value;

- Dead definitions - variables that are assigned a value but never referenced;

- Ambiguous definitions - variables that are assigned values in multiple tasks whose execution order is non-deterministic; therefore, other tasks referencing the variable are not assured of consistent results.

Criteria Addressed

The Concurrency Checker addresses the following criteria in the ways shown:

Consistency - The CC parses the input to assure that it is consistent with the formal definition of the structures allowed.

Fault tolerance - The CC checks the state tables to provide information on any possibility for a deadlock.

Distributedness - The CC helps the designer/programmer assure that his distributed structure is sound.

Distributed Processing Considerations

In the area of Defense C^3 computing environments, it has been decided that most future efforts will employ languages that support concurrent programming structures. The CC analyzes these concurrent structures, both in source or PDL, and aids the designer in developing better code for the distributed systems environment.

3. BRIEF DESCRIPTION OF EXISTING TOOL EXHIBITING SIMILAR FUNCTIONALITY

N/A - No commercial tools available

4. SUMMARY OF IMPROVEMENTS

N/A

5. TOOL SPECIFICATION

A. Identification of I/O Elements

Input
- The design analyst may enter PDL or the programmer may enter a supported high-level language.

Output
- The analyst/programmer receives the state diagrams (both individual module and system level) as well as annotated listing from the CC.

B. Form

Inputs

Pseudo-code - The pseudo-code is an abstraction of the eventual source code and must include parsable constructs expressing concurrency. These constructs, as well as all of the control constructs, must be identical to those of the eventual source code.

Source Code - The source must include constructs supporting concurrency (i.e. Ada, Concurrent Pascal, Modula).

Outputs

Annotated listings - The input is annotated with messages produced by the tool. These messages point out errors and possible problem errors identified by the tool.

State Diagrams - The CC provides both individual module and system level state tables. These tables are derived from analysis of the concurrency constructs expressed in the input. The state tables are exhaustive listings of all possible states the program can achieve. The user of the tool is made aware of possible problem areas as well as the blatant errors flagged by the tool.

C. Logical Functional of the I/O Elements

Input through concurrency constructs defines the parallelism of the application. The output provides the tool's feedback to the designer/programmer. The state diagrams provide a pictorial representation of the structures described. Finally, the anomalies detected by the CC are output in the listings.

CONCURRENCY CHECKER

INPUT

PDL, PSUEDO CODE, OR SOURCE CODE: MUST INCLUDE FORMAL SYNTAX CONCURRENCY CONSTRUCTS

ex. PDL (SUBSET OF SOURCE CODE LANGUAGE), ADA, MODULA, CONCURRENT PASCAL

PROCESS

PARSE CONCURRENCY CONSTRUCTS: ASSURE CORRECTNESS AND CONSISTENCY

CONSTRUCT TASK STATE TABLES

CONSTRUCT SYSTEM STATE TABLE

CHECK STATE TABLE FOR ANOMALIES & POSSIBLE PITFALLS

IDENTIFY DATA SHARED BY MULTIPLE TASKS

ex. NONE AVAILABLE (ADA COMPILERS WILL PERFORM PARSE)

OUTPUT

STATE TABLES

ANNOTATED LISTINGS OF INPUT

SET/USE LISTINGS OF SHARED DATA

ex. NONE AVAILABLE (ADA COMPILERS WILL PROVIDE SET/ USE LISTINGS)

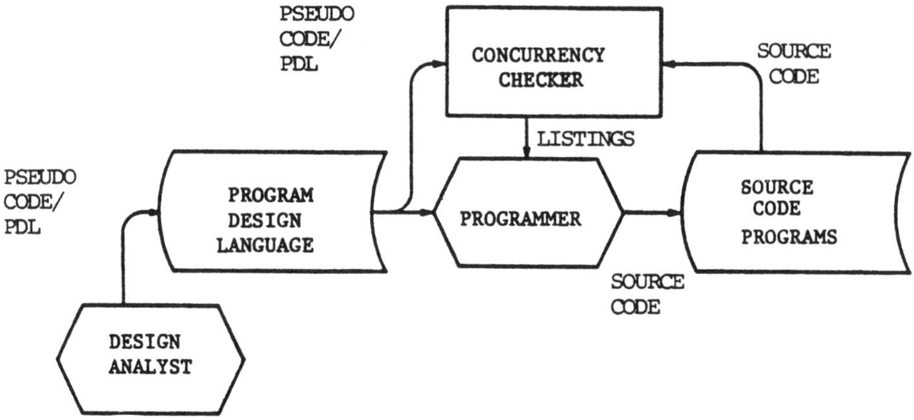
PSEUDO
CODE/
PDL
CONCURRENCY
CHECKER
SOURCE
CODE
LISTINGS
PSEUDO
CODE/
PDL
PROGRAM
DESIGN
LANGUAGE
PROGRAMMER
SOURCE
CODE
PROGRAMS
SOURCE
CODE
DESIGN
ANALYST

3.2.2.1.11 PATH GRAPH BUILDER

1. INTRODUCTION

The Path Graph Builder is for use during the testing, and maintenance and phases of the software lifecycle. Its main function is to build finite state diagrams from one of two sources: the source code or the specification of the allowable ordering of operators being used in that source code. The result of the former is to be called the program path graph and the latter will be referred to as the allowable operator sequence (AOS) graph. A list of abbreviations used is given below.

A list of abbreviations used is given below:

PGB	Path Graph Builder
OSA	Operation Sequence Analyzer
VHM	Variable History Mapper
RA	Reachability Analyzer
ISSE	Integrated Systems Support Environment
OAS	Operator's Allowable Sequence

2. FUNCTIONAL SUMMARY

The PGB receives input from two places and outputs to three. It's input comes from the programmer/maintainer, the source code and the symbol table information as produced by the compiler (see connectivity diagram at the end of this section).

Its output, the pathgraphs, is forwarded to the OSA, the VM and the RA. In all these output cases, the data produced is of the same form, but varies in content depending on which tool requested the information. The PGB is evoked by the programmer/maintainer and provides the option of specifying for which particular variables or operators the pathgraph is to be built for. The term operator is taken here to mean a line or group of lines of code that implement an operation on a shared data object. If the shared data object and the operators that operate on it are packaged and the details of the code are hidden from the user, that package is an implementation of an abstract data type.

After the PGB receives instructions from the programmer/maintainer, it goes into one of two modes: path graph generation operator's allowable sequence graph generation. The characteristics of these two modes are discussed below.

If the PGB is placed in the OAS graph generation mode, it must look at only the OAS input and as others (see figure) Simply stated, when the programmer wants the OAS graph, he tells the PGB to read the sequence information from a file and generate a graph which is both machine-readable and human-readable. When generating the OAS graph, the PGB will seem the input file in which the programmer/maintainer has specified all the allowable sequences of operators (or unallowable sequences, depending on implementation decisions) and generate a linked list in which the nodes represent the states of the data types and the arcs represent the operators that operate on those data types (the two together constitute the abstract data types.)

If the programmer puts the PGB in the pathgraph generation mode, the PGB scans different input files and outputs different information (though in the same format). In this mode, the PGB must use the source code, symbol table information, abstract data type definitions, and the set of variables or operators of interest as specified by the programmer to generate the finite state diagram of the program.

The inputs including a description of the PGBs operation on those inputs, are listed below.

- Set of variables or operators of interest. This input tells the PGB what kind of path graph to build. If a list of variables is provided, the PGB must locate occurences at those variables in the code by symbol table lookup, and using these statements along with branching and joining statements, the PGB builds the finite state diagram with the nodes being the states of the variables entered.

  If operators are provided, the PGB must build the path graph slightly differently. In this case, the PGB must first identify the source code that implements the high level operators named in the input list and then proceed as described above.The identification of the source code that implements a given operator will not be difficult if that operator is implemented as a procedure-like structure with the procedure having the same name of the operator. If the operator is not implemented in this way, the task of generating the path graph becomes more difficult and the PGB becomes more expensive to build. The cost estimate presented in the appendix was calculated assuming operators would be implemented by their name as procedures.

- Abstract Data Type Descriptions, Source Code and Symbol Table Information. The abstract data type definitions input to the PGB describes the shared data types and the operators that operate on them. A simple example appears in figure 3-20.

  Figure 3-20 shows a possible input format to specify the abstract data types of interest to the programmer. Given this input, the PGB can math the names of operators (e.g. push, pop)in the input list to their symbol table entries to determine where in the program to find the code that implements that operator. The PGB then scans the source looking for only those lines of code that implement the specified operators plus branching and joining code (e.g. "if"statements, "end/if" statements). From this scan, the PGB creates the finite state diagram requested by the programmer. This process is depicted in figure 3-21.

- Operator's Allowable Sequence. The presence of this input tells the PGB that it is to generate the OAS graph as discussed earlier. This input simply lists abstract data objects and their operators in legal order of appearance (or illegal order of appearance, depending on design) in a case-statement like format. The PGB then simply generates the OAS graph without having to reference any other information.

In summary, then the PGB utilizes one of four distinct inputs; source code and symbol table information, operator's allowable sequence, abstract data type descriptions, and variables/operators of interest, and generates either a finite state diagram of the program (the path graph) or the OAS graph.

The method of PGB uses to actually construct a requested finite state diagram is really a matter for implementation. Suffice it to say that the state diagram can be produced by techniques analogons to basic flowcharting techniques used to construct the flow-graph, as the state diagram is simply the graph complement of the flow-graph.

```
package STACKS is
    type STACK is limited private;
    procedure PUSH(S: in out STACK; X: in INTEGER);
    procedure POP(S: in out STACK; X: out INTEGER);
private
    type CELL;
    type STACK is access CELL;
    type CELL is
        record
            VALUE: INTEGER;
            NEXT: STACK;
        end record;
end;
package body STACKS is
    procedure PUSH(S: in out STACK; in INTEGER) is
    begin
        S:=new CELL(X, S);
    end;
    procedure POP(S: in out STACK; X: out INTEGER) is
    begin
        X:=S.VALUE;
        S:=S.NEXT;
    end;
end STACKS;
```

When the user declares a stack

```
S: STACK;
```

Figure 3-20(a). Example of abstract data type as it would appear in source.

```
OBJECTS         (* list of all objects which are   *)
-------         (* declared  of the type listed    *)
                (* below                           *)

                STACK1
                STACK2

TYPES           PACKAGE STACKS    (* this is the abstract data*)
-----                             (* object                   *)

OPERATORS       PUSH
---------       POP
```

Figure 3-20(b). Example of programmer/maintainer's specification of abstract data type of interest

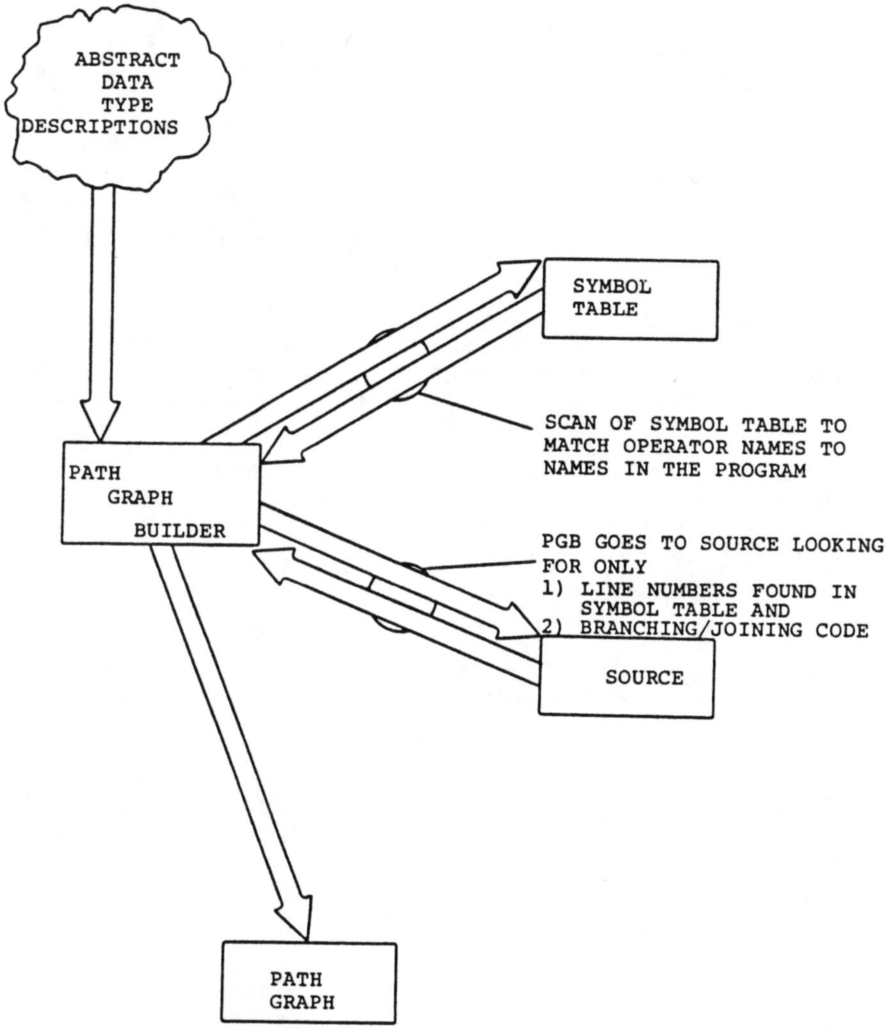

FIGURE 3-21 BUILDING OF PATH GRAPH FOR OSA

Distributed Processing Impacts.

When two or more processes are to be running in some distributed environment, the difficulty of constructing the path graphs increases by an order of magnitude. The process of forming a compound state diagram (one that depicts a number of independent processes) requires the notion of a control state. A control state is the product of the individual states of all the processes represented in the compound state diagram. The complete definition of a compound state diagram from the individual state tables is presented in Appendix B.

The important impact of distributed systems is the expression of synchronization mechanisms in the compound state diagram for the distributed application. The compound state diagram is in the same form as the individual state diagrams, with the extension of having synchronization points (e.g. send and waits, rendevouz) expressed as edges just like other operators. The ordering of these operators and synchronizations (again, represented by edges in the compound state diagram) is an issue for the operator Sequence Analyzer (OSA).

Criteria Addressed

Traceability - the PGB enhances traceability of the final product by establishing a thread from the final product back to the requirements statement. The path graph and the OAS graph serve as an excellent form of documentation and design strategy.

Simplicity - This criteria is enhanced because the data structures which are addressed by the PGB (the abstract data types) are guaranteed to be operated on correctly by various operators. If this operator-data structure relationship is clearly defined (as this tool forces), the final product becomes simplier to use.

Control of Data Access - The requirement of restricted access to sensitive data can be demonstrated by the PGB. That is, the application may have limitations placed on it by requirements in terms of order or type of data access, and the PGB demonstrates graphically whether or not the implementation of the application's design conformed to that requirement.

3. BRIEF DESCRIPTION OF TOOLS EXHIBITING SIMILAR FUNCTIONALITY.

Many version of flow-charters exist in industry and academia today. This function, which is a basic function of the PGB, is not complicated to program and although the implementations vary the techniques are becoming fairly standardized. Basically, a scan of the source code takes place with the knowledge of the language incorporated into the flowcharter, and some form of graphical output is produced.

4. SUMMARY OF IMPROVEMENTS

The PGBs ability to construct the compound state diagram is a new function. This task as discussed in Section 2, involves building the finite state diagram for a group of independent processes which constitute the distributed application software. This technique is not complicated except for the expression of synchronization mechanisms between processes. The PGB must also build the OAS graphs which not only express the operation sequences but also the synchronization order to be imposed on the system. These improvements, although they have not yet been implemented, do not involve the development of any complex new techniques. Therefore, the effort required to develop these improvements will take the form of implementing existing theories for the first time (see Appendix B).

5. TOOL SPECIFICATION.

A. Identification of I/O Elements

Inputs

Programmer/Maintainer. The programmer/maintainer initiates the tool and places it in one of the two modes described earlier. If he desires the path graph and the source be constructed, he must also supply a list of the variables or operators of interest. This list will simply be specified on an input file readable by the PGB.

Abstract Data Types. These are supplied by the programmer, maintainer in a separate file from the other inputs. An example of their form was given in Figure 3-20.

Allowable operator sequence. Again specified by the P/M in tool-readable file.

Source Code and Symbol Table. The PGB makes references to these after initiation. The tool should be provided read-only access to these databases.

Outputs

Path Graphs. These will be dumped to the provided file system and used by either the VM, the OSA or the RA. The path graph will probably be in linked list form, but this is a detail for implementation.

B. Form of I/O Elements. (See Section 2.)

C. Logical Form of I/O Elements. (See Section 2.)

PATH GRAPH BUILDER

INPUT

SOURCE CODE AND SYMBOL TABLE INFORMATION

SET OF VARIABLES OR OPERATORS OF INTEREST SPECIFYING WHAT THINGS TO LOOK FOR IN THE SOURCE

ABSTRACT DATA TYPE DEFINITIONS FROM THE PROGRAMMER

ALLOWABLE OPERATOR SEQUENCE FROM THE PROGRAMMER

PROCESS

PROCESS INPUT AND LOOK UP IDENTIFIERS IN SYMBOL TABLE

CONSTRUCT FINITE STATE DIAGRAM FROM IDENTIFIERS OF INTEREST AND BRANCHING/JOINING STATEMENTS

COMPLEMENT FINITE STATE DIAGRAM TO OBTAIN PATH GRAPH

OUTPUT

PATH GRAPH, PROBABLY IN LINKED-LIST FORM, FOR EITHER THE VM, RA, OR OSA

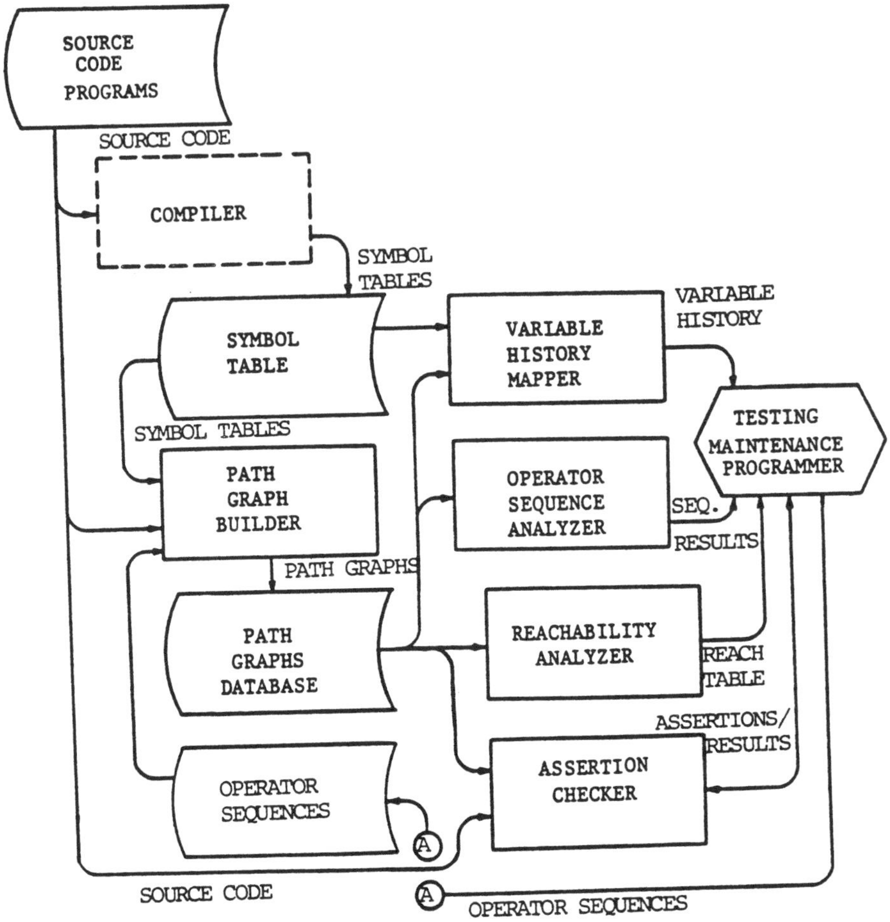
SOURCE CODE PROGRAMS
SOURCE CODE
COMPILER
SYMBOL TABLES
SYMBOL TABLE
VARIABLE HISTORY MAPPER
VARIABLE HISTORY
TESTING MAINTENANCE PROGRAMMER
SYMBOL TABLES
PATH GRAPH BUILDER
OPERATOR SEQUENCE ANALYZER
SEQ.
RESULTS
PATH GRAPHS
PATH GRAPHS DATABASE
REACHABILITY ANALYZER
REACH TABLE
ASSERTIONS/ RESULTS
OPERATOR SEQUENCES
ASSERTION CHECKER
A
SOURCE CODE
A
OPERATOR SEQUENCES

3.2.2.1.12 CROSS REFERENCE GENERATOR

1. INTRODUCTION

The Cross Reference Generator (CRG) is used during the implementation, testing, operation, and maintenance phases of the software lifecycle. It provides various requested cross reference listings from data available in the Symbol Table (ST) and the Source Code (SC). It can limit the information provided in these, listing in accordance with restrictions specified by the requestor. The following abbreviations are used:

CRG Cross Reference Generator
SC Source Code
ST Symbol Table

2. FUNCTIONAL SUMMARY

The Cross Reference Generator (CRG) processes source code in conjunction with symbol table information in response to cross referencing requests from programmers, testers, or maintainers. The source code provides the context in which the symbols being cross referenced reside. The symbol table information supplies the data accumulated by the compiler on each symbol. This enables the CRG to provide a great depth of information in its cross reference without duplicating the effort put forth by the compiler. This dependence on information supplied by a compiler reflects the dependence on the formal language of the source code. Thus the particular language involved will influence the details available for inclusion in the CRG output. The general information included, however, will address where symbols are declared, set, referenced, and located. Particulars about declaraton would include compilation unit, design unit, and full expansion of names. The expansion of names is used in some of the new languages, which permit overloading, to select a specific honograph. A means of expanding a name is to prefix it with the name of its enclosing parental unit, and use a special character, which does not appear in names, as a separator. When units are nested within units to multiple levels, the full expansion of a name reflects the names of all the outer enclosing levels. Setting particulars would include default initialization if supported by the language, initialization during declaration if supported by the language, first executable assignment, and a tabulation of all subsequent assignments. Referencing details would include names of modules in which the referencing occurs and would attempt to associate each reference with the set that precedes it. Location would include a symbol's name and address within the node where it is located and also its extended name and address for access from other nodes (depending on naming scheme being used). References which cross nodal boundaries must be highlighted in listing output. These internodal references normally incur an overhead cost which must be carefully evaluated. Additionally, such references may be inconspicuous in the source code when implementations spread the software scope supported by the language across hardware node boundaries.

Another aspect involved with software scope is the topic of overloading the multiple use of a symbol. In languages supporting overloading of names the CRG must be capable of indicating overloaded names for clarification. Additionally, the CRG should also be capable of detecting out of scope overloading, which is no problem for compilers, but occasionally a point of confusion for human readers. Also for ease of use, the CRG should be capable of restricting its processing to a subset of the system modules as specified by the requestor. Special listings providing information on related modules can be of great assistance when making decisions about node assignments or particularly when attempting to modify node assignments. These can answer questions such as: what are the external references made by a set of modules assigned to or proposed for assignment to a node; what modules reference a set of symbols assigned to or proposed for assignment to a node; etc. Qualification on sets should also be available so that conditionals such as "all" or "one of any" could be used in the descriptions of the desired listings.

The criteria affected by the CRG include consistency, clarity, and distributedness. Consistency in respect to the use of symbols is improved by the availability of listings showing where specific terms are utilized. This enables programmers to ensure that their use of terms is consistent throughout the system software. These listings also enable programmers to be discriminating in their selection of names. Therefore, they can select distinct sets of names for different areas of code and avoid confusing overlap, thus improving clarity. Distributedness is impacted by the CRG capability to reflect location information which it gleans from the ST.

The CRG ability to produce listings of external references or internodal references provides information needed when making decisions about nodal positioning of software elements within a distributed environment. The added capability of providing special listings to provide information on specified sets of elements can be pivotal in making the best decisions.

3. BRIEF DESCRIPTION OF EXISTING TOOLS EXHIBITING SIMILAR FUNCTIONALITY

Existing tools are too numerous to attempt selecting specific ones to mention. Additionally, many tools, such as compilers, have a cross referencing capability incorporated into them. General capabilities available include listings in a standard format on a module basis. Some older tools provide address assignments, some newer tools provide set/used information.

4. SUMMARY OF IMPROVEMENTS

A. Functional Improvements

A significant improvement is needed for providing distributed information about symbols in the cross reference listings. The nodal location of elements must be available as well as a capability to highlight referencing which crosses nodal boundaries. Also needed is extensive means of specifying restrictions on what elements are to appear on specially requested listings. Specialized listings provide a quick means of evaluating proposed nodal assignment adjustments during implementation, operation, and maintenance. These listings may call for listings of elements referenced by all modules of a specified set or by at least one of a specified set. A reverse type request may be for listings of modules which reference all elements of a specified set or at least one of a specified set. Set member specification for these requests needs to be quite flexible. Some desired sets may be all elements appearing in a module, or in a specific statement, or in a selected line of source code, or within an alphabetical range of names, or within a list of names.

B. Existing Desirable Capabilities

Current capabilities available are uniprocessor oriented but are none the less applicable, as all those capabilities still need to be applied on a node by node basis in a distributed environment.

C. Elimination or Reduction of Existing Capabilities No Longer Needed

There are no cross referencing capabilities to be eliminated from ISSE. However, by consolidating the capabilities into the CRG they may be eliminated from other tools, such as compilers. This makes a clean division between the functions to be carried out by different tools in the ISSE. This does not mean that presently existing tools must be modified but that new tools developed for the ISSE should be designed to avoid undesirable overlap with other tools in the ISSE.

5. TOOL SPECIFICATION

A. Identification of I/O Elements

Symbol Table information is available throughout an ISSE database after a compiler has processed the source code.

Source code files are established by the user and available throughout the underlying file management support of the ISSE.

Cross Reference listings are provided by the CRG as output to the user.

B. Form of I/O Elements

Symbol Table information is stored in a data base. Its detailed form will be dependent on the language supported. There must be constructs to support the data associated with the distributed target environment included in this detailed form. Care must be taken in the design of this database to ensure that sufficient flexibility is in these constructs so that all desired targets can be supported. Details of location information and internodal information and internodal referencing data are examples of such items.

Source Code is a textual programming language which follows formal syntax rules. FORTRAN, COBAL, and Ada are examples.

Cross Referencing listings are formatted output of the requested information which may be provided to the user through whatever means are supported by the ISSE host environment. Interactive display and printed listings are examples of possible means.

C. LOGICAL FUNCTION OF I/O ELEMENTS

Symbol Table information provides the pre-processed details from the compiler on each sybmol. This enables the CRG to rapidly assemble a great depth of information in response to a request without having to duplicate effort expended by a compiler. Included in these details are the location assignments of each symbol. This location information enables the CRG to answer questions concerned with distributedness.

Source Code provides the context of the symbols in the ST. Thus the user can make his requests by referring to the SC as a framework.

Cross Reference listings provide the resultant information in response to a users request.

CROSS REFERENCE GENERATOR

INPUT

SYMBOL TABLE INFORMATION INCLUDES FULL QUALIFICATION, ALIAS, PARENT, SIBLING, OFFSPRING, LOCATION, SIZE, ETC.

SOURCE CODE - PROVIDES CONTEXT OF SYMBOLS

INITIATING REQUEST INCLUDING SPECIFICATION OF DATA TO BE REFERENCED AND INFORMATION TO BE LISTED

PROCESS

EXTRACT, CORRELATE AND TABULATE DATA FROM SOURCES IN ACCORDANCE WITH REQUEST FOR OUTPUT

OUTPUT

CROSS REFERENCE - LISTINGS IN RESPONSE TO REQUEST

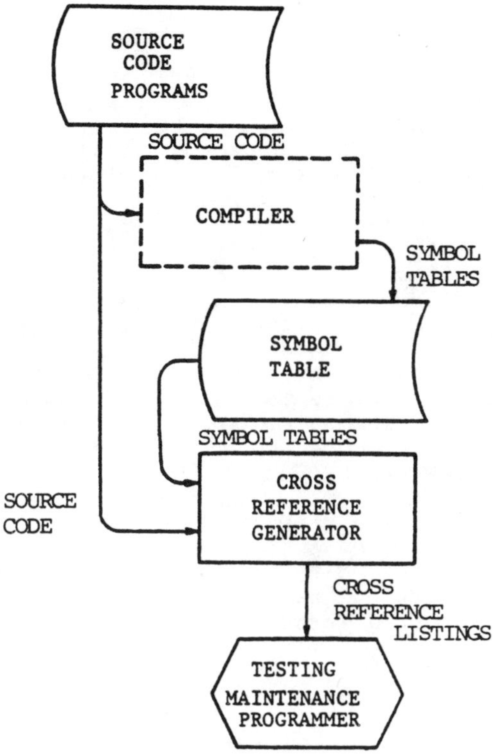
SOURCE CODE PROGRAMS
SOURCE CODE
COMPILER
SYMBOL TABLES
SYMBOL TABLE
SYMBOL TABLES
SOURCE CODE
CROSS REFERENCE GENERATOR
CROSS REFERENCE LISTINGS
TESTING MAINTENANCE PROGRAMMER

3.2.2.1.13 INTERFACE MAPPER

1. INTRODUCTION

The Interface Mapper is designed for use in the testing and maintenance phases of the software lifecycle. It uses the source code of a particular architecture as input. Each module within that architecture is examined individually by the Interface Mapper. Specific attention is paid to the interfaces between modules. Each interface between modules is characterized in terms of data abstractions transmitted and received. Using these characterizations, a testing and maintenance programmer can assess whether the degree of modularization is sufficiently functional. The mapping of interfaces produced by the Interface Mapper is used as input to the Integrated System Support Environment Completion Analyzer.

List of abbreviations include:

IM	Interface Mapper
CA	Completion Analyzer
ISSE	Integrated System Support Environment
AC	Assertion Checker
MT	Mutation Tester

2. FUNCTIONAL SUMMARY

The IM examines the source code produced by the programmer from the standpoint of functional modularity. Such modularity is closely related to the particular architecture being implemented to satisfy design specifications. Each program module produced by the programmer should satisfy the architectural specifications of the design analyst. Furthermore, each architectural node established during the design phase should have a corresponding program module during the implementation or coding phase. The coding itself represents an implementation detail not addressed during the design phase. Consequently, the IM examines these implementation details (i.e., the programming modularity) to determine a software architecture which should satisfy the functional modularity required by the design analyst. A decision concerning adequacy is reached by the testing and maintenance programmer using the output produced by the IM. Such output is also available to other tools within the ISSE. One such tool is the CA which can be used by the testing and maintenance programmer to help determine adequacy. The IM characterizes all interfaces between program modules in terms of data abstractions sent and received by those modules. The characterizations are used by the testing and maintenance programmer to determine if the software modules are sufficiently functional. Functionality of the IM itself is divided into three parts. First, the IM must access the program source code files on the basis of requirements functions. Such access capability is also exercised by AC and MT. Second, the IM must be able to discern software modules from the source code for a particular application under examination. Included in such a discernment is the characterization of interfaces between source modules in terms of data abstractions sent and received. Third, the IM must be able to present its characterizations to the testing and maintenance programmer for determination of functional sufficiency. The capability for presenting interface characterizations to other tools within the ISSE is included in such functionality.

Several software quality criteria of a product under development within the ISSE are addressed by the IM. The criterion of traceability is enhanced through the linking of software architecture to the functional modularity required by the design analyst. The linkage itself is determined by the testing and maintenance programmer and is based upon information generated by the IM. The criterion of modularity is enhanced through the reconciliation of program modules produced by the programmer to architectural specifications generated by the design analyst. The reconciliation itself is performed by the testing and maintenance programmer and is based upon information generated by the IM. The criterion of commonality is enhanced by the characterization of data abstractions transmitted and received between functional modules of the product under development. The IM produces the characterizations but subsequent commonality depends upon action taken by the testing and maintenance programmer. When that programmer is sufficiently experienced, a standardized set of interfaces between modules within a particular product can be implemented. The criterion of distributedness can be enhanced through linking the program modules of a product to the hardware architecture specified by a design analyst. The IM can support any logical or geographic separation required by the design analyst of the product under development.

The IM addresses distributed processing through the design architectures it can analyze. Such architectures are developed from the analysis of product source code. As a consequence, these architectures are independent verifications that programmers understand product specifications delineated by design analysts. Whether all product specifications have been satisfied depends upon the characterizations produced by the IM and subsequent analysis by the testing and maintenance programmer using the CA.

3. BRIEF DESCRIPTION OF EXISTING TOOLS EXHIBITING SIMILAR FUNCTIONALITY

Static analysis tools exhibit the closest functionality to the IM. The IM can be viewed as a special case of static analysis since it involves the examination of program source code. The static analysis implemented by General Research Corporation for Rome Air Development Center specificially addresses software module interface conflicts where actual and formal parameters may be mismatched. The static analysis for FORTRAN, COBOL, JOVIAL, and J73 source code has been implemented by General Research Corporation. As a consequence, the allowable syntax within the respective compilers determines what interface conflicts can be detected between software modules. In effect, such determinations depend less upon the final source code product under development and more upon the allowable syntax of the source code, i.e., FORTRAN, COBOL, JOVIAL, and J73. Petri net analysis tools also approach the functionality of the IM but from a different direction. Whereas static analysis tools examine program source code to detect software module interface conflicts, Petri net tools model these interface possibilities during the design phase. In general, Petri net modeling is performed in such a way that network transitions correspond to executable program source code modules. The places within the Petri network correspond to decision processes which also correspond to subsequent program source code modules. The Petri net tools are valuable in representing process synchronization and mutual exclusion. Such representations designate specifications which must be met by the final source code products. As a consequence, the application of Petri net tools is problem dependent while static analysis tools are problem independent since they necessarily emphasize source code syntax. In summary, Petri net tools have the correct emphasis but are applied too soon while static analysis tools emphasize problem independent syntax and are applied at the proper time.

4. SUMMARY OF IMPROVEMENTS

A. Functional Improvements (new capabilities)

The IM is a specialized use of an existing static analysis capability. Within existing static analysis tools such capability has been coupled with the detection of structurally infinite loops, recursive procedure calls, uninitialized variables, and structural deadlock. The IM would decouple itself from such capability and become a stand-alone tool within the ISSE. The reason for such decoupling is based upon the orientation of large static analysis tools, e.g., FAVS, JAVS, CAVS, and AAVS. Without deocupling an IM from such tools, the orientation is toward problem independent properties evident in the source code syntax of a product. When an IM is decoupled and used as an ISSE too, the orientation is toward problem dependent properties. Such properties originate within the design phase and are evident as implementation details during the implementation or coding phase. The IM examines source code modules to determine a software architecture which should satisfy the functional modularity required by a design analyst. Using the output produced by the IM, a testing and maintenance programmer can decide if a product software architecture satisfies the functional modularity established during the design phase and implemented during the coding phase.

B. Existing Desirable Capabilities

The static analysis tools which are currently available (e.g., FAVS, JAVS, CAVS, and AAVS) emphasize problem independent properties like structurally infinite loops, recursive procedure calls, uninitialized variables, structural deadlock, and module interface conflicts. Such tools can detect a significant number of source program errors. The program independent properties which can be detected by such tools are most applicable to single programs with program operators which interact with shared data objects. The extent to which such tools apply to distributed environments varies as a function of source language. FORTRAN and COBOL languages support single programs with program operators. Two or more independent processes running concurrently and in parallel are not easily supported in either FORTRAN or COBOL. These independent processes running concurrently and in parallel are characteristic of the distributed environment. JOVIAL language is capable of supporting such characteristics but has difficulty when processes run in parallel and contain operators interfacing with data objects shared by more than one of the processes. Ada is capable of addressing interacting operators through the implementation of rendezvous but a validated Ada compiler is currently not available. In the short run, a general purpose static analysis tool set can be developed for doing code-oriented and design-oriented analyses. However, such development is not without cost and must compete with the alternative of more specialized and less costly tools, e.g., the IM.

Currently existing static analysis tools perform code-oriented analysis. With the exception of FORTRAN, empirical studies of product source code have not been performed to establish the efficiency of such code-oriented analysis. For FORTRAN, a study of 100 scientific source code programs detected 14% of the errors using only uninitialized variables and structural deadlock properties of static analysis. Efficiency levels within distributed environments have not been determined.

C. Elimination or Reduction of Existing Capabilties no Longer Needed

Existing static analysis tools need to be closely examined from the standpoint of an ISSE. Capabilities offered by each tool should be closely coordinated with software system lifecycle phases supported by the ISSE. Under such an examination much of the code-oriented analysis of present tools is no longer needed or is best accomplished by other tools within the ISSE. The ultimate benefit of such an examination is a set of scaled-down tools within the ISSE thereby making the ISSE easier to implement.

5. TOOL SPECIFICATION

A. Identification of I/O Elements

Input to the IM by the testing and maintenance programmer is exercised when the initiation command is issued. In addition to the initiation command, the testing and maintenance programmer must also input information concerning which program source code is to be examined by the IM. Such information about program source code is an indirect reference to Program Design Language Descriptions previously generated by the design analyst and known to the testing and maintenance programmer. Based upon the initiation command and information submitted by the testing and maintenance programmer, the IM retrieves the designated source code program from a file maintained by the ISSE during the implementation or coding phase.

Output from the IM is a consolidated mapping of data abstractions being transmitted and received within a designated source program to specific module interfaces in that program. The consolidated mapping is presented to the testing and maintenance programmer as well as other tools within the ISSE, e.g., the CA. As in the case of the CA, these other tools within the ISSE are general in nature. They apply to uniprocessor as well as distributed processing architectures. Some of these tools are not necessary for the initialization of an ISSE for distributed processing architectures. However, the IM produces a consolidated mapping for them in case they are implemented.

B. Form of I/O Elements

Input supplied by the testing and maintenance programmer to the IM has two forms. First is an initialization command structure characterized by a string of characters. Second is information concerning the specific source code program to be examined by the IM. Such information exhibits the identification characteristics of specific programs previously stored during the implementation or coding phase. Input to the IM from the previously stored source code programs is in terms of source code and its embedded delineators.

Output produced by the IM for either the testing and maintenance programmer or other tools within the ISSE is primarily tabular in nature. Within the tables are identifiers for specific data abstractions and specific module interfaces contained in the program source code specified by the testing and maintenance programmer.

C. Logical Function of I/O Elements

Input supplied to the IM by the testing and maintenance programmer references a specific source code program to be examined plus an initiation command. The reference to a specific source code program is also a logically indirect reference to a specific set of Program Design Language Descriptions previously generated by a design analyst. This logically indirect reference to a set of Program Design Language Descriptions is itself a logically indirect reference to a set of System Specifications established by a requirements analyst.

Output mapping information produced by the IM is a very specialized application of static analysis techniques to the program source code designated by the testing and maintenance programmer. Specific identifications of transmitted or received data abstractions and module interfaces included in the designated program source are generated by the IM.

INTERFACE MAPPER

INPUT

USER INSTRUCTIONS - IDENTIFY SOURCE CODE TO BE PROCESSED AND INITIATES TOOL

SOURCE CODE - PROVIDES INTERFACES IN CONTEXT OF THEIR USE

PROCESS

PROCESSES SPECIFIED SOURCE CODE IDENTIFYING THE DATA ABSTRACTIONS WHICH ARE TRANSMITTED AND RECEIVED VIA THE INTERFACES

OUTPUT

OUTPUT REPORT PROVIDES THE MAPPING OF THE IDENTIFIED DATA ABSTRACTIONS TO THE PROGRAM INTERFACES

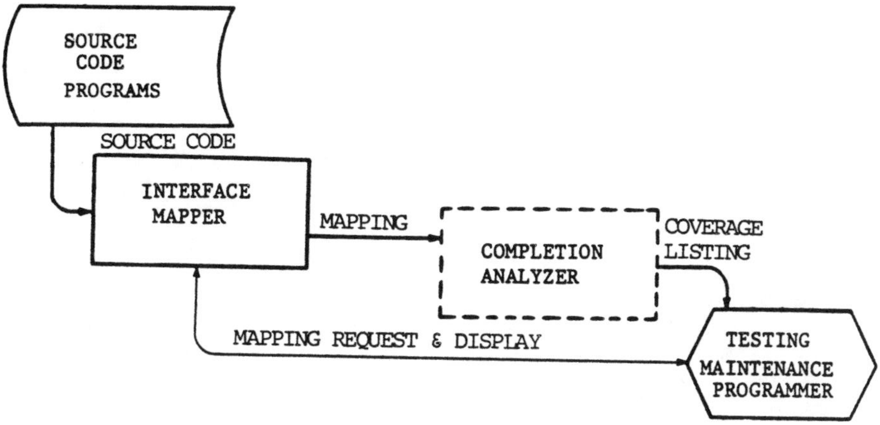
SOURCE
CODE
PROGRAMS
SOURCE CODE
INTERFACE
MAPPER
MAPPING
COMPLETION
ANALYZER
COVERAGE
LISTING
MAPPING REQUEST & DISPLAY
TESTING
MAINTENANCE
PROGRAMMER

3.2.2.1.14 ASSERTION CHECKER

1. INTRODUCTION

The Assertion Checker is designed for use during the testing and maintenance phases of the software development lifecycle. It operates on the source code of a program selected by a testing and maintenance programmer. Its analysis of source code uses the concept of predicate testing. Under its approach, assertions in the form of predicates are inserted in the Program Design Language Descriptions produced during the design phase. As Program Design Language Descriptions are implemented in source code, the previously inserted assertion predicates remain unchanged. These unchanged predicates represent testing sites within the implemented source code. Each site is subsequently exercised by the Assertion Checker when it analyzes the source code. Such activity is made possible through the composition of the assertion predicates themselves. Each assertion predicate is a Boolean expression which is evaluated when the Assertion Checker performs its analysis of source code. The order in which assertion predicates are evaluated is a function of the processing path(s) perceived by the Assertion Checker as it proceeds through the source code. Procession is from the source code starting point to the source code ending point. The testing and maintenance programmer can apply the Assertion Checker repeatedly to the same source code by inserting additional assertion predicates and/or modifying those predicates already inserted.

The list of abbreviations include:

AC	Assertion Checker
ISSE	Integrated System Support Environment
PDL	Program Design Language
PGB	Path Graph Builder
ANSI	American National Standards Institute

2. FUNCTIONAL SUMMARY

The AC examines the source code produced by the programmer from the standpoint of processing paths. To accomplish such an examination requires source code with assertions inserted and knowledge of the processing flow when that source code is executed. The assertions themselves are in the form of Boolean expressions which are executed by the AC as it proceeds along the processing path(s) between a source code beginning point and a source code ending point. The insertion of assertions into program source code is performed by the AC under the directon of the testing and maintenance programmer. Placement of the Boolean assertions requires the programmer to know significant processing points specified by the PDL descriptions before the source code was written. Applying this knowledge after the source code has been written enables Boolean assertions to be inserted at the appropriate locations. Knowledge of processing flow when the source program is executed is obtained from path graphs produced by the PGB. Such path graphs require previous compilation of the program source code. The compilation produces a symbol table necessary to the PGB in its production of path graphs. In general, the insertions of Boolean assertions is an activity taking place before compilation while establishing process flow is an activity taking place after compilation. Functionally the AC requires access to program source code before compilation and information generated from the same program source code after compilation. In effect, the AC performs a symbolic execution of the source program as it either validates or disproves each inserted Boolean expression.

Functionality of the AC is subdivided into several parts. The most obvious subdivision deals with the insertion of Boolean expressions into designated program source code. Each inserted expression can be viewed as a predicate which will be used to verify the transformation of PDL specifications into source code modules. The verification is accomplished through the subsequent evaluation of the inserted Boolean expressions by the AC after execution information is obtained from the PGB. Actually obtaining that execution information from the PGB is another distinct function performed by the AC. The quality of the information obtained depends upon the compiler being applied to the source code. Of course the precise compiler selected is dictated by the language used by the programmer when source code was being implemented. In any case, assuming the appropriate match between program source code and subsequent compiler selection has been made, the quality of information available to the PGB varies as a function of compiler selected. Compilers differ as to the source code checks they provide. These source code checks are evolutionary in nature. Older languages like FORTRAN and COBOL offer few constraints on the way program source code is used. As a consequence, the functionality of the AC to these older languages is most applicable. However, new languages like Ada enforce many constraints on the way program source code is used. These constraints examine the same conditions addressed by the Boolean expressions inserted by the AC. As a consequence, the anticipated role for an AC with a language like Ada undergoes change.

Final resolution of such an issue awaits the introduction of the first validated Ada compiler. Languages like PASCAL and JOVIAL bridge the gap between languages providing few constraints (e.g., FORTRAN and COBOL) and languages enforcing many constraints (e.g.,Ada). In summary, the current evolutionary trend in compilers is producing tighter controls on the use of source code which, in turn, impacts the applicability of assertion checking to such source code.

Assuming the AC has exercised its functionality of inserting Boolean expressions into source code and has obtained sufficient execution information from the PGB, it performs the symbolic execution of the source code program. During symbolic execution the previously inserted Boolean expressions are evaluated. The final function performed by the AC is the production of a table containing which Boolean expressions have been validated and which have been disproven. Such a table is used by the programmer to determine what modifications need to be made to the source code. Several software quality criteria of a product under development within the ISSE are addressed by the AC. The criterion of traceability is enhanced by the AC since it cannot be used unless traceability is present in the source code. The required traceability applies to the transformation or mapping of PDL specifications into program source code implementations. The criterion of consistency is enhanced by the AC since its absence would preclude use of the AC. The required traceability referred to the mapping of the PDL specifications into source code. However, the programmer which initiates the AC must also have knowledge of the mapping of requirements specifications into the appropriate PDL specifications. Such knowledge spans the requirements, design, and implementation or coding phases, i.e., such knowledge enforces consistency before the AC can be applied. The criterion of compliance is encouraged by the AC. In effect, the Boolean expressions inserted into source code by the AC attempts to validate compliance. If compliance is not present and the Boolean insertions are adequate, the AC should not validate the designated source code.

The AC addresses distributed processing through the software architectures which can be addressed by the PGB. Such architectures depend upon the capability of the source code compiler to support distributed processing structures, e.g., concurrent execution and parallel operation. Older languages like FORTRAN and COBOL do not support such structures. Newer languages like MODULA, Concurrent PASCAL, and Ada do. However, the AC neither extends nor detracts the capability of a particular compiler to support distributed processing structures. Instead, the AC is constrained to information provided by the PGB.

3. BRIEF DESCRIPTION OF EXISTING TOOLS EXHIBITING SIMILAR FUNCTIONALITY

A variety of tools already exist with functionality similar to the AC. Some support assertion constructs as an integral part of the program source code. Others allow a testing and maintenance programmr to insert Boolean statements into program source code already generated. Both types of asserton checkers require compilation of the source code before the AC can perform its analysis.

An existing assertion checking tool called ACES is available at the University of California at Berkeley. It emphasizes execution path flow with FORTRAN source programs implemented in either the IBM or CDC mainframe environment. The tool itself is written in CENTRAN (a language similar to FORTRAN) and constrains the ranges of variables within FORTRAN source code programs. ACES is not available commercially.

Another assertion checking tool is called DISSECT which has been implemented at the University of California at San Diego. Originally the tool was developed by McDonnel Douglas under a grant from the National Bureau of Standards. It emphasizes symbolic execution of an ANSI FORTRAN source program. The tool itself is written in LISP and operates within a DEC-10 mainframe environment. DISSECT is not available commercially.

Another assertion checking tool is called EFFIGY which has been implemented by IBM. It emphasizes symbolic execution of PL/I source programs written for the IBM/370 environment under the VM/370 operating system. The tool allows for the insertion of formal ASSERT statements into the PL/I source code. The tool itself is not commercially available.

Yet another assertion checking tool is called JAVS and has been developed by General Research Corp. under contract with RADC. It validates and tests JOVAIAL J3 source programs and is written in JOVIAL J3 and FORTRAN. It runs in a CDC 6400 environment as well as a Honeywell 6080/6180 environment. The user supplies executable assertions which are used to check predicate computations, constraining the ranges on variables, and trapping special conditions. The tool itself is owned by the U.S. Air Force. Another assertion checking tool is PET which has been implemented at McDonnell Douglas Astronautics Co. It is written in FORTRAN and examines FORTRAN source programs. It inserts Boolean expressions into source code prior to compilation. It operates within the CDC 6000/7000, IBM 360/370 OS, and Univac 1100 machine environments. The tool is commercially available.

The Computer Science Group of the Standard Research Institute has implemented an assertion checking tool called SELECT. It emphasizes execution path analysis and is written in LISP. It validates assertions inserted into LISP source code programs. The tool itself is not commercially available.

Under contract with the U. S. Army, General Research Corporation has developed an assertion checking tool called SQLAB. It formally verifies assertions entered into source programs of FORTRAN, IFTRAN (an extension of FORTRAN), PASCAL, and JOVIAL J3 B-2. The tool itself is written in IFTRAN and resides in a CDC 6400/7600 environment. The tool is not commercially available. However, a similar tool developed by General Research Corporation is commercially available. The tool itself is called V-IFTRAN and verifies FORTRAN source code through the assertion of executable statements. It contains a preprocessor to transform those executable assertions into FORTRAN source code statements for subsequent compilation. The tool is transportable and can be used on any computer offering FORTRAN capability.

A final assertion checking tool is called TPL and has been implemented by General Electric Co. It analyzes FORTRAN source code programs and is itself written in FORTRAN. Logical expressions written in FORTRAN-like syntax comprise the assertions and are inserted into the source code under examination. A formal VERIFY statement is used to specify assertions which must be validated during execution. The tool itself is not commercially available.

4. SUMMARY OF IMPROVEMENTS

A. Functional Improvements (new capabilities)

The functionality of an AC is most important to older programming languages like FORTRAN and COBOL. Newer languages like Ada offer a related functionality through the source code constraints they support. Distributed processing impacts both assertion checking and the language applied to source code. The capability to analyze concurrency constructs is needed. However, such capability introduces complexity into either the AC or compiler language used. If the compiler does not address such complexity, the Boolean expressions inserted by the AC must accommodate the required complexity. Such accommodation by an AC is non-trivial. The current generation of ACs do not exceed the analytical capability of their accompanying compilers. Extensions to Ada must be undertaken to accommodate all distributed processing constructs, e.g., the assignments of nodes. Currently such extensions are not underway. An alternative is the implementation of an AC which inserts Boolean expressions which can be evaluated during symbolic execution to provide information about distributed processing constructs. The decision to undertake such an AC should be based upon a negative decision concerning the extended capability of an associated compiler, e.g., Ada. Whether the AC can accommodate distributed processing constructs while an associated compiler cannot is an unanswered question.

B. Existing Desirable Capabilities

The assertion checking capability of existing tools is extremely useful within the context of specific compilers. However, new compilers like Ada are being introduced and the capabilities they offer with respect to assertion checking are also very useful. The ability to accommodate all distributed processing constructs is presently lacking in both the existing tools and the new compilers.

C. Elimination or Reduction of Existing Capabilities No Longer Needed

New compilers like Ada are subsuming existing capability offered by current ACs. When such compilers are validated and introduced, currently available tools which perform assertion checking may no longer be needed with respect to such compilers. However, the accommodation of distributed processing constructs is not being fully addressed by either these new compilers or existing assertion checking tools.

5. TOOL SPECIFICATION

A. Identification of I/O Element

The AC is initiated by the testing and maintenance programmer. Prior to the initiation command, the programmer inserts assertions into the appropriate sections of source code under examination and designates the particular source code which is to be symbolically executed. Subsequent retrieval of the designated source code accounts for a second source of input to the AC. However, the AC also needs input from the PGB before symbolic execution is undertaken. This latter input provides necessary information concerning the flow of execution within the subject source code. The PGB is able to provide such information to the AC because it accesses symbol table information already generated from previous compilation of the subject source code.

Output from the AC is in terms of validation and/or violations of the previously entered insertions. The validations and/or violations are determined by symbolic execution of the source code by the AC. Such information is provided the testing and maintenance programmer. Such information can also be provided other tools within the ISSE.

B. Form of I/O Elements

Input to the AC falls into five categories: inserting assertions, designating code, retrieving code, retrieving execution data, and initiating execution. Inserting assertions involves the textual insertion of Boolean expressions into specified sections of source code. Designating code involves the identification of source program blocking factors previously established by PDL specifications prior to the implementation of the source code under examination. Retrieval is based upon accessing factors generated as a consequence of the designated blocks of program source code. Whether the previous insertions are included in such program source code blocks is a function of the particular source code compiler. If the compiler can accommodate inserted Boolean expressions, a degree of preprocessing must be performed before the AC initiates its analysis. The degree of preprocessing is particularly important when the retrieval of execution data is considered. If the compiler can accommodate the Boolean insertions, the source program must be recompiled to establish an appropriate symbol table for the PGB. In either instance, execution data is supplied the AC in the form of an execution table based upon the source code structure established during PDL specifications. The initiation command has the form of a START instruction, i.e., a string of characters followed by a end-of-text indicator.

Output from the AC is in the form of an assertion table in which individual assertions are identified and the subsequent verification or violation is denoted.

C. Logical Function of the I/O Elements

The insertion of assertions and the subsequent generation of a resultant assertion table by the AC address the requirement for interaction with the testing and maintenance programmer. The designation and retrieval of program source code logically relates the program structures being studied by the AC to the previous implementation of PDL specifications produced during the design phase. Knowledge of such relationships must be supplied by the testing and maintenance programmer through interaction with the AC. The execution information supplied to the AC by the PGB is developed from previous compilation of the designated source code under examination. The amount of preprocessing required before compilation depends upon the specific source code compilers. The output of an assertion table by the AC depends upon the symbolic execution of the designated source code with the appropriate Boolean expressions already inserted.

ASSERTION CHECKER

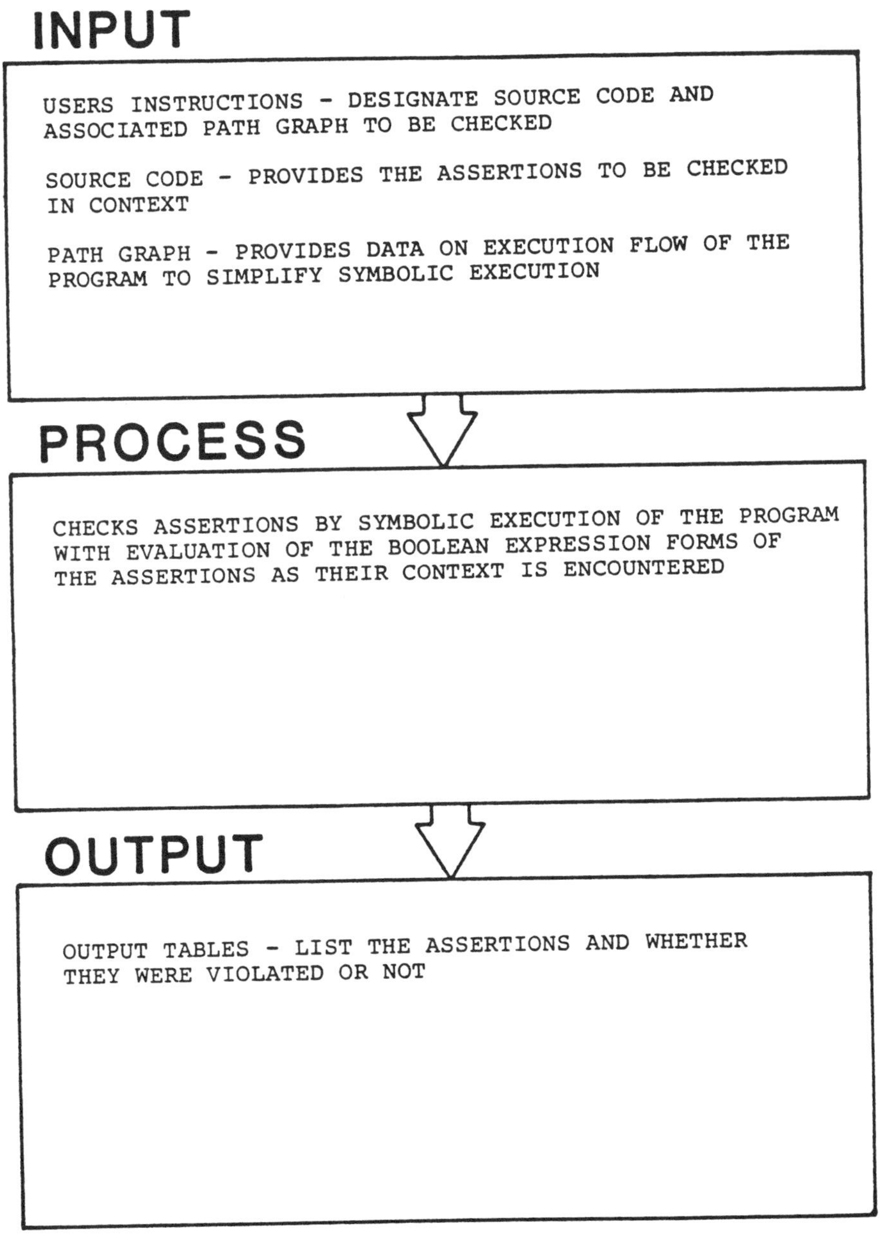
INPUT
USERS INSTRUCTIONS - DESIGNATE SOURCE CODE AND ASSOCIATED PATH GRAPH TO BE CHECKED
SOURCE CODE - PROVIDES THE ASSERTIONS TO BE CHECKED IN CONTEXT
PATH GRAPH - PROVIDES DATA ON EXECUTION FLOW OF THE PROGRAM TO SIMPLIFY SYMBOLIC EXECUTION
PROCESS
CHECKS ASSERTIONS BY SYMBOLIC EXECUTION OF THE PROGRAM WITH EVALUATION OF THE BOOLEAN EXPRESSION FORMS OF THE ASSERTIONS AS THEIR CONTEXT IS ENCOUNTERED
OUTPUT
OUTPUT TABLES - LIST THE ASSERTIONS AND WHETHER THEY WERE VIOLATED OR NOT

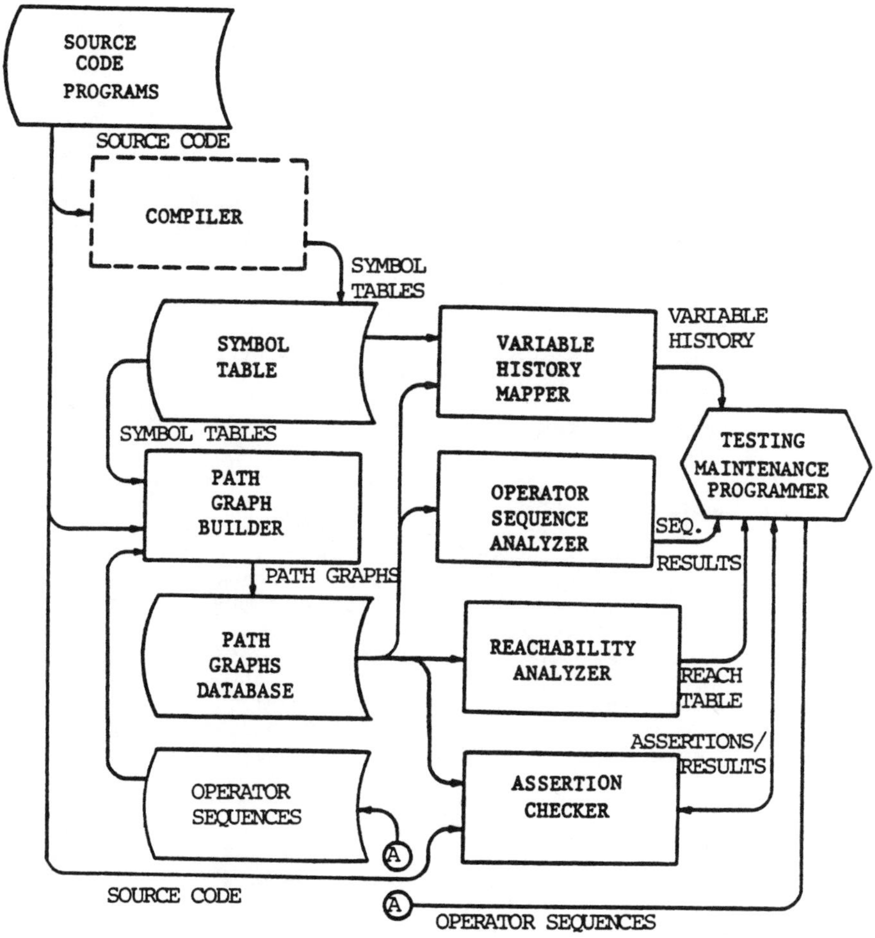
SOURCE CODE PROGRAMS
SOURCE CODE
COMPILER
SYMBOL TABLES
SYMBOL TABLE
VARIABLE HISTORY MAPPER
VARIABLE HISTORY
SYMBOL TABLES
TESTING MAINTENANCE PROGRAMMER
PATH GRAPH BUILDER
OPERATOR SEQUENCE ANALYZER
SEQ. RESULTS
PATH GRAPHS
PATH GRAPHS DATABASE
REACHABILITY ANALYZER
REACH TABLE
ASSERTIONS/ RESULTS
OPERATOR SEQUENCES
ASSERTION CHECKER
A
SOURCE CODE
A
OPERATOR SEQUENCES

3.2.2.1.15 CONFIGURATION BUILDER

1. INTRODUCTION

The Configuration Builder (CB) is for use during the coding, testing, and maintenance phase of the software lifecycle. The tool functions basically as a configuration manager, but is also capable of putting commands together for other tools to "build" configurations -- hence, the name. A list of the abbreviations used in this writeup appear below:

CB Configuration Builder
C^3I Communications, Command, Control and Intelligence
ISSE Integrated Systems Support Environment

2. FUNCTIONAL SUMMARY

The CB will derive its input from the relocatable object modules produced by the compilers of the ISSE. These object modules will contain the lists of external references and globally accessible symbols declared in each module as a separate part of their arrangement. The CB will operate as a post-processor to the compilers and may or may not require explicit invocation by the programmer. The object of the CB takes the form of a system dependency table which expresses the external dependencies (i.e., reference) of each module. This table will be resident in the file system of the ISSE and accessible by the programmer for inspection. The CB will also output several different entities derived from the dependency table upon programmer request. The programmer will need access to the dependency data in order to discern which modules are affected (and must therefore be modified) by a particular change to a particular module. Programmers must also construct instructions to the linker, and when modules are dependent on other modules in different libraries, the formulating of these linking instructions can become quite difficult. Using the CB, the programmer can request that the linking instructions (more particularly the names of the libraries in which the linker will find the references) be created for him in the form of command procedures or shell-type constructs, thereby saving much programmer time.

To build the dependency table, the CB must scan the information in the "external" portion of the object modules. Both the external information and each module's global variables are explicitly expressed in separate, predetermined blocks within each object module. It is these sections of the object modules that the CB scans for names of external references to be resolved and the symbols to which they refer. First the CB scans modules local to the same libraries making the external reference, then related libraries, and finally the remaining libraries and system libraries until a reference is resolved. Figure 3-22 depicts this table building and look-up activity.

After the initial construction of the dependency tables, the CB must provide the programmer access to the configuration information. There are two main circumstances under which the programmer might request this information: source configuration control and command generation. These two functions are discussed in the following paragraphs.

The CB administers configuration control for the source libraries as one of its most important functions. After the initial run of a compiler against a library of modules (i.e., after unit testing), or a library containing a combination of coded modules and stubbed modules (i.e., during unit testing), the system dependency tables are created and stored automatically on the ISSE file system by the CB. If an error is found during testing and a particular module must be changed, that change can be made and all references to that changed section can be identified by the CB. The programmer making the change can then inform others to change their code to accomodate for the change due to the original error. It should be noted here that not all resultant errors can be avoided when changing a particular section of software; but all errors of a data-dependent nature can be avoided and considerable time and effort saved by the use of the CB as a configuration manager.

The building of commands to the linker is the other major function of the CB. Upon programmer request, the CB can determine the libraries in which modules being referred to reside. The CB does this by simply looking up the reference in the previously built dependency tables. The search for the location of external references (performed when a new or revised object module is to be incorporated into a load module by the linker) by the CB starts in the object library hosting the referencing module, and continues to the other user and system object libraries until the reference is resolved or the libraries are exhausted. If the latter is the case, the CB will inform the programmer that certain modules necessary for successful linking are not present and must be produced (compiled) before the linking can commence. If all external references are resolved, the CB will prepare the command sequence for

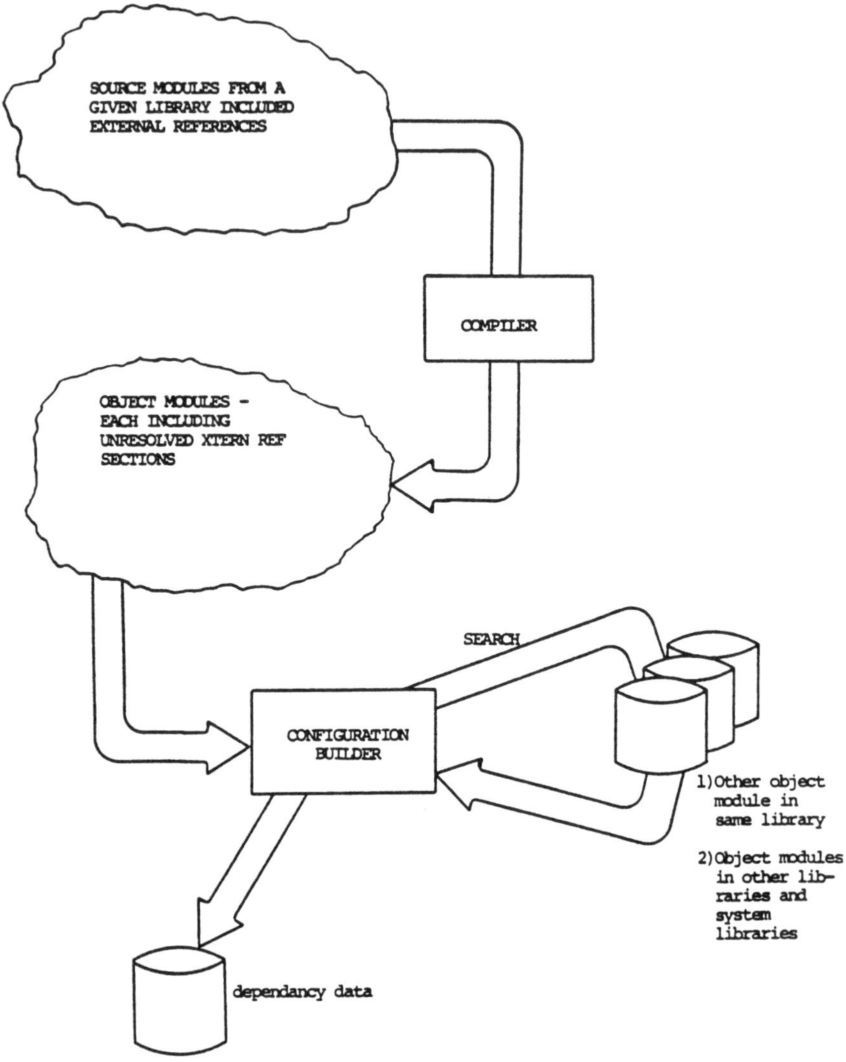
SOURCE MODULES FROM A
GIVEN LIBRARY INCLUDED
EXTERNAL REFERENCES
COMPILER
OBJECT MODULES -
EACH INCLUDING
UNRESOLVED XTERN REF
SECTIONS
SEARCH
CONFIGURATION
BUILDER
1)Other object
module in
same library
2)Object modules
in other lib-
raries and
system
libraries
dependancy data

FIGURE 3-22

linking by naming the libraries to be searched by the linker. It should be noted that the CB does not actually resolve external references, but simplifies the linker's job by telling it what libraries to search in order to resolve the external references. Figure 3-23 illustrates the use of the CB in building linking commands.

Criteria Addressed by the Tool

The CB enhances several software quality criteria pertaining to the products to be produced by the ISSE. These criteria and the way in which they are affected by the CB are listed below.

- Modularity. The CB reduces the human overhead time required to handle the module configuration.

- Simplicity. The CB allows each individual module to be coded in an understandable manner without having to be environment specific, i.e., the programmer need not know specifics of each configuration and program.

- Expandability. The CB facilitates the addition of new modules to load modules without requiring the programmers to examine tedious software interfaces.

Distributed Processing Considerations

The development of distributed systems mandates the use of the CB. The major reason for this is the good possibility of having several different compilers (e.g., Pascal, Fortran) generating code targeted for different nodes in the same network. The problem arises here when two modules, coded in different source languages and residing in two different processors, must communicate with one another. When this is the case, programmers have a particularly hard time trying to keep module interpendencies straight both for coding and maintenance. They must be fluent in both languages or work together extremely closely; this either damages productivity or increases the level of expertise needed to staff the project and results in cost increases and overruns.

3. BRIEF DESCRIPTION OF EXISTING TOOLS EXHIBITING SIMILAR FUNCTIONALITY

To our knowledge, there are no commercially available tools with the full functionality of the CB. However, many large development environments do have some automatic configuration management tools. One example is the MAKE facility provided as part of the IS/1 workbench from

PROGRAMMER	CONFIGURATION BUILDER
Builds commands to link mods A&B	
	Which libraries and versions?
Libl,6:LibD,4	
	Consults Dependancy Table--writes "Link Libl.A.6:LibD.B.4: Lib6,Libl/ Syslib 3"
	Into formatted command file
	Completion message with name of command file

DEPENDANCY TABLE

MODULE	LIBRARY	VERSION#	XTERN REFS	WHICH LIB. LOCATED IN?
A	LIBl	6	IDl	LIB6
			TYPE 2	LIB6
			SUBROUTINE X	LIBl
B	LIBD	4	FUNCTION XX	SYSLIB 3
C	LIBD	5	TYPE 3	NOT FOUND

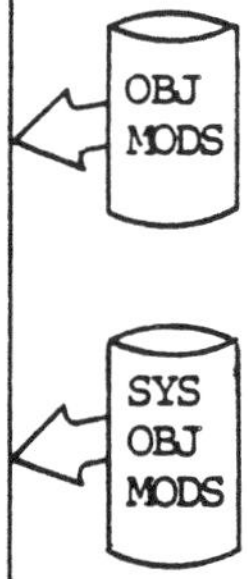

Figure 3-23. ILLUSTRATION OF CB BUILDING LINK COMMANDS FROM DEPENDENCY TABLE

Interactive Systems, Inc. MAKE has the all-important ability to maintain the system dependency charts which aid the software engineers in their maintenance efforts. However, MAKE does not generate command files for linking and does not attempt to resolve external references to appropriate libraries.

4. SUMMARY OF IMPROVEMENTS

It seems, then, that the techniques needed to build the CB exist (although they are somewhat fragmented) in industry currently; the major effort in implementing the CB will be one of integrating existing functionalities and expanding library searching methods in order to accomodate the increased number of modules that come with large C^3I applications development.

5. TOOL SPECIFICATION

A. Identification of the I/O Elements

The CB derives as input the information in the "unresolved external references" and "globally available symbols" sections of the object modules. The CB is initiated either automatically by the compiler (on option on compiler invocation) or explicitly by the programmer. The tool is then allowed read-access to the libraries it needs to scan and proceeds without further interaction.

The CB outputs its information to the file system of the ISSE for subsequent use by the programmer.

B. Form of I/O Elements

INPUTS - Object libraries - the CB must read the data derived above as stored by the compiler. The exact format of this data is a detail for the design of the compiler.

OUTPUTS - Dependency Table Information - Formatted pieces of the dependency table in human-readable form. The specific content of the output depends on exactly what was requested by the analyst.

- Formatted Commands - Commands to the linker instructing it on which libraries to search for unresolved references

CONFIGURATION BUILDER

INPUT

USERS INSTRUCTIONS - PROVIDES GENERAL DESCRIPTION OF DESIRED CONFIGURATION

OBJECT LIBRARIES - PROVIDE DETAILED DATA FROM WHICH CONFIGURATION IS BUILT

PROCESS

USING THE USERS INSTRUCTIONS AS STARTING POINT, ACCESSES NEEDED OBJECT MODULES AND TRACKS DOWN ALL EXTERNAL REFERENCES, CASCADING THRU MODULES IN WHICH REFERENCES ARE DEFINED

OUTPUT

DEPENDENCY TABLE - PROVIDES USER THE INTERMODULE DEPENDIES IN THE BUILT CONFIGURATION

FORMATTED COMMANDS - PROVIDES LINKER INSTRUCTIONS FOR COMPOSING THE BUILT CONFIGURATION FOR LOADING

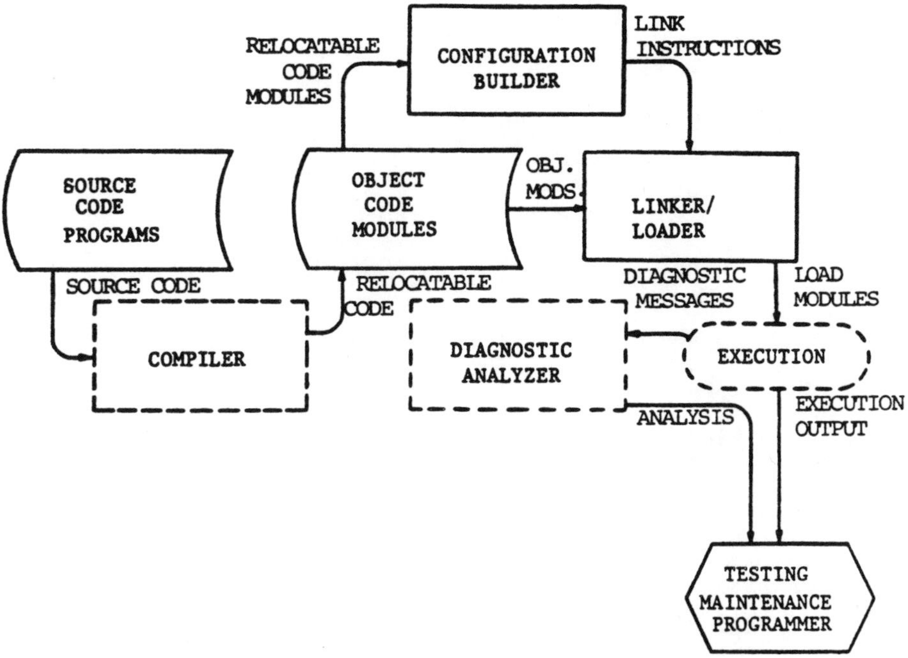
CONFIGURATION BUILDER
RELOCATABLE CODE MODULES
LINK INSTRUCTIONS
SOURCE CODE PROGRAMS
OBJECT CODE MODULES
OBJ. MODS.
LINKER/ LOADER
SOURCE CODE
RELOCATABLE CODE
DIAGNOSTIC MESSAGES
LOAD MODULES
COMPILER
DIAGNOSTIC ANALYZER
EXECUTION
ANALYSIS
EXECUTION OUTPUT
TESTING MAINTENANCE PROGRAMMER

3.2.2.1.16 VARIABLE HISTORY MAPPER

1. INTRODUCTION

The Variable History Mapper (VHM) is used during the implementation, testing and maintenance phases of the software lifecycle. The programmer, tester, or maintainer may invoke it to examine variable usage and the history of variable values within a specified program. The following abbreviations are used in this description:

PGB Path Graph Builder

VHM Variable History Mapper

2. FUNCTIONAL SUMMARY

An invocation of the VHM, the requestor specifies the path graph and any limitations to be utilized in the mapping. The path graph can be any graph previously generated by the Path Graph Builder (PGB). The VHM will obtain details on variables from the symbol table corresponding to the source code used by the PGB to build the graph. Limitations may be expressed in terms of subsets of the pertinent variables for a graph or in terms of the depth of history to be mapped. The VHM maps the requested variables by recording each operation on a variable and where it occurs. Each segment of the path graph is limited to a single operation on a variable. Thus each occurrence of any operation maps to a unique segment of the path graph. All operations on variables can be classed as either setting the variable or as only using the variable. Setting operations derive the value to which the variable is set from some source. This source may include a combination of variable values. The VHM records the source of the value for each occurrence of a setting operation. It further maps the variables if any that were combined to produce the value. The depth to which the VHM maps the variable values is dependent on the limits specified upon invocation of the VHM. For use operations, if the value of the variable is used in a setting operation of a variable, the VHM further maps that variable. The depth for these cascading maps is also determined by the limit specified upon invocation. The results of these maps is a symbolic history of the values for each variable.

The VHM must take into consideration the possibility of parallel processes concurrently accessing shared variables. The order of concurrent accesses to shared variables by parallel processes may be indeterminant. As long as these concurrent accesses are only use operations there is no problem, however if a set operation is involved an ambiguity might be introduced. The VHM must recognize the possibility for such ambiguities and flag them for special attention. Another characteristic introduced by distributed processing which the VHM must support is distributed locations. In distributed processing different sets of variables reside at each node. Processes on one node may reference variables located on another node. These internodal references may generate nodal dependencies that impact fault tolerance. Since fault tolerance is quite often an important quality in distributed processing, it is important to be able to obtain information about internodal references. The VHM should be capable of flagging all internodal references in its reports, and/or restricting a report to internodal references or variables which are associated with internodal references.

The product criteria affected by the VHM include consistency and fault tolerance. Through its reports which provide a detailed history of where a variable's value is derived and where a variable's value is used, the VHM provides the data necessary to detect any inconsistency concerning a variable. This assists the programmer or maintainer in assuring consistency. By the flagging of internodal references, the VHM alerts programmers and maintainers of areas which may require special treatment in order to provide fault tolerance. This enables the effort to establish fault tolerance to be more efficiently expended.

Distributed processing is addressed by the VHM in a couple of ways. By its highlighting of internodal references it helps isolate information about distributed interaction. This information is important when making decisions about the support needed for distributed data and about the support needed for particular connections between nodes. Its highlighting of concurrent accesses to data which may introduce ambiguities, isolates significant information about parallel process interaction. This information may impact decisions about the sequencing and synchronization of parallel processes.

3. BRIEF DESCRIPTION OF EXISTING TOOLS EXHIBITING SIMILAR FUNCTIONALITY

There are several compilers which include the capability to produce variable listings with set/used information. Other static analysis tools such as DATFLOW also exist which provide variable set/used information. These provide the capability to list all occurences of setting a program variable and of using a program variable. Some designate the location of set and use occurences by refering to statement numbers or line numbers of the source code. Others designate locations by refering to segments in the control flow graph of the program. Some tools provide simply an alphabetical listing of program variables with a list of reference numbers for all sets and a list for all users. Others add the capability to associate with each setting the subsequent uses which would access that value. They may also provide the converse, to associate with each use the prior settings which supplied the value accessed by the use. An additional capability may be to identify "live" variable definitions given a specific location in the program. The location being designated on invocation of the tool according to its scheme. A "live" variable definition refers to a variable whose value has been set prior to the designated location and for which there is a subsequent use.

4. SUMMARY OF IMPROVEMENTS

A. Functional Improvements

The extension to recognize internodal references information in the symbol table and note them in reports is needed. The capability to recognize parallel processes referencing shared data and to detect whether an ambiguity is introduced is a needed support for distributed processing.

B. Existing Desirable Capabilities

The variable set/use analysis capabilities that are currently available are still applicable in distributed processing and should be retained.

5. TOOL SPECIFICATION

A. Identification of I/O Elements

The path graph is supplied by the PGB. The symbol table is generated by the compiler. The invocation instructions are provided by the programmer or maintainer. The output is a report of the information on each variable formatted for display to the programmer or maintainer.

B. Form of I/O Elements

The path graph is stored in a file or database by the PGB, to be accessed as needed. The symbol table generated by the compiler is stored in a datebase available to other tools. The invocation instructions are generated in an interactive session with the programmer or maintainer. The output report may be interactively displayed or directed to a file or printer.

C. Logical Function of I/O Elements

The path graph provides a graphical form of the program. The graph segments are limited to a single operation on a variable, thus providing unique coordinates for referencing. The symbol table provides the information accumulated by the compiler on each variable, thus reducing the effort which must be put forth by the VHM. This information provides the VHM basic data on where the variable is defined and the location it has been allocated within the system. The invocation instructions direct the VHM in its actions. The output report provides the selected information to the programmer or maintainer.

VARIABLE HISTORY MAPPER

INPUT

PATH GRAPH - PROVIDES REFERENCE FOR LOCATIONS AND SEQUENCING OF OPERATIONS

SYMBOL TABLE - PROVIDES DETAILS ON EACH VARIABLE

INVOCATION INSTRUCTIONS - PROVIDE THE BOUNDS ON THE DESIRED PROCESSING

PROCESS

EXTRACT VARIABLE HISTORIES FROM PATH GRAPH AND SYMBOL TABLE INFORMATION AS REQUESTED IN THE INVOICING INSTRUCTIONS

OUTPUT

REPORT - PROVIDES SYMBOLIC HISTORY OF EACH VARIABLE, HIGHLIGHTING INTERNODAL REFERENCES AND CONCURRENT ACCESS AMBIGUITIES

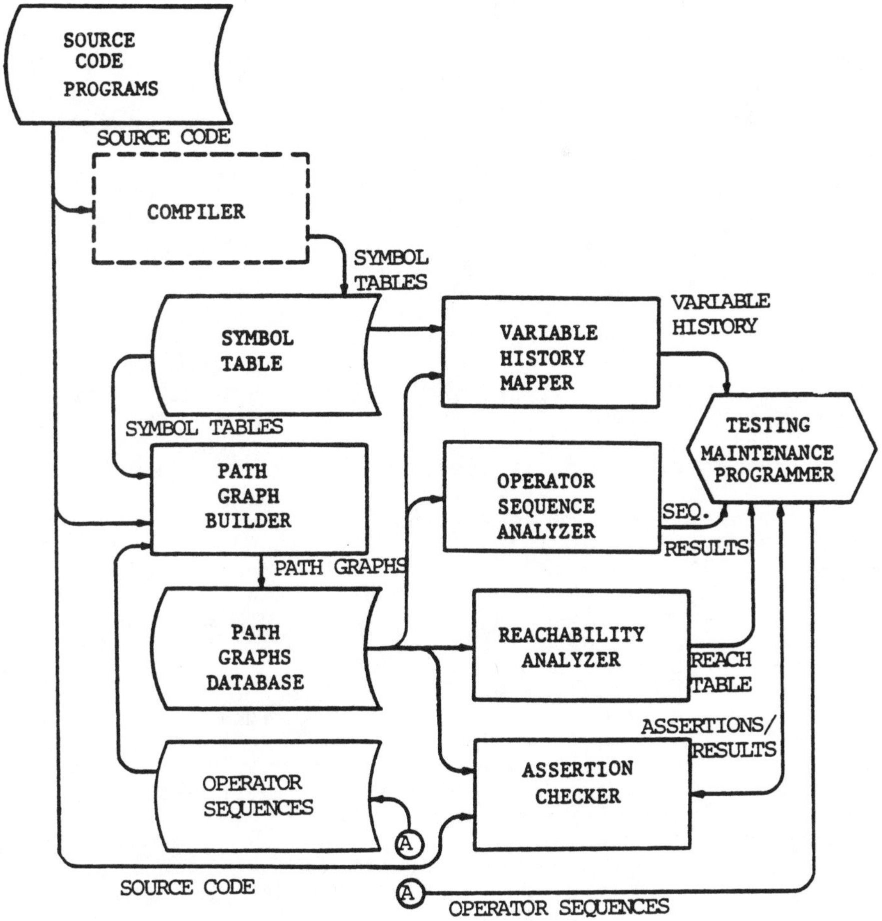
SOURCE
CODE
PROGRAMS
SOURCE CODE
COMPILER
SYMBOL
TABLES
SYMBOL
TABLE
VARIABLE
HISTORY
MAPPER
VARIABLE
HISTORY
TESTING
MAINTENANCE
PROGRAMMER
SYMBOL TABLES
PATH
GRAPH
BUILDER
OPERATOR
SEQUENCE
ANALYZER
SEQ.
RESULTS
PATH GRAPHS
PATH
GRAPHS
DATABASE
REACHABILITY
ANALYZER
REACH
TABLE
ASSERTIONS/
RESULTS
OPERATOR
SEQUENCES
ASSERTION
CHECKER
A
SOURCE CODE
A
OPERATOR SEQUENCES

3.2.2.1.17 REACHABILITY ANALYZER

1. INTRODUCTION

The Reachability Analyzer (RA) is used during implementation, testing, operation, and maintenance phases to examine questions about execution paths. These questions arise during debugging, validating, verifying, or modifying.

PGB	Path Graph Builer
RA	Reachability Analyzer
JAVS	JOVIAL Automated Verification System

2. FUNCTIONAL SUMMARY

The Reachability Analyzer (RA) takes the path graph generated by the Path Graph Builder (PGB) as its major resource for information with which to address the users questions about execution paths. The user may request information about what variables control the execution flow from one specified segment in the program path to another. The segments which can be referenced by the user include those established by the PGB which have a single entry point and single exit point. A significant concern of the RA are the conditions on exit which determine the next segment in the execution flow. Also of interest to the RA are the various possible conditions which could exist on entry to a segment dependent on which path of segments has been executed prior to the current segment. Another category of segments which can be referenced by the user are those which can be formed through interval analysis. In the path graph the connections between segments are nodes. An interval is a maximal subgraph of the path graph generated by the PGB, which has a single entry node and in which all closed paths contain the entry node (Fig. 3-24). Intervals derived directly from the path graph are considered to be first order or basic intervals. Higher order intervals may be derived by considering graphs in which the current order intervals are the nodes and the segments are only the exit segments of these intervals. The major concerns of the RA are still the conditions on entry and exit. It is through the analysis of these conditions, using such techniques as predicate testing, that the RA is able to respond to some reachability questions.

Since a complete, exhaustive reachability analysis may be rather expensive in terms of time and computer resources, and quite often is not desired, it is necessary to have the capability to restrict the analysis. This need for

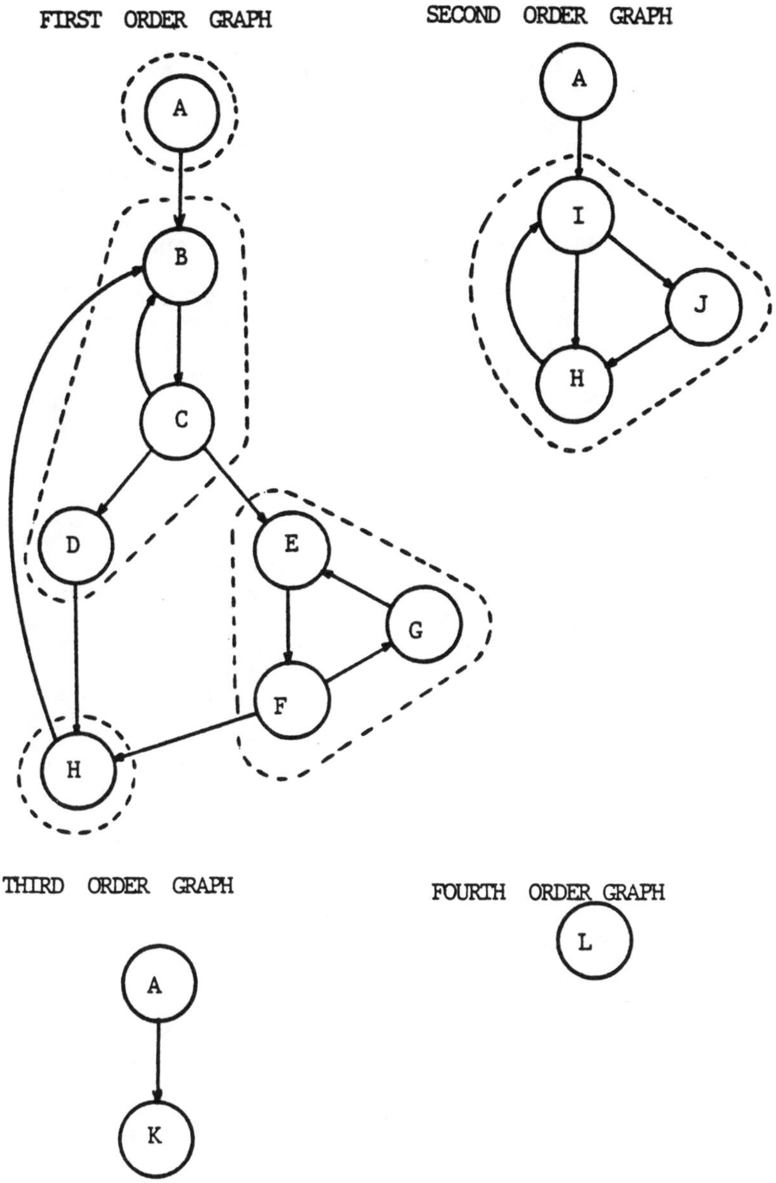

Fig. 3-24 Path Graph Intervals

restriction necessitates the ability to describe the state of conditions for any segment in the graph. Other restrictions which must be specifiable are the starting and ending nodes for analysis, any limitations on the nodes to be considered, such as include or exclude nodes in parallel paths, and any simplifications such as treating a previously analyzed subgraph as a single node. Other limitations may restrict analysis to derived graphs, in which the only segments from the original graph that are of interest are those which include an operation on a specific data object or group of objects. The RA should be very flexible concerning the manner in which the operations of interest can be designated. It should support designation by object or objects acted on, and by general class of operation, and by where defined, and by where used, and by a specific listing of operations. The more flexible the RA is in the ways that its analysis may be restricted, the easier it will be for the user to direct its analysis toward a specific are of interest.

The product criteria addressed by the RA include fault tolerance and modularity. The RA by its testing of reachability can reveal erroneous branching. This can lead to the discovery of uncovered conditions. The correction of these errors yields more complete coverage in the product, thus improving its fault tolerance. Also, by restricting analysis to exclude paths on a specific processor, an analyst can examine the effect of the loss of that processor. This can reveal the need of additional paths when the specified processor has failed. Thus the RA can be used to directly analyze fault tolerance to faults which eliminated a processor. Modularity can be affected by the interval analysis supported by the RA. Intervals are excellent candidates for modules. Forming modules from intervals helps to establish modules with a single entry point. There are other properties that must be examined when selecting modules, such as data referencing requirements. Interval boundaries do have good execution flow properties which make them good module boundaries.

Distributed processing requires special consideration in an RA due to the possibility of parallel paths. A unique feature that may be present with parallel paths is synchronization points. The RA must do its analysis in terms of a compound node composed of the nodes of each individual parallel process. The number of compound nodes is bounded by the product of the number of nodes for each process. Synchronization points can also have an effect on the number of possible compound nodes. Synchronization forms pairs of nodes from parallel processes and requires that the first process reaching its node in the pair, wait until the other process reaches its paired node. Thus synchronization may segregate the node of processes into subsets which may execute in parallel only with corresponding subsets of the other processes. This ability of synchronization to segregate the nodes into subsets can be adversely affected by loop structures. Reachability questions in distributed processing may include questions which span processes. Given that process one has reached a specified node, can process two reach a specified node? The RA must address these questions by referring to a composite path graph composed of the compound nodes and segments which correspond to segments in the individual process path graphs. Thus, connected compound nodes can only differ in their node for only one process.

3. FUNCTIONAL DESCRIPTION OF EXISTING TOOLS EXHIBITING SIMILAR FUNCTIONALITY

There are several static analysis tools, such as JAVS, which include the uniprocess function of reachability analysis within their capabilities. They can determine the set of paths between specified statements. They can also generate sets of branches that reach a specified statement. These capabilities are still applicable in distributed processing as paths and branches in each process are the same as those in a uniprocess. Therefore, the techniques currently in use are appplicable to the majority of the analysis required in distributed processing.

4. SUMMARY OF IMPROVEMENTS

A. Functional Improvements

Distributed processing requires the capabilities of reachability analysis be expanded to handle the compound nodes which reflect the fact that processes are executing in parallel. Another extension which will help control the size growth of the analysis task is the capability to analyze derived graphs. These graphs may be formed by restricting interest to only a specific set of operations, such as those acting on one or more shared data objects.

B. Existing Desirable Capabilities

The path analysis techniques currently in use for uniprocess analysis are still applicable to distributed processes. The major difference is that they must be applied simultaneously to parallel processes.

5. TOOL SPECIFICATION

A. Identification of I/O Elements

The RA receives the path graph built by the PGB and in response to users questions or requests produces a report of its analysis results.

B. Form of I/O Elements

The path graph is provided from the PGB in a file or database form. The users questions and requests take the form of direct interactive commands. The report may be output interactively or directly to a file or printer.

C. Logical Function of I/O Elements

Path Graph provides a graphical form of the program, resolved into single entry single exit segments. These segments may also be restricted to a single operation on a data object. The nodes or connections of these segments represent the state of a data object or a combination of states of several objects.

User's commands provide the directions for carrying out an analysis of the graph. They indicate the portion of the graph of interest and specify any restrictions or limitations on the scope of the analysis.

The report provides the results of the analysis to the user.

REACHABILITY ANALYZER

INPUT

PATH GRAPH - PROVIDES PROGRAM TO BE ANALYZED AS A GRAPH RESOLVED INTO SINGLE OPERATION SEGMENTS WITH SINGLE ENTRY AND SINGLE EXIT.

USER'S COMMANDS - PROVIDE DIRECTIONS AS TO WHAT PORTION OF THE GRAPH IS TO BE ANALYZED

PROCESS

ANALYZE THE PATH GRAPH AS TO WHAT NODES ARE REACHABLE AND WHICH VARIABLES CONTROL THE EXECUTION FLOW TO REACH THE NODES OF INTEREST

OUTPUT

REPORT DELINEATES NODES WITHIN BOUNDS OF ANALYSIS WHICH ARE NOT REACHABLE UNDER GIVEN CONDITIONS, DENOTES CONTROLING VARIABLES FOR EACH PATH OF INTEREST

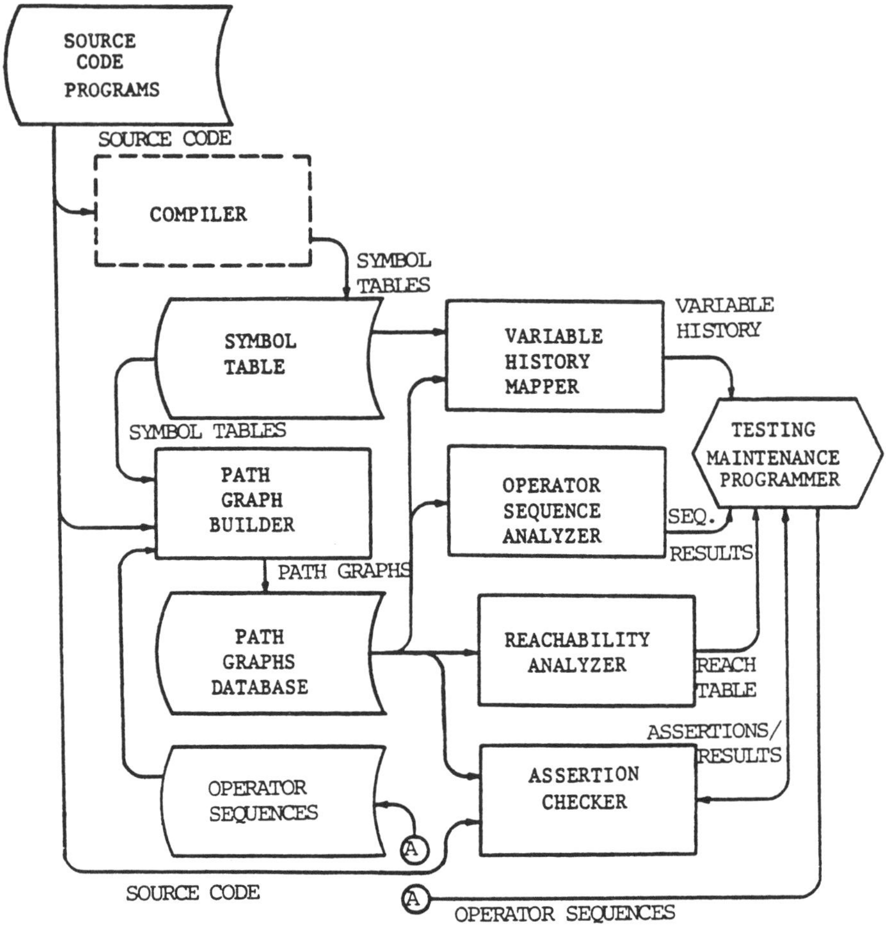
SOURCE CODE PROGRAMS
SOURCE CODE
COMPILER
SYMBOL TABLES
SYMBOL TABLE
VARIABLE HISTORY MAPPER
VARIABLE HISTORY
TESTING MAINTENANCE PROGRAMMER
SYMBOL TABLES
PATH GRAPH BUILDER
OPERATOR SEQUENCE ANALYZER
SEQ.
RESULTS
PATH GRAPHS
PATH GRAPHS DATABASE
REACHABILITY ANALYZER
REACH TABLE
ASSERTIONS/ RESULTS
OPERATOR SEQUENCES
ASSERTION CHECKER
A
SOURCE CODE
A
OPERATOR SEQUENCES

3.2.2.1.18 OPERATOR SEQUENCE ANALYZER

I. INTRODUCTION

The Operator Sequence Analyzer (OSA) is used during the implementation, testing, and maintenance phases of the software lifecycle. Given an operators' allowable sequence graph and a program path graph, both generated by the Path Graph Builder (PGB), the OSA analyzes the program graph to determine if all operator orderings in the program are included in the operators' allowable sequence graph. The following abbreviations are used in this description:

OSA	Operator Sequence Analyzer
PGB	Path Graph Builder
RA	Reachability Analyzer
VHM	Variable History Mapper

2. FUNCTIONAL SUMMARY

The OSA takes paired graphs, one program path graph and one operators' allowable sequence graph, both generated by the PGB as its input. Which pair of graphs it is to take must be specified upon invocation. An implementation should support user friendly ways of specifying the pair of graphs. An example would be, the user specify an abstract data type which would generate a database lookup to provide the pair of applicable graphs to the OSA. If either or both graphs were not available, the proper command to cause their generation should be provided in the failure response.

The graphs generated by the PGB are doubly linked list with entries for each node and each arc of the graph. With nodes representing object states and arcs representing operators, the entries are sufficient for the description of the graph of a single process. For distributed processing, with its parallel processes, there will need to be synchronization information for each entry or in special entries which connect the graphs of separate processes.

The OSA will process the program graph by applying the algorithm for distributed systems discussed by Howden in "A General Model for Static Analysis and Its Application to Distributed Systems", included as an appendix to this report. As he cautions, the number of compound states for a distributed system is only bounded exponentially. Therefore an implementation must exercise care in applying the algorithm. One way to attempt to avoid exponential storage requirements is to only maintain data for the current path. This does not guarantee avoidance but will provide a significant reduction in most cases.

Another detail for consideration in the implementation of the algorithm is the action to be taken when an illegal sequence of operators is found. One tack would be to generate a message specifying the arc and corresponding source code statements, and then continue processing the node from which that arc came. Additionally, an implementation may choose to accummulate a list of illegal arcs and mark legally processed entries. Upon completion of the traversal of the graph, a composite listing of all illegal code could be generated by using the accumulated list of illegal arcs as starting points and searching out unmarked entries in the program graph

Other kindred tools in the ISSE that also process path graphs are the Variable History Mapper (VHM) and the Reachability Analyzer (RA). When the VHM is constrained to analyze the variables on which a set of operators act, it produces the histories for the origin of values of those variables as a complement to the analysis of the OSA, which ascertains whether the operators have been applied in a proper sequence. The RA will discover paths in a program graph which will never be executed due to the values which the controlling variables can assume, in contrast the OSA discovers paths which should not be executed as they introduce an improper sequence of operators. Thus these three tools the OSA, VHM, and RA, all analyzing path graphs provide complimentary views of the program.

The OSA addresses both consistency and compliance in the produced software. Since the OSA analyzes the sequence in which operators are used, it tests both that the usage of the operators is consistent throughout the program and that the usage complies with any specified sequencing restrictions.

Distributed processing is addressed in the OSA by the fact that its analysis is carried out with compound states describing parallel processes. For this analysis to be successful the input graphs generated by the PGB must include synchronization information.

3. BRIEF DESCRIPTION OF EXISTING TOOLS EXHIBITING SIMILAR FUNCTIONALITY

There are a number of static analysis tools currently on the market. The algorithms they use apply to single processes. The extension of those algorithms to parallel processes requires significant modifications to the tools. An example is the algorithm described by Howden. In the extension to distributed processes, an exponential in the number of processes plays a role in describing the size of the resultant compound graph. Since the algorithm traverses the graph, the exponential also impacts the implementation of the algorithm for distributed processes.

4. SUMMARY OF IMPROVEMENTS

A. Functional improvements

Needed improvements to accommodate distributed processing, include the addition of synchronization information to the graphs analyzed by the OSA. With this synchronization information available, the analysis must then be carried out using compound states which are needed to describe the combined states of parallel processes. The analysis can then be capable of handling operator sequences which span several processes thru synchronization. This capability is necessary with complex distributed systems.

B. Existing Desirable Capabilities

The existing capability to analyze operator sequences within a single process is still necessary and included within the extended algorithm.

5. TOOL SPECIFICATION

A. Identification of I/O Elements

Interactive instructions from the programmer or maintainer direct the OSA to the two graphs it is to use in its analysis. Both the program path graph and the operators' allowable sequence graph are obtained from the database where they were stored upon generation by the PGB. The output report may be interactively displayed to the user or directed to a file or printer.

B. Form of I/O Elements

The users instructions are on interactive command line. The graphs are a doubly linked list stored in a graph database. The output report is formatted test for display.

C. Logical Function of I/O Elements

The users instructions provide the information needed to identify the graphs to be analyzed. They may directly name the graphs or provide a description which must be looked up in the database in order to identify the pertinent graphs. The graphs provide the sequencing of operators which are to be compared by the algorithm. Also included in the graphs is synchronization information which defines the set of reachable compound states of the combined graphs of parallel processes. The output reports pass the results of the analysis back to the user, informing the user of all occurences of illegal sequences and relating those to sections of code.

OPERATOR SEQUENCE ANALYZER

INPUT

USER INSTRUCTIONS - SPECIFY GRAPHS FOR ANALYSIS

PROGRAM PATH GRAPH - PROVIDES SEQUENCING OF OPERATORS IN THE PROGRAM

OPERATOR ALLOWABLE SEQUENCE GRAPH - PROVIDES PERMISSIBLE SEQUENCES OF OPERATORS

PROCESS

ANALYSIS - COMPARE SEQUENCES APPEARING IN PROGRAM GRAPH AGAINST SEQUENCES SPECIFIED IN ALLOWABLE SEQUENCE GRAPH, RECOGNIZING ALL ILLEGAL SEQUENCES

OUTPUT

REPORT - PROVIDES ALL ILLEGAL SEQUENCES OF OPERATORS FOUND AND CORRELATES THEM TO SOURCE CODE STATEMENTS

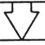

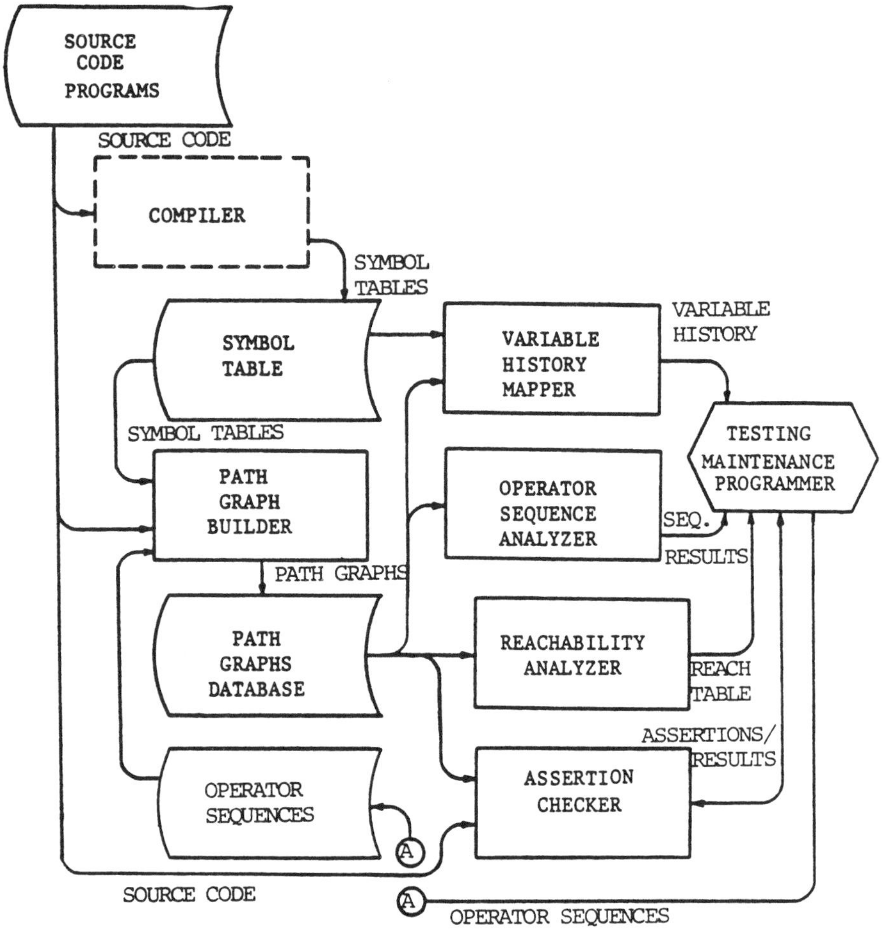
SOURCE
CODE
PROGRAMS
SOURCE CODE
COMPILER
SYMBOL
TABLES
SYMBOL
TABLE
VARIABLE
HISTORY
MAPPER
VARIABLE
HISTORY
SYMBOL TABLES
TESTING
MAINTENANCE
PROGRAMMER
PATH
GRAPH
BUILDER
OPERATOR
SEQUENCE
ANALYZER
SEQ.
RESULTS
PATH GRAPHS
PATH
GRAPHS
DATABASE
REACHABILITY
ANALYZER
REACH
TABLE
ASSERTIONS/
RESULTS
OPERATOR
SEQUENCES
ASSERTION
CHECKER
A
SOURCE CODE
A
OPERATOR SEQUENCES

3.2.2.1.19 LINKER/LOADER

1. INTRODUCTION

The Linker/Loader is designed for use in the implementation, testing, and maintenance phases of the software lifecycle. It transforms the relocatable object modules produced by a compiler into executable object code modules for a specific target using the system dependency table produced by the Configuration Builder. It is initiated by commands for the testing and maintenance programmer.

List of abbreviations include:

LL Linker/Loader
CB Configuration Builder
ISSE Integrated System Support Environment

2. FUNCTIONAL SUMMARY

The LL uses the system dependency table produced by the CB to map relocatable object code into executable code segments for a specific target architecture. That relocatable object code was previously generated through compilation of program source code. Information concerning the specific target architecture was previously entered by the testing and maintenance programmer. Each module of relocatable object code which serves as input to the CB is produced through independent compilation. Consequently, the CB accesses all independently compiled relocatable object code modules to construct a subset associated with the particular architecture under examination. Using this subset, the CB produces a system dependency table based upon the external references contained in each relocatable object code module. Using the system dependency table, the LL is able to access specific relocatable object code modules and prepare them for a specific target architecture. Each module or relocatable object code is prepared independently by the LL for its location within the target architecture being implemented. How these independently produced executable target modules are placed within the pertinent target architecture is beyond the scope of an ISSE. Such activity occurs during the operational phase of a target architecture and can only be simulated by an ISSE.

The LL characterizes a specific architecture in terms of linkages between nodal processors. Various processors can be accommodated at individual nodes within the specific architecture, e.g., Single Instruction Multiple Data

(SIMD) and Multiple Instruction Multiple Data (MIMD). The LL prepares an executable object code module for each nodal processor within the architecture. Space constraints within specific nodes can be addressed through modular overlays by the LL. However, these constraints must be entered into the LL by the testing and maintenance programmer before the LL produces its executable object code modules for the specific architecture.

Since executable object code modules are produced independently by the LL, a mechanism to accommodate internodal references within a specific architecture must also be provided by the LL. That particular mechanism is closely related to the types of references between architectural nodes, e.g., one node requires data located at another node or an executable object code module uses a procedure call that requires parameter passing. All types of references between nodes must be accommodated by the LL.

After a particular architecture and its references between nodes has been accommodated by the LL, a set of executable object code modules has been produced on a node-by-node basis for that architecture. If a particular module requires overlaying, that overlaying of the executable object code has already been accomplished. When the target architecture has been loaded with these executable products of the LL, that target architecture requires initialization to begin its operation. Such initialization is outside the scope of an ISSE. The actual target initialization activity occurs during the operational phase of a target architecture and can only be simulated by an ISSE.

The structure of a LL can be subdivided into several separate functions. The most obvious concerns interaction with the testing and maintenance programmer. Of course the programmer must be able to enter commands but he must also be able to enter architectural descriptions of the target. Included in such architectural descriptions is information concerning overlays and communication between nodes. These are subtle issues requiring innovation if the interface provided the testing and maintenance programmer is to remain user-friendly. Another function of the LL concerns the retrieval of the independently compiled relocatable object code modules specified by the system dependency table of the CB. This retrieval capability must equal the retrieval capability of the CB. The third and final function of the LL concerns the production of executable object code modules for a particular target architecture. Included in such information is how the target architecture is to initialize itself.

The subsequent loading and initialization of the target architecture occurs during the target operation phase and is beyond the scope of an ISSE.

Several software quality criteria of a product under development within the ISSE are addressed by the LL. The criterion of traceability is implemented in the target architecture by the LL. That implementation is introduced through the linking of executable object code modules to a particular target architecture. The criterion of modularity is enhanced by the LL since the executable object code modules are produced independently for the processing nodes within a specific target architecture under examination. The implementation within that architecture addresses the distribution of control, the interconnect architectures, and pertinent databases.

The LL addresses distributed processing through the implementation of target architectures. Such architectures can exhibit distributed processing characteristics and pose issues which are resolved through the use of the LL, e.g., overlaying nodal software and orchestrating the references between nodes of a distributed architecture. How successfully these characteristics and issues are resolved depends upon the expertise of the testing and maintenance programmer. Performance of the LL does not exceed the information provided by the testing and maintenance programmer.

3. BRIEF DESCRIPTION OF EXISTING TOOLS EXHIBITING SIMILAR FUNCTIONALITY

The LL is an established tool within currently available software environments. Every vendor typically supplies a LL with its minimal software system. Their capabilities include linking specific object modules to target runtime routines. The target executable object code produced by a LL is directed toward single nodes within the target architecture. More sophisticated LLs provide additional capability such as specially linking for overlays in specific nodes within a target architecture. In such instances, the sophisticated LL is often reclassified to a Linkage Editor. However, such capability is rare within the distributed processing environment. Many emerging architectures simply require sophistication beyond the current LLs and their more sophisticated Linkage Editors. An example is offered by intelligent communication satellites. Viewed as targets, these devices require development LLs in the traditional sense. However, if one of these targets begin to malfunction, the previously generated LL needs to generate an upline load of its communication information prior to shutdown. Consequently, the basic definition of a LL has been extended within such an architecture. When upline loading is considered, the basic definition of a Linkage Editor has also been extended. The current situation within hardware architectures is that these sophisticated architectures are outdistancing some of the software tools that support them. One of the software tools which is lagging behind is the LL.

4. SUMMARY OF IMPROVEMENTS

A. Functional Improvements (new capabilities)

The functionality of a LL within emerging distributed software environments is becoming increasingly important. The production of target executable object code on a nodal basis within a distributed architecture is becoming increasingly sophisticated. A development tool like a LL must accommodate such increasing sophistication within the framework of an ISSE. However, the level of sophistication available within a LL should not exceed the level of sophistication exhibited by the using testing and maintenance programmer.In other words, an unsophisticated programmer should be provided a relatively modest capability by the LL. On the other hand, a highly-experienced programmer should be provided as sophisticated a linkage/loading capability as he can require from the LL. In effect, the functional improvement for a LL is to raise or lower its capability as a function of the demand placed upon it.

B. Existing Desirable Capabilities

The existing capability for linking specific object modules to target runtime routines must still be offered. Such current capability is closely related to specific vendor softwre environments, e.g., DEC and IBM. This present capability needs transported to an ISSE which, in turn, can be transported to a variety of vendor software environments. The level of capability offered by an ISSE should meet or exceed the requirements originated by a testing and maintenance programmer.

C. Elimination or Reduction of Existing Capabilities no Longer Needed

None of the capability offered by existing LLs should be eliminated or reduced when transported to the framework of an ISSE. In fact, extensions and additions should be made to accommodate the increasing sophistication of distributed processing architectures.

5. TOOL SPECIFICATION

A. Identification of I/O Elements

The LL is initiated by the testing and maintenance programmer. Prior to initiation, the programmer specifies what object code modules are to be retrieved and converted into executable code segments for a specific target architecture. The format (e.g., direct storage or overlays) of each executable code segment must be specified and directed to appropriate nodes within the target architecture. To accomplish some of this activity, the programmer relies upon the system dependency table produced by the CB. Acting upon the input information and initiation supplied by the testing and maintenance programmer, the LL retrieves the specified object code modules and produces output patterned for the specific target architecture. Output is in a medium which can be transported and loaded into the target architecture.

B. Form of the I/O Elements

Input to the LL is straightforward and originates from two different directions.The first and most obvious source of input is the testing and maintenance programmer. Textual information is supplied to describe the target architecture and the various alternatives associated with loading that architecture. File identifiers and location information is supplied concerning the object code modules which are to be retrieved and prepared by the LL. The second source of input originates from the retrieval process. Strings of object code are retrieved by identifier and location for preparation of executable target object code.

Output by the LL is in terms of precisely packaged executable object code modules associated with the specified target architecture. Such modules are strings of executable object code which are placed on a transport medium capable of being loaded by the target architecture itself.

C. Logical Function of the I/O Elements

The source of logical input for the LL is the testing and maintenance programmer. The mapping of object code modules into executable target code segments is specified by the programmer. According to these instructions produced by the programmer, the LL retrieves and outputs the target code segments. No independent logic is exercised by the LL.

LINKER/LOADER

INPUT

USER INSTRUCTIONS - IDENTIFIES OBJECT MODULES TO BE PREPARED FOR LOADING IN A SPECIFIED TARGET ARCHITECTURE

OBJECT MODULES - PROVIDES OBJECT CODE TO BE PREPARED FOR LOADING

TARGET ARCHITECTURE - PROVIDES SPECIFICS ABOUT REQUIRED CHARACTERISTICS OF THE LOAD MODULE

PROCESS

PROCESSES OBJECT CODE IN THE OBJECT MODULES, RESOLVING EXTERNAL REFERENCES AND INSERTING ADDRESSING DATA FOR RUNTIME RESOLUTION OF REFERENCES IN ACCORDANCE WITH THE SPECIFIC CHARACTERISTICS OF THE TARGET ARCHITECTURE

OUTPUT

OUTPUT LOAD MODULE - IS PRODUCED ON A MEDIA WHICH IS READILY TRANSPORTED TO TARGET ARCHITECTURE FOR EXECUTION

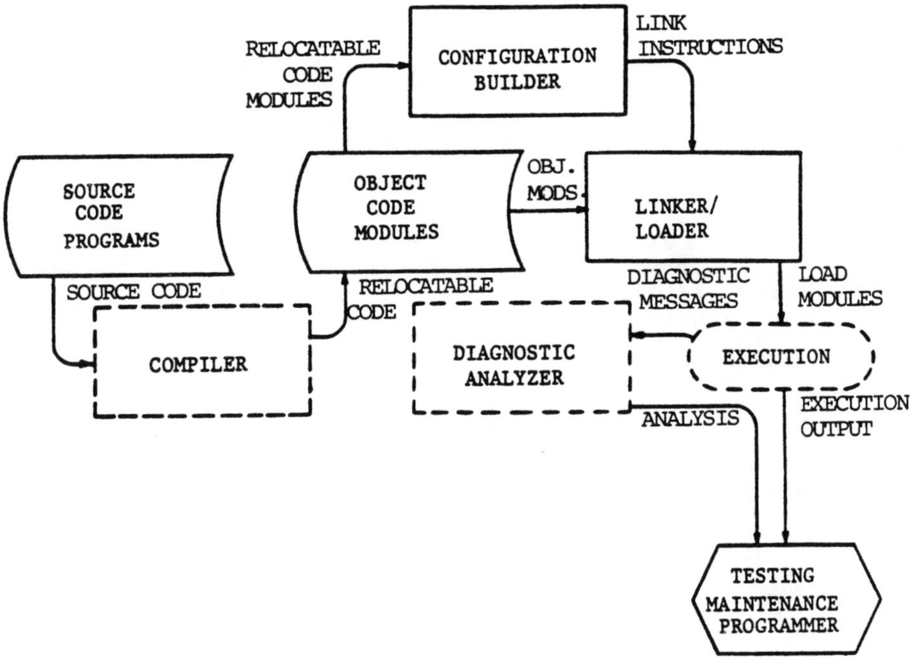
RELOCATABLE CODE MODULES
CONFIGURATION BUILDER
LINK INSTRUCTIONS
SOURCE CODE PROGRAMS
OBJECT CODE MODULES
OBJ. MODS.
LINKER/ LOADER
SOURCE CODE
RELOCATABLE CODE
DIAGNOSTIC MESSAGES
LOAD MODULES
COMPILER
DIAGNOSTIC ANALYZER
EXECUTION
ANALYSIS
EXECUTION OUTPUT
TESTING MAINTENANCE PROGRAMMER

3.2.2.2 DISTRIBUTED PROCESSING IMPACTED TOOL PRIORITIES AND BENEFITS

An initial analysis of an ISSE has been completed. Approximately 45 tools comprise the ISSE. Of those tools, 19 directly benefit the implementation of distributed processing software. Priorities within the 19 tools have not yet been addressed. More analysis needs to be performed before priorities are established.

As a first step, the 19 tools are grouped by lifecycle phase. Within each phase the tools are ranked in order of importance to distributed processing. The following lifecycle rankings result.

Requirements Phase

1) Requirements Interface Processor (RIP)
2) Functional Requirements Interpreter (FRI)
3) Static Requirements Analyzer (SRA)
4) Automatic Language Translator (ALT)

Design Phase

1) Design Interface Processor (DIP)
2) Hardware Simulator (HS) or Control Simulator (CS)
3) Serialization Analyzer (SA)
4) Performance Analyzer (PA)

Coding, Testing, Maintenance Phases

1) Path Graph Builder (PGB)
2) Reachability Analyzer (RA)
3) Operator Sequence Analyzer (OSA)
4) Variable History Mapper (VHM)
5) Assertion Checker (AC)
6) Concurrency Checker (CC)
7) Configuration Builder (CB)
8) Linker/Loader (LL)
9) Cross Reference Generator (CRG)
10) Interface Mapper (IM)

From the above ranking procedure, three candidates for more important tool are evident, i.e., the RIP, the DIP, and the PGB.

As a second step, preference is shown tools which work at a high level of abstraction and which condition information for other tools to use. As a consequence the RIP is ranked ahead of the DIP which, in turn, is ranked ahead of the PGB. However, such a ranking is misleading because tools of second order importance to the RIP and DIP could be more important than the PGB. To address such issues, the following considerations were performed. Weight was given to tools which supported design feasibility. Of such tools, the ones providing feedback for evaluation purposes were assigned greater importance. Such a decision was felt justified on the basis of information provided concerning expectations. Whether a software product met or exceeded expectations was deemed very important early in the lifecycle phases. Next in importance was the establishment of static analysis during the implementation or coding phase. Once the software has had it validity verified, a check of its consistency in meeting requirements was valued. The importance of extending the previous static analysis and consistency checking to distributed processing should be emphasized. Upon completion of such considerations, a ranked listing of the 19 tools and their benefits is produced. The most important tool is ranked first.

Ranking	Tool	Benefit
1)	RIP	Automates the entry of requirements.
2)	DIP	Automates the entry of design.
3)	HS	Provides direct feedback for design feasibility on a nodal basis.
4)	CS	Integrates HS support of nodes with design feasibility feedback.
5)	FRI	Provides requirements feedback to determine if expectations are met.
6)	SA	Addresses distributed proessing design.
7)	PGB	Provides breakdown for static analysis.
8)	RA	Accomplishes basic static analysis.
9)	OSA	Accomplishes sophisticated static analysis.
10)	SRA	Provides requirements consistency feedback.
11)	PA	Provides automated analysis of feasibility simulation statistics.
12)	VHM	Extends static analysis to implementation phase.
13)	AC	Provides symbolic execution of implementation phase.
14)	CC	Constructs and traverses state tables.
15)	CB	Expedites product implementation.
16)	LL	Defines implicit internodal communication.
17)	CRG	Extends traditional support to distributed processing.
18)	IM	Extends traditional support to distributed processing.
19)	ALT	Provides alternate means for checking requirements against expectations.

3.2.3 Tools Not Impacted by Distributed Processing

To complete a full complement of software development tools to support the full life cycle of distributed processing applications, an ISSE will need to include a number of tools which are not impacted by distributed processing issues. The criteria for whether a tool should be included in an ISSE for distributed processing is whether the tool is needed to support the development and production of a product which operates in a distributed processing architecture. The tools impacted by distributed processing issues were described in a previous section of this report. Many of the tools which are not impacted by distributed processing issues fall in the category of basic software development support tools. Others deal with documentation or administrative support of the software life cycle.

3.2.3.1 Tool Descriptions

The following paragraphs are brief descriptions of tools that are not impacted by distributed processing issues but may be needed to complete an ISSE supporting the development of distributed processing applications.

3.2.3.1.1 Text Editor. The backbone of any computer supported software development system is the text editing support provided. This may be accomplished with a powerful, flexible, easy-to-use general purpose editor. Other options include specialized support such as word processing for document writing and program editors for entry or modification of source code or pseudo code. There is a multitude of editors commercially available from which to select. Opinions as to which are best tend to vary due to varied experience with different editors. One desirable characteristic is simple, straight-forward commands for basic edit functions. A desirable feature to support more complex commands is interactively available documentation to explain commands, their use and syntax.

3.2.3.1.2 Document Generator. Document generators are just starting to appear in conglomerate tools or integrated support systems. Their function is usually to process the information accumulated in a database and produce in a prescribed format a readable document. Depending upon the detail available in the database and the format specification, the document may be fully worded or only an outline. Usage seems to be gravitating toward the earlier phases of the life cycle, with applications converting database stored requirements specifications into a standard format readable form. The latter phases of the life cycle are tending toward high level languages with self documenting quality.

3.2.3.1.3 Document Management System. The requirements for a document management system are highly dependent on both the volume of documents and the size of documents which must be managed. In low volume, small size documents, a simple file system may be satisfactory. If high volume or large documents are involved, a more complex management system is required. Desirable capabilities include management of versions and editors. Versions are usually copies of an identical program except for limited specific differences for an application with a minor requirements variation. Editions are copies of an identical program which have been updated with corrections or modifications. Some management schemes address the matrix of versions versus editions. The need for this addressal varies with the amount of interdependencies amont the versions or editions. It is important that the document management system selected be at least sufficient to maintain all the needed data. If it is later determined that new capabilities are needed and an upgrade of the management system is undertaken, it is very difficult to regenerate any previously discarded data.

3.2.3.1.4 Account Management System. An account management system is a very important tool in a software development environment. It is a tool by which management maintains control over the expenditure of resources. The most desirable characteristic is that it not place a significant burden upon the technical talent involved in the actual development.

3.2.3.1.5 Work Scheduling System. A work scheduling system is usually only needed for the development of very large systems on which several diverse groups will be working with minimal interaction. The work scheduling system combines the data supplied for each assignment which includes groups involved, effort required of each group, resources required, inputs required from other assignments, other outputs, and time estimates. From this combined data plus overall information such as desired start and ending dates, and work load capacity of each group, the work scheduling system can calculate the feasible schedules of assignments. Many work scheduling systems are quite elaborate and expensive to run; therefore, their usage is only cost effective when applied to large expensive systems.

3.2.3.1.6 Structure Checker. A structure checker is usually designed to deal with PDL or a structured language description of functional specifications. Its advantage is that it can be applied early in the design to coding transition to catch errors in the writeup of functional specifications. It normally only recognizes specific structure keywords, and is therefore, limited in the errors it can recognize; however, the correction of these errors greatly improves the correctness and clarity of the functional specifications passed into the coding phase.

3.2.3.1.7 Standards Auditor. A standards auditor is used to enforce standards prescribed by supervision throughout the software life cycle. They must be customized to enforce the selected standard. Most often they are used to enforce coding standards in order to improve readability and clarity, and thereby reduce maintenance costs. Usage in the earlier phases of software development with textual requirements, PDL or pseudo code is also possible.

3.2.3.1.8 Menu Generator. A menu generator is a rather specialized tool which assists in the development of interactive applications using screen displays of menu options. It provides support to quickly and easily design screen formats and define input fields within screen formats. This can greatly reduce the needed effort both in the initial development of applications interactive screens and when modifications to those screens are needed.

3.2.3.1.9 Report Generator. A report generator is a specialized tool which assists in the development of formatted output reports of an application. It provides support to quickly and easily design the page formats and define the content of specific fields within the formats. It also supports defining which pages are to be included in particular copies of reports and to whom they are to be routed. This greatly eases the development of applications which produce written reports.

3.2.3.1.10 Formatter. A formatter is a "nice-to-have" tool for improving printed output in the system software development environment. Its availability enables technically oriented writers to input their textual material disregarding details of format. The formatter can combine material input by different personnel and eliminate any idiosyncrasies of format details, and produce a printed output that conforms to a specified format.

3.2.3.1.11 <u>Instrumenter</u>. An instrumenter is a useful tool during debug and testing efforts. It provides support for the insertion of code into a program in order to answer particular questions or collect specific data. The most useful instrumenters are those that supply very flexible support for the specification of where code is to be inserted. Another feature that increases its usefulness is the availability of standard or library routines for gathering statistics which can be readily inserted.

3.2.3.1.12 <u>Stub Generator</u>. Stub generators are useful during module testing. They provide an automated means of generating brief or null substitutes for other referenced modules which are not available or not to be exercised. This is useful for testing modules prior to integration or during maintenance when isolating a module for testing is desired.

3.2.3.1.13 <u>Version Generator</u>. A version generator is used to develop the definition of versions of software that arise during the life cycle of a software system. The maintenance of multiple versions must be handled by a supporting management system such as the document management system previously described. The version generator must support the development of initial definitions by providing a capability to determine if a definition includes all necessary modules. It should also support changes to a version with detection of whether changes are consistent with dependencies determined by other tools.

3.2.3.1.14 <u>Historical File Generator</u>. An historical file generator provides automated support for the accumulation of execution statistics for multiple test runs. Care must be exercised in the design of such a tool as the ability to segregate the statistics out by which run may be important for certain types of analysis of some applications.

3.2.3.1.15 <u>Timing Analyzer</u>. A timing analyzer is used to calculate the time required to execute specific segments of code from data collected on executions of the program. By specifying segments which correspond to time constrained functions delineated in the requirements, it is possible to examine the program's ability to comply with the required time constraints.

3.2.3.1.16 Usage Counter. The usage counter is used to collect the execution statistics for individual program objects. Depending on the instrumentation and its relation to the objects for which usage is desired, this may be a trivial task or require a significant amount of deduction.

3.2.3.1.17 Completion Analyzer. A completion analyzer is used to examine the thoroughness of testing that has been accomplished. It is usually designed to work in concert with other tools such as an instrumenter and historical file generator.

3.2.3.1.18 Storage Dumper. The storage dumper is a necessary tool for saving program status. For debug purposes it is often needed so that it can be invoked in response to a catastrophic error which defies other debugging techniques. It is most helpful if it can provide a formatted output in a human readable form. This includes such niceties as instructions in assembler mnemonics, data in character or applicable numeric form. As many systems cannot distinguish the proper form, the storage dumper may provide multiple form interpretations of the same storage elements.

3.2.3.1.19 Symbolic Debugger. The symbolic debugger provides support for referencing loaded program elements by their source code symbolic name. The various actions that need support in this form include status snapshots of program elements, breakpoint insertion relative to symbolic locations, and tracing of operations involving program elements.

3.2.3.1.20 Resource Management Analyzer. A resource management analyzer is used to support the evaluation of resource management in the target environment for the application. The data needed by this tool for its analysis is accumulated during execution of the application. The results of its analysis are used to determine if the application will be able to function sufficiently to meet requirements or whether a different resource management scheme will be necessary.

3.2.3.1.21 Emulator. An emulator is used to mimic the target hardware so that the software developed can be exercised as it will be executed during operation. Some emulators are implemented in software which provides an opportunity to include additional debug support. If real-time or near real-time emulation is necessary, the emulator is implemented in hardware, sometimes special faster hardware is utilized to provide additional debug support. To support distributed processing, it is necessary to have emulators for each element of the system to be included in the emulation and to link them in the same fashion as the target architecture.

3.2.3.1.22 Compiler. A compiler is a necessary support tool for software development in a high level language. It provides the transformation of high level language source code text into relocatable object code suitable for processing by a system builder or linker/loader. There is a wide variation in the capabilities included in compilers. This can be attributed to the differences in expectations of organizations which have had compilers constructed and the intended usages of the compilers. Some compilers devote a significant effort to diagnostic analysis of programs in order to provide meaningful error messages to inexperienced programmers. Others devote significant effort to optimization of the code they generate in order to produce a high quality product. Some varieties of compilers generate code for hardware other than the system they reside on.

3.2.3.1.23 Mutation Tester. A mutation tester is a specialized testing tool which attempts to uncover errors in a program by constructing variations of that program. These variations are constructed by making changes in a program in a manner similar to a correction. The assumption is that the current variation of the program contains an error of a type correctable by the mutation tester's algorithms.

3.2.3.1.24 Diagnostic Analyzer. The diagnostic analyzer is a tool used to address errors which occur during the operation phase. This requires the tool to either reside in the target system or obtain data from the target system. Since the diagnostic analyzer's main purpose is to isolate in the source code text the correction to be made, if it resides in the target it must be supported there by a significant amount of data about the source code text. The tradeoff on which direction to transfer the large amount of data to support a diagnostic analyzer is usually determined by the capabilities available in the target system.

3.2.3.1.25 Calling Tree Generator. A calling tree generator is used to produce a hierarchy of the sequence of execution of modules. This information is useful for understanding how a module fits into the whole system. From a graph of this information it is easy to deduce which modules are necessary to support a particular module. It is also possible to deduce which modules are indirectly supported by a particular module; however, this requires a full search of the graph for every occurrence of the supporting module.

3.2.3.1.26 Correctness Analyzer. A correctness analyzer is used to compare the implemented source code against the specified requirements. Its analysis reflects the traceability of functional requirements to code. This comparison is used to verify that a program's response is compliant with the response stated in the functional requirements. As formal proof techniques are not yet practical for the treatment of large programs, most correctness analyzers implement informal techniques to improve confidence in the produced program.

3.2.3.1.27 Data Base Simulator. Data base simulators are used to support feasibility studies in the design phase. Current simulators are only known for single nodes. To support distributed processing, a simulator would be needed to each node to be simulated. The control simulator for distributed processing would handle the distributed aspects affecting the data bases.

3.2.3.2 Priority Assignments of Tools Not Impacted by Distributed Processing

From the 27 tools not impacted by distributed processing in the ISSE, the following ranking is produced. The most important tool is ranked first.

Ranking	Tool
1	Text Editor
2	Compiler
3	Data Base Simulator
4	Timing Analyzer
5	Usage Counter
6	Historical File Generator
7	Resource Management Analyzer
8	Completion Analyzer
9	Storage Dumper
10	Symbolic Debugger
11	Emulator
12	Document Management System
13	Document Generator
14	Calling Tree Generator
15	Structure Checker
16	Instrumenter
17	Version Generator
18	Stub Generator
19	Standard Auditor
20	Formatter
21	Correctness Analyzer
22	Diagnostic Analyzer
23	Mutation Tester
24	Report Generator
25	Menu Generator
26	Account Management System
27	Work Scheduling System

The above ranking is based upon the following considerations. The highest priority is assigned tools which produce results useful to distributed processing, e.g., the compiler and text editor. Lowest priority is associated with highly restrictive tools with limited capability, e.g., administrative management tools. Between these two extremes, the tools are ranked on the basis of important to the software development cycle.

3.2.4 ISSE Issues

The ISSE must provide all of the functions necessary for full development of distributed systems. Section 3.2.2 discussed the impacts of distributed systems on the ISSE tools themselves; this section addresses the remaining considerations for design and implementation of an ISSE for distributed C³I systems. Some of these considerations fall beyond the scope of this report, but a high-level treatment of all the pertinent issues is still necessary for a full understanding of an ISSE. The major issues for consideration other than the tools themselves can be placed in one of three areas: interconnection of the tools, database organization and management, and issues surrounding the eventual target environment. The interconnection of the tools as well as the tools' interface with the host operating system must be strictly specified before the attempt to design or integrate the first tool is made. This is the subject of section 3.2.4.1. Section 3.2.4.2 is a discussion of database issues. These issues are highly environment dependent; that is, the vendor must be identified before final database interfaces can be described. However, possible conceptual databases can be evaluated prior to vendor selection. Finally, section 3.2.4.3 deals with issues concerning the final target machines and their interface to the ISSE.

3.2.4.1 Tool Interconnections

When the tools eventually decided upon are to be implemented, a great deal of attention must be paid to the overall arrangement of the support environment. The individual descriptions of the tools in section 3.2.2.1 dealt with the workings of the tools themselves. But these tools must work and exist together in the same environment, and they cannot simply be thrown together. Some of the most important considerations for tool interconnections are command languages, interfaces between tools and data sequencing/protection. These are the issues addressed in the following paragraphs.

The command language, which is part of the host's operating system, is an integral part of the configuration of the set of tools in an integrated environment. Figure 3-25 depicts a tool's interface to the command language and the human user. The human interacts with the tools through (1) a human interface built into the tool, (2) user defined command procedures built from the command language, or (3) the command language itself. The structure of the commands the tools accept, then, must be the same as the structure of the command language itself. This will make the interaction with all the tools more consistent, and therefore, easier to understand and remember. An example of structure might be the ordering of commands and parameters. If the command language of the host operating system uses the convention of command before parameters, and a particular tool reverses this order, confusion is introduced. To minimize difficulty when trying to implement many tools together, the tool should be built only after the command language is precisely defined. This will reduce the amount of inte-

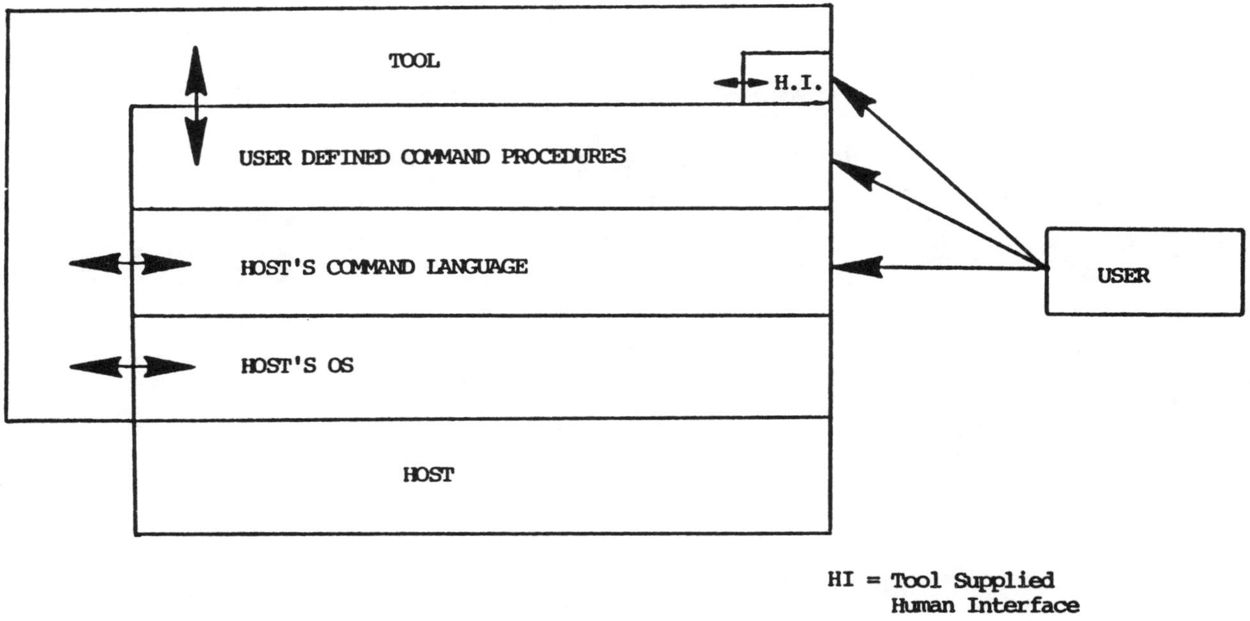

FIGURE 3-25 A Tool's interface with the user and the host

grating code needed to install tools as well as make them simpler to use.

The tool-to-tool interfaces are also very important for adequate performance of an integrated set of tools. Most obvious here is the fact that outputs must be structurally identical to inputs when tools are strung together. This implies that tools that process each others information, i.e., closely coupled tools, should be designed in parallel or have their I/O specifications done before design takes place. If this is not done, much effort is needed to pre-process inputs in order to make them compatible for particular tools.

The sequencing and partitioning of data is one of the hardest elements of integration to define and control. Much of this depends on two things: (1) the DBMS on the host environment and (2) the architecture of the host itself. Item (1) is discussed in the following section on databases. Item (2) is one of the first things known about an Integrated Systems Support Environment. If the host is a uniprocessor based system which is fairly standard, no real considerations for tool interconnections arise. However, if the host is distributed, the communications strategies between nodes must be considered. In this case, the tools may have to be designed with some knowledge of the architecture on which it is running. This host architecture must accommodate the data sequencing and partitioning required by the tools or the tools must be altered to limit their realm of data access.

In summary, the host environment and the tools' relationship to each other, the host, and the human user must be carefully defined (if not existing) or examined (if existing) before the design specifications are produced.

3.2.4.2 Databases

Database organization of the host system is a crucial consideration. Since most of the intertool I/O interfaces are accommodated by data buffering and not direct coupling, this is another issue to be considered prior to tool design. As a result of this fact, the prioritization of the tools presented in sections 3.2.2.2 and 3.2.3.2 were made under the assumption that an adequate DBMS will exist on the machine(s) which will host the tools. The definition of "adequate" DBMS is the subject of the rest of this section.

The most important consideration is assuring that the database subscheme, or the conceptual view of the physical database, is capable of supporting the different views required by the tool set. By "supporting" the different views we mean that a database design language (DDL) exists with which we can express the characteristics of the view to the subscheme. Figure 3-26 illustrates this relationship between views, subscheme and physical database. The different tool groups that use a common database (the term database was used throughout this document for simplicity--they are really database views) must each have these databases implemented by the same physical and conceptual database. If the conceptual view of the database is capable of implementing the DDL descriptions of all of the various views, then the DBMS is adequate for the needs of the tool set.

If the eventual host environment is implemented as a network, several extenuating points for consideration arise. Research on the design of distributed databases indicates that it is possible to design and build DBMSs that span nodal boundaries. This would be a requirements for any integrated tool set if it was to be distributed. Determining the best data model for this system (relational, network, hierarchical) is a sizable effort and care should be taken with regards to data integrity, ease of access, and data security. At any rate, the implemented data model should be invisible to the tool; indeed, the installation should be able to change the actual data model without having to alter the tool's use of their respective database views.

3.2.4.3 Target Issues

The relationship of the targets to the host is a dynamic one which must be examined before the tools of the support environment are designed and integrated. The target is obviously the eventual host for the products that are developed on the host, and the transition line for the product between target and host is fuzzy at best. This impacts the tools at the lower end of the life cycle phases heavily but only slightly at the upper end. For instance, is the loading process accommodated by host or target? How is symbolic debug accomplished between host and target? How are uploaded diagnostics handled by the host? These questions are complicated, of course, when the target is a distributed architecture. It is impossible to precisely answer these questions without knowing the precise nature of the target, but the integrated tool set can be designed to minimize the customized program for each product.

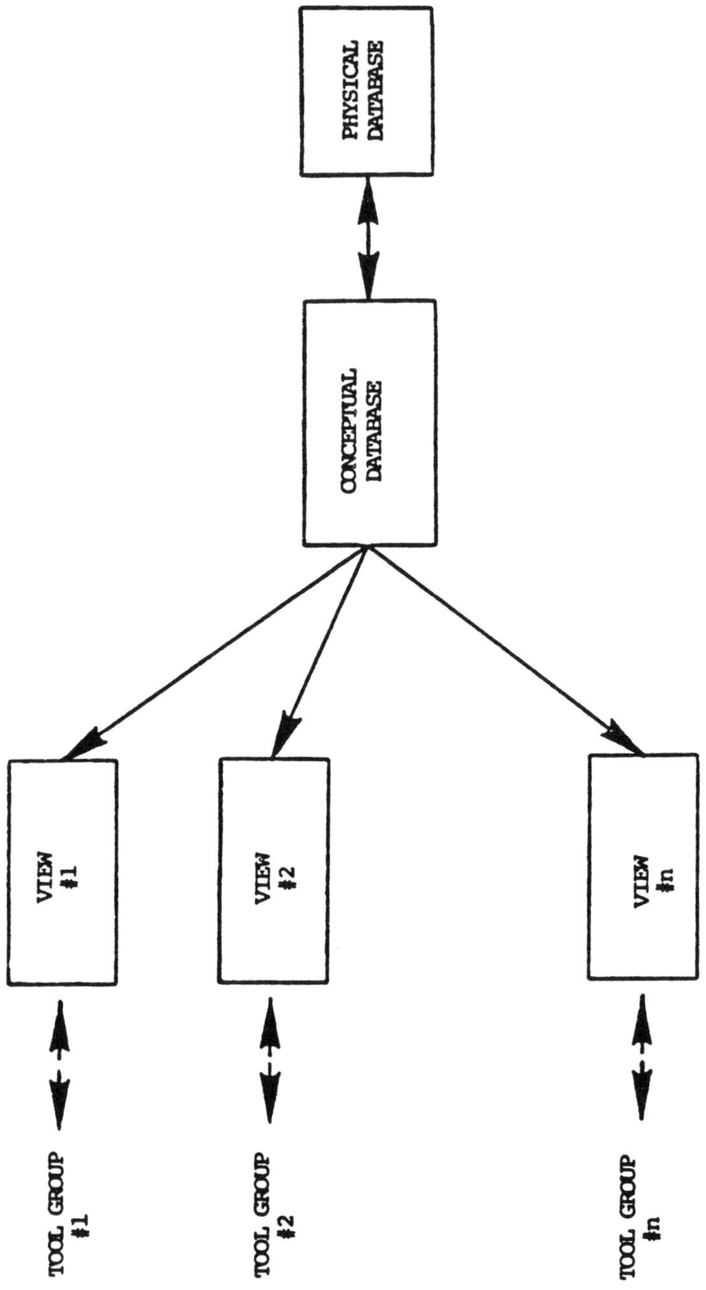

FIGURE 3-26 Levels of abstraction in a database system

Flexibility of tools at the low end of the software life cycle (testing, maintenance) phases is the best way to minimize customized programming. For example, the linker/loader described in section 3.2.2.1.19 will accommodate multiple target architectures or yield to a vendor supplied loader. Symbolic debugging can also be accomplished regardless of target architectures if the design is flexible.

Many of the host-target interactions, though, must be coded as part of the application and cannot by accommodated by the tool set. Run time diagnostics, for example, differ from application to application and must be produced by the running product. The analysis of these statistics is the responsibility of the host environment when the target is embedded, and this software must be designed in parallel with the application.

The functions wholly dependent on the target configuration, then, must be accommodated by the software developed for that target. If a software tool is dependent on the target only to a partial degree, a tool can be made flexible by design to accommodate the wide variety of architectures encountered in distributed C³I processing. The range of the types of architectures that the development environment will be used for must be specified as precisely as possible before dollars are spent on tool design. The more specifically the target environments can be described and the narrower their range is found to be (that is, the closer the possible target architectures are to one another), the more specific the tools with direct interfaces to the targets can be made.

Appendix A: Tool Cost, Manpower, and Schedule Estimates

This appendix presents the results of the effort to arrive at good estimates of calendar schedule and cost for the nineteen distributed processing-impacted tools described in 3.2.2.1. Throughout this section, the reader should bear in mind two important facts about the nature of software estimating: (1) if an estimation of any kind is to be done previous to detailed design (as was the case here), the estimates should be taken as "ball park" figures at best and (2) the estimation is only as good as the empirical data used to drive the model or method. These two points for consideration are discussed in more detail in the following paragraphs.

The estimation of the characteristics of software products before they have been designed is a very inaccurate science at best. Quite simply, not enough is known about the proposed product to arrive at hard and fast estimates. Basically then, the estimation of schedule and cost of software prior to design provides two distinct benefits: (1) it forces the consideration of elements of the task that might have otherwise been overlooked until a later, more critical point in the product's lifecycle and (2) it provides management with "ballpark" estimates which can be used as a basis for feasibility of "bid-no bid" decisions. The data that are used to drive the method or model are the most important single consideration of the estimate. If the product being estimated is of a completely new and complex nature, it is very difficult to describe the characteristics of the task in terms of past experience; a key part of the estimating process. On the other hand, if the project is being done by a group of people who have experience with the development of similar products, empirical data about those products drive the estimate of the new project to a greater degree of accuracy.

In general, two factors positively impact the accuracy of the estimate; the amount of detail we have about the project and the amount of past experience we have with similar efforts. The remainder of this appendix is divided into four sections; the first presents the method used to arrive at the estimates, the second shows the reader the form the data are displayed in and how to interpret them, the third section contains the estimations themselves and the fourth summarizes the estimates in tabular form.

A.1 Method

The method that was used to arrive at the cost and schedule estimates for the nineteen different tools involved 3 steps.

1. Study internal and outside products to determine average size ranges for different classes of tools. This included examining existing tools that had similar functionality to the ones we identifed and described. As a result of this study, we named categories that most tools fall into and identified upper and lower limits (for the number of executable, machine language instructions) for each category.

2. We looked at each tool individually and determined its appropriate placement within its groups. To do this, a list of eight factors which contribute to the magnitude of software was used. For each tool, we estimated the relative amount of each of these eight criteria. Then we simply summed the product of the criteria and the percentage of that criteria possessed by the tool under evaluation. This process resulted in a magnitude estimate that fell somewhere within the ranges arrived at in step (1).

3. Using the magnitude estimates resulting from step (2) as well as empirical data gained from our knowledge of similar development efforts, we described the task to an automated parametric software estimating model (namely PRICE Software Cost Estimating Model, RCA). With the parameters fully described, the model then produced the actual cost and scheduling estimates. These are presently in the following section. A diagram of this procedure appears in figure A-1.

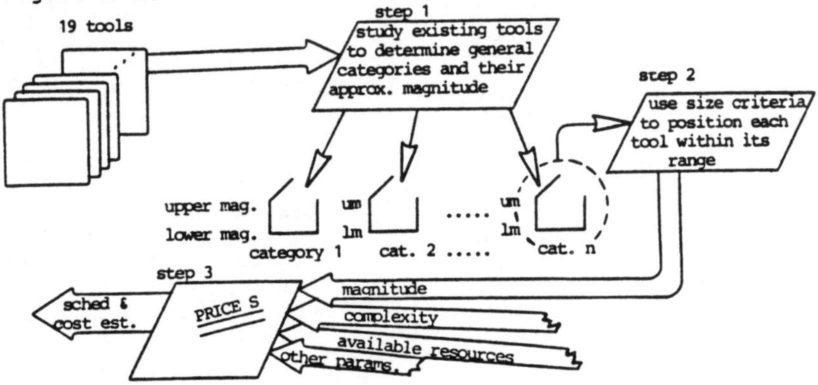

Figure A-1 Process Used for Estimating

We believe that this method applied to General Dynamics' excellent pool of experience and the functional descriptions of the tools as presented in Section 3.2.2.1, resulted in the most realistic estimates possible. To improve on these estimates, preliminary design must be carried out on a tool-by-tool basis to expand our knowledge of the tools.

A.2 Estimates

This section presents the cost and schedule estimates obtained using the method described in section A-1 of this appendix. For each of the 19 tools, the set of input parameters and the pertinent output parameters to/from the PRICE S model are presented. A brief description of the typical range and meaning of the parameters appears below.

INSTRUCTIONS is the total number of deliverable, executable, machine-level instructions which describe the size of the software development effort. The method used to arrive at this number is detailed in section A.1 of this appendix.

APPLICATION is a single parameter that summarizes the application mix of instructions. Its normal range is from 0.866 to 10.952. Values toward the lower end of the range describe programs that are predominately math and string manipulation. Values toward the higher end represent greater emphasis on real-time command and control and interactive applications. In general, the larger the value of APPLICATION the more difficult the programming task.

RESOURCE is an empirically derived parameter which includes such items as skill level, productivity, efficiency, computer operating charges, labor and overhead rates. The RESOURCE of 3.50 used in these PRICE S runs was empirically derived from similar development efforts conducted here at General Dynamics.

UTILIZATION is the fraction of available hardware or total memory capacity to be used in the target machine. It describes the extra effort needed to adapt software to operate within limited processor capabilities. Since the tools being costed in these estimates are for use in a support role, a value of 0.5 was entered for UTILIZATION. This value will not effect the model's output.

PLATFORM is the variable which describes the customer's requirements stemming from his planned operating environment. It is a measure of the portability, reliability, structuring, testing and documentation required for acceptable contract performance. Table A-1 below summarizes typical values for PLATFORM.

Operating Environment	PLTFM
Production Center Internally Developed S/W	0.6 - 0.8
Production Center Contracted S/W	1.0
MIL-Spec Ground	1.2
Military Mobile (Van or Shipboard)	1.4
Commercial Avionics	1.7
MIL-Spec Avionics	1.8
Unmanned Space	2.0
Manned Space	2.5

Table A-1 Typical Platform Values

A PLATFORM value of 1.20 was used for these estimates due to the level of documentation required for a military software development effort.

COMPLEXITY is the variable which provides a quantitative description of the relative effect of complicating factors on the design task. Factors entering into COMPLEXITY are product familiarity, personnel skills, hardware/software design interactions, and any unusual factors present in the development environment that affect the development schedule. Table A-2 summarizes the adjustments which, when applied to a base of 1.0, yield the COMPLEXITY value for the task.

	CPLX ADJUSTMENT
PERSONNEL	
OUTSTANDING CREW, AMONG BEST IN INDUSTRY	-0.2
EXTENSIVE EXPERIENCE, SOME TOP TALENT	-0.1
NORMAL CREW, EXPERIENCED	0
MIXED EXPERIENCE, SOME NEW HIRES	+0.1
RELATIVELY INEXPERIENCED, MANY NEW HIRES	+0.2
PRODUCT FAMILIARITY	
OLD HAT, REDO OF PREVIOUS WORK	-0.2
FAMILIAR TYPE OF PROJECT	-0.1
NORMAL NEW PROJECT, NORMAL LINE OF BUSINESS	0
NEW LINE OF BUSINESS	+0.2
COMPLICATING FACTORS	
FIRST TIME WITH LANGUAGE	+0.1
FIRST TIME WITH PROCESSOR	+0.1
NEW LANGUAGE	+0.2 to +0.3
NEW HARDWARE	+0.2 to +0.3
MORE THAN ONE LOCATION/ORGANIZATION	+0.2
MULTINATIONAL PROJECT	+0.4
HARDWARE DEVELOPED IN PARALLEL OR MANY CHANGING REQUIREMENTS	+0.2 to +0.3

Table A-2 Typical COMPLEXITY Adjustments

For the tool estimates, the value of COMPLEXITY was computed as follows:

	1.0
CPLX=first time with language	(+0.1)
new language	(+0.3)
new line of business	(+0.2)
	1.60

NEW DESIGN and NEW CODE are composite values (weighted averages) for the total amount of new design and new code respectively. NEW DESIGN and NEWCODE values are set to values between 0 and 1, where:

0 = no effort (the design or code exists)
1 = 100% (all new task)
0.7 = 70% new task (30% exists)

For these estimates, the value of NEW CODE was always set to 1.0, while the value of new DESIGN varied depending on the technology involved when designing the tool.

TOOL: REQUIREMENTS INTERFACE PROCESSOR

DESCRIPTORS		COST ($ PER 1,000)	
INSTRUCTIONS:	28000	SYSTEMS ENGINEERING:	350
APPLICATION:	5.26	PROGRAMMING:	220
RESOURCE:	3.50	CONFIG.CONTROL,Q/A:	146
UTILIZATION:	0.50	DOCUMENTATION:	62
PLATFORM:	1.20	PROGRAM MANAGEMENT:	49
COMPLEXITY:	1.60	TOTAL:	827
NEW DESIGN:	0.50		
NEW CODE:	1.00		

SCHEDULE	DESIGN	IMPLEMENTATION	T&I
START WORK	JAN 83	APR 83	JUN 83
END WORK	JUL 83	NOV 83	JUN 84

TOOL: AUTOMATIC LANGUAGE TRANSLATOR

DESCRIPTORS		COST ($ PER 1,000)	
INSTRUCTIONS	172400	SYSTEMS ENGINEERING:	1569
APPLICATION:	4.24	PROGRAMMING:	931
RESOURCE:	3.50	CONFIG.CONTROL,Q/A:	753
UTILIZATION:	0.50	DOCUMENTATION:	334
PLATFORM:	1.20	PROGRAM MANAGEMENT:	263
COMPLEXITY:	1.60	TOTAL:	3850
NEW DESIGN:	0.50		
NEW CODE:	1.00		

SCHEDULE	DESIGN	IMPLEMENTATION	T&I
START WORK	JAN 83	JUN 83	OCT 83
END WORK	JAN 84	AUG 84	AUG 85

TOOL: STATIC REQUIREMENTS ANALYZER

DESCRIPTORS		COST ($ PER 1,000)	
INSTRUCTIONS	135500	SYSTEMS ENGINEERING:	1303
APPLICATION:	3.19	PROGRAMMING:	682
RESOURCE:	3.50	CONFIG.CONTROL,Q/A:	535
UTILIZATION:	0.50	DOCUMENTATION:	250
PLATFORM:	1.20	PROGRAM MANAGEMENT:	204
COMPLEXITY:	1.60	TOTAL:	2974
NEW DESIGN:	1.00		
NEW CODE	1.00		

SCHEDULE	DESIGN	IMPLEMENTATION	T&E
START WORK	JAN 83	JUN 83	OCT 83
END WORK	JAN 84	JUL 84	MAY 85

TOOL: FUNCTIONAL REQUIREMENTS INTERPRETER

DESCRIPTORS		COST ($ PER 1,000)	
INSTRUCTIONS:	87000	SYSTEMS ENGINEERING:	1490
APPLICATION:	5.55	PROGRAMMING:	772
RESOURCE:	3.50	CONFIG.CONTROL,Q/A:	613
UTILIZATION:	0.50	DOCUMENTATION:	288
PLATFORM:	1.20	PROGRAM MANAGEMENT:	236
COMPLEXITY:	1.60	TOTAL:	3398
NEW DESIGN:	1.00		
NEW CODE:	1.00		

SCHEDULE	DESIGN	IMPLEMENTATION	T&I
START WORK	JAN 83	JUL 83	NOV 83
END WORK	FEB 84	JUL 84	JUN 85

TOOL: SERIALIZATION ANALYZER

DESCRIPTORS		COST ($ PER 1,000)	
INSTRUCTIONS	53000	SYSTEMS ENGINEERING:	664
APPLICATION:	4.41	PROGRAMMING:	374
RESOURCE:	3.50	CONFIG.CONTROL,Q/A:	269
UTILIZATION:	0.50	DOCUMENTATION:	121
PLATFORM:	1.20	PROGRAM MANAGEMENT:	97
COMPLEXITY:	1.60	TOTAL:	1524
NEW DESIGN:	0.80		
NEW CODE:	1.00		

SCHEDULE	DESIGN	IMPLEMENTATION	T&I
START WORK	JAN 83	MAY 83	AUG 83
END WORK	OCT 83	FEB 84	NOV 84

TOOL: PERFORMANCE ANALYZER

DESCRIPTORS		COST ($ PER 1,000)	
INSTRUCTIONS	55330	SYSTEMS ENGINEERING:	358
APPLICATION:	2.17	PROGRAMMING:	210
RESOURCE:	3.50	CONFIG.CONTROL,Q/A:	138
UTILIZATION:	0.50	DOCUMENTATION:	60
PLATFORM:	1.20	PROGRAM MANAGEMENT:	49
COMPLEXITY:	1.60	TOTAL:	815
NEW DESIGN:	0.80		
NEW CODE	1.00		

SCHEDULE	DESIGN	IMPLEMENTATION	T&E
START WORK	JAN 83	APR 83	JUL 83
END WORK	AUG 83	NOV 83	JUN 84

TOOL: HARDWARE SIMULATOR

DESCRIPTORS		COST ($ PER 1,000)	
INSTRUCTIONS:	57970	SYSTEMS ENGINEERING:	928
APPLICATION:	5.09	PROGRAMMING:	491
RESOURCE:	3.50	CONFIG.CONTROL,Q/A:	367
UTILIZATION:	0.50	DOCUMENTATION:	170
PLATFORM:	1.20	PROGRAM MANAGEMENT:	139
COMPLEXITY:	1.60	TOTAL:	2095
NEW DESIGN:	1.00		
NEW CODE:	1.00		

SCHEDULE	DESIGN	IMPLEMENTATION	T&I
START WORK	JAN 83	JUN 83	SEP 83
END WORK	DEC 83	APR 84	JAN 85

TOOL: CONTROL SIMULATOR

DESCRIPTORS		COST ($ PER 1,000)	
INSTRUCTIONS	54175	SYSTEMS ENGINEERING:	900
APPLICATION:	5.27	PROGRAMMING:	476
RESOURCE:	3.50	CONFIG.CONTROL,Q/A:	355
UTILIZATION:	0.50	DOCUMENTATION:	164
PLATFORM:	1.20	PROGRAM MANAGEMENT:	134
COMPLEXITY:	1.60	TOTAL:	2030
NEW DESIGN:	1.00		
NEW CODE:	1.00		

SCHEDULE	DESIGN	IMPLEMENTATION	T&I
START WORK	JAN 83	JUN 83	SEP 83
END WORK	NOV 83	APR 84	JAN 85

TOOL: DESIGN INTERFACE PROCESSOR

DESCRIPTORS		COST ($ PER 1,000)	
INSTRUCTIONS	31163	SYSTEMS ENGINEERING:	592
APPLICATION:	6.64	PROGRAMMING:	332
RESOURCE:	3.50	CONFIG.CONTROL,Q/A:	235
UTILIZATION:	0.50	DOCUMENTATION:	106
PLATFORM:	1.20	PROGRAM MANAGEMENT:	86
COMPLEXITY:	1.60	TOTAL:	1350
NEW DESIGN:	0.80		
NEW CODE	1.00		

SCHEDULE	DESIGN	IMPLEMENTATION	T&E
START WORK	JAN 83	MAY 83	AUG 83
END WORK	SEP 83	FEB 84	SEP 84

TOOL: CONCURRENCY CHECKER

DESCRIPTORS		COST ($ PER 1,000)	
INSTRUCTIONS:	35115	SYSTEMS ENGINEERING:	323
APPLICATION:	3.54	PROGRAMMING:	200
RESOURCE:	3.50	CONFIG.CONTROL,Q/A:	130
UTILIZATION:	0.50	DOCUMENTATION:	56
PLATFORM:	1.20	PROGRAM MANAGEMENT:	44
COMPLEXITY:	1.60	TOTAL:	753
NEW DESIGN:	0.60		
NEW CODE:	1.00		

SCHEDULE	DESIGN	IMPLEMENTATION	T&I
START WORK	JAN 83	APR 83	JUN 83
END WORK	JUL 83	NOV 83	MAY 84

TOOL: PATH GRAPH BUILDER

DESCRIPTORS		COST ($ PER 1,000)	
INSTRUCTIONS	56130	SYSTEMS ENGINEERING:	298
APPLICATION:	2.19	PROGRAMMING:	193
RESOURCE:	3.50	CONFIG.CONTROL,Q/A:	125
UTILIZATION:	0.50	DOCUMENTATION:	52
PLATFORM:	1.20	PROGRAM MANAGEMENT:	41
COMPLEXITY:	1.60	TOTAL:	709
NEW DESIGN:	0.50		
NEW CODE:	1.00		

SCHEDULE	DESIGN	IMPLEMENTATION	T&I
START WORK	JAN 83	APR 83	JUN 83
END WORK	JUL 83	OCT 83	MAY 84

TOOL: CROSS REFERENCE GENERATOR

DESCRIPTORS		COST ($ PER 1,000)	
INSTRUCTIONS	30488	SYSTEMS ENGINEERING:	180
APPLICATION:	3.21	PROGRAMMING:	134
RESOURCE:	3.50	CONFIG.CONTROL,Q/A:	82
UTILIZATION:	0.50	DOCUMENTATION:	32
PLATFORM:	1.20	PROGRAM MANAGEMENT:	24
COMPLEXITY:	1.60	TOTAL:	452
NEW DESIGN:	0.20		
NEW CODE	1.00		

SCHEDULE	DESIGN	IMPLEMENTATION	T&E
START WORK	JAN 83	MAR 83	MAY 83
END WORK	MAY 83	AUG 83	FEB 84

TOOL: INTERFACE MAPPER

DESCRIPTORS		COST ($ PER 1,000)	
INSTRUCTIONS:	33130	SYSTEMS ENGINEERING:	224
APPLICATION:	2.49	PROGRAMMING:	142
RESOURCE:	3.50	CONFIG.CONTROL,Q/A:	88
UTILIZATION:	0.50	DOCUMENTATION:	37
PLATFORM:	1.20	PROGRAM MANAGEMENT:	29
COMPLEXITY:	1.60	TOTAL:	519
NEW DESIGN:	0.60		
NEW CODE:	1.00		

SCHEDULE	DESIGN	IMPLEMENTATION	T&I
START WORK	JAN 83	APR 83	MAY 83
END WORK	JUN 83	SEP 83	MAR 84

TOOL: ASSERTION CHECKER

DESCRIPTORS		COST ($ PER 1,000)	
INSTRUCTIONS	150000	SYSTEMS ENGINEERING:	1177
APPLICATION:	3.13	PROGRAMMING:	668
RESOURCE:	3.50	CONFIG.CONTROL,Q/A:	520
UTILIZATION:	0.50	DOCUMENTATION:	234
PLATFORM:	1.20	PROGRAM MANAGEMENT:	187
COMPLEXITY:	1.60	TOTAL:	2786
NEW DESIGN:	0.70		
NEW CODE:	1.00		

SCHEDULE	DESIGN	IMPLEMENTATION	T&I
START WORK	JAN 83	JUN 83	OCT 83
END WORK	DEC 83	JUN 84	MAY 85

TOOL: CONFIGURATION BUILDER

DESCRIPTORS		COST ($ PER 1,000)	
INSTRUCTIONS	12665	SYSTEMS ENGINEERING:	124
APPLICATION:	4.61	PROGRAMMING:	89
RESOURCE:	3.50	CONFIG.CONTROL,Q/A:	51
UTILIZATION:	0.50	DOCUMENTATION:	20
PLATFORM:	1.20	PROGRAM MANAGEMENT:	16
COMPLEXITY:	1.60	TOTAL:	299
NEW DESIGN:	0.30		
NEW CODE	1.00		

SCHEDULE	DESIGN	IMPLEMENTATION	T&E
START WORK	JAN 83	MAR 83	APR 83
END WORK	MAY 83	JUL 83	DEC 83

TOOL: VARIABLE HISTORY MAPPER

DESCRIPTORS		COST ($ PER 1,000)	
INSTRUCTIONS:	65040	SYSTEMS ENGINEERING:	632
APPLICATION:	3.66	PROGRAMMING:	367
RESOURCE:	3.50	CONFIG.CONTROL,Q/A:	263
UTILIZATION:	0.50	DOCUMENTATION:	116
PLATFORM:	1.20	PROGRAM MANAGEMENT:	93
COMPLEXITY:	1.60	TOTAL:	1472
NEW DESIGN:	0.70		
NEW CODE:	1.00		

SCHEDULE	DESIGN	IMPLEMENTATION	T&I
START WORK	JAN 83	MAY 83	AUG 83
END WORK	OCT 83	FEB 84	OCT 84

TOOL: REACHABILITY ANALYZER

DESCRIPTORS		COST ($ PER 1,000)	
INSTRUCTIONS	55000	SYSTEMS ENGINEERING:	439
APPLICATION:	3.74	PROGRAMMING:	285
RESOURCE:	3.50	CONFIG.CONTROL,Q/A:	197
UTILIZATION:	0.50	DOCUMENTATION:	82
PLATFORM:	1.20	PROGRAM MANAGEMENT:	64
COMPLEXITY:	1.60	TOTAL:	1067
NEW DESIGN:	0.40		
NEW CODE:	1.00		

SCHEDULE	DESIGN	IMPLEMENTATION	T&I
START WORK	JAN 83	APR 83	JUL 83
END WORK	AUG 83	DEC 83	AUG 84

TOOL: OPERATOR SEQUENCE ANALYZER

DESCRIPTORS		COST ($ PER 1,000)	
INSTRUCTIONS	38870	SYSTEMS ENGINEERING:	734
APPLICATION:	3.84	PROGRAMMING:	409
RESOURCE:	5.00	CONFIG.CONTROL,Q/A:	283
UTILIZATION:	0.50	DOCUMENTATION:	126
PLATFORM:	1.20	PROGRAM MANAGEMENT:	101
COMPLEXITY:	1.60	TOTAL:	1653
NEW DESIGN:	0.80		
NEW CODE	1.00		

SCHEDULE	DESIGN	IMPLEMENTATION	T&E
START WORK	JAN 83	MAY 83	JUL 83
END WORK	SEP 83	JAN 84	AUG 84

TOOL: LINKER/LOADER

DESCRIPTORS	
INSTRUCTIONS:	13920
APPLICATION:	2.91
RESOURCE:	3.50
UTILIZATION:	0.50
PLATFORM:	1.20
COMPLEXITY:	1.60
NEW DESIGN:	0.30
NEW CODE:	1.00

COST ($ PER 1,000)	
SYSTEMS ENGINEERING:	90
PROGRAMMING:	67
CONFIG.CONTROL,Q/A:	36
DOCUMENTATION:	14
PROGRAM MANAGEMENT:	11
TOTAL:	219

SCHEDULE	DESIGN	IMPLEMENTATION	T&I
START WORK	JAN 83	MAR 83	APR 83
END WORK	APR 83	JUN 83	NOV 83

RANK	TOOL	COST (x$1,000)	Sched (Mos.)
1	Automatic Language Translator	$3,850	32.5
2	Functional Requirements Interpreter	3,398	30.1
3	Static Requirements Analyst	2,974	29.4
4	Assertion Checker	2,786	28.8
5	Hardware Simulator	2,095	25.2
6	Control Simulator	2,030	24.8
7	Operator Sequence Analyzer	1,653	20.3
8	Serialization Analyzer	1,524	22.5
9	Variable History Mapper	1,472	22.4
10	Design Interface Processor	1,350	21.2
11	Reachability Analyzer	1,067	19.9
12	Requirements Interface Processor	827	17.9
13	Performance Analyzer	815	17.8
14	Concurrency Checker	753	17.3
15	Path Graph Builder	709	16.9
16	Interface Mapper	519	14.9
17	Cross Reference Generator	452	14.2
18	Configuration Builder	299	12.1
19	Linker/Loader	219	10.6

Figure A-3. Tools' Rank by Cost

A.4 Summary

The estimates have been summarized tabularly in Figure A-3. This representation shows the tools ranked from lowest cost to highest cost as well as the estimated calendar months to complete. As explained in Section A.1, these estimates should not be treated as absolutes but rather as estimates to serve as management and budgeting aids.

Appendix B: Consultation by Howden

Permission has been granted by William E. Howden to publish the following:

A GENERAL MODEL FOR STATIC ANALYSIS AND ITS APPLICATION TO DISTRIBUTED SYSTEMS

William E. Howden

1. Introduction.

The term *static analysis* is used to refer to program validation methods which can be used to analyze programs for the presence of errors without actually executing the programs. It is also sometimes used to refer to the analysis of other software development documents, such as design specifications, for possible errors.

The oldest and most widely studied form of static analysis is that in which programs are analyzed to determine whether or not certain kinds of operations occurring in the program can be executed in an *illegal* order. The classic case is the referencing of an uninitialized variable [1]. Two operations are involved: assigning a value to a variable and referencing the variable. If, along some program path, a referencing operation is carried out before an assignment operation, a potential error exists. This paper is concerned with analysis of out of sequence operations.

A general model for static analysis is presented. The analysis of programs for reference/initialization problems is only one, simple example of the type of analysis that can be described and discussed using the model. The model can be used to specify static analysis rules not only for the ordering of code level operations, but for higher level abstract operations that occur as part of a program's design or its specifications. The model can also be used to investigate and describe the application of static analysis to distributed systems. The paper begins with a short discussion of higher level static analysis and its use in detecting errors. This is followed by the description of the general model for static analysis and the general purpose static analysis algorithm. The paper concludes with a discussion of the application of static analysis to distributed systems.

2. Sequencing of operators and data states.

At the code level computer programs are constructed from low level operators such as referencing a value of a variable, assigning a value, and arithmetic and logical operations on a variable. Some of these operations have problem independent properties which limit the circumstances in which they may be applied. Division by zero, for example, is undefined. This is because division is a *partial operator*. Other operators may not be partial operators, but can only be applied after some other operation has been performed. Uninitialized variables, for example, can be referenced but it may be desirable to prohibit this by requiring that a variable may be referenced only after it has been assigned a value. This restriction can also be modeled using the notion of a partial operation, but there are other, more intuitive approaches. One involves the notion of a *state*. Variables can be in one of two states: initialized or uninitialized. Assignment operations can be applied to a variable regardless of its state. If a variable is in the unintialized state, assigning a value to it causes it to enter the initialized state. Referencing can be restricted to variables which are in the initialized state.

In addition to the code level operations, programs may also contain design or specifications level operators which are "higher level" and which are *problem dependent*. Problem dependent operators may be defined for a class of problems, or even a single program. Unlike assignment and reference they do not occur in all kinds of programs. Consider, for example, a data processing problem in which a file of account records is to be processed. Suppose that the file is ordered by account number and that there may be more than one record with the same account number. The processing is to include the totaling of one of the number fields in the records in such a way that subtotals are to be reported for each account group. The following design level operators can be used in the design and implementation of a program: *getrecord* (get next record from file), *checkgroup* (see if this is a new account number), *addtogroup* (add to total for account group), *processgroup* (generate a subtotal for a completed account group, zero out subtotal, and remember account number for this new group of accounts). There are several implicit restrictions on the sequence in which these operators may be applied. The *getrecord* operation, for example, should not be applied twice in a row without an intervening *checkgroup*. *Subtotal* can only be applied after *checkgroup*, and there should not be any intervening *addtogroup* operator.

The ordering of problem dependent operators can be described using object states. In the data processing example, the "current record" can be either in the "processed" state or the "unprocessed" state. It is illegal to apply the *getrecord* operator if the current record is in the unprocessed state.

3. Shared data objects and abstract data types.

Sequencing restrictions hold for operators that operate on common objects. In the simplest cases, a group of operators and their shared object is an instance of an abstract data type. The operators are used for accessing the data structure. Additional constructor operators may be introduced which make it possible to formally define the type using algebraic axioms. In more complicated cases, the ordering restrictions may apply to operators acting on several different, unshared or loosely-shared objects. These may be examples of collections of abstract data types whose only relationship is the restrictions on the sequencing of their operators in the program.

Although most operators that are studied in static analysis act on data objects, they may also involve other kinds of objects. Suppose it is possible for one process to *schedule* and *wait* for another, or to *terminate* itself. The legal sequencing of these operators within a collection of processes can be determined using static analysis.

4. Static analysis and program errors.

Empirical studies have been carried out which indicate that a significant number of program errors occur which can be readily detected even by the simpliest form of static analysis: assignment reference analysis. In a study of approximately 100 scientific programs, it was found that 14% of the errors could be found [2].

Additional error analyses of data processing systems have revealed that many "hard to detect" errors in programs are detectable using static analysis for out of order operations like the *getrecord*, *checkgroup*, *etc.* mentioned above. "Easy" errors involve code that does the wrong thing because the code has bugs in it. "Hard" errors involve "missing cases" and "missing code." Many hard errors can be detected by requiring legal ordering information for program design or specifications level operators. If a missing case or missing code error corresponds to a missing operator, then this error will often result in an out of sequence execution of other operators and can be detected by static analysis.

Static analysis of the type which is described in this paper is particularly valuable for large complex or distributed systems in which it is difficult to keep track of the interaction of operations and shared data objects. Its applicability to design and specification level operations, as well as code level instructions, makes it a technique of powerful general applicability.

5. Finite state diagrams and ordering of operators.

The general model for static analysis that will be used is based on finite state diagrams. Each node in a diagram stands for a data object state. It may represent the state of a single data object or a combination of states of several related objects. The arcs in the diagram correspond to operators. They indicate the change in state that can occur when an operator is applied to an object in some state. Figure 1 contains a finite state diagram which describes the legal sequencing of assignment and referencing operations.

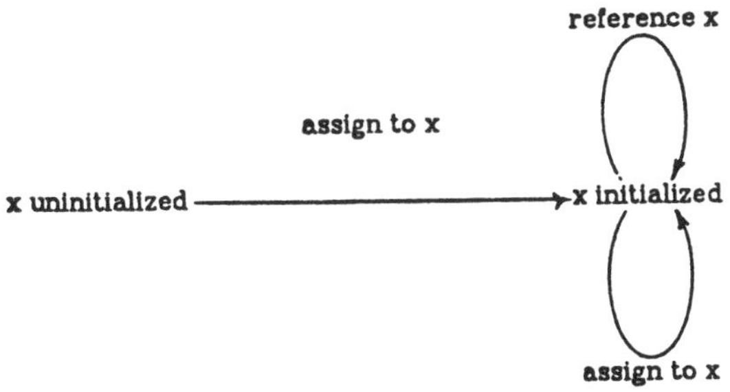

Figure 1. Assign-reference state diagram.

In the diagram in Figure 1, the simple application of an operator may cause a state change. In some applications the state change depends on a value returned by the operator. Figure 2 contains a finite state diagram for the account subtotals example. In this case, some of the state changes depend on the value returned by the *checkgroup* operator. Note that the diagram and its prose equivalent in Section Two are incomplete. It is necessary to also describe what happens when an *end-of-file* operator indicates there are no more records.

6. Finite state diagrams and programs.

The order in which operators are executed in programs can also be represented by a finite state diagram. The diagram is closely related to the graph-complement of the program's flowgraph (i.e., arcs in the state diagram correspond to nodes in the flow graph and nodes in the state diagram correspond to arcs in the flow graph). Each arc in the finite state diagram corresponds to a line or section of code which implements an operator. A line or section of code may result in the generation of several state diagram arcs. The construction of an algorithm for converting a program and a set of operator-code correspondences to a state-diagram is not difficult and will not be discussed here.

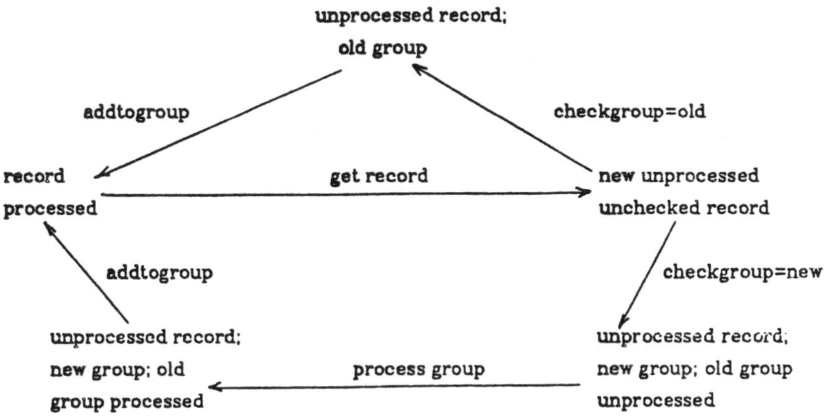

Figure 2. Account groups state diagram.

7. Equivalence of finite state diagrams.

The problem of determining whether or not the sequencing of operators in a program (or of the code corresponding to those operators) is consistent with a state diagram description of legal operator sequences and can be represented as an equivalence problem for finite state diagrams. Algorithms for determining equivalence have been constructed and it is possible to build a static analysis tool which could process any program and any set of operator-ordering restrictions, as modeled by a finite state diagram, and determine whether or not the ordering of operations in the program corresponds to that specified in the finite state diagram.

In general, the goal in static analysis is to determine whether or not the set of possible operator orderings in a program is *included in*, rather than equivalent to, the set of orderings specified in an operator-ordering finite state diagram. The following algorithm can be used to determine this.

8. General purpose static analysis algorithm.

The algorithm operates by performing a depth-first search over the program-operator graph. Suppose that P and S are the program and allowable operator sequencing graphs. Note that each arc on each graph contains exactly one operator. Assume that P and S have a single start state and that P has one or more termination states. Each node in P will have a stack associated with it called its node-set stack. Each entry on the stack for a node n in P is of the form (a,M,U) where a denotes one of the arcs which lead into n, M is a set of nodes in S, and U is the set of "unused" arcs leading out of n.

Let n_0 and m_0 be the start nodes in P and S. Initialize the stack for n_0 with the entry $(\phi, \{m_0\}, \{a_1,a_2,...,a_k\})$ where a_i, $1 \leq i \leq k$, are the arcs which lead out of n_0 and ϕ is the "null arc". Choose an arc a_i from the unused arc set for n_0 and delete it from the set. Suppose α is the operator on arc a_i, and a_i leads from n_0 to n_1. Let M be the set of all nodes in S which can be reached from m_0 along an arc in S with operator α. If M is not empty, push $(a, M, \{b_1,b_2,...,b_k\})$ on the stack for n_1 and continue processing at n_1. b_i, $1 \leq i \leq k$, are the arcs which lead out of n_1.

Let n_i be some node in P to be processed. Suppose its top stack entry is (a, M_i, U_i). If $U_i \neq \phi$, select an arc b from the set U_i and delete it. Let α be the operator on b and suppose n_{i+1} is the node in P_i at the end of the arc. Let M_{i+1} be the set of all nodes in S which can be reached from a node in M_i along an arc labelled with α. If M_{i+1} is empty, terminate. If M_{i+1} is not empty, look at the stack for n_{i+1}. If it is not empty, it has been previously encountered along the current path in P (i.e., it is part of a loop).

Examine the other node sets on the stack to determine if there is a previous node set M' which contains the same nodes as M_{i+1}. If there is no such M', push (b, M_{i+1}, U_{i+1}) onto the stack for n_{i+1}, where U_{i+1} is the set of arcs which lead out of n_{i+1}, and continue processing at n_{i+1}. If there is an $M' = M_{i+1}$, do not push anything on the stack for n_{i+1}. Instead, continue processing n_i using another unused arc in the set U_i. If $U_i = \phi$, backup. If the stack for n_{i+1} is empty, push (b, M_{i+1}, U_{i+1}) and continue processing at n_{i+1}.

Backing up is achieved as follows. Suppose it is necessary to back up from node n_i. Let (a,S,U) be the top stack entry for n_i and let n_{i-1} be the node at the tail of arc a. Delete this stack entry from the stack for n_i and resume processing at node n_{i-1}.

There are several ways in which the algorithm can terminate. If an attempt is made to back up from the root node, then it is possible to conclude that all paths through P result in legal sequences of operators. If the algorithm terminates because a node set M was empty, then an illegal sequence of operators has been found in P.

9. Distributed systems.

The above discussion is limited to single programs in which program operators interact with shared data objects. In a distributed system, two or more "independent" processes running in parallel may contain operators which interact with data objects shared by more than one of the processes. Processes may also be synchronized in some way so that the order in which operators from different processes are executed is not completely random. Distributed systems will differ in the kind of interaction they have with shared data objects and in the kind of process synchronization (if any) that is present.

It will be assumed that each process in a distributed system is modeled using a finite state diagram of the type that was used for a single program. The arcs on the diagrams are each labelled with a single operator from the collection of operators that act on shared data. All other code in the program is ignored, except for possibly synchronization operations.

The complexity of static analysis for distributed systems will be discussed by first considering the case in which there is no synchronization between processes. It is assumed that there are k processes P_i, $1 \le i \le k$, all running completely independent of each other. The only restriction is that it is assumed that two operators cannot be executed simultaneously. Sequencing of operators is determined only by sequencing in individual processes.

The possible orderings of operators in a set of independent processes can be modeled by a single finite state diagram using the notion of a control state. Let $n_1, n_2, \ldots, n_k$ be nodes in processes $P_1, P_2, \ldots, P_k$. Suppose the operators in the P_i, $1 \le i \le k$, are executed in such a way that at some point the next operator to be executed in P_i, $1 \le i \le k$, will lie on an arc out of n_i, $1 \le i \le k$. Then $(n_1, n_2, \ldots, n_k)$ is the current control state.

From the purely structural point of view, it is possible for any control state $(n_1, n_2, \ldots, n_k)$ to occur, provided each node in P_i is reachable along a path from the beginning of P_i to n_i, $1 \le i \le k$. Construct therefore a compound finite state diagram in which there is a node corresponding to every possible control state. Suppose $N = (n_1, n_2, \ldots, n_k)$ and $M = (m_1, m_2, \ldots, m_k)$ are two nodes in the compound finite state diagram. Then there is an arc from N to M in the diagram if for some j, $1 \le j \le k$,

(i) $n_i = m_i$ for $i \ne j$, $1 \le i \le k$; and

(ii) there is an arc from n_j to m_j in the state diagram for P_j. If α is the operator on the arc from n_j to m_j, then the corresponding arc in the compound state diagram is also labelled with operator α.

If the state diagram for each process P_i has c_i nodes, then the number of nodes in the compound state diagram is $\prod_{i=1}^{k} c_i$. If the processes have on the average c nodes, then the compound diagram has c^k nodes. This indicates that the cost of static analysis for k distributed processes is going to be exponential in the number of processes.

10. Complexity of Distributed Systems Static Analysis and Synchronization.

In order to make static analysis tractable for distributed systems it is necessary to deal with the exponential factor in its cost. There are several possibilities.

(a) Small factors. If c and k are small, the exponential nature of the cost of doing static analysis will not make static analysis impossible. This is not unlikely because c, the number of nodes in a program's state diagram, is determined by the number of occurrences of operators in the program and not the number of branches or statements. In addition, the number of processes k will not, in general, be large.

The state diagrams which describe allowable operator sequences contain operators which act on one or more shared data objects. It is possible to carry out a separate static analysis for each non-interacting set of operators. A very rough approximation of reduced computational costs can be calculated as follows. Suppose P_i, $1 \le i \le k$, are the set of processes and that when all operators are considered together, the state diagram for each P_i has c nodes. Suppose that the operators can be divided into h non-interacting groups and that the state diagrams for each P_i for each group has on the order of c/h nodes. This will result in the need to consider h compound state diagrams having $(c/h)^k$ nodes, rather than the consideration of one diagram with c^k nodes. The difference in processing costs is c^k/h^{k-1} versus c^k.

(b) Impossible paths. Many of the paths through a program's finite state diagram may be infeasible in the sense that they correspond to paths through the program which are never executed for any choice of input data. This is because the paths contain contradictory branch conditions. The same is true of a compound state diagram.

It can contain paths which, corresponding to interleaved traversals of individual program paths, are either individually or jointly infeasible. One approach to the exponential problem is to find a static analysis procedure which is capable of recognizing and ignoring impossible paths. This would involve symbolic evaluation and solution of arbitrary systems of relationships, a problem which is itself intractable. It may be possible to carry out a more modest, incomplete weeding out of infeasible paths. But, without any data on how many paths can be weeded out, the use of such a procedure would be questionable. This problem is studied in [3] for certain classes of synchronized processes.

(c) Lock step synchronization. One way of reducing the combinatorial interleaving of operations between processes is to require that processes be synchronized in such a way that many of the possible orderings are eliminated. Several simple possibilities will be considered.

The first kind of synchronization is the extreme case where processes are scheduled in a round robin fashion so that first an operator in P_1 is executed, then one in P_2, and so on until an operator in P_k is executed. Then it is P_1's turn again, and so on. The reduction in combinatorial possibilities that this type of synchronization will result in can be studied by considering the different control states that can occur for the k parallel processes.

If there are no loops in the process state diagrams, and each of the k state diagrams has c nodes, then the number of different control states is kc rather than c^k; a significant reduction. If the diagrams have loops, then the savings may be far less. Consider, for example, the two process state diagrams in Figure 3.

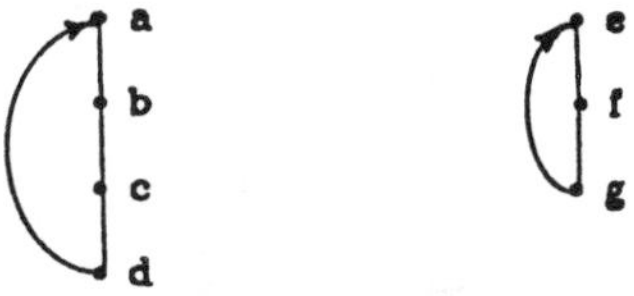

Figure 3. Out of Synchronization State Diagrams.

It is easy to determine that, even with lock step synchronization, all possible control states (x,y) can occur, where x is a node in the first process diagram and y is a node in the second. It should be noted that it is not possible to construct a compound state diagram for the two processes simply by considering all state pairs (x,y) and filling in arcs between the pairs as appropriate. This is because the history of the state transitions that have been followed during an execution of the processes determines which arc to follow next. Suppose the processes are in state (x,y). Then the allowable operator (arc transition) that can be used next depends on whether it was the first or second element of the ordered pair in the process state that was changed in getting to state (x,y). This implies that lock step synchronization may, in general, increase the number of states in a compound state diagram rather than decrease it. It will be necessary to consider states of the form (x,y,z) where x and y are any states in the two original processes and z is a state in one of the processes which has an arc to x or to y in the state diagram for that process.

(d) Multiple Lock-Step Synchronization. Suppose each process is allowed to execute up to c (for some constant c) operators before operators in another process are executed. The same problems that occur for single step synchronization can occur.

(e) User Specified State Coordination. The number of state combinations that must be considered can be effectively reduced by "segmenting" process state diagrams. In this approach it is required that users include assertions at different places in their programs which declare what state (with respect to operator sequencing diagrams) they expect the programs to be in at that point.

Suppose $n_{1,0}$, $n_{2,0}$, ..., $n_{k,0}$ are the start nodes for a set of distributed processes $P_1, P_2, \ldots, P_k$. It is required that each path from $n_{i,0}$ in $P_{i,0}$, $1 \le i \le k$, lead to an "assert s_1" statement, where s_1 is a state in the operator sequencing state diagram. The state s_1 must be the same on each of these paths for each process. The paths from each of these nodes must also lead to an identical state assertion, and so on. If the processes satisfy this condition, then it is only necessary to do static analysis on collections of path segments that begin and end with the same state assertions. If these are "small enough" (in terms of the number of nodes or operators they contain) then static analysis will be feasible.

(f) Classes of Operator Sequences. For certain special kinds of operator sequences in parallel processes it is possible to do a less general form of static analysis that avoids the exponential state explosion. Consider the diagram in Figure 4. It indicates that any sequence of α and β operations is allowable, provided that an "initialization" α is always done first. This implies that every β in every process graph must be preceded by an α along every path leading to that β. If this condition holds, then every possible ordering of the execution of the α and β operators in the processes will satisfy the operator sequencing finite state diagram. Hence, it is sufficient to analyze each process state graph independently to determine if the processes jointly satisfy the initialization state diagram.

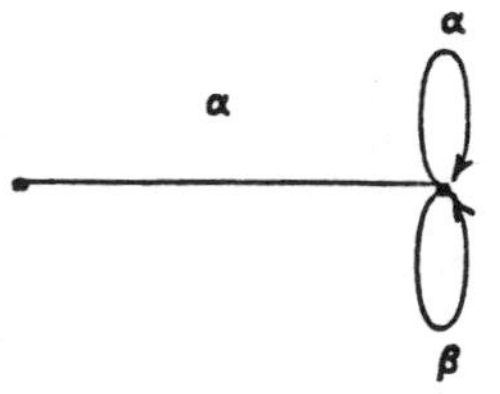

Figure 4. Initialization State Diagram.

In general, some paths through a state graph will be infeasible and it will be desirable to check if the application of a β is legal even if it is not preceded by an α along some path leading to β because that path is infeasible, and it is expected that the required α is done in some other process. In order to analyze for this kind of situation it will be necessary to have some way of eliminating certain program paths from consideration by the static analyzer.

11. Summary and Future Work.

A general model for static analysis has been introduced which can be used to discuss all forms of static analysis of both simple programs and distributed systems. A general purpose static analysis algorithm was described. The complexity of static analysis for distributed systems has been identified with the exponential number of states in the compound operator state diagram for the processes. Suggestions for dealing with the exponential problem were indicated.

This paper indicates that it is possible, in the short run, to construct a general purpose static analysis system for doing both code and design-oriented analyses. Error studies indicate that it can be used to reveal the presence of difficult, significant classes of errors, some of which are not readily discoverable by alternative techniques. The paper indicates that it is also feasible to carry out static analysis for distributed systems, provided that some restrictions on the number of interacting processes, the number of interacting operators in processes, and the amount of random interaction are used to make the problem tractable. Of the limitations that were suggested, several are both computationally tractable and intuitively reasonable.

REFERENCES

[1] L. J. Osterweil and L. Fosdick, DAVE - A Validation Error Detection and Documentation System for FORTRAN Programs, *Software - Practice and Experience*, *Vol. 6*, 1976.

[2] W. E. Howden, Applicability of Software Validation Techniques to Scientific Programs, *ACM Transactions on Programming Languages and Systems*, *Vol. 2, No. 3*, July 1980.

[3] R.N. Taylor, Complexity of Analyzing Synchronization Structure of Concurrent Programs, *ACTA INFORMATICA* (to appear).

[4] William E. Howden, A Survey of Static Analysis Methods, in E. Miller and W. E. Howden, *Software Testing and Validation Techniques*, IEEE, 1981.

[5] William E. Howden, Validation of Scientific Programs, *ACM Computing Surveys*, June 1982.

Appendix: General Research Corporation Third Interim Technical Report.

The document contains a standard survey of program-based static analysis, i.e. analysis of source code, rather than specifications or design documents. The document concentrates on "problem independent" static analysis, in which the errors that are looked for are general, and not related to information in specifications or design.

The methods that are suggested in the GRC report fall into one of three classes: standards checking, augmented programming language syntax checking, and data flow analysis. Data flow analysis is restricted to searching for references to uninitialized variables, and failure to reference an assigned variable value.

Standards checking or augmented syntax checking has not been discussed above, since they do not depend on the development of new ideas or advanced technology. Both have been previously discussed in the literature [2,3] and the ideas in the GRC report are a subset of material in these published papers. One topic covered in the papers, but not in the GRC report, is the notion of an extensible static analysis tool for implementing purely syntactic standards and augmented syntax checking. This would allow the user to add and delete new rules. Development in this area, including its application to distributed systems, involves the assembly of collections of rules which describe the desired syntactic limitations and extensions to the host programming language. These rules should be derived on the basis of error studies [e.g., 1].

The generalization of reference-initialization errors to operator ordering state diagrams which is described above or anything like it, is not touched on at all in the GRC report. This concept is probably the most important for the extension of static analysis to distributed systems, since the critical complex feature of a distributed system is the loss of determinism in the ordering of operations. Some way of detecting unintended combinations of these operations is critical. Empirical studies indicate that the technique is also important for the detection of difficult errors in single synchronous programs.

In summary, the GRC report is a relatively complete survey of a limited set of source code based static analysis methods. It contains no information on static analysis of distributed systems and no information on fundamental, general approaches to static analysis concepts.

Appendix C: Consultation by Browne

Permission has been granted by Information Research Associates to publish the following:

FEASIBILITY TESTBED CONCEPTS

A Report to

General Dynamics

From

Information Research Associates

EXECUTIVE SUMMARY

The feasibility of a software system is determined by its ability to meet its performance specifications for executing its functionality on a given hardware configuration under its expected workload. This report establishes the importance of demonstration of feasibility at system design time, defines the requirements for a capability for feasibility testing and discusses how such a capability can be assembled and integrated into an Ada Programming Support Environment.

The conclusions of this report are that:

1. A feasibility testbed is an essential element of a development support environment for embedded distributed data systems.

2. The current minimal Ada support environments will have to be given extended data management capabilities in order to effectively integrate a feasibility testbed into these systems.

3. A separate but effective experimental feasibility testbed can and should be developed to give experience with the use of this concept. A system to support experimental use can be readily synthesized by combining the existing ADEPT feasibility testbed system with the PAWS computer system simulation system.

1. Overview

This report is a detailed exposition of the feasibility testbed concept and its role in the development of embedded distributed data systems. The topic coverage includes:

a. Establishment of the need for feasibility testing of embedded systems.

b. Definition of the feasibility testbed concepts.

c. Definition of the data and functional requirements for implementation of a feasibility testbed.

d. Inventory of the available components from which to construct a feasibility testbed.

e. Extensions required to STONEMAN concepts for an Ada Programming Support Environment (APSE) for effective implementation of a feasibility testbed.

The conclusions of the report are that feasibility testbeds are not only important but are essential, that feasibility testbeds can be for the most part assembled from existing technology and that a prototype capable of supporting experimental use should be constructed.

2. The Need for Feasibility Validation

Embedded computer systems have intrinsic limitations on hardware capabilities. Embedding places explicit bounds on the hardware resources which can be made available to meet performance and reliability specifications. Application systems executing on embedded hardware must nonetheless execute their functionality at the specified levels of performance and reliability within these resource constraints. These constraints on hardware configuration make the resource usage of the implementation of the required functionality as vital to system validity as is the correctness of the functionality. This fact has significant implications for the facilities which must be available in a complete support environment for the development of embedded systems. Determination of the feasibility of a given implementation for use in an embedded context depends not only upon the software system but upon the workload for the system and the execution environment for the system. A radar tracking unit which must follow only a limited number of objects at low speeds over a small segment of solid angle has a very different workload to that of a system which must search and follow a large number of rapidly moving objects over the entire horizon. The same implementation is clearly not appropriate even if the hardware environments are scaled appropriately to the tasks.

The traditional approach in total system development has been to partition the development process into functional and performance phases. The system design and specification procedures are normally based entirely on functionality considerations. Concern for performance is considered only after the system reaches integration testing since performance problems, if sufficiently severe, will often make their first appearances at that time. It is seldom the case that response times or other performance properties are even specified in a requirements analysis.

Resource usage is often strongly determined by decisions taken at early design time. It is often possible to make drastic changes in functionality by addition in the later stages of development. This is difficult if not impossible in the case of performance. The early binding of resource usage by design decisions forces feasibility analysis to begin at an early stage of design if it is to be effective.

The usual solutions to performance problems when they are detected in system integration or later are two-fold. Either additional hardware resources are added to the proposed configuration or else a search is made to identify the high resource consumption sections of the code. In the latter case efforts to enhance the code to give lower levels of resource consumption are usually attempted. The first solution is not possible to any large measure for embedded systems. The second approach often leads to poorly organized and/or poorly structured code. Major modifications at this point tend to lead to the Belady-Lehman [BEL79] syndrome that further modifications have a high propagation across the entire system. This effect is based on the fact that a large fraction of performance problems are founded on either excessive or improper modularization or data organizations which do not conform well to the processing structure.

A third solution and the only one with long term viability, redesign with due consideration of performance properties in the new design, is seldom undertaken because of cost and time.

The true solution is clearly to incorporate performance specification and validation into the basic design process. A feasibility testbed is the basic vehicle for supporting performance validation.

3. Operational Definition of a Feasibility Testbed

A feasibility testbed is a capability for "execution" of a software system design on a given hardware resource configuration with its execution being driven by its expected workload of transactions. The "execution" of a design is obtained by evaluation of a model of the system in which each of the components of an "execution": software system design, workload and hardware configuration, are all explicitly represented. The "execution" may be carried out at any stage of design where a meaningful mapping of workload to system interfaces and the resulting processing to resources can be resolved. The execution behavior is measured and the resource requirements to process the transactions of the workload are established for the given level of design resolution. The response times of the transactions are compared to the performance specifications for the total system to determine the feasibility of the given design with respect to the proposed hardware configuration.

There can be several results from the analysis of the performance characteristics obtained for the model execution.

a. The total system performed satisfactorily. In this case the development process can proceed.

b. The system failed to meet the performance specifications for the workload on the proposed hardware. Then there are two options. The execution can be modelled with an extended set of hardware resources or the design for the software system can be analyzed for elements leading to excessive resource usage and redesigned accordingly.

Pilot tests [SMI82] of the feasibility testbed concept have shown that it is possible to produce assessments of feasibility even at early stages of the design of software systems if the workload is reasonably well-specified.

4. Functional Specification of a Feasibility Testbed

The validation of feasibility at design time requires the ability to construct and evaluate a faithful model representation of the execution of the total system. The evaluation of the model of execution should return both external metrics such as response times and also internal metrics such as hardware resource usage broken out by transaction.

A model which can represent execution behavior must integrate representation of system designs, hardware configurations and the workload which is to drive execution. Thus the data required for a feasibility analysis goes far beyond what is required for analysis of functional properties. Functional validation can be done independently of hardware configurations and actual workload but these must be combined for validation of feasibility.

It is a requirement for the modeling system that resolved measurement of execution behavior be obtainable. The model representation basis must be one which allows observation and recording of the continuous mapping of workload to resources by the processes and algorithms of a given design.

The procedure which has been followed in previous work and that which is proposed herein is to combine the software system design with workload to yield a model of abstract execution and to then map this abstract execution behavior to a model basis which represents physical hardware resources.

The hardware representational capabilities must be able to support system executions resolved at levels of abstraction ranging from complete transactions as units of execution to instructions as units of execution. It must be able to specify resources at levels of granularity conforming to the abstract units of execution. Time must be explicitly resolved in the execution model since embedded systems will often have transactions which have time constraints. It is also clear that explicit programming of each representation to carry out a feasibility validation would pose an intractable burden of additional work. One conclusion which can be drawn from these requirements and constraints is that the models of hardware execution will need to be data structure defined rather than explicitly programmed.

The power and flexibility of queueing networks (QN) to represent the execution behavior of computer systems with very many devices executing many processes and communication systems coupling the computer systems has been well-established [KLE75, CHA80, KOB78]. It has also become clear that while very reliable estimates of execution behavior for systems represented at high levels of abstraction can be obtained from those classes of QN's which are analytically soluble or approximately analytically soluble that faithful representations at high levels of resolution of algorithms and details requires the specification of the queue/server pairs and the properties of the connecting arcs yielding networks which can be evaluated for execution properties only be discrete event simulation. The modeling system thus proposed is the use of a state-of-the-art queueing network modeling package which can utilize analytical or approximate analytical solution techniques when convenient but which has the representational power to require the use of discrete event simulation evaluation when appropriate.

Integration of the design and workload to obtain abstract execution models and mapping of the resulting single thread execution structure to the queueing network model for evaluation of total system behavior is the other major problem. A graphical representation suggests itself for many reasons. System execution of single processes is naturally represented as a flow of control and data through a sequence of modules. The sequence of modules representing a single execution thread is normally selected from a graph of possibilities on the basis of some set of parameters. Representation of modules and their individual execution properties as the nodes of a graph with the arcs representing the flow of control and data and carrying the parameters which are path determining is therefore a straightforward representation of single threads of execution. The execution behavior of a given traversal of a graph in a dedicated hardware environment can be evaluated by following a path through such a graph.

The mapping of the graphs to a QN model representation is the next problem. The execution behavior in the graph representation is given in terms of logical units or processing while the queue/server pairs of the QN model are normally formulated to represent hardware devices. The mapping of the processing steps of the graph representation to the hardware representation in the queueing network model is straightforward. Each node representing a logical unit of processing will use some set of hardware devices to accomplish its processing. Processing is mapped to the devices following the path through the graph representing the execution of some transaction. The QN model representational capability must therefore have the ability to retain the identity of each process which is mapped to a device if detailed resolution of processing is required.

5. Components Inventory for a Feasibility Testbed

There actually exists a feasibility testbed prototype whose effectiveness in resolving performance behavior at a high level of abstraction (application in early design) has already been demonstrated [SMI82]. This feasibility testbed is the Automatic Design Evaluation and Performance Testing system (ADEPT) developed by Information Research Associates [SMI80]. The ADEPT system is a proof-of-concept system and is not suitable for use by staff without in-depth training in performance evaluation. There can, however, be a major transfer of technology from ADEPT to an experimentally usable system. The execution graph concepts have been realized in prototype form in the ADEPT system. ADEPT takes a functional specification in terms of procedures, functions, etc. as one of its primary inputs. Execution graphs are created by following the trace of a given transaction through the set of functions and procedures.

Smith and Browne did an extensive study of the problems of integration of system design and workloads to produce abstract representations of execution. These authors introduced the concept of execution graphs. An execution graph is a graph model of execution behavior which includes blocking and probabilistic aspects of execution. An execution graph also carries specifications for the usage of specific resources by the logical processing units of the software system. The execution graph concept is detailed in the references to the work of Smith and Browne [SMI79a,79b]. Execution graphs have all of the power necessary to handle establishment of mappable abstract execution representations.

The crucial problem of mapping from the graphs to queueing network models is accomplished by specification of queueing networks where the queue/server pairs represent the devices of the system but with the parameters represented only as slots on parameter templates. The parameters are determined by the properties of the single thread execution paths through the execution graphs.

The ADEPT system maps its abstract representation of execution onto the structures representable in the Computer Analysis and Design System (CADS). CADS implements only those queueing network structures which are analytically soluble. This is a substantial limitation of representations and thus ADEPT is only applicable to rather abstract levels of design. A more powerful queueing network representational system is needed for a fully usable feasibility testbed. These are IBM's RESQ [SAU79] and Information Research Associates Performance Analyst's Workbench System (PAWS) [IRA82]. The two systems are similar in concepts and capabilities. PAWS is one generation of development beyond RESQ in a development cycle which started with QSIM [FOS74]. PAWS allows a software system to be modeled directly in terms of its logical processing units with PAWS handling the mapping to physical resources. PAWS is implemented as a user level program for most common operating systems and can thus be straightforwardly integrated into APSE's for the support of feasibility testbed implementation.

The Performance Analyst's Workbench System (PAWS) supports representation and evaluation of a spectrum of queueing network models adequate for almost all levels of resolution of detail down to the instruction level. As would be expected model evaluation or so powerful a representational capability requires the application of discrete event simulation. PAWS does have the critical capability of retaining the identity of processing for processes which are multiplexed upon a given resource for ech burst of execution. In PAWS both the specification of models and the evaluation of models is accomplished through specification of data structures. The PAWS translator effectively maps these data structures to a simulation program in standard ANSI Fortran 66. Thus the faithfulness and accuracy of simulation based modeling is combined with the convenience and ease of use commonly associated only with analytically soluble models. The power of the PAWS representation of QN's also greatly simplifies the task of mapping execution graphs to the QN's.

The execution graph technology of ADEPT and the representational power of PAWS offer a direct path to the implementation of a feasibility testbed.

6. Applicability and Benefits of Use

A feasibility testbed with the capabilities described herein can be applied at several stages of development and for several purposes. The focus of application can be any of the three system elements of design, execution environment or workload.

It can be used to assess the effectiveness of a hardware environment at any stage of development of a design. It can, for example, suggest needs for changes in execution environment such as moving a set of critical instructions to microcode or replacing software interpreted floating point by a floating point chip set. It can be used to identify the resource patterns of a design on a given hardware configuration to isolate potential trouble spots. It can be used to determine the amount of work which can be accomplished by a given design on a given hardware configuration.

Feasibility analysis should be begun at early design since design flaws not identified at this stage may lead to costly investment in work which must be discarded and/or repeated when the flaws surface at a later stage of development. The resolution of detail possible with data-specified event-driven simulation systems allows the application of feasibility analysis down to the procedure level. It should probably not be carried below this level because actual execution should become cheaper at this point. It may still be desireable to do some feasibility analysis even after the system is implemented in order to explore the effects of different hardware environments.

There are also important fringe benefits to including feasibility analysis in the development process. The execution of the feasibility analysis forces consideration of system integration issues at all phases of development since the abstract execution model generated by the execution graphs focuses attention on the interfaces between modules. The execution graphs are also extremely good hierarchical documentation for the system itself. The execution graphs at different levels of resolution give a clear picture of the structure of the system.

7. Extensions to Components Required for Testbed Use

We now examine the shortcomings of PAWS and ADEPT and the added capabilities which are needed for implementation of a testbed based on PAWS and ADEPT. The major deficiency of PAWS with respect to its use in a feasibility testbed is a need for a more selective and powerful recording and instrumentation capability. The current recording capability focuses primarily on physical devices and is deficient with respect to accounting for resource usage in terms of logical execution structures. The development of a production quality execution graph management system is a more substantial task. ADEPT is built upon a sophisticated commercial data base management system. Such a capability will have to be present in the APSE or the task of generating execution graphs from functional specifications and mapping them to QN's will be quite cumbersome.

8. Extensions to APSE Specifications for Feasibility Testbed Implementation

Extension of APSE to include a feasibility testbed capability will require extension to STONEMAN specifications only in the area of data management. A data management capability capable of representing complex relationships between program units and necessary structures to represent abstract execution is essential. Separate coding of the complex representations in the proposed MAPS defined in STONEMAN would be excessively tedious and burdensome.

The current STONEMAN concepts call for the ability to integrate additional tools and processors into the PSE. The execution graph generator and the QN modeling system would merely be additional tools for the PSE tool set under this definition. It may be that suitable data base management capabilities can be added in this same fashion since many DBMS are available on several operating systems. The process linking capabilities defined in STONEMAN provide a reasonable structure for the integration of the rather complex sequencing steps necessary to produce feasibility analysis of total system designs.

9. Conclusions

There are three principal conclusions.

1. A feasibility testbed is an essential element of a development support environment for embedded distributed data systems.

2. The current minimal Ada support environments will have to be given extended data management capabilities in order to effectively integrate a feasibility testbed into these systems.

3. A separate but effective experimental feasibility testbed can and should be developed to give experience with the use of this concept. A system to support experimental use can be readily synthesized by combining the existing ADEPT feasibility testbed system with the PAWS computer system simulation system.

REFERENCES

[BEL79] Belady, L. A. and Lehman, M. M., "The Characteristics of Large Systems" in Research Directions in Software Technology (MIT Press, Cambridge, 1979) pp. 106-138.

[CHA81] Chandy, K. M. and Sauer, C. H., "Computer Systems Performance Modeling," (Prentice-Hall, 1981).

[FOS74] Foster, D. V., McGehearty, P. F., Sauer, C. H. and Waggoner, C. N., "A Language for Analysis of Queueing Models," Proc. 5th Pittsburgh Modelling and Simulation Conference, 1976, pp. 381-386.

[IRA82] Information Research Associates, User's Reference Manual for the Performance Analyst's Workbench System (Austin, Texas, 1982).

[KLE75] Kleinroch, L., Queueing Systems: Volume 1: Theory; Volume 2: Applications (John Wiley & Sons, 1975).

[KOB78] Kobayashi, H., Modeling and Analysis: An Introduction to Performance Evaluation Methodology (Addison-Wesley, 1978).

[SAU80] Sauer, C. H., MacNair and Salza, S., "A Language for Extended Queueing Networks," IBM Journal of Research and Development 24, 6 (November 1980).

[SMI79a] Smith, C. U. and Browne, J. C., "Performance Specifications and Analysis of Software Designs," Proc. of Conf. on Simulation, Measurement and Modeling of Computer Systems (Boulder, CO, August, 1979).

[SMI79b] Smith, C. U. and Browne, J. C., "Modeling Software Systems for Performance Predictions," Proc. CMG X (Dallas, TX, Dec., 1979).

[SMI80] Smith, C. U., "The Prediction and Evaluation of Software Performance from Extended Design Specifications," (IPAD Report #2, Information Research Associates, Austin, TX, 1980).

[SMI82] Smith, C. U. and Browne, J. C., "Performance Engineering of Software Systesm: A Case Study," Proc. NCC 51, pp. 217-224 (1982).

Appendix D: Consultation by Enslow

Permission has been granted by Philip H. Enslow, Jr. of Georgia Institute of Technology to publish the following:

MODELLING PARALLEL CONTROL IN DISTRIBUTED SYSTEMS
PHILIP H. ENSLOW, JR.

SUMMARY

Parallel processing has been a popular approach to improving system performance through several generatons of computer systems design. Although it is not usually characterized as a "parallel" processing system, a distributed processing system has the inherent capability for highly parallel operation. In order to capitalize on the potential performance improvements achievable by a distributed system, major parallel control problems must be solved. Central to the issue of parallel control is the design and implementation of distributed and decentralized control. A study of models for decentralized control has been initiated with this survey.

1 BACKGROUND

1.1 Goals of computer system development

It is somewhat remarkable that the goals motivating most computer system development projects have remained basically unchanged since the earliest days of digital computers. Perhaps the most important of these long-sought-after improvements are the following:

1) Increased system productivity
    - Greater capacity
    - Shorter response time
    - Increased throughput
2) Improved reliability and availability
3) Ease of expansion
4) Graceful growth and degradation
5) Improved ability to share system resources

These goals are not expressed in absolute numbers, so it is not surprising that they continue to apply even though phenomenal advances have been made in many of the areas such as speed, capacity, and reliability. What is noteworthy is how little progress has been made in areas such as modular growth, availability, adaptability, etc.

It seems that each new major systems concept or development (e.g., multi-programming, multiprocessing, networking, etc.) has been presented as "the answer" to achieving all of these goals. "Distributed Processing" is no exception to this rule. In fact, many salesmen have dusted off their old lists of benefits and are marketing today's distributed systems as the answer to all of them. Although some forms of distributed processing appear to offer great promise as a means of making significant advances in many of the areas listed, the state of the art, particularly in system control software, is far from being able to deliver even a significant proportion of these benefits today.

1.2 Parallel Processing Systems

An important theme of computer system development work at both the "system organization" and "system software" levels has been parallel processing. It is important to note that parallel processing has been supported by both hardware and software.

Since the early days of computing a direction of research that has offered high promise has been that of "parallel computing". Work in this area dates from the late 1950s which saw the development of the PILOT system at the National Bureau of Standards. The PILOT system consisted of "three independently operating computers that could work in cooperation" (Ensl74). It is interesting to note that the development of parallel systems led to the development of other tightly-coupled systems such as the Burroughs B-825 and B-5000, the earliest examples of the classical multiprocessor. Other development paths saw the introduction of systems such as SOLOMON adn the ILLIAC IV, examples of other forms of tightly-coupled processors.

1.2.1 Tightly-coupled computer systems

During the 1960s and 1970s activities in the development of parallel computing, specifically multiple computer systems, were focused primarily on the development of tightly-coupled systems. These tightly-coupled systems took the form of classical multiprocessors (i.e. shared main memory) as well as specialized computation systems such as vector and array processors. There was also significant activity in the development of loosely-coupled multiple computer systems as exemplified by the attached support processor concept. In the latter part of the 1970s vector and array processors were being connected to general computational systems and utilized as "attached support processors" in any event the specialized nature of the services provided by these "ASP" systems exclude them from consideration as possible approaches to providing general-purpose computational support such as that available from tightly-coupled processors functioning as multiprocessors.

Although the concept of tightly-coupled multiprocessor systems seems like a valid approach to achieving almost unlimited improvements in performance with the addition of more processors, such has not been the result obtained with implemented systems. It is the very nature of tight-coupling that results in limitations on the improvements achievable. These limitations manifest themselves in the following ways:

1. The direct sharing of resources (memory and input/output primarily) results in access conflicts and delays in obtaining use of the shared resource.

2. User programming languages that support the effective utilization of tightly-coupled systems have not been adequately developed.

3. Any inefficiencies present in the operating system seem to be greatly exaggerated in a tightly-coupled system.

4. The development of "optimal" schedules for the utilization of the processors is very difficult except in trivial or static situations. Also, the inability to maintain perfect synchronization between all processors often invalidates an "optimal" schedule soon after it has been prepared.

Tightly-coupled systems certainly do have a role to play in the total spectrum of computer systems organization; however, their limitations should certainly be considered.

1.2.2 Loosely-coupled systems

Loosely-coupled systems are multiple computer systems in which the individual processors communicate with one another at the input/output level. There is no direct sharing of primary memory, although there may be sharing of an on-line storage device such as a disk in the input/output communication path. The important characteristic of this type of system is that all data transfer operations between the two systems are performed as input/output operations. The unit of data transferred is whatever is permissible on the particular input/output channel being utilized, and, in order to complete a transfer, the active cooperation of both processors is required (i.e., one must execute a READ operation in order to accommodate another's WRITE operation).

An important characteristic of loosely-coupled systems is that one processor does not have the capability to "force" another processor to do something. It can deliver data across the interconnecting I/O path; however, even if that data is a request (or demand) for a service to be performed, the receiving processor, theoretically, has the full autonomous right to refuse that request. The reaction of processors to such requests for service is established by the operating system rules of the receiving processor, not by the transmitter. It is possible to have a system which is physically loosely-coupled but logically tightly-coupled due to the rules embodied in the operating system, e.g., a permanent master/slave relationship is defined.

1.2.3 Computer networks

A computer network can be characterized as a loosely-coupled multiple computer system in which the interconnection paths have been extended by the inclusion of data communications links. Fundamentally there are no differences between the basic characteristics of computer network systems and other loosely-coupled systems other than the data transfer rates normally provided. The transfer of data between two nodes still requires the cooperation of both parties and there is no inherent cooperation required between processors other than that which they wish to provide.

1.2.4 Distributed systems

Although there is a large amount of confusion, and often controversy, over exactly what is a "distributed system", it is generally accepted that a distributed system is a computer network designed with some unity of purpose in mind. The components included in the system have been interconnected for the accomplishment of some identified common goal.

2 INTRODUCTION TO FDPS

2.1 Definition of an FDPS

A Fully Distributed Processing System (FDPS) as defined by Enslow (Ensl78) is distinguished by the following characteristics. First, an FDPS is composed of a multiplicity of general-purpose processors (i.e., processors that can be freely assigned to various tasks as required) physically connected by a network providing communication by means of a two-party protocol. The executive control in an FDPS must unify all logical and physical resources providing system transparency (i.e., services are requested by "service name" rather than by a network address). System transparency is designed to aid rather than inhibit and, therefore, can be overridden. In other words, a user who is concerned about the performance of a particular application can provide system-specific information in order to guide its control. Finally, both the logical and physical components of an FDPS should interact in a manner described as "cooperative autonomy" (Clar80, Ensl78). This means that the components operate in an autonomous fashion requiring cooperation among processes for the exchange of information. In a cooperatively autonomous environment, the components are afforded the ability to refuse requests for services. This could result in anarchy except for the fact that all components follow a common master plan expressed by the philosophy of the executive control.

2.2 Implications of the FDPS Definition

2.2.1 Nature of an FDPS

Several characteristics of an FDPS have an impact on the design of the executive control, including system transparency, cooperative autonomy and extremely loose coupling. System transparency means that the FDPS appears to a user as a large uniprocessor which has available a variety of services. Services may be obtained by naming the desired service without specifying any information concerning the details of its physical location. The result is that the control is left with the task of locating all instances of a particular resource and choosing the instance to be utilized.

Cooperative autonomy is another characteristic of an FDPS affecting executive control. Both the logical and physical resource components of an FDPS are designed to operate in a cooperatively autonomous fashion. Thus, the control must be designed in such a manner that any resources is able to refuse a request even though it may have accepted the message containing the request. Degeneration into fully anarchy is prevented by the criteria followed by all resources in the determination of whether a request may be rejected.

Another important FDPS characteristic that affects the design of the executive control is the extremely loose coupling of both physical and logical resources. The processors of an FDPS are connected by communication paths of relatively low bandwidth. (The direct sharing of memory between processors is prohibited.) This implies that the sharing of information among components on different processors is greatly curtailed, and the control is forced to work with information that is often out of date or inaccurate.

2.2.2 Why not a centralized control?

One of the first questions that comes to mind in the discussion of an FDPS is why a centralized method of control is not appropriate. In centralized systems the processes comprising the control share a coherent and deterministic view of the entire system state. An FDPS, though, contains only loosely-coupled components, and the communication among these components is variable and subjected to time delays. This means that one cannot guarantee that all processes will have the same view of the system state (Jens78).

A centralized control also presents problems in the area of fault-tolerance in the form of a single critical element, the control itself. This obstacle, though is not insurmountable for strategies do exist for providing fault-tolerance in centralized applications. For example, Garcia-Molina (Garc79) describes a scheme for providing fault-tolerance in a distributed data base management system with a centralized control. These approaches typically assume that failures are extremely rare events and that the system can tolerate the dedication of a relatively long interval of time to configuration. These restrictions are usually unacceptable to the basic control mechanism.

Finally, the issue of performance must be addressed. An application utilizing distributed resources is expected to utilize a large quantity of resources for control purposes. If control is realized in a centralized manner a large bottleneck will be created in the form of the node housing the control. A distributed and decentralized approach enables the bottleneck to be broken by dispersing the control decisions among multiple components on different nodes.

2.2.3 Distributed versus decentralized

This paper advocates utilizing a distributed and decentralized approach to control in an FDPS. There is a very important distinction between the terms "distributed" and "decentralized". A distributed control is characterized by the location of its physical components on different nodes. This means there are multiple loci of activity. In a decentralized control, on the other hand, control decisions are made independently by different components. In other words, there are multiple loci of control. A distributed and decentralized control thus has physical components located on different nodes that are capable of making independent control decisions.

3 FDPS SYSTEM MODELS

3.1 Introduction

Models serve extremely important, if not essential, roles in the development of complex systems. This is especially true for systems in which the effects of complexity are further complicated by inconsistencies, ambiguities, and incompleteness in the use of the terms that are employed to describe the structure, as well as the operation of the systems involved and the components thereof. Suitable models are valuable tools to support and clarify such discussions. When examining or using any model it is equally important to recognize that it may have been prepared or developed for a specific purpose (e.g., logical or physical description, simulator design, implementation guide, etc.) and may not be totally sutiable for other uses.

3.1.1 Why a new model?

Since the concepts of "full distribution" were first conceived over four years ago members of the FDPS project have been plagued by severe problems in explaining the significance of various aspects of the definition of an FDPS. Most of these problems have been caused by the difficulties in clearly communicating the extremely important differences between "fully" distributed systems and those that are merely "distributed". These problems in understanding often appear to result from the "listener" incorrectly equating certain aspects of FDPS operation with those of a "similarly appearing" distributed system. Such misunderstandings are not totally unreasonable, for some of the most significant differences are quite subtle. One highly desirable effect anticipated from "new" sytem models is to prevent, or at least make more difficult, these undesirable associations with existing system concepts.

3.1.2 Approaches to modelling

There are a number of approaches that may be followed in the development of a system model, and the selection of the approach to be taken is based on intended uses for the model and the nature of the system being modelled.

There are basically six different types of models:

1) Physical structure model: Depicts the manner in which the various hardware and software components are partitioned and packaged.

2) Logical structure model: Focuses on the functionality provided by the hardware and software components and how they may be logically organized into modules.

3) Scenario or flow chart model: Depicts the sequence of processing actions taken on the data .

4) Interaction model: Focuses on the interactions between processing entities - services provided to or received from adjacent layer entities and the protocols governing the communication and negotiations that can occur between nonadjacent layers (see figure 1).

5) Analytic model: Focuses on the performance of complete systems or subsystems. Often the external performance characteristics of the system being modelled are available.

6) Simulation model: Depicts a system or subsystem by modelling as close as possible the operations that it performs. Provides more internal detail than an analytic model.

The various types of models discussed above do not represent different ways to accomplish the same task. Although there is some common information found in or derivable from two or more, each is actually focused on quite different aspects of the system description.

3.2 Other models

Although the work on FDPS models has certainly been strongly influenced by the numerous existing "models" of

Figure 1. Protocols and interfaces.

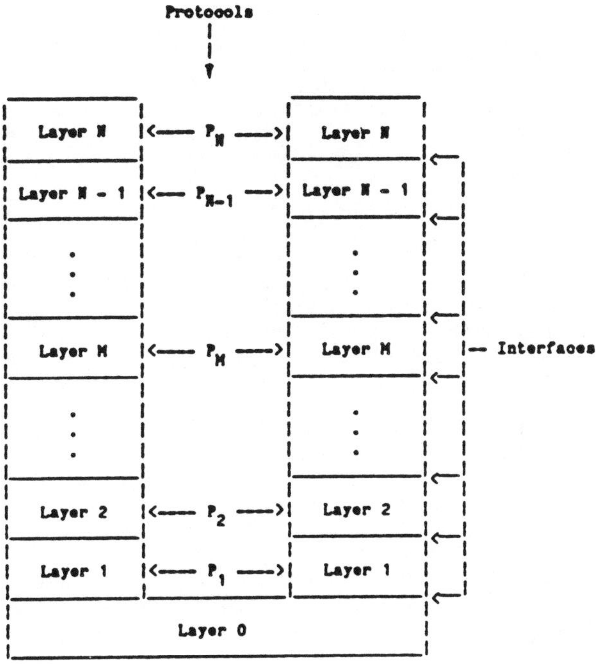

multiprocessors, multiple computer systems, and computer networks, there has been very little influence from other "distributed system" models since few have been developed to the point that they can be closely analyzed. One model that has had a great deal of influence on the development of the FDPS models, at least in guiding the manner in which these models are presented, is the "Reference Model for Open System Interconnection" developed by the International Standards Organization (ISO) Study Committee 16.

3.2.1 The ISO Reference Model for OSI

The ISO Reference Model, a layered-interaction model, is being prepared to establish a framework for the development of standard protocols and interfaces as appropriate for the interconnection of heterogeneous nodes in a computer network. The ISO model is a 7-layer structure as shown in figure 2.

Although the ISO Reference Model has been influential in providing ideas and concepts applicable to a layered model of an FDPS, there are two major factors limiting its direct applicability:

> The ISO model is almost totally concerned with communication between the nodes of a network. Some references are made to higher level protocols in the applications layer, but these are not a part of the OSI model.
>
> Although it is not explicitly stated there appears to be a general assumption in the OSI model of a degree of coupling that is tighter than that anticipated for an FDPS. (This comment also applies to nearly all of the current network architectures - even those that include application layer protocols.)

3.2.2 Protocol hierarchies

As stated above, the ISO Reference Model addresses only a subset of the protocols and interfaces that will be found in a complete distributed system. A more complete picture is shown in figure 3.

3.3 The FDPS Models

3.3.1 The FDPS logical model

Figure 2. The ISO Reference Model for OSI.

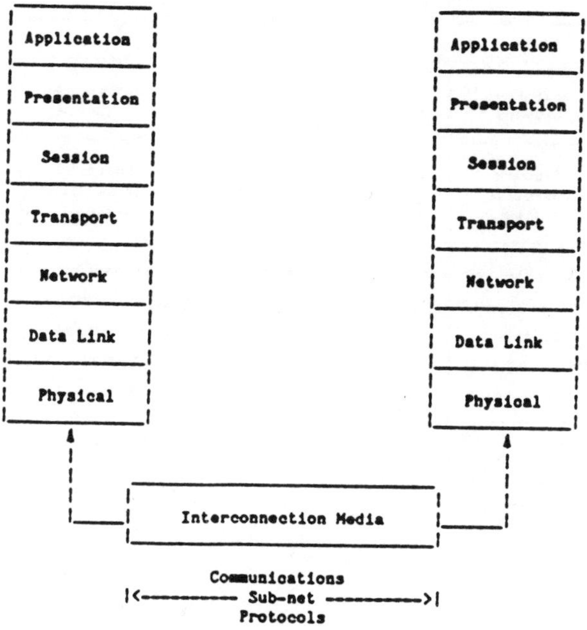

Figure 3. A complete protocol hierarchy.

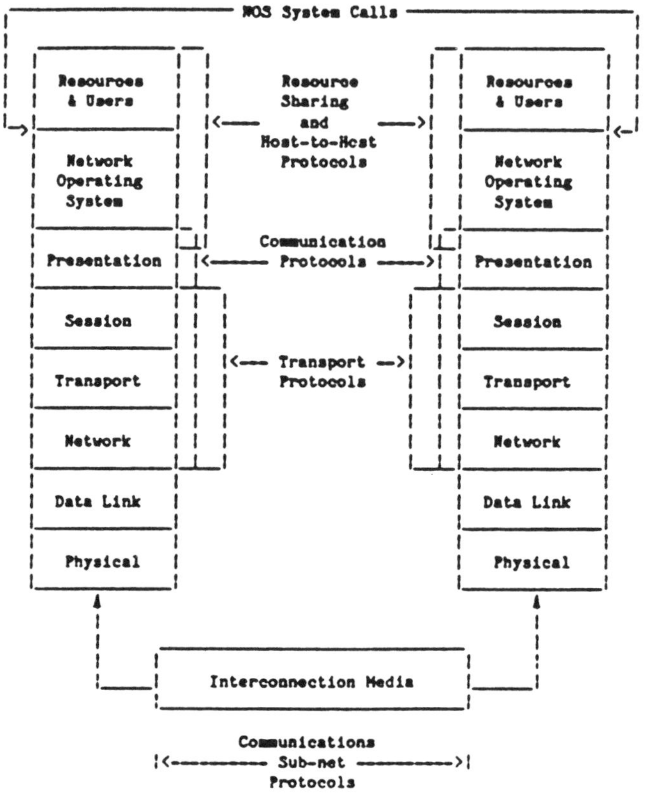

The current version of the FDPS logical model is organized into five layers above the "physical interconnection" layer (figure 4). The important or significant characteristics of this logical model are:

1. It is also a rudimentary layered-interaction model; however, to be useful, the interaction model must delineate more layers.

2. The network operating system has been divided into two parts based on functionality and responsibilities:

   (a) The local operating system (LOS) is responsible for the detailed control and management of the users and resources at that node.

   (b) The distributed operating system (DOS) is responsible for interactions between this node and all others.

3. The correlation of FDPS layers and ISO layers is:

FDPS layers	ISO layers
Users and resources	
Local operating system	Application
Distributed operating system	
Message handler	Presentation
	Session
	Transport
Message transporter	Network
	Data link
	Physical

3.3.2 The FDPS physical model

Figure 4. Logical model of a control.

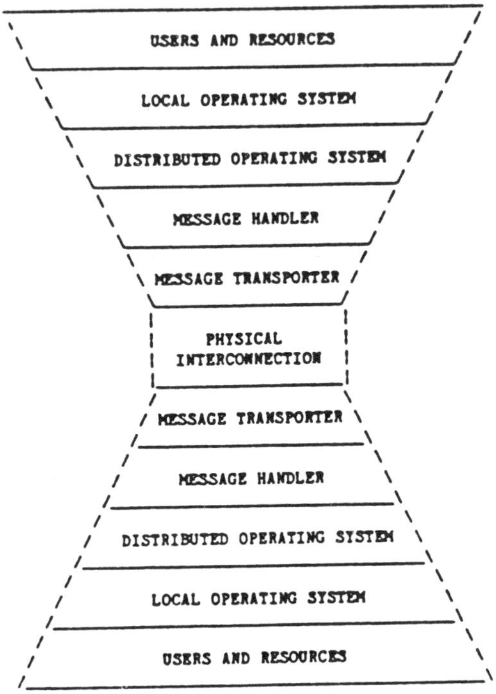

A physical model for the FDPS operating systems is shown in figure 5. This is a good example of how logical models and physical models may differ. In figure 5 the division between the LOS and DOS layers of the logical model runs horizontally through the MANAGERS.

3.3.3 FPDS Interaction model

All the individual layers of the FDPS interaction model have not yet been identified; however, a more detailed list of the protocols that may be loosely related to figure 3 is given in figure 6. This list of protocols is especially significant to the FDPS research project since it identifies those specific area in which design work must be done.

4 Issues of Control

Before examining specific aspects of control in an FDPS, a look at various issues of control is appropriate. There are basically three issues that need examining; the effect of the dynamics of an FDPS on the control, the nature of the information the control element must maintain, and the principles to be utilized in the design of the control.

4.1 Dynamics

Dynamics is an inherent characteristic of the operation of an FDPS. Aspects of dynamics can be found in the workload presented to the system, the availability of resources, and the individual work requests submitted. The dynamic nature of each of these provides the control with many unique problems.

4.1.1 Workload presented to the system

In an FDPS work requests can be generated either by users or active processes and can arrive at any processor. Such work requests can potentially require the use of resources on any processor. Thus, the control must be able to respond to requests arriving at a variety of locations from a variety of sources. Each request may require system resources located on any node. One of the goals of the system is to respond to these requests in such a manner that the load on the entire system is balanced.

4.1.2 Availability of resources

Another dynamic aspect of the FDPS environment concerns the availability of the resources of the system. As men-

Figure 5. Physical model of an FDPS network operating system.

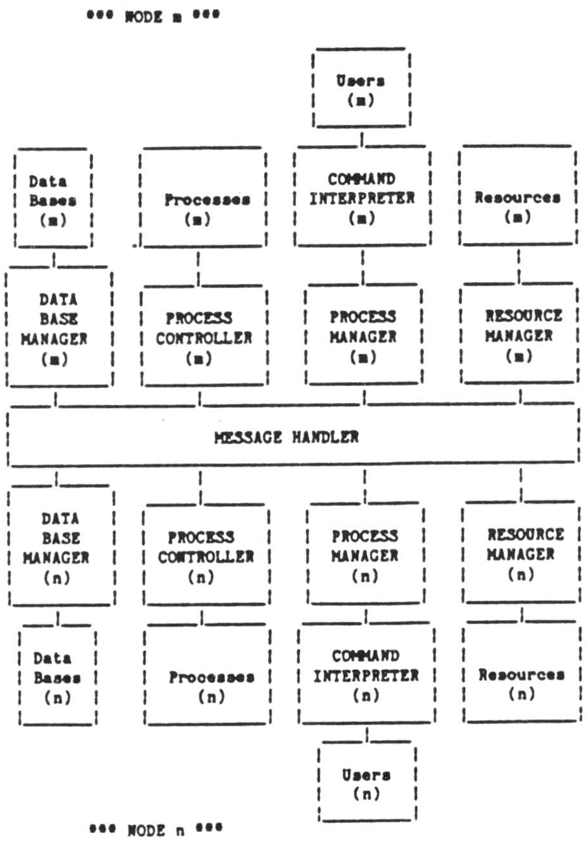

Figure 6. Classifications of computer network protocols.

```
                 Computer Network Protocols
                           |
           ________________|________________
          |                                 |
          |                                 |
          |                                 |
     Communications                    Resource
     Protocols                         Sharing
          |                            Protocols**
          |-(Processing                     |
          |  Communication)                 |-(Data Base Control)
          |  |-Message Formatting           |  |-File naming
          |  |-Addressing                   |  |-File access
          |                                 |  |-File transfer
          |-(Message Handling)              |  |-Update concurrency
          |  |-Destination                  |     control
          |  |  resolution                  |
          |  |-Connection                   |-(Access)
          |  |  establishment               |  |-Virtual terminal
          |  |-Message transfer             |  |-Access control
          |                                 |  |-User interface
          |-(End-to-end)                    |     |-Human
          |  |-Presentation*                |     |-Internal
          |  |-Session*                     |
          |                                 |-(Work Request Processing)
          |-(Transport Subsystem)              |-Resource management
          |  |-Transport*                      |  |-Identification of
          |  |-Network control*                |  |  resource requirements
          |  |-Data link*                      |  |-Resource location
          |  |-Physical*                       |  |-Resource selection
          |                                    |  |-Resource allocation
          |-(Communications Subnet)            |  |-Resource deallocation
          |  |-Network control                 |-Task management
          |  |  |-Routing                         |-Execution control
          |  |  |-Broadcast                       |-Synchronization
          |  |-Data link                          |-Failure recovery
          |  |-Physical
```

* Classifications (layers) defined by the ISO and CCITT Network Architecture Models

** A preliminary list for FDPS's

tioned above, a request for a system resource can originate from any location in the system. In addition, there may be multiple copies of a resource or possibly multiple resources that provide the same functionality (e.g., there may be functionally equivalent FORTRAN compilers on several nodes). Since resources are not immune to failures, the possibility of losing existing resources or gaining both new and old resources exists. Therefore, the control must be able to manage system resources in a dynamic environment in which the availability of a resource is unpredictable.

4.1.3 Individual work requests

Finally, there is the dynamic nature of the individual work requests. As mentioned above, these work requests define, either directly or indirectly, a set of cooperating processes to be invoked. Any of these processes may be command files which contain additional work requests. The main problem is to control these processes and do so in such a manner that the inherent parallelism of the operation is exploited to the maximum. In addition, the control must also handle the situation in which one or more of the processes fail.

4.2 Information

All control systems require information in order to function and perform their mission. The characteristics of the available information is one aspect of fully distributed systems that results in the following somewhat unique control problems:

> Because of the nature of the interconnection links information on hand is always out of date.
>
> Because of the autonomous nature of the operation of all components each processor can make "its own decision" as to how to reply to an inquiry; therefore, there is always the possibility that information received is incomplete or inaccurate.

5 CHARACTERISTICS OF A CONTROL MODEL

5.1 Basic Operations of the Control

The applications to be considered here are presented to the control in terms of a work request that specifies a series of tasks and their connectivity. The tasks to be executed may consist of either executable programs or command files. The control has three basic operations to perform: (1) information gathering, (2) work distribution and resource allocation, and (3) task execution. These operations need not be executed in a purely serial fashion but may take a more complex form with operations executed simultaneously or concurrently as the opportunity arises.

Examination of the basic operations in further detail (figure 7) reveals possible variations in the handling of work requests. Two steps exist in information gathering-(1) collecting information about task requirements for the work request and (2) identifying the resources available for satisfying the request. Information gathering is followed by the task of distributing the work and allocating resources. If this operation is not successful, three alternatives are available. First, more information can be gathered in an attempt to formulate a new work distribution. Second, more information can be gathered as above, but this time the requester will indicate a willingness to "pay more" for the resources (this is referred to as bidding to a higher level). Finally, the user can simply be informed that it is impossible to satisfy his work request.

5.2 Information Requirements

In accomplishing the operations mentioned above, the control must maintain two types of information: information about system resources and information about the structure of the set of tasks required to satisfy the work request. System resource information records the utilization of the system's resources. The task set information is specific to each individual work request and identifies the task identified in the work request and the connectivity of these tasks.

Each work request identifies a set of cooperating processes to be used to satisfy the request. These processes are referred to as "tasks", and the collection of these tasks is called a task set. The task set control information is collected in a structure, the task graph, which contains information describing the needed resources (files, processors, and special peripheral devices) and the connectivity (for purposes of interprocess communication)of the individual tasks comprising the task set.

The control must also maintain information on all system resources (processors, communication lines, files, and special peripheral devices). This information will include

Figure 7. Work request processing.

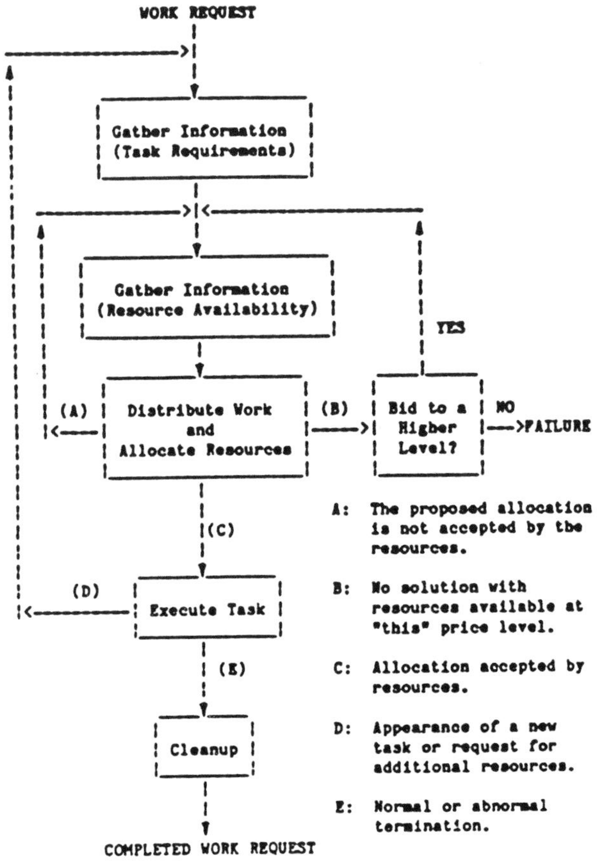

at a minimum an indication of the availability of resources (available, reserved, or assigned). Pre-emptible resources (e.g., processors and communication lines) capable of accommodating more than one user at a time may also have associated with them utilization information designed to guide the control in its effort to perform load balancing.

5.3 Information Gathering

Upon receiving a work request the first task of the control is to gather information on the resources needed to satisfy the work request (figure 8) and the resources available to fill these needs (figure 9). Each work request includes a description of a series of tasks and the connectivity of those tasks. Associated with each task is a series of files. One is distinguished as the execution file and the rest are input/outfiles. The control must first determine which files are needed. It must then examine each of the execution files to determine the nature of its contents (executable code or commands). Each task will need a processor resource, and those tasks containing command files will also require a command interpreter.

The control must also determine which of the system resources are available. For non-pre-emptible resources the status of a resource can be "available", "reserved", or "assigned". A reservation indicates that a resource may be used in the future and that it should not be given to another user. Typically, there is a time-out associated with a reservation that will result in the release of the reservation if an assignment is not made within a specified time interval. An assignment, on the other hand, indicates that a resource is dedicated to a user until the user explicitly releases the assignment. Pre-emptible resources may be accessed by more than one concurrent user and thus can be treated in a different manner. For these resources the status may be indicated by continuous values (e.g., the utilization of the resource) rather than the discrete values described above.

5.4 Work Distribution and Resource Allocation

Another decision of the control concerns the allocation of system resources (figures 10 and 11). This process involves choosing from the available resources those that are to be utilized. This decision is designed to achieve several goals including load balancing, maximum throughput, and minimum response time. It can be viewed

Figure 8. Information gathering (resources required).

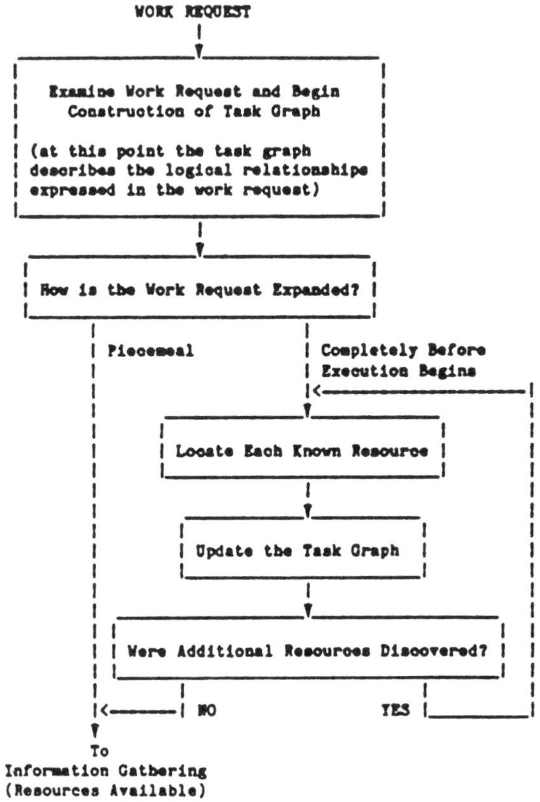

Figure 9. Information gathering (resources available). 1: Resources reserved during information gathering. 2: No resources reserved. 3: Some resources may be reserved. A: General, for all resources. B: To meet specific task/job requirements. C: Replies cover information on resources available only. D: Replies cover information on the total status. E: Broadcast only significant changes. F: Periodic broadcasts at regular intervals.

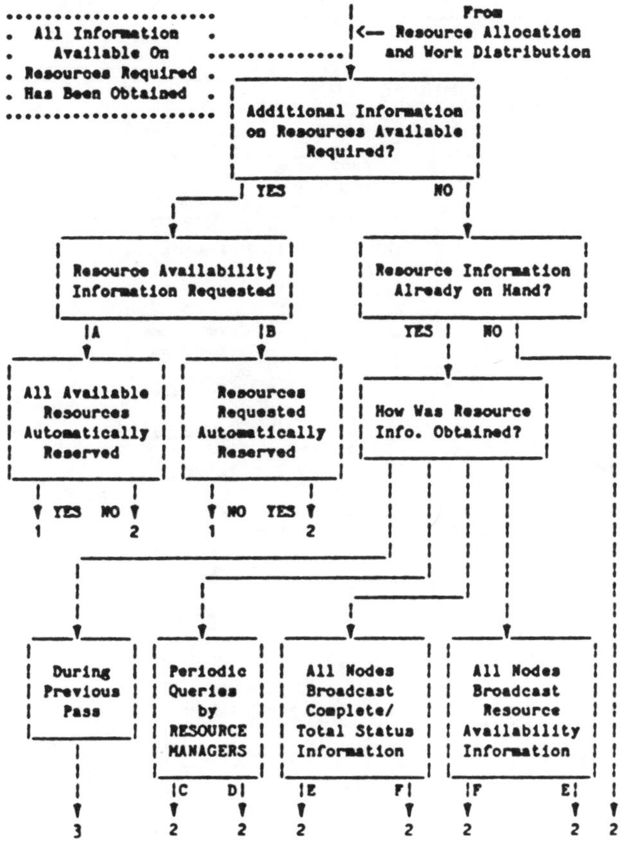

Figure 10. Resource allocation and work distribution.

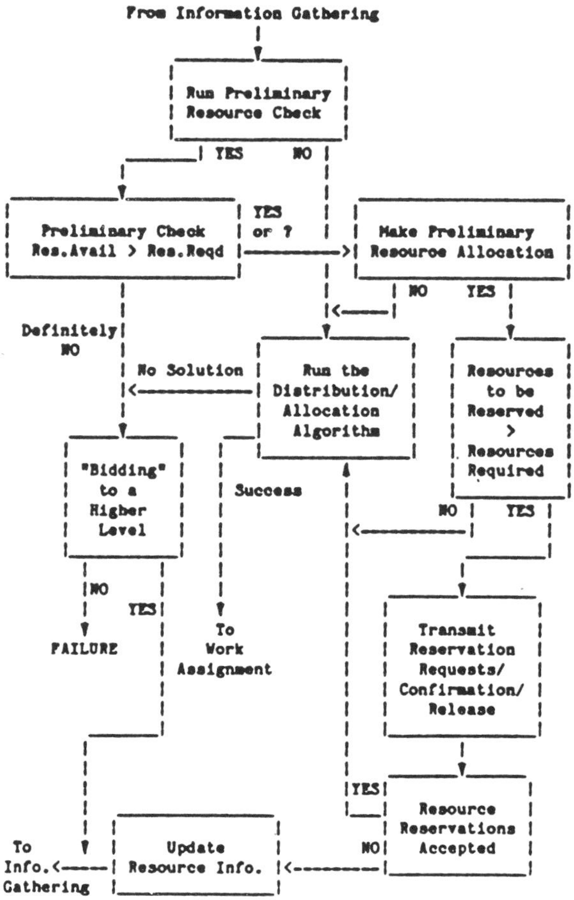

Figure 11. Work assignment.

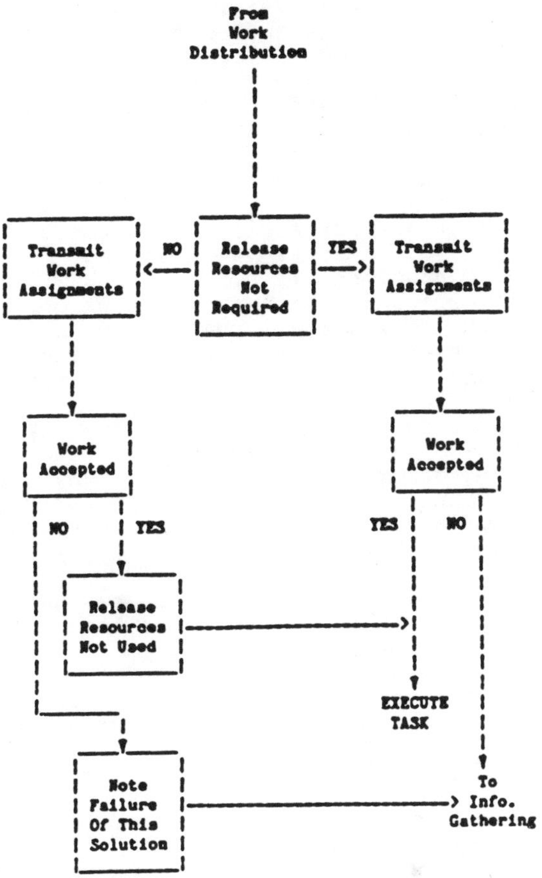

as an optimization problem similar in many respects to that discussed by Morgan (Morg77).

Once an allocation has been determined, the processes comprising the task set are scheduled and initiated. If a process cannot be scheduled immediately it may be queued and scheduled at a later time. When it is scheduled, a process control block and any other execution-time data structures must be created.

5.5 Task Execution

Finally, the control must monitor the execution of active processes. This includes providing interprocess communication, handling requests from the active processes, and performing process termination. The tasks associated with interprocess communication include buffering messages and synchronizing communicating processes. The latter task is necessary to protect the system from processes that flood the system with messages before another process has time to absorb the messages. Active processes may also make requests of the control. These may take the form of requests for additional resources or possibly additional work requests. Work requests may originate from either command files or files containing executable code.

The termination of processes must be detected by the control. This includes both normal and abnormal termination. Any process needing to be informed of the termination must be so notified, open files closed, and other loose ends cleaned up. When the last of the processes of a work request has been terminated, the control must inform the originator of the request of its completion.

5.6 Fault Recovery

If portions (tasks) of the work request are being performed on different processors, there is inherently a certain degree of fault recovery possible. The problem is in exploiting that capability. The ability to utilize "good" work remaining after the failure of one or more of the processors executing a work request depends on the recovery agent having knowledge of the location of that work and the ability of the recovery agent to re-establish the appropriate linkages to the new locations for the portions of the work that were being executed on the failed processor.

6 CHARACTERIZATION OF WORK REQUESTS

One of the goals of an FDPS is the ability to provide a hospitable environment for solving problems that allows one to utilize the natural distribution of data to obtain a solution which may take the form of an algorithm consisting of concurrent subalgorithms. The expression of the solution will be in terms of a work request that describes a series of cooperating processes, the connectivity of the processes (how the processes communicate), and the data files utilized by the processes. The description of the processes and data files reference logical entities and thus do not contain any node-specific information. By formulating work requests in this manner, a user can express a solution in terms of logical, configuration-independent subalgorithms that may potentially be executed concurrently.

6.1 Characteristics

The nature of work requests determines to a large extent the functionality of the control. Therefore, it is important to examine the characteristics of work requests and further to see how variations in these characteristics impact the strategies of control.

Five basic characteristics of work requests have been identified: (1) the visibility of references to resources; (2) the presence of an interprocess communication specification; (3) the relative distribution of the resources comprising the work request; (4) the presence of a reference to a redundantly maintained resource;and (5) the absolute distribution of resources.

6.1.1 Visibility of references to resources

References to the resources required to satisfy a work request may either be visible prior to the execution of any process associated with the work request or embedded in such a manner that some part of the work request must be executed to reveal the reference to a particular resource. The visibility of a resource reference results either from the explicit statement of the reference in the work request or a declaration describing the reference that may be located with little effort over that needed to locate the resource containing the reference. An example of the latter means of visibility is a file system in which external references made from a particular file are identified and stored in the "header" portion of the file.

The identity of a reference can be obtained by simply accessing the first portion of the file.

The greatest impact of the resource reference visibility characteristic occurs in the construction of task graphs and the distribution of work. The timing of resource reference resolution determines when the various parts of a task graph can be constructed and which processes are required to take part in the construction procedure. Similarly, some work cannot be distributed until certain details are resolved. For example, consider a system where resource references are not resolved until execution time. If process X calls process Y, the control will not be able to consider Y in the work distribution decision that must be made before X can begin execution. The significance of this constraint imposed by characteristics of the work requests is that certain work distribution decisions may not be "optimal" because total information is not available at the time the decision is made.

6.1.2 Interprocess communication

Another characteristic of the work requests is the presence or absence of interprocess communication. The presence of interprocess communication will affect both the work distribution decision and the control required during execution. Experience has demonstrated that communication costs can be high, and therefore the presence of interprocess communication is an important fact that must be considered in a work distribution decision. In addition, if there is communication between the processes of a work request, the control will have to provide the means for passing messages, buffering messages, and providing synchronization to insure that a reader does not underflow and a writer does not overflow the message buffers.

6.1.3 The relative distribution of resources

How the resources of a work request are distributed (on the nodes of the FDPS) relative to each other affects both the construction of task graphs and the control required during execution. In certain models the presence of distributed resources results in the construction of task graphs, which pertain to a particular work request, on multiple nodes. These task graphs may be replicated versions of the same task graph or multiple task graphs that, taken together, describe the complete work request.

This distribution also affects how execution control is provided. The important issues here are controlling the activation of processes, controlling the termination of processes and the associated cleanup operations, detecting failures and then recovering, and reporting results to users and processes requiring termination information. Each of these issues can be approached in a variety of ways resulting in a number of different control models.

6.1.4 References to resources with redundant copies

In an FDPS certain resources may exist as redundant copies for reasons of performance or fault-tolerance. The presence of reference to these resources in a work request affects the work distribution decision by providing alternative choices for certain resources. In addition, the presence of redundant resources introduces the problem of maintaining the consistency of the resources. This may be accomplished by a concurrency control or a simple resource locking scheme

6.1.5 The absolute distribution of resources

The final work distribution characteristic to be considered concerns the absolute distribution of the resources referenced in the work request. The concern here is whether the resources that are referenced reside on the same node where the work request arrived or on another node or nodes. These differences lead to variations in task graph building as well as work distribution and execution control.

6.1.6 Summary of work request characteristics

There are thirty-two different combinations possible for the characteristics discussed above. It should be noticed, however, that several of these combinations are impossible because they contain conflicting characteristics. These conflicts demonstrate that the characteristics are not independent, but they do represent distinct issues that significantly affect the design and operation of the control. Therefore, their study is important to achieving a better understanding of control in an FDPS.

7 VARIATIONS IN CONTROL MODELS

Having described the functionality required of a control for an FDPS, we can now investigate the different variations available for realizing that functionality.

The basic issues upon which different models can be based include the nature of how and when a task graph is constructed, the maintenance resource availability information, the allocation of resources, process initiation, and process monitoring.

7.1 Task Graph Construction

The task graph is a data structure used to maintain information about a task set. The nodes of a task graph represent the tasks of the task set, and the arcs represent the hierarchical relationships between tasks and the connectivity or flow of information between tasks. There are basically three issues in task graph construction: (1) who builds the task graph, (2) where the copies of the task graph are stored, and (3) when the task graph is built.

The identity of the component or components involved in the construction of a task graph is an issue that presents three basic choices. First, a central node can be responsible for the construction of all task graphs for all work requests. Another choice is for the control component on the node receiving the work request to construct the task graph. Finally, the job of building the task graph can be distributed among several components. In particular, the nodes involved in executing individual tasks of the work request can be responsible for constructing those parts of the task graph which they are processing.

Another issue of task graph construction concerns the location of the copies of the task graph. One possibility is to maintain a task graph representing the complete task set. This may be stored on only one node or redundant copies may be maintained on several nodes. The nodes containing the copies may be nodes specifically assigned the responsibility of maintaining task graphs or they may be the nodes that are executing part of the work request. Alternatively, the task graph could be divided into several subgraphs and these maintained on several nodes that may or may not be involved in the execution of the work request. Thus, there are basically two different issues: (1) a task graph can be maintained either as a single unit or as a series of subgraphs, and (2) a task graph or its subgraphs can be maintained either on nodes specializing in the maintenance of task graphs or nodes involved in receiving, or executing parts of a work request.

Finally, there is the issue concerning the timing of task graph construction in the sequence of work request processing. Two choices are available: (1) the task graph can be constructed completely, as far as possible, before execution is begun, or (2) the task graph can be constructed incrementally as execution progresses.

7.2 Resource Availability Information

Another issue upon which control models may vary is the maintenance of resource availability information. The main issues here are concerned with which components maintain this information and where it is maintained. The latter question includes the possibility of maintaining redundant availability information. A particular model need not uniformly apply the same technique for maintaining resource availability information on all resources. Rather, the technique best suited to a particular resource class may be utilized.

The responsibility for maintaining resource availability information can be delegated in a variety of ways. The centralized approach involves assigning a single component this responsibility. In this situation, requests and releases of resources flow through this specialized component which maintains the complete resource availability information in one location.

A variation of this technique maintains complete copies of the resource availability information at several locations (Caba79a,b). Components at each of these locations are responsible for updating their copy of the resource availability information. This requires a protocol that insures the consistent operation of all components. For example, two components should not release a file for writing to different users at the same time To provide this control, messages containing updates for the information tables must be exchanged among the components. In addition, a strategy for synchronizing the release of resources (e.g., passing a baton which permits the holder to release resources (Caba79a,b) is required.

Another approach exhibiting more decentralization requires dividing the collection of resources into subsets or classes and assigning separate components to each subset. Each component is responsible for maintaining resource availability information on a particular subset. In this case, requests for resources can only be serviced by the control component responsible for that resource. Resources may either be named in such a manner that the desired manager is readily identifiable or a search for the appropriate manager can be utilized where control is passed from component to component until a component capable of providing service is discovered.

Pre-emptible resources which can be shared by multiple concurrent users (e.g., processors and communication lines) do not necessarily require the maintenance of precise availability information. For these resources, it is reasonable to maintain only approximate availability information because such resources are rarely exhausted. The primary concern in these instances is degraded performance.

7.3 Allocating Resources

A major issue in allocating resources is concurrency control. It is possible in a hospitable environment to ignore concurrence control. In other environments this becomes an important issue that is made even more difficult in the FDPS case due to the loose-coupling inherent in this type of system. The control has basically two approaches to solving this problem. One is to introduce the concept of a reservation, which entails allowing a user to reserve a resource prior to the actual allocation and thus provide the work distribution component with reserved resources. The other technique involves making the work distribution without any reservations. In the latter case if the chosen resources cannot be allocated, the control can either wait until they can be alloated or attempt a new work distribution.

7.4 Process Initiation

Several issues arise in process initiation. Chief among these is the distribution of responsibility. One possibility is to place a single component in complete charge of the entire task graph. It supervises separate components that are responsible for the execution of individual processes comprising the task graph. This hierarchy can be carried one step further to provide a control in which the component assuming responsibility for the complete task graph supervises components responsible for disjoint pieces of the task graph that further supervise components in charge of individual processes. The distribution of responsibility need not necessarily take a hierarchical form. For example, there may be no single component assuming responsible for the complete task graph, but rather multiple components may exist that take charge of disjoint subgraphs of the complete task graph.

Regardless of the distribution, at some point a request for the assumption of responsibility by a component will be made. A component may reasonably deny such a request for two reasons: (1) the component does not possess enough resources to satisfy the request (e.g., there may not be enough space to place a new process on an input queue), or (2) the component may not be functioning. The question that arises concerns how this denial is handled. One solution is to keep trying the request either until it is accepted or until a certain number of attempts have failed. It is also possible to attempt to formulate a new work distribution decision that is made with the new knowledge that a certain component failed to accept a previous request.

7.5 Process Monitoring

The task of monitoring the progress of the processes comprising the task set consists of two parts, providing interprocess communication (IPC) and handling requests. It is assumed that IPC is provided by means of ports (Balz71, Have78,Suns77,Zuck77) and that special control components called port managers are responsible for managing IPC. The issues here include the buffering of messages and the synchronization of communicators. To allow communicators the opportunity to execute in parallel, there needs to be some buffer space associated with each port. The nature and location of this space leads to different control designs. Another problem facing the control is that of synchronizing the communicators. This is necessary to prevent an overactive writer from utilizing a large amount of buffer space before its corresponding reader can remove some of the messages.

The task of monitoring processes also involves processing requests generated by the executing tasks. These may be either requests for additional resources (e.g., an additional file) or new work requests. One question concerns the selection of the control component to receive the request and assume responsibility for seeing that the request is satisfied. If the request is a work request, there is also the question of how the new task set is to be associated with the existing task set. The new task set could be combined with the old one creating a new and larger task set, or it could be kept separate from the old set with the only connection to the old set being the task that originated the new work request.

7.6 Process Termination

When a process terminates there is always some cleanup work that must be accomplished (e.g., closing files, returning memory space, and deleting records concerning the process from the control's work space). In addition, depending on the reason for termination (normal or abnormal) other control components may need to be informed of the termination. The nature of the cleanup and the identity of the control components that must be informed of the termination is determined from the design decisions resulting from the issues discussed above.

8 THE LIFE CYCLE OF DISTRIBUTED SYSTEMS

One important aspect in considering the requirements for support capabilities is the specific environment in which a given support capability is to be employed. For the purpose of this study, the application environment will be identified by reference to a phase or a set of phases in the overall life cycle of a distributed system.

In this study the various phases or activities of the life cycle are, in chronological order,

Problem Analysis and Functional Design

Logical System Design

Program Implementation

Unit Test

System Integration

System Test

Program Distribution and Installation

System Operation and Utilization

System Maintenance

Just as with centralized systems, to which this list is equally applicable, there are a number of feedback paths present in the complete life cycle.

8.1 Categories of Support Capabilities and their Application

As this study has progressed, a large number of different system support capabilities applicable to the total life cycle of distributed systems have been identified. As the list expanded, it became obvious that confusion was being created by a lack of clear definition of the relationships between the various capabilities and their specific applicability. A major cause of this confusion was the absence of a clear distinction between the major categories of support capabilities.

In addressing this particular problem, three major types of support capabilities have been identified:

Software Development Support Tools

System Design Support Facilities

Operational Support Capabilities

8.1.1 Software Development Support Tools

The primary purpose of software development support tools are the production, maintenance, and management of the operational software systems, both operating systems and applications programs--i.e., the production of software. Some confusion is caused by the word "software" in the title. It should be noted the software applies to the application of the tool or support capability, not the nature of the tool itself since nearly all of the support capabilities will be implemented in software, at least in part.

It is unfortunate that the desiginations "tool" and "support capability" have been used almost totally interchangeably. (We have been as guilty of this as anyone else.) However, using the terms in this manner was one of the major factors creating the confusion referred to above.

Because of the wide variety of support capabilities found within this single category, further subcategories are useful in examing the characterization and applicability of software support tools. The subcategories identified thus far are:

- o Software Requirements/Specification Tools

- o Software Design Tools
- o Software Implementation (Programming) Tools
- o Software Quality Assurance Tools
- o Software Maintenance Tools
- o Software Cross-Environment Tools
- o Miscellaneous Software Utility Tools
- o Software Management Tools

It should be noted that these subcategories are equally applicable to tools supporting centralized systems.

The list of subcategories given above will be utilized during this study when such subdivisions are required; however, that is not the only set that has been proposed. William Howden in discussing software development environments presents a five-way categorizaton (Howden).

- o Requirements Tools and Methods
- o Design Tools and Methods
- o Coding Tools and Methods
- o Verification Tools
- o Management Tools and Techniques

Also, A.N. Haberman in (Riddle & Fairley) discusses his two-part classification

- o Program Development Tools
- o System Construction Tools

where examples of the first are the "classical tools such as compilers and editors" while the latter "emphasizes the importance of specifications and system version maintenance."

Another categorization methodology for software development tools has been proposed by the Software Tools Project of the Institute for Computer Sciences and Technology at the National Bureau of Standards. This methodology is based on a multi-dimensional taxonomy of tool features describing the characteristics of the input, the function, and the output of the tool. These three major features are further divided into two or three dimensions. In all there are seven dimensions.

In the list below the following notation is employed:

- o Basic processes of a tool
  - Classes of tool features - Classification dimensions.
    - Specific tool features - multiple features in a single class may apply to a given tool.

- o Input
  - Subject (main input)
    - Text
    - VHLL
    - Code
    - Data
  - Control Input
    - Commands
    - Parameters

- o Function
  - Transformation (how is the subject manipulated)
    - Editing
    - Formatting
    - Instrumentation
    - Optimization
    - Restructing
    - Translation
  - Static Analysis (operations on the subject)
    - Auditing
    - Comparison
    - Complexity Measurement
    - Completeness Checking
    - Consistency Checking
    - Cost Estimation
    - Cross Reference
    - Data Flow Analysis
    - Error Checking
    - Interface Analysis
    - Management
    - Resource Estimation
    - Scanning
    - Scheduling
    - Statistical Analysis
    - Structure Checking
    - Tracking

Type Analysis
Units Analysis
Dynamic Analysis (operations during or after execution)
Assertion Checking
Constraint Evaluation
Coverage Analysis
Resource Utilization
Simulation
Symbolic Execution
Timing
Tracing
Tuning

- Output
  - User Output
    - Computational Results
    - Diagnostics
    - Graphics
    - Listings
    - Text
    - Tables
  - Machine Output
    - Data
    - Intermediate Code
    - Object Code
    - Prompts
    - Source Code
    - Text

Although this classification methodology was developed primarily to support, or force, complete descriptions of tools, it has also been useful in the context of this study to check for completeness of coverage in our consideration of the need for various software development tools.

8.1.2 Examples of Software Development Support Tools

Implementation tools such as compilers and editors are certainly the most common; however, there is beginning to be significant activity in the development of support capabilities in the other categories as well. In the initial edition of the "Software Engineering Automated Tools Index" published by Software Research Associates the breakdown was as follows:

Category	Number of Tools	Percentage of Total
Requirements/Spec. Tools	20	3
Design Tools	47	7
Implementation Tools	210	32
Quality Assurance Tools	132	20
Maintenance Tools	119	18
Project Management Tools	57	9
Cross-Environment Tools	16	2
Miscellaneous Utility Systems	40	6
Research and Development Systems	7	1
Maintenance Tools	119	18
Project Mgmt. Tools	57	9
Cross-Environment Tools	16	2
Miscellaneous Utility Sys.	40	6
Research and Development Systems	7	1

Examples of specific tools that fall in each subcategory are given below.

- Requirement/Specification Tools
  - Requirement/Specification Languages
  - Charts and Diagrams (both formal and informal) (e.g., HIPO. SADT, Dataflow, etc.)
  - Specification Cross-Reference Analyzer
  - Archiver/retriever for requirements specification

- Design Tools
  - Formal Design Tools/Methodologies (e.g., PDL, Structured Design)
  - Automated Data Dictionary
  - Distributed Data Base and Transactions Processing

Design Language
Module Interface Checker
Module Cross-Reference Analyzer
Automated Simulator Builder
Automated Archiver for Design Specifications

- Implementation Tools
  - Distributed Applications Programming Languages
  - Distributed Systems Implementation Languages
  - Editors
  - Text Managers (source and object code file systems)
  - Source Code Manager
  - Program Code-Reference Analyzer
  - Language Processors
  - Compiler Development Tools (???)

- Quality Assurance Tools
  - Flow Charter
  - Test Harnesses
  - Test Coverage Analyzer
  - Test Data Generator
  - Control Flow Analyzer
  - Data Flow Analyzer

- Maintenance Tools
  - Source Code Debugging
  - Trouble Report and Comment Tracking System

- Cross-Environment Tools
  - Cross Compilers
  - Environment Simulators

- Miscellaneous Utility Tools
  - Program Archiver

- Management Tools
  - Project Status Control
  - Project Status Report Generators
  - Build Plan Recorders
  - Configuration Manager
  - Cost Estimator
  - Version Manager

8.2 Applicability of Software Support Tools

The applicability of the various subcategories of tools to the different phases in the overall life cycle is fairly obvious from the name of each subcategory.

- Software Requirements/Specification Tools

Problem Analysis and Functional Design

- Software Design tools
  Logical System Design

- Software Implementation Tools
  Program Implementation

- Software Quality Assurance Tools
  Unit Test
  System Test
  System Maintenance

- Software Maintenance Tools
  System Maintenance

- Cross-Environment Tools
  Program Distribution and Installation

- Miscellaneous Software Utility Tools
  System Maintenance

- Software Management Tools
  System Integration
  Program Distribution and Installation

REFERENCES

Balz71 Balzer R.M., "PORTS - A method for dynamics interprogram communication and job control", in AFIPS Conference Proceedings Vol. 38 (1971 Spring Joint Computer Conference):pp.485-9.

Caba79a Cabanal, J. P., Marouane, M.N., Besbes, R., Sazbon, E.D., and Diarra, A.K., "A decentralized OS model for ARAMIS distributed computer system", in Proceedings of the First International Conference on Distributed Computing Systems (October, 1979):pp.529-35.

Caba79b Cabanel, J.P.,Sazbon, R. D., Diarra, A.K. Marouane, M.N., and Besbes, R.,"A decentralized control method in a distributed system", in Proceedings of the First International Conference on Distributed Computing Systems (October, 1979):pp.651-9.

Clar80 Clark, David D., and Svobodova, Liba, "Design of distributed systems support local autonomy", in COMPCON Spring 80 (February 1980):pp.438-44.

Ensl74 Enslow, Philip H., Jr. (ed.), Multiprocessors and Parallel Processing, New York:John Wiley and Sons, 1974.

Encl78 Enslow, Philip H., Jr., "What is a "distributed" data processing system?" Computer (January, 1978):13-21.

Garc79 Garcia-Molina, H., Performance Comparison of Update Algorithms for Distributed Database,Crash Recovery in the Centralized Locking Algorithm, Progress Report No. 7, Stanford University, 1979.

Have78 Haverty, J.F., and Rettberg, R.D., "Inter-process communications for a server in UNIX", in COMPCON Fall 78 (September, 1978):pp.312-15.

Hopp79 Hoppr, K., Kugler, H. J., and Unger, C., "Abstract machines modelling network control systems', Operating Systems Review 13 (January 1979): 10-24.

Jens78 Jensen, E. Douglas, "The Honeywell experimental distributed processors-An overview", Computer (January, 1978):28-38.

Morg77 Morgan, Howard L., and Levin, K. Dan, "Optimal program and data locations in computer networks", Communications of the ACM 20 (May, 1977):315-22.

Suns77 Sunshine, Carl, Interprocess Communication Extensions for the UNIX Operating System: I. Design Considerations, Rand Technical Report R-2064/1-AF, June 1977.

Zuck77 Zucker, Steven, Interprocess Communication Extensions for the UNIX Operating System: II. Implementation, Rand Technical Report R-2064/2-Af, June 1977.

Appendix E: Consultation by Cook

Permission has been granted by Robert P. Cook to publish the following:

KERNEL DESIGN
FOR
CONCURRENT PROGRAMMING

1. Introduction

A growing number of application programmers are starting to realize that the use of multiple processes in a program does not require the support of a traditional operating system. Therefore, the construction of an efficient kernel which supports concurrent programming is of interest. This paper summarizes the author's experiences with respect to the implementation of bare machine kernels on the Intel 8086, Digital Equipment PDP-11, and Motorola 68000 computers for the StarMod[1] programming language.

Our design philosophy is one which forces the processor to imitate the language, as opposed to having the language mimic the machine. Also, clarity and program correctness are of prime importance. In the following sections, we will discuss how to virtualize a given processor, how to handle devices, how to provide for synchronization and mutual exclusion, and how to implement error recovery mechanisms.

2. Virtual Processor Construction

Assume that your supervisor walks into your office one day, removes a new processor from his pocket, and tells you to make it work. What do you do first? The first step is to choose a concurrent programming language such as Ada[2], Modula[3], Edison[4], Mesa[5], etc. The compiler will either generate code for your processor or interpretive code for a virtual processor.

We will also assume for the sake of simplicity that the programming language calls runtime routines to implement the following:

Function	Name
Program Start	_start
Program Stop	_stop
Procedure Entry	_procin
Procedure Exit	_procout

Thus, a sample StarMod program might have the following machine language translation:

```
module main;
                                        JUMP  main
var a:integer;
procedure p;
   begin
                                        CALL  _procin
   (*do nothing*)
end p;
                                        CALL  _procout
begin
                                 main:  CALL  _start
   a:=a+1;
                                        INC   a
   p;
                                        CALL  p
end main.
                                        CALL  _stop
```

The "_start" routine initializes the machine and sets up the activation record stack for the programming language. The stack size is usually restricted to be a constant. The "_procin" and "_procout" routines create and delete activation records for procedure call and return, respectively. These two entry points can also be used to implement a procedure breakpoint facility for debugging. If necessary, stack overflow and underflow are checked to provide error detection. At this point, we should be able to make the statement that an incorrect program manifests an error as one of the following:

1. incorrect results
2. an infinite loop
3. a program fault (subscript, case, pointer error, etc.)

Point 3 is especially important with respect to detecting errors, as testing "is hopelessly inadequate for showing their absence"[6]. The work on the kernel can begin once procedures are implemented.

Next, a module should be created which encapsulates any useful, machine-dependent instructions such as "enable interrupt" or "set privileged mode". It is also easy to include any absolute addressing capability that might be needed for kernel construction. Consider the following example:

Virtual Module	Real Module
module cpu; export enable, device_reg;	DEF enable, device_reg
procedure enable; end enable;	enable: ENABLE RETURN
var device_reg: array 0:2047 of integer;	device_reg=14000o
end cpu.	

The assembly language program defines values which are declared as language elements by the kernel implementor. The "export" specification is equivalent to the "DEF"inition of a symbol in assembly language. Note that the "device_reg" symbol is equated with an absolute value; therefore, the array declaration acts as a template for the specified memory locations. This technique can be used to manipulate device registers on machines such as the PDP-11.

Even though some systems programming languages include the capability to refer to device registers, we do not recommend its use, ever. The reason is that most device registers do not obey the axioms associated with variables. In particular, it is possible to

1) assign to a device register and have the resulting value be different.

2) read from a device register and get a different value each time.

These anomalies can sometimes cause a "smart" compiler to optimize operations in such a way that programs fail inexplicably. Thus, we currently use procedure calls to control devices. Before discussing I/O programming in more detail, the implementation of kernel processes will be outlined.

3. Kernel Processes

A processor executes instructions, a procedure is a sequence of instructions for a processor, and a process is a collection of procedures together with a context block which defines its current state of execution. A process can be thought of as the logical environment for the execution of a collection of procedures, as contrasted to the physical environment which is a hardware processor.

In order to switch the physical processor from one process to another, certain information must be saved. When control is removed from a process or when control is restored to a process, the following information must be saved.

(1) The process must know which instruction to execute next when it resumes control of the physical processor. Therefore, the program counter must be saved and restored.

(2) The contents of the physical processor's registers must be saved so that they can be restored before proceeding.

(3) For a stack machine, the current frame and stack pointers must be saved.

Additional information may be required to define a virtual processor--the number and type of I/O devices it can access, the amount of memory or CPU time it can use, and any other capabilities it will be given.

That minimal part of the context block which must be copied to the hardware processor to start execution of a process is called the state vector. The size of the state vector should be minimized in order to be able to switch a processor from one process to another as quickly as possible.

For concurrent programming at the kernel level, efficiency is a primary concern. Therefore, we will impose the following restrictions.

1) all processes share code and global data.
2) the stack size is a constant for each process.

We also assume that the code is write-protected. The context block for a kernel process could then be defined as follows:

```
type context_block = record
        next: ^context_block;
        status: (RUNNING,READY,BLOCKED);
        sp: ^state_vector;
        stack_base, stack_limit: ^integer;
end; (*context_block*)
```

"next" can be used to link a context block into various queues, while "status" is used to indicate the type of queue. "sp" is the stack pointer and we assume that the state vector is always at the top of the stack for a BLOCKED or READY process. "stack_base" and "stack_limit" define the boundaries for the private stack of a process. The next step is to implement process execution.

We will assume the following syntax for a process declaration:

```
process IDENT(FORMALS);
   LOCAL_DECLARATIONS
begin
                                 IDENT:     PUSH  size(FORMALS)
                                            CALL  _prosin

   STATEMENT_LIST
end IDENT;
                                            CALL  _prosout
```

A process is created by a "process call" statement which has the same syntax as a Pascal procedure call, but different semantics. For a procedure call, the caller waits until execution of the procedure is completed. For a process call, the caller continues executing. In addition, the only effect of a process exit is to free a context block and to cause control of the processor to be passed on to the next READY process.

The generated code for a process pushes the size of the argument list on the caller's stack and calls a runtime routine to allocate a new context block and to initialize a stack for the new process. At the end of the process, "_prosout" is called to free the context block. Figures 1 and 2 illustrate the implementation of these routines.

The stack and its limits are kept in the context block. We also assume that the stack grows from high addresses to low. Obviously, these choices must be varied depending upon the architecture. Another convention is that the top of stack for a non-executing process contains the state vector and that the pointer(sp) to the state vector is kept in the context block. To start a process, the state vector is moved into the hardware

```
module _processes;
export _initialize, _process_in, _process_out, pause, state_type;
import _switch;

    const MAXIMUM_PROCESSES = 5;
          MAX_STACK_SIZE = 1000;

    type stack_type = array 1:MAX_STACK_SIZE of integer;

    type context_block_type = record
                status : (READY, RUNNING, BLOCKED, FREE);
                sp : ^state_vector;
                stack_base, stack_limit : ^integer;
         end; (* context_block_type *)

    type state_type = record
                next : ^state_type;
                context_block : context_block_type;
                stack : stack_type
         end; (* state_type *)

    var process_state : array 1:MAXIMUM_PROCESSES of state_type;
        ready_list : ^state_type;
        free_list : ^state_type;
        who_is_running : ^state_type;

procedure _initialize : ^stack_type;
    var i : integer;
begin (*initialize the data structures*)
    who_is_running:=addr(process_state[1]);
    with process_state[1] do (* reserved for "main" *)
        next:=nil;
        with context_block do
            status:=RUNNING;
            stack_base:=addr(stack[1]);
            stack_limit:=addr(stack[MAX_STACK_SIZE);
            _initialize:=stack_limit;(* assume stack grows towards 0 *)
        end; (* with *)
    end; (* with *)
    ready_list:=nil;   free_list:=nil;
    i:=2;
    repeat
        with process_state[i] do
            next:=free_list;
            free_list:=addr(process_state[i]);
            with context_block do
                status:=FREE;
                stack_base:=addr(stack[i]);
                stack_limit:=addr(stack[MAX_STACK_SIZE]);
            end; (* with *)
        end; (* with *)
        inc(i);
    until i > MAXIMUM_PROCESSES;
end _initialize;
```

Figure 1. Process Initialization

```
type stack_in_type = record
        process_start_address : ^instruction;
        argument_size : integer;
        callers_return_address : ^instruction;
        arguments : array 1:argument_size of integer;
     end; (* stack_in_type *)

procedure _process_in(stack_in : stack_in_type);
    var cp : ^state_type;
begin
    cp:=free_list;
    if cp = nil then
        (* error--too many processes *)
    end;
    with cp^ do
        free_list:=next;   next:=ready_list;
        ready_list:=cp;
        (* stack := stack_in.arguments                   *)
        (* dec(top_of_stack,size(stack_in.arguments))    *)
        (* stack := first activation record              *)
        (* dec(top_of_stack,size(activation record))     *)
        (* initial state_vector.pc :=
                   stack_in.process_start_address *)
        (* stack := initial state_vector                 *)
        (* dec(top_of_stack,size(state_vector))          *)
        with context_block do
            status:=READY;
            sp:=top_of_stack;
        end; (* with *)
    end; (* with *)
end _process_in;

procedure _switch(from_process, to_process : ^state_type);
   (* imported from the assembly language runtime to
      save the state_vector and set sp in the context_block
      of the from_process and to restore the state_vector
      of the to_process.  sets status to RUNNING.        *)

procedure _process_out;
    var previous : ^state_type;
begin
    previous:=who_is_running;
    with who_is_running^ do
        next:=free_list;
        free_list:=who_is_running;
        context_block.status:=FREE;
    end; (* with *)
    who_is_running:=ready_list;
    if who_is_running = nil then
        (* error--no process to run *)
    end;
    ready_list:=ready_list^.next;
    _switch(previous,who_is_running);
end _process_out;
```

Figure 2. Process Start and Stop

```
procedure pause;
    var previous : ^state_type;
begin
    if ready_list <> nil then
        previous:=who_is_running;
        who_is_running:=ready_list;
        ready_list:=ready_list^.next;
        previous^.context_block.status:=READY;
        _switch(previous,who_is_running);
    end; (* if *)
end pause;
end _processes.
```

```
module main;
import pause;
procedure pause;
    (*part of the kernel*)
process p;
begin
                          PUSH  0
                          CALL  _prosin
end p;
                          CALL  _prosout
begin
                    main: CALL  _start
    p;
                          CALL  p
    pause;
                          CALL  pause
end main.
                          CALL  _stop
```

EXECUTION RESULTS

```
 1. Initialize processor
 2. CALL _initialize to set up the context blocks
 3. Set up an initial activation record at the returned address
 4. JUMP main
 5. _start just returns
 6. CALL p
 7. CALL _prosin
 8. CALL _process_in
 9. On return, _prosin clears the stack back to Step 6 and exits
10. CALL pause
11. Process p starts executing
12. CALL _prosout
13. Control reurns to the main program
14. CALL _stop
15. The program halts
```

Figure 3. The Pause Operation and An Example

registers, while to stop a process, the state vector must be saved on the stack and sp must be saved in the context block.

The "_initialize" routine is used to transform the "main" part of a user's program into a process. The "_process_in" and "_process_out" routines in Figure 2 create and delete processes based on process invocation and termination calls. Note that "_process_in" declares its argument list so that it overlaps the portion of the stack which sets up the process invocation. The "_prosin" routine consists of a few assembly language statements to call "_process_in" and to clean up the stack on its return. This involves transferring control back to the point of process invocation.

Figure 3 traces the execution sequence for a sample program. The pause procedure is provided so that a process can temporarily release control of the processor. It places the current process at the end of the ready list. Thus, a process can create a number of worker processes and then "pause" to let them execute. In the next section, the kernel will be augmented with primitives to control process execution.

4. Process Control

The bane of concurrent programming is interference among a group of processes. Interference can occur in the following ways between two processes:

1. Some of the input variables of process 1 are the same as some of the output variables of process 2.
2. Some of the input variables of process 2 are the same as some of the output variables of process 1.
3. Both process 1 and process 2 share some of the same output variables.
4. The execution of process 1 causes process 2 to miss a deadline, or vice versa.

The problem with conditions 1, 2 and 3 is that it becomes increasingly difficult to verify the results of a given statement. Writing programs without being able to state what each statement does is a dangerous occupation. Condition 4 is more subtle and is usually present in real-time programs. To solve these problems, we will discuss the implementation of mutual exclusion and priority.

After identifying the critical sections of the program which exhibit conditions 1, 2 and 3, the programmer can use mutual exclusion primitives to guarantee indivisible execution. Indivisible execution serializes the use of shared variables and allows the use of sequential programming proof techniques. We should note, however, that greater efficiency can often be obtained by eliminating mutual exclusion and spending more time on a proof which includes concurrency. If we assume that deadlines are missed due to insufficient processor time, then priority can be used to order execution.

4.1 Mutual Exclusion and Synchronization

The first problem is how to execute a section of code indivisibly. The building blocks on most machines can be classified as either processor synchronous (disabling interrupts) or memory synchronous (test and set instruction). Disabling interrupts should be used with caution since indivisibility is not guaranteed for multiprocessor systems. In addition, disabling interrupts can affect the responsiveness of a program to external events. Therefore, the disable operation will be used sparingly. Figure 4 illustrates the construction of a semaphore[7] type which can be used to implement a critical section as follows:

```
var s : semaphore;
initsem(s);

wait(s);        (* start critical section *)

send(s);        (* end critical section   *)
```

Note that the "send" operation always performs a context switch, as opposed to just adding the target process to the ready list. The rationale for this choice is that a critical section is a resource which should be allocated and released as quickly as possible to avoid queuing delays. Based on system design goals, the semaphore module can be modified as desired.

The use of semaphores to implement critical sections has, however, been subjected to the following criticisms[8,9]:

1. The programmer must place them in the correct sections of code and in the right order, operations which are subject to error.
2. Direct or indirect recursion can cause deadlocks.
3. Nesting of critical region entries does not release access when a wait occurs, thus creating potential unexpected delays.

These problems were solved, in part, with the introduction of the monitor concept by Brinch Hansen[10] and Hoare[11].

A monitor is a module which encapsulates a data abstraction and the procedures which operate on the abstraction. The procedures are automatically implemented as mutually exclusive critical sections by a combination of compiled code and kernel routines. We will assume that a module prefix of "monitor" denotes this abstraction. We will also assume that the procedures which define an abstraction can be partitioned into mutually disjoint subsets where each subset either is, or is not, a monitor. Consider the following example:

```
module abstraction;
export (* for use by others *);
import (* for use by the abstraction *);

    (* define global data structures and types *)

    [monitor INTEGER] module one;
    end one;

    [monitor INTEGER] module N;
    end N;
begin (* initialization *)
end abstraction.
```

Each sub-module encapsulates part of the definition. Thus, mutual exclusion is used only where necessary by using the "monitor" prefix. The INTEGER constants must be unique for each monitor declaration and are used to avoid deadlock by using a hierarchical resource allocation scheme[12]. When executing in monitor _i_, the program is only allowed to call monitors _j_, j>i. In practice, we have never encountered an example where such an assignment of INTEGERs did not exist. Furthermore, the procedures within a monitor are allowed to be recursive. Next, the code generated for a monitor will be discussed.

```
monitor INTEGER module name;
export p;
procedure p;
begin
                              p:  PUSH  INTEGER
                                  CALL  _monprocin
end p;
                                  PUSH  INTEGER
                                  CALL  _monprocout
begin
                                  PUSH  INTEGER
                                  CALL  _moninit
end name.
```

A semaphore is used to control entry to the monitor and the INTEGER represents the array index of the semaphore. It is also necessary to change procedure entry and exit to acquire and release exclusive control of the monitor. Two fields were added to each process' context block; "in_mon" is a bit vector which remembers monitor entries and the array "nesting_level" which counts recursive procedure calls for each possible INTEGER. On procedure exit, if the recursion count is zero, control of the monitor is released. Figure 5 illustrates the monitor implementation.

The monitor procedure entry routine, "_mon_procedure_in", first checks that the entry is following the hierarchical ordering. Next, the owner of the monitor is compared to the caller; if equal, the user is executing a recursive call so the nesting level is incremented. In the normal case, the user waits on the semaphore, initializes the nesting level, and marks "in_mon" to indicate the monitor selected. The monitor exit subroutine, "_mon_procedure_out", just decrements the nesting level and releases the monitor, if necessary. In addition to solving most of the problems with semaphores, the implementation has the advantage that the information on the status of all monitors is centralized, which is useful for debugging and for error recovery.

The one problem that has not been addressed concerns the release of exclusion when a process delays. We have chosen not to release exclusion when a process delays on monitor entry. The reason is that we expect the execution time in the monitor to be short. The delay time, however, may be long. With semaphores alone, there is no easy way to distinguish between semaphores used for long-term delay and those used for short delays. In the next section, the definition of semaphores in Figure 4 will be

```
module semaphores;
export semaphore, initsem, wait, send;
import state_type, enable, disable, who_is_running, _switch;
    type semaphore = record
              owner, head, tail : ^state_type;
         end; (* semaphore *)
procedure initsem(var s : semaphore);
begin
    with s do
        owner:=nil;  head:=nil;   tail:=nil;
    end; (* with *)
end initsem;
procedure wait(var s : semaphore);
    var previous : ^state_type;
begin
    with s do
        disable;
        if owner <> nil then
            if head = nil then
                head:=who_is_running;
            else
                tail^.next:=who_is_running;
            end; (* if *)
            tail:=who_is_running;
            previous:=who_is_running;  who_is_running:=ready_list;
            if who_is_running = nil then
                (* error--no process to run *)
            end;
            ready_list:=ready_list^.next;
            previous^.context_block.status:=BLOCKED;
            _switch(previous,who_is_running);
        end; (* if *)
        owner:=who_is_running;
        enable;
    end; (* with *)
end wait;
procedure send(var s : semaphore);
    var previous : ^state_type;
begin
    with s do
        disable;
        if head = nil then
            owner:=nil;
        else
            previous:=who_is_running;   who_is_running:=head;
            previous^.next:=ready_list; ready_list:=previous;
            previous^.context_block.status:=READY;
            head:=head^.next;   owner:=who_is_running;
            _switch(previous,who_is_running);
        end; (* if *)
        enable;
    end; (* with *)
end send;
end semaphores.
```

Figure 4. A Semaphore Implementation

```
module monitors;
export _mon_procedure_in, _mon_procedure_out, _moninit;
import Initsem, who_is_running, wait, send;
    const MAXIMUM_MONITORS = 5;  (*limit of 15 processes*)
    var monitor_control : array 1:MAXIMUM_MONITORS of semaphore;

    var error_tab : array 1:MAXIMUM_MONITORS of bits;
    value error_tab = (0fffex, 0fffcx, 0fff8x, 0fff0x,
                       0ffe0x, 0ffc0x, 0ff80x, 0ff00x,
                       0fe00x, 0fc00x, 0f800x, 0f000x,
                       0e000x, 0c000x, 08000x, 00000x);

procedure _moninit(index:integer);
begin
    if (index<1) or (index>MAXIMUM_MONITORS) then
        (* error--compiler error *)
    end;
    initsem(monitor_control[index]);
end _moninit;

procedure _mon_procedure_in(index:integer);
    var b : bits;
begin
    if (index<1) or (index>MAXIMUM_MONITORS) then
        (* error--compiler error *)
    end;
    with who_is_running^.context_block do
        b:=in_mon;
        if error_tab[index] and b then
            (* error--illegal nesting of monitors *)
        elsif monitor_control[index].owner = who_is_running then
            inc(nesting_level[index]);
        else
            wait(monitor_control[index]);
            nesting_level[index]:=1;
            in_mon:=in_mon or [index];
        end; (* if *)
    end; (* with *)
end _mon_procedure_in;

procedure _mon_procedure_out(index:integer);
begin
    if (index<1) or (index>MAXIMUM_MONITORS) then
        (* error--compiler error *)
    end;
    with who_is_running^.context_block do
        dec(nesting_level[index]);
        if nesting_level[index] = 0 then
            in_mon:=in_mon and not [index];
            send(monitor_control[index]);
        end; (* if *)
    end; (*with*)
end _mon_procedure_out;
end monitors.
```

Figure 5. A Monitor Implementation

augmented to provide long-term scheduling capabilities. As a result, we will assume that the no-release implementation in Figure 4 is used only for monitor control.

4.2 Scheduling

Scheduling involves the ordering of the assignment of resources to processes. If the number of resources equals the number requested by processes, scheduling is superfluous. Otherwise, the ordering is usually based on a process' attributes.

In the simplest case, the order of arrival is used to control access. Other possibilities are to order the assignment list at the point of request or to order the list at the point at which the resource is granted. If a semaphore is considered as a representative name for a process, the following methodology can be used to implement general scheduling operations.

```
type schedule = record
     forward_link, backward_link : ^schedule;
     attributes : attribute_type;
     process_name : semaphore;
end; (* schedule *)
```

By creating lists of the "schedule" type, algorithms to perform arbitrary scheduling can be created. The "attributes" are used to order a process on the resource request list while "wait" and "send" operations on the semaphore control the associated process. However, these semaphore operations must be modified such that all of the "in_mon" monitors are released on a "wait" and are reacquired on a "send". Figure 6 contains the necessary modifications.

When a process starts to "wait", the monitors that it controls are released from high to low values of INTEGER. This has

```
procedure wait(var s : semaphore);
    var previous, t : ^state_type;
        b, c : bits;
        i    : integer;
begin
    with s do
        disable;
        if owner <> nil then
            if head = nil then
                head:=who_is_running;
            else
                tail^.next:=who_is_running;
            end; (* if *)
            tail:=who_is_running;
            b:=who_is_running^.context_block.in_mon;
            c:=b;   i:=MAXIMUM_MONITORS;
 (* RELEASE ALL MONITORS FROM HIGH TO LOW *)
            while b and (i>0) do
                if b and [i] then
                    b:=b and not [i];
                    with monitor_control[i] do
                        if head = nil then
                            owner:=nil;
                        else
                            t:=head;  head:=head^.next;
                            t^.next:=ready_list;
                            ready_list:=t;
                            t^.context_block.status:=READY;
                        end; (* if *)
                    end; (* with *)
                end; (* if *)
                dec(i);
            end; (* while *)
 (* WAIT FOR THIS SEMAPHORE TO SEND *)
            previous:=who_is_running;  who_is_running:=ready_list;
            if who_is_running = nil then
                (* error--no process to run *)
            end;
            ready_list:=ready_list^.next;
            previous^.context_block.status:=BLOCKED;
            _switch(previous,who_is_running);
            enable;    i:=1;
 (* REACQUIRE ALL MONITORS FROM LOW TO HIGH *)
            while c and (i<=MAXIMUM_MONITORS) do
                if c and [i] then
                    Figure_4_wait(monitor_control[i]);
                end; (* if *)
                inc(i);
            end; (* while *)
        else
            owner:=who_is_running;
            enable;
        end; (* if *)
    end; (* with *)
end wait;
```

Figure 6. Wait Extended to Release Monitor Control

two benefits. First, since monitors must be acquired from low to high, delayed processes are more likely to find a "clear" path in a monitor call sequence. Secondly, the ready list is ordered so that the processes with "low" requests will execute first, thus minimizing context switches.

When the corresponding "send" occurs, the monitors must be reacquired. The reacquisition takes place on low to high values of INTEGER to maintain the hierarchical ordering. As long as no infinite loops exist inside monitors, the reacquisition is guaranteed to complete.

4.3 Priority

Priority is an attribute which is usually associated with the assignment of processes to processors. Normally, it should only be used to improve the ability of a concurrent program to handle real-time events. Priority is implemented in the kernel by the addition of a "priority" field to the context block of each process. In addition, the ready list is implemented as a priority queue. A further use would be to order monitor entry and semaphore queues by priority, but at the cost of additional complexity. As Lampson[13] points out, it is difficult to implement guaranteed priority service. Another property of our system is that hardware priority is never used. More will be said about this decision in the next section on I/O programming.

5. I/O Programming

Two implementation choices for I/O programming are busy-wait and interrupt driven routines. The first method is illustrated by the following program segment.

```
loop (* program *)
        b:=get_buffer;
        (* compute until buffer is full *)
        (* build command list *)
        (* start device *);
        while (* device is BUSY *) do
                (* busy wait *)
        end;
end; (* loop *)
```

The buffer program contains a "busy wait" loop which wastes CPU time that could be applied to a computation. If the I/O device signaled the CPU on completion, the time which had been spent in the loop could now be applied to any of the processes in the program. Such an I/O completion signal is called an interrupt, which can be defined as follows (assuming a stack machine).

```
procedure interrupt(location,status:integer);
begin
        while DISABLE do  end;
        PUSH(state_vector)
        PUSH(status)
        state_vector:=memory[location]
end interrupt;
```

The interrupt routine, which is built into the CPU, saves the current state vector and loads a new one from the interrupt location. Interrupts are usually recognized by the CPU at the beginning or at the end of the instruction cycle. Most CPUs also include instructions to disable interrupts (remember but don't let the action happen) and to enable (action as in the example). If two interrupts to the same location arrive while the CPU is disabled, one is lost. Interrupts to different locations are usually remembered, but now the problem exists of how to decide which one should be processed first.

Most CPUs allow interrupts at different priority levels with interrupts at higher levels recognized first. Simultaneous interrupts at the same priority level are first-come-first-served. As lower priority routines are interrupted, their state is saved in a first-in-last-out order on the stack. The following discussion reviews some of the aspects of interrupt-driven programming[14].

It is customary to associate a process with each device (or array of identical devices). If a separate processor is available for this purpose, the process is called a <u>driver</u>. If a general processor has to be shared, it is called an <u>interrupt handler</u>. In either case, both the device itself and the associated routine effectively constitute a pair of cooperating sequential processes. Typical examples of the process and procedural models are listed below.

<u>Process</u>

```
process driver(p:^device);
begin
(* initialize device *)
loop
     (* get next request *)

     p^.cpusem:=0;
     (* start device *)
     wait(p^.cpusem);
     (* remove request *)
end (* loop *);
end driver;
```

<u>Procedure</u>

```
procedure front(p:^device);
begin
if not active then
    if (* request present *) then
       active:=true; (* start device *)
    end;
end;
end front;
procedure back;
(* assumes p is known *)
begin
if active then
       active:=false;
       (* remove request *)
       front(p);
end;
end back;
```

In the procedural example, the "front" procedure is called to start the device, if necessary, by the procedure which queues requests. The "back" procedure is "called" from the interrupt location. Once the device is started, interrupts will cause queued I/O requests to be removed until the queue is empty.

Interrupts which arrive with "active" false are ignored.

In the driver model, a separate process exists for each I/O device. Whereas "front" is called by the request queuing procedure, driver must check for a request, waiting if necessary, each time through the loop. We have also introduced a special "semaphore" type which is used only by the I/O system. "cpusem" has the following properties:

<u>INTERRUPT</u>

1)	cpusem=0	an interrupt sets it to 1
2)	cpusem=1	an interrupt causes an error
3)	cpusem=2	an interrupt sets it to 2
4)	cpusem=pid	an interrupt wakes up the process

<u>WAIT FOR INTERRUPT</u>

5)	cpusem=0,2	cpusem:=pid; process goes to sleep
6)	cpusem=1	cpusem:=0; process continues
7)	cpusem=pid	an error condition

"cpusem" is intended to model the two process communication which is typical of I/O operations. Conditions 4 and 5 represent the most common occurrence; that is, the process goes to sleep until the interrupt arrives. Conditions 1 and 6 illustrate what happens when the interrupt arrives before the process goes to sleep. This can happen when dealing with very fast devices, for example. Setting "cpusem" to 2 causes all interrupts to be ignored. Condition 2 catches device overrun situations in which an interrupt arrives before a prior interrupt has been handled. Finally, condition 7 checks for a violation of the one-to-one communication restriction. We should also point out that neither example detects the failure of a device to send an interrupt, but a time-out could easily be incorporated in the semaphore definition.

The handler has a speed advantage on most architectures since a procedure call is normally faster than a context switch. However, the procedure model has the disadvantage that when the interrupt occurs, the frame must be jammed onto the stack of some random process. The victim cannot continue until the information is removed. If the victim controls any resource which the "back" procedure needs to complete, deadlock results. Therefore, the process model is recommended.

When the interrupt occurs, a context switch occurs only if the driver has a higher priority than the running process; otherwise, it is just added to the ready list. As we mentioned previously, hardware priority is not used. The result is a high availability of the CPU for I/O processing. Furthermore, our approach is machine independent. The drawback is that a high-priority process may have an arbitrary amount of cycle-stealing by interrupts to lower priority processes. Since the I/O semaphore is designed to minimize execution time, we have never found this to be a disadvantage. The final example is a driver for a disk device.

The head of the disk request queue contains information describing the attributes and address of the disk, the semaphores to be used for user and device communication, and the drive, sector, and track request parameters. The driver attempts to overlap the I/O operation with both the request setup and the "send" operation to the client process.

```
type disk = record
     attributes : disk_attribute_type;
     disk_queue : queue_type;
     disk_request : disk_request_type;
     cpusem : IO_semaphore_type;
     usersem : semaphore;
end; (* disk *)

process disk_driver(p:^disk);
var r : disk_request_type;
    abp, bp : ^buf_header;
begin
    with p^ do
         (* set up device queue *)
         bp:=nil;  (* try to overlap setup with I/O *)
         loop      (* forever *)
             if bp = nil then
                 bp:=get_dq(p,dr,WAIT);
                 (* start device *)
             end;
             abp:=bp;
             bp:=get_dq(p,r,NO_WAIT);
             wait(cpusem);
             if bp <> nil then (* start immediately *)
                 (* start device *)
             end;
             send(usersem);
         end; (* loop *)
    end; (* with *)
end disk_driver;
```

6. Exception Handling

In a large hierarchical software system, it is often desirable to have each subroutine return an error indication. Thus, each call must be followed by a check for correctness. This methodology is tedious and error prone. An alternative is to provide a simple exception handling mechanism as part of the language kernel. At the minimum three functions are required:

1. The ability to "catch" an error.
2. The ability to "raise" an error condition.
3. The ability to discover which error has occurred.

A programmer might use an exception handler as follows:

```
        if ERROR then
                error_number:=get_ERROR;
                case error_number of
        OVERFLOW:       begin
                        end;
        UNDERFLOW:      begin
                        end;
        otherwise:      begin  (* let someone else see it *)
                        set_ERROR(error_number);
                        exit_procedure;
                        end;
                end;  (* case *)
        end;  (* error handler *)
```

"ERROR", "set_ERROR", and "get_ERROR" are exported from the assembly language kernel. Each activation record for a procedure is augmented with an error number cell and two locations to save the stack pointer and program counter. On procedure entry, the error number is set to zero and the saved stack pointer to "nil". An ERROR call, sets the two save locations and returns "false". On procedure exit, a non-zero error number causes a search of the call chain for a non-"nil" save location. When a handler is found, the stack pointer and program counter are restored and a value of "true" is returned from ERROR.

When an error is detected, the user performs a "set_ERROR" with an error code which would normally be a named constant. On procedure exit, if the error cell in the activation record is non-zero, the activation record of the caller is checked for the presence of an exception handler. If a handler is present, the stack pointer and program counter are adjusted to execute the handler. When the error number is retrieved, the error cell is automatically set to zero. Thus, the programmer must explicitly propagate errors.

If a handler is not present, several actions are possible. Normally, the next call frame is checked until a handler is found. If no handler is found, the program is terminated. Also, if the process is in a monitor, a handler must always be present or the program is terminated. The presence of error handlers could be enforced by the compiler.

7. An Operating Systems Kernel

The algorithms presented so far implement the kernel for a concurrent programming environment which supports a fixed number of processes that execute in the same address space. The next step might be to implement an operating system kernel. Figures 7 and 8 present an outline of a simple scheduler which handles system calls and a timer process which is used to multiplex process execution. Since we are, in essence, creating a new virtual processor, a new context block format is required with a state vector for the virtual machine.

The scheduler searches for a READY user process. At that point, it calls the assembly language routine "user_go" to implement a coroutine[15] swap with the user. The context block of the kernel becomes the context block for the user process. The argument to "user_go" is used to retrieve the state vector for the user process. In addition, the "user_go" routine has the side effect of setting "u" to the address of the user's "machine_dependent" record. Any trap which occurs when "u" is not "nil" will cause a coroutine swap back to "scheduler" with a return value which indicates the condition. The example implements TIMEOUT(quantum expiration) and SYSCALL(request for operating system services).

Each user process is limited to "quantum" units of execution by the "timer" process. If a user is executing(u not equal

```
module phoenix;
export u, time;
import cpusem, user_go, user_stop, pause, CLOCKINT;

const QUANTUM=5;           (*number of clock ticks per time slice*)
      NPROC=15;            (*number of user processes*)
        (*PROCESS STATES *)
      READY=1;             (*in core and waiting for a processor*)
      RUNNING=2;           (*assigned to a processor*)
      SYSCALLS=3;          (*set to indicate system call*)

type termtype=(BADINST,TIMEOUT,SYSCALL,SEGERR,STKOVF,STKUNF);
     userpnt=^user;
     user=record           (*PHOENIX process descriptor*)
        state:integer;             (*current process state*)
        pid:integer;               (*unique process id*)
        parentid:integer;          (*id of parent process*)
        opcode:integer;            (*opcode for the system call*)
        args:array 5 of integer;  (*arguments to sys calls*)
        error:integer;             (*completion code on sys calls*)
        result:long;               (*result of system call*)
        machine_dependent:record
           s:user_state_vector_type; (*state_vector for cpu*)
           csize,dsize:integer;      (*code and data segment sizes*)
           quantum:integer;          (*ticks left to execute*)
        end; (*machine_dependent*)
     end; (*user*)

var cpusem:array 255 of semaphore;
    u:^machine_dependent_type;  (*NIL or current USER's structure*)
    ua:array NPROC of user;     (*one structure per USER process*)
    time:long;                  (*counts seconds since 1970*)

procedure xsyscall(u:userpnt);
begin
with u^ do
    error:=0;  result:=0;
    (* copy opcode and arguments from the user's address space *)
    case opcode of
TIME:
        begin
        result:=time;
        end; (* TIME *)
GETPID:
        begin
        result:=long(pid);
        end; (* GETPID *)
     end; (*case*)
     (* copy error and result to the user's address space *)
     state:=READY;
end; (* with *)
end xsyscall;
```

Figure 7. System Call Processing and Data Structures

```
process scheduler;
var i:integer;
    j:termtype;
begin
i:=0;
loop   (* FIND A READY PROCESS *)
    if i > NPROC then
        i:=0;
    end;
    with ua[i] do
        if state = READY then
            (* F O U N D  O N E *)
            quantum:=QUANTUM;   state:=RUNNING;
            j:=user_go(machine_dependent);
            case j of
    TIMEOUT:    begin  (* QUANTUM EXPIRED *)
                state:=READY;
                end;   (* TIMEOUT *)
    SYSCALL:    begin  (* SYSTEM CALL *)
                state:=SYSCALLS;
                xsyscall(addr(ua[i]));
                dec(i);
                end;   (* SYSCALL *)
    otherwise:  begin
                (* error--user exit not implemented *)
                end;
            end; (* case *)
        end; (* if *)
    end; (* with *)
    inc(i);
end; (* loop *)
end scheduler;

process timer;
var sixty:integer;
begin
sixty:=60;
loop (* clock interrupt every 1/60 of a second *)
    P(cpusem[CLOCKINT]);   dec(sixty);
    if sixty <= 0 then
        sixty:=60;   inc(time);
    end;
    if u <> nil then
        dec(u^.quantum);
        if u^.quantum <= 0 then
            user_stop(TIMEOUT);
        end;
    end; (* if *)
end; (* loop *)
end timer;

begin    (* MAIN PROGRAM *)
timer;   scheduler;   pause;
end phoenix.
```

Figure 8. An Operating System Kernel

"nil") when a clock interrupt occurs, the "quantum" value is decremented. When time expires, the "user_stop" routine is called to perform a coroutine swap from the user to the "scheduler" process with a return value of TIMEOUT.

The SYSCALL procedure is responsible for communication between the operating system and the user. By convention, each system call reurns a "result" value and an "error" indication. Any system call which can be implemented without blocking is executed by the scheduler. System calls, such as I/O operations, are handled by other kernel processes.

8. Conclusions

Obviously, kernel design is replete with religious convictions. For example, we didn't even mention message-based kernels. The intention was to present a complete set of primitives which should be usable across language and machine boundaries. We encourage others who might have alternative experiences to present different implementations which maintain the same functionality.

REFERENCES

[1] Cook, R.P., "StarMod--A Language for Distributed Programming", IEEE Transactions on Software Engineering SE-6, 6(Nov. 1980) 563-571.

[2] Honeywell, Inc. and Cii Honeywell Bull, "Reference Manual for the ADA Programming Language", SIGPLAN Notices 14, 6(June 1979) Part A.

[3] Wirth, N., "Modula: A language for Modular Multiprogramming", Software- Practice and Experience 7, 1(1977) 3-35.

[4] Brinch Hansen, P., "Edison--A Multiprocessor Language", Altadena, California, (Sept. 1980).

[5] Mitchell, J.G., Maybury, W. and R. Sweet, "Mesa Language Manual", Xerox PARC Technical Report CSL-79-3, (April 1979).

[6] Dijkstra, E.W., "The Humble Programmer", Communications of the ACM 15, 10(Oct. 1972).

[7] Dijkstra, E.W., "Cooperating Sequential Processes", in Programming Languages (F. Genuys ed.), Academic Press, (1968) 43-112.

[8] Keedy, J.L. On structuring operating systems with monitors. Operating System Review 13, 1(Jan. 1979), 5-9.

[9] Lister, A.M. and Maynard, K.J. An implementation of monitors. Software-Practice and Experience 6, 3(July 1976), 377-385.

[10] Hoare, C.A.R., "Monitors: An Operating System Structuring Concept", Communications of the ACM 17, 10(Oct. 1974) 549-557.

[11] Brinch Hansen, P., "Structured multiprogramming", Communications of the ACM 15, 7(July 1972), 574-578.

[12] Havender, J.W., "Avoiding Deadlock in Multitasking Systems", IBM Systems Journal 7, 2(1968) 74-84.

[13] Lampson, B.W. and D.D. Redell, "Experience with Processes and Monitors in Mesa", Communications of the ACM 23, 2(Feb. 1980) 105-117.

[14] Wirth, N., "Toward a Discipline of Real-Time Programming", Communications of the ACM 20, 8(Aug. 1977) 577-583.

[15] Conway, M.E., "Design of a Separable Transition-Diagram Compiler", Communications of the ACM 6, 7(July 1963) 396-408.

List of Abbreviations

AAVS	Ada Automated Verification System
AC	Assertion Checker
ADGE	Air Defense Ground Environment
AI	Artificial Intelligence
ALU	Arithmetic Logic Unit
ALT	Automatic Language Translator
ANSI	American National Standards Institute
APSE	Ada Programming Support Environment
CA	Completion Analyzer
CAVS	COBOL Automated Verification System
CB	Configuration Builder
CC	Concurrency Checker
C&I	Command Control Communication Intelligence
CK	Configuration Kernel
COS	Constituent Operating System
CRG	Cross Reference Generator
CS	Control Simulator
DA	Diagnostic Analyzer
DBMS	Data Base Management System
DECNET	Digital Equipment Corporation Network
DIP	Design Interface Processor
DoD	Department of Defense
DOS	Distributed Operating System
DSSL	Distributed System Specification Language
FAVS	FORTRAN Automated Verification System

FRI	Functional Requirements Interpreter
HS	Hardware Simulator
IA	Interconnect Architectures
IEEE	Institute of Electrical and Electronic Engineers
IM	Interface Mapper
I/O	Input/Output
IPO	Input Process Output
ISSE	Integrated Software Support Environment
JAVS	Jovial Automated Verification System
KAPSE	Kernel Ada Program Support Environment
KBS	Knowledge Based System
KIT	KAPSE Interface Team
LAN	Local Area Network
LL	Linker/Loader
MAPSE	Minimal Ada Program Support Environment
MCMD	Multi-Center, Multi-Drop
MDMS	Multi-Center, Multi-Star
MMI	Man Machine Interface
MST	Minimal Spanning Tree
MT	Mutation Tester
NOS	Network Operating System
OAS	Operator's Allowable Sequence
OSA	Operator Sequence Analyzer
PA	Performance Analyzer
PDL	Program Design Language
PGB	Path GraphBuilder

PSA	Problem Statement Analyzer
RA	Reachability Analyzer
RADC	Rome Air Development Center
RAT	Resource Allocation Tool
REVS	Requirements Engineering and Validation System
RIP	Requirements Interface Processor
RLP	Requirements Language Processor
ROM	Read Only Memory
RPS	Requirements Processing System
RSDB	Raw Statistics Database
RSL	Requirements Statement Language
SA	Serialization Analyzer
SC	Source Code
SCMD	Single-Center, Multi-Drop
SCSS	Single-Center, Single-Star
SNA	Systems Network Architecture
SRA	Static Requirements Analyzer
SREM	Software Requirements Engineering Methodology
SSDB	System Specification Database
ST	Symbol Table
VHM	Variable History Mapper

Bibliography

1. Andrews, D. M. and Melton, R. A., FAVS: FORTRAN Automated Verification System User's Manual, General Research Corp. Report CR-1-754/1, April, 1980.

2. Baklovich, E., Decentralized Systems. Computer Science Technical Report, University of Connecticut, AD/A099 195, Storrs, Connecticut, 1980.

3. Barr, A. and Feigenbaum, E. A., editors, The Handbook of Artificial Intelligence, Los Altos, CA, William Kaufman, 1981.

4. Bell, Thomas E., Bixler, David C. and Dyer, Margaret E. An Extendable Approach to Computer-Aided Software Requirements Engineering, Transactions on Software Engineering, Vol. SE-3, No. 1, January 1977.

5. Benoit, John W. and Selander, J. Michael, Knowledge-Based Systems as Command Decision Aids, First U.S. Army Conference on Knowledge-Based Systems for C&I, 1981.

6. Clark, Lori A. et al, Toward Feedback-Directed Development of Complex Software Systems, University of Massachusetts, Amherst, Massachusetts.

7. Cook, R. P., A Review of the Stoneman APSE Specification, Consulting Report, June, 1982.

8. Cook, R. P., How To Write a Distributed Program, Consulting Report, June, 1982.

9. Cook, R. P., Kernel Design for Concurrent Programming, Consulting Report, June, 1982.

10. Daley, P., Modeling of Distributed Command/Communication/Control Intelligence Systems, RADC Distributed Processing Technology Exchange, May, 1982.

11. Department of Defense, Reference Manual for the Ada Programming Language, July, 1980.

12. Donahoo, J. D. and Swearinger, D., A Review of Software Technology, RADC-TR-80-13, February, 1980.

13. Drazovich, Robert J. and Payne, J. Roland, Artificial Intelligence Approaches to Information Fusion, First U.S. Army Conference on Knowledge-Based Systems for C&I, 1981.

14. Enslow, P., Performance of Distributed and Decentralized Control Models for Fully Distributed Processing Systems, RADC-TR-82-105, May, 1982.

15. Enslow, P., Support for Loosely-Coupled Distributed Processing Systems, RADC Distributed Processing Technology Exchange, May, 1982.

16. Feng, Tse-Yun and Wu, Chuan-lin, Interconnection Networks in Multiple-Processor Systems, RADC-TR-79-304, December, 1979.

17. Findler, N. V., editor, Associative Networks: The Representation and Use of Knowledge by Computers, New York, Academic Press, 1979.

18. First U.S. Army Conference on "Knowledge-Based Systems for C&I", Ft. Leavenworth, Kansas, 4-5 November, 1981.

19. Forsdick, Harry C., et al, Distributed Operating System Design Study, RADC-TR-81-384, January, 1982.

20. Fortier, P. J. and Leary, R. G., A General Simulation Model for the Evaluation of Distributed Processing Systems, Annual Simulation Symposium, November, 1981.

21. Gannon, C. and Brooks, N. B., JOVIAL J73 Automated Verification System Functional Description, General Research Corp. Report CR-1-947, March, 1980.

22. Giese, C., Research and Development Plan for Ada Target Machine Operating System (ATMOS) for the Ada Bare Target Machine, AJPO/U.S. Army AIRMICS, April, 1982.

23. Gorney, L., Queueing Theory: A Problem Solving Approach, Petrocelli Books, 1982.

24. Green, Cordell, A Knowledge-Based Approach to Rapid Prototyping, Software Engineering Symposium: Rapid Prototyping, 1982.

25. Hayes-Roth, Frederick, Artificial Intelligence and Expert Systems, A Tutorial, First U.S. Army Conference on Knowledge-Based Systems for C&I, 1981.

26. Jensen, D., Decentralized System Control, RADC Distributed Processing Technology Exchange, May, 1982.

27. Jensen, E. Douglas, The ARCHONS Project, RADC Distributed Processing Exchange, October, 1981.

28. Joobbani, R. and Siewiorek, D. P., Reliability Modeling of Multiprocessor Architectures, Carnegie-Mellon University, Pittsburg, PA, 1979.

29. Kemp, G. H., Debugging Embedded Computer Programs, GDPD Technical Memorandum, March, 1980.

30. McCall, J. A. and Matsumoto, M. T., Software Quality Metrics Enhancements, RADC-TR-80-109, Volumes I and II, April, 1980.

31. Melton, R., Grunburg, G. and Sharp, M., COBOL Automated Verification System: Study Phase, RADC-TR-81-11, March,1981.

32. Post, J., Quality Metrics for Distributed Systems, RADC Distributed Processing Technology Exchange, May, 1982.

33. Reinstein, H. C. and Hollander, C. R., A Knowledge-Based Approach to Application Development for Non-Programmers, IBM Palo Alto Scientific Center, July, 1979.

34. Saponas, T. G., Distributed and Decentralized Control in Fully Distributed Processing Systems, GIT-ITC-81/18, December, 1981.

35. Sharma, R. L., deSousa, P. J. T., and Ingle, A. D., Network Systems, Van Nostrand Reinhold Data Processing Services, 1982.

36. Sharp, M., Melton, R. and Greenburg, G., COBOL Automated Verification System Functional Description, General Research Corp. Report CR-2-970, November, 1980.

37. Stenning, V., et al, The Ada Environment: A Perspective, Computer, June, 1981.

38. Tanenbaum, A. S., Computer Networks, Prentice-Hall, Englewood Cliffs, NJ, 1981.

39. Taylor, R. N., Complexity of Analyzing the Structure of Concurrent Programs, University of Victoria Department of Computer Science, 1981.

40. Taylor, R. N. and Osterweil, L. J., Anomaly Detection in Concurrent Software by Static Data Flow Analysis, IEEE Transactions on Software Engineering, Volume 6, 1980.

41. Teichroew, Daniel and Hershey, Ernest A. III, PSL/PSA: A Computer-Aided Technique for Structured Documentation and Analysis of Information Processing Systems, Transaction on Software Engineering, Vol. SE-3, No. 1, January 1977.

42. Thomas, R., Distributed Personal Computer-Based Information Systems, RADC Distributed Processing Technology Exchange, May, 1982.

43. Wolfe, M. I., et al, The Ada Language System, Computer, June, 1981.

44. Ziegler, K., A Distributed Information System Study, IBM System Journal, Volume 18, Number 3, 1979.

Other Noyes Publications

ROBOTICS AND FLEXIBLE MANUFACTURING TECHNOLOGIES

Assessment, Impacts and Forecast

by

Robert U. Ayres and Steven M. Miller
Department of Engineering and Public Policy
Carnegie-Mellon University

James Just, Keith King, Michael Osheroff, George Berke, Peter Spidaliere, Tran Ngoc
DHR, Incorporated

A critical assessment of current robotics and flexible manufacturing technolgies, their impacts on the industrial base, and a forecast of future functional capabilities and emerging applications areas are presented in this book.

Nearly three times as many robots were installed in industry in 1984 as in 1979, and the prospects for the future can only increase, probably by orders of magnitude.

Part I of the book reviews the role of tools, machines and controls in our society; the extensions of capabilities of commercially available robots, integration of sensory information processing with robotic devices, and the integration of robots, machine tools, parts handling and transport devices and computers into flexible manufacturing systems (FMSs). Analyses are given on changes in unit costs and production labor requirements which will accompany the more widespread use of industrial robots and FMSs.

Part II reviews key worldwide R&D activities and discusses the principal thrusts and trends in robotics development. It provides a technological forecast addressing future directions of robotics producers and end-users.

The condensed table of contents listed below includes **part and chapter titles and selected subtitles.**

ISBN 0-8155-1043-8 (1985) **443 pages**

Other Noyes Publications

ARTIFICIAL INTELLIGENCE IN MAINTENANCE

Edited by

J. Jeffrey Richardson

Denver Research Institute
University of Denver

Theoretical and practical research and development, and applications issues in the use of artificial intelligence in maintenance are identified here. Based on a Joint-Services-sponsored workshop, this book provides an exchange of technical information for managers, engineers, and other personnel involved in ongoing R&D in artificial intelligence applicable to automatic testing, maintenance aiding, and maintenance training.

AI research in problem solving and expert systems provides us with new tools and techniques to be refined for practical applications. The material presented covers the state of the science of artificial intelligence, specific efforts in expert systems and knowledge engineering, the psychologies of technical devices and fault diagnosis, and the future of AI.

The information is presented in four parts: Overview, The Science, Department of Defense Programs and Projects, and Commercial and Industrial Development Projects.

A condensed table of contents listing **part titles and 27 selections of the 36 chapter titles** is given below.

ISBN 0-8155-1042-X (1985) **485 pages**

Other Noyes Publications

ARTIFICIAL INTELLIGENCE EXPERT SYSTEMS, COMPUTER VISION AND NATURAL LANGUAGE PROCESSING

by

William B. Gevarter
National Aeronautics and Space Administration

An overview of artificial intelligence (AI), its core ingredients, and its applications is presented in this volume. AI is a field with over a quarter century of history; however, it wasn't until the 1980s that AI received economic and popular acclaim and went through the transition from a primary research area to potential commercial applications. The full impact of AI's transition has yet to be felt. Recently, AI was made the basic thrust of Japan's Fifth Generation computer research effort. Success in this venture could project the Japanese into a dominant position in information sciences in the 1990s. Similar importance has been placed on AI by the U.S., Great Britain, and France.

The real payoff for AI will be in applications. Intelligent computer programs are now emerging from the laboratory into practical applications. This book presents overviews of key application areas—expert systems, computer vision, natural language processing, speech interfaces, and problem solving and planning. Basic approaches to these systems, the state of the art, existing systems, participants, and future trends are detailed. The book should be useful to engineering and research managers, potential users and others seeking a basic understanding of the rapidly evolving area of artificial intelligence and its applications.

A condensed table of contents listing **part and chapter titles and selected subtitles** is given below.

ISBN 0-8155-0994-4 (1984) **226 pages**